Radical Roots

Radical Roots

PUBLIC HISTORY AND A TRADITION
OF SOCIAL JUSTICE ACTIVISM

Editor
Denise D. Meringolo

Amherst College Press

Copyright © 2021 by Denise D. Meringolo
Some rights reserved

This work is licensed under the Creative Commons Attribution-NonCommercial 4.0 International License. To view a copy of this license, visit http://creativecommons.org/licenses/by-nc/4.0/ or send a letter to Creative Commons, PO Box 1866, Mountain View, CA 94042, USA.

Published in the United States of America by
Amherst College Press
Manufactured in the United States of America

DOI: http://dx.doi.org/10.3998/mpub.12366495

ISBN 978-1-943208-20-3 (paper)
ISBN 978-1-943208-21-0 (OA)

The complete proposal of this work was subjected to a fully closed ("double blind") review process; the complete manuscript was subjected to a partly closed ("single blind") review process. For more information, please see our Peer Review Commitments and Guidelines at https://acpress.amherst.edu/peerreview/.

Contents

Acknowledgments ix

Introduction: Social Justice and Public History: The Networks, Goals, and Practices That Shaped Our Noble Dream 1
   Denise D. Meringolo

RAISING CONSCIOUSNESS OR RAISING HELL: NEW NARRATIVES FOR ORAL HISTORY

Allan Nevins Is Not My Grandfather: The Roots of Radical Oral History Practice in the United States 23
   Daniel R. Kerr

Helen Matthews Lewis: Oral History and Social Change in Appalachia 53
   Judith Jennings

"Recalling Our Bitter Experiences": Consciousness Raising, Feminism, and Women's Oral History 75
   Anne M. Valk

Pushing Boundaries Onstage: Culture Clash, Oral History Theater, and the Influence of El Teatro Campesino 97
   Kristen Ana La Follette

What Are the Roots of Your Radical Oral History Practice? 119
   Shane Bernardo, Maria E. Cotera, Fernanda Espinosa, and Amy Starecheski

"We're All Bozos on This Bus": An Oral History with Jeremy Brecher . . 153
   Daniel R. Kerr

PLACE-BASED PEDAGOGIES: ORIGINS OF PUBLIC HISTORY EDUCATION

The People's Camp: The Progressive Pedagogy of Camp Woodland . . . 191
  Rachel Donaldson

Carter G. Woodson: A Century of Making Black Lives Matter. 219
  Burnis Morris

Louis C. Jones and the Cooperstown Model: Working at the Nexus
of Public Folklore and Public History. 247
  William S. Walker

The American Civilization Institute of Morristown:
Education and Inclusive Community Building. 271
  Denise D. Meringolo

Radical Futures: Teaching Public History as Social Justice. 295
  Elizabeth Belanger

Radical Is a Process: Public History Pedagogy in Urban Universities. . . 325
  Rebecca Amato, Gabrielle Bendiner-Viani, Dipti Desai,
  Denise D. Meringolo, and Mary Rizzo

SITES OF DISCORD AND DIALOGUE: MUSEUMS IN PROGRESS

Imperfectly Progressive: The Social Mission of Museums in the 1930s . . . 363
  Clarissa J. Ceglio

What to Do with Heritage: The Museum of Jewish
Ceremonial Objects, 1931–43 395
  Laura Schiavo

Exhibiting Ourselves: The Making of a Community Museum in
a National Institution. 427
  Michèle Gates Moresi

Crossing the Gentrification Frontier: The Lower East Side Tenement
Museum and the Blind Spots of Social History 455
  Rebecca Amato

Recollections on Interpreting Slave Life and Falling into Your Purpose . . . 483
  Nicole A. Moore

PUBLIC HISTORY FROM THE GROUND UP:
CULTURAL HERITAGE AS COMMUNITY BUILDING

Unintentional Public Historians: Collective Memory
and Identity Production in the American Indian and
LGBTQ Liberation Movements 503
   Lara Kelland

Reflections on Black Public History: Past, Present, Future. 525
   Pero Gaglo Dagbovie

What Happens Next? Institutionalizing Grassroots Success
in Selma, Alabama. 541
   Abigail Gautreau

Getting to the Heart of Preservation: The Place of Grassroots Efforts
in the Contemporary Preservation Movement. 555
   Kristen Baldwin Deathridge

Philadelphia's Original Social Justice Warriors: The Little Big Story of
Germantown and the Germantown Mennonites 575
   Craig Stutman

Conclusion: The Uneasy Relationship between Civic Engagement
and Social Justice 609
   Denise D. Meringolo

Further Reading 615
Contributor Biographies 619

Acknowledgments

This project would not have been possible without the sustained support of a variety of individuals and organizations. We are grateful for every word of advice, every penny of research funding, and every opportunity to present our work. The project editor would particularly like to acknowledge three sources of assistance. Jessica Berman, director of the Dresher Center for the Humanities at the University of Maryland, Baltimore County, and the members of the advisory board provided financial support and work space for development of the Radical Roots project. While a Dresher Center Faculty Fellow, Denise D. Meringolo wrote a grant proposal that, while unsuccessful in winning large-scale funding, became the foundation for the original book proposal as well as materials used to recruit new authors. Stephanie Rowe, executive director of the National Council on Public History, helped us organize a mini symposium as part of the 2017 annual meeting. We ran four conference sessions in which participants presented their findings and asked specific questions to the audience. We gathered significant peer review, including anonymous feedback in a series of open Google documents. This event helped shape the project research and findings in meaningful ways. Finally, Linda Shopes, the accomplished and respected oral historian, was a dedicated member of the Radical Roots project from the beginning. She played a significant leadership role on the oral history research team. She organized several conference sessions on the project, and she provided ongoing, meaningful intellectual and practical support to the project editor.

INTRODUCTION

Social Justice and Public History

The Networks, Goals, and Practices That Shaped Our Noble Dream

Denise D. Meringolo

This volume critically examines an activist thread—a conscious effort to connect history-making to the promotion of social justice—which runs through the profession of public history as it has evolved in the United States. While it may be argued that all history has the potential to be political, particularly when historians conduct research and produce interpretations that challenge deeply held beliefs about the past, public history is uniquely political. Public historians are engaged in historical inquiry outside the bubble of scholarly discourse. In the words of Cathy Stanton, "Whether we intentionally locate ourselves in controversial settings, have something blow up in our faces, or encounter less-spectacular kinds of resistance or misunderstanding, we are always on the edge of the political, even when we don't set out to be."[1] Although, as Stanton suggests, public historians cannot deny the political aspects of their work, some are reluctant to assume an overtly political posture. They believe the conventions of the discipline require a kind of objectivity and intellectual rigor that are undermined when they align their work with a particular political position. Others are constrained by the conditions of their employment in government or quasi-government agencies from advancing historical interpretations that might be labeled as "biased" or politically motivated. Nonetheless, there is a consistent if often overlooked tradition of political engagement that runs through the history of the profession. A significant minority of public historians see rigorous scholarship as entirely compatible with—even necessary for—productive political discourse, and they embrace the potential of their work to promote change.

The authors assembled here have identified precedents, antecedents, and contemporary examples of what we have loosely termed *radical public history*, which we define as public history that is future-focused, committed to the advancement of social justice, and engaged in the creation of a more inclusive material record. Taken as a whole, the essays suggest that examples of radical public history become more visible to researchers and practitioners alike when we invert our understanding of professionalism, placing less emphasis on the outcomes and products of historical inquiry and more emphasis on social networks, political goals, practices, and habits of mind that distinguish public history from the larger discipline.[2] In this, our work follows the path established by Rebecca Conard. In her introduction to a 2006 special issue of the *Public Historian*, she argued there had been no sustained, influential effort to theorize and define public history as a distinct field. Adopting the philosophy of reflective practice developed by the oral historian Donald Schon, Conard called for new histories and theories of public history that emphasize shared inquiry, interdisciplinary cooperation, attention to real-world conditions, dedication to problem solving, and self-reflection, and that valued intuition and artistry as much as research and logic.[3] Contributors to the issue advanced a thorough description of a public history approach defined by reflective practice, shared inquiry, shared authority, and reflection in action. The public history approach they identified has become broadly accepted by educators and practitioners alike, and it manifests in a variety of practices, including dialogic interpretation, community-based collaborative research, and crowdsourced collecting. It also encourages public historians to define their field not as strictly rooted in the discipline of history but rather as broadly interdisciplinary and inclusive of both formal knowledge and knowledge acquired through firsthand experience. This understanding of public history practice serves as the foundation for the lines of inquiry framing *Radical Roots*. Contributors to this volume have looked for evidence that the community-focused and community-rooted practices that define public history are not recent developments. Rather, they have been put to use—in the past and today—to advance social justice and promote change.

The initial inquiry that lead to this volume took shape in the summer of 2013. I have long been interested in identifying points of origin for the ideas about community service, dialogue, and collaboration that run through the field of public history.[4] I sought out scholars with similar research interests and entered into a series of conversations with Daniel R. Kerr, assistant professor of public history at American University. As an activist himself, Kerr's work explores the ways in which practitioners have understood and negotiated the intersection between scholarly inquiry and political action.[5] Together, we put out a call for research collaborators and found a dozen public history practitioners willing to join in a series of online and in-person discussions during the fall of 2013. These initial conversations culminated in a working group session at the 2014 annual meeting of the National Council on Public History, during which participants began to map a historical time line for the development of an activist branch of public history practice. Together, we identified key research themes and organized working group participants into interest groups, each of which made recommendations about how to organize a collaborative research project to fully examine the relationship between social justice activism and public history practice.[6]

The *Radical Roots* research project began in earnest immediately after this meeting. Four research groups emerged: one examining experimentation with radical practices in museums, a second focused on the intersection between oral history and social justice activism, a third tasked with identifying the ways in which grassroots preservation practices have served movements for equality, and a fourth focused on identifying the emergence of collaboration, community-based learning, and shared inquiry as strategies in public history education. The members of these four research collectives provided support and feedback to one another, and—as volume editor—I reviewed each contribution. Between 2015 and 2018, we sought external commentary from our professional peers, presenting at the annual meetings of the Oral History Association, the National Council on Public History, and the National Humanities Conference. In addition, several contributors have presented their work to the communities directly impacted by or analyzed in their research.

Ultimately our efforts produced the twenty-three essays collected here. Though diverse in approach to context, methodology, and analysis, they are united by their attention to several interrelated questions designed to address both historical roots and contemporary articulations of radical public history practice: What core practices have shaped radical public history? How have these core practices changed over time? How, when, and by whom have these core practices been mobilized for the purpose of promoting social justice? What larger trends in history, education, museum studies, oral history, preservation, and other fields (formal or vernacular in nature) led some groups or individuals to mobilize core public history practices for the purpose of facilitating civic discourse and promoting social justice? Can we make a case for claiming as part of the genealogy of radical public history incidents, individuals, and/or groups that have been marginalized in the standard history of the field? What do radical public history practices look like today? How effective are they? What constitutes success?

Taken as a whole, the essays in this volume shed new light on two interrelated issues that have restricted our understanding of the distinctive roots and professional practices that define public history. First, while radical forms of public history practice have evolved over time in the United States, they have been rendered invisible by the accepted genealogy of the field. Second, and related, the potentially radical strategies of public history as reflective practice can be (and often have been) co-opted and neutralized by processes of professionalization, institutionalization, and standardization. We do not presume that the work of this inquiry is finished. Rather, we hope this volume will generate new research. Drawing attention to both the persistence of a radical public history agenda and the forces that have undermined its influence opens up important new questions about the history and the direction of our field and provides a framework for reevaluating historical and contemporary tensions in museums, in historic sites, in commemorative spaces, and elsewhere.

Broadly speaking, the accepted historiography of the field took shape during the 1980s and 1990s. Peter Novick's influential 1988 book, *That Noble Dream: The "Objectivity Question" and the American Historical Profession*, tracked historians' aspiration to document the past accurately and without bias, initially framing the discipline as more science than art. Novick suggests that the pursuit of objectivity shaped the practice of history over time, even as it proved impossible to achieve fully. The pursuit of objectivity has, of course, produced well-documented, carefully researched, complex narratives that have established a meaningful foundation for understanding and analyzing

American history. But historians' effort to capture an unvarnished past has also—at times—constrained creativity and rendered particular historical experiences invisible. This effort also created a rift between university-based and public-oriented historians that proved difficult to overcome. Arguably, it was not until the end of the twentieth century that historians housed primarily in the academy began more fully and frequently to connect with public historians as peers and colleagues. The culture wars of the 1990s forced professional associations like the Organization of American Historians (OAH) to recognize and address the particular challenges faced by public practitioners. The OAH created a working partnership with the National Park Service in 1994 and hired a public history manager in 2002 to facilitate the organization's outreach and support for practitioners working outside of university settings.[7]

Novick's book helped shed light on the differences in perspective that set history and public history on separate paths toward professionalization. Since its publication, dozens of scholars have examined the roots of public history, drawing necessary, critical attention to the values that shaped the field over time. This important body of scholarship has identified public history as having emerged from several points of origin, including the preservation of historic structures, commemoration of historic events, development of museums and historic sites, acquisition of collections, and interpretation of the past for a broad public. Identifying the motivations and values of each group of founders in this history has made clear that most sought to protect, collect, and interpret the past in order to inhibit social and political change. While academic historians sought objectivity, however imperfectly, the earliest public historians manufactured a past populated by apparently infallible role models of patriotism and morality. For example, Ann Pamela Cunningham established the Mount Vernon Ladies' Association (MVLA) in the 1850s to preserve the historic plantation owned by George Washington. Cunningham, a Southerner, believed that saving symbols of Americans' common heritage could stave off Civil War. MVLA perceived the historic homes of founding fathers as incubators of shared American values. In order to advance this interpretation, they eliminated reference to the presence of enslaved people at Mount Vernon. Acknowledging the centrality of slavery to the establishment of the nation would mean admitting to the profound contradictions and tensions at the heart of American identity and enflame the sectional conflicts the MVLA hoped to extinguish.[8]

Similarly, Maria Denning Van Rensselaer established the Colonial Dames of America in 1890. By then, commentators, policy makers, and nativists had begun to remark on the arrival of "new" kinds of immigrants to the United States: Eastern and Southern Europeans whose cultural traditions, religious beliefs, and habits of work seemed to make them unfit for American citizenship and potentially threatening to the American way of life. The Colonial Dames believed historic structures representing the establishment of the original colonies and the birthplace of American democracy could become spaces for moral education and Americanization. By describing the members of the nation's founding generation as individuals who had cast off "Old World" values, the Colonial Dames sought to normalize and promote assimilation. The sites they preserved became spaces for reinforcing a narrow set of American traditions.[9] Other influential organizations—including the Confederate Memorial Literary Society, the Daughters of the Confederacy, and the Association for the Preservation of Virginia Antiquities—sought to prevent businessmen and relic hunters from removing Civil War materials from the South and, more broadly, to defend against Northern influence on the South's economy, politics, and culture.[10] Their work included the preservation of historic sites, the memorialization of the Confederate dead, and the commemoration of Southern patriotism from Yorktown to Manassas, and it established White Southern identity as a stabilizing and civilizing force that could prevent African Americans from reshaping political and cultural norms. By the early decades of the twentieth century, national agencies were similarly engaged in assembling collections that could promote patriotism. National Park Service superintendents and Smithsonian curators believed that national collections could "Americanize" visitors, preventing them from asserting any alternative interpretations of the past that might challenge the nation's identity and values.[11] The practice of assembling museum collections reflected a broader cultural imperialism, and the organization and display of these collections tended to reinforce a belief in the superiority of Western Europeans and in the unassimilability of non-White and non-Western peoples.[12]

With the emergence of formal disciplines in the United States during the early twentieth century, historians, anthropologists, and others began to argue that scientific objectivity was the marker of academic rigor. The emphasis on patriotism and cultural purity that had justified preservation and influenced early collections revealed historic sites and museums as inherently subjective, damaging their evidentiary value. This subjectivity was compounded by the fact that women's voluntary associations had pioneered preservation, collecting, and historic site interpretation, the very practices that established public history as a field. They had justified their participation in this very public work by defining it as an extension of women's private sphere; they preserved houses and homes and collected Americana as part of their duty to protect America's moral center. Museum curators, hoping to position themselves within burgeoning professions, tended to organize their scientific specimens as study collections, emphasizing their use by students and scholars and displaying them as proof of scientific objectivity.

Historical artifacts proved problematic for advancing professionalism. Some were assembled as anthropological or ethnographic study collections, but materials associated with particular individuals were identified as "Americana" and curators found them difficult to categorize. This task often fell to women volunteers rather than the professional and typically male curatorial staff. At the Smithsonian, volunteers Rose Gouverneur Hoes and Cassie Myers Julian-James collected and displayed clothing worn by the various "hostesses" of the White House in order to inspire visitors to replicate good taste and good manners. By the turn of the twentieth century, academics interested in staking a claim to authority and cultural standing on the basis of scientific rather than emotional or moral measures of significance distanced themselves from museum collections as well as from historical societies, historic sites, and museums.[13] At the same time, curators and interpreters sought to defend their professionalism by concentrating on research and distancing themselves from the needs and interests of audiences. During the late twentieth century, as public historians worked to bring new audiences and new interpretations to historic sites and collections, they encountered resistance and found themselves embroiled in controversy. Such controversy, often dismissed as evidence of audience ignorance, can be better explained as a symptom of the extent to which these mutually constituting impulses to resist change and to protect authority had defined the landscape of public history and shaped organizational and institutional structures over time.[14]

The contributors to this volume do not deny the validity of the well-established histories of the field, broadly defined. Indeed, the existing scholarship has illuminated the origins of problems and tensions that continue to trouble public history practice. Our goal is to identify alternative pathways that can help historicize the smaller but no less significant impact that forward-looking, community-focused preservationists, collectors, educators, and others have had on the field. While it is tempting to try to identify a straight and consistent line from past to present-day radical practices, our work suggests this is often a fragmentary history, replicated and advanced not necessarily through formal institutionalization or professionalization but through personal friendships and social networks.[15] Our work attempts to connect the fragments, drawing attention to strands of influence that are woven deeply into the history of radical public history practices.

The volume is formally organized into four sections, each of which contains the work of one of the original thematic research groups. Reading these sections as organized provides a window into the concerns, conflicts, and innovations that shaped radical practices in specific fields. It also illuminates the particular approach taken by each *Radical Roots* research team. The members of the Oral History collaborative worked closely from a set of questions and observations advanced by Linda Shopes and Daniel R. Kerr and eloquently articulated in Kerr's piece, "Allan Nevins Is Not My Grandfather."[16] Kerr argues that the widely accepted historiography of oral history has promoted a "simplistic view of what oral history is" and has misrepresented its development over time. Kerr draws attention to a deeper history for the field, one rooted in the belief that collecting personal narratives could play a pivotal role in fostering political action and promoting social change. The essays that follow provide historical and contemporary examples of the precise oral history tradition Kerr's work illuminates. Judith Jennings highlights the work of Helen Matthews Lewis, who worked actively to connect oral history, research, and teaching with political organizing and advocacy. Anne M. Valk examines the role of feminist consciousness raising techniques in the evolution of oral history and explores the complex power relationships that shaped its use over time. Kristen Ana La Follette analyzes a tradition of politically aware theatrical uses of oral history in the Latinx community and demonstrates that verbatim scripts have been used to engage audiences and actors in conversation about pressing political issues. Her work not only makes a case for the inclusion of oral history–based theater as part of the field's radical tradition but also argues that the inclusion of Latinx oral history practices broadens our definition of the field. The final two contributions to the oral history section bring voices of contemporary practitioners into the project of defining radical practice, creating a dialogue among oral historians about the political value and community-based relevance of their work.

The next section of this volume explores the evolution of public history pedagogy. Contributors identified and analyzed the emergence of politically oriented and community-grounded approaches to teaching and learning both inside and outside of traditional educational spaces. Their efforts challenge the notion that public history education began in the 1970s, when the University of California, Santa Barbara, established its program. Rachel Donaldson argues that the oral history training at Camp Woodland in the Catskill Mountains was both enjoyable and politically significant, providing a vehicle for young campers to actively promote social justice. Burnis Morris examines Carter G. Woodson's political influence, arguing that his intellectual endeavors were driven by a deep concern about the devaluation of Black lives. Woodson's work illustrates the potential of inclusive pedagogical practices to foster a variety of movements for social justice. William S. Walker analyzes the pivotal role that Louis C. Jones played in twentieth-century museum studies. In aftermath of World War II, Jones argued that museum professionals must challenge elitism. His personal commitment to antiracism became an essential element of education in the Cooperstown Graduate Program and created the foundation for contemporary demands for inclusive approaches to museum staffing, collection, and interpretation. Denise D. Meringolo examines a short-lived experiment in public history education, the American Civilization Institute of Morristown, New Jersey (ACIM), as a point of origin for community-based, politically engaged pedagogy. She notes that the "radical" nature of public history training is defined as much by its context as by its intent. Elizabeth Belanger describes the contemporary resonance of projects like the ACIM and argues that not only must public history educators provide practical training; they must guide students through the emotional aspects—and discomfort—of community-based work. Her case study explores the ways in which community-university partnerships invite reflection on epistemology and process, and raises questions about how public history educators might acknowledge and diffuse the unequal power relationships that engaged learning can expose. The critical conversation that ends the section addresses some of the very questions Belanger raises. The participants suggest that success in community-based pedagogy is less about completing a deliverable and more about creating truly collaborative space, fostering meaningful dialogue, and addressing the systemic inequalities that can dampen creativity and restrict social justice.

The third section of this volume identifies and analyzes examples of experimentation in museum practice, offering a direct challenge to the widely accepted museum studies historiography. Clarissa J. Ceglio tracks the evolution of museums as visitor-centered social actors. Her contribution provides both a theoretical definition of radical museum work as socially aware and community-focused work and a close and critical examination of what that work looked like in practice during the 1930s. In that context, proponents expressed concern about how to differentiate persuasive social action in the cultural sector from more pernicious forms of propaganda. Today, public historians and their colleagues across related disciplines express similar worries about what it means to advance particular political perspectives. While Ceglio is examining large-scale trends in United States museums, Laura Schiavo's study recovers the neglected story of a single curator in an ethnically specific institution. She argues that a critical reexamination of small museums can reveal meaningful counternarrative histories and illuminate important, if not always successful, efforts to resist conservative ideas about collections, their potential meaning, and their appropriate use. Michèle Gates Moresi argues that the founding of the Anacostia Neighborhood Museum brought a Black political sensibility into the realm of the Smithsonian Institution. Museum staff engaged in a deeply collaborative process, enabling local residents to become partners in exhibition creation. The institution was, at least in its early years, both overtly politically engaged and profoundly responsive to the needs and interests of local people. Rebecca Amato analyzes the difficulty of maintaining a social justice–oriented museum agenda across time and through multiple contexts. Her work describes and critiques the Tenement Museum's unintentional but no less impactful role in gentrification during the early years of the twenty-first century. The final contributor to this section, Nicole A. Moore, reflects on her own experience interpreting slavery at plantation sites in the South. She describes both the personal sense of mission and the intense intellectual and emotional labor required to make radical interventions that can dismantle damaging and popular, romantic narratives about the past.

The fourth section of this volume examines the impact that amateurs and history buffs have made in the realms of collecting, protecting, and commemorating the past. These essays demonstrate that the act of preservation has long had radical potential. Lara Kelland offers a critical reexamination of the intersection between social justice organizing and community-authored history. While other scholars have identified the significance of this work in shaping the scholarship of social history, Kelland analyzes its impact in establishing social justice as a concern of public history. Her work suggests that public history can indeed serve the political interests of self-identified communities. Examining a similar trend from the opposite angle, Pero Dagbovie suggests that Black history as an academic discipline and a subject of formal scholarship has embodied qualities of radical public history. Shaped by both recognized scholars and those outside of the academy, Black history has been committed to establishing a firm foundation for collective action. To this end, the founders of Black history tended to place community-oriented history and the strategies of civic engagement at the center of their scholarship. Abigail Gautreau complicates this notion by examining the ways in which formal preservation—defined by policy and effected through official procedures of site nomination and approval—can create both opportunities and points of friction. By examining the case of a grassroots organization that became integrated into an established preservation organization, she raises important questions about the extent to which formal institutions can successfully counter dominant narratives and promote inclusive practices. Kristen Baldwin Deathridge offers something of a counterpoint. She argues that the history of preservation has been unnecessarily divided into two camps: one that took shape at the intersection where economic and governmental concerns meet and another that grew out of vernacular community needs. Her case studies suggest that preservation best serves the needs of local people when such impulses strike a balance between the interests of development and the interests of local people. Craig Stutman's essay traces the history and impact of a specific commemorative decision. The Germantown Mennonite Community in Pennsylvania issued one of the earliest protests against slavery in North America. The document became embedded in both the community's sense of identity and the larger memory of German immigrant history in the United States. In Germantown, preservation of the document and its memory enabled a commitment to social justice to flower and fostered the emergence over time of powerfully self-reflective and inclusive local public history practices even as national attitudes toward German heritage, the historic protest, and antiracist activism fluctuated wildly over time.

In addition to reading within each thematic section, the digital format encourages readers to approach this volume nonlinearly. Reading selections from across the volume reveals additional themes and points of intersection among the articles. For example, several authors in this volume identify connections between the progressive education movement, which emerged in Chicago in the late nineteenth century, and radical public history practices. First defined and tested by John Dewey, progressive education emphasized community engagement and insisted on respect for diversity. Through the first half of the twentieth century, progressive educators adapted Dewey's ideas to suit the needs and conditions of specific learning communities. During the 1920s, the members of the Progressive Education Association (founded in 1919) opposed the growing emphasis on data collection as a way to quantify learning. They saw intelligence tests and cost-benefit analysis as potentially undermining their efforts to foster emotional and creative development and as a threat to diversity and inclusion. Several authors in this volume have identified the values of progressive education in general and the influence of John Dewey in particular as having shaped core aspects of radical public history practice. Dewey's influence is evident in both Daniel R. Kerr's and Judith Jennings's work to trace the emergence of radical oral history practices, as well as in the efforts by Rachel Donaldson and Denise D. Meringolo to trace the development of public history pedagogy. These articles demonstrate that oral historians, folklorists, and teachers translated Dewey's emphasis on the civic value of education as a call to put historical inquiry to work to address the questions and concerns of local communities. Several authors in this collection follow these roots to the Highlander Folk School and its founder, Myles Horton, as well as to the social movements his work helped advance (see, for example, Kerr, Jennings, Kelland, and Donaldson). Horton's development of oral history practices and his use of personal narrative for political organizing bridged practices of collecting to social justice aims. Progressive educators and the radical public historians they inspired recognized embodied knowledge and firsthand experiences as relevant both for shaping an understanding of the past and for fostering productive political action. For most of the twentieth century, and certainly in the years prior to the culture wars of the 1990s, this element of radical practice did not really include practices of shared authority. There is an undeniable thread of elitism running through the history of progressivism. In the past, most reformers, educators, museum professionals, and others positioned themselves as saviors whose expert knowledge could "rescue" marginalized and disenfranchised people. Today, radical public historians practice self-reflection and reflection in action as a way to keep authority balanced and to honor various forms of expertise, from disciplinary to experiential. Nonetheless, progressive educators' understanding that intellectual learning must also include attention to emotional development and respect creativity was revolutionary, and it survives in contemporary radical public historians' efforts to promote empathy, facilitate dialogue, and diversify the delivery of historical interpretation well beyond the monograph.

Another selection of authors points to 1930s-era social experimentation as having shaped some of the beliefs and practices of radical public history. The influence of New Deal programs in the realm of public history has been well documented. The Civilian Conservation Corps transformed national parks and national forests, not only implementing protection measures but also building the roads, visitor centers, and comfort stations that made federal and state lands more visitor friendly. The Federal Writers' Project sought to document everyday life, collecting oral histories from average Americans, including people who had been born into slavery. The Historical Records Project and the Historic American Buildings Survey documented and organized a variety of collections across the country.[17] For the purposes of our inquiry, reexamining program-specific outcomes like these is less important than identifying and analyzing shifts in philosophy and practice. Clarissa J. Ceglio argues that the crisis of the Depression and the sense of urgency that drove New Deal collection and conservation projects also inspired museum professionals to experiment with civic engagement. In the 1930s, leaders in the American Association of Museums began to reimagine museums as social spaces, less dedicated to the reproduction of exclusive knowledge and more attentive to contemporary social concerns and focused on visitor needs. Their work, disrupted by World War II, has too often been dismissed as "biased" and overlooked by scholars. Yet the significance of such experimentation for theorizing radical public history practice is made evident by Laura Schiavo's study of innovations in the Museum of Jewish Ceremonial Objects during the 1930s. Curator Paul Romanoff and his wife, Bertha, promoted the museum and its collections as useful for countering anti-Semitism and promoting empathy and mutual understanding. Their efforts to attract a broad public audience were not appreciated by the museum board, and Romanoff paid a high personal cost for his radical vision. Nonetheless, these essays suggest that the American cultural front gave shape to radical forms of public history practice during the 1930s.[18] While it failed to completely replace the racism, sexism, and ethnocentrism deeply embedded in American political and cultural institutions, it did create moments in which educators, oral historians, folklorists, and museum professionals could foster small realignments of power. While many—if not most—of these realignments were temporary, William S. Walker identifies at least one important, permanent site of influence that continues to advance radical museum practices. The dialogic, collaborative, antiracist, and activist model of museum practice that defines the mission and values of the Cooperstown Graduate Program emerged from early efforts to frame museums as social spaces.

Several scholars in this volume identify the roots of radical public history practice in a variety of social movements, particularly—but not exclusively—those that emerged in the United States after World War II. Grassroots activists in the African American civil rights movement, the women's rights movement, and the American Indian Movement as well as in Latinx, LGBTQ, and other social and political movements understood efforts to collect and interpret a communal past as crucial for the development of a viable political identity. Lara Kelland argues that not only did community-centered and community-based preservation and history-making projects serve to counter white supremacist, male-dominated, heteronormative narratives; they also enabled communities to assert authority over their own past and control over their own future. If we recognize this dual agenda as central to the evolution of radical public history practice, we must also denounce the extent to which White practitioners have been placed at the center of our field's historiography. Pero Dagbovie argues that it is reasonable to identify the origins of public history in the emergence of Black history. He and Burnis Morris both argue that Carter G. Woodson must be acknowledged as a founder of radical public history, because Woodson's work was shaped by the dual goal of challenging White racism and empowering Black communities. Michèle Gates Moresi explores the effort to institutionalize this agenda at the Anacostia Neighborhood Museum, tracking the success of early efforts to engage the community. Daniel R. Kerr explores the ways in which a commitment to social justice shaped the particular form of oral history practiced and advanced by Jeremy Brecher. Kristen Ana La Follette argues that culturally specific traditions within the Latinx community established oral history performance as a tool for political communication and organizing. Yet these articles suggest that as self-identified communities and the radical practices they adopt move away from the margins and closer to the center of American culture, their work can lose some of its counternarrative power. As a result, practices designed and implemented with radical intent became less viable and therefore less visible over time, and their influence has been difficult for many researchers to recognize and trace.

Despite this difficulty, the essays in this collection suggest that important values and habits of mind worthy of both closer examination and better articulation define radical public history practice. It seems evident that this work is built on a foundation of optimism, however foolish. Abigail Gautreau argues that individuals and communities that engage in preservation are in a unique position to transform the field and that the resistance to—and failure of—these efforts at transformation is a sign of the power and potential of such work. Craig Stutman demonstrates that histories of slavery and abolition, often ignored because they are too "difficult" to reconcile with ideals of contemporary life, can become powerful sites for the creation of inclusive communities. Kristen Ana La Follette, Shane Bernardo, Maria E. Cotera, Fernanda Espinosa, and Amy Starecheski suggest that gathering firsthand accounts of both everyday life and political organizing from marginalized communities is an assertion of power that can create emotional connections and build viable political movements. Nicole A. Moore draws attention to the small interactions between interpreters and audiences that allow dialogue to flourish. Together, these contributors highlight the belief, essential for motivating radical public historians, that the work of collecting, analyzing, and interpreting the past can have a powerful, positive impact on contemporary life, providing clarity and direction for those working to understand and address injustice. At the same time, radical public historians remain wary of the exclusive practices of cultural institutions. Many resist efforts to diminish the radical potential of stories, artifacts, and experiences through the quantifying acts of cataloging and transcribing. Questions about how to ensure broad accessibility and actively counter both the further marginalization of particular histories and communities and the diminishment of the political potential inscribed in collections are evident throughout this volume.[19]

Those questions are amplified by contributors whose work exposes deep and unchallenged inequality in public history broadly and in radical public history in particular. All the contributors to this volume suggest that a profoundly antiracist and antisexist world view lends a sense of urgency to radical public history practices in both their historical and their contemporary articulations. Whether it is the founders of the American Civilization Institute described by Denise D. Meringolo, the actors and oral historians animated by Kristen Ana La Follette, the community-based historians illuminated by Lara Kelland, or the founders of Black history highlighted by Burnis Morris and Pero Dagbovie, these pages are full of individuals and organizations dedicated to harnessing history-making for the dual purpose of creating an inclusive historical record and countering immediate oppression. At the same time, the combination of unexamined privilege and the racist, misogynist, and heteronormative belief systems deeply embedded in American social, political, and cultural structures continually undermines the impact of radical public history and its civic engagement strategies. Anne M. Valk points to the influence of feminist "consciousness raising" on radical oral history. Designed to help individuals recognize private experiences as part of a larger misogyny in order to foster political action, in actual practice, consciousness raising was troubled by questions about power: Who dictated the terms of the discussion? Who determined which experiences women had in common and which were racially or ethnically or religiously specific and therefore outside the realm of feminism? Who controlled the preservation, use, and distribution of women's personal experiences? Kristen Baldwin Deathridge recognizes that preservation has long served middle-class interests and endangered the political interests of less affluent communities. She argues that preservationists must shift their focus to the protection of broadly inclusive historical landscapes. Rebecca Amato demonstrates the difficulty of this task. The creation of a politically viable counternarrative is undermined when preservation freezes time, cutting off the past from the present materially as well as narratively. Her work suggests that it may be impossible to protect both the political interests of marginalized communities and the economic interests courted by preservationists. Taken together, these authors suggest social justice is only served when public historians are willing to facilitate dialogue about persistent inequality, connecting past to present in unpredictable and perhaps ahistorical ways. The authors also remind us that radical public history requires radical self-reflection and responsiveness.

Despite these shortcomings, radical public history is grounded in the belief that history-making must be broadly relevant. Long before Roy Rosenzweig and David Thelen produced their landmark study, *Presence of the Past*, radical museum professionals, preservationists, oral historians, and educators conceptualized history as a well of experience from which we might learn rather than as a model we should emulate. As a result, they were comfortable illuminating difficult or uncomfortable pasts in order to help identify persistent social ills and to articulate viable political platforms. For this reason, the pioneers of radical practice advanced the idea that personal experiences are historically and politically significant, and efforts to collect, record, and share personal experiences are necessary for advancing social justice. Working from these beliefs, radical public historians in the past—as today—have worked to build empathy and understanding by fostering dialogue, not by constructing "definitive" narratives. Given this, Elizabeth Belanger argues that public history education must help students develop skills like mindfulness, empathy, self-awareness, and openness so that the next generation of professionals is prepared for work that can be as uncomfortable as it is rewarding. In their conversation about public history pedagogy, Rebecca Amato, Gabrielle Bendiner-Viani, Dipti Desai, Denise D. Meringolo, and Mary Rizzo explore the challenges of developing pedagogical approaches to public history that are sustainable, actively engaged with community interests, and valuable to both the intellectual and emotional development of our students.

Recognizing and reclaiming a past for radical public history is made complicated by the fact that "radical" can only be understood in context. Projects and practices that were designed to challenge injustice in the late nineteenth century, the early twentieth century, the 1930s, the 1960s, and even the 1990s now appear shortsighted. But both scholars and practitioners have been too quick to criticize the failures and limitations of some early practitioners, missing the opportunity to learn from their experiments. Tracing the genealogy of a field—like the genealogy of a family—presumes longevity and generational continuity, but the work of radical public history has often been ephemeral. It has resisted institutionalization and often failed to attract sustainable financial and intellectual support. Its strategies persisted somewhat haphazardly. To some extent, this transient quality is central to radicalism: it emphasizes immediacy and acknowledges that needs and interests change over time. Our volume suggests that the ideals expressed in radical public history have survived and evolved not through the establishment of permanent structures but through the creation and nurturance of social networks of practice. Further, these networks can be difficult to identify because they exist outside the boundaries of disciplines. The discipline of history remains central to public history practice because we are applying historical methods and advancing understandings of the past. However, the contributors to this volume remind us that we must look to other fields—including folklore, education, and oral history—to find our radical roots. Radical public historians are not simply interdisciplinary in practice. We are interdisciplinary in origin.

Some final notes: First, following the lead of the Chicago Manual of Style, we have decided to capitalize *Black* and *White* to refer to race or ethnicity throughout this volume. However, when writing *white supremacy* we do not capitalize *white*. We also capitalize *Brown* when referring to *Brown people*.

Second, we are acutely aware of the silences and absences in this volume. Despite our efforts during 2017 and 2018 to recruit additional contributors—with an eye toward expanding geographical scope and incorporating a more broadly inclusive set of contributors and topics—there is no ignoring the fact that many perspectives are absent. We do not pretend otherwise. Our hope is that this project will inspire others to engage in similar research that can deepen, complicate, and even contradict our arguments. While the production of this volume needed to reach an end, the research is ongoing.

Notes

1. Cathy Stanton, "Hardball History: On the Edge of Politics, Advocacy, and Activism," *History@Work: A Public History Commons*, National Council on Public History, March 25, 2015, accessed August 29, 2021, https://ncph.org/history-at-work/hardball-history-stanton.
2. William Adair, Benjamin Filene, and Laura Koloski, eds., *Letting Go? Sharing Historical Authority in a User-Generated World* (New York: Routledge, 2011).
3. Rebecca Conard, "Public History as Reflective Practice: An Introduction," *Public Historian* 25, no. 1 (Winter 2006): 9–13.
4. Denise D. Meringolo, *Museums, Monuments, and National Parks: Toward a New Genealogy of Public History* (Amherst: University of Massachusetts Press, 2012).
5. Josh Halprin, "Oral History and Homelessness," American University, College of Arts and Sciences, November 4, 2011, http://www.american.edu/cas/news/daniel-kerr-homelessness-oral-history.cfm; Daniel R. Kerr, *Derelict Paradise: Homelessness and Urban Development in Cleveland, Ohio* (Amherst: University of Massachusetts Press, 2011).
6. The members of the 2014 working group, facilitated by Daniel R. Kerr and Denise D. Meringolo, were Elizabeth Belanger, Christopher Benning, Peter Bunten, Julie Davis, Abigail Gautreau, Jodi Giesbrecht, Lara Kelland, Kristen La Follette, Laura Schiavo, Linda Shopes, and Craig Stutman. In addition, meeting attendees who joined the working group as members of the audience were fully integrated into our discussion and several—including Kristen Baldwin Deathridge—stayed with the project. I regret that I did not preserve a complete list of attendees. Daniel R. Kerr remained with the project as a key member of the oral history interest group, but he opted not to serve as coeditor of the larger project. While not all of the working group participants submitted an article for this volume, they were instrumental in shaping the project inquiry. Linda Shopes played a particularly critical role. She stayed with the project for its entirety, leading the oral history inquiry, organizing panel discussions at meetings of the Oral History Association, and serving as a true partner in facilitating communication and deepening analysis. We are all in her debt.
7. "OAH/NPS Projects (1994–Present)," Organization of American Historians, accessed November 15, 2018, accessed August 29, 2021, https://www.oah.org/the-oah-national-park-service-collaboration/; Susan Ferentinos, *History in Service of*

the Future, accessed November 12, 2018, http://susanferentinos.com/wpblog/ (see specifically her CV).

8   Patricia West, *Domesticating History: The Political Origins of America's House Museums* (Washington, DC: Smithsonian Books, 1999).

9   James M. Lindgren, *Preserving Historic New England: Preservation, Progressivism, and the Remaking of Memory* (New York: Oxford University Press, 1995).

10 Reiko Hillyer, "Relics of Reconciliation: The Confederate Museum and Civil War Memory in the New South," *Public Historian* 33, no. 4 (November 2011): 35–62; James Lindgren, "'Virginia Needs Living Heroes': Historic Preservation in the Progressive Era," *Public Historian* 13, no. 1 (Winter 1991): 9–24.

11 These are ideas I discussed at length in my book *Museums, Monuments, and National Parks: Toward a New Genealogy of Public History* (Amherst: University of Massachusetts Press, 2012).

12 Steven Conn, *Museums and American Intellectual Life, 1876–1926* (Chicago: University of Chicago Press, 1998).

13 Conn. See also Peter Novick, *That Noble Dream: The "Objectivity Question" and the American Historical Profession* (Cambridge: Cambridge University Press, 1988).

14 James Oliver Horton and Lois Horton, eds., *Slavery and Public History: The Tough Stuff of American Memory* (Chapel Hill: University of North Carolina Press, 2008); Richard Handler and Eric Gable, *The New History in an Old Museum: Creating the Past at Colonial Williamsburg* (Durham, NC: Duke University Press, 1997); Edward T. Linenthal and Tom Englehardt, eds., *History Wars: The Enola Gay and Other Battles for the American Past* (New York: Holt Paperbacks, 1996).

15 This finding echoes the notion of public history as a social practice articulated by Keith A. Erekson, *Everybody's History: Indiana's Lincoln Inquiry and the Quest to Reclaim a President's Past* (Amherst: University of Massachusetts Press, 2013).

16 This article was previously published in *Oral History Review* 43, no. 2 (2016): 367–91. It is reprinted with permission.

17 There is significant project-specific literature each of these programs. For broader program analysis, see, for example, Neil M. Mahar, *Nature's New Deal: The Civilian Conservation Corps and the Roots of the American Environmental Movement* (New York: Oxford University Press, 2009); Jerrold Hirsch, *Portrait of America: A Cultural History of the Federal Writers' Project* (Chapel Hill: University of North Carolina Press, 2003).

18 Michael Denning, *The Cultural Front: The Laboring of American Culture in the Twentieth Century*, new ed. (New York: Verso, 2011).

19 There is a movement among archivists, librarians, museum professionals, and others to address these questions. Some have adopted terms like "decolonizing collections" and "abolitionist archives" to describe work that can do more than simply increase diversity in collections but also create more broadly inclusive practices that transform our understanding of what collections are and do. See, for example, Bergis Jules, "Architecting Sustainable Futures: Exploring Funding Models in Community Based Archives," *Medium*, June 19, 2018, https://medium.com/

community-archives/architecting-sustainable-futures-exploring-funding-models-in-community-based-archives-da9a7a856cbe; Jarrett M. Drake and Stacie M. Williams, "Power to the People: Documenting Police Violence in Cleveland," *Journal of Critical Library and Information Studies* 1, no. 2 (2017), https://doi.org/10.24242/jclis.v1i2.33; Amy Lonetree, *Decolonizing Museums: Representing Native America in National and Tribal Museums* (Chapel Hill: University of North Carolina Press, 2012).

RAISING CONSCIOUSNESS OR RAISING HELL

NEW NARRATIVES FOR ORAL HISTORY

Allan Nevins Is Not My Grandfather

The Roots of Radical Oral History Practice in the United States

Daniel R. Kerr

> People know the basic answers to their problems, but they need to go further than that, and you can, by asking questions and getting them stimulated, coax them to move, in discussion, beyond their experience.... And when you begin to expand the experience and share your own, people will ask each other questions.... If you listen to people and work from what they tell you, within a few days their ideas get bigger and bigger. They go back in time, ahead in their imagination. You just continue to build on people's own experience; it is the basis for their learning.
> —Myles Horton, *The Long Haul*

In the fall of 1996, I brought a recorder to Public Square in Cleveland, Ohio, to interview people experiencing homelessness.[1] At the time, I had no idea who Allan Nevins was, nor did I have any formal training in oral history. Rather, the works of popular educators such as Paulo Freire, Myles Horton, and Augusto Boal inspired my decision to use a recorder to listen to people reflect on their own experiences.[2] Each of these educators embraced a pedagogy that emphasized working with oppressed communities, drawing on people's personal experiences as a starting point, relating these experiences to others within the community, and then moving beyond them to gain a greater understanding of structural oppression. For me, popular education was a process that was related to, but distinct from, the radical housing activism that I had participated in in the preceding years as a squatter in New York City. Rather than explain to people what the issues were that impacted their lives and then attempt to organize them to join an action that they had not planned, I would begin by listening. I ended up spending the next decade working on the Cleveland Homeless Oral History Project (CHOHP). I interviewed nearly two hundred people about their experiences with homelessness and, even more important, their analysis of its causes. The narrators defined the issues that shaped their lives and developed the strategies that they would use to address the issues of day-labor exploitation, the criminalization of homelessness, and miserable shelter conditions. When the narrators arrived at their strategies for making changes, I supported and joined in with their mobilizations. Reflection and action became intertwined; oral history proved to be a powerful tool for initiating change.

As I presented and published this work, I received a warm reception from other oral historians.[3] I came to see myself as an oral historian, immersed myself in the literature of "the field," and eventually taught graduate-level courses that trained others in the methods of oral history. By then I had learned who Allan Nevins was, and his name made its way onto my syllabus as the founder of oral history. Until I started researching more deeply for this article, I viewed my professional success as a product of fortuitous timing: I was lucky enough to bridge oral history practice with pedagogies drawn from popular education just at the moment when the field was ready for it. I believed the histories of oral history that traced a progressive advance in the field from an original fixation on elites and archives to one that had become more democratic, theoretically sophisticated, and ethically grounded. What neither I nor the existing histories of our field had taken into account, however, was that the very embrace of bottom-up oral history had in fact sprung from the same sources of inspiration that informed my work. It is, in fact, deeply inaccurate to assume that oral history originated in a concern with archival documentation and only later came to focus on social justice.

In every iteration I have encountered, the genealogy of oral history in North America begins with Allan Nevins. While many versions cursorily point to examples of earlier endeavors that drew upon oral accounts, such as the work of Herodotus, the Zhou dynasty's scribes, African griots, Hubert Howe Bancroft, and the Federal Writers' Project of the New Deal, these examples are treated as prehistories.⁴ The official history begins with Allan Nevins establishing "the oral history project" at Columbia University in 1948, the same year the first American-made tape recorders were sold.⁵ With our identification of Nevins as the founder of our field, we position the archival and technological aspects of oral history at the core of our practice. As the story goes, Nevins turned to recording interviews with elite men because he feared that the rise of the telephone age posed significant threats to the historical record as oral communication displaced letter writing. For Nevins, oral histories were evidentiary documents that needed to be preserved so that future historians could draw on them to produce better histories. His emphasis on oral history's evidentiary value, as well as his fixation on elites, have come to define what we consider to be the relevant past of oral history in the 1950s.⁶

Casting Allan Nevins as the founder of oral history promotes a simplistic view of what oral history is; it also misrepresents its development over time. In the first place, the focus on Nevins ignores the development of other contemporaneous practices that I will address here and thus makes the interest in interviewing everyday people in the 1960s and 1970s appear to be a major shift in the field. Second, our conventional origin story misrepresents that shift, in turn, by arguing that, while the practitioners in those decades broadened the pool of narrators by interviewing the working class, women, people of color, and LGBTQ people, they continued to have a positivistic fixation and defined their oral histories solely as archival documents. Not yet understanding the concept of shared authority, they tasked themselves only with interpreting these documents as evidence. Finally, these oral historians' supposedly limited understanding of subjective narratives set the stage for what is presented as the next great shift in the field: by the late 1970s and 1980s, as the argument goes, oral historians began moving away from seeing their interviews as documents and began to view them as texts. They turned away from their earlier embrace of objectivity and positivism as they recognized the interpretive value of the intersubjective dimensions of the oral history interview.⁷

Linda Shopes has challenged the neatness and totality of these presumed shifts, arguing that some oral historians recognized the narrative elements of their interviews much earlier than this broadly accepted time line would suggest. Furthermore, she points out that a substantial majority of oral history publications still utilize oral histories as documents rather than texts.⁸ Joan Sangster has also urged us to move beyond this "onward and upward story in which each new academic orientation theoretically surpasses the one before." This framing of oral history's past precludes us from seeing the "acuity of previous work" and "the limitations of current writing."[9] These critiques by Sangster and Shopes suggest that we may in fact have simply imagined that there ever was a "theoretical turn in oral history." Many practitioners thought more complexly about narratives prior to the so-called turn, and others continue to think in a positivist fashion even today. The construct of an earlier turn away from a fixation on elites is just as troublesome. It ignores a whole body of work done by radicals outside of academia. While British oral historians have embraced their socialist and radical forbearers, those of us in the United States have erased our own.[10]

Our founding myth served a purpose that is no longer helpful. Identifying Nevins as our founder and making a case for our newfound theoretical rigor helped legitimate the field of oral history within the halls of academia. Intriguingly, those whose contributions have either been erased or devalued by this narrative principally worked outside of academia or had been blacklisted from academia. Today, however, we have other more pressing needs than legitimating oral history in academia. We live in a historic moment marked by profound economic instabilities and dislocations, deepening inequalities, anti-immigrant attacks, and public displays of police violence. We also live amid the emergence of new social movements and a flourishing of radical oral history projects that seek to do more than document the world; they seek to play a role in transforming it. The time has come to reclaim our more radical past so that we can as oral historians more effectively address our present.

With this article I do not intend to replace our founding mythology; doing so will require a collaborative endeavor, as there are many traditions that shape the practices of those of us who envision oral history as a powerful tool that can support movement building. The tradition I draw on is the one that comes out of the pedagogies of popular education, where change and social transformation begin with personal reflection. What I seek to do here is reflect on the sources of inspiration for my own work and use that understanding to trace one now largely forgotten branch of our genealogy. My hope is that others will do the same and that together we can create a robust new family tree.

Recovering a Lost Branch of Oral History's Past

Our fixation on recording technologies, archives, and academia has prompted us to ignore substantial portions of what oral history is. More central to our practice than our production of recordings, transcripts, collections, articles, and monographs is the fact that we facilitate dialogues grounded in personal experiences and interpretive reflections on the past. If we positioned that work at the center of what we do as oral historians, we could then look back and identify the people who have inspired this aspect of our practice, regardless of whether they considered themselves to be oral historians. When the Phillips Company introduced the portable cassette recorder in 1963, there was already a well-established social movement that recognized the power that grew out of reflections on personal experience.

This movement can be traced back to at least the 1930s, when Myles Horton, the founder of the Highlander Folk School, began to develop the practices for working with personal narratives that would play a pivotal role in the work of oral historians who followed in his footsteps. Horton began working on his vision to create a school for adult education in the mountains of Tennessee in 1931. The school, Horton argued, would need to be "yeasty," one where small groups "could have the potential to multiply themselves and fundamentally change society." Its principal goal would be to teach people to "value their own experience, to analyze their own experience, and to know how to make decisions."[11] Horton had been an active Socialist and had studied with Socialist theologian Reinhold Niebuhr at Union Theological Seminary. He later went on to the University of Chicago, where he thought more deeply about conflict and social change through his discussions with sociologist Robert E. Park, drew upon ideas about progressive education from reading John Dewey, and reflected on the ideals of participatory democracy with Jane Addams. Horton himself was inspired by his predecessors and was unstinting in his efforts to understand all he could about past practices that could make his own future work more consequential. Through his connections to the Socialist Party of America, he raised funds to start the Highlander Folk School in the mountains west of Chattanooga, Tennessee, in 1932.[12]

From the 1930s through the 1960s, Highlander played a significant role in two major social movements: the industrial union movement and the civil rights movement. Highlander's earliest workshops included miners and workers from the textile, upholstery, and furniture industries. After the Congress of Industrial Organizations formed in 1935, it designated Highlander as its official educational training center for the South. Highlander continued in that capacity until 1949, when it severed ties with the CIO as the union embraced anticommunism and banished left-wing unions from its fold. As its interest in working with unions waned, Highlander decided to focus on antiracist work in the South. Over the next decade and a half, figures such as Martin Luther King Jr., Rosa Parks, Andrew Young, Julian Bond, and Stokely Carmichael all attended workshops at the school.[13]

The workshops, which lasted from a weekend to several weeks, were always fluid and grounded in the realities of those who participated. Horton argued, "There is no method to learn from Highlander. What we do involves trusting people and believing in their ability to think for themselves."[14] While the participants designed the program and agenda, Highlander staff shaped the workshops by choosing the people to invite. The staff only invited grassroots leaders who represented the organizations that they belonged to back in their home communities. Thus when working with unions, they invited the shop stewards, people who worked directly with the rank and file. And during the civil rights movement in the early sixties, they led a series of workshops for Black beauticians, barbers, and schoolteachers—people who were economically independent of Whites and who were viewed as having the potential for grassroots leadership. Throughout, they only invited people deemed to be dealing with big problems, who were seeking "basic changes in the structure of society."[15]

Myles Horton drew upon what he termed "a two-eye" theory of teaching, keeping one eye on the point people started from while focusing the other eye on where they might arrive. As part of this approach, he sought to create "circles of learners" comprised of people who shared similar problems. The term *circle* was used intentionally, highlighting the fact that there was no lead educator: the goal of the staff was not to direct the learning but to create a relaxed atmosphere in which participants could share their personal experiences freely. The circle required participants to listen to each other's stories and thus to stretch their thinking and put their own experiences in the context of others'. Drawing on the group members' knowledge, they then analyzed their problems and learned how to transform their society from the bottom up. Importantly, for Horton, the foundation of social transformation rested on narratives of personal experience. But these narratives were starting points, not ending points. And they were not seen as static, but emergent in the midst of collective dialogue. The goal was for learners to "*go beyond* their [current] state of thinking."[16]

Highlander primarily envisioned its role as a retreat center where grassroots leaders came to reflect on their experiences from their home communities. By the mid-1950s, however, several workshop participants, including Septima Clark, a Black schoolteacher from Charleston, South Carolina, called on Highlander to build a program of Citizenship Schools. Their goal was to bring the Highlander workshop approach to Black people in the communities they lived in across the South. These schools would not only teach people to read and write so that they could register to vote but also seek to cultivate activists. Rather than bring a program to people, Horton argued that the Citizenship Schools, if they were to be successful, needed to "start listening to the people themselves." Horton turned the project over to Clark, who joined the Highlander staff.[17]

As the schools expanded in number under Clark's direction, they drew the attention of the Southern Christian Leadership Conference (SCLC). Ella Baker, a Socialist who had a long history as a community organizer, was then working with the SCLC and convinced Martin Luther King Jr. to partner with Highlander to run the schools.[18] Worried about the growing size of the Citizenship Schools program, Horton turned it over entirely to SCLC in 1961. That same year, the state of Tennessee revoked Highlander's charter and seized the school, arguing that it was a communist organization. It would be a decade before Highlander would get a new charter and start over as the Highlander Research and Education Center.[19]

Septima Clark continued to run the Citizenship Schools under the SCLC, which ultimately trained over ten thousand teachers for the program.[20] Implicitly critiquing the charismatic leadership style of Martin Luther King Jr., Baker argued, "Strong people don't need strong leaders."[21] After the student-led sit-in movement spread across the South in 1960, she organized the conference of sit-in leaders at Shaw University that led to the creation of the Student Nonviolent Coordinating Committee (SNCC). She inspired them to embrace a radical and democratic approach to community organizing. And Baker and Clark would subsequently shape the curriculum of the Freedom Schools that SNCC established as the foundation of its efforts to organize sharecroppers in Mississippi in the mid-1960s. Mirroring Horton's approach, Baker believed "firmly in the right of the people who were under the heel to be the ones to decide what action they were going to take to get [out] from under their oppression."[22] The Freedom Schools would provide the spaces where people could draw on their experiences to think strategically about how they could transform the world around them. While Horton had focused on establishing a retreat for grassroots leaders, Baker and Clark extended the principles of popular education to base communities across the South.[23]

Staughton Lynd, who served as the director of SNCC's Freedom Schools in 1964, played a pivotal role in translating the core principles of adult popular education into the field of oral history. He and his wife, Alice Lynd, engaged in one of the earliest efforts to incorporate the portable cassette recorder into popular education practice.[24] They also had the audacity to call what they did oral history, and our failure to understand how their methodology drew upon ideas from Horton, Clark, and Baker has impeded our ability to recognize their theoretical sophistication.

The Lynds' most significant contributions to the field of oral history happened after the history department at Yale University denied Staughton Lynd tenure as a result of his visit to Hanoi during the Vietnam War. His antiwar activities led to him being blacklisted in academia.[25] Since Staughton was unable to gain a university position, the Lynds moved to Chicago, where Staughton taught in Saul Alinsky's school for radicals in the late 1960s. It was during this period that they engaged in what they termed a "guerilla history" project in Gary, Indiana, in which they conducted oral histories with older rank-and-file workers in hopes of building cross-generational dialogues that could empower young working-class people.[26] Sharing Horton's interest in working with grassroots leaders, they also engaged self-identified organizers in a series of community forums and writers' workshops.[27]

Their project had clear parallels to the structure of learning circles at Highlander. Recognizing the project participants as "equals" who had "expert knowledge," the Lynds sought to start with personal reflections from people who shared an experience of oppression in common: "Experience was the heart of the matter."[28] Through collective telling and listening, narrators put their individual experiences into the context of others' experiences and used their dialogue as a lens to understand structures of power. What was new, however, was that the Lynds explicitly sought to generate cross-generational discussions by interviewing elders and sharing the content of these interviews with a new generation of workers. Furthermore, they introduced the idea of recording these reflections and publishing edited portions of the interviews in a book, *Rank and File: Personal Histories by Working-Class Organizers*.

Staughton Lynd, who would become a leading figure in the bottom-up history movement, approached oral history in a very different way than our reductionist critique of the era suggests. Our histories of oral history credit bottom-up historians with including new voices in the historical record, but they also criticize the practitioners of that era for supposedly viewing oral histories simplistically as unmediated evidence that required no interpretation. In response to criticisms that their approach lacked sophistication, however, Staughton Lynd emphasized that they were not concerned with "rescuing the voices of the people 'below'" in order to enrich the archives and benefit future academic historians.[29] Both he and Alice Lynd saw *Rank and File* as a means to extend the listening circle that was a central component of the pedagogical principles of popular education. The intended audience for their "oral history from the bottom up," as they envisioned it, comprised other industrial workers: they conceived of the book less as an end product and more as a tool to facilitate further dialogue among workers who were geographically isolated from one another.[30] They thus made a deliberate choice not to offer their conclusive interpretations of the interviews; rather, they saw their role as that of "a catalyst, and organizer."[31] They also intended to unsettle the reader, as the narratives contained perspectives that were contradictory and had stark political and interpretive differences. The question was not whether the oral histories should be further interpreted, but rather who should be doing the interpreting. Recognizing their effort to decenter intellectual authority as a methodological contribution, Lynd argued that radical historians should embrace oral history, which was "like history from the bottom up carried a step further because it's people at the bottom doing their own history."[32]

The Lynds' work inspired a whole new generation of oral historians, and they introduced many of the ideas we associate with oral history's theoretical turn. For example, in an essay published in *Oral History Review* in 1976, Alice Hoffman argued that the importance of the Lynds was not that they interviewed people from below, but rather that they had redefined what it meant to be a historian: "The oral history process unearths many natural historians in many settings, from steel towns to rural Appalachia."[33] The Lynds' work explicitly acknowledged the shared authority embedded within the oral histories they had conducted. The Lynds also thoughtfully worked out a resolution to the problems posed by power imbalances within the interview. They called for embracing a concept of "accompaniment," where two people seeking to bridge a divide come together as they are, not pretending they are something they are not; recognize each other's expertise; and walk "side by side with one another on a common journey." Foreshadowing Alessandro Portelli's essay, "Research as an Experiment in Equality," Staughton Lynd concluded, "'Accompaniment' thus understood presupposes, not uncritical deference, but equality."[34]

Paulo Freire further translated the core principles of popular education with the publication of *Pedagogy of the Oppressed*, which came out in English for the first time in 1970. While Freire—like Horton, Baker, and Clark—did not identify as an oral historian, his ideas would be quickly embraced by those who did. Freire, a Brazilian educator and Christian Socialist, had established literacy learning circles with sugarcane workers in Recife, Brazil, at the same time Septima Clark was directing the literacy campaigns of the Citizenship Schools. As the state of Tennessee shuttered Highlander, a military coup in Brazil led to Freire's imprisonment and eventual exile. While facing severe persecution in Brazil, he was offered a position as a visiting professor at Harvard in 1969. Unlike Staughton Lynd, who had been blacklisted from academia, Freire was uniquely positioned to lend academic credibility to many of the same pedagogical principles that informed the work of Horton, Baker, Clark, and the Lynds.[35]

In *Pedagogy of the Oppressed*, Freire argued that in critical pedagogy, oppression and its causes were the "objects of reflection by the oppressed." Like Horton, Freire envisioned this process of reflection beginning with the oppressed examining their own "concrete situation" and doing so in dialogue with others who shared a similar situation. Reality, for Freire, was not something that independently existed in a static state and merely needed to be observed. Rather, people socially constituted "reality in process, in transformation" through their experiences, perceptions, and dialogue. For the popular educator, the goal was to work with the oppressed to identify the "generative themes" that were found within "the thought-language with which men refer to reality, the levels at which they perceive that reality, and their view of the world." Through intervening in that socially and linguistically constituted reality, the oppressed gained historical awareness and consciousness.[36]

Freire distinguished his popular education approach both from traditional research practices and from top-down political approaches. He warned that there was a significant danger that the educator might shift the focus of investigation away from identifying "generative themes" toward a focus on the people themselves, "thereby treating the people as objects of investigation." Popular educators should neither manipulate people's ideas nor naïvely adopt those ideas as their own. Rather, Freire proposed a synthesis whereby educators identified with people's ideas *and* posed them as a problem for consideration by the people themselves. In a formulation similar to the Lynds' conception of accompaniment, he argued that the popular educator "does not consider himself the proprietor of history or of men, or the liberator of the oppressed; but he does commit himself, within history, to fight at their side."[37]

Helen Matthews Lewis, the "grandmother of Appalachian studies," one of the founders of the field of participatory action research and a self-proclaimed oral historian, became one of the first United States–based popular educators to draw on Freire's work. When the newly named Highlander School for Research and Education reopened in 1971, Lewis also became a pivotal figure within that organization and played a role in widening its social justice work to include environmental and community health issues. Furthermore, she emphasized the importance of understanding regional change in a global context. These issues came to the forefront in the early 1970s as the coal industry initiated strip mining in Appalachia, prompting major social and environmental disruptions in the region.[38]

Helen Lewis drew upon oral history as the starting point for the economics education curriculum she developed at Highlander and brought two long-term projects she worked on in Jellico, Tennessee, and Ivanhoe, Virginia. Rooted in participatory action research, this curriculum taught community members how to assess their community needs and recognize their existing resources as they began to conceive potential development strategies that would allow them to build sustainable economies for their own benefit. For Lewis, grounding the process in people's personal experiences was essential, and initiating the research with an oral history project served that purpose. Community-based researchers interviewed each other, as well as hundreds of other members of their community, and they drew upon these interviews to analyze the economic changes that impacted their lives. In addition to gathering information, the interviews served as an important tool to mobilize widespread discussion about the economic problems that the community was facing. The project participants Lewis worked with produced theatrical performances that drew from the oral histories, developed history books and museum exhibits, and wrote poems and songs inspired by the interviews. Collective analysis of the interviews helped the local groups recognize common issues they were facing so that they could prioritize development strategies.[39]

Like Freire, as well as a growing number of oral historians who would follow her in the 1980s, Lewis acknowledged the issue of unequal power relations in research. Whereas anxieties about exploitation in research would prove to be immobilizing for oral historians in the 1990s, Lewis identified community action research as an effective means to address these inequities. She argued that "the process of gaining control over knowledge and skills normally considered to be the monopoly of the experts is an empowering one, which produces much more than just the information in question."[40] She also critiqued academic experts who studied communities without being accountable to them: "Experts are not objective," and their research is often "not accountable and responsible to the needs of ordinary people, but serves the power holders." Participatory research sought to give "validity to people's knowledge," allowing communities to systematize and analyze their own knowledge while also gathering additional information that spoke to their problems. Lewis urged all researchers working in communities to ask themselves who determined the need for and controlled the process and dissemination of research. "Where," she asked, "does accountability lie?"[41]

The Era of People's History

In the late 1970s and early 1980s, a growing movement of historians drew inspiration from Myles Horton, Septima Clark, Ella Baker, Staughton Lynd, Paulo Freire, and Helen Matthews Lewis as they organized dozens of people's history projects across the United States. The people's history movement sought to share the tools of historical production with people in communities outside of the halls of academia. The people were more than sources; they were "their own historians" who could draw on their power to interpret the past as a means to shape the future.[42] The historians at the forefront of these projects turned to oral history, which was the primary tool they used to engage the broader public in a collaborative and democratic exercise in history-making. Much of this work also benefited from access to significant funding streams during President Jimmy Carter's administration through the Comprehensive Employment Training Act and the National Endowment for the Humanities (NEH).[43]

While not all the projects had a foot in academic institutions, a significant number of professional historians began to embrace the radical collaborative practices that had been forged outside of universities. Academic historians' embrace of the people's history movement heralded many changes within the discipline of history as these professionals began reflecting and writing about methodological issues that were at the center of Lewis, Freire, Lynd, Clark, and Horton's work. What were the ethical implications of working across differences marked by social inequalities? How did one balance one's own interpretive authority while working collaboratively with others? Who were the people who would be invited to participate in these projects? Who were the audiences that the work would seek to engage? These questions were not new; rather, they emerged from the popular education tradition, which drew upon personal narratives as a starting point for movement building.

One of the earliest and most influential projects of the people's history era, the Massachusetts History Workshop, explicitly drew inspiration from the work of the Highlander Folk School. James Green—a professor at the University of Massachusetts Boston and one of the group's founders, along with Marty Blatt and Susan Reverby—saw himself as a movement educator working in the footsteps of Myles Horton.[44] Like Helen Matthews Lewis, he turned to oral history as a tool to facilitate community dialogue: "Oral history projects were the medium we used to begin individual and group dialogues with working people. These experiences enabled us to expand the dialogue in less private settings, to experiment with a movement inspired version of public history."[45] Green was not primarily interested in collecting oral testimony "as raw evidence of experience" but rather as a "record of how people told their stories and made their own interpretations."[46] He understood that this new work was innovative precisely because the historians organizing the project worked for academic institutions. Even so, he was not entirely convinced that it "was possible to be a movement historian in the university."[47]

The Massachusetts History Workshop projects in Lynn and Lawrence did not adequately resolve the dilemma of whether it was possible to successfully translate methods drawn from movements to an academic setting. Green, Blatt, and Reverby organized well-attended reunions of retired mill hands, where historians presented their research and workers offered up recollections on their past experiences in both oral histories and public forums. As the projects came to a close, Green observed that they had put "activist historians" in "collaborative community settings" where they encountered agendas among the project participants that were at times at odds with their own. For example, the academic historians wanted to understand more about the everyday life experiences of workers, while many of the participants wanted to highlight their participation in dramatic struggles. These tensions came to a head in Lawrence in the spring of 1980 when the academic historians decided not to get involved with a commemorative Bread and Roses pageant that was being organized by a local hospital workers' union. The organizers sought to celebrate the unity and solidarity of the famous 1912 strike, but from the perspective of the historians, the pageant organizers had failed "to explore the social history of mill worker communities, which was the workshop's main concern."[48] Rather than meet the workers where they were and find creative ways to raise these differences as problems for discussion, as Freire might have advised, the historians decided to preserve their integrity by not participating in the planned festivities. The historians thus lost an opportunity to engage a larger working-class audience, as the pageant went on to become a huge success that was held annually and that was embraced by young and retired workers alike.

The Massachusetts History Workshop did not immediately result in the kinds of dramatic social change we associate with Highlander or the Freedom Schools. It must be remembered, however, that Highlander conducted workshops for decades rather than for a few short years, and there were many years that Highlander worked unremittingly without any immediate signs of structural change to the conditions that African Americans and industrial workers had experienced. Furthermore, without devaluing the dire economic conditions of the Great Depression, when Highlander was founded, the realities of deindustrialization that shaped the lives of Massachusetts' workers in the 1980s were unique. Lynn and Lawrence had become industrial graveyards as factory owners shut down their remaining mills and moved production elsewhere. Doing their projects in the midst of this dislocation, the organizers of the Massachusetts History Workshop were taken aback by the level of "cynicism and defeatism" expressed by the mill workers they interviewed.[49]

While the Massachusetts History Workshop disbanded without any clear victories, it inspired other projects and served as a testing ground for the collaborative research practices that James Green would continue to embrace throughout his career as a labor educator at the University of Massachusetts Boston and at the Harvard Trade Union Program. In his memoir, *Taking History to Heart*, Green documented his decades of work teaching labor history to union members using a "problem-posing approach" inspired by Horton and Freire.[50] Green referred to his approach as a "kind of oral history" that "involves a dialogue about the past, conversations in shared spaces, public and private."[51] The younger "worker students" in his classes—who engaged in dialogue with one another about their own personal experiences and who interviewed and organized workshops with older labor activists—did end up playing major roles in the labor union revival in the 1990s. Green argued that this cross-generational work of union members had resulted in a "consciousness raising process" that informed a new social movement that democratized and radicalized labor unions.[52] Radical work rooted in the traditions of popular education, grounded in personal experiences, and drawing upon the tools of oral history could in fact be done with a foot firmly inside an academic institution.

In the late 1970s, the National Endowment for the Humanities funded Jeremy Brecher, Jan Stackhouse, and Jerry Lombardi to do the Brass Workers History Project, another endeavor that would demonstrate oral history's potential to effect social change in the context of deindustrialization. The participatory project sought to bring together workers in the declining brass industry in Naugatuck Valley to discuss the past and present conditions they were experiencing at work and in their communities. It would continue through 1984, leading to the production of a feature-length documentary and a book, both titled *Brass Valley*. In 1984, Brecher wrote, "Perhaps the greatest lesson we have to pass on to future projects is that participation takes time—plan your project with plenty of it."[53] Brecher would continue his work in the same community for the next twenty-five years. The participants in the Brass Workers History Project would go on to form the Naugatuck Valley Project (NVP), a group that spearheaded countless creative projects to address issues related to affordable housing, health care, and the environment. NVP also organized several employee-owned factories as a response to the plant closings that ravaged the region in the 1980s. In 2011, Brecher would publish a second book, *Banded Together*, this time documenting the history of the NVP.[54]

Brecher, Lombardi, and Stackhouse rooted their approach to people's history in oral history, and they understood that what they were doing entailed much more than recovering voices from below. They came to depend on oral history as a foundational organizing tool after their initial efforts to organize a history collaborative proved ineffective: "We initially defined the project as a way we could help people in the community tell their own history. Thus, we offered to help people do things: collect the history of their own organization, set up a history committee, or learn how to operate video equipment. We rapidly learned that most people defined participation very differently: as them helping us. I believe now that our initial approach was rather arrogant, and that theirs represented a more realistic picture of the situation."[55]

Brecher discovered it was much more appropriate to begin the project by asking community members to participate in oral history interviews, an approach that entailed listening and learning from community members in the earliest encounters. The interviews helped further deepen relationships and eventually did facilitate the creation of a robust community and labor advisory panel.

In conducting the oral history interviews with factory workers, Brecher, Lombardi, and Stackhouse envisioned their narrators as experts rather than merely as sources. And in editing the *Brass Valley* volume, they explicitly acknowledged the shared authority within the interviews; the excerpts were much more than what "a traditional historian would regard as raw sources." Rather, the narrators offered descriptions of events from the past as well as "their own interpretations of their meaning."[56] Like the Lynds before them, their role was to function as organizers and editors. They understood that the accounts they recorded were not just laden with facts but were rich with interpretation, and they prized the subjective elements: "The value of the materials is enhanced by the fact that they shed light, not only on what happened, but on the ways the various people organized their understandings of what happened."

In accepting the narrators' authority, the coordinators also "learned to be comfortable" with the fact that people who participated brought their own agendas and divergent interpretations to the project. Staking claim to an identity as "pet outsiders," they navigated through intercommunity conflict and were careful to respect but move across antagonistic lines within the community. While they could play a role in helping people to see the larger context of their experience and perhaps gain an understanding of the commonalities they shared with their antagonists, they acknowledged that they could not presume that their work would reconcile long-standing divisions.[57] What they hoped to do instead was to generate a "dialogue between individual experiences, as lived and thought about by the participants, and their lives as viewed in a larger historical context."[58] They hoped that participants and readers alike would gain a greater appreciation of their role as historical actors. As evidenced by the project's role in facilitating the emergence of the Naugatuck Valley Project, it remains one of the most significant models demonstrating the potential for people's history to play a role in mobilizing communities to further social change from the bottom up.[59]

A plethora of people's history projects flourished during the 1980s. Collectively, they made significant contributions to the way many historians and activists think about the past, and they informed a broad array of social justice movements. Projects such as the Baltimore Neighborhood Heritage Project, the New York Chinatown History Project, and Philadelphia's Historymobile focused on specific urban neighborhoods and the marginalized working-class and ethnic residents that lived within them.[60] The Black community museums that sprang up in places like Detroit, Chicago, Philadelphia, and Cleveland drew inspiration from SNCC's Freedom Schools, engaged in oral history projects, and encouraged Black communities to produce their own histories.[61] The feminist oral history movement also flourished during this same period, coming together in 1977 with the founding of the National Women's Studies Association and the subsequent special issue of *Frontiers* that focused on women's oral history. While many feminist oral history projects had a foot in academia, they also sustained a broader commitment to the contemporary feminist movement.[62] The period also saw the emergence of oral history projects that focused on lesbian and gay communities across the United States, such as the Lesbian Herstory Archives, the Buffalo Oral History Project, the Boston Area History Project, and the New York Lesbian and Gay Historical Society.[63] Collectively these projects redefined the very meaning of community, as they helped broaden the concept of oppression and social justice. By focusing on narratives of personal experience by people from communities experiencing marginalization, exploitation, and oppression, they have pushed forward our understanding of how different forms of oppression intersect in the lives of individuals.

With the election of Reagan and the appointment of William Bennet as the head of NEH in 1982, however, funding for community projects began to dry up. In the mid-1980s, Susan Porter Benson, Stephen Brier, and Roy Rosenzweig concluded, "The most expensive efforts, such as films and large-scale community and oral history projects, face an uncertain future without federal funding."[64] Heavily staffed projects, such as the Baltimore Neighborhood History Project, collapsed when the grant funding disappeared.[65] In the wake of austerity, John "Jack" Tchen, the founder of the New York Chinatown History Project, asked, "Can a participatory social history be fostered in this era of flat public-sector support and the growing dependence on benevolent donor wealth?" Tchen's response was, "We do our best. We work with limited time and limited resources. We do what we can."[66]

Paralysis and Movement

By the early 1990s, the flourishing moment of people's history projects had come to a close. Funding for community oral history projects dried up, and by the late 1980s and early 1990s, the tone of publications reflecting on people's history had dramatically changed from the earlier visionary calls to action to more pessimistic critiques that sought to address the shortcomings of this work. Undoubtedly, there needed to be an assessment of the projects as they came to a close, and many of the people who critically reflected on the work from this era supported the larger aims of the movement. A growing number of scholars, however, published critiques that were hostile to the aims of people's history and even went so far as to claim it had a greater potential to be exploitative than traditional scholarship.

After funding dried up and the Baltimore Neighborhood Heritage Project (BNHP) came to an end in 1982, one of the project's lead organizers, Linda Shopes, offered a critique of its shortcomings. Initially the BNHP had sought to facilitate cross-generational dialogue within working-class ethnic neighborhoods that could "nurture the self respect of senior citizens" and communicate to younger residents that their communities were "worth something." She hoped that in revaluing their communities, the residents could "be so moved to take a more activist, critical stance with respect to their social and economic circumstances." With the project completed, however, she lamented that the collection of oral histories consisted primarily of sentimental and nostalgic memories that "ultimately go nowhere." Rather than put "individual memories into social context," the senior citizens she worked with sought to communicate an individual sense of survival. The project failed to build relationships with established community organizations that would allow for it to continue after the funding and the organizers' enthusiasm had run out. Even with her recommendation that projects be more grounded in the communities within which they worked, Shopes forthrightly concluded, "I am surer of the problems than the way to solve them."[67] Her frustration may have been born more from the structural difficulty of building social movements in the communities that she worked with rather than from the methodological limitations of oral history.

Susan Porter Benson, Stephen Brier, and Roy Rosenzweig also contended that people's history projects, drawing on "pluralist and populist" notions of American history, had avoided difficult historical questions and needed to "sharpen their modes of historical analysis." They did not give up on people's history but argued that collaborations needed to be deeper and projects should make a greater effort to facilitate the "diffusion of skills of writing history." Rather than seeing critical perspective emerging out of community dialogue, as Freire and Horton had called for, Benson, Brier, and Rosenzweig identified a need to merge "a nonhierarchical, democratic, and community-based historical practice" with a "theoretical understanding of class, racial, and sexual oppression." However, other than stating that this merger required the "energy and vision" of the organizers of people's history projects, they offered no clear guidance on how the synthesis between democratic practice and critical perspectives might take place.[68]

While Shopes, Benson, Brier, and Rosenzweig were clearly sympathetic to people's history, other scholars embraced an explicitly hostile critique that falsely characterized the approach as "facile democratization" and "complacent populism."[69] Rather than understanding the significance of seeing narrators as historians who had interpretive authority, the growing critique of people's history viewed it as merely seeking to encourage oppressed groups to "speak for themselves" in an effort to obtain history "pure . . . directly from people without the intervening ideology" of professional historians.[70]

In their articles published in 1991 in the feminist collection of essays, *Women's Words*, Judith Stacey and Daphne Patai advanced the pessimistic critique further and argued that nontraditional approaches that embraced empathy, mutuality, and collaboration in research were fraught with an even greater risk of producing exploitation than traditional, hierarchical research models that were "positivist" and "impersonal." Judith Stacey questioned whether "the appearance of greater respect for and equality with research subjects in the ethnographic approach masks a deeper, more dangerous form of exploitation." By delving into challenging and potentially explosive topics related to gender and sexuality, the researcher, who had the power to leave when the project was over, intruded upon and unduly threatened the system of relationships that were integral to a community's survival. The embrace of mutuality functioned as a disguise that would ultimately lead to treachery and betrayal when the researcher got what she wanted and left. Stacey continued, "And the greater the intimacy—the greater the apparent mutuality of the researcher/researched relationship—the greater is the danger."[71] Patai also argued that promoting emotional intimacy and a sense of friendship or "spurious identification" in an interview was a form of manipulation that was even more troublesome when interviewing "down" (that is, interviewing less powerful groups). In addition to personal betrayals resulting from insincere promises of friendship, researchers also blundered when they implicitly or explicitly offered a false "expectation of positive intervention" to assist the informants in their daily struggles. These promises, she argued, were frequently unkept and further led to feelings of betrayal and injury. She rejected the notion of using oral history as a consciousness raising tool, and she represented the process as one where researchers "turn interviews with other women into opportunities for imposing our own politically correct analysis." For her, this was a form of "savage social therapy" that required "an arrogance incompatible with genuine respect for others."[72] Patai's extreme framing of the narrator as a victim of ideologically driven feminists left her unable to acknowledge that the narrator could reflect on her own narrative, examine it dialogically in relationship to others, and come to her own new understandings through that process. Stacey and Patai's critical framing of community-based research was paralyzing and offered no possibility that these kinds of projects could have any value.

Patai and Stacey appropriated a concern about exploitation in research that had long been addressed by popular educators and scholars interested in participatory research. Patai and Stacey, however, turned the critique on its head and argued that participatory research was more dangerous than traditional research. In the 1960s and 1970s, both Paulo Freire and Helen Matthews Lewis critiqued as exploitative the work of academic experts who were only interested in studying communities for their own scholarly purposes and not interested in working with these communities to address the communities' needs and ends. In the early 1980s, the British Popular Memory Group further articulated this critique as they specifically addressed the dynamics of power in "bottom-up" oral history. They worried that research that did not address the needs of a community and that was not carried out in an equal alliance with that community threatened to deepen "social divisions which are also relations of power and inequality." Research not rooted in communities risked being exploitative because the returns for the academic would be "grossly unequal" in contrast to the lack of any return to the community.[73] These analyses of research exploitation, unlike Patai's and Stacey's, buttressed the call to fully include communities in interpreting their past just as the people's history movement had sought to do.

Linda Shopes and Karen Olson, who were very forthright and critical of their own community-based work, pushed back against Stacey's and Patai's despairing outlook in an essay they coauthored that also appeared in *Women's Words*. While they did not dismiss all concerns about exploitation in research, they argued that the threat had been exaggerated: "In our own sensitivities to inequality, we indulge ourselves a bit and perhaps overestimate our own privilege, even our own importance, in the eyes of the people we interview. Most in fact, seem not especially overwhelmed, intimidated, or impressed with us at all."[74] Given the constellation of forces that threatened communities, academics were relatively inconsequential.

While Olson and Shopes put the power of the interviewer into perspective, Michael Frisch and Alessandro Portelli highlighted the agency of the narrator within the interview process itself. Together they helped move the field of oral history beyond the state of anxiety over whether research exploitation was impossible to escape. Frisch argued that the process of oral history inherently produced "a shared authority." Emphasizing the distinction between "sharing authority" and "a shared authority," Frisch argued, "'Sharing Authority' suggests this is something we do—that in some important sense 'we' have the authority, and that we need or ought to share it." He countered, "We don't have the authority to give away, really, to the extent we might assume." In contrast, "a shared authority" recognizes that "the interpretive and meaning making process is shared by definition—it is inherent in the dialogic nature of an interview."[75] Narrators were neither vessels to be manipulated nor sources simply to be mined—a fact that had been recognized by the Lynds, the Massachusetts History Workshop, and the Brass Valley project.

Portelli, for his part, contended that the power differential between the researcher and researched was not something we should turn away from, as Stacey and Patai suggested. Rather, this inequality could lead to an uncomfortable and painful critical self-awareness on both sides that was a necessary part of building solidarity. For Portelli, fieldwork was "an experiment in equality." "There is no need," he argued, "to stoop to propaganda in order to use the fact itself of the interview as an opportunity to stimulate others, as well as ourselves, to a higher degree of self-scrutiny and self-awareness; to help them grow more aware of the relevance and meaning of their culture and knowledge; and to raise the question of the senselessness and injustice of the inequality between them and us." Indeed, consciousness raising was not a "savage" top-down affair; narrators were not victims but active historical agents who could consider questions of inequality, conceive of new strategies, mobilize new movements, and transform the world around them.[76] Frisch and Portelli brought the field back from paralysis to movement once again.

Groundswell

When I came down to Cleveland's Public Square in 1996 to begin my oral history project with those experiencing homelessness, I did so at a moment when people's history was at a nadir; funding had dried up and enthusiasm had waned. Even though Frisch and Portelli had helpfully reenvisioned the interview as a radical, democratic space, both were vague on how that dialogical space could inform a collective transformative process. Specifically, they focused on the dynamic between the oral historian and narrator and did not address how oral histories might mobilize communities outside of the interview process itself. Those I interviewed—people who faced daily degradations checking in and out of shelters, police harassment on the street, and ongoing exploitation in their work as day laborers—had a palpable sense that something in their world needed to change. I came with no answers and brought no promises. I brought audio and video recorders and a question: How had the phenomenon of homelessness become so entrenched in Cleveland, Ohio? The object of inquiry was not the lives of the people I interviewed but the structures of power and oppression that shaped their lives.

Between 1999 and 2004, I interviewed over one hundred narrators and facilitated dozens of workshops with people experiencing homelessness. Initially, I conducted the oral histories on Public Square; then, over time, I did interviews in encampments, in shelters, and eventually live, on-air over the radio. The interviews, in which people drew on their personal experience to present their analysis of structural changes in housing and job markets and the welfare and criminal justice systems, were starting points for further group dialogue. I organized workshops in shelters and at meal sites where project participants watched and listened to one another's interviews and identified shared "generative themes" that ran through the interviews. Organizing these dialogues required identifying points and times in which narrators gathered; negotiating access to rooms where we could host workshops; producing and distributing flyers announcing the gatherings; obtaining necessary supplies for the meetings; supplying the television, the VCR, the recorders, and the recordings; crafting an agenda; and facilitating discussion at the meetings. While authority was inherently shared within the frame of the interview as well as the workshops, my work as a popular educator entailed doing the background work that enabled those dialogic spaces to exist in the first place. The willingness to do that work was an important part of what I had to offer.

The expressed needs and desires of the narrators shaped the focus of the interviews, as well as the products that emerged from the overall project.

The iterative process of conducting interviews, reflecting on those interviews in workshops, and then going back to do new interviews led to numerous shifts in the project's direction and objectives. Early on, the interviews were broad and relatively unfocused, covering a wide range of significant issues. But as the narrators began to discuss the interviews, they focused on stories about their working lives, experiences with the shelters, and difficulties they had sustaining their encampments outside of the shelters. They did not shy away from interpretive disagreements, nor did they ever reach a single consensus on what the most important issues were. But through discussion, clusters of narrators began to mobilize around aspects of their shared experience. Some organized to prevent the demolition of encampments, and they protested police campaigns to "clean the streets" and arrest people for the act of sleeping on the sidewalk. Others sought to improve the horrific conditions within the shelters and confront the organizations responsible for those circumstances. Still others focused their attention on the abuses they faced in their working lives while employed by day-labor agencies. In response to these mobilizations, I was able to draw on the interviews to quickly design low-budget end products. The multiplicity of end products included edited videos, flyers and pamphlets, petitions, press releases, an ongoing weekly radio show, organized protests and public hearings, and reports for public officials. Project participants formed the Day Laborers' Organizing Committee and established a Community Hiring Hall, both of which effectively addressed issues of exploitation the narrators faced in their working lives. Furthermore, their actions ended the city's practice of arresting people on the street and prompted the Salvation Army's removal from operating the city's emergency shelters. As a result, conditions within the shelters significantly improved.

I began this project in 1996, and then at my first Oral History Association (OHA) conference in 1998, I discovered a community of committed people who were also very interested in the possibility that oral history could be an effective tool to strengthen movements for social change. These people, like myself, lacked funding and were working in marginalized communities that had largely been ignored by the earlier NEH-funded people's history projects, which predominately focused on industrial workers and their communities. For example, Wendy Rickard led a collaborative oral history project with sex workers, Alicia Rouverol organized an oral history and performance project with people experiencing incarceration, Alisa del Tufo used oral history in her work with survivors of domestic violence, Terry Easton focused on day laborers in Atlanta, Ellen Griffith Spears worked with activists confronting environmental racism, Horacio Roque Ramírez orchestrated a project with queer Latinos in San Francisco, and Amy Starecheski had an ongoing project with squatters in New York City. Each of these projects sought to do more than document the communities under siege; they sought to further empower them.

This bubbling of activity led to the formation of a threaded discussion at the 2009 OHA annual meeting in Louisville, Kentucky, entitled "Oral History as Activism and Social Justice." Participants in the concluding discussion agreed to form the OHA affinity group Oral Historians for Social Justice, and in 2011, a group of fifteen activist oral historians brought together by Sarah Loose and Alisa del Tufo formed an independent collective, Groundswell: Oral History for Social Change. The group coalesced around the idea that "oral history can be a source of power, knowledge and strength" as communities engage in their "struggles for justice": "Oral history provides a unique space for those most impacted by injustice to speak and be heard in our own voices."[77] Through speaking and hearing, people experiencing oppression and exploitation might gain a better understanding of how their subjective personal experience relates to others' and how their lives are shaped by structures of power. Personal narratives could function as a starting point for social change, just as Myles Horton had argued over eighty years earlier.

We live amid a new groundswell of radical oral history practice. While this practice needs to be rooted in the needs, passions, and desires of communities today, it would be a mistake to discount the work of those who have come before us. The prevailing way we tell the history of oral history does just that. It ignores the important contributions of the field of popular education on radical oral history practice, and it dismisses as naïve the work that stemmed from the people's history moment. Rather, we should learn what we can and draw on the effective practices from that past as they resonate in the communities we work with in the present. People in communities under siege can reflect upon and interpret their own experiences, envision themselves as historical actors, and transform the world around them. And we, as radical oral historians, can accompany them along the way.

Notes

This article was previously published in *Oral History Review* 43, no. 2 (2016): 367–91. It is reprinted with minor edits and with the permission of the *Oral History Review*.

1. Epigraph: Myles Horton, *The Long Haul* (New York: Doubleday, 1990), 136–37.
2. Most notably, I read Paulo Freire, *Pedagogy of the Oppressed* (New York: Continuum, 1990); Myles Horton and Paulo Freire, *We Make the Road by Walking: Conversations on Education and Social Change* (Philadelphia: Temple University Press, 1990); and Augusto Boal, *Theater of the Oppressed* (New York: Theatre Communications Group, 1985).
3. An article I published about this work in *Oral History Review* in 2003 has since been included in the second and third editions of *The Oral History Reader* in its section titled "Advocacy and Empowerment." Robert Perks and Alistair Thomson drew upon my work as an example for how oral history "can play a significant role in movement building." Robert Perks and Alistair Thomson, eds., *The Oral History Reader*, 2nd ed. (London: Routledge, 1996), 448. For more on my work, see Daniel R. Kerr, "We Know What the Problem Is," *Oral History Review* 30, no. 1 (2003): 27–45; "Countering Corporate Narratives from the Streets: The Cleveland Homeless Oral History Project," in *Oral History and Public Memories*, ed. Paula Hamilton and Linda Shopes (Philadelphia: Temple University Press, 2008), 231–51; and *Derelict Paradise*.
4. For one example of how this prehistory is dealt with, see Rebecca Sharpless, "The History of Oral History," in *History of Oral History*, ed. Thomas L. Charlton, Lois E. Myers, and Rebecca Sharpless (Lanham, MD: AltaMira, 2007), 14–16.
5. Sharpless, 12.
6. See Ronald J. Grele, "Reflections on the Practice of Oral History: Retrieving What We Can from an Earlier Critique," *Suomen Antropologi* 4 (2007): 11–12.
7. Remarkably similar versions of this narrative of our past can be found in Donald Ritchie, *Doing Oral History*, 3rd ed. (Oxford: Oxford University Press, 2015), 5–7; Valerie Yow, *Recording Oral History*, 3rd ed. (Lanham, MD: Rowman & Littlefield, 2015), 3; Perks and Thomson, *Oral History Reader*, 2; Lynn Abrams, *Oral History Theory* (London: Routledge, 2010), 4–8; Ronald Grele, *Envelopes of Sound*, 2nd ed. (Chicago: Greenwood, 1991), 196–211; and Alistair Thomson, "Four Paradigm Transformations in Oral History," *Oral History Review* 34, no. 1 (2006): 49–70. After the 1980s, the histories of oral history became a bit more muddled as the consensus of what has happened to the field became less clear, other than a general acknowledgement that we have entered a "digital age."
8. Linda Shopes, "'Insights and Oversights': Reflections on the Documentary Tradition and the Theoretical Turn in Oral History," *Oral History Review* 41, no. 2 (2014): 260.
9. Joan Sangster, "Politics and Praxis in Canadian Working-Class History," in *Oral History Off the Record*, ed. Anna Sheftel and Stacey Zembrzycki (New York: Palgrave Macmillan, 2013), 64.

10 The argument draws on Luisa Passerini's essay "Mythbiography in Oral History," in *The Myths We Live By*, ed. Ralph Samuel and Paul Thompson (London: Routledge, 1990). For an example of how British oral historians tell a very different story about their past, see Alistair Thomson, "Oral History and Community History in Britain," *Oral History* 36 (Spring 2008): 95–104. Interestingly, Thomson draws on the established US narrative while contrasting it with the British history of oral history. Thomson argues, "By the end of the 1980s community oral history was arguably *the* dominant presence in the British oral history movement. That contrasts with other countries. In the United States oral history started as an elite and archive-based movement, which then broadened out to include people's history work in the seventies." Thomson, 96.

11 Horton, *Long Haul*, 57.

12 Horton, 44–62.

13 Horton, 86–87, 96–97.

14 Horton, 157.

15 Horton, 147.

16 Horton and Freire, *We Make the Road*, 98.

17 Horton, *Long Haul*, 100, 102, 104–5.

18 Horton, 100, 104–5; Todd Moye, *Ella Baker: Community Organizer of the Civil Rights Movement* (Lanham, MD: Rowman & Littlefield, 2013).

19 Horton, *Long Haul*, 108–12. For more on the schools, see Charles Payne, *I've Got the Light of Freedom: The Organizing Tradition and the Mississippi Freedom Struggle* (Berkeley: University of California Press, 1997).

20 Septima Poinsette Clark, *Ready from Within: Septima Clark and the Civil Rights Movement* (Navarro, CA: Wild Trees, 1986), 77.

21 Barbara Ransby, *Ella Baker and the Black Freedom Movement* (Chapel Hill: University of North Carolina Press, 2003), 188.

22 Ransby, 92.

23 Ransby, 242–49.

24 In 1964, another historian, Howard Zinn, introduced Staughton Lynd to the potential of the portable cassette recorder (released in 1963) when Lynd stumbled upon Zinn conducting an interview of two SNCC field secretaries for his book, *SNCC: The New Abolitionists* (Boston: Beacon, 1964). Andrej Grubacic, ed., *From Here to There: The Staughton Lynd Reader* (Oakland, CA: PM, 2010), 120.

25 Carl Mirra, *The Admirable Radical: Staughton Lynd and Cold War Dissent, 1945–1970* (Kent, OH: Kent State University Press, 2010).

26 Grubacic, *From Here to There*, 152–58.

27 Alice Lynd and Staughton Lynd, eds., *Rank and File: Personal Histories by Working-Class Organizers* (Boston: Beacon, 1973), 7.

28 Alice Lynd and Staughton Lynd, *Stepping Stones: Memoir of a Life Together* (New York: Lexington Books, 2009), 61–64; Lynd and Lynd, *Rank and File*, 7.

29 Staughton Lynd, "The Battle over Radical History," *New Republic*, August 4, 2010, https://newrepublic.com/article/76687/the-battle-over-radical-history-part-2.

30 Grubacic, *From Here to There*, 160–62.

31 Lynd and Lynd, *Rank and File*, 7.

32 Grubacic, *From Here to There*, 161.

33 Alice Hoffman, "Who Are the Elite and What Is a Non-elitest?," *Oral History Review* 4 (1976): 4.

34 Grubacic, *From Here to There*, 18–20. In his essay, Alessandro Portelli makes a remarkably similar argument: "Field work is meaningful as the encounter of two subjects who recognize each other as subjects, and therefore separate, and seek to build their equality upon their difference in order to work together." Portelli, *The Death of Luigi Trastulli and Other Stories* (Albany, NY: SUNY Press, 1991), 43.

35 James D. Kirylo, *Paulo Freire: The Man from Recife* (New York: Peter Lang, 2011), 50–59.

36 Freire, *Pedagogy of the Oppressed*, 33, 52–53, 70–71, 86, 101.

37 Freire, 23–24, 99, 184.

38 Helen Matthews Lewis, *Helen Matthews Lewis: Living Social Justice in Appalachia*, ed. Patricia D. Beaver and Judith Jennings (Lexington: University Press of Kentucky, 2014), 5–6, 63, 74–75.

39 Lewis, 142–44. For more on Lewis's project in Ivanhoe, Virginia, see Mary Ann Hinsdale, Helen Lewis, and Maxine Waller, *It Comes from the People: Community Development and Local Theology* (Philadelphia: Temple University Press, 1995).

40 Lewis, 143.

41 Lewis, 144.

42 Ronald Grele, "Whose Public? Whose History? What Is the Goal of a Public Historian?," *Public Historian* 3, no. 1 (Winter 1981): 48.

43 Linda Shopes, "Oral History and Community Involvement," in *Presenting the Past*, ed. Susan Porter Benson, Stephen Brier, and Roy Rosenzweig (Philadelphia: Temple University Press, 1986), 254.

44 James Green, *Taking History to Heart* (Amherst: University of Massachusetts Press, 2000), 81.

45 Green, 54.

46 Green, 64.

47 Green, 31.

48 Green, 54–55, 60. The Massachusetts History Workshop regrouped and learned from these setbacks when it engaged in a clerical workers project in Boston, which more fully embraced collaborative history-making. See Green, 65–68.

49 Green, 60.

50 Green, 96.

51 Green, 3.

52 Green, 279.

53 Jeremy Brecher, "How I Learned to Quit Worrying and Love Community History: A 'Pet Outsider's' Report on the Brass Workers History Project," *Radical History Review*, nos. 28–30 (1984): 201.

54 Jeremy Brecher, *Banded Together* (Urbana: University of Illinois Press, 2011), xiv–xv.

55 Brecher, "How I Learned," 199.
56 Jeremy Brecher, Jerry Lombardi, and Jan Stackhouse, eds., *Brass Valley: The Story of Working People's Lives and Struggles in an American Industrial Region* (Philadelphia: Temple University Press, 1982), 275–76.
57 Brecher, "How I Learned," 193.
58 Brecher, Lombardi, and Stackhouse, *Brass Valley*, 275.
59 In a review of *Brass Valley*, Ron Grele referred to the project as "genius" and "so much better than anything yet produced." Ronald Grele, review of *Brass Valley: The Story of Working People's Lives and Struggles in an American Industrial Region*, ed. Jeremy Brecher, Jerry Lombardi, and Jan Stackhouse, *Radical America* 17, no. 5 (1983): 48, 53.
60 Linda Shopes, "Community Oral History," *Oral History* 43, no. 1 (Spring 2015): 97–106; Michael Frisch, *A Shared Authority: Essays on the Craft and Meaning of Oral and Public History* (Albany, NY: SUNY Press, 1990), 225–38; John Kuo Wei Tchen, and Liz Ševčenko, "The 'Dialogic Museum' Revisited," in *Letting Go? Sharing Historical Authority in a User-Generated World*, ed. Bill Adair, Benjamin Filene, and Laura Koloski (Philadelphia: Pew Center for Arts and Heritage, 2011), 82.
61 Jeffrey C. Stewart and Fath Davis Ruffins, "A Faithful Witness: Afro-American Public History in Historical Perspective, 1828–1984," in Benson, Brier, and Rosenzweig, *Presenting the Past*, 328–32; Samir Meghelli, "Remixing the Historical Record: Revolutions in Hip Hop Historiography," *Western Journal of Black Studies* 37, no. 2 (2013): 95–97.
62 Sherna Berger Gluck, "What's So Special about Women? Women's Oral History," *Frontiers* 2, no. 2 (Summer 1977): 5; Sherna Berger Gluck, "Has Feminist Oral History Lost Its Radical/Subversive Edge?," *Oral History* 39, no. 2 (Autumn 2011): 64–65.
63 Lisa Duggan, "History's Gay Ghetto," in Benson, Brier, and Rosenzweig, *Presenting the Past*, 282.
64 Benson, Brier, and Rosenzweig, introduction to *Presenting the Past*, xxvii.
65 Shopes, "Community Oral History," 105.
66 Tchen and Ševčenko, "'Dialogic Museum' Revisited," 86; John Kuo Wei Tchen, *Homeland Insecurities: Teaching and the Intercultural Communication*, Foreseeable Futures 5, Position Papers from: Imagining America: Artists and Scholars in Public Life, November 22, 2005, 8. https://imaginingamerica.org/wp-content/uploads/Forseeable-Futures-5-Tchen.pdf.
67 Shopes, "Oral History and Community Involvement," 249–50, 252–53, 260.
68 Benson, Brier, and Rosenzweig, *Presenting the Past*, xxii–xxiii.
69 Thomson, "Four Paradigm Transformations," 56.
70 Thomson, 56; Ronald Grele, "Oral History as Evidence," in Charlton, Myers, and Sharpless, *History of Oral History*, 45.
71 Judith Stacey, "Can There Be a Feminist Ethnography?," in *Women's Words*, ed. Sherna Berger Gluck and Daphne Patai (New York: Routledge, 1991), 113–14.

72 Daphne Patai, "U.S. Academics and Third World Women," in Gluck and Patai, *Women's Words*, 137, 142, 144–45, 148.

73 Popular Memory Group, "Popular Memory: Theory, Politics, Method," in Perks and Thomson, *Oral History Reader*, 52.

74 Karen Olson and Linda Shopes, "Crossing Boundaries, Building Bridges," in Gluck and Patai, *Women's Words*, 196.

75 Frisch, *Shared Authority*, xx, xxii; Michael Frisch, "From *A Shared Authority* to the Digital Kitchen, and Back," in Adair, Filene, and Koloski, *Letting Go?*, 127.

76 Portelli, *Death of Luigi Trastulli*, 44.

77 "About," Groundswell: Oral History for Social Change, accessed June 11, 2015, http://www.oralhistoryforsocialchange.org/about/.

Helen Matthews Lewis

Oral History and Social Change in Appalachia

Judith Jennings

What can the life story of a "self-proclaimed oral historian,"[1] also known as the grandmother of Appalachian studies, reveal about public history's radical roots? Born in 1924, Helen Matthews Lewis created new pathways for radical analysis and oral history practices over seven decades of teaching, research, and activism, mainly in the coalfields of Appalachia. Her story raises new questions about the radical origins of oral history.

Can and should the process of investigating radical roots expand the criteria for what counts as oral history? If so, what are the similarities and differences between practicing oral history as a tool for community change rather than as a subset of social or political history? What is the role of oral interviews in knowledge production where social justice goals and collective action, not publication or archival preservation, are the primary priorities?

This chapter approaches Lewis's life chronologically through her body of work collected in *Helen Matthews Lewis: Living Social Justice in Appalachia*.[2] This approach links the development of her oral history principles and practices to the social contexts so important to her as an activist. Juxtaposing her first-person narration with her scholarship, teaching methods, and community organizing demonstrates the relationship of her oral interviews to individual agency and collective social change. Taken as a whole, her life story provides a case study in the radical roots of oral history.

Helen Matthews Lewis attending an Appalshop event in Whitesburg, Kentucky, 2010. Courtesy of Helen Matthews Lewis Collection located in the Appalachian State University Library Special Collections.

There's No Going Back after That

In oral history interviews conducted with her, Lewis stresses how her early life experiences and education influenced her later work. Raised in small towns in north Georgia, she witnessed racial segregation, although her postman father taught her to respect all people. In 1941, she entered the all-White Bessie Tift College in Forsyth, Georgia. Her first year there, she vividly recalls learning about structural racism from Southern Baptist preacher, Clarence Jordan.[3] In Cotton Patch sermons throughout the South, Jordan powerfully combined New Testament parables with analysis of racial and economic inequalities.

In Jordan's version of the Good Samaritan parable, an older Black man helps a badly injured White man found lying on a road. Lewis still vividly recalls Jordan's words: "He tries to put him in the hospital, and they won't let him in because this black man had brought him. . . . And he's the Good Samaritan. I'm sitting there listening, and it's kind of like, My God that is it, that is it!" Lewis often tells this story as a touchstone experience for her. Jordan's sermon opened her eyes to the racial injustice around her: "And there's no going back after that. I mean it just turned my mind. From then on."[4]

In another story of her social awakening, Lewis tells how she became radicalized at the all-White Georgia State College for Women (GSCW) in

Milledgeville, where she completed her undergraduate education between 1943 and 1946. She explains, "At GSCW, we still had a lot of older spinster-suffragette teachers; strong independent women who were among the first generation to vote. They not only provided models but also brought us ideas from the earlier women's movement." As Lewis recognizes, "The 1940s were a time of great change [because] World War II opened up the world for all of us." She describes how, "combined with liberal ideas about political and social change from the new faculty, the ideas of older teachers produced at GSCW what might be called today . . . education for social change along with informal women's studies."[5]

Despite Lewis's emerging commitment to feminism, heteronormative social expectations of marriage remained strong. After graduating college, she married Judd Lewis, then studying economics at Duke University, because, as she says, she was expected to marry someone. Yet GSCW students were also encouraged to enter professions or attend graduate school. When her husband accepted a job teaching at the University of Virginia, she enrolled in graduate school there.

She studied sociology and anthropology with Floyd Nelson House. He had served as chair of anthropology and sociology at the legendary University of Chicago School of Sociology.[6] At the University of Virginia, House specialized in studying race and culture. He introduced Lewis to Gunnar Myrdal's influential work *An American Dilemma: The Negro Problem and Modern Democracy*.[7] The Carnegie Corporation had commissioned Myrdal, a Swedish political economist, to analyze past and contemporary race relations in the US. Many hailed its 1944 publication for critiquing the long-standing segregationist doctrine that racially separate social institutions could be equal. Yet others, most notably Ralph Ellison, argue that Myrdal failed to recognize African American agency.[8]

Combining her knowledge of women's activism with this racial analysis, Lewis completed her master's thesis in 1949, examining "The Woman Movement and the Negro Movement—Parallel Struggles for Rights." Her purpose was "to point out . . . similarities and interrelations in the status and history of both groups . . . it is hoped that in concentrating on the similarities of the two that it will thereby give perspective to both problems." Exploring common experiences of economic, social, and paternalistic oppression, she also recognized the conflicts and tensions between the two movements.

In her thesis, Lewis began constructing what became a lifelong focus on social change, which would undergird all her work and subsequently lead her to emphasize the importance of oral interviews. "The chief task of all social movements," she wrote, "must be at first to impress upon the rest of society the right of unsatisfied and unrepresented human impulses to constitute a real problem worthy of attention." To do this, however, required purposeful interaction: "This they will never bring about until there is a sufficient number of people who are so socially sensitive and adaptable that they feel within themselves as their own the impulses and points of view of both races and both sexes."

While she described race and sex in the stark binaries of her own experience, her understanding of human rights was more inclusive. Citing the recent work of Eleanor Roosevelt on the United Nation's Universal Declaration of Human Rights, she argues that "everyone is entitled to all the rights and freedoms set forth in the Declaration, without distinction of any kind, such as race, color, sex, language, religion, political or other opinion, national or social origin, property, birth, or other status."[9]

The post–World War II era and focus on human rights remain an important era for further research on the origins of radical roots as suggested by oral historian Ronald Grele in his article "Oral History as Evidence." As Grele observes, there is a link between human rights and "histories of oppression," including colonialism.[10]

For Lewis, social change would not come from the top down, but only when individuals of all identities and backgrounds recognized common concerns and formed social movements. Linking individual oppressions to collective action for social justice would inform her future work as a scholar, oral history interviewer, and activist. Recognizing the value of her work, the University of Virginia selected her thesis for publication.

Finding Her Place in Appalachia

In 1955, Lewis and her husband moved to southwest Virginia when he joined the faculty at the newly established Clinch Valley College, now the University of Virginia at Wise. The then all-White college prohibited wives from being hired as faculty. These systems of segregation and paternalism were familiar to Lewis, but the geography and social conditions were different from the agrarian South where she grew up. Barred from teaching, Lewis focused on learning all she could about the place where she now lived.

Wise is part of the Appalachian coalfields, where geography had long been a determining factor because of the presence of coal. As the nation's railroads and steel mills boomed at the turn of the twentieth century, the region's large deposits of coal attracted speculators and international corporations. The coal could be cheaply, if not safely, extracted by low-paid miners and sold nationally at a large profit for owners. This outside ownership of land and natural resources shaped not only the history but also the economy, culture, and power dynamics of the coalfields in ways still being debated by scholars and activists today.[11]

When Lewis arrived in Wise in the mid-1950s, she found "the coal industry was being mechanized and half the population of the coalfield counties were leaving for northern industrial centers." As portrayed in the documentary film *Long Journey Home*, Appalachian coal miners who could no longer find work in their home region went to urban centers like Detroit, Akron, and Chicago for factory jobs.[12] Lewis wanted to know more about the workers who stayed and what options were available for them. So the first thing she did "was go down to the United Mine Workers to talk to them about what was going on and why there weren't retraining programs."

Exploring the links between geography and economic development, she "became very interested in trying to understand what happens to a rural region . . . when it is industrialized by outside ownership, by an extractive industry." Initially, her efforts were stymied by the lack of research on the coal industry in general and on rural working people in Appalachia in particular. She addressed this problem by connecting the students at Clinch Valley College with regional residents to create new sources of knowledge.

Allowed to teach part time, Lewis explains how she "started working with the students to get the coalfield history . . . because these coal camps were being demolished and depleted and people were going everywhere." Scattered outside the town of Wise, the coal companies built camps with poorly constructed houses lacking basic services where rural workers with their families lived while working in the mining operations. Although most of her students were local, few had ever visited the coal camps.

Lewis directed the students to select a coal camp to research, visit homes there, conduct interviews with the families about their lives and work, and write a community history. Her first use of oral history—though not specifically identified as such—proved to be a pedagogical success. Through the interviews, the students learned firsthand about what coal camp life was like. They also asked the camp residents what they wanted most in their communities. The residents identified a water system, improvements in the houses,

Helen Matthews Lewis visiting a coal mine in southwestern Virginia, 1960s. Courtesy of Helen Matthews Lewis Collection located in the Appalachian State University Library Special Collections.

garbage collection, and a playground. Lewis proudly points to an archival component for the histories as well: "We collected a huge book, which is still in the library at Clinch Valley."[13]

In the mid-1960s, Lewis teamed up with Edward Knipe, a fellow sociologist on the Clinch Valley College faculty, to develop oral history interviews as a research methodology to study coal mining. She and Knipe obtained funds from the national bureau of mines for the innovative work described in their final report, *Toward a Methodology of Studying Coal Mining*. Their first priority was to build trusting relationships among the faculty and student interview teams and the miners and their families. Only then could the interviews proceed as mutually beneficial exchanges.

Reflecting Lewis's interest in women's roles, she and Knipe directed that "the interviewers worked in male-female teams. The male would interview the husband, and the female would interview the wife. In this manner, the interviewee answers as a friend or acquaintance rather than a subject." The gender-specific interviewers mirrored the family structure rather than acting as disassociated observers and interpreters.

The interviewer teams gained a wider understanding of the family's socio-economic and cultural contexts as well as the male-centered work of coal mining. The interviewees, including male and female family heads, gained affirmation as experts of their own histories and opportunities for mutual reflection with the interviewers. The interviews ended by presenting the participants with a family photograph as a concrete representation of the mutual benefit of the time spent together.[14]

In 1964, Lewis entered the PhD program in sociology at the University of Kentucky, eager to continue her research on the socioeconomic impact of coal in Appalachia. Still teaching part time in western Virginia, she focused on her own place-based research. Her dissertation, completed in 1970, examines "Occupational Roles and Family Roles: A Study of Coal Mining Families in the Southern Appalachians." Here again, she successfully used interviews as a research methodology for interactive learning, engaging both males and females. The research topics and methods used by Lewis and Knipe in the 1960s point to the need for further investigation of the radical roots of oral history in the field of sociology, especially studies of social movements.

Challenging the Academy, or The Academy Strikes Back

In 1967, while completing her graduate work, Lewis joined the faculty at East Tennessee State University (ETSU), an hour's drive from Clinch Valley and still in the Appalachian coalfields. Her job combined teaching and further collaborative grant-funded research projects led by her colleague Edward Knipe. At that time, students there, like many across the country, questioned the United States' involvement in the Vietnam War. At ETSU, as in other rural areas where options were scarce, many students were returning veterans.

"It was one of the most exciting teaching opportunities I ever had," she recalls. "The sociology department was growing, and we attracted all these interesting students." Lewis encouraged the students to speak and act on their views. One of them, a Vietnam veteran, started a petition for a referendum on whether Reserve Officers' Training Corps (ROTC) membership should be compulsory for males on campus.

In the summer of 1969, the dean who oversaw the sociology department unexpectedly notified Lewis and Knipe that their contracts would not be renewed. His reason? They were "nurturing radical students." According to Lewis, when students protested by conducting a mock funeral for the department of sociology, the university president "cut off all money to our department," Stunned, she says, "[I] just went back to my house [in Wise], and I didn't have a job."[15]

By then, Clinch Valley College in Wise had changed their gender-restrictive policies, and they hired her as a full-time faculty member. There, she started a social work program and also began designing what is now recognized as the first Appalachian studies classes. Drawing on the work of Paulo Freire's *Pedagogy of the Oppressed*, she created an alternative curriculum with oral interviews and active learning at its heart. Lewis envisioned that "the area, itself, should become a learning laboratory and students should see the area as a learning environment."

For Lewis, the primary purpose of Appalachian studies was to be a tool for social change, not just a new field for academic study. Place-based community histories and oral history interviews as social interactions remained her primary pedagogies. She arranged class field trips to coal mines and student interviews with miners as well as collecting data and studying local land ownership.

Her curriculum was decidedly interdisciplinary. She emphasized oral traditions, music, social conditions, and economic development in the region. She encouraged students to organize local music festivals as a source of cultural pride and self-expression. She gladly shared her curricula with high school and college teachers throughout Appalachia. Mimeographed copies of her syllabi passed from hand to hand across the region, used both as teaching and social change tools for knowledge building and action.

By then, academics and activists inside and outside the region were hotly debating the causes of the debilitating social and economic conditions there. Was Appalachia an isolated American subculture bypassed by progress, or was it an internal American colony exploited for the benefit of national and international corporations? In 1970, Lewis and Edward Knipe took a strong stand by presenting "The Colonialism Model: The Appalachian Case" for the national American Anthropological Association. They argued there was an urgent need to advance grassroots research strategies that would recognize first-person interviews as a vehicle for establishing collective agency and promoting social change.

Lewis and Knipe argued that "the subculture model . . . blame[s] the underdevelopment of the region on the Appalachian character rather than the exploitative conditions institutionalized in the region" Instead, they identified the causes of poverty as "the processes of colonialism and exploitation. Those who control the resources preserve their advantages by discrimination." Lewis, Knipe, and other scholars further developed this theory in *Colonialism in Modern America: The Appalachian Case*, published in 1980.

As anthropologist Patricia Beaver points out, the "application of the internal colonialism model to the Appalachian coalfields . . . altered the direction in which regional activists and educators set their course and provided new ways to begin thinking about regional culture and class." Beaver describes Lewis's work as "an essential piece in the movement of cultural workers and scholars away from the Appalachian subculture and deficiency models toward a broader analysis that took into consideration global industrial forces."[16]

Lewis's articulation of the colonialism model not only helped change research about the region but also inspired individual resistance to the social and economic dominance of coal and the creation of new frameworks for social change. The theory shifted the focus away from academics and experts analyzing and describing Appalachian deficiencies and instead to listening to what Appalachians had to say for themselves. This often meant conducting oral history interviews with community members as a form of empowerment. As Daniel R. Kerr observes, a defining characteristic of radical oral history is the conviction that "through speaking and hearing, people experiencing oppression and exploitation might gain a better understanding of how their subjective personal experience related to others and how their lives were shaped by structures of power. Personal narratives could function as a starting point for social change."[17]

Advocating for Appalachia as an internal colony also changed the course of Lewis's life by bringing her into direct conflict with local coal companies as she pushed for better wages, working conditions, and environmental safeguards. Corporate coal leaders were donors and trustees of the college so they joined forces with repressive academic authorities. By 1977, Lewis faced intense pressure from "a new dean who started trying to put clamps on everything." She explains, "The coal operators got upset with me because I decided when I got fired at ETSU that . . . if you just pussy foot around and try to be safe, you won't get anything done, and they'll still fire you."

Lewis resolved, "Might as well accomplish all you can," assigning her students to examine the local land records of the mining companies and interview workers about their conditions, wages, and health risks. The college administrators kept the pressure on too: for example, by relocating her office to a janitor's closet while she was away on a trip. When scholars and activists across Appalachia met for the first time in 1977 to exchange knowledge, consider the region's assets and challenges, and support one another's work, the embattled Lewis could not attend. Yet the group built on her curricula and

Helen Matthews Lewis speaking at Clinch Valley College graduation, 1977. Courtesy of Helen Matthews Lewis Collection located in the Appalachian State University Library Special Collections.

community-based oral history practices to begin planning annual meetings that grew into the Appalachian Studies Association.

In 1977, as Lewis recounts, "I actually resigned from Clinch Valley College," underscoring, "I was not fired."[18] In this defining moment of her academic teaching career, she took decisive and self-determined action in the face of certain financial consequences and an uncertain future. She chose preserving her independence as a community-based teacher and activist over the economic and social security of a faculty position.

A Circuit-Riding Humanities Scholar, 1977–97

For the next twenty years, from age fifty-three to seventy-three, Lewis described herself as a circuit-riding humanities scholar. By then divorced, she traveled frequently from her River Farm home in southwest Virginia to the Highlander Research and Education Center in east Tennessee and to Appalshop, a media arts and education center in Whitesburg, southeastern

Kentucky. She created an economically independent career as a community-based change agent and public intellectual, often serving as a scholar on various grant-funded projects, sometimes simultaneously and sometimes serially. She also interspersed this work with occasional teaching and administrative positions at regional colleges and universities.

Over these two decades, Lewis served in several capacities at the Highlander Research and Education Center in the foothills of the Smokey Mountains. As shown in the documentary film, *You Got to Move: Stories of Change in the South*, Highlander, founded in 1932 as a folk school on the Danish model of citizen education, played a crucial role in both the southern labor and civil rights movements. By the 1970s, Highlander became a national leader in addressing social inequities in Appalachia at the community level.[19] Lewis already knew and respected director Myles Horton. The two shared a deep friendship based on values and core beliefs about grassroots change and corporate domination of the region.

Like her, Horton supported the popular education methodology pioneered by Paulo Freire and the practice of using oral history interviews to inspire

Helen Matthews Lewis with Myles Horton, founder of the Highlander Research and Education Center. Courtesy of Helen Matthews Lewis Collection located in the Appalachian State University Library Special Collections.

social change through collective grassroots actions. She and Horton both saw community-based interviews as valuable opportunities for individual and collective knowledge building and reflection, essential precursors to positive collective action. Both shared heartfelt commitments to the belief that people must be the experts and authors of their own social change.

When Lewis joined the staff, her first assignment was to focus on regional health programs and community clinics. She quickly applied her oral history research practices to learn from new communities about their public health, a subject rarely discussed in the region. She never doubted that lasting health improvements must be led by the grassroots expertise gained from oral interviews.

First, she identified medical professionalism as a class barrier to communication about public health in a region characterized by educational inequities. In a public presentation entitled "Medicos and Mountaineers," she observed that mountain people don't want "to know the [medical] doctor's degrees, but . . . who he is, what he is like as a person, is he honest, does he really care?" Speaking directly to medical workers, she continued, "If I had some advice for professionals coming to the mountains or to mountaineers turning professional, I would say 'Listen *to people*, Learn from *people*.' . . . Unlearn your 'professional' training; be unprofessional, be human."[20]

She also defended community-based standards for evidence in interviews about the health and environmental damage caused by surface coal mining then taking place. In a 1978 Highlander publication, *"It Shakes You Up": The Social and Psychological Effects of Surface Mine Blasting*, Lewis began "with a set of definitions, which set the perspectives from which I come."

She started with "gossip—to talk mostly about other people's affairs, to go about tattling, to tell tales." She explained, "As a sociologist that is what I do. . . . I have been a gossip of surface mining for some time and will draw on interviews and observations during the past 10 years to show psychological and social impacts." Lewis arranged public forums where community members, many of whom were women, recruited through oral history interviews, effectively testified to health experts about how large-scale surface mining affected their family's health, such as by causing mental stress and damaging water sources.

"Local people have learned that the coal industry does not want or plan to meet the social costs of mining, but expects residents to meet those costs and thus subsidize their operations," she writes in *It Shakes You Up*. Through sharing their stories in first-person interviews, "They have learned the value of joining in protest and the power of organized resistance. They have learned the need to effect political change, the need for constant monitoring of both business and government agencies to prevent collusion and continued destruction."[21]

In 1979, she won a National Science Foundation grant through their Science for Citizens Program to organize public forums on environmental health problems in Appalachia. In her 1980 final report, she wrote frankly about the power differentials between the coal companies and the communities. "The NSF point of view seems to assume that all groups in a community are equal," she observes. "This does not admit to the power relationships within a community, the gaps of information, the dominance and control over the life choices within the community." She expressed a clear vision of her own role as a community-based researcher: learning about grassroots conditions through oral histories, sharing that information, "and bringing balance through power equalization, making scientific information available to those with the least access."[22]

In 1979, Lewis also began teaming up with filmmakers at Appalshop in a series of partnerships that continue to this day. Established ten years earlier as the Film Workshop of Appalachia, the young people there were well aware of the potential of locally produced media to capture stories that could advance social change and address the negative impacts of coal mining.[23] With surface or "strip" mining devastating the surrounding mountains, one of their first film projects was *Strip Mining: Energy, Environment and Economics*, featuring Lewis explaining the environmental and economic impacts of coal on southeastern Kentucky.[24]

After that, she became the project director for an ambitious proposed six-part film series on the history of Appalachia. *Strangers and Kin*, the first in the proposed series, was completed in 1983 with funding from the National Endowment for the Humanities. Lewis served as the primary humanities scholar.

Strangers and Kin traces the history of harmful Appalachian stereotypes by juxtaposing negative images from popular culture with young Appalshop actors telling their personal stories. In this way, the film reveals and challenges stereotypes through first-person stories presented directly to viewers, unmediated by experts and professionals. For example, the Appalshop actors grew up in the region during President Lyndon Baines Johnson's media-laden War on Poverty. In the film, they share stories of seeing local children, some of whom they knew by name, being portrayed as icons of poverty in *Life Magazine*.[25]

Moving past teaching through texts and spoken words, Lewis saw the power of visual images integrating community education and media production. "One of the things that has been interesting to me," she wrote, "is trying to learn to see things visually and understanding visual images and what you can do with them. We learned a lot."[26] First-person interviews focusing on the primacy of voice and using video interviews to communicate visual information became a staple of Appalshop films and also of emerging oral history practices, enabled by new technology like lightweight cameras.[27]

Popular Education, Participatory Research, and Appalachian Studies

During her twenty years as an itinerant scholar, Lewis balanced multiple part-time or time-limited projects in different states. From 1985 through 1990, supported by the Fund for the Improvement of Postsecondary Education, Lewis led a Highlander participatory action research project with women in east Tennessee. As mechanized surface mining became more prevalent, hundreds of men in the coalfields lost their jobs. Lewis developed an action research project centered on economic education with women in some of the rural communities devastated by coal mechanization. With high rates of male unemployment, Lewis noted that "there is something of a social movement led by women in these communities."

Drawing on her long experience with interactive interviews, social analysis, and focused actions, she and the women first discussed then wrote down their work histories. Then they analyzed changing economic variables and identified home-based skills with potential for generating income. Working together, the women discussed how they could create viable cottage industries or form cooperatives. They then combined their first-person narratives with individual and collective reflections about paid and unpaid work. "The stories were so powerful that we put them together in a booklet," Lewis explains, as a way to inform and inspire women to see their own economic potential.

Thus began the Highlander Economics Education Program, which still exists today. According to Lewis, "The goals of the Highlander Economics Education Program are to help people in rural Appalachian communities understand the changing economy and be able to develop ways of dealing with the economy and community economic development." She outlines four ways she used participatory action research in the program: "1. The starting point is the experience and knowledge of the participant. 2. The methods are participatory. 3. The relationship with participants is based on mutual respect and shared responsibility. 4. The activities end up with action." In this way, Lewis clearly connects popular education and radical oral history practices, such as focusing on first-person lived experiences as a pathway to collective action for social change.[28]

During this time too, Lewis co-led a community economic development project in the small town of Ivanhoe in the southwest Virginia coalfields. The Ivanhoe Civic League had requested help from Highlander in attracting a new factory to their town, the most common concept of community economic development in the coalfields then and oftentimes still now. She writes, "The participatory research project began in June 1987, when I visited Ivanhoe as a community educator to help the year-old Ivanhoe Civic League assess their efforts and understand the economic change of which they were a part."

An unlikely partnership developed when she met two more women with direct interest in community economic development in Ivanhoe: Maxine Waller, president of the Ivanhoe Civic League, and Mary Ann Hinton, a former Glenmary nun studying feminist theology. The three strong women worked together over a five-year period to learn not only about the history of Ivanhoe and its economic prospects but also about the nature of civic leadership and the role of religious faith in local social change.

Lewis later describes the partners participating in "an exciting, on-going educational and development process." Together, the women were "interviewing and being interviewed, discussing, arguing, crying, laughing." Through it all, they were "trying to understand and pass on this understanding to others so that they also might learn from [their] experiences."[29]

As described by oral historian Donald Ritchie in *Doing Oral History*, "Their 'participatory research project' combined outside researchers, educators, grassroots community groups, and community members who collectively designed the project and analyzed the results. Their 'history group' of volunteers interviewed people at the post office, in the Civic League office, on the street, and in stores, collecting, transcribing, and editing fifty-three interviews and over eight hundred photographs."[30]

In 1990, the first volume of the history project, *Remembering Our Past, Building Our Future* won Berea College's prestigious W. D. Weatherford Award for best book on Appalachia. Consistent with her lifelong practice

Helen Matthews Lewis leading Highlander economics education workshop, 1980s. Courtesy of Helen Matthews Lewis Collection located in the Appalachian State University Library Special Collections.

of honest self-reflection, Lewis openly discussed the power dynamics and the difficulties of working as a community-change agent in Ivanhoe. She vividly but respectfully explained her differences—for example, access to higher education—with local leader Maxine Waller. "I was not a value-free neutral observer," Lewis recognized. "I pushed people, especially Maxine. And she would respond, sometimes very forcefully. In a recent exchange, she responded, 'Damn it, Helen! You drive me crazy! You have educated me too damn much.'"[31]

Despite these differences, Lewis and Waller worked successfully together with Hinton to cowrite *It Comes from the People: Community Development and Local Theology*. This is Lewis's best-known and most widely respected national contribution to oral history as an experienced community-based researcher working over a long period of time. The concept of *local theology* and how it relates to grassroots social change has not been as widely recognized, however.

Lewis, Waller, and Hinsdale understood the power of religion to inspire hope and a vision of the possibility of change in the face of daunting structural inequities. Working together at Ivanhoe, the three women integrated Bible study and religious fellowship into their community development work, underscoring the importance of local theology in shaping both individual narratives and collective reflections. Their incorporation of local theology into community history is worth further investigation because it recognizes faith as a factor in catalyzing grassroots change in places where religion is a strong part of daily life.

In 1997, at age seventy-three, Lewis ended her twenty-year stint as a traveling sociologist, including her work on large projects with Appalshop and Highlander, and returned to her family home in north Georgia. Over those twenty years, the Appalachian Studies Association had matured into a strong region-wide organization. By then, ASA was holding annual conferences reflecting Lewis's values and oral history practices. The annual gatherings include community practitioners, such as the history group in Ivanhoe, along with interdisciplinary researchers and students, providing scholarships for youth leaders and community members, and always sharing food and celebrating culture.

In 2002, the Appalachian Studies Association recognized her contributions by naming her as president and holding their twenty-fifth annual conference in Unicoi, Georgia, near her family home. There, she presided over the presentation of the first Helen M. Lewis Community Service Award. The award recognizes how Lewis "shaped the field of Appalachian studies by emphasizing community participation and challenging traditional perceptions of the region and its people."[32]

In 2007, Lewis, ever self-reflecting, issued a powerful critique of her own place in Appalachian studies. In a talk to Morehead State University undergraduates in Kentucky, she asked whether she and others in the field were

"Telling the Truth or Preserving the Myths?" She then went on to contest her own unofficial title of mother—or, as she says now, grandmother—of Appalachian studies.

She pointed to early local color writers, educators and missionaries, regional novelists like Harriette Arnow and Wilma Dykeman, and the social movements of the 1960s as some of the forerunners of modern Appalachian studies. She reminded the students and faculty, "My original vision of Appalachian studies required a change in academic structure, teaching methods, curricula design and learning about and from the region, which leads to action. But this type of action through Appalachian studies was very hard to do and led to my leaving academe."

Lewis looked unflinchingly at the changing paradigms around her. "We must be willing to accept when our truths are declared myths and are no longer useful to describe reality as we see it now," Lewis urged. Yet her bedrock optimism about the future remains intact. In her talk, she affirmed that Appalachian studies can be a resource for positive social change in the region, but it requires a commitment from the institution to provide services to the region and to collaborate with communities to deal with social and economic problems.[33]

Conclusion

Throughout her eighties and into her nineties, Lewis has continued to work for social change. She served as a key humanities scholar (once again) for After Coal: Stories of Survival in Appalachia and Wales, a multimedia project directed by Tom Hansell at the Center for Appalachian Studies at Appalachian State University.[34] Based on a miners exchange program, Lewis helped initiate in the 1960s, the project investigates how these two regions are coping with the effects of past deindustrialization and working for a better future.

In this way, she continues to inspire thinking and action about Appalachia's challenges and potentials in the postcoal era. In a video interview, for example, she reflects on creating and maintaining healthy communities, the necessary role of governments, and how the depletion of natural resources has become a global concern with lessons to be learned from the coalfields of Appalachia and Wales.[35]

Lewis revisited Appalshop in 2012 to participate in a reading from the collection of her edited works. She selected one of her poems, explaining that she used to protest by sitting down in front of coal trucks but

Lewis giving the presidential address at the Appalachian Studies Conference, 2002. Courtesy of Helen Matthews Lewis Collection Appalachian State University.

now she protests by writing verses. In the poem, she expresses her concerns about the future of elders as caretakers of culture.[36] Yet her faith in social change is unshaken, and she ended the evening by celebrating Appalachian music and dancing.[37]

The research, educational, and social justice contributions of Helen Matthews Lewis are widely respected throughout the Appalachian region, as well as nationally and internationally among popular educators and participatory action researchers. Appalachian State University Library is the main repository for her papers, which are well cataloged. East Tennessee State University, which once fired her, now has a Center for Appalachian Studies and Services acknowledging her contributions. Many of her key works on community development now have new life as digital resources on the After Coal website, bringing Lewis's insights to new generations of learners.

Placing her life and work in the context of the radical genealogy of oral history answers some questions. For example, how community-based oral historians, like Lewis, recognize the importance of capturing and preserving firsthand accounts of lived experiences as an integral part of history.

How these sources are too often missing in public life, past and present. And how individual stories can lead to collective change.

Her life story also opens up new areas of inquiry not yet fully explored. For example, what relationship, if any, does Lewis's community-based practice of oral interviews for social change have with current university-based programs for community engagement? Is it still, or was it ever, the role of a public university to support research and teaching focused on social change? If so, how are unequal power dynamics negotiated and shared authority established with people in a community? What about the radical roots of oral history that are entirely community led and may not be recorded or preserved at all?

These questions and Lewis's work outside the oral history mainstream indicate the need to establish new criteria for what oral history is and to develop new ways to assess its impact on social change. How can a practice with roots in history recognize compatible roots and branches in other fields, practices, and professions?[38] What is gained and what is lost in that process?

While Lewis's life stories raise many questions for further exploration, her work and writings clearly demonstrate her unshakable conviction that social change comes from the people and oral history interviews can be starting points for action. Her life demonstrates her clear-eyed self-reflection, imagination in creating new visions of the future, and dedication to social interactions and oral history practices that advance grassroots social change.

Notes

1 Daniel R. Kerr, "Allan Nevins Is Not My Grandfather: The Roots of Radical Oral History Practice in the United States," *Oral History Review* 34, no. 2 (Summer/Fall 2016): 371.

2 Helen Matthews Lewis, *Helen Matthews Lewis: Living Social Justice in Appalachia*, ed. Patricia D. Beaver and Judith Jennings (Lexington: University Press of Kentucky, 2012).

3 *New Georgia Encyclopedia*, s.v. "Clarence Jordan," accessed April 1, 2020, https://www.georgiaencyclopedia.org/articles/arts-culture/clarence-jordan-1912-1969.

4 Beaver and Jennings, *Helen Matthews Lewis*, 18–19.

5 Beaver and Jennings, 20–21. See also Jessica Wilkerson and David Cline, "Mountain Feminist: Helen Matthews Lewis, Appalachian Studies, and the Long Women's Movement," Southern Cultures, accessed April 1, 2020, http://www.southerncultures.org/article/mountain-feminist-helen-matthews-lewis-appalachian-studies-and-the-long-womens-movement/.

6 Anthony J. Cortese, "The Rise, Hegemony and Decline of the Chicago School of Sociology, 1891–1945," *Social Science Journal* 32, no. 3 (1995): 235–54.

7 Gunnar Myrdal, *An American Dilemma: The Negro Problem and Modern Democracy*, vol. 1 (Abingdon, UK: Routledge, 2017).
8 Ralph Ellison, review of *An American Dilemma*, by Gunnar Myrdal, 1944, available at http://teachingamericanhistory.org/library/document/an-american-dilemma-a-review/.
9 Beaver and Jennings, *Helen Matthews Lewis*, 34–42.
10 Ronald Grele, "Oral History as Evidence," in *Handbook of Oral History*, ed. Thomas L. Charlton, Lois E. Meyers, and Rebecca Sharpless (New York: AltaMira, 2006), 43–104.
11 See, for example, Anthony Harkins and Meredith McCarroll, eds., *Appalachian Reckoning: A Region Responds to* Hillbilly Elegy (Morgantown: West Virginia University Press, 2019).
12 *Long Journey Home*, directed by Elizabeth Barret (Appalshop Film, 1987), https://appalshop.org/shop/long-journey-home.
13 Beaver and Jennings, *Helen Matthews Lewis*, 47–51.
14 Beaver and Jennings, 54–56.
15 Beaver and Jennings, 59–60.
16 Beaver and Jennings, 64–70.
17 Kerr, "Allan Nevins," 371.
18 Beaver and Jennings, *Helen Matthews Lewis*, 78.
19 *You Got to Move: Stories of Change in the South*, directed by Lucy Massie Phenix (Milliarum Zero, 1985), https://vimeo.com/channels/828884/125290703.
20 Beaver and Jennings, *Helen Matthews Lewis*, 98–100.
21 Beaver and Jennings, 104–7.
22 Beaver and Jennings, 112.
23 *Long Journey Home*.
24 *Strip Mining: Energy, Environment and Economics*, directed by Frances Morton and Gene DuBey (Appalshop, 1979).
25 *Strangers and Kin*, Appalshop Film clip, accessed on April 1, 2020, https://www.youtube.com/watch?v=GP5-RRfKXDY.
26 Beaver and Jennings, *Helen Matthews Lewis*, 119–21.
27 Linda Shopes, email to author, March 30, 2020.
28 Beaver and Jennings, *Helen Matthews Lewis*, 138–41.
29 Beaver and Jennings, 153–55.
30 Donald A. Ritchie, *Doing Oral History*, 3rd ed. (New York: Oxford University Press, 2015), 243.
31 Beaver and Jennings, *Helen Matthews Lewis*, 157.
32 "Awards," Appalachian Studies Association, accessed on April 1, 2020, http://appalachianstudies.org/awards/.
33 Beaver and Jennings, *Helen Matthews Lewis*, 186–90.
34 Tom Hansell, After Coal: Stories of Survival in Appalachia and Wales, accessed on April 1, 2020, http://aftercoal.com/.
35 Tom Hansell, "Helen Lewis Interview Excerpt," Vimeo, April 2, 2020, https://vimeo.com/403347192/8e60537399.

36 Tom Hansell, "Helen Lewis Poetry Reading," Vimeo, April 2, 2020, https://vimeo.com/403350798/cf07b7b789.

37 Tom Hansell, "Helen Lewis Dancing at Appalshop's Seedtime Festival," Vimeo, April 2, 2020, https://vimeo.com/403347772/e4ce90ffac.

38 Shopes, email to author.

"Recalling Our Bitter Experiences"

Consciousness Raising, Feminism, and Women's Oral History

Anne M. Valk

In 1983, Cindy Cohen described the Cambridge Women's Oral History Project (CWOHP) in the women's studies journal *Frontiers*. As project director, Cohen collaborated with community women to preserve and amplify the stories of everyday working women. High school–aged girls recorded interviews with women in their sixties and older and then worked together to produce *Let Life Be Yours: Voices of Cambridge Working Women*, a short slide-tape presentation and an exhibit. The project hoped to positively impact local residents in multiple ways. Working women would benefit from telling their stories, high school students would gain interviewing skills, and both groups would meet new people and gain insight into the place they lived. Scholars could access new research materials. And the hundreds of individuals who attended CWOHP's public gatherings would more fully understand the city and, perhaps, become inspired to begin their own oral history projects. On these many levels, the CWOHP showed that "oral history can function as a form of community consciousness raising. . . . For the individual who is telling about her life, being listened to and having her life documented are validating experiences in themselves. For those of us who are doing the interviewing or listening to the tapes, the active, nonjudgmental inquiry, the experiences and perceptions of another individual become material for analysis and reflection." The outcomes of this kind of multigenerational public oral history project might extend even further. "Within a community," Cohen argued, "the study of history can help the group to become more conscious of itself and of the forces that have shaped its present circumstances." With this greater historical awareness, community members would recognize their shared interests and understand how race, class, and age have kept women apart.[1]

The CWOHP represented one of the many women's oral history projects launched in the 1970s and the early 1980s that aimed to awaken individual women to the importance of their history and provoke collective social change. In this decade, the new field of women's oral history grew like wildfire, ignited by sparks of feminist activism, kindled by public historians' efforts to preserve community, and stoked by academics' insistence that women's lives were worthy of documentation and analysis. Articles like Cohen's—which detailed the project goals, described its methods, assessed its outcomes, and then shared project information in a new scholarly journal—helped spread the fire. Moreover, Cohen's evocation of "consciousness raising" connected her project to feminist organizing. Her terminology linked women's oral history to a feminist practice through which millions of American women had experienced their own "aha moment" when they realized that the personal is political.

By 1970, thanks to the notion of consciousness raising, feminist organizers had begun to build a movement for women's equality that relied on women sharing stories from their own lives, past and present, to explore how sex, class, race, and other factors shaped their identities and opportunities.[2] The process of consciousness raising, speak-outs and other forms of testimony generated evidence that could heighten activists' comprehension of patriarchy, connect women through appreciation of their shared experiences, and insert women's voices into policy-making arenas. Consciousness raising also served more academic purposes, as it moved from the streets, living rooms, and public venues where activists met into classrooms, libraries, and archives. Throughout the 1970s, women's studies classrooms and women's centers became sites where consciousness raising and oral history intersected and generated new forms of public history.

The links between oral history and consciousness raising are direct and indirect, explicit and implicit, personal and pedagogical. Rosalyn Baxandall, a women's liberation activist and historian, described oral history as an "offshoot" of consciousness raising, categorizing both methods as "part of a wider philosophical emphasis on experience as a source of knowing in radical circles."[3] Sherna Berger Gluck, part of the "first generation of feminist oral historians," recalled that "ties to local groups where we were organizing and engaged in consciousness raising influenced how we used [oral history]."[4] Gluck, Baxandall, and other feminists simultaneously occupied roles as teachers, scholars, and activists, and they carried ideas and inspiration from one realm into another, sometimes blurring the distinctions between the sites and methods that nurtured political change. Indeed, in these years, women's studies operated as an academic arm of the women's movement. Although they did not characterize themselves as public historians, these scholar-activists resembled the "proto-public historians" whom historian Lara Kelland has described as employing a variety of "memory practices" to create historical projects that would help build collective experience and construct new political identities.[5] Fueled by anger and analyses produced through consciousness raising, they proceeded to transform research and teaching and the institutions in which both took place. Through this synergetic activity, women's studies and women's oral history both ignited and were kindled by feminists' uses of personal testimony.

This article argues that the methods of and motivations for consciousness raising became woven into the rationales and practices adopted by a generation of feminist oral historians, public history practitioners, and other scholars in the 1970s and 1980s. After introducing the process of consciousness raising, including the more specific practice of women's consciousness raising groups, the essay describes several feminist public and oral history projects. For scholars, teachers, and activists, women's oral history provided a methodology that paralleled consciousness raising in movement circles. Incorporated into women's studies classes and public history projects, practitioners argued that women's oral history could generate new sources of insight into women's experiences and help build the movement. These efforts were enhanced by women's studies' growing institutionalization, which provided new classes, programs, and publications through which teachers and organizers exchanged information about ways that oral history could advance feminist pedagogy and activism. Even as women's studies' academic position solidified, its practitioners tried to remain connected to a broader (female) public that could inspire the ongoing movement for women's equality. Recovering the role that consciousness raising played in the evolution of oral history illuminates one way in which activists connected personal testimony with their social change goals.

Speaking Bitterness

The concept of consciousness raising synthesized analyses of oppression and social movement tactics drawn from a variety of sources. However, as a feminist practice, it is typically attributed to Kathie Sarachild. An activist who had spent the summer of 1964 volunteering on civil rights projects in Mississippi, Sarachild later helped to found New York Radical Women and Redstockings, both New York City–based women's liberation groups. These experiences convinced her that women, like other subordinate groups, had internalized their own oppression, succumbing to a sense of inferiority that led them to accept pervasive economic, political, and social inequalities. In order to act against their oppression, women needed to understand that their problems were not only individual but collective and structural. They could gain this awareness by talking with each other about intensely personal experiences, especially those they considered too shameful, embarrassing, trivial, or unusual to discuss. Based on techniques honed within New York Radical Women, Sarachild urged feminists to form small "'bitch session' cell group(s)" in which they could discuss personal, gender-related experiences. As they became aware of the "concrete reality" of their lives, women would establish a sense of community with one another and a theoretical understanding of oppression that could lead to action. Thus by helping women to understand that the personal is political, these groups would help energize a larger women's movement.

In 1968, at the first National Women's Liberation Conference, Sarachild presented her "Program for Feminist 'Consciousness Raising.'" Activists from women's liberation groups traveled from around the country to attend this conference near Chicago; returning home, they helped to swiftly spread consciousness raising through feminist groups, which began to coalesce into a national movement. In 1970, New York Radical Women reprinted the program in its newspaper, *Notes from the Second Year: Women's Liberation,* and this publication ensured its continuing impact.[6]

One activist called consciousness raising one of the "sparks that would help light the prairie fire of women's liberation" and the "primary organizing tool of our movement."[7] Activists—and later, historians—described consciousness raising as both "the backbone" and the "cornerstone" of the surging women's liberation movement in the US.[8] As these descriptions suggest, consciousness raising represented both a means of personal enlightenment and a way to mobilize women to take action. Most importantly, its adherents believed consciousness raising contained seeds for radical change and offered a way of "carrying theory about women further than it had ever been carried before."[9] Feminists drew inspiration from other revolutionary movements that used similar processes, such as that of the peasants in communist China described in William Hinton's 1966 book, *Fanshen: A Documentary of Revolution in a Chinese Village*. According to Hinton, women fought against the oppression of their husbands and their domestic roles through "speaking pains to recall pains."[10] "Speak Bitterness" meetings also gave peasant farmers a chance to testify publicly against—and in front of—their landlords and describe the injustices done against them. In the Chinese Revolution, as in American feminism, the act of "recalling their bitter experiences" was intended to "raise the consciousness" of participants, making them newly cognizant of the politics of their lives. Philosophers of Black liberation informed consciousness raising as well. In his book *Black Skin / White Masks*, for example, Frantz Fanon described how the phenomenon of internalized oppression blinded people from realizing, let alone challenging, cultural and political systems that kept them subordinate. Consciousness raising promised to aid women in identifying such systems, strengthening their resolve and newfound confidence to speak truth to power, and using their personal testimony to confront political and economic inequalities.[11]

In feminist practice in the US, the term originally described a social change *process* more than a specific method. In a 1973 talk, Kathie Sarachild explained, "From the beginning of consciousness-raising . . . there has been no one method of raising consciousness. What really counts in consciousness-raising are not methods, but results. The only 'methods' of consciousness raising are essentially principles. They are the basic radical political principles of going to the original sources, both historic and personal, going to people—women themselves, and going to experience for theory and strategy."[12] As it spread, however, a more standardized form developed, aided by the distribution of guidelines that appeared in magazines, newsletters, and mimeographed booklets. Consciousness raising became synonymous with the small, structured groups in which women discussed topics that could illuminate the workings of patriarchy: childhood memories of sex roles in the family, relationships with their mothers and other women, sexuality, sexual oppression and violence, racism and privilege, and paid and unpaid work.[13] The authors of one set of guidelines explained, "The group should plan to spend a substantial amount of time sharing personal histories and feelings in order to build trust, especially at the beginning. It is good to pose questions constantly that make women backtrack and remember their own pasts."[14] Likewise, Rosalyn Baxandall recalled, "We would pick apart each other's memories, compare and interrogate them, and start to recast memory as theories about the forms taken by sexism. We wanted to create an open-ended, fluid approach to politics that would lead to change and to a new theory of causes of female oppression."[15]

To achieve these ends, groups needed to encourage all women's participation and to dedicate adequate time to explore the complexities of each issue. Although groups might have an organizer or coordinator, that person was not a leader; instead, groups aspired to be nonhierarchical, with women seated in a circle, and everyone was expected to speak but none would be required to do so. Including many voices enlarged the "common pool of knowledge."[16] When they had learned to trust and respect each other, participants would build a community based around their shared experiences of oppression. The point was not to create friendships (although this often occurred) or to function as a support group but to nurture action and organizing.

In practice, however, activists discovered the hard way that consciousness raising did not necessarily lead to action. One critic asserted that "consciousness raising groups too often stayed at the level of recounting personal experiences of oppression. That is the place we all have to begin," she explained, "but if we don't try to bring those experiences together and figure out what is common to them, our movement will stay at the level of individual struggle."[17] Others recognized that consciousness raising did not negate the differences that separated women. Economic, educational, racial, and other disparities shaped dynamics within consciousness raising groups; indeed, distinctions in status, privilege, and other forms of power often were accentuated. Thus for some activists, consciousness raising highlighted the limitations of personal storytelling as a route toward political mobilization and provided important lessons about the ways that power dynamics shaped interpersonal interactions even when equality was a goal.[18]

Consciousness raising also inspired public testimonial gatherings, starting with an abortion speak-out in 1969 organized by Sarachild and other feminists from New York's women's liberation group Redstockings. After being excluded from hearings to consider the state's abortion laws, activists demanded they should have a voice in legal reforms.[19] At their speak-out, women activists recounted the logistical, financial, and emotional difficulty of seeking or obtaining what was then an illegal procedure; women in the audience shared even more stories. Talking publicly about an issue that was typically cloaked in secrecy and shame, the speak-out emboldened women to break their silence in order to influence public policy. The Redstockings' speak-out inspired similar actions on topics including the birth control pill, rape, and the Equal Rights Amendment. At these speak-outs, women insisted that they were "the true experts, the only experts," as those with firsthand experience, not politicians or health care professionals. Thus speak-outs, like consciousness raising, provided a way for women to counter or correct misinformation and elevate their personal experience as a form of knowledge.[20]

From Living Rooms to Classrooms

By the start of the 1970s, feminism had begun to transform academic institutions and practices. In 1966, the year that the Oral History Association held its inaugural meeting in southern California, two activists offered a course on women at the community Free School in New Orleans. Students who sought academic credit could enroll in new women-centered classes at the University of Chicago and Barnard College.[21] In 1970, San Diego State University established the country's first women's studies department. Other universities and even high schools soon followed, and by 1975, at least 150 new women's studies programs were underway across the US.

Historian Marilyn Boxer explained, "From the beginning, the goal of women's studies was not merely to study women's position in the world but to change it."[22] The lines between activism and academics blurred in the goals, methods, and subjects that formed the core of the new women's studies programs. In many places, activists from the community taught classes and most of the new programs reached out with classes and programs intended for a broader feminist public.[23] Through these inclusionary practices, women's studies courses became organizing spaces for the feminist movement. In addition to offering novel content, women's studies sought to democratize the classroom and decenter authority in order to increase the sense of power that women students felt over their education and, by extension, their lives. Teachers often rearranged their classrooms to resemble consciousness raising groups or feminist meetings, with chairs arrayed in circles and preferred nonhierarchical discussions to lectures.[24] The similarities to consciousness raising extended into course goals and content too. Women's studies operated with an explicitly feminist agenda to use new research to challenge male bias and to instigate activism. This disruption was premised on feminists' understanding of how knowledge is constructed, especially repudiation of the goal, and the possibility, of neutrality and objectivity. Women's studies aimed to present women as they saw themselves, not filtered through the gaze of men.[25] As the poet and essayist Adrienne Rich put it, "We are not 'the woman question' asked by somebody else; we are the women who ask the questions."[26]

Consciousness raising and oral history were ideally suited for courses that rejected the impossible ideal of academic objectivity. In particular, oral history offered a way to learn about women's experiences while honoring women's subjectivity as a source of knowledge and expertise. Many women's studies courses, using a variety of disciplinary approaches, incorporated oral history assignments to awaken students to the realities of women's lives, past and present. Used along with other autobiographical sources—journal writing, first-person essays, and so on—oral history gave students insight into women's experiences in the past and revealed how sexism shaped their choices. Oral history interviews additionally became a foundation for some research in women's studies courses, adding first-person experiences as evidence that could challenge traditional disciplines. Women's oral history (later "feminist oral history"), oral history within women's studies classes, and consciousness raising remained distinct, however. Feminist consciousness raising, for example, prioritized political activism rather than education, although activists recognized that one was a necessary precondition for the other. In addition, activists never intended that testimony shared within consciousness raising groups would be recorded, preserved, or shared outside in its raw form. Testimony provided during public speak-outs sometimes was reported by journalists but because they intended primarily to influence policy, activists did not record it in a more systematic manner. Finally, although activists had discovered that consciousness raising could magnify women's differences and cause dissension within their groups, they approached oral history believing that it could establish connections and continuity.

Despite these differences, feminists turned to oral history with motives similar to those that inspired consciousness raising. Both consciousness raising and oral history promised to address the inadequacy of existing documentation of women's lives in the past and present.[27] In addition, both processes valued the insights gained from women's daily experiences and their inner lives to understand how patriarchal power worked. Consciousness raising used this knowledge in order to identify social biases and structural inequities that shaped women's lives; oral history used testimony to document these processes. As one teacher explained, "The primary value of oral history in this context [women's studies classroom] is in showing the living, human reality that must be understood and accounted for."[28]

Mostly, women's studies teachers emphasized that oral history could raise the consciousness of both narrators and interviewers. Many courses asked students to conduct their own interviews, aiming to replicate the sense of discovery and connections that emerged when women shared their experiences within consciousness raising groups. Family history projects were frequently assigned. In a Massachusetts high school class on women and society, for example, students were encouraged to ask their grandmothers and mothers about "their upbringing, mores, role in the house, other work, etc."[29] Along with giving students a means to understand historical change and continuity, these family history assignments emphasized cross-generational conversations. An early women's studies class at the University of Massachusetts Boston assigned students to interview female relatives. According to the instructors, this encouraged students to "celebrate the strengths of their unnoticed, unrewarded female relatives, whose heroism in simply living their hard daily lives may never before have struck their friends and relatives" and whose revelations might inspire students and heighten their self-understanding.[30] Whether interviewing relatives or women from outside their family, teachers emphasized how young women students could think about their own futures differently as a result of their interviews. One teacher remarked that she wanted oral history to "provide our daughters not with heroines, but with models."[31] A class called Surviving Female at the University of North Carolina at Charlotte used autobiography and oral history to offer "practical self-help for women,"[32] and students in a Massachusetts high school course, Woman Working, conducted interviews to learn about challenges that women faced in various jobs and how they had "dealt with issues, overcome obstacles, etc."[33]

Mostly the interviews conducted in fulfillment of these assignments did not result in archived collections of interviews, nor were they intended to: teachers stressed the value of process over the finished product, such as the worthiness of the relationships nurtured in an interview. Indeed, some teachers argued that students would benefit more if not impeded by having to record their interviews. Marge Grevatt of the University of Minnesota Duluth relied on oral history as a key pedagogical source in her course, Women of the Western Reserve. She found that "teaching proper oral history techniques and . . . producing acceptable oral history research" interfered with her ultimate goal to establish "a personal connection between students and women of a different time period." For one thing, some students could not afford to buy a tape recorder. Grevatt discounted this dilemma, arguing that "once the goal of the course is reasserted, it becomes clear that the key to the course need not be the production of tape recordings but can rather be the use of interviewing techniques to establish personal connections." Keeping this objective in mind, Grevatt preferred group interviews and other methods that would augment the learning and relationships developed through oral history.[34]

Unlike Grevatt, others argued that recording interviews was essential to produce resources that could be used in future classes and challenge the male domination of history (and other) classes. Tapes and transcripts of interviews conducted in women's studies classes at Harvard were donated to the Schlesinger Library on the History of Women in America, where they became the library's first oral history collection. And oral history offered a solution to parents of children at one elementary school interested in curricular changes. After participating in their own consciousness raising group, the parents (both men and women), sought to minimize the sex biases inherent in history classes. As an alternative, they advised the school to create oral history sources that could be used to educate students about women's lives and to validate the importance of such a topic.[35]

Along with the important impact of oral history on student interviewers, scholars and teachers believed the method could help nurture and sustain feminist activism off campus. For example, oral history seemed well suited to advance women's studies' mission to link the community with universities. Scholars posited that oral history would have a consciousness raising benefit for those who were interviewed. One scholar explained, "The oral historian can raise the self-esteem of the woman interviewed, for in talking about themselves women can recognize the worth of their roles, their efforts, their contributions, their lives. Through the medium of oral history other women can identify with their sisters, mothers, grandmothers, daughters."[36]

Whether raising the consciousness of women participating in interviews or creating materials to teach women's history in classes, women's studies teachers solidified oral history's unique means of connecting activism, pedagogy, and scholarship. Oral history could produce empirical information that would raise the consciousness of women, and participants on both sides of the microphone could experience a raised consciousness as a result of their encounter. At a time when oral history still struggled for legitimacy within the field of history, women's studies teachers and scholars embraced the interview process for such tangible and intangible outcomes.

Feminist Encounters

In 1977, two journals published special issues focused on women's oral history. *Oral History*, published by the British Oral History Society, dedicated a volume to papers presented at a 1976 women's history / oral history conference at Essex University in England. In the US, *Frontiers*, a new women's studies publication, produced a volume focused on women's oral history that included Sherna Berger Gluck's pathbreaking 1977 article, "What's So Special about Women? Women's Oral History." In it, Gluck applauded oral history's potential to change scholarship and advance the women's movement. "Women's oral history is a feminist encounter," Gluck explained, "even if the interviewee is not herself a feminist. It is the creation of a new type of material on women; it is the validation of women's experiences; it is the communication among women of different generations; it is the discovery of our own roots and the development of a continuity that has been denied us in traditional historical accounts."[37]

The dedicated journal issues were a sign of scholars' enthusiasm for women's oral history and their assertion that it constituted something "special."[38] Like women's studies, women's oral history practitioners argued that the process should be *by*, *about*, and *for* women. This included the women who were interviewed, the interviewers (assumed to be women), and the audience of activists, scholars, teachers, students, and others ready to consume the histories that were uncovered. Women's oral history methods differed from other forms of oral history too, advocates stressed. Rather than emphasizing public and political life, Gluck and other practitioners advocated developing questions that could make women's lives and consciousness visible. As Gluck explained, women's oral history should explore intimate matters that could reveal the "rhythm of women's lives." Interviewers should ask about women's biological, reproductive, and sexual activities, for example, along with their relationships with families and friends, their intellectual and working lives, household work, and more. Not surprisingly, given their centrality to women's experiences across the life-span, this list of topics aligned closely with subjects often pursued within consciousness raising groups. Although it departed from the format employed in consciousness raising groups, women's oral history benefited from feminists' insistence that women's narratives could serve as a foundation for political organizing and evidence of women's historical agency.[39]

By producing new archives and publishing interviews, women's oral history projects intended to accelerate the transformation of scholarship and knowledge production that feminists desired. Several projects interviewed woman suffrage activists in order to restore women's public and civic activities to the historical record. They also aimed to uncover information about strategies and organizational approaches that might direct current and future activism. In 1972, for example, Sherna Berger Gluck and Ann Forfreedom initiated the Feminist History Research Project (FHRP) at the Westside Women's Center in Los Angeles. The FHRP prioritized interviews with women who had joined in the early twentieth-century movement for the vote. When she published these interviews, Gluck explained that even though suffrage offered an incomplete path to gender equality, knowledge of that movement's accomplishments was important to younger women and to the larger feminist cause. She explained, "That shared effort, that defiance of entrenched male authority, that glimpse of possible triumph, could and should become part of the consciousness of all women. The oral-history interviews with five unknown suffragists presented here will, I hope, contribute to that consciousness."[40]

Whereas the suffrage project included women prominent as a result of their political activities, other early projects focused on daily life and work. Initiatives across the West and the South, for example, documented the regional diversity of women's experiences.[41] Others focused on representing diversity that came from race and ethnic differences. The Black Women's Oral History Project, organized in 1977 by the Schlesinger Library at Radcliffe College, interviewed an astonishingly diverse group of narrators, including many individuals recognized as "the first" in their fields, those who headed national organizations, and those who founded and sustained community organizations and local movements across the country. The University of Michigan and Wayne State University initiated a large labor history project to interview women from the trade union movement, resulting in an archival collection, at least one book, and an original performance, developed by the Labor Theater, that brought some of those interviews to life.[42]

Like the ones named above, most women's oral history projects straddled academic, public, and activist realms and emphasized the value of preserving and sharing oral histories through the creation of publicly accessible archives and presentations for general audiences. Public programs were obligatory if support came from state humanities councils or the National Endowment for the Humanities. Beyond a funding requirement, however, women's oral historians considered it essential to their movement-building goals to share their research with women outside the academy. Katherine Jensen, an advisor for a Wyoming women's oral history project, insisted that feminist oral historians had a political obligation "to avoid exploiting our sisters for professional purposes." Presenting research back to the public was seen as one important means of meeting this obligation. Public programming also could extend consciousness raising to a broader audience, Jensen argued, by "mak[ing] women subjects rather than objects of women's history. When we take the project back to the community, the audience adds to and critiques the presentation, and, more importantly, participates in the creation of their own historical memory."[43] A Portland, Oregon, project that interviewed women who had built ships and aircraft carriers during World War II demonstrated these values. Interviews with these "Rosie the Riveters" revealed their pride in their accomplishments and highlighted how women were quickly pushed out of their jobs after the war ended.[44] The Oregon project shared the histories of women's work in the shipyards through a public slide-tape show, giving interviewees the chance to gather and rekindle old friendships while others in the audience could reflect on the significance of their work.

Slide-tape shows represented state-of-the-art technology and promised an engaging way to use both audio and visual images to narrate history. Sadly, few of these slide-tape shows are still available, but one created for the suffragists oral history project mentioned above is online.[45] Documentary films, radio stories, and live performances were also popular ways to incorporate women's interviews into public programs.[46] For many researchers, however, the original interviewees constituted the most important audience. Mary Aickin Rothschild, director of *Lives of Arizona Women: Past and Present*, incorporated that project's interviews into a readers-theater-style performance and slide show. After having finished twelve performances around the state, Rothschild recounted that the "most gratifying" of the many "heartwarming" responses the actors received came from the interviewees who indicated that she and the performers "had captured their interviews correctly." Thus in addition to enriching the historical record by recording and preserving women's memories of life, work, family, and community, Rothschild and other oral historians believed that public sharing of those accounts offered to women an important form of validation that their experiences mattered.[47]

Many projects sought to uncover the diversity of women's experiences and to positively document the complexity of their personal and private lives, however, they sometimes essentialized women's commonalities and failed to critically analyze those differences. The Arizona project, for example, was framed around the experience of the "common woman," and coordinators worked hard to include Anglo, Native American, Latina, and African American women and employ interviewers who could speak Spanish. But instead of offering a critical analysis of the ways that race, ethnicity, and immigration status shaped women's social roles or economic opportunities, the culminating slide-tape show celebrated women's contributions to the state, their labor and willingness to do "what the day brought." The groundbreaking Buffalo Lesbian Community Research Project was an exception. Elizabeth Kennedy, the anthropologist who organized the research, interviewed members of a community bonded by both place and sexual identity. For this project, oral history offered a means to understand diversity within this place-based community and to give "voice to the invisible." As Kennedy and her collaborators explained, "An analytic focus on documenting the history of a *community*, in addition to compiling individual life stories, zeroes in on the lives of the unnoticed lesbians." This approach brought visibility to the "common" women who "risked exposure and propelled group survival." But Kennedy and her collaborators also emphasized that "researchers must be cognizant of the sub-communities which developed along race and class lines, and develop adequate research methods to capture and express this reality." Thus rather than aggregate or celebrate universality in women's experiences, the project uncovered the complexity of lesbian identities by revealing how sexuality, gender, race, and socioeconomic class shaped the social experiences of lesbians in Buffalo.[48]

Mainstreaming Consciousness Raising

In 1983, when *Frontiers* published the second special issue focused on women's oral history, the volume included a "Directory of Women's Oral History Projects and Collections." The list described projects in twenty-six states and the District of Columbia on topics as diverse as "Hoosier Homemakers through the Years," a collection of 250 interviews of rural women conducted by volunteers from the Indiana Extension Homemakers Association, and a much smaller effort to interview "Hispanic Women Folk Artists of the San Luis Valley" in Colorado. As the compilation detailed, projects conducted through public libraries, community radio stations, college and university archives, local women's centers, and grassroots history organizations had yielded thousands of hours of tape and thousands of pages of transcripts, plus radio and slide shows, performances, booklets, exhibits, and celebratory public programs. In addition to homemakers and artists, projects recorded the memories of government employees, factory workers, rural women, college alumnae, lesbians, strikebreakers, suffragists, doctors, and more.[49]

Along with providing ample evidence of the popularity of women's oral history and its tangible output, this listing suggests how consciousness raising contributed to the growth of a radical feminist public history practice. This practice was firmly rooted in the principle that by taking seriously accounts of their own lives, women—whether students, scholars, activists, historians, or "everyday women"—could learn to understand present-day political, social, and economic structures and work to change the future. In addition, women's oral history accentuated the power of the process of shared discovery, as narrators and interviewers established relationships through the face-to-face encounter of the interview, ideally followed by public gatherings.

A decade of efforts had taught women's oral historians, however, to question the limitations of such collaborative and often celebratory projects to generate change beyond the individual participants. By the early 1980s, methodological challenges considered unique to this practice, particularly those related to the scholar's responsibility and authority, assumed greater attention.[50] Researchers sought to work with narrators to collectively interpret and make meaning of their sources—what Michael Frisch would call "sharing authority"—while also introducing historical contexts and an understanding of the conditions under which the interview was produced.[51] But how much critical context could be introduced before an interview no longer belonged to the woman who had shared it? And who had the authority to make those determinations?

More specifically, women's oral historians sought to uncover both oppression and women's resistance to it. Historian Susan Armitage contended that women's oral historians "can do much more than simply illuminate neglected lives." She explained, "We can push ahead to the harder job of analysis and connection. To move from the single story to the whole picture requires that we be systematic and critical—while remaining caring and appreciative." This balance necessitated scholarly distance without abandoning the desire to affirm narrators through their participation in the interview process. Marge Grevatt and her students, for example, noticed that "women whose lives appeared to have been stunted and dulled by marriage and motherhood told us that the best thing that could happen to young women today was marriage and motherhood. Did we have the right to challenge them with the apparent contradiction between their own lives and what they were saying to us?" they asked. The answer to such questions, according to Armitage, lay in the practice of interviews that encouraged narrators to "discover and explore" their lives, followed by reflection and questions "about meaning, about comparability, about context. These *are* two steps," Armitage expressed, "but they must connect. If we stop at the first, we have not realized the full potential of women's history; if we do the second carelessly, we misrepresent the women we have interviewed."[52]

The conservative backlash that ushered in the Reagan revolution also made it hard for many women's oral historians to continue their activist work. Public funders for large-scale oral history projects declined and conservative ideologies accentuated economic and racial disparities and reversed many gains made by the 1960s generation. The institutionalization of women's studies strained its community ties. Cindy Cohen mused that for these reasons, the radical practice of women's oral history was both more difficult and more vital. The CWOHP faced numerous challenges, she acknowledged, but she maintained, "We have become more convinced of the importance of this work because it combines so many divergent interests and groups. Finding vocabularies in which we can communicate across our differences and explore common interests is becoming more essential, particularly during a time when the political climate becomes increasingly less supportive for all of the groups involved."[53]

These goals now motivate many public historians interested in social change and their counterparts in the community. As the history of oral history and public history gets rewritten, we should not forget the practitioners from outside the academy and outside the historical profession who birthed women's oral history. For these pioneers, the academic, public, and activist worlds were intimately connected both in practice and in principle.[54]

Notes

1 Cindy Cohen, "Building Multicultural and Intergenerational Networks through Oral History," *Frontiers* 7, no. 1 (1983): 99.
2 The 1960s–70s feminist movement was characterized by internal differences in philosophy and politics. Although they shared an interest in ending women's oppression, activists differed in their analysis of its causes and strategies for social change. Activists across the political spectrum tended to embrace consciousness raising as a process, however. For clarity, in this essay, I use the general terms "feminism" and "women's liberation" unless a more specific reference is required. See also Alice Echols, *Daring to Be Bad* (Minneapolis: University of Minnesota Press, 1989); Stephanie Gilmore, *Groundswell: Grassroots Feminist Activism in Postwar America* (New York: Routledge, 2013).
3 Rosalyn Baxandall, "Historical Life Stories," *Feminist Studies* 34, no. 3 (Fall 2008): 415.
4 Sherna Berger Gluck, "Has Feminist Oral History Lost Its Radical/Subversive Edge?," *Oral History* 39, no. 2 (Autumn 2011): 63–64.
5 Lara Leigh Kelland, *Clio's Foot Soldiers: Twentieth-Century U.S. Social Movements and Collective Memory* (Amherst: University of Massachusetts Press, 2018).
6 Kathie Sarachild, "A Program for Feminist 'Consciousness Raising,'" *Notes from the Second Year: Women's Liberation*, 1970, 78–80, http://library.duke.edu/digitalcollections/wlmpc_wlmms01039/. Splits between radicals who viewed women's liberation as part of a larger socialist struggle and "wildcats"—women who argued in favor of a separate women's movement—occurred at this conference and affected how activists responded to consciousness raising as an organizing tool. See Marlene Dixon, "On Women's Liberation," *Radical America* 4, no. 2 (February 1970): 26–34, reprinted at https://libcom.org/library/radical-america-0402-women.
7 Carol Hanisch, "A Women's Liberation Tribute to William Hinton and the Women of Long Bow" (speech), Understanding China's Revolution: A Celebration of the Lifework of William Hinton. Columbia University, April 3, 1999, http://www.carolhanisch.org/Speeches/HintonSpeech/HintonTribSpeech.html.
8 Chicago Women's Liberation Union, "How to Start Your Own Consciousness-Raising Group," 1971, available at https://www.cwluherstory.org/conscious/how-to-start-your-own-consciousness-raising-group?rq=consciousness-raising; Claudia Dreifus, *Women's Fate: Raps from a Feminist Consciousness-Raising Group* (New York: Bantam Books, 1973), 5.

9. Kathie Sarachild, "Consciousness-Raising: A Radical Weapon," in *Feminist Revolution* (New York: Random House, 1973), 140–50, available at https://womenwhatistobedone.files.wordpress.com/2013/09/1973-consciousness-raising-radical-weapon-k-sarachild-redstockings.pdf.
10. William Hinton, *Fanshen: A Documentary of Revolution in a Chinese Village* (Berkeley: University of California Press, 1966), 157.
11. Sarachild notes these influences in "Consciousness-Raising: A Radical Weapon."
12. Sarachild, 147–48.
13. Letty Cottin Pogrebin, "Rap Groups: The Feminist Connection," *Ms.* 1, no. 9 (March 1973): 80–83, 98–100.
14. Tia Cross et al., "Face-to-Face, Day-to-Day—Racism CR," in *All the Women Are White, All the Blacks Are Men, but Some of Us Are Brave: Black Women's Studies*, ed. Gloria T. Hull, Patricia Bell Scott, and Barbara Smith (New York: Feminist, 1982), 53.
15. Baxandall, "Historical Life Stories," 414.
16. Sarachild, "Consciousness-Raising: A Radical Weapon," 148; "Consciousness Raising," in *Radical Feminism*, ed. Anne Koedt, Ellen Levine, and Anita Rapone (New York: Quadrangle, 1973), 280–81.
17. Coletta Reid, "Ideology: Guide to Action," *Furies* 1, no. 3 (March–April 1972): 6.
18. For example, see Joreen, "The Tyranny of Structurelessness," in Koedt, Levine, and Rapone, *Radical Feminism*, 285–99; Brooke, "Woman's Fate: Raps from a Feminist Consciousness-Raising Group," *Off Our Backs* 5, no. 1 (January 1975): 18.
19. A February 1969 New York State legislative committee hearing on abortion law reforms only included one woman, a nun, who was called to testify regarding the impact of proposed changes. A recording of the speak-out organized by Redstockings the next month is available on the Internet Archive at https://archive.org/details/RedstockingsAbortionSpeakoutNewYork1969March21/Part+1+-+Redstockings+Abortion+Speakout+New+York+1969+March+21.m4a. See also the Redstockings website, http://redstockings.org.
20. Flora Davis, *Moving the Mountain: The Women's Movement in America since 1960* (New York: Simon & Schuster, 1991), 87–90.
21. Sara Evans, *Personal Politics: The Roots of Women's Liberation in the Civil Rights Movement and the New Left* (New York: Alfred A. Knopf, 1980), 183, 185–86; Janice Law Trecker, "Woman's Place Is in the Curriculum," *Saturday Review*, October 16, 1971, 85.
22. Marilyn Boxer, *When Women Ask the Questions: Creating Women's Studies in America* (Baltimore: Johns Hopkins University Press, 1998), 13. See also Alice E. Ginsberg, ed., *The Evolution of American Women's Studies: Reflections on Triumphs, Controversies, and Change* (New York: Palgrave Macmillan, 2008); Florence Howe, ed., *The Politics of Women's Studies: Testimony from 30 Founding Mothers* (New York: Feminist, 2000). The personal profiles that scholars contributed to these volumes reveal how many of the "founding mothers" cited the importance of their own participation in consciousness raising groups on their teaching and research. On the growth of women's

history, see Judith P. Zinsser, *History and Feminism: A Glass Half Full* (New York: Twayne, 1993); Judith M. Bennett, *History Matters: Patriarchy and the Challenge of Feminism* (Philadelphia: University of Pennsylvania Press, 2006).

23 Florence Howe, "Women's Studies in the United States: Growth and Institutionalization," in *Women's Studies International: Nairobi and Beyond*, ed. Aruna Rao (New York: Feminist, 1991), 104. See also articles in the tenth-anniversary issue, "The Women's Studies Movement: A Decade inside the Academy," *Frontiers* 8, no. 3 (1986).

24 Elizabeth Lapovsky Kennedy, "Dreams of Social Justice," in Howe, *Politics of Women's Studies*, 257.

25 Paula Rothenberg, "Women's Studies—the Early Years," in Ginsberg, *Evolution of American Women's Studies*, 71.

26 Adrienne Rich, *Blood, Bread, and Poetry: Selected Prose 1979–1985* (New York: W. W. Norton, 1986), 216.

27 Ann Froines, "Materials for Basic Women's Studies Courses," *Radical Teacher*, no. 17 (November 1980): 32. See also American Association of University Women, *Liberating Our Children, Ourselves: A Handbook of Women's Studies Course Materials for Teacher Educators* (Washington, DC: AAUW, 1975), 36–40; Miriam Wolf-Wasserman and Linda Hutchinson, *Teaching Human Dignity: Social Change Lessons for Every Teacher* (Minneapolis: Education Exploration Center, 1978), 36–44.

28 Jean M. Humez and Laurie Crumpacker, "Oral History in Teaching Women's Studies," *Oral History Review* 7 (1979): 53.

29 June Slavin, "Notes on Women and Society," in *Female Studies*, vol. 3, ed. Florence Howe and Carol Ahlum (Pittsburgh, PA: KNOW, 1971), 139.

30 Humez and Crumpacker, "Oral History in Teaching."

31 Barbara Harrison, "Feminist Experiment in Education," *New Republic*, March 11, 1972, 16.

32 Mollie C. Davis, "Grass Roots Women's Studies: Piedmont, North Carolina," *Women's Studies Newsletter* 60, no. 1 (Winter 1978): 24; Barbara Hillyer Davis, "Finding New Forms: Student Autonomy in a Patriarchal University," *Women's Studies Newsletter* 7, no. 2 (Spring 1979): 22–24.

33 Gene Thompson, "Notes on Teaching 'Women Working,'" *Radical Teacher*, no. 25 (November 1983): 15. For other descriptions of oral history–based classes, see Sherna Berger Gluck, Sue Armitage, and Joan Jensen, "Women's Oral History in the Classroom: Three Views on Sources," *Frontiers* 7, no. 1 (1983): 109–11.

34 Marge Grevatt, "Oral History as a Resource in Teaching Women's Studies," *Radical Teacher*, no. 10 (December 1978): 22. Grevatt also published a book based on her interviews with Lillian Craig, a Cleveland welfare rights activist, that was intended to document and bolster that movement. Grevatt, *Just a Woman* (Cleveland: Legal Aid Society, 1981).

35 Eva Moseley, "Documenting the History of Women in America," *American Archivist* 36, no. 2 (April 1973): 220; Harrison, "Feminist Experiment in Education."

36 Lynn Z. Bloom, "Listen! Women Speaking," *Frontiers* 2 (Summer 1977): 2.

37 Sherna Berger Gluck, "What's So Special about Women? Women's Oral History," *Frontiers* 2, no. 2 (Summer 1977): 5.

38 Gluck, 4.

39 Gluck, 3–4.

40 Sherna Berger Gluck, *From Parlor to Prison: Five American Suffragists Talk about Their Lives* (New York: Monthly Review, 1985), 43. The FHRP interviews are now part of the collection at California State University, Long Beach. See also Amelia R. Fry, "Suffragist Alice Paul's Memoirs: Pros and Cons of Oral History," *Frontiers* 2 (Summer 1977): 82–86; Sally Roesch Wagner, "Oral History as a Biographical Tool," *Frontiers* 2 (Summer 1977): 70–74; and the woman suffrage project coordinated by the Regional Oral History Office at Berkeley.

41 Jacquelyn Dowd Hall, "Documenting Diversity: The Southern Experience," *Oral History Review* 4 (1976): 26–27; Susan Armitage, "Here's to the Women: Western Women Speak Up," *Journal of American History* 83 (September 1996): 551–59. For projects outside the US, see Joanna Bornat, "Women's History and Oral History: An Outline Bibliography," *Oral History* 5, no. 2 (Autumn 1977): 124–35.

42 Bette Craig and Joyce Kornbluh, *I Just Wanted Someone to Know: A Documentary Play* (Brooklyn, NY: Smyrna, 1981). Project files and interviews are at "Trade Union Women Oral History Project: 1978–1979," Bentley Historical Library, accessed November 20, 2020, https://quod.lib.umich.edu/b/bhlead/umich-bhl-85223?rgn=main;view=text.

43 Katherine Jensen, "Woman as Subject, Oral History as Method," *Frontiers* 7, no. 1 (1983): 86.

44 Amy Kesselman, Tina Tau, and Karen Wickre, "Good Work, Sister! The Making of an Oral History Production," *Frontiers* 7, no. 1 (1983): 64–70. See also Craig and Kornbluh, *I Just Wanted*.

45 The project can be found here: http://jukebox.uaf.edu/site7/suffragists.

46 In the 1970s, a number of pioneering women began to produce and distribute feminist documentary films. Although these fall outside the scope of this article, they represented important explorations of aspects of women's lives and, like the public programs discussed above, could be used to support the consciousness raising and social change goals of the movement. A selective list includes *It Happens to Us* (1972) in support of abortion rights and a portrait of three generations of women, *Nana, Mom, and Me* (1974), both directed by Amalie Rothschild; *Union Maids* (1976) by Julia Reichert, which profiled women labor activists from the 1930s; and *With Babies and Banners* (1979) by Lorraine Grey, documenting women's support for the 1937 sit-down strike by auto workers.

47 Mary Aickin Rothschild, "Using Oral History to Find the 'Common Woman': An Arizona Project," *Frontiers* 7, no. 1 (1983): 89.

48 Rothschild. On the Buffalo project, see Judith Schwarz, "Questionnaire on Issues in Lesbian History," *Frontiers* 4, no. 3 (Autumn 1979): 6. See also Elizabeth Lapovsky Kennedy, "Dreams of Social Justice: Building Women's Studies at the State University

of New York, Buffalo," in Howe, *Politics of Women's Studies*, 243–63; Kennedy and Madeline Davis, *Boots of Leather, Slippers of Gold: The History of a Lesbian Community* (New York: Routledge, 1993).

49 Nancy D. Mann, "Directory of Women's Oral History Projects and Collections," *Frontiers* 7, no. 1 (1983): 114–21.

50 Mary Chamberlain and Paul Thompson, "International Conference on Oral History and Women's History," *Oral History* 12, no. 1 (Spring 1984): 8–12; Sherna Berger Gluck and Daphne Patai, eds., *Women's Words: The Feminist Practice of Oral History* (New York: Routledge, 1991).

51 Michael H. Frisch, *A Shared Authority: Essays on the Craft and Meaning of Oral and Public History* (Albany, NY: SUNY Press, 1990).

52 Grevatt, "Oral History as a Resource," 24; Susan H. Armitage, "The Next Step," *Frontiers* 7, no. 1 (1983): 3–4. See also Katherine Borland, "That's Not What I Said: Interpretive Conflict in Oral Narrative Research," in Gluck and Patai, *Women's Words*, 63–76.

53 Cindy Cohen, "Building Multicultural and Intergenerational Networks," 102. On the transformation of women's oral history away from its earlier collaborative, community approach to an increasingly solitary academic endeavor due to the conservative backlash of the Reagan era and the disappearance of public funding for large-scale oral history projects, see Armitage, "Here's to the Women," 558.

54 See also Daniel R. Kerr, "Allan Nevins Is Not My Grandfather: The Roots of Radical Oral History Practice in the United States," *Oral History Review* 43, no. 2 (2016): 367–91 and in this volume.

Pushing Boundaries Onstage

Culture Clash, Oral History Theater, and the Influence of El Teatro Campesino

Kristen Ana La Follette

Oral history has been viewed as subversive and revolutionary as a research method in many academic circles. For years, traditional history departments questioned and often rejected the legitimacy of interview-based research. Oral sources were deemed inherently unreliable and oral historians ill-equipped to determine the veracity of their sources. In acknowledging subjectivity, the field posed a threat to established interpreters of history. Additionally, valuing multiple voices challenged written records. Oral historians also recognized that great value lay in the analytical potential of inconsistencies and faulty memory.[1] The discipline persisted despite marginalization by academic circles. Today, movements to decolonize the practice continue to adapt methodology toward more inclusive practices within and outside of academia.[2]

The interview exchange is the heart of oral history, where interviewer and narrator converge. The resulting recording and transcript are rich with information via setting, behavioral cues, what is spoken, and silences surrounding words unspoken. This generates ideal source material for stage performance. Verbatim theater therefore seems an intuitive outcome of the oral history process.[3] It offers the possibility to reanimate the orality of the interview for a live audience. Scripts often also replicate humans' ingrained tendency to organize life events in narrative form.[4] Individuals who would never be in one room together can be placed side by side onstage. This creates space to imagine them in conversation with one another.⁵ As actors employ the words uttered by multiple narrators, they interrogate social structures, highlight incongruence, and reveal connections between people who may seem completely disconnected on the surface. The spoken word infuses energy into oral history and theater. Both are uniquely positioned to heighten the perception of what it means to be human.

Yet the historiography of verbatim theater still largely privileges few to create a small central group of lauded performers. In predominant overviews of the genre, one will see the same names and plays mentioned over and over. The dynamic contributions of Chicanx and Latinx theater companies are frequently left out of mainstream theatrical recognition. However, they successfully disrupt narratives traditionally presented on the American stage. Culture Clash was a notable troupe that infused oral history theater with their satirical perspective and biting social critique. They leaned into the subjectivity of actors to profile Latinx communities in site-specific plays. Culture Clash drew upon the Mexican carpa tent show tradition, rasquache aesthetics, and popular culture to wield comedy against social inequity. This politically aware theater also traces back to the work of El Teatro Campesino. Culture Clash presented diverse and discordant voices onstage, propelling oral history theater forward.

Pre–Culture Clash

Herbert Sigüenza, Richard Montoya, and Ricardo "Ric" Salinas were performers who all came to live in San Francisco's Mission District. Before the 1970s, though in the same neighborhood, their creative paths had not yet collided. Sigüenza was born in San Francisco and raised for a time in El Salvador. He returned to spend his teenage years in the United States at the height of the Chicanx movement. Sigüenza was eventually trained in visual arts but was then drawn to theater and performed with the company Teatro Gusto.⁶ Salinas, also from El Salvador, moved to San Francisco as a child. He attended San Francisco State University, where he was involved in theater and later joined Teatro Latino.⁷ Montoya grew up in the heart of the Chicanx movement. His father was the well-known poet and activist José Montoya, whose collaborations with Luis Valdez during his early days with the UFW (United Farm Workers of America), influenced and inspired his son. Valdez was a founding member of El Teatro Campesino, which was intimately connected to the farmworker struggle. The early impact of Valdez laid the groundwork for Culture Clash. Montoya was trained in acting at the American Conservatory Theater and moved to San Francisco after attending California State University, Sacramento.[8] From their varied backgrounds, Sigüenza, Salinas, and Montoya shared comedic styling, integrating stand-up, politics, and humor in their work. To further trace the path of their influences and how the three came together as a troupe, El Teatro Campesino plays an important role.

El Teatro Campesino as the Forerunner

In late 1965, a flatbed truck pulls up beside a grape field in California's Central Valley. A banner hangs across the back of the truck with the words, El Teatro Campesino, which translates to "The Farmworkers' Theater." Farmworkers begin to gather alongside to view the show as several actors stand atop this moveable stage. One performer wears a large sign with the title Esquirol, denoting a strikebreaker or scab. Another is Patroncito, the boss, and dons a papier-mâché pig mask. Through the mask he loudly chides Esquirol for wanting to join the emerging farmworker strike. Then Patroncito insists they switch roles so the worker can experience how difficult it is to be a boss. Soon the reversal turns as both Patroncito and Esquirol realize they share a common humanity as they both suffer under the unequal farming structure that places them at odds. In the end, Patroncito is dragged offstage as he is mistaken for a farmworker. "Where's Cesar Chavez [a prominent union leader]? Help! Huelga! Huelgaaaaa!" he calls out, using the strikers' common rally cry.[9] On traveling open-air stages, El Teatro Campesino imbued the acto, or short skit, with humor to encourage laborers to join the emerging UFW union and strike.

Drawing from diverse theater traditions, El Teatro Campesino would evolve into the most widely known and commercially successful Chicanx theater troupe of the 1960s and 1970s. Its accomplishments opened possibilities for contemporary Latinx theater companies whose success is a credit to their aesthetic style, commitment to social change, and tenacity in bringing visibility to the community.[10] The troupe would go on to inspire and directly train new generations of performers and companies as it provided the most well-known representations of Latinxs onstage, created by Latinx writers. Actors found opportunities to work in El Teatro's ensemble and were trained in workshops that showcased their performance theory.

Culture Clash was one of the next generation of acting troupes to emerge from the path forged by El Teatro. Culture Clash pushed their common aesthetic further, eventually using oral history theater to examine specific Latinx communities throughout the United States. Both companies draw from similar roots to create unique performance forms and share stylistic elements of humor embedded in social commentary. Each can trace back to Mexican popular theater, as well as Brechtian notions of abstraction, to bring larger societal truths into focus. El Teatro broke ground for Chicanx theater as a whole, and Culture Clash would continue to shift the boundaries of theater and oral history.

Farmworkers labored in Central Valley vineyards under dismal and dangerous working conditions. The farming system in California was also highly stratified, and attempts to organize unions in the early 1900s were squelched by employers. However, in the 1960s, organizers were able to form broader coalitions to more successfully advocate for unionization. In 1965, the UFW was formed in an alliance between the Filipinx-led Agricultural Workers Organizing Committee (AWOC) and the National Farmworkers Association, a largely Mexican American organization. They led a series of grape strikes and boycotts to draw attention to their emerging movement. In reading about the strikes, Luis Valdez was inspired to join their efforts. The child of migrant laborers, Valdez, who trained in theater for years, felt performance was the ideal medium to speak to workers.[11] He envisioned plays staged directly in the fields that would energize laborers to get behind the emerging movement. Valdez approached the organizers, Dolores Huerta and Cesar Chavez, to propose his idea.[12] With their blessing, Valdez invited the community to help develop the ensemble, offering opportunities to previously untrained actors. Fresh from his collaboration with the San Francisco Mime Troupe, Valdez had honed skills in commedia dell'arte. Because of this experience, outdoor performances, improvisation, and the use of masks would figure centrally in the early stages of El Teatro and influence later work.[13]

Valdez held a series of meetings in Delano, California, at the center of the strike effort. An ensemble cast soon evolved and the troupe took its performances out to the fields. They staged actos on top of flatbed trucks parked near Latinx and Filipinx farmworkers. Performers hung large signs around their necks denoting their roles, erected minimal sets, and used masks and symbolic props. Improvisation and feedback facilitated the influence of the audience, who would shout, cheer, and loudly boo. The characters symbolically represented the class struggle between farmworkers and grape growers. As in the scene described earlier, farmworkers were underdogs whose plight was exacerbated by the unjust farming system enforced by growers and facilitated by strikebreakers. Presented alongside vignettes—songs and other performances—the skits gave the workers' situation urgency and proposed a solution: to organize and join the union.

While El Teatro's plays began to develop an audience, the strikes and boycotts also gained momentum, garnering support from national allies such as the American Federation of Labor and Congress of Industrial Organizations (AFL-CIO) and United Agricultural Workers. The UFW decided to march in 1966, and thousands of laborers walked some 340 miles to Sacramento to jump-start a larger farmworker rights movement. El Teatro followed the march, invigorating crowds along the route, which helped maintain energy for the strike. Word of their work spread, and soon the company was invited to perform for universities and audiences abroad. El Teatro's aims and notoriety then seemed to come into conflict with the UFW. The two parted ways. In the decades that followed its divergence from the union, El Teatro established itself as the premiere Chicanx theater company, developing beyond the acto to create full-length plays.[14]

El Teatro's large body of work eventually included published scripts and Theatre of the Sphere, their own distinct performance theory based on Aztec and Mayan philosophy.[15] This theory encouraged actors to think dimensionally not only about how they functioned onstage but about their greater relationship to the world. It was "a multidimensional pedagogy that included the intense program of the Veinte Pasos (Twenty Steps); participation in platicás (teachings) by indigenous maestros; danza; interaction with different indigenous communities in the United States and Mexico; a program of readings and discussion; and the work of stage performance and community involvement."[16] El Teatro therefore trained actors in a revolutionary world view. This nurturing of Chicanx theater, with the explicit aim to change mind-sets and affect social issues, led directly to the next generation of performers. Many trained individuals, including members of Culture Clash, would take the original impetus for Chicanx theater further, employing oral history–based performance to continue El Teatro's tradition of advocacy grounded in community.

In 1978, El Teatro gained a Rockefeller grant to create *Zoot Suit* for the Mark Taper Forum in Los Angeles. The troupe's inaugural wide-scale production was the first time a Chicanx play had been produced on a main stage. The script was based on the Sleepy Lagoon murder trial and subsequent Zoot Suit Riots in Los Angeles in 1943, in which hundreds of pachucos, or Latinx zoot suiters, were rounded up after a gang-related murder. The trial convicted twenty-two men to life in prison for their ties to the gang. At the same time, anti-Latinx fervor sparked riots in which White sailors stripped and attacked pachucos in LA. Police refused to intervene. The play highlights the discrimination faced by the defendants during the trial while illuminating racial tension, power inequity, and Latinx community identity in the midst of sanctioned marginalization. *Zoot Suit* became a smashing success, selling out an eleven-month run in LA. It then made its way to Broadway, the first Chicanx play to ever do so, before finally becoming a major motion picture.[17] While in LA, *Zoot Suit* connected with diverse theatergoers, many of whom were attending their very first play. El Pachuco, the omniscient narrator of the piece, is especially striking. Wearing the ultimate zoot suit—including a crisp hat, chain, and large pleated pants—he represents the Greek chorus. He is also alter ego to the protagonist, Henry Reyna. El Pachuco notes Reyna's dire situation and prods him to examine his misfortune, all while exuding the ultimate cool exterior.

El Teatro's revolutionary act as Latinx writers profiling Latinx characters onstage cannot be understated. The portrayals and styling of *Zoot Suit*'s characters inspired performers to imagine that Chicanx plays could and should be staged with high production value and vibrant visuals. Herbert Sigüenza, Richard Montoya, and Ricardo "Ric" Salinas were among those invigorated by the play.

The Formation of Culture Clash

In 1978, after hearing positive reviews of *Zoot Suit*, Sigüenza traveled to Los Angeles to view a performance. The experience—especially that of witnessing El Pachuco—was transformative. Of the opening scene, Sigüenza said, "The minute the knife goes down that giant newspaper and El Pachuco comes out, I was sold. I knew from that day on that I was going to do theatre the rest of my life. Because I saw people that looked like me doing world class, professional theatre at a really high level, and that was my goal."[18] *Zoot Suit* became one of the catalysts that set Culture Clash, and their later oral history work, in motion. Yet the influence of El Teatro on the formation of the group would extend further.

El Teatro Campesino convened several Chicanx theater festivals in the early 1970s to showcase and encourage new groups to take up performance.[19] At various points, Montoya, Salinas, and Sigüenza separately came to perform with El Teatro. In early 1984, Valdez convened the Concilio de Arte Popular at El Teatro's headquarters in San Juan Bautista, California. The meeting brought together Chicanx artists of various genres to form a coalition. They intended to organize a board to further collaboration among artists, seek shared financial support, and facilitate Chicanx advocacy through the arts. During this initial meeting, the need for comedy and levity to reinvigorate the Chicanx movement was emphasized. Visual artist Rene Yañez agreed with this sentiment. Just a month later, he assembled a performance showcase in San Francisco's Mission District. Held on Cinco de Mayo at Galeria de la Raza, the event provided the occasion for Comedy Fiesta to come together, thus creating the forerunner of Culture Clash.[20]

As Comedy Fiesta, six performers—Montoya, Sigüenza, and Salinas along with José Antonio Burciaga, Marga Goméz, and Monica Palacios—assembled their stand-up routines to form a new ensemble group.[21] Each actor's extensive stage experience facilitated their use of comedy and short skits as vehicles for social criticism. After this original gig, the troupe decided to continue on together, though each still sought individual side work. Two years later, Goméz and Palacios left Comedy Fiesta to continue fully on their own. The remaining members renamed the group Culture Clash. This new title represented their intention to confront the tension between dominant culture and Chicanx identity while referencing mainstream films and television. Popular entertainment mostly ignored Latinx people. When infrequently represented, depictions relied on stock characters, reinforcing stereotypes that glossed over nuances within the community.[22] Culture Clash also wished to confront divisions within the Chicanx movement, such as those between activists and "armchair" Chicanxs, who espoused ideas but did not join efforts.[23] After defining this more focused identity, Burciaga eventually also departed. The three remaining members developed a signature style: they combined sharp wit with satire, calling on Latinx theater traditions and pop culture references to confront Chicanx issues.[24]

A Style Develops

Early on, Culture Clash used their work as an outlet for their frustration as Latinx actors. Despite formal training, Montoya, Salinas, and Sigüenza continually met with rejection auditioning for roles. In 1988, exasperation with limited opportunities and representation led to their first full script, *The Mission*.[25] Focused on San Francisco's Mission District, the trio traveled back in time to relive and reimagine the history of their neighborhood. Every role was played by one of the three actors, which led to some creative maneuvering when all were expected to be onstage. The play begins at Mission Dolores, which gave the neighborhood its name. In the 1700s, Father Junípero Serra, a Spaniard, founded twenty-one Catholic missions throughout California in an attempt to convert American Indians. The scene opens with the trio playing indigenous people as Serra flogs and criticizes them. It highlights individual and systemic maltreatment of indigenous people within the mission system. As the scene shifts to present time, this harm is linked to contemporary marginalization of Latinxs, who share mixed indigenous and colonial Spanish origins. In the next sequence, the actors are living together in an apartment. They lament the ridiculous roles in which they are cast and the need to take on unsavory jobs to pay the bills. They soon hear that a performance showcase is to be held on the mission grounds. Culture Clash audition but are immediately rejected. The trio decides the only way for their work to be seen is to kidnap the event's main performer, the famous Spanish singer Julio Iglesias, and hold him hostage until they are given a slot. A similar fusion between pop culture references and comedic social critique is woven throughout the piece. In touching upon MTV, Mel Brooks, and sitcoms of the 1960s and '70s, their humor both reflects the era the actors grew up in and makes fresh references from the present time.[26]

In "The Auditions" scene, the actors stage vignettes lampooning, while simultaneously drawing critical attention to, the superficial ways Latinx actors are represented in entertainment:

(Lights up. Richard walks into the light.)

RICHARD: Hi, thank you for the audition. Yes, I just got the script, my Spanish is great. (*Holding product. With Anglo accent:*) Hola, su baño tiene mal olor? Es usted embarasado con sus visitas? No se preocupee-pee. Usted necesita "2000 Flushes." Deja su baño especta . . . culo, culo? Oh, espectáculo! Dísfrutalo, hoy!

(Blackout. Lights up. Herbert, dressed like Frida Kahlo, stands in a spotlight.)

HERBERT: First of all, let me congratulate the producers at ABC-TV for doing the mini-series on "The Life and Times of Frida Kahlo."

Excuse me? Am I willing to connect my eyebrows? For two-grand, I'll make love to Diego Rivera!

(Blackout. Lights up. Ric does elaborate Bob Fosse–type dance. Lights black out in the middle of his dance. Lights up. Richard enters.)

RICHARD: I have prepared a song for the audition today. Here goes. (*Blows tune whistle. Sings:*) "Yo soy como el chile verde, Llorona, picante, pero sabroso . . ." What? You want it in English? Yes I can do that. "I am tender chunks of pork in a light, zesty green sauce. Spicy . . . but not hot."

(Blackout. Lights up. Herbert is the sleepy Mexican, complete with sombrero, serape and cactus. He lifts his head slowly and points offstage.)

HERBERT: Señor . . . Indiana Jones went that way.

(Blackout. Lights up, Ric does a line from "La Bamba.")

Ric: Ritchie!

(Blackout. Lights up. Richard stares straight ahead; he holds a spear and speaks with his very best Shakespearean accent.)

Richard: Is it for fear to wet a widow's eye
That thou consum'st thyself in single life?
Ah! If thou issueless shalt hap to die
The world will wail thee like a makeless wife.
The world will be thy widow, and still weep
That thou no form of thee has left behind.

(Blackout. Richard continues in black.)[27]

This scene tackles shallow nods to diversity in commercialism and limited depictions in brief television specials. In light of the dearth of roles offered, Salinas stated that even writing scripts was a political act. He said, "As Latino actors, we knew that we had to write our own roles, our own stories. There are millions of Latinos, like us, who are bilingual, bicultural and proud of both their American and Latino roots, who are not being represented."[28] In acknowledging biculturalism, the scene also challenges assumptions that all Latinxs speak Spanish. Importantly as well, in the brief nod to *La Bamba*, the trio takes on commercially successful representations of Latinxs. The biographical film, written and directed by Valdez in 1987, was criticized by the Chicanx community for whitewashing the story of musician Ritchie Valens, born Richard Valenzuela, in order to appeal to a mostly Anglo audience. Even Valdez was not spared from the critical eye of Culture Clash's no-holds-barred farce.

Humor cut to the heart of social issues. As the troupe found, "With comedy, we could address socially relevant issues but disguise them with wit."[29] Comedy could both disarm the audience, making viewers more receptive to the critique offered, and release tension that arose when dealing with challenging topics confronting social hierarchy. The comedic roots of Culture Clash can be attributed both to its predecessor El Teatro Campesino and older theatrical traditions. Both companies share a rasquache aesthetic, a rough-edged, underdog style reminiscent of traveling Mexican tent shows. Despite the jab at *La Bamba*, the relationship between the companies remained good natured and *The Mission* was soon staged at El Teatro Campesino's home in San Juan Bautista, with director Tony Curiel further developing the piece.[30]

Culture Clash's next play, *A Bowl of Beings*, premiered in 1991. It offered an array of satirical sketches, all confronting Chicanx identity. The script took on a deeply personal tone, featuring several emotionally intimate sketches. This direction was attributed to Salinas's brush with death in 1989. One evening, after a party the three attended in San Francisco, Salinas attempted to break up a fight. Instead, he was shot by an assailant. His struggle to survive induced a new perspective on life and death. He addressed this directly in the poignant monologue "Ricflections."[31] The combination of depth and levity resonated with audiences, and *A Bowl of Beings* toured more widely than *The Mission*. The attention it gained led to a PBS Great Performances special, which soon set the stage for their oral history–based work. After the special aired, the nonprofit Miami Light Project asked the group to bring *A Bowl of Beings* to Miami.[32] Impressed by the reception the play received, Miami Light Project commissioned Culture Clash to return and profile the city by interviewing its residents. In many ways, this new play would present a creative departure and evolution of Culture Clash's form.

Oral History Theater

The early 1990s brought oral history theater to the fore. In 1991, riots broke out between Lubavitch Hasidic Jewish residents and the Caribbean American and Black communities in Crown Heights, Brooklyn. Tensions concerning social and economic separations between the groups boiled over when a Lubavitch motorcade struck and killed the young Gavin Cato. Yankel Rosenbaum, a Jewish student, was then killed in retaliation. Anna Deavere Smith soon interviewed and personally portrayed myriad community members, civil rights leaders, and eyewitnesses to create *Fires in the Mirror*. Prior, she wrote the series *On the Road: A Search for American Character*, for which she interviewed individuals in various communities and embodied each onstage. In Crown Heights, her interviews covered not only the riots but the distinct cultural identities and histories that influenced how the groups interacted and failed to connect with each other. In 1992, she used a similar technique in response to the Los Angeles Riots, which flared up after four White police officers were acquitted for the beating of Rodney King, a Black male, despite video recorded evidence.[33] Smith's interest in collisions between social groups influenced by historic marginalization connects clearly to Culture Clash's work. However, the latter would not focus on violent flash points.

In order to approach Miami from the inside, a board of over twenty Miamians was compiled by Miami Light Project to offer advice and a pool of narrators. As Sigüenza noted, "Since we were outsiders, it was important for there to be a structure to facilitate our relationship with, and truthful understanding of, the community."[34] The board provided this link, drawing from a broad slice of Miami's community, suggesting two hundred potential interviewees who represented widely differing socioeconomic groups and opinions. From this list, Culture Clash decided upon seventy city residents to ultimately interview over a two-month period. They also observed life in Miami, as ethnographers would, to more accurately portray its vibrancy and contradictions.[35] The troupe's writing process was unique as a three-part collaboration among the actors. After interviews, they would transcribe recordings and work separately on their monologues. Together they would then identify similar themes, create composite characters when it seemed messages were similar, and decide which interviews to represent in verbatim monologues.[36] Culture Clash created this site-specific theater through interviews to showcase Miami as a particular location.

In 1994, *Radio Mambo: Culture Clash Invades Miami* premiered at the Colony Theatre in Miami Beach, Florida.[37] The play begins with a monologue by Sigüenza that explains how and why the piece was created. He also provides context for the conflicting views that would be presented. Sigüenza includes his positive take on Cuba, formed after an artistic residency there. As he speaks, two shadowy figures enter the stage and approached him in an obvious show of intimidation. They represent the perspectives of conservative Cubans who left the nation in exile, vehemently opposing Fidel Castro. Their world view looms large in Miami society. After Sigüenza is chased offstage, a slew of other characters emerge in a series of monologues. Some speak alone. Others are presented together to reenact conversations or link themes that emerged from interviews. Characters include Haitians, several waves of Cuban exiles and their children, Black residents, drag queens, and Jewish individuals.

The predicament in revealing contradictions was significant. As Sigüenza noted, "Our greatest challenge in creating this work was to ensure that we played these people realistically and with dignity, avoiding broad stereotypes and shallow characterizations."[38] The juxtaposition and interaction of these voices lend the play vibrancy. These divergent and sometimes contradictory perspectives not only document a textured story of modern Miami through opinions about its residents by its residents but reenact the historic and social dynamics influencing their positions in Miami hierarchy.

The script interweaves the history of the city with a discussion of current issues. Culture Clash does not shy away from economic divides. They note when they found contrasting groups. They observe that White residents and exiles often attain strong financial security through business, while others, like many Haitians, live with limited job prospects and social mobility. Racial tension aimed at, and between, marginalized groups was also addressed. The actors include asides and gestures by characters revealing the distrust among Miami's groups. They explore de facto segregation. In the scene "Tea for Two," two Black women sit in a café to discuss the history of the area. They reveal their own oppression and existing tensions:

> **DOROTHY:** When Miami became a city, we became second-class citizens. When we built the railroad, we were placed adjacent to downtown. Back then they called it Colored Town, or the Central Negro District, or Overtown; that's what the people called it. And later, when white downtown wanted to expand, it couldn't go east because it would go into the bay and west was the Miami River, so they expanded right

into Overtown. And they built their big old expressway which further divided the community. And I don't think they understood what a flourishing, vibrant community it was. It was self-contained, self-operated. We were treated like first-class citizens in Overtown. No ma'am. Most local history books still tend to sugarcoat the founding of Miami and the building of the railroad. Yes, indeed, I would have to say that people in this country have amnesia.

(The Cuban waiter comes back and pours more tea.)

MARGO: That's very interesting, Dorothy, but my experience here in Miami has been totally different, coming from New York. The retirement lifestyle, living on the beach is great, but from what I see of Miami, what we call Miami, not Bell Harbor or Sunny Isles, I don't see any mixing here at all. (*She dismisses the Cuban waiter with disdain.*) There are definitely divisions worse here than I have seen in a long, long time.

Way back in segregation days, what we call Blacks now, they lived in one section or two sections. Now you have Black Haitians living in Little Haiti, or Black Cubans living in Wildwood, or some name I can't think of. And then you have people who live in, uhm, Oak . . . oh you were just talking about it.

DOROTHY: Overtown.

MARGO: Overtown! Those people don't meet other people. Now you're going to have to pardon me, Dorothy, but these are just my observations.[39]

In this scene, and throughout the play, the script includes sidebars. These are moments that interrupt characters and narrative flow, such as when the Cuban waiter enters to pour tea. They are reminders that the monologues are based on actual interviews conducted with real people in real time. Culture Clash also uses sidebars to highlight the opinions that exist between social groups about each other.[40]

Importantly, Culture Clash's choice to create staged performance around oral histories while amplifying dissonance took *Radio Mambo* beyond a simple retelling of individual stories. It did not seek to leave existing relations as they were—to smooth over the distinct and strong opinions of community members to emphasize connections rather than disunity. Some have critiqued verbatim theater pieces such as Moisés Kaufman and the Tectonic Theater Project's *The Laramie Project*, surrounding the violent death of Matthew Shepard, in which incongruous voices were somewhat muffled to instead highlight similarities between characters. As performance scholar Della Pollock noted, "Wherein some may aestheticize stories on stage, as Walter Benjamin coined the term, this striving toward beauty removes discourse and discord, rendering political discontent mute and serving the purposes of the elite."[41] The potentiality for political change inherent in portraying stories for an audience may be dulled as lines are blurred, rather than drawing a magnifying glass to the very issues that created the overarching conflict.[42] Culture Clash certainly does not run this risk, as it tackles political issues directly.

While making conflict and typically invisible populations visible, *Radio Mambo* also brought voices into hypothetical dialogue. Juxtaposing conflicting viewpoints in a way that did not happen in physical reality, it laid disagreements bare and opened possibilities for discussion. As Ryan Claycomb remarked, "In short, while various characters place blame on one another, many also often acknowledge the complicity of their own community, and when placed up against one another, they create a dialogue unlike what is typically heard in the streets."[43] In seeing stories side by side, the audience could pick up on their commonalities and imagine how, if these people and groups did have a conversation, they may find ways to alleviate the issues that kept them apart. In her own experience with oral history theater, reenacting the stories of southern mill workers onstage, Pollock found, "By telling the told, it seemed performance could 'dialogize' the mill world—it could be a nexus of perspectives, a point of contest and intersecting visions."[44] *Radio Mambo* staged a similar intersection. It was not just a retelling of the history of Miami but an act of dialogic creation and history-making.

In 1996, Culture Clash brought *Radio Mambo* to the San Diego Repertory Theatre after its initial run in Florida. Roger Guenveur Smith directed the play and helped the trio reshape their performance. Smith is a renowned stage performer and his familiarity in presenting historically grounded documentary theater facilitated his work with the script. He also frequently acted in and collaborated on Spike Lee's films. That same year, Smith portrayed Black Panther Huey P. Newton in a one-man show. His nuanced and complex performance was featured on PBS and eventually led to an award-winning film with

Lee. With *Radio Mambo*, Smith helped the troupe whittle away extraneous scenes to allow the narrative power of each monologue to come into focus. The original script included Culture Clash mounting a guerrilla takeover of a radio station, but the resulting adaptation in San Diego removed this.[45] Audiences reacted positively to the genuine nature of the monologues, whose specificity lent them a universal quality. Early on, Culture Clash's members worried the play's confrontation of attitudes toward Castro and Cuba may alienate audiences. Instead, their honest portrayals drew viewers in. *Radio Mambo* became one of their most successful and widely toured works. It led to a series of four additional site-specific plays commissioned by other cities. These would include profiles of the interplay between San Diego and Tijuana in *Bordertown*, as well as *Nuyorican Stories* of New York, *The Mission Magic Mystery Tour* in their return to San Francisco, and of Washington, DC, *Anthems: Culture Clash in the District*.[46]

While the group continued their site-specific work, projects by Montoya, Salinas, and Sigüenza also expanded, as each continued to branch out, performing their own individual pieces. Their brand of social commentary pushed audiences to confront divided social structures. Culture Clash's method for documenting communities through oral history interviews, blending pop culture and satire, circles back to the influence of El Teatro Campesino and the stylistic roots both theater companies share.

Stylistic Connections and Shared Influences

Parallels between El Teatro Campesino and Culture Clash run deep. In an interview with the Mark Taper Forum, Montoya noted, "Our rhythm, our iambic pentameter, our language" was absorbed from viewing and working with El Teatro.[47] Both troupes can trace several stylistic motifs to carpa, and popular theater. Carpa companies toured Mexico and border communities in the American Southwest, employing elements dating back to the 1700s. The form reached the height of its popularity in the decades after the Mexican Revolution.[48] As carpa troupes moved from town to town, entire families would attend. They presented a mixture of formats including dance numbers, song, political satire, and dramatic poetry to entertain audiences ranging from young children to grandparents. Sometimes clowns or even acrobats performed. El Teatro's early work reflects this varied arrangement, with vignettes featuring acto, music, or dance. Culture Clash's plays also switched rapidly between dramatic monologues, humorous sketches, and poetry. Though El

Teatro eventually moved to full-length plays, it still frequently incorporates elements of dance and music.

Another hallmark of carpa was over-the-top humor. Comedy worked in tandem with audience participation and became the vehicle to connect with largely working-class spectators. Crowds loudly laughed and applauded performances they enjoyed. However, if skits were not up to par, actors were instead met with roars of boos and jeers. Therefore, performers frequently improvised, adjusting their style to elicit a positive audience response. Fueled by the pressure to meet the scrutiny of live viewers, actors relied on quick wit and physicality to amplify humor onstage. Pacing was rapid, movements were large, slapstick humor became a staple, and stock characters built on established audience expectations.[49] Eventually, the carpa style transmuted to film and television. By the time Valdez and El Teatro began their shows in Delano, many audience members were accustomed to this responsive theatrical form. El Teatro actors magnified performances in turn. Their goal clearly was not just to entertain but to use heightened audience energy to inspire individuals to join the UFW strike. In 1967, Valdez explained how humor enhanced the social message of El Teatro's pieces: "We use comedy because it stems from a necessary situation—the necessity of lifting the morale of our strikers, who have been on strike for seventeen months. When they go to a meeting it's long and drawn out; so we do comedy, with the intention of making them laugh-but with a purpose. We try to make social points, not in spite of the comedy, but through it. This leads us into satire and slapstick, and sometimes very close to the underlying tragedy of it all—the fact that human beings have been wasted in farm labor for generations."[50] Comedy made heavy issues more digestible. It neutralized threatening and overwhelming circumstances that farmworkers lived through. Simultaneously, it buoyed crowds so that enthusiasm remained high even during the most challenging portrayals.

For Culture Clash, humor also led the way. As Salinas has said, "Despite the cultural, social and political implications of our subject matter, the emphasis was always on the funny, the satirical, what would invoke the biggest laugh, which pratfall would work best."[51] This responsiveness to audiences via comedy was also a tool for drawing attention to the absurdity of social inequity. In articulating critique through farce, the painful bite of conflict was somewhat lessened. Notably for both Culture Clash and El Teatro, humor could communicate to the audience that actors understood their pain. In poking fun at unjust circumstances, a sense of power and possibility could also be restored to those who outwardly lacked agency.

The rasquache aesthetic is another offshoot of carpa tradition. Rasquachismo is an artistic sensibility that addresses the plight of the underdog, or the oppressed, while critiquing power structures that produce injustice. It is also a scrappy make-do attitude, when artists use what is available to them to create. As El Teatro Campesino began performing, they lacked financial backing. They staged sets and costumes out of what was near so minimal backdrops were used. Props and flags were made from burlap, signs around actors' necks were cardboard, commedia dell'arte masks were papier-mâché, and the performance space itself was the back of a truck. This approach was financially practical and another signal to the audience that performers understood their lived experience and recognized their oppression. In rasquache, even if scenes depicted are not literal retellings, visual representation employs symbols that identify with historical marginalization.

Cantinflas, the performer most popular in Mexican and American films of the 1940s and 1950s, rose to prominence through carpa and is a prime example of rasquache. He took on the pelado persona, that of a street or slum dweller. Dressed in exaggeratedly ill-fitting clothes, he emulated the struggles of the working class and used wit to outsmart those in power. His wide appeal and ability to cross over into mainstream entertainment illustrate how deeply his methods resonated with audiences of various backgrounds. El Teatro embodied a similar rasquache ethos as it continually reflected the plight of the underdog. The farmworker with little economic power could use the union to poke holes in the authority of the grower through actos. For Culture Clash, the underdog spoke back to the invisibility of Latinxs.

Site-Specific Theater Today

In 2007, Montoya, Salinas, and Sigüenza collaborated with the Social History in Performance Art seminar at UCLA led by Professor David G. Garcia, a scholar on Culture Clash's history. Students examined Culture Clash's aesthetic and Chicanx theater's potential for social impact. The class created their own actos to teach material to one another. They then identified individuals to interview who represented different generations and experiences within the Latinx community. Culture Clash held a series of workshops with the students that were instructive in their methods and fostered reciprocal sharing. The trio would perform monologues from a site-specific play, discuss how these were constructed and help the class shape work in progress. To culminate the experience, Culture Clash and the students held an evening showcase of their monologues. Afterward, Garcia noted, "Our exploration of

Culture Clash's work generated much discussion around the power of teatro as a form of public revisionist history. In reflecting on the use of satire as a tool of resistance, I asked students to identify how the theatre productions from ETC [El Teatro Campesino] to Culture Clash also illuminated the sociopolitical conditions of the particular time and place of their creation."[52]

Though Culture Clash performances today frequently employ fictional scripts, Montoya, Salinas, and Sigüenza still individually examine communities through oral history source material. In October 2016, Montoya staged *Nogales: Storytellers in Cartel Country* with director Sean San José and filmmaker Jean Osato of Campo Santo theater company. Campo Santo's ensemble is one of the next generation to spring from Culture Clash and therefore El Teatro Campesino. San José is cofounder of Campo Santo and grew up in the Mission District. He was inspired by *A Bowl of Beings* to write representations of multicultural neighborhoods, and the company focuses its work on communities of color. *Nogales* was performed at both the Borderlands Theater in Arizona and Magic Theatre in San Francisco. It centers on the 2012 death of José Antonio Elena Rodriquez, a teen shot by American border patrol as he stood on the Mexican side of the US boundary with Arizona. Montoya and San José interviewed a variety of characters on both sides of the border, while Osato filmed the encounters and landscape. Interviewees included immigrant rights advocates, undocumented individuals who detailed the perils of crossing the border, law enforcement, and even Rodriguez's mother.

At the height of the piece, Montoya and San José take the stage to re-create their interview with controversial Arizona sheriff Joe Arpaio. The sheriff became notorious for his large persona and dogged pursuit of undocumented immigrants in Arizona. In defiance of a court order to cease the practice of racial profiling, Arpaio directed officers to question suspected immigrants' status during traffic stops. He gained notoriety for housing Maricopa County Jail inmates outdoors, even under the beating desert sun. He bragged about issuing pink jumpsuits and surplus bologna sandwiches that turned green in the unrelenting heat.[53]

Montoya embodies the rambling energy of Arpaio in transfixing fashion. San José repeatedly attempts to regain hold of the interview and presses Arpaio to discuss what he knows of the case. The sheriff sidesteps and redirects, continually shifting back to his persona and ideas. He never answers a question directly. This portrait of Arpaio indicts broader complacency. It reveals how power and politics shape which events are buried, especially when they challenge concepts of national sovereignty, race, and the authority of law enforcement. The play juxtaposes Arpaio's egoism with an overall examination of the border as a physical and political location that keeps lopsided power structures intact.[54] Montoya's portrayal harkens back to Cantinflas's use of empty language to lampoon political demagoguery in post-revolution Mexico.[55]

While oral history theater cannot solve the issues it illuminates onstage, the conversation it develops shapes the ways history is imagined and reimagined: "More specifically, in choosing to create a dialogue of actual voices from the pages of the past, staged oral histories do not attempt to change the substance of what we know about, say, the Los Angeles riots. But they do change how we look at them. By reframing the past not as a series of individually held views, but rather as the kind of dialogue that can prevent future misunderstanding, these plays are revising the discourse around the past."[56] Culture Clash has built a body of work to shift interpretation of events and the lenses through which communities are viewed. Equipped by El Teatro Campesino's innovative legacy, Montoya, Salinas, and Sigüenza confront the biases and blinders that maintain the unequal present. Building upon forms laid down by Mexican carpa theater, both companies have woven their own influences to create their brands of Chicanx performance. El Teatro Campesino and Culture Clash both intended to embolden audiences to view themselves as potential agents of change. Culture Clash then went further to replay community voices back, reinterpreting what may be possible onstage.

Notes

1 Alessandro Portelli, "What Makes Oral History Different?," in *The Oral History Reader*, ed. Robert Perks and Alistair Thomson (New York: Routledge, 2006), 32–42.

2 Ioana Radu, "Blurred Boundaries, Feminisms, and Indigenisms: Cocreating an Indigenous Oral History for Decolonization," *Oral History Review* 45, no. 1 (2018): 32.

3 *Verbatim theater* and *oral history theater* are used interchangeably in this chapter.

4 Jonathan Gottschall, *The Storytelling Animal: How Stories Make Us Human* (Boston: Houghton Mifflin Harcourt, 2013), 103.

5 Ryan Claycomb, "(Ch)oral History: Documentary Theatre, the Communal Subject and Progressive Politics," *Journal of Dramatic Theory and Criticism* 17, no. 2 (2003): 97.

6 James Hebert, "A New Stage for Herbert Siguenza," *San Diego Union-Tribune*, October 5, 2012.

7 Richard Montoya, *Culture Clash: Life, Death and Revolutionary Comedy* (New York: Theatre Communications Group, 1998), xii.

8 Montoya, xiii.

9. Luis Valdez, "Las Dos Caras del Patroncito," in *Luis Valdez—Early Works: Actos, Bernabé, and Pensamiento Serpentino*, ed. Luis Valdez and El Teatro Campesino (Houston: Arte Publico Press, 1990), 27.
10. Yolanda Broyles-González, *El Teatro Campesino: Theatre in the Chicano Movement* (Austin: University of Texas Press, 1994), xii.
11. Broyles-González, xi.
12. Broyles-González, 74.
13. Beth Bagby and Luis Valdez, "El Teatro Campesino Interviews with Luis Valdez," *Tulane Drama Review* 11, no. 4 (1967): 73.
14. Broyles-González, *El Teatro Campesino*, 84.
15. Broyles-González, 56.
16. Broyles-González, 88.
17. "Our History," El Teatro Campesino, last modified 2015, http://elteatrocampesino.com/our-history/.
18. Luis Valdez, Richard Montoya, Ricardo Salinas, and Herbert Sigüenza, "Passing the Baton of Art and Activism," interview by Michael Ritchie, Center Theatre Group, Mark Taper Forum, February 1, 2017.
19. Jorge Huerta, "The Legacy of Luis Valdez and El Teatro Campesino: The First Fifty Years / El Legado de Luis Valdez y El Teatro Campesino: Los Primeros Cincuenta Años," *Howlround*, accessed July 3, 2017, http://howlround.com/the-legacy-of-luis-valdez-and-el-teatro-campesino-the-first-fifty-years.
20. Valdez, Montoya, Salinas, and Sigüenza, "Passing the Baton."
21. "20 Years of Culture Clash," California State University Northridge Oviatt Library, last modified October 15, 2012, https://digital-library.csun.edu/20-years-culture-clash-exhibit.
22. Montoya, *Culture Clash*, 3.
23. Brent Beltrán, "Latino Playwright Herbert Siguenza Talks Culture Clash, Perceptions and Legacy," *San Diego Free Press*, June 26, 2014, https://sandiegofreepress.org/2014/06/latino-playwright-herbert-siguenza-talks-culture-clash-perceptions-and-legacy/.
24. Montoya, *Culture Clash*, 4.
25. Montoya, 3.
26. Montoya, 5.
27. Montoya, 32–33.
28. Montoya, 6.
29. Montoya, 4.
30. Montoya, 3.
31. Montoya, 61.
32. Montoya, 110.
33. "Anna Deavere Smith," National Endowment for the Humanities (NEH), accessed April 14, 2020, https://www.neh.gov/about/awards/jefferson-lecture/anna-deavere-smith-biography.
34. Montoya, *Culture Clash*, 110.

35 David G. Garcia, "Culture Clash Invades Miami: Oral Histories and Ethnography Center Stage," *Qualitative Inquiry* 14, no. 6 (2008): 872.
36 David G. Garcia, "Transformations through 'Teatro': Culture Clash in a Chicana/o History Classroom," *Radical History Review*, no. 102 (2008): 116.
37 Montoya, *Culture Clash*, 113.
38 Montoya, 109.
39 Montoya, 126–27.
40 Garcia, "Transformations through 'Teatro,'" 119.
41 Della Pollock, "Telling the Told: Performing 'Like a Family' (Oral History Theatre and Performance)," *Oral History Review* 18, no. 2 (1990): 7.
42 Pollock, 8.
43 Claycomb, "(Ch)oral History," 101.
44 Pollock, "Telling the Told," 16.
45 Montoya, *Culture Clash*, 112.
46 "20 Years of Culture Clash."
47 Valdez, Montoya, Salinas, and Sigüenza, "Passing the Baton."
48 Broyles-González, *El Teatro Campesino*, 7.
49 Broyles-González, 28.
50 Bagby and Valdez, "El Teatro Campesino Interviews," 77.
51 Montoya, *Culture Clash*, 4.
52 Garcia, "Transformations through 'Teatro,'" 123.
53 Sue Anne Pressley, "Sheriff's Specialty: Making Jail Miserable," *Washington Post*, August 25, 1997.
54 *Nogales: Storytellers in Cartel Country*, written by Richard Montoya, directed by Sean San José, Magic Theatre, San Francisco, CA, October 12, 2016.
55 Broyles-González, *El Teatro Campesino*, 54.
56 Claycomb, "(Ch)oral History," 110.

What Are the Roots of Your Radical Oral History Practice?

Shane Bernardo, Maria E. Cotera,
Fernanda Espinosa, and Amy Starecheski

A key part of the project of documenting the radical roots of oral history is imagining what the new shoots on the various branches of our reimagined family tree might look like. And so we (Amy and Fernanda) interviewed two radical oral historians working today (Shane and Maria) about their own roots as well as the future of oral history as they practice it. Of course, the very earliest stages of planning this project led us immediately to a need to define our terms. Who were we counting as an oral historian? What did we mean by *radical*? And what kinds of roots were we seeking? We sought people doing work that emphasized the telling of life stories, whether or not they defined themselves as oral historians. We sought work that was radical in the sense that it aimed to challenge the structural forces that create oppression, including colonialism, white supremacy, capitalism, and patriarchy. As oral historians, we approached these interviews as collaborations in which we brought our own ideas and frameworks for analysis to the table but were committed to building a conversation around the narrator's analysis and point of view. We told them that research conducted as part of our collective project so far had focused on feminist consciousness raising, testimonio, and popular education as relevant roots for radical oral history work. As always happens in a good oral history interview, our narrators surprised us with what they had to say, and their descriptions of their roots were simultaneously broader and more specific than we expected. They were also often intensely personal.

Our analysis of these interviews has been influenced by our own engagement with many other radical oral history projects, especially those developed through Groundswell: Oral History for Social Change, a network of activists, scholars, and cultural workers using oral history for social justice. The narrators we chose for our contribution to this volume are only two of the many radical oral historians we talked to and researched as part of this project. Our intention is to continue to build this line of inquiry and analysis.

Maria E. Cotera is an associate professor at the University of Michigan and the cofounder of the Chicana por mi Raza Digital Memory Collective, "a group of historians, educators, researchers, archivists and technologists dedicated to preserving imperiled Chicanx and Latinx histories of the long Civil Rights Era" through oral history and the digitization of personal archives.[1] Shane Bernardo is a Detroit-born-and-raised food and environmental justice activist and a cofounder of the Swimming in the Detroit River storytelling project.

While Shane and Maria's work differ in many ways, several strands link them together. Both value embodied knowledge, and each emphasizes the spread of knowledge through living people. Both speak about decolonizing the archive. Both Swimming in the Detroit River and Chicana por mi Raza are collective projects in which the forging of relationships between participants in the oral history process is one of the major products of the work. Maria articulates a vision of "cocreation with cafecito," a specifically Chicana practice of oral history interviewing based on deep affective ties and shared cultural knowledge that builds on but is distinct from mainstream oral history.

There are also important differences between these two narrators. While Maria is a tenured professor who works in and on the margins of the university and the library, whose work focuses on the lives of other Chicana intellectuals, Shane's work promotes knowledge-making practices that are completely independent of the university. From these different positions, each articulates a model of archiving that does not rely on institutional support. Maria acknowledges the power of institutional archives to legitimize and preserve knowledge while recognizing that this power is too often withheld from projects that focus on the knowledge of women, people of color, and other marginalized groups. She worries about the long-term preservation of the materials collected in the Chicana por mi Raza collection at the same time as she is excited by the radical potential of the embodied and social archive the collective is producing together. Shane aims specifically to decolonize the practice of oral history by finding legitimacy in the bodies, histories, and people that contain stories, and formulating practices of collective storytelling and self-respect that depart from institutionalized, often White, ways of knowing and appreciation. Both seek to share the knowledge they produce, but not without constraints: Maria asks those who want to use the archive to become members of the collective and contribute to the curation or preservation of the collection, while Shane's work emphasizes person-to-person storytelling that is not reproduced online or in an institutional archive at all.

Maria's two-hour-long interview was conducted as more of a life history and is presented here as a collection of selected and edited clips and transcripts. Shane's interview was shorter and more focused, and the outcome includes an edited interview accompanied by audio highlights, which are included in the open access version of this text on Fulcrum. Listen to their voices; much nuance is lost in the process of transcription.

Maria E. Cotera, Interviewed by Amy Starecheski: The Chicana por mi Raza Digital Memory Collective as a Space of Encuentro

> For audio highlights and all other media, please visit the open access version of this text at https://www.fulcrum.org/amherst.

I interviewed Maria E. Cotera on a hot afternoon in Detroit in June 2017. I was in town for the Allied Media Conference (AMC), an annual gathering of people using media to create radical social change. Maria, who teaches at the University of Michigan in Ann Arbor, drove over to Detroit to meet me. I had heard her speak the year before at the AMC about the central role her mother, a Chicana feminist and activist named Martha P. Cotera, played in her work, and so I started off by asking her to tell me about her mom. Martha Cotera, a bookworm, was born in 1964 in Chihuahua, Mexico, and raised in El Paso, Texas. In the late 1960s, when Maria was still little, the family moved to Crystal City, Texas, where the Mexican majority was in the process of taking political power through the Raza Unida Party.[2]

"My Consciousness Had Been Raised since the Time I Was a Little Baby"

Amy Starecheski: And then at what point in your mom's life did you come into the picture?

Maria E. Cotera: I was born when [my parents] were like in the thick of the struggle around the housing rights issues [in Austin, Texas].

So I was very young when they were involved in these kind of extremely radical spaces, which also, you know—it's hard for people to wrap their heads around that so many of those activists in that generation are young, and they had small children and they were like—those kids went to meetings. Those kids did everything, and that was before we had, like, these massive SUV stroller things with, like, so many entertainment devices. We got paper clips. "Here's some Post-its." We didn't even have Post-its! "Here's a legal pad, a pen, and paper clips." And you were lucky if you got binder clips. Sometimes we got those. Yeah, a different time. Raised by wolves. That's kind of how I describe it.

When I went to school in Crystal City, for example—that would have been in 1969, '70, right in the thick of the transformation of that small town. When I arrived to first grade, they had switched out all the pictures of presidents that lined the classroom wall above the chalkboard with pictures of, like, Che Guevara, Emiliano Zapata. It was like these radical transformations, political transformations that were impacting not just at the political level but the children, all the way down, the whole family had this radical consciousness. It was really intense.

You know, so when we moved back to Austin, still a very White space and extremely racist still, in the early 1970s. I was like, what? fourth grade, I guess, when we moved back, and I wasn't taking anything from anyone. Like when the lunch lady wouldn't punch my lunch card unless I said my name in English. You know, I was like, "I just won't eat lunch. Fuck you. I'm *Maria Cotera*." She's like, "Say it in English!" I'm like, "That isn't—that, that's the only way to say it." You know, that kind of thing, like, just tiny little—I think we call them today "microaggressions," but they would happen a lot. And I had been so—my consciousness had been raised since the time I was little baby, so I was not having it.

Maria was a punk rock teenager, one of few people of color in the local punk scene. After going to college at the University of Texas at Austin, she spent a few years working for her mom in the Chicana Research and Learning Center, a grassroots research and advocacy center her mom had founded in Austin in 1974. Maria began to realize that she loved doing research but could make much more money doing so with a PhD. She was accepted into the English MA program at UT Austin and then went on to get her PhD at Stanford, where she found Condoleezza Rice, then university provost (later secretary of state under President George W. Bush), actively dismantling the structures of ethnic studies and affirmative action that had been supporting students and faculty of color. The contradictions she encountered as a student entering academia after a lifetime's immersion in alternative, people of color–led spaces of knowledge production have continued to shape her work today.

The Power and the Disciplining of Ethnic Studies

Maria E. Cotera: Being in the institution really kind of introduced me to the power of institutional knowledge forms and the contradictions of people of color in institutions studying ethnic studies and the way institutions can use people of color as cover.

And so that kind of really made me aware of the really paradoxical position faculty of color have in institutions that ultimately exist to reinforce relations as they are. Like, there's no academic institution, no scholarly institution that is not meant to uphold as much as possible social relations. Ironically, they're filled with people who critique them, decolonize them, and you know, otherwise want to subvert them in the most mild way possible, which is through publishing books. But it's a confusing and highly politicized space to kind of carve out life in and especially for women, minorities—so-called minorities—sexual dissidents, and anyone trying to mess with the status quo. And oddly they're attracted to the university.

It's the contradictions in a given moment that kind of push one to either analyze them—I mean, there's two ways you can go: You can push them under the rug and just carry on and try to just make it through your life reasonably unscathed. Or you can think about them deeply and try and figure out ways to work around them. *Or* you can leave. And those are your choices, you know.

And I think that the particular contradictions of the academic-industrial complex and people of color and other dissidents who are actively trying to engage those power relations—those contradictions lead you to potentially more and more radical positions.

Amy Starecheski: Can you give me an example of how those contradictions became apparent to you as you were reentering the academy?

Maria E. Cotera: Yeah, thanks for that excellent question. It's a really good one! [*Laughs.*]

For most of my master's and PhD, I was really focused on Chicano studies and Latino studies and ethnic studies writ large. And in those spaces, we were actively producing knowledge for this kind of audience that was highly literate, and basically for classrooms and other professors to use the knowledge we produce to produce more knowledge for a certain sector of the population. And because I had grown up in the Chicano movement and in such a radical space and because my mom had been involved in the establishment of the Center for Mexican American Studies at UT Austin, I knew that the early versions of those institutional formations were very radical.

And by the time I got to my PhD in the '90s, it was like, they looked like everything else. So they had been disciplined. We were writing books that were decolonizing and challenging and doing all this, but our practices, the way we were actually engaging in our scholarship and the people we were talking to and the way we were organizing our institutions, departments, programs, what have you, looked exactly like an English department. I knew that, for example, in the first Chicano studies department at Northridge, they were tenuring people without PhDs, and there were community members on tenure committees. They were tenuring people for their—you know, they were counting, in fact, as a major element of a tenure case, the nature and the quality of your community activism. And they got that passed. I mean, the administration agreed to that, right? So for me it was sort of like we were producing all of this academic work, this scholarly work, but our formations were totally hierarchical and completely separated from communities around us. There was a weird way in which we had been kind of allowed into the door, but then once you accept that and you rely on it, then you're kind of stuck.

In her first book, *Native Speakers: Ella Deloria, Zora Neale Hurston, Jovita Gonzalez, and the Poetics of Culture* (2008), Maria excavated the lives and writing of three women intellectuals of color in order to extend the genealogy of women of color theory into the early twentieth century.[3] Her current project, the Chicana por mi Raza Digital Memory Collective, fills in the gap between this early generation and the rise of women of color anthologies like *This Bridge Called My Back* in the 1980s, essentially turning her attention to her mother's generation.[4] It was this move toward studying the next generation of women of color intellectuals that led Maria to oral history. Her first set of interviews for the project that became Chicana por mi Raza included her mom, Martha P. Cotera.

"She Would Escape from Us"

Amy Starecheski: It sounds like from what you're saying that you were somewhat familiar with her work before you started working with her. When you actually were, like, in the trenches, at that point was there anything that surprised you about what she was actually doing or what the Chicana Research and Learning Center was actually like or what—? Anything—?

Maria E. Cotera: I think, you know, because I was always so involved in my mother's work—like, she wrote *Diosa y Hembra*, her profile of Mexican American women, in the McDonald's.[5] And we would play like at the playscape. She wrote it in longhand, of course, in the '70s. And it was the only McDonald's with a playscape. So she would take my brother and I to the playscape, and we would play there for hours and she would just sit there and write. So I had always associated her with her work. They were really forged together.

I guess it wasn't until I interviewed her and then I interviewed other women who spoke of the importance of those books to them that I understood how important she was to a certain generation, and her work was to a certain generation of women. Like, I didn't fully understand that. I mean I understood her work as *something*, like sometimes she would take me to New York or to Washington when I was really young, or with her on trips, you know, and she would have meetings. It was all very abstract to me. But it was really when I started out with the project that I'm doing now that I kind of understood.

And also when I wrote my book, actually. Because when I wrote my book, and I had—I was finishing up my book, and Penelope was, my daughter was . . . Oh god, when was my book published? 2008, so she was around six when my book was published.[6] And so I was constantly locking her out of my office. And I remember in those moments how my mother would do that. Well, she never had an office. But like she would escape from us, you know. And why she would do that.

Maria and her friend Linda Garcia Merchant, an Afro-Chicana filmmaker whose mother was involved in many of the same political projects as Maria's, launched the Chicana por mi Raza Digital Memory Collective in 2009. When Maria began doing oral histories with Chicana feminists of her mother's generation after years working in more traditional archives, she started by reading some books—*Doing Oral History*, by Donald Ritchie, and *Women's Words: The Feminist Practice of Oral History*, edited by Sherna Gluck and Daphne Patai.[7] Much of their advice was useful, but it was more of a jumping-off point than a blueprint for the methods Maria and her team developed. They did many of the standard things oral historians do—making sure narrators had a clear understanding of the project's goals, giving the narrator the chance to review and edit the transcript, starting with a life story and asking lots of follow-up questions—but they also developed some unique tools of their own.

"I Always Think of Them as like My Aunties"

Maria E. Cotera: Each engagement with an interview subject is really so particular. But for us we developed over time a set of practices that we are very consistent with. And they're very basic. But then there's these sort of more affective things that—like, for example, when we arrive we always arrive with . . . Usually we go to their homes, and that's partially because they feel more comfortable that way. But it's also because many times, they have things in their homes that we can photograph or scan that become part of their story. And a lot of times, it's not just the comfort of being in the home and the freedom that they feel, but they don't—they don't always want to talk. Right. And so sometimes we begin—when we sense that, we begin by having them take us around the house. "Well, let's just take some pictures of your different stuff and things that are important to you." And then stories began to kind of roll out. Right, so a lot of people need objects to tell stories. I've just found many of the women bring notes, have written notes for themselves, which they need only as a kind of strange, like a, like a security blanket, right, because they never look at their notes! You know, but still.

The other thing is, we bring food, lots of food, and we are always prepared to feed the women, whether it be breakfast or lunch or lots of snacks. Again, these are older women. They like their snacks. Jolly Ranchers, carrots, things like that. Lots of water. And we make food there. A lot of times, we'll make food after. Have dinner. Like, we'll bring stuff for tacos or whatever. We're prepared to—it's a full day. It's not like an in and out. Or we'll go out to dinner. Because it's really a social experience, and part of this is like my mother—the first women we interviewed were women who knew my mother. And I will just say that my mother is—this is funny—my mother is, like, absolutely obsessed with, whenever I go to someone's house, you must always take food. It's something that she just drilled into me. So when we did our first interviews, of course she was like, "Make sure you take them out to eat. Make sure you take them food."

And we took her on our second set of interviews to California, actually. So we used her for the first two years as a kind of like a—I used to joke it was like, you know how they sometimes put goats or donkeys into barns when there's a thunderstorm because they keep the other animals calm? So we used my mom as a kind of, like, introductory token. *Everyone* was so excited to see her again. In most cases, they had seen her at conferences forty years or fifty years before, and so there was a big reunion and so—but that really kind of shaped how we engage with the participants.

But really it's the affective dimension of engaging with elders who have a kind of, I would say a familial connection to me through my mother, really. And that is why she was so instrumental in the beginning. Her physical presence was necessary in many cases, I will say, because these women also felt very burned. In many cases, the women that we interviewed have been interviewed before, or people have borrowed their archives to write books and never returned them. And they're extremely suspicious, and they feel like they've been misrepresented. And so they feel like they've been actively used for knowledge-making in the academy, and they're very suspicious of academic knowledge makers. And so, you know, working around and through that suspicion involves something more than a kind of very pragmatic or practical approach to ensuring that everything is caught on tape, that ignores, like, all the affective dimensions of everything that comes before and after.

And this affective dimension was really intense. Like, my students found it incredibly tiring, right. Because Linda and I knew this history because we'd grown up in this history, and both of our mothers were involved in different parts of it. Right. And were involved with each other. So when we're engaging—and we're closer in age to the women—and so when we're engaging with the women, there's a lot of talk that happens before, during, and after that frankly exhausts our students. Because we continue the conversation into dinner and sometimes late into the night.

It requires a kind of—I mean, I always think of them as like my aunties. I know you're not supposed—you're supposed to have distance. I absolutely cannot. I would not be able to do anything with them if I did. So I understood very early on, mainly because my mom also nagged me about it a lot, but that there are respect relations that have to be always at the forefront. That you can have intimacy and respect, and all of those things have to be articulated through gestures.

Having a gin and tonic with them if that's what they want at the end of the day, which one of the women we interviewed did. Several gin and tonics. [*Laughs.*] Stopping for a cafecito. You know, not rushing through. Having that time for things to unroll or, you know, kind of—there's a word in Spanish: desarrollar, "to develop." So these are all the things you don't find really in books that much.

Over time, Maria and her team continued to develop their unique methodology for doing oral history. They became more comfortable switching back and forth between English and Spanish or allowing a narrator to play a guitar or sing in the interview. They recognized that they needed to turn the camera off, though, if the women being interviewed began to cry. Maria frames all these ethical, affective, and intellectual practices as part of a practice of decolonizing the archive, reimagining the work of the scholar as collaborative, de-centered, and politically engaged.

"Cocreation with Cafecito"

Amy Starecheski: Can you tell me more about how the way that you're doing oral history is a feminist and specifically a Chicana feminist approach?

Maria E. Cotera: The typical way that scholars produce knowledge, either from archives or oral histories or interviews is, you amass an archive. It's your evidence. You keep the archive to yourself because you don't want anyone scooping you. You produce your account of what happened, and sometimes you hold on to the archive for a really long time, and then maybe you give it to a library. Sometimes you put a hold on it in a library. Right? So there's this kind of possessiveness that happens with the knowledge that is very much about a kind of individualist approach to scholarship and scholarly production. And when I started this project, I started it in large part to honor the collectivist labors of women who wanted to transform the world. And I thought if I just turn this into my project, this is actively dishonoring their narratives.

So I feel it was a risk, and it remains a risk, because you know the institution absolutely does not recognize the value of this, right? But what I would say is that the impetus behind the collection is one that is collectivist. It is not for my individual gain. Although certainly I have gained and certainly I will write something, that was never the main point. The main point was to preserve Chicana history. These women are in their seventies and eighties. And to make it available to scholars and community members because I think it's valuable.

Scholars write about decolonizing this and decolonizing that and decolonial practice, but they very rarely do things in their practice that are really challenging some of the primary assumptions of scholarly knowledge production. It's individualized. It's competitive. It's transforming radical knowledges into exchangeable commodities. And so I was not interested in doing that. And so that is what constitutes the major intervention of the project, a feminist or decolonial intervention in a more kind of practical way.

We try as much as possible to kind of create a situation in which there is a cocreation of knowledge. A lot of oral history practice talks about this, and it's central to a lot of oral history practice. And so what I would say is that that's our particular version of that. Right. So I wouldn't say that "oh, people talk about cocreation; they don't really do it." I think they do. I do think they do. And I think this is our particular way of doing it, but it has a Chicana spin on it because we're Chicanas and we have a certain way of doing things. And like I said, you know, maybe I would say the cocreation with cafecito—or the sense that that the person that you're cocreating with becomes a part of the project, the family of the project, that they continue to engage with it. That they have access to it. That they control who sees it, you know.

We call the project—we started calling it the Digital Memory Collective. And part of the reason why we called it that is because when we were calling it an archive, people just wanted to use it. And so now we say, "Well if you want access to the primary materials in this archive"—because we have a website too that has clips of oral histories and other stuff—but "if you want to, you have to join the collective. You have to help build it. So what are you going to do?" So that again, this is a process, it's envisioned much less as a kind of top-down knowledge-delivery model than a coequal exchange with responsibilities. Because too many people just come in and use it, and then they don't do anything, you know, and we're just trying to survive.

Inspired by the Women Who Rock project at the University of Washington, which uses a collaborative and community-based "feminist archivista practice" to document the role of women of color in popular music and movement building, Maria began thinking of her work using the idea of encuentro. This shifts the focus onto the process of doing oral history, from the intimate space of the interview to the larger digital encuentro of the online archive.

"Shadowed by Precarity": Encuentro in the Archive

Amy Starecheski: You've written about the archive as a space of relationship building and of encuentro. Can you talk a little bit about the idea of *encuentro* and how that's different from *encounter*? What is the specificity and the history of that idea?

Maria E. Cotera: When I talk about encuentro in the more intimate space of the interview, what I'm really trying to get at is a way of thinking about the interview as something other than just artifact. Right. So we do oral history interviews to preserve oral history. At the heart of that process is a kind of archival mind-set, right, which would say, "Well, it's important to preserve these histories because we may use them in the future to reimagine the past." And it's important to preserve knowledges. And even if we're doing radical oral history work and really uncovering subjugated knowledges, there is still a sense in which that encounter always has a kind of futurity or a future use built into it.

And with our project—which is so precarious, right. It's so poorly funded; it's so poorly supported. It's a project of the heart that Linda and I have been doing with the help of students who've worked for us, not for free but paid for by the university. But again, every trip is kind of shadowed by precarity. Our resource is not necessarily permanent. Our server space is not permanent. Our platform is not permanent. Digital archives themselves are shadowed by impermanence. And so it leads to, or it can lead to, a fear that we're doing all this work and trying to preserve these histories and we don't have the resources to sustain that process of preservation, and nobody seems all that interested in helping us.

So sometimes in the shower, I have time to think about these things, and I start to have an anxiety attack. And so the idea of encuentro borrowed from this UW project actually came as a result of one of these anxiety attacks, when I was just like, "What am I doing? I'm saying I'm going to preserve all this stuff, and I don't know that I can. I can't."

But then I started thinking about this idea of futurity that's implicit in the process and the idea of the archive that's implicit in the process, which is a very institutional understanding of the archive. The archive as a kind of house for the papers of the state or those in power, right, that must be preserved for the preservation of capital—really, that's where it comes from. And so I thought, "Well, what if we reimagine the archive not as this site of preservation for these papers to preserve power structures, but if we thought of it as an active site of exchange?"

Now what does that mean? OK, well, you know, I say occasionally when I'm in a bad humor that it's like the classic colonial trick where they say, "Well, you know, you're only an archive if you can guarantee sustainability and preservation," and then deny you the things you need for sustainability and preservation. So I said, "You know, what if we reject that idea of the archive and think of the archive as something that's constituted in the exchange of stories and memories in the space for that time? And what if we think of the archive as every single individual who walks away from that engagement in that encounter and carries with them some knowledge seed, right, that even if the archive disappears, that can't? That doesn't disappear." So when we talk about the ephemeral archive or our archive as encuentro, it's because in many ways, we've been placed in this position where we must make something, you know, we must claim something. And this, this may be—I mean this really sounds depressing—but I think that is a transformation. That engagement, right—multigenerational, from spaces of difference—that engagement is something that is a kind of result of the encuentro. It's not really, it's not a classic archive. Right. But it is an archive that's living.

Students have played a critical and core role in the Chicana por mi Raza project. Often outsiders to Chicana feminism, they come on research trips, scan materials, curate the website, and help with research, but they don't do interviews. While oral histories are often assumed to be done one-on-one, in this project, there are always many people in the room. Students watching the interview play the roles of "critical witnesses," an audience that reminds the narrator of the broader world that will encounter their interviews as they begin to circulate.

The Critical Witness

Amy Starecheski: In thinking about the relationships of oral history, you've kind of added a new relationship into the mix, I think: that idea of the critical witness. And can you tell me about that role and what it looks like and where it came from?

Maria E. Cotera: Well, I mean, it comes from our experience of the students that we've worked with. So we've worked from the very beginning with students, and they always come away from interviews, even when they're not conducting them, completely exhausted. And so, you know, I've been thinking a lot about this and what is so exhausting about listening. Right.

You know, we've had students who have nothing to do with Chicana feminism, students from Bloomfield Hills in Michigan, you know, who have not really had much of an engagement with difference, but what they've taken away from the experience is a deeper understanding of like Cherrie Moraga's conceptualization of "theories in the flesh," right—embodied knowledges.[8] So what deepens and expands for them is not necessarily first and foremost their understanding of feminism or the Chicano movement, but something else. Right. And also something about the process of knowledge-making, you know, and the stakes of knowledge-making and disrupting the hierarchies of knowledge-making too. So yeah, that's what the encuentro does.

And I think that's kind of where the idea of critical witness comes from—but also obviously from other people who've written about critical witness—but also from this idea of, you know, when I take students to these interviews or to these oral histories, sort of encuentros, the students are there really to help, but they don't do the interviews.[9] And there's lots of reasons for that. Mainly, they don't have the sort of embedded knowledge that it takes to ask good follow-up questions. They don't have the years to engage with someone who's in their seventies.

I mean, it's just a whole different relationship, right? But when they're there witnessing, something interesting happens for the people that we're talking to. One would think they'd clam up more, right, with other people in the room, but they don't. And there is something about the youth of the students that I think brings out a kind of storytelling impetus in the women we interview that's really interesting to watch. But the students are also—when they enter into that space, they don't enter in without any prior knowledge, right? They read about the practice of radical oral history. They read about Chicana feminism. They read about feminism and the Chicano movement. So they have this kind of knowledge that they enter into this thing with that makes them not just witnesses but critical witnesses, witnesses who are taking in the sort of particularities of the story they're listening to and kind of having an encounter with what they bring to the table, what they understand of the history. And that kind of act of critical witness, I think, deepens their experience of it. But also I think it shifts, right—they're not just an audience. Right. They're putting these stories into place into a kind of field of knowledge that they come with.

And yeah, I think at least that's how I justify not letting them interview. Because I can't. Not just because I'm controlling either.

The audience for these interviews now stretches far beyond those in the room while they were conducted. As the archive opens, the space of encuentro grows.

"It's Absolutely Beautiful": The Living Archive

Amy Starecheski: Now that the archive has been open to the public in the way that you've described—it's not totally open, right?—for a couple of years now, what has that been like? You imagine this thing going out in the world, and now it's out there.

Maria E. Cotera: So the archive itself is some six thousand items with another, you know, two or three thousand to still be processed and put up on there. And it's absolutely beautiful, actually. I love just opening it up and looking. It is available to scholars via login. One of the wonderful things that we've been doing is we have our students and other students at other universities—we give them access to the archive to find stories in the archive. These could either be biographies of women who have not been written about that use some of their materials to illustrate them and oral history clips, but they could also be like stories that are—

Like one student was really intrigued by these photos taken in the seventies, by one of the people who donated to the archive, of this police brutality march in Austin, Texas, and she became really interested in this, and so she used the archive to—it was a case that involved a man named Jose Torres. And she searched for other images in the archive and was able to trace back the story to where it happened in Houston and why this police brutality march was happening in Austin. Use these photographs, use materials from other parts of the archive, and then go on the web and find oral histories on the web and clips from reports about the case from the 1970s and put together an essay on that for our website.[10] To me, this is really exciting.

I love looking at the archive because there's all these beautiful women's faces, you know, because it's a video archive. But then it's also like their materials and these amazing posters. And it's just this kind of explosion of history that's super messy. But you can still tag search it, which is really exciting to me because then you see these confluences. A lot of the oral histories are tagged and metadataed. So that means that you could attach clips to evidence that's more archival in nature in other collections, and you can start seeing connections and women who remember being at the same places at the same time.

So that's like—the messiness of that, I find just incredible, incredible. And if I had to reduce all that messiness to a book about Chicana feminism, it would make me crazy. So I love that, and I love the fact that it's a resource. I think we have achieved what we wanted to achieve, which was to create a resource that filmmakers and scholars and students and teachers could kind of go into and just discover things that really are intriguing inside that resource and then use that to produce knowledge that's new. And so our website has become a site for that. We have a biographies page, and we have a page called Historias, stories from the archive, and we've only got a few essays up, but those essays to me are, like, incredible—they realize the potential of the archive to be a source of knowledge. And they're written by students, and they're beautiful. They're short. They're beautiful, and they're beautifully illustrated from our archives. So I get really excited about that.

The messy, collaborative model of history-making Maria has envisioned is still resource-intensive. Lacking institutional support, the project is chronically short of server space. And it takes time—time that is hard to find—to do the organizational and affective work of growing the collective.

"I Am *Very* Busy": The Collective Model in Practice

Amy Starecheski: How has the model of having people who want to use the archive come in as members of a collective worked, in practice?

Maria E. Cotera: Not so great. Because I am *very* busy, and I realize that, like, *a lot* of people want to join the collective when they go to the website. And then there's a bit of a logjam in terms of resources to get those people plugged into things they can do for the archive that will sustain the archive while also protecting the archive. And so I have a backlog of about twenty people who want to join our collective. I don't know how to manage the collective quite yet, so I think that's still a bit of a learning curve. But I think that the impetus behind the collective was simply, like, we're not creating a resource to be mined for your scholarship. We're creating an encuentro. We want this to become a site of a kind of digital encuentro, if you will. But if you can add metadata based on your research, or you can create a story for "Historias," or write a bio if you listen to an oral history—this is a kind of simple goal that we're trying to achieve.

But I'm really busy so I need to find someone that will just handle that part of it, you know. Yeah. But the idea, I think, will work. It's just a matter of finding the time to bring all these people together and to start thinking about what that looks like on the site.

Even with these very real limitations, the impact of the archive, beginning with the impact on the narrators, is real.

"Not Just Being the Speaking Subjects of Chicana Feminist History"

Amy Starecheski: You've written and talked about the feeling that a book has such a limited political impact and that knowledge production in the university is, like, deeply depoliticized. What kind of political impact have you seen from this work, in whatever way you define it? If any, you know, and maybe it's ephemeral.

Maria E. Cotera: First and most important for me is, my encuentro with this generation of women has really reinforced for me and the other participants in the project, who have come and gone, that knowledge production—we tend to think that however knowledge is produced now has been how it's always been produced. And one of the things that has really come to light for me at least is the ways in which knowledge—alternative spaces for knowledge production were so central to the 1960s and '70s and are still viable today. Right. I think that those spaces—makers' spaces, things like Allied Media Conference—there's still viable sites that are really important in the contemporary moment.

Politically, I think that one of the other really interesting things is that while none of the women that we've interviewed ever stopped being active, what we have noticed is that in interviewing them, in bringing them together for various events, we've kind of generated an interesting intergenerational space that is a kind of what I would say is that encuentro, the echoing out of that encuentro from the single site of the interview into a kind of networked space so that, you know, we've had, for example, a few roundtables and organized a few events in which women have come together and spoken of their experience.

And that's bringing their voices—in many ways, bringing them back to life. In some cases, these women experienced tremendous political marginalization and have trauma really from that period. But they're coming into their own in some way by being acknowledged and by having their stories listened to. So my mom, for example, has been invited to do all these lectures all over the place, and I don't credit that to the project, but I credit it to a valorization of her voice as a historical subject that the project has pushed.

We are publishing an anthology where several of the women that we've interviewed are included, and they're not writing testimonios, they're not writing autobiographical pieces, they're writing critical pieces about different things that they were involved in in this historical moment.[11] So that I think is a very interesting thing because these women are often—in as much as they are brought into more scholarly anthologies, like the one I'm working on, they're often brought in as speaking subjects that are going to speak their truth of their time, which is important. I mean, I'm not discounting that. But what I found interesting about some of the essayists who contributed to our volume, who we've interviewed for the project, is they've kind of gotten beyond that positionality. And so, for example, my mother wrote a piece on how women in the Chicana caucus organized at the 1977 IWY, International Women's Year, conference in Houston; and Anna Nieto Gomez, who we also interviewed, wrote about Francisca Flores, a woman who mentored her, who came from a generation before, right. I think that's an incredibly important turn for both of them because they are not just being the speaking subjects of Chicana feminist history; they're writing and producing Chicana feminist history.

And so I just think these intergenerational—listening to these stories has done something really profound for both sides, or all three sides: the critical witness; the interviewer or the recorder, Linda and I, you know; and for the women who were part of it. Yeah. It's not only brought attention to what they did and why it's important to know about them, but it's brought them into public life in a certain way that's really profound.

Another practice that shaped the project, in more implicit and limited ways than the very robust concept of encuentro is that of testimonio, a Latin American tradition of telling first-person stories in public to raise consciousness and prompt action.[12]

"The I Story": Testimonio and Its Limits

Amy Starecheski: That reminds me, I wanted to ask, How if at all do you see this work in relation to testimonios traditions?

Maria E. Cotera: I mean, I think we're definitely pulling from the tradition of testimonio because our interview is really more geared toward the life history. So we're asking them to narrate their political development. And that implicitly involves a contextualization of their individual experience inside of larger structures of power and inside of larger movements, social movement activities. And the nature of our questioning is precisely to get at that. Not that we need to really push them in that direction, because there is a strong tendency, in fact, for all of these women to narrate their coming to consciousness in and through experiences of structural racism and sexism and heterosexism and also in and through collective activity. So these are the two aspects of testimonio that I think are organically produced in the interaction between their already politicized point of view and our questions that try to get them to talk about political development. Right. So we don't ever use the word *testimonio*, but our questions are very influenced obviously by the idea of *conscientization*, right, and how it comes about.

Amy Starecheski: Is there a reason not to use that word?

Maria E. Cotera: Yeah, because it's kind of overused, I guess. No. There's just my particular reasons. There's not like a strong philosophical or political reason not to. I just think, you know—yeah. I mean, I think we—with women, we basically speak of political development. I also think testimonio has become a little bit about personal narrative. And so some of the aspects of testimonio that are collectivist in nature kind of get forgotten. Right. Because we think of it as "the I story," right.

As we prepared to close the interview, I asked Maria if she had anything to add. She shared one part of her vision for how the archive can continue to function as a space for deep, collaborative, generative thinking about Chicana feminist history and for a grounded practice of radical knowledge production.

"What Would It Mean to Unify a Dispersed Network of Activists?" Making New Knowledge

Maria E. Cotera: I think one aspect of encuentro that I think could just be reinforced is that there is a kind of scaling of it that I think is important. Like, that there's the encuentro of the actual active storytelling and listening. And then there's the encuentro between people who use the archive and produce knowledge from it that did not exist before. But they're encountering the sort of recorded versions of that smaller encuentro. And then there's the much larger encuentro that develops in the community of scholars, practitioners and women who are actively engaged in the archive to differing degrees. Right.

And that to me is what encuentro means, so beyond just the space of the archive there, there's kind of digital encuentro and then, you know, a kind of broader network that is—I used to talk a lot about archival reunification projects, like these projects that reunify dispersed archives. And you know, at the heart of this project when we started it was, "What would it mean to unify a dispersed network of activists?" And to think of their archive not as a collection of individual archives but an archive, right, that needs to be reunified to make sense of what happened in this particular moment. And what would happen when that archive is reunified? Does it just become like a regular archive that sits in a repository or in multiple repositories, linked by the wonders of the digital age? Or does it become a field of knowledge that's active and not just in the past but that's making new knowledge?

And so that's kind of how I think of encuentro throughout these different scales and in these different spaces, some of them real and intimate and some of them sort of larger and networked and mediated.

And a perfect example of this is Anna Nieto Gomez, who regularly sends me little pieces from her personal archive. I told her what kind of scanner to buy. And she'll send me these sort of "Here is my syllabus from 1972. This is the first class on la Chicana that I know was ever taught." And she'll send me these little essays on them. To me, that kind of archive is just so interesting to think about because she's actively framing historically the object, right, and curating it to a certain extent.

And we've even talked about what it would mean to take her syllabus, which she just discovered, you know, and this is a syllabus of Chicana feminism before there was such a thing really in the university curriculum. So it includes things like Marx and Engels. You know, the *Structure of the Family* and these really—*Our Bodies, Ourselves*—like it's really fascinating.[13] And we've talked about, "What if we co-taught, you know, a master class in Chicana feminism and taught this syllabus and then combined an oral history with you for each of the weeks that we do it, and what your thinking was, why you assigned these things. What was it like to teach this?" And that's going inside—deep in the archive.

That's not just like surveying her archive and figuring out a story of her life. That's like looking at this one archival object. And talking to her and reading it through with her, doing that reading. And to me, that is the archive. That's what I mean by archive as encuentro, as an exchange and not as a kind of repository or something filed away.

You can read more about the Chicana por mi Raza Digital Memory Collective in this article with Maria.[14] The full interview excerpted above will be available through Chicana por mi Raza.

Shane Bernardo, Interviewed by Fernanda Espinosa: Deprofessionalizing Oral History and Living the Archive

> For audio highlights and all other media, please visit the open access version of this text at https://www.fulcrum.org/amherst.

Shane Bernardo grew up working in his family's grocery store on the westside of Detroit. For more than thirteen years, the family helped cultivate a nourishing environment for the community's Southeast Asian, West African, and Afro-Caribbean ethnic groups by providing a space for sharing culturally relevant foods, recipes, stories, and traditions. Shane has been active in grassroots efforts for social and food justice, most recently as the outreach coordinator and farm stand manager at Earthworks Urban Farm, a project that strives to restore human connection to the environment and community, and as a facilitator for Uprooting Racism Planting Justice, a volunteer-run monthly convening of individuals desiring to participate as change agents in addressing the injustice of racism in the Detroit food system.

Shane has approached oral history through his work as a core working group member of Groundswell: Oral History for Social Change, and as a cofounder and active member of Swimming in the Detroit River, an environmental justice storytelling collective. They describe the project in their collective statement: "'Swimming in the Detroit River' is an initiative to collectivize the history of social justice as it relates to Earth and the human connection to nature. We center storytelling as the primary way of bringing justice into a space and realizing the power of truth. To be graceful, fierce, to be compassionate and brutally honest in storytelling, such that truth is revealed to cultivate a stronger movement for the generation that will inherit the Climate Crisis as a defining fact of life itself."[15]

The goal of the group is to expand the narrative around environmental justice in Detroit. The members realized that the narratives often used by mainstream environmentalists around green energy, recycling, or sustainability were not speaking to the experiences of people of color such as the environment of overpolicing, deportations, foreclosures, water shutoffs, and gentrification—issues that, according to Shane, are facilitated by policies of austerity and privatization. Founded in 2014, the collective sought to use their own life stories to shift mainstream narratives of environmental justice. In this context, they have a unique approach to oral history that manifests in organized storytelling events where a specific prompt is offered for participants to respond to in writing. The individual narratives are then woven together to generate a collective narrative that can be circulated among the members themselves, participants, and grassroots movements. They have also worked on some recordings with the idea of generating an audio piece that can be circulated more broadly and on the radio. Because the sharing of these narratives often happens person to person, such as in the storytelling events, not much can be found about the group on the internet, but Shane did share with me that the name "Swimming in the Detroit River" comes from the experience of Detroiters of being surrounded by water and yet not able to have a relationship with it. The name was their way of talking about the issues of environmental racism and omitted narratives of their experiences.

I conducted a short interview with Shane in his home city in June 2017. He was fairly busy organizing gatherings for the Allied Media Conference and, although an oral history was not the chosen format for this encounter, I learned a lot about Shane's life and his intentions in the context of his life by trying to understand his work during our short but rich interview and the exchanges that followed. Shane is a second-generation, lifelong Detroiter and sees the work of oral history, food justice, and his own history and ancestral traditions as inextricably related and personal. During our exchange, we discussed ancestral roots, justice, the embodied archive, decolonial intergenerational healing, and why these involve reclaiming spaces that have become professionalized and, often, inaccessible to many—especially to those they presumably are about. Please, click on the audio links to listen to some highlights in Shane's own voice. These selections of audio can be listened to on their own or to accompany the reading. The written piece is an edited interview based on the full transcript.

Fernanda Espinosa: Thank you for doing this interview! I know you have a lot of things going on. Can you introduce yourself and then tell me a little bit about the work that you do here, in Detroit?

Shane Bernardo: Sure! My name is Shane Bernardo and I am the second generation of my family here in Detroit. I'm a long-life Detroiter and grew up on the east side. The work that I do now is around oral history as it relates to food. Food is one of the ways that I practice my oral history work because there's a lot of stories embedded within the food that I grew up eating and where I draw a sense of identity from.

Oral history work and my food work is really personal to me.

Fernanda Espinosa: This interview is about the radical roots of oral history, and that can be interpreted in many ways. Can you say more about how you think of *radical* in the context of your oral history work?

Shane Bernardo: Sure. There's a couple of ways that I think of *radical* in regards to my oral history work. One of the ways is through my work as a founding member of an environmental justice storytelling group called Swimming in the Detroit River. We've been around for a couple of years now, and we came together under the premise that we were very disenfranchised by how environmental justice was being framed. It was being framed by well-intended White folks that seemed to focus a lot on sustainability and not where environmental racism impacted communities of color, immigrant, Indigenous, refugee, and low-income communities. We wanted to interject a different narrative into the mainstream environmental justice movement.

We brought up issues like gentrification, xenophobia, Islamophobia, foreclosures, water shutoffs, land grabbing, emergency management, austerity, and state-sanctioned violence. These are issues that aren't generally associated with sustainability, and that is because the folks that are driving the mainstream environmental justice movement don't have that lived experience.

In terms of radicalizing the environmental justice movement and our work around oral history, we are challenging the dominant mainstream sentiment within the environmental justice movement. This is one of the primary ways I practice radical oral history.

The other way that I look at radical oral history, or the roots of my radical history, is through an ancestral perspective. After my father passed away in 2010 from chronic health disease, I started looking at how his personal health and well-being—not just his physical health, but his emotional and spiritual health—were connected to his proximity to Earth-based culture and, in particular, to the land that my ancestors are from in the Philippines. My dad's side of the family is from Bayombong, in the province of Nueva Vizcaya, which is in the northernmost island of the Philippines. He used to tell me a lot of different stories about growing up in a household with thirteen other siblings and not really having a job, per se. You just hustled and you lived off the land, and that was just the way that you lived. No one really questioned it. There wasn't a regular job that you went to work from nine to five and you derived a paycheck and benefits and paid your taxes. You just made do with what you had, with what was around you: you lived off the land, you foraged, you hunted, you fished, you grew your own food, you raised animals, you traded, you bartered. So that's where my dad comes from. We don't have the same level of chronic health disease that we do here in the US.

Looking back at his own life and comparing the stories of how he was raised and was brought up to be more subsistent compared to the way that I was brought up and my relation to food here in the western part of the world, in the United States, Detroit, Michigan, I saw how our connection to Earth impacts our physical, emotional, and spiritual health. So when I talk about oral history, I talk about it from that place of deep belonging, from a deep place of knowing, and I talk about it from a longer practice of tradition—cultural tradition—that existed prior to even our written language.

Oral history, again, is something that's very personal to me and helped shape who I am as part of the Filipinx diaspora here on the land mass that I'm still, in some ways, trying to get to know, and trying to gain some type of footing in. Being within the diaspora in a predominantly Black city, and not identifying as Black but also experiencing structural racism, is something that speaks to the longer history around displacement that my family and ancestors have experienced.

Oral history for me is an ancestral practice, and it's also one that is rooted in healing from intergenerational trauma—from that displacement of being physically and culturally displaced. Not being physically in the place where my ancestors are from inhibits my way of practicing my cultural traditions. By not having that firsthand experience, I'm relegated to the stories that my grandmother or my father told me when I was growing up. Storytelling is a way for me to connect to my ancestors, to my tradition, and to my own sense of identity, and it can be very healing, nurturing, and affirming.

Fernanda Espinosa: You said that you also use oral history in the work you do with other people; can you tell me more about what that process looks like?

Shane Bernardo: Part of the work that we are doing with Swimming in the Detroit River is about building a collective narrative out of our own personal stories. We are sharing stories from our own lived experience about being a person of color that is on the margins, outside of the mainstream environmental justice movement. In doing so, we are honoring the humanity in our own stories and we're building a collective narrative that challenges the mainstream one. The way that I tend to do that in practice is by talking about my relationship to food, my relationship to my family, my relationship to my ancestors, and how that has been complicated by the legacy of displacement and the impact that has on our physical, emotional, and spiritual health.

Fernanda Espinosa: When you say that you do oral histories, how does that look like? Do you interview each other, or do you have more open story-sharing moments?

Shane: For us, there isn't a divide between the interviewer and the narrator. We are really interviewing ourselves. There is an interplay between the individual and the collective. What stories are embedded within our own persons? It is like seeing our own bodies, our own beings, as an archive of stories that have been embedded within our

DNA over multiple generations. It gets into some of the thought around intergenerational trauma and how that can be inherited. I found that the same way that we can inherit intergenerational trauma, we can also inherit intergenerational wisdom, and intergenerational creativity. We may not sometimes have cognitive awareness or knowledge of these things, but they're there because I know that their presence manifests as anxiety, post-traumatic stress disorder, chronic health disease, or some addictive behaviors that we use as coping mechanisms to this historic oppression that we've experienced and my ancestors have experienced and they have passed on to me.

The interplay between uncovering and unearthing the stories that live within us is part of the practice of oral history as a healing modality not just to heal ourselves but also healing our ancestors. We are a living embodiment of our ancestors, their stories and their intentions, and their dreams. My practice around oral history comes from the sense that these struggles live within us, but also the possibility for healing lives within us. By telling the stories and naming them, we allow healing to happen.

Fernanda Espinosa: Shane, you mentioned the idea of the archive that we carry in our bodies and the stories that we carry with us throughout the generations. Can you tell me more about how you think of the archive? I've noticed institutions talk about the importance of preserving the stories for a future public; this seemed like a very abstract idea to me. I wonder how that affects change and who that public is. For example, when we say "public," who are people actually talking of? White, male researchers? Or who we are talking about?

Shane Bernardo: I see our bodies, psyche, memory, and imagination as part of a living archive. It's a living universe. The idea that it's living is a very critical one, as opposed to the more institutional way that we look at archiving. By the time that a story is recorded, and archived, it's locked into this state of the past where time doesn't exist. In some way, it's sort of commodified. It becomes a product for academic researchers and administrators to gaze upon without the opportunity to interact with the person who told it. The idea that we are a living archive is that when we tell our own stories, we are always in relationship to it. We can see, we can feel, we can experience and express the humanity of our own stories in a way that an institutionally archived oral history cannot. It's in constant relationship to ourselves and to our lived experience, it's in constant relationship to our ancestors that helped shape us in our experiences, and it is constantly evolving. It's generative, it's iterative, and it speaks to the way that we walk in this world and who we are as people.

I kind of struggle with the way that stories are archived within institutions. In my own practice of decolonizing oral history, seeing ourselves as living archives and living institutions are ways of doing that.

Fernanda Espinosa: One thing that I struggle with in terms of its decolonial potential is thinking that the colonizers have used the record to preserve untrue stories that then get told again and again. I wonder if you have any more thoughts about this—about the importance of circulating stories, the living archive and transmission, but then also about the record as a tool of oppression.

Shane Bernardo: In terms of decolonizing oral history, looking at ourselves as a living archive is certainly one way of doing that and looking at the actual record of an oral history as a way of decolonizing as well. The way that that is practiced within my own work is by challenging narratives about Detroit. There is a certain way that mainstream media presents Detroit. Some of the more contemporary stories being told are about "the comeback city." In terms of settler colonialism, and its neocolonial form of gentrification, the story sees Detroit from a scarcity perspective, already doing without. From which standpoint does Detroit need to come back from? And where did it go during that time?

We have to be really careful about how these dominant narratives shape us and shape our stories because it's from a much different perspective than the way that we would tell it. I use oral history as a way of challenging them and the colonial mind-set that's inherent within. They are looking at the city, looking at the people that live here from a standpoint of scarcity, versus a standpoint of abundance. That narrative about "comeback city" mainly revolves around material wealth, and it connects capitalism and an extractive economy to this idea of the city coming back. I find that really hurtful because it reduces us to the haves and have-nots, and seeing the city from this scarcity perspective is the same one that has led to the emergency management, neoliberal rule, austerity politics, state-sanctioned violence, the over-policing of our communities, the water shutoffs, the largest municipal bankruptcy in the country, the Flint water crisis, environmental racism—all these things happen because the residents here are seen from a scarcity perspective, which implies that it's our fault for the city being in the condition that it's in.

Therefore, when I tell stories about Detroit, it's one from abundance, it's one from resilience, it's one that recognizes our beings as being the main assets, not material assets. This perspective of valuing our own self-worth—and it comes from taking back our stories from the colonizer, from the gentrifiers, and from the profiteers that seek to derive a material benefit from this new story being told about Detroit.

Fernanda Espinosa: Do you have some reflections more specific to how you see this field, method, or practice of oral history in your future and how you want to continue using it? Or do you have any observations about the field in general? I know that's a really open question, so feel free to elaborate however you want.

Shane Bernardo: In terms of my oral history work going forth, I see that as a model and a practice of healing myself by reclaiming my stories and rewriting ourselves as victors and champions of our stories. I see it much in the same light as I do food. I have a very personal relationship with food because embedded within our food are some of those things that I just talked about: some of those struggles around food as it pertains to displacement, Western imperialism, and settler colonialism. And as someone that identifies within the Filipinx diaspora, it's a really important one in terms of my own identity because the Philippines is and was the first US colonial possession. That came after 375 years of settler colonialism of Spain. A lot of our foodways were impacted by their presence. Some of our ingredients and the ways that we prepare food was based on who we were colonized by because they traded with other places around the world, places where they could derive wealth from, where they could enslave people from, where they could sell some of their goods. And because of where the Philippines is in the world, we are a very strategic location for them to do that to access the Far East. In terms of going forward, I'm challenging the notions of this Western gaze upon folks that similarly identify as me, and I am placing our narrative within this larger historical context of Western imperialism and how that impacts us still today. Seeing food as a platform for doing that is talking about how these stories are embedded within our food, the ingredients, the foodways, and the ways that we prepare and celebrate food. So that is a form of oral history to me: it's my connection to food.

Fernanda Espinosa: In the same way that you think about food, I think a lot about language. Do you have any thoughts about the traces that are embedded in the languages that we speak, or that we don't speak (or that we remember, or don't remember)?

Shane Bernardo: It's important when we look at our language to see what is present, what is dominant, what is suppressed. English is the second-most spoken language in the Philippines. Everyone in school learns English, and even the national language, which is Tagalog, was greatly influenced by the Spanish presence in the Philippines. The point that I'm getting to is that both of these languages are very gendered. These Eurocentric ideals around gender have also shaped how we think of ourselves within the context of heteronormativity. In our indigenous language, we looked at gender much differently. We didn't have these gendered ways of referring to ourselves, and inherent within that is this binary thinking of right and wrong, Black and White, good and bad. This was a way of dividing people that were different based on how you presented as a person, physically. When we look at our indigenous language, gender was not based on your sex organs, it was based on what you did. And to a greater degree, as it relates to heteronormativity, language also placed women and femme-identified people in a subordinate position to male-identified people. I find it really interesting how language normalizes that and invisibilized the ongoing systemic oppression of women, women-identified people, and femme-identified people.

Part of my oral history practice is about looking at the historic legacy of not just settler colonialism but heteronormativity and patriarchy and how that still continues to live within myself and the stories that I tell.

Fernanda Espinosa: Do you want to share anything else or any reflections before we conclude?

Shane Bernardo: Yeah, I think you had a question about how I look at oral history, just in general? One thing that I would like to say about oral history is that I'm explicitly attempting to deprofessionalize it. When I started looking at oral history more closely, I saw that the people that were found as being credible in this field were professionals, academics, people who had letters behind their name. I have a big problem with that because this is a tradition that my ancestors practiced before any of that was around. This was the primary way that we handed down our traditions and our knowledge to our descendants to preserve them. I see my work around storytelling and oral history as a way of decolonizing and deprofessionalizing the work in the field and taking back that power from institutions that benefit from white supremacy, heteropatriarchy, and institutional racism. The idea is to value the social capital that exists within our stories and see ourselves as the primary purveyors of that, as the culture creators, as culture preservers, as the knowledge keepers.

I appreciate the work that folks are doing within the ivory tower to challenge those powers, and at the same time, I'm encouraging myself and others to do our own work around reclaiming our own power and stories that exist within us, reclaiming ourselves as living archives and reclaiming the record as a way of decolonizing ourselves and healing ourselves and our communities.

Fernanda Espinosa: Going back to language, there is this separation—or naming—of *oral history* differently from *oral tradition*, in the same way that *art* is named differently from *craft*—all these ways of calling things so that they gain status. What I'm hearing from you is that oral tradition and things that have been passed on to you are not separate from oral history. Would you say that's how you look at it?

Shane Bernardo: I look at oral history and oral tradition being very much connected, if not the same thing. The reason why I see it that way is that there is no longer a power dynamic that exists because I'm telling my own story, someone's not telling it for me. Someone is not coming in with the prescribed agenda and telling me how to tell my own story. I'm choosing to do that. I have my own agency, and because I'm not playing a subordinate position to somebody else who has their own agenda around their research or their academic work, there isn't a distinction between those two things.

Sometimes I find that within the professionalization of oral history, that oral history can be—the practice of it—can be seen as very elitist. We think that in order to do this oral history project, we need to write a grant, we need IRB [Institutional Review Board] approval, we need all this fancy equipment. Whereas when I'm telling my own story, I'm telling it in a way that preserves its humanity and dignity and seeing the story as a living being unto itself. Being in deep relationship and having a deep sense of intimacy with myself and my stories and my ancestors helps shape these stories. I'm addressing the power differentials that exist within mainstream institutional relationships that say that they're doing oral history. I don't make a distinction between oral history and oral tradition because I'm defining that for myself.

I'm not allowing the mainstream culture to define that for me because these traditions lived before all of that existed. They existed before empire, they existed before fascism, they existed before the colonial oppressors showed up and displaced my people from their cultural land-based traditions, before we were displaced from our way of sustaining and subsisting upon the earth. In the same way that I talk about oral history and oral tradition, that's much in the same way that my ancestors lived and practiced, and self-identified.

Fernanda Espinosa: I don't know if I recorded your name at the beginning, but just in case, can you just say your name, your age, and where are you from?

Shane Bernardo: My name is Shane Bernardo. I'm a long-life Detroiter, second generation of my family here in Detroit. My ancestors are from the Philippines. I'm the son of Edgardo Bernardo and Lita Bernardo and grandson of Paulita Natividad and Florido Natividad.

Fernanda Espinosa: Thank you, Shane.

Notes

1. "About," Chicana por mi Raza, accessed August 17, 2017, http://chicanapormiraza.org/about.
2. Audio clips and transcripts have been edited for length and clarity. Transcripts may not exactly match the audio, as they have been edited for readability in print. In a few cases, a clarifying word or phrase has been added to the transcript. Maria E. Cotera and Shane Bernardo both reviewed and edited their transcripts.
3. María Eugenia Cotera, *Native Speakers: Ella Deloria, Zora Neale Hurston, Jovita Gonzalez, and the Poetics of Culture* (Austin: University of Texas Press, 2008).
4. Cherrie Moraga, Gloria Anzaldua, and Toni Cade Bambara, eds., *This Bridge Called My Back: Writings by Radical Women of Color*, 2nd ed. (New York: Kitchen Table / Women of Color Press, 1983).
5. Martha P. Cotera, *Diosa y Hembra: The History and Heritage of Chicanas in the U.S.* (Austin, TX: Information Systems Development, 1976).
6. The book she refers to is *Native Speakers*.
7. Sherna Berger Gluck and Daphne Patai, eds., *Women's Words: The Feminist Practice of Oral History* (New York: Routledge, 1991); Donald A. Ritchie, *Doing Oral History*, 2nd ed. (Oxford: Oxford University Press, 2003).
8. Moraga, Anzaldua, and Bambara, *This Bridge Called My Back*.
9. See, for example, Elizabeth Dutro, "Writing Wounded: Trauma, Testimony, and Critical Witness in Literacy Classrooms," *English Education* 43, no. 2 (2011): 193–211, http://www.jstor.org/stable/23017070.
10. Taylor Davidson, "The Death of Joe Torres and the Continued Fight against Police Brutality," Chicana por mi Raza, accessed March 5, 2021.
11. Maria Cotera, Dionne Espinoza, and Maylei Blackwell, eds., *Chicana Movidas: New Narratives of Activism and Feminism in the Movement Era* (Austin: University of Texas Press, 2018).
12. Latina Feminist Group, *Telling to Live: Latina Feminist Testimonios* (Durham, NC: Duke University Press, 2001).
13. Boston Women's Health Book Collective and Judy Norsigian, *Our Bodies, Ourselves: A New Edition for a New Era*, 4th ed. (New York: Touchstone, 2005); Frederick Engels, *Origin of the Family, Private Property, and the State*, intro. Eleanor Burke Leacock (New York: International Publishers, 1972).
14. Maria Cotera, "'Invisibility Is an Unnatural Disaster': Feminist Archival Praxis after the Digital Turn," *South Atlantic Quarterly* 114, no. 4 (October 1, 2015): 781–801, https://doi.org/10.1215/00382876-3157133; "The Academic Feminist: Summer at the Archives with Chicana por mi Raza," Feministing, September 4, 2013, accessed June 30, 2017, http://feministing.com/2013/09/04/the-academic-feminist-summer-at-the-archives-with-chicana-por-mi-raza/.
15. Language from an event flyer provided by Shane.

"We're All Bozos on This Bus"

An Oral History with Jeremy Brecher

Daniel R. Kerr

I first reached out to Jeremy Brecher in 2015 as I was doing research for "Allan Nevins Is Not My Grandfather." Brecher had been the lead oral historian for the Brass Valley History Project, widely considered the most significant project that came out of the People's History movement of the late 1970s and early 1980s. Ron Grele referred to the project as "genius" and "so much better than anything yet produced."[1] The more I learned about the project and others from the period, the more I agreed with Grele. Not only had Brecher produced a groundbreaking work in the field of "New Labor History"; the project had played a significant role in fostering a workers' movement that led to what may have been the only successful workers' buyout of an industrial plant in the United States. This oral history is an in-depth exploration of Brecher's sources of inspiration—his radical roots.

The interview took place over two sittings a year apart, on January 30, 2016, and January 24, 2017. The first sitting focused primarily on the period before the Brass Workers History Project, and the second one picked up from there. The interview does not undermine the argument I made in "Allan Nevins Is Not My Grandfather"; rather it complicates it. Oral history, of course, is rather good at that. As the interview makes clear, Brecher situates himself in a genealogy that does not nest neatly with the one I trace. He includes well-known figures such as John Dewey, Jean Piaget, and Alan Lomax as sources of inspiration, as well as figures who may not be as well known, such as Tim Costello and Dorothy Lee.

While Brecher productively complicates the genealogy, the interview solidifies my understanding of Brecher's work as breaking new theoretical ground in the field of oral history. His innovations should be taken into account by anyone interested in doing a radical community history project.

DK: What inspired you to think about using oral history as a tool in your work?[2]

JB: Well, I think there are a lot of things that were in the air at various points in my life. There was a woman named Dorothy Lee [Dorothy Demetracapoulou Lee],[3] who was a professor of anthropology, who came to Yelping Hill, my little community, and spent summers next to me. I probably first got to know her when I was about ten. So it would have been around 1956. She called herself an experiential/existential anthropologist. The idea of trying to get at people's experience through what they said or what they wrote was amplified and held up as an important way of knowing for me. She was a huge influence and mentor for me. As I became a teenager, she gave me a book called *Metamorphosis* by a German maverick psychoanalyst Ernest Schachtel.[4] He was drawing on phenomenological approaches, experiential approaches. So how do you get at experience, and how do you get some understanding of other people's experience?

And I was certainly aware in some vague way of the Freedman's Bureau slave narratives and the WPA [Works Progress Administration] oral histories. In my family, I don't know if there's anyone who had been in the WPA oral history projects, but there certainly were people who knew all about them and talked about them. They regarded it as part of their cultural background from the 1930s.

There was a series of pamphlets on methodology of using personal documents that was done by someone with a name like Social Science Research Council.[5] They actually did a series of sort of manuals, sort of critical guides to using personal documents in the social sciences, which I acquired at some early age. I have no idea how I found out about them, but I read them.

Another strand that flew into this for me, and I think for a lot of other people of my generation really, was folk music and folklore. You had the Folkways Records, with their massive booklet of notes inside, which were mostly oral histories of the people who were the performers and their stories about the songs, and about the background of them and their family and community backgrounds. I read the pamphlet by Alan Lomax called "Folk Song Style" very early.[6] What does it mean as a folklorist to capture the things that are the social experience that the song comes out of? Eventually, I ended up doing ethnic music collecting in Waterbury and Naugatuck Valley after the Brass Workers History Project. I would go in like an oral historian, get people's story throughout, the culture of the community, the family history, et cetera, and embed the songs in that milieu.

So that gets us to the point when I actually started doing history. I went to Reed College from 1961 to 1965—dropped out. I started the SDS [Students for a Democratic Society] chapter at Reed. The sense was strong that the radical student movement and the antiwar movement were cut off from the working class. We were in a sort of situation where the radical student movement and the movements associated with it were at loggerheads with the established White working-class and trade union movement. It was a split about racial questions and above all about nationalism and the war. And at the same time, we were kind of at a dead end from a power point of view. We had pretty much won the population to be against the Vietnam War and had all kinds of direct action and mass action going on against it, and it seemed to not change anything.

I got a bunch of the early issues of the *New Left Review* from England, and they had a big influence on my early politics. The *New Left Review* at that time was quite different from the hyperintellectual publication that it became. It had a special issue on workers' control,[7] which I devoured. It said basically, "This is participatory democracy in the workplace, and why the heck isn't our participatory democracy movement propounding the idea of participatory democracy in the workplace and reaching out to working people?" That has been a central theme of my thinking and writing ever sense, and it was motivated both by the same values that motivated participatory democracy in general—why should somebody else be telling people what to do, why can't they get together and figure out themselves what to do, and why shouldn't they? At the same time, if we are going to build a political movement, antiwar, antiracist, for democracy, that obviously has to have at its core working people, organized working people. And yet that's not happening, and how can we move that forward?

Raising the question of workers' power in the workplace seems like a no-brainer; to me, it seemed like a no-brainer. I discovered the very short labor history shelf in the school library at Reed and read everything, and I was pretty dissatisfied with it and wanted to know much more and didn't find it out there. And so I eventually just continued pursuing it on my own.

My first book, *Strike!*[8] was really politically motivated by two concerns: Could you connect with radical traditions in the working class and stories from working-class history that would both be a vehicle for the means to assist the self-transformation of the working class and also a way to create some kind of common dialect and sense of common experience and common objectives between the radical movement of the day, which was student and youth based, and the more mainstream working class? To write *Strike!*, I basically researched by sitting in the stacks of the Yale library and reading the old labor journals and whatever sources I could find without doing serious primary research, because it just covered too huge, too vast a canvas to do that. When I was done, although I liked the book and I still like the book, I realized there was something fucked about the way it was done: I didn't talk to a single worker who had experienced the things that I was writing about.

There's an enormous amount that you couldn't get at from that distance, so I became very interested in trying to find one community where I could really sink some roots in and where I could talk with the people who had experienced the stuff I was writing about. It wasn't something I had an action plan to pursue. But that year, just before *Strike!* came out, I was helping develop a tiny homemade magazine project called *Root and Branch*.[9] Hovering around the fringes of it was a guy name Tim Costello, who was a young worker intellectual. We both needed a place to live, so we rented an apartment together. Tim and I became fast friends and writing collaborators for forty years starting then.[10]

There was a highly publicized young workers revolt at that point in Lordstown, Ohio. The publicized flash point of it was worker resistance, young worker resistance in the auto plant. So we decided we would take a trip across the country in the summer, and interview young workers, and do a book about it, which became *Common Sense for Hard*

Times.[11] We really didn't know anything about oral history—I mean, I probably had heard about the Columbia Oral History Office. I probably had heard of it as an elite thing. But it wasn't really in the air yet. I was aware of Staughton Lynd's work in Chicago through his article on the writer's workshop that was in *Radical America*.[12] That definitely had an influence on the Brass Valley work when we get there. But the thing about Tim was that he had always interviewed the people he worked with and got their stories and tried to understand their way of thinking and the background of it. He was, from the time I met him, basically trying to reinvent working-class consciousness and the working-class movement. We had very similar views. We had always been a faction of two basically.

That was really our takeoff point in *Common Sense for Hard Times* and that trip we did. We would go into and set up formal interviews. I mean, they weren't very formal; we didn't record them. We must have known that people did record these things. Partially we just didn't have any experience with that. We didn't know anyone who was doing that, but we also wanted to talk about sabotage and various forms of on-the-job resistance. That was what we were trying to get at, which Tim was an expert at on his job, and so we didn't think that people would want to record that. So we would just sit down with people and take notes, and then write it up as much as possible immediately afterward. But we were making this up as we went along; we had no guidance about how to do any of this. Somebody who sat in on one of our early interviews said, when they saw our write-up, he said, "They're going to think you smuggled a tape recorder in there." So that was reassuring. Although somebody else said, "The problem with this book is that every worker talks in exactly the same way." So between those two sides, we probably made a pretty accurate capturing of the content of what people said, but the nuance of the expression, we probably were very poor at; it all sounded like us. But I think we did what we set out to do, which was to collect those stories and put them in a book and a framework that informed it with historical perspectives of working-class experience. So that's really the start of doing oral history.

DK: Was your vision that by collecting the stories and putting out the book, that would then generate dialogue? Who was the perceived audience for the book?

JB: Right, good questions, because those aspects of it are very germane to my later Brass Valley work and the participatory approach to doing community history. So we definitely saw it as a book for young workers, and we said that. Some academic wants to learn something about the current working class, that's the secondary purpose. But the main purpose is that we are part of this young working-class world and our exploration of it is to amplify a dialogue that's going on within that community. I knew nothing about Freire [Paulo Freire], and I knew of John Dewey,[13] but everyone was influenced by John Dewey. He was the Stalin after 1956, permeated the atmosphere even though no one really talked about him by the time I came along. But he had been such a dominant force in the culture and politics of America. So Deweyian, reflexive learning-by-doing permeated everything. As well it should.

DK: And then the agenda of talking about sabotage and some of the—

JB: Yeah, well we were talking about on-the-job resistance. We were talking about sabotage in the broad Wobbly [Industrial Workers of the World] conception of it, not necessarily machine breaking, but all the things—stealing work time was the main thing that people were doing.[14] Any specific sabotage that was being done was a means to just getting a little more freedom on the job. Everybody we talked to talked about it. They sometimes would say to us, "Why are you concentrating on this? There's other important things going on: we've got pollution, we've got war. Why is this informal resistance on the job so important?" But we had no problems getting people to talk about it.

DK: You said Tim had a lot of experience interviewing before that.

JB: Yeah, and that was what we built on. He had done this very similar kind of thing with similar questions. He would ask his gang of fuel oil drivers—which was the job he had when I knew him in New York and in Boston, and they would have incredibly long hours. But the job had to get done. They had very elaborated techniques for soldiering, informal job control. Everybody knew how much time you could take to do job X, and nobody would do it in the shorter time. And that left a couple hours to go have a cup of coffee or go hang out with your buddies. In Tim's case, he set up a desk in the back of his truck and he would go hide out for a couple hours and study, and maybe he would go back and make the next delivery. But you could only do this if you've got an informal network that protects people and makes sure nobody does a nine-hour job in six hours. He was the total master of that and was raised up in it. His father was a railroad worker, and that was part of the tradition.

By that time, a friend of mine, Steve Sapolsky, had gone out to study with Dave Montgomery at the University of Pittsburgh. Dave had done a series of papers that hadn't been published that were circulating among his grad students about soldiering, job resistance, Taylorism, and all of the nitty-gritty of workplace struggle at that level, especially in the late nineteenth and early twentieth centuries.[15] So we had historical background for this and got more of it when we came back and were writing a book. So we took these troubles that people were telling us about and put them in a historical context in *Common Sense for Hard Times*, and that was kind of the fun of it.

DK: Was the essential understanding that this form of everyday resistance was the foundation for what a larger working-class struggle could be built off of?

JB: Yes, exactly, and you'll find that motif in *Strike!*, where it talks about the cell unit of the mass strike being the day-to-day job struggle and the struggle over conditions of work, informal, usually not through the union, although often interpenetrated with the union. So that was very much what it was, and because I think we (not just Tim and me, but our wider peer group) tended to view the trade union movement as more or less a uniform reactionary monolith, which was probably not too far from the truth. Even if it was a little overdrawn—it didn't have enough room for exceptions. So we saw the creation of the independent working-class movement that was independent although not totally opposed to the existing trade union movement as the course forward for working-class self-organization. And you can see that in *Strike!*

DK: You talked about your dissatisfaction after producing *Strike!*; what was your assessment at that point, after publishing *Common Sense for Hard Times*?

JB: Well, first of all the book came out at an economic crisis point. It was the peak of 1973–75 crisis, and our publisher was shut down when the book was in something called mechanicals, which was the final stage of production. It's beyond page proofs, literally ready to have the things put on the press. And it was years before we got it out, like two or three years. The magic moment was missed. So in terms of any impact it might have had for the audience that it was aimed for, it was greatly reduced by that. We essentially self-published it, and then it got picked up by South End when I think South End was on the first press list. So if it had come out at the time that it was ready to go, it might have had a very different impact, because young workers were hot, hard times were hot, but as it was, I think it had a very limited impact.

The Woody Guthrie line about "let me be known as a man who tells you something you almost already knew"—that was definitely our intent, and I think we were trying to invent how to do that. I think we made a noble effort at doing it. I don't think that we completely solved all the problems in doing that. Staughton Lynd didn't like the book at all. He wrote and he said he loves *Strike!*, but we raised so many questions that we didn't answer, but that might be the virtue of the book. I think, for me personally in terms of my own development, *Strike!* is still a lefty book in the sense that it has a lot of the underlying paradigms of what social democracy and communism have in common. It's a very cleaned-up version of socialism. *Common Sense for Hard Times* is much more dialogic, much more assuming that there's not that much gap between the audience and the writers. It's not that we know the truth and we're bringing enlightenment to the masses. It's we've hung out with the masses, and we're taking what we've learned there with some things we've learned in the library and made our best synthesis. And now we're putting that out for people to do the next round—what they can make of this. I think you'll find that pretty explicitly articulated in the book, a Hortonian [referencing Myles Horton] approach, even though we didn't know his full rap on that.

DK: So you've got the two-year delay, things have changed over that time, and now you're in about 1975, 1976?

JB: I have the idea of wanting to find a place, one working-class town where I can dig in, get to know people, and have people involved.

First of all, do labor history in a way that's drawing on the experience of workers with some kind of collaboration with the people that are being studied. The people whose story is being told being part of telling the story was definitely part of what my thinking was. I knew that the people that I would want to interview would know a tremendous amount and have a tremendous amount of insight into the history that we were developing. So it was in a way a no-brainer to assume that they would in some way be involved, not just as the object of study but also as cointerpreters. I didn't have that language fully developed then, but certainly the idea. It wouldn't have occurred to me not to do it that way by then.

DK: One quick question: so right in this early stage, you've thought that this was more than just a study to better understand the conditions, that this was about some form of radical mobilization?

JB: So it is all grounded in having a very unfavorable view of organizing society based on a very small number of people bossing everyone else around. And it all one way or another comes out of the idea that the people who are subjected to those conditions need to find some way to get together and make things happen in a way that's more fair and favorable to themselves—so some very broad notions of class struggle and class self-organization.

DK: Participatory democracy in the workplace?

JB: Yup, and then I tried to find more concrete ways that that's been manifested, that people have done that, and then what can you learn from that, what can they learn from that, how can that be developed to a further extent? It always comes out of that, just about everything I do. I could attempt to justify it, but probably the explanation is that everything in my background, and my experience, and also the world that I look at—but that's obviously shaped by the categories that I look at it in. So the answer is yes, and it's definitely all some contribution to working people being able to get the understandings that are necessary, to get more cooperative control over their conditions of life. After *Strike!*, it became less guided by a left paradigm of "The masses are going to be organized and then storm the barricades and destroy capitalism." I became more agnostic about that whole historical paradigm. It became more Deweyian in the sense of "Here's problems the working people are facing." Addressing them requires getting together in some way and addressing them collectively and formulating objectives about how to do it, what needs to be done, and how it ends. So that's got to grow out of people's experience. So let's look at people's experience, what they've done with that experience before, and draw and put that out not in a way that "Here's the solution," but put it out in a way that says, "Here's the experience, here's some lessons that maybe we should draw from it, what's the next phase of problem solving that we need to look at?" Maybe if I see some hypotheses that are reasonable, I don't try to hide them, but they're presented as things we might explore in addressing a current phase of the problem we face. So everything comes out of some version of that paradigm.

So the origin myth for the Brass Workers History Project is one day I got a call from Peter Marcuse, son of Herbert Marcuse, who I didn't know at all but who turned out to live in Waterbury. And he was having a party, and Rob Burlage, who I had known forever at SDS, was a friend of his and was coming up for the party. Rob said he should get in touch with me, so he invited me and Jill. And I went to this party at his house in Waterbury where there were a bunch of old left of various kinds, the older Waterbury radicals.

There was an old Italian guy who had been an organizer for smelters in the 1930s and actually remembered as a young immigrant kid the general strikes of 1919 and 1920. And so I was back in the corner, interviewing the Italian guy for an hour—I mean we were at a party, but I was just sitting and asking him questions—and it occurred to me, maybe this town is the place to do a study with participation by workers who had experienced the history that I wanted to tell about.

I started doing research, and I discovered more about these two general strikes, so there was a fantastic story here, and other pieces of the story I began gleaning. Then two things happened. I heard about two young filmmakers, Jan Stackhouse and Jerry Lombardi, who were making community videos about unemployment in the lower part of Naugatuck Valley. And this was a time when the brass industry was hitting the skids. It was very hard hit but not totally gone, but everyone was kind of expecting it to be gone. And there was very large unemployment in the towns where the brass mills were already starting to close and cutback. They were making videos and showing them in the local library or community centers. I saw an announcement of one of their showings, and I just went down and met them. So we had kind of the idea of collaborating on something because we were doing similar things. It struck me that doing video would be a great way to put some of this back into the community.

We're in the Carter administration, which started in 1977, and this is in the lead-up to the reelection campaign. We were told they're bringing money to the labor movement around New England in saddlebags, and they're looking for any way to give money to labor. And there was a guy who was making the rounds for the National Endowment for the Humanities, going from state to state and doing presentations through the state labor councils to say that the NEH wanted to fund labor projects. Somehow, I got invited to this, and Jan and Jerry got invited to it also. So he gave us a presentation, and I thought, "This is kind of weird," and I was much too radical and alienated to think of actually doing something like this. But we found out that they couldn't directly fund unions to do these projects, because it wasn't scholarly, respectable, to have people studying themselves. So they had this weird situation where they wanted to do labor projects, but they needed somebody to do labor projects where labor would look favorably on it but where the people who were doing it had some kind of scholarly cover for what they were doing. So if you look at the string of projects that you have identified in that period,[16] many of them are the result of this odd political reality.

DK: So they ended up giving the more radical guys the money because you didn't believe in the unions.

JB: That's exactly right. And I think you'll find a similar pattern to half a dozen other projects like this.

DK: How did you pitch yourself as a scholar?

JB: I kind of suppressed my lack of academic background. I didn't have—and I'm forgetting the chronology here, maybe I already had my mail-order PhD. Actually, yeah, I did. *Common Sense for Hard Times* was my dissertation equivalent, as they said, PDE (Project Demonstrating Excellence). So yes, I had a PhD from the Union Graduate School, and somewhere after I got it, Union Graduate School actually got accredited.

We talked to Hank Murray, a UAW organizer and rep in Connecticut. We said we wanted to do some kind of project, and he said, "You're going to do it on the brass workers, the brass industry is going down, it's not going to be here anymore, it has an incredibly rich labor history. What you should do is the history of the brass workers of the Naugatuck Valley." And that made perfect sense. I realized that there was a confluence between the themes of the new labor history as they were being developed by Herbert Gutman and David Montgomery, and the idea of worker self-organization, and the idea of a community-based history project. These things fit together very well. Now we had the video component so that we could produce materials that would be useful to local working-class communities and people like them elsewhere.

So we did the proposal, and we got funded and had to look for models and some idea of what to do. There had been various city histories: *Yankee City*[17] and so on, done by sociologists from Middletown[18] and so on. *Middletown* has all kinds of oral history in it, although they used whatever statistical data they could get. And it has a sort of people's history of Middletown—migration patterns and stuff like that largely come from interviews. We vaguely knew about the History Workshop in England, although not very much. But Jim Greene, Susan Reverby, and Marty Blatt were just starting the Massachusetts History Workshop.[19] I missed the first event they did in Lowell. But the second one was in Lynn, and I went to it.

That was really all of the background that we had for doing this. So we faked about a lot of things. We did the best we could to talk like we knew what we were doing. Actually, we had no clue what we were doing.

DK: When you went to this workshop in Lynn, what was your thought—

JB: First of all, it validated the basic premise that workers can tell most of the story of working-class and labor history. The people who had worked in the shoe industry were perfectly capable of laying out the main lines of their history, and they argued with each other over points of interpretation and so on. So it completely validated that premise that there would be interest. It also taught me that we would have to learn the right approach to engaging participation. We weren't just going to hand out a flier and people were going to say, "Oh, how wonderful, they're doing the history of the workers in the brass industry. Let's go to the meeting that's announced in this flier." It required much more of a process of figuring out how you were going to do it, how to make it be meaningful to people, how to get rid of the barriers that prevented people from participating.

What happened in Lynn was that they connected with a woman who was the administrative person for the retirees' unit of the old shoe workers' union, who knew everyone who was still alive who worked in the industry. She was a wonderful person, understood exactly what they were trying to do, and would pitch it to people who would come in for whatever kind of events they were running. She was seeing large swathes of the retirees. And over time, she started calling it a reunion. People suddenly said, "Of course I have to come to the reunion." It redefined what was going on, not "Are you coming to the history workshop?" but "Are you coming to the reunion?" She also made it clear that having food was really an important thing. If they knew that they were going to get a free meal and see their friends, they would have a really strong motive to come. What I learned from that was not so much the specifics of reunion or food or whatever, but that you have to think strategically/humanly about what it is that's going to draw people in and get over all the reasons that they might not want to do it. Our approach involved a lot on the participation side.

The Brass Workers History Project was basically three people. Jerry was really the video person, and Jan was basically an organizer, a union and community organizer. Jan also had some administrative skills, had done some fund-raising, and knew how to budget a project. God knows what I was—sort of a historian, definitely a writer, but not someone who was either big organizational or had any video experience. None of us were really local in Waterbury. We rented an office with a little apartment upstairs where I lived; they were living in the lower valley. The next day, we opened the office and looked at each other and said, "What do we do now?"

Because we didn't know until the last minute whether we were going to get the grant, we were very reluctant to get people excited and draw people from the community into the process until we knew it was really going to happen. We didn't want to disappoint people. We really had to hit the ground running. We hadn't been able to recruit people into working on this project.

Over the course of several weeks, we didn't know what to do. So we made some rounds of the retiree organizations and the union locals and anyone else that we could talk to and explain what we were doing. We kept a very low profile, mostly because of the political situation. Extreme anticommunist and nationalist views were widespread. There was a minuteman center. There was Ku Klux Klan, not in Waterbury but in Sheldon, in the lower valley. We were afraid of getting shot out of the water by the right-wing local paper. We assumed that if anybody found out about our crazy project and that the government is paying for this, it would be a total setup for some kind of extreme red-baiting response. That meant we couldn't do a big article in the local paper as a way of contacting people, and we avoided that all the way to the end. As a matter of fact, I was told that the people with the local paper, when they saw the books, said, "How could this have been going on in our community and we didn't even know about it?" So that's how low our profile was. We made the rounds of all the organizations we knew about and our union contacts were helpful for that.

So at a certain point, I just said, well, we can't just keep spinning our wheels like this. We need to go out and start doing interviews, and do audio interviews; we'll get to the video later. We'll identify the people that we want, but we need to go out and start getting the story. I'm somebody who had, at that time, an aversion to making a cold call, so it was very difficult for me to telephone somebody who I had been told about and chum them up and end up with an appointment for an interview. I made myself do it, but it's not the kind of thing I was particularly comfortable with. Where we had contacts to go through was much more comfortable and worked much better, and it was much easier to get people's trust.

And so we just basically worked the network that we had and asked people, "Who should we go see?" By that time, I knew a fair number of people, and I knew the outlines of the historical story of the labor movement there and of the industry. So we just started doing interviews. It immediately opened up everything; I mean, it was extremely exciting and revealing and just great. So that was really my role; my initial approach to things was just a lot of interviewing. And we went around to senior centers to build up our network. We found a woman who ran one of the senior centers and knew everybody. It was a labor-based senior center started by the UAW, and so she would say to people, "We have these nice young people who are doing these interviews. Would you be interested in playing the intermediary role that way?"

We also had some internal tension. Jan felt very strongly that we should be targeting the interviewing pretty carefully around what now we call diversity issues. I don't even know if we were even using the term that way at that time, but the representation of women, of African Americans, and I was for that, but I was probably more oriented toward the how are we going to have people from different occupations, different generations, the different companies—get the different stories in those kinds of terms, people with different union experiences, organizing experiences. In particular, how are we going to get some of the accounts of the events, notable strikes, starting with, as I thought, 1919? And how are we going to find people who had participated in the various labor struggles? We ended up with a pretty good variety of people. What we basically did was come around at the end and fill in the holes. And of course, this community is so ethnically complex. We aren't just talking about Black and White; that's a small bit of diversity in a place like Waterbury at that time.

We had a description of what we were doing, and we worked up a rap to explain why we were asking people to be interviewed and what the project was about. Along the way, not very far in, I realized we were saying to people, "We want to help you tell your story." I realized, no matter how much we said that, people thought, "Oh, well, here are these nice young people, and we'll help them with their project." It was definitely a question of they're helping us, not our helping them. And that actually reoriented the way we thought about the personal and community dynamics quite a lot. And that was the same when we started asking people to be on the advisory committee. We learned that we weren't helping them; they were helping us. If they got some benefit from it one way or another, that was gravy.

We were originally planning to have people participating with us and doing interviews and all the activity of the project. We rapidly learned that that was not going to happen easily. One of the things is that in the original proposal, we had a slot for an organizer, because Hank Murray said, "You need to have an organizer. That's really what you need to make this project go," and that got cut out in the budget. And so that was part of why we didn't have an outreach operation unless we did it ourselves, even though that wasn't what I was good at. That meant that our original participation plan wasn't staffed, didn't have anywhere to go. Gradually, we created an advisory committee, and that was largely Jan's work, in sort of pulling people in as we got to know people. If it seemed appropriate for them, we asked them would they be on it.

Very early on, before we even started doing the interviews, I did a lot of archival research to try and find out what the heck the story was. Because there's also a very complex intraunion conflict within this—a line that runs right through the history of the brass workers union history. And we were going to have to deal with that. I went out to University of Colorado library in Boulder, which is where the papers of Mine, Mill and Smelter Workers were—which was the first union in the thirties, forties, and fifties—and copied a vast amount of stuff. Then I went and spent a lot of time at Harvard Business School library, which had the collection of the Scovill Manufacturing Company, which was absolutely fantastic. The written research both helped orient us toward how to deal with it as a piece of history and also added another level to the products that was very complimentary to what we were doing with oral history and video documentation. It also allowed us to have a much better sense of what the story was when we went in. People that we were interviewing and working with appreciated the fact that we actually knew something about the history of labor and the history of the valley. It also helped us know where the minefields were. You needed to know this guy and that guy had run against each other in a union election and it had turned to almost fisticuffs—that kind of stuff.

Explaining to people what we were doing turned out to be a very important part of the lead-in to the interviews. We had a short presentation of what it was about and why we were doing it and how the material would be used, because that was always the question. What's going to happen to this stuff? And we were very clear that they'll be stored in a local repository, future generations, including your descendants, will be able to access them. This is not somebody who's going to go someplace and write their PhD and become a professor. This is something that's being done for the local community. But what we very rapidly learned was that people would make their own interpretations about what we were doing. We came to realize that was actually the way it should be, and we stopped trying to set people straight about what we were doing. We'd give them our basic rap and then let them watch us, let them talk to their friends who had already been interviewed by us, and make their own judgment of what it was we were doing. That became a much more comfortable and equal way of relating. Like yeah, we're another type of animal that wandered in here, and you know you can look at us and say, "Oh, they're so sweet. We don't believe for a minute that this project is ever going to happen, but we're certainly going to help them have a nice experience doing this." When we came out with the book and the movie, I remember one person we did several interviews with being absolutely flabbergasted and saying, "We never thought this was going to happen. We thought that this was all just like some fantasy of yours, that anything would get produced out of this. We played along because you were nice." And different people had very different takes on what we were doing. Our coming to accept that was I think an important milestone in the development of this as a human project.

So we started doing the interviews, and we ended up doing over a hundred before we were done, and that really was a very, very big part of the initial work. When we interviewed people, we were not just collecting the stories of the events and what happened. We would ask people what they thought it meant and to put things into historical context. We really said, "The people that we're approaching are the experts, and they're the theorists." They had spent their entire lifetimes watching, listening, analyzing, trying to figure out what was going on. There were people who were just spectacular as far as their depth of understanding and reflection on what this whole experience meant.

I did a lot of what would be fairly conventional oral history: "Tell me about your background and your family, where you come from, and how did you get to the valley, and if you went to school there, what was it like?"—that type of thing. Then leading into "How did you get to be a brass worker, what was it like, what happened when times got slow?" all those kinds of questions that reflect aspects of working-class life and would allow people to talk about what it meant to them and how they lived it. But then we would go to the union and organizing and that kind of thing, and "When did you first hear about the union, and what did you think when you first heard; well, what did your parents think about that?" et cetera. The questions directed what the subject matters were, but they were opened-ended and encouraged people to make their own story of what it is and their own interpretation of what that's about.

When we did the videos, we assembled the first draft of the book. Making a video was a huge task. I don't actually remember their using razor blades to cut tape. But they must have, I don't know how else they could have done it. It wasn't easy. Jan made an alliance with Connecticut Public Television to make the documentary, and that really made it possible. They gave us a huge amount of editing time in their studio and let us just keep going. This would not be nearly as big an issue today, but in that time, if you didn't have that, you couldn't make a movie.

So we took the rough edit of the movie and the rough edit of the book and we had our advisory panels that were really involved, who read them, looked at them, and gave us feedback. And we revised a fair amount based on that. That was another part of treating the community people as interpreters. One of the first things that was said to us is "In the old days, Waterbury was all sectioned off and people didn't mingle too good." *Mingle* and *sectioned off*, I learned, were local words for "segregation" and "integration." And they said, "If you treat this just as a labor story, you're never going to understand it. The ethnic dimension of this was overwhelmingly the most important dimension, and the whole labor piece of it was secondary. And you won't understand the labor part if you don't understand and put front and center the ethnic part." And after the tenth person told us more or less the same thing, we realized we were dealing with people who were more capable of interpreting what all this meant than we were.

Then the actual process of making the book and video went forward. We held shows of the video in each of the main valley towns. The union did an edition of the book and distributed it to all their locals in the state, certainly in the valley.[20] They made a lot of copies available and put it in all the school libraries and public libraries. I think that we could've done better with distribution and outreach, but we were out of money. We had one guy who was selling copies of the book from his locker at American Brass. There were things like that that could've made it much more adopted by the community as its own. We could have gone on with an organizing strategy for the distribution part of this but didn't, partially resources, partially we didn't have the right imagination for how to do that, and partially we all had to go on with our lives. And there's a certain burnout factor to it that meant that we didn't do as well with it as we could have.

The movie was shown on public television repeatedly all over the state and in the valley and in local showings in the libraries and stuff like that for forever. A better job happened with that almost osmotically rather than through a conscious design on our part. And I did two subsequent shorter documentaries on the valley, and I think both of them gave a new lease on life to the Brass Valley documentary.

There were tensions among the three of us as a team, but I don't know how germane they were. They were on the one hand roles and on the other personalities. There were some things where we had disagreements about what the subject matters were and who to interview. There were political or intellectual differences that were not really part of the personality difficulties. I don't think we really need to go into that.

DK: The personality part. What about the political part?

JB: Jan was pretty much a conventional leftist. And Jerry was a less politically experienced person who took her lead. And I am what I am, a radically participatory democratic, anti-Leninist type. We were on a somewhat different wavelength politically, within basically a broad agreement that the working class should organize itself to get treated better. In a broad sense, our politics were the same, but within that, they were somewhat different. I think that Jan would have gone for a more conventional, leftist interpretation of the internal fights within the Mine, Mill and Smelter Workers and subsequent labor movement. She would've had us tell a story that was more certain of who were the good guys and who were the bad guys. Whereas my inclination was to try and let all the different factions present their versions of what happened and then try to make some kind of sense out of it that was not mainly about who was right and who was wrong, but more about understanding how this came to be and how this local working class came to be divided around issues that probably 90 percent of the people had no idea what they were about even.

This is what was known at the time as a left-right fight, although I question even that characterization of it. But it was around the question of communist leadership in Mine, Mill and Smelter Workers, and then it filtered down to battles between different local leadership groups. The ones who were identified as the left, as far as I could see, were not by any reasonable criteria that much to the left of those who were identified as the right. But they were allied with the Communist Party group, and so it got to be called the left-right division. And it was certainly a very festering sectarian division within organized labor in the valley. One of the reasons that the valley was a political minefield for this project was that when we came in, the people who had been on the two sides of that battle were still very antagonistic to each other, in a lot of cases didn't talk to each other. This is thirty years later maybe, and it was particularly horrifying to me because they're all like heroes as far as I was concerned. They were all people who took tremendous risks to fight for the same things. I think we ended up not disagreeing about how we would present things. Maybe the movie emphasized some things a little bit more, the book something else, because we had a somewhat different story in our heads about it. I don't think it was of major significance.

Another disagreement we had had to do with the decline of the industry. Initially that was not part of how we saw the story, but as we did this over a couple of years and the industry was literally hitting the fan as we were doing it, we became more aware of it. As we started working on the later part of the story, Jan said, "We have to deal with international capitalism." I said, "Get off it, we're trying to tell a local story, we're trying to do something that no one has really done in terms of this level of depth and intimacy of understanding the local community." "Well, yeah, but you can't understand what's going on unless you look at the broader picture." And as we went on, again the people we were interviewing would say, "Well, the companies are moving their plants all over the world, and that's why nobody has a job in Waterbury anymore." Eventually it began penetrating my brain that she was right. So we ended up putting it in the context of the concentration and centralization of capital. We didn't use those words, but the way in which the local brass mills went through a concentration process, and they became the big three from many different small plants. Then the brass companies were acquired by national copper companies, and they in turn were acquired by international oil companies. The decisions about these local plants were being made by the people who were sitting in a boardroom somewhere, for whom they were specs on a balance sheet.

There was a strong community identification with these industries, separate from the class questions. They had built the brass industry, and this was their thing. The fact that these distant companies that weren't even brass companies were making their community be puppets of their economic interest was a theme that people were very responsive to. It was very different from the usual picture widely propagated and believed, even by a lot of workers, that the greedy demands of the working class and the unions were what were responsible for the decline of the industry. We told a different story.

DK: You said you set out for this not to be a project about the book and film, and clearly, as you've laid out the story, that was a big portion of what it was about. But what was that other part that it was about, and do you think that was actually a successful component?

JB: Good question. I mean the book and movie were always conceived as what we would be producing out of this project and out of the process, but I would say we had a very optimistic concept of what the community participation part would look like. Our original conception was, we would have an organizer and the organizer would organize a history committee in each of the locals and the retiree organizations. There were a lot of senior centers in Waterbury whose main people in them were former brass workers or their wives. We expected we'd have committees in them. The original concept was that there would be like twenty committees that would be researching each of these subareas. Retirees of one company would work on the history of the workers in that company. It was just overambitious, both because we didn't have the organizer to do it and because we didn't understand the process which people would need to go through before they were interested in participating at that kind of level. We had people who were extremely interested in participating, for whom it was a very meaningful thing to do. But other people were more interested in fixing their car. And that was something else we had to learn to accept. If we really thought that somebody was an important person for us to talk to, being on our committee was not more important than working on their car, but taking an hour and a half to talk with us was really important, and they should take the time out to do it. We had to learn how to manage our expectations of what it was reasonable to ask people. The original vision of it was a mass participation community research project, even in the scaled-down version.

We had a hundred people involved with being interviewed. A lot of those people were involved in other ways. We had scores of people in the network around the project. That's where I learned about building a network around your project. We thought about it as organizing committees and organization. But what really worked was to have an informal network around it where we could go to so-and-so and say, "We don't have anybody from Cape Verdean community; can you steer us toward someone that we could talk to who was a Cape Verdean brass worker? We've got these pictures from nineteen twenty of Cape Verdean brass workers, we haven't found any of them or their families." People steered us to a Cape Verdean family. And we had great stories from it, and there's a section in the book. And then there were the meetings, the events where we showed the products and had discussions. What it was, was a sector of a community participating in making a construction of its history. And then that process was incorporated in the products that three people, who happen to be professionals at making these types of products, made. But they were profoundly influenced and guided from what we had learned from the people in the community. And then those products became available over the longer term for the community to understand its history, and for younger people to be able to learn something about it, and as a way also of saying, "This is meaningful. This is important, this is worth recording."

The quality of the products I think really impressed people. They really thought it was valuable, worthwhile to do something like that! I'm reminded of Jack Tchen's project with Chinese laundry workers. He was going around saying, "I'm researching the history of Chinese laundries in New York," and this guy slammed down his iron and said, "Laundries have no history." That emphasized that sense of, we're nothing. I think that in many ways what we've done has had an impact on that community, countering that and saying, "This is valuable and important." That's gone way beyond the book and the movie as the outcome. I think the whole work of the Mattatuck Museum, the ethnic music project, the Naugatuck Valley project—all are outgrowths of the work of the Brass Workers History Project.

DK: Did you have a sense that crafting this own history was more than just kind of a democratizing history but kind of a radical project that would potentially make some form of positive intervention in everyday lives?

JB: I saw it in that framework but not in a way that I wanted to have overdefined. I wanted it to be an exploration: we'll talk with people about what they have experienced and how they see it, and we'll have a dialogue. I come with certain things that I have come to think are important. A lot of people have found it weird that I was so interested in informal, on-the-job resistance, for example. I went in and asked a lot of questions about that and how do people get time to themselves on the job and so on. I was very much confirmed in the importance of that, and it turned out that there was a lot of informal class struggle over the generations around piecework and control of piecework. It was almost so much part of ordinary life that people might not have told us about it because they wouldn't have thought of it. But because we came in with a sense of that as an important thing, we were able to ask questions that brought it out. I didn't go in with a tabula rasa, thinking, "I will just listen to what the workers have to say about their lives." But I tried not to go in with an assumption that I already knew what was important and what it meant. And so, it was "Let's see what happens if we do this. And then as we finish it, let's see in what way this is useful." I think we did always have a sense of being part of the new labor history movement—the idea of participatory history about working people as a sort of a movement.

I don't think that we believed the workers would occupy the factories because they read about what the people did in 1919. I had the participatory democracy sort of view, and obviously from the subject matter we chose and the way we approached it, a strong sense of the important and collective roles of class in understanding American life and American history. We were interested in the experience of working people and also the importance of class in terms of working-class self-organization as a crucial dimension of trying to make a better life for people who so far have not had possession of the means of production. We saw class specifically as a shaping feature of the actual society and actual economy we're dealing with, which is why it was a workers' project, not a community history one.

DK: When the project was over, why did you decide to stay?

JB: So first of all, my home was about thirty-five or forty miles from the valley. I was there; I wasn't going to go and live in some other place for any extended period of time. Although I'm not a valley person, and I regard myself as a pet outsider.[21] I've been there so long now that I'm more of a valley person. It's more part of my identity than it certainly started out being, and I think I'm viewed as a little more than a pet outsider now. It's like, "Well, he's not exactly one of us, but he's kind of part of us." If I had said, "Well, OK, I did that, now I'm going to go on and do something completely different and unrelated to that," it would have been totally alien to me. It would have been like getting into a forest and starting another family somewhere else. We wanted to go on with it. I actually designed an oral history project for ethnic communities to do their own histories. We went to get a grant for it from the humanities council. It was shot down, and I was told it was on the grounds that oral history wasn't something for community people to do. It required people with professional training.

I had a Fulbright to New Zealand for six months. When I came back, I had no means of livelihood. I quickly designed the Waterbury ethnic music project, and it got funded. And so that was the next big project I did, and that's what I was doing for a couple years. And then we did the collecting project, which was totally a development of the Brass Workers History Project. That was phase two of the same work. We did five festivals after that annually, or every two years, so for the next seven years, I was involved with doing that. Although they were ethnic music festivals, they were organizing projects in the sense that we organized within the ethnic communities. They were organizing projects in terms of building the audience, and they were also very much historical projects. When we did the music recording, we did extensive interviews on the history of the ethnic communities and how the music and the culture fitted into them. When we presented the material, it was encased in the local cultural context as well as what it meant in the old country. And we featured people from those ethnic groups as the interpreters, much to the chagrin of the National Endowment for the Humanities. By then we had pretty much brainwashed the state humanities council to accept our community experts as the real experts. But the question of whether we would have licensed humanologists or licensed folklorists to oversee the presenting of the folk was a continual struggle. We were never able to make an institutional home for this work that could be an ongoing occupation. I've gone on to having the center of my attention be other things. But I've kept a hand in the valley and its history and movements down to the present.

DK: Could you tell me a little bit about NVP [Naugatuck Valley Project] and its relationship to the Brass Workers History Project?

JB: The plants were collapsing, sort of serial shutdowns, as we started the project. The valley was extremely hard hit. I referred to it as an outpost of the Rust Belt. It was very much the same generation of closings as Youngstown, and Lorain, and all the Midwest steel shutdowns. It was very much a question of international competition and a question of the plants being bought and milked and shut down by international corporations. It was more a sense of runaway plants than of competing foreign companies, although that was also a factor. When we did *Brass Valley*, there was a strong elegiacal quality to what we did in both the book and the movie. It was not so much elegies for the brass industry as for the working-class communities and the incredibly dense social networks and cultural networks that they had developed. There's no way that you could envision something that would be next. There was a labor community that was formed to try to oppose plant closings, but not with any significant reach. That was it. It looked like there wasn't anything that looked like the next piece of this story.

Then I got a call from a guy named Ken Goldstein who had become a student radical as a result of the Vietnam War, gotten interested in worker co-ops, gotten interested in community organizing, and went and spent a number of years with the Alinsky organization. He originally studied with Alinsky [Saul Alinsky] himself and then eventually became a lead organizer in Buffalo and various other places. He then went to Yale School of Organization and Management, which is basically the Yale business school. I got a phone call from him, and he said he was looking at what could be done to save jobs in the valley, and people told him he should talk to me. And I thought, what kind of Yale asshole was this going to be? But I went and met with him, and he was going around doing interviews, talking to people and trying to find out whether something could be done here. He had been in Buffalo while the huge plant closings were going on, and they were doing typical community organizing things—trying to get a traffic light fixed or something like that. Meanwhile, the parishioners of the churches he was working with were all losing their jobs, and he realized that something needed to be done that was different. He went to Yale School of Organization and Management to explore whether you could apply these techniques, community organizing techniques, to more fundamental economic problems like plant closings. This was something that Alinsky had totally opposed doing. So I gave Ken a copy of *Brass Valley* and tried not to discourage him, but everybody who talked with him walked away thinking, "He wants to do what?"

A month or two later, I got another call; he had his organizing committee, and they had their first community meeting, and they were launched. I got a call from the union at Seymour Specialty Wire—Bridgeport Brass—which was one of the oldest mills. If you look at *Brass Valley*, there's lots and lots from people that worked there. The workers had snuck me through on a secret tour while the managers were away. We had a lot of relationships there. And they said, "We hear the plant's going to be sold, what can we do?" And Ken said, "You ought to tell them that you want to be considered as a bidder." And that was the beginning of what became Seymour Specialty Wire—workers bought the plant. And there's at least two, maybe three, chapters about it in *Banded Together*.[22] I became involved with it and supportive of it and wrote about it a lot and always assumed that eventually I would have to do a book about it. I started doing interviews at the beginning. And I did a hundred interviews along the way, with all kinds of participants, leaders, all the executive directors. Every six months, I did a long debriefing interview. I had massive documentation on it. As far as my role was, I was a resource that people could call on.

Very often, they would say, "Well, we got a call, this plant is being threatened with being closed down, what's the background of this plant?" And I would talk with them about the history of it. In Ken's initial round of talks to community groups, he'd put up a newssheet on the wall, and he'd ask about the companies that were threatened with closing. And then he would say, "OK who owns this, who owned it before, what was it?" And he would trace the genealogy. And of course, everyone knew well, "That's the clock shop, and that was started by so-and-so, and originally employed all the Italians who were new greenhorns" and so on. And he would do the industrial genealogy exactly along the way that I was describing it and ending with the fact that they were controlled by distant corporations that had no concern for the people of Waterbury whatsoever. And basically, we need to organize ourselves to resist that and get some control back over our economy. Their idea was that they would organize on a community-wide basis and that local small businesses and churches would all be part of the coalition to try to save their local economies. He picked up what we had written in the later parts of *Brass Valley*. Unbeknownst to me until I started tracking the NVP, the alternate paradigm we had presented had actually permeated. And then when they began using that for organizing, it became quite central to the people who were doing that. So that was not due to our thoughtful, brilliant insight into where things should go. It was not strategic on our part. It was just our attempting to tell an alternative story that fit better with people's experience.

That was probably the biggest impact of the Brass Workers History Project on the subsequent development of working-class organization in the valley. For quite a big time, the NVP was very lively, they had like sixty organizations, they had regular meetings with hundreds of people up and down the valley, changed a lot over the years and decades. It was a significant player in its glory period. And it still plays a role, but the fighting and the plant closings was a huge mobilizing issue that there's not really any equivalent to.

Seymour Specialty Wire, the one the workers bought out, was one of the places that we had spent the most time and written about a lot in *Brass Valley*. And the people there knew probably as much as any group of workers in the valley about what we had done and the story that we had told about them. After the buyout was well under way, somebody said to us, "Of course this is happening because of what you guys did." I said, "No, what's the connection?" And they said, "Well, that's why they thought it was worth saving. They didn't accept the notion 'we're going to lose.' They didn't just see it as this old falling-down plant. They had some sense of it as something with a heritage, of value that went beyond a purely economic value. It was of value as part of a community, as part of the life inheritance of these people." And that kind of rocked me back to my heels, because I hadn't thought of it that way. That was something you can never measure. But I think the fact that somebody had said, "OK, you guys are important, you matter; what you've done, what your ancestors did, that's part of history. It's part of the heritage of people today."

Throughout, I always did some consulting and projects in cooperation with the Mannatech Museum, which is the local art and culture museum in Waterbury. We had numerous exhibits, participatory oral history projects that were done out of there. I was the writer and historian for the two big permanent exhibits. The first one was really like *Brass Valley* in an exhibit form; it very much drew on it. And the second one not so much, but it too was deeply influenced by the *Brass Valley* work. So we had a museum that was visited by thousands of people every year. School kids that went to the Waterbury schools went to those exhibits.

We had an evaluation and planning meeting for the Mannatech Museum around the time that we were starting to think about what the new exhibits should be like. The director asked basically, "What are we really trying to do here, what's really our mission?" I finally said something like, "Everything that people who live in Waterbury and in the Naugatuck Valley hear and are told about themselves is that they're worthless. There are different layers of disrespect for them in cultural terms—'Oh, they're just dirty immigrants. In education, people at other places, they all go to college, but these people don't; in the political system, they're a stepchild; and on and on of the different ways in which they're denigrated. What this museum does, because of the kinds of exhibits it runs and kinds of programs it runs, is fundamentally about giving respect to the people of the valley and treating their history and their experience with respect, and making a loud statement thereby that they are worthy of respect." That's a continuing legacy of the Brass Workers History Project and its sequels. I think it contributed to the idea that it was right to think of people in the valley and people like them as people who are worthy of respect and therefore whose institutions and ways of life were worthy of respect.

DK: What role does oral history play in terms of community mobilization and social justice work?

JB: At one pole are the broad reflective things that have a community coming to create a sense of itself as worthy of respect, revivifying and understanding things that people have done to make a better life for themselves, for each other, sacrifices people have made for that reason, and artistic cultural contributions that people have made that are worthy of respect. That's sort of at one pole. In the center is maybe a broad sense of "people can win stuff if they get together and fight for it." And sometimes you have to stick up for yourselves and your group in ways you're told not to, sometimes you have to strike, sometimes you have to be ornery and refuse to go along with it. People learn about sit-down strikes from reading about sit-down strikes. The occupation that was done by the mine workers in the Pittston strike was led by a guy who was a labor history buff. He knew about the Flint sit-down strikes. You can trace the effect of labor history on labor struggles of the last twenty or thirty years pretty well. I mention a few examples of that in the updates of *Strike!* So that's a kind of a midpiece, still in the sense of learning about possibilities and so on. Then there's a part of it that's very directly connected to current social struggles, where it blends over from history to current social engagement. The history of the Naugatuck Valley Project that we did was directly empowering for the Naugatuck Valley Project, and it was also a valuable way to explain what the project was to the wider community. It got full-page stories in the local newspaper and a lot of people coming through to see the exhibit. It drew a fairly direct contribution in that way.

There's a place for all of those. You don't want to reduce the reflective dimension of oral history to propagandizing, and at the same time, it's completely legitimate to take people's experiences and learnings and identities and make that be a part of and a vehicle for struggles that they themselves and people associated with them are involved with. It was a way for them to tell their stories, in a way that's germane to the things that they're fighting for right now. But I wouldn't want to have it be all one or all the other. I don't feel like any one point on that continuum should subsume the others. I wouldn't be interested doing something that was all reflection and no relevance, or that was all relevance and no reflection. I think that almost anything you do of this kind should have an element of both. The radical side of Deweyian thinking is always hovering back there somewhere.

DK: Staughton Lynd does not use the word *organizing*, whereas you do use the word. Why?

JB: I think our critiques of that would be aligned. I usually use *cooperation*, or *learning to cooperate*, or *coordinating activity* more than *organizing*. Or I use *self-organization*. I mean, the main problem I have about the organizing concept is that as it's usually used in the Alinsky tradition and the trade union tradition and a lot of other traditions; the idea of who's the subject and who's the object is all too clear. There's the organizer, who is the subject, and there is the organized, or the disorganized, who are going to be organized by the organizer, and it's often used with inherently elitist bias. When I use it, it's almost always in terms of self-organization. It's either self-organization or it's negative.

DK: You use the term *pet outsider* and also referred to the folks you're working with as experts of their experiences. But I'm wondering how you go about being an outsider, given your critique of the outsider organizer.

JB: I have moved away from the idea of whatever group, the valley, the working class, whatever it is, as a totally enclosed object in which the people in it are all part of one common unified experience and identity. I have come to see overlap and the nonnesting of social groups and individuals in social groups as a much more important part of the story. So the fact that someone is a worker and also Black and also a woman and also gay or straight, and they're all those things, and they had a grandmother who came from Italy, and grandfather who came from Poland—the reality is very, very complex.

That doesn't mean that social groups and collective identities aren't important, they're enormously important, but they are things that are constructed and reconstructed all the time out of the past experience and the preceding definitions of identity and role. And so the challenge is to make those experiences as creative and constructive as possible, but it is all a construction. Which is not to say that it's not a reality, but it's a constructed reality.

As you've probably picked up, I'm very influenced by Piaget, who was another person influenced by Dewey, which is not well-known but profoundly important for him. Everything is an inside-and-outside question, everyone is always negotiating the fact that they're both part of a group and an outsider to the group, or they're partially in the group but they're also a part of other things. And the group itself has divisions within it so somebody may be part of the group in one way or not in another. These are fraught matters. You could say, "Well, they're all just working class," or you could say, "They're all just Black, or green, or Latino," or whatever it was. Both in the practice and in the understanding, the inside-outside division is not meaningless. But it's only one aspect. The first thing that I would say to anyone is if you don't respect the people you're doing stuff with, you have a problem at a human level. That goes with insider group, outsider group, and in between. On the other hand, if you treat the people that you're dealing with with respect, the question of being insider and outsider is not as fraught.

I guess another part of the critique that goes along with this is the etic-emic thing, where there's this ideology that the insider has a certain type of knowledge that's not accessible to the outsider. Well, there are people who have common experiences, and that is important in terms of who they are and their group and how they function and what they might be able to do in terms of a common practice, but it can't be reduced to that. It's one set of things out of many, and it's important to recognize that, but it's also important to recognize that it's not an absolute. In my case, because I've been there so long, I'm like the repository, the residual—I've interviewed hundreds of people in that community who have died. As the person who talked to them, there is something that is in me that makes—I wouldn't say I'm a valley person, because in all kinds of ways I'm not, but I'm not really an outsider. To say I'm an outsider would be going too far in the other way, or it would be a reductionist statement in the opposite direction.

DK: One of the unusual aspects of your work is the extent of how long you have been committed to different iterations of it within a local area. Could you describe why there's some significance or importance to that longevity?

JB: When I was younger, people would say, "Are you going to do Bristol next or Hartford next?" I've only scratched the surface of Waterbury and the valley, and I could do ten more projects, each one of which would add to my understanding and the available understanding of that community as the brass workers project or ethnic music project. When I was working on the *History from Below*, one of the main things that I realized was that we did parachute into this community; we knew a few people there beforehand, but it was a bad thing in relative to what it should have been.[23] Jan and Jerry had lived there more than a couple years, but we weren't people with deep roots.

And I started saying to people after that that the ideal person to do this kind of work is a librarian, a teacher, a curator in the local museum, somebody who has an organic connection to the community, and a functional connection, and a long-term involvement, and a long-term basis for interacting and taking in knowledge and information and understanding and giving it back out. While I haven't achieved that, the appeal of doing that and the benefit of doing that has certainly been part of what's kept me deeply engaged with this community.

I think it's a labor of love. Love is never an unambiguous emotion; I certainly wouldn't say I have no feelings about the valley other than love. I hate what the kind of life that people in the valley are forced to live does to them. What it makes them into is like what any of us get made by our circumstances—not always good or what people in their better selves would want to be. So I don't dote on the valley, but my engagement with it is a labor of love. I've never used those words for it before, I don't think, until this minute, but it is that.

DK: I think you've thrown in some complexities in terms of looking at the fissures and the ways in which there are different groups, and insiders and outsiders, and ways in which when you're walking alongside people who are arguing with each other sometimes. Would you characterize, at least what you're striving to do, as kind of a form of accompaniment, a walking alongside?

JB: I wouldn't. It's not the way I think about it. Because actually, it's still too close to the subject-object thing. I think about it as, we're all bozos on this bus. We're all just people trying to figure out what the heck is going on and what the heck we can do about it. And at the most fundamental, epistemological level, none of us has any privileged, epistemologically privileged position of any kind. And the same goes for politics—none of us has a moral or superior place to stand. We're all just swimming in this confusing sea and trying to figure out what's the right thing to do. My problem with the accompaniment, it's not the way I feel about it, because it's not me accompanying them. It may be at one particular moment that I know something, and I have something to share with somebody. But the next moment, they may have something to share with me. Unless it's that at this particular moment, I'm the accompanier and they're the accompanied, but tomorrow it may be that I'm the one that's drowning and they're the one that has to throw the rope to help me—unless it's strongly qualified by that, I'm not comfortable with it. I also think it's unnecessary. I find it more comfortable to be a bozo on the bus.

Actually, Freddy Gardner, who I won't try to explain, but there's a great song which is called "The Vanguard Song," and actually, if I may, I'll sing a verse instead of just reciting it, and it goes:

> I don't know nothing,
> Neither do you.
> We don't know nothing,
> Let us not pretend we do.
> He don't know nothing,
> Neither does she.
> They don't know nothing,
> They don't any more than we.

> I don't know where my elbow is,
> From where my ass is.
> Don't look for me in the vanguard,
> Baby, look for me in the masses.

And I guess the bottom line of this is that the masses are not a "they" for me, I'm just another one. And either they aren't the masses, or I'm not the not-masses.

Notes

1 Ronald Grele, review of *Brass Valley: The Story of Working People's Lives and Struggles in an American Industrial Region*, ed. Jeremy Brecher, Jerry Lombardi, and Jan Stackhouse, *Radical America* 17, no. 5 (1983): 48, 53.

2 Editing transcripts for print is an act of translation, as the spoken word loses its coherence with literal transcription. All words and meanings in the excerpts are the narrators own. Through editing, we have removed false starts, digressions, and redundancies. The order of sections has been changed and similar accounts of the same story have been combined. These editing practices draw upon the best practices in the field of oral history. See Linda Shopes, "Editing Oral History for Publication," in *The Oral History Reader*, 3rd ed., ed. Robert Perks and Alistair Thomson (New York: Routledge, 2016), 470–89. The unedited transcripts and original audio are housed in the Humanities Truck Community Archive, https://dra.american.edu/islandora/object/humanitiestruck%3A1.

3 For an example of her work, see Dorothy Lee, *Valuing the Self: What We Can Learn from Other Cultures* (Upper Saddle River, NJ: Prentice Hall, 1976).

4 Ernest Schachtel, *Metamorphosis: On the Development of Affect, Perception, Attention, and Memory* (New York: Basic Books, 1959).

5 G. W. Allport, "The Use of Personal Documents in Psychological Science," *Social Science Research Council Bulletin* 49 (1942), available at https://archive.org/details/useofpersonaldoc00allprich.

6 Alan Lomax, "Folk Song Style," *American Anthropologist* 61, no. 6 (December 1959).

7 Special issue, *New Left Review*, no. 10 (July–August 1961).

8 Jeremy Brecher, *Strike!* (New York: Straight Arrow Books, 1972).

9 A partial archive of this libertarian socialist journal can be found at https://libcom.org/library/root-branch-libertarian-socialist-journal, accessed September 28, 2018.

10 For a more recent example of a publication that lays out their shared political commitments, see Jeremy Brecher, Tim Costello, and Brendan Smith, *Globalization from Below: The Power of Solidarity* (Cambridge, MA: South End, 2000).

11 Jeremy Brecher and Tim Costello, *Common Sense for Hard Times* (Montreal: Black Rose Books, 1982).

12 Staughton Lynd, ed., "Personal Histories of the Early C.I.O.," *Radical America* 5 (May–June 1971).

13 For more on John Dewey, see his work *Democracy and Education* (Norwood, MA: Macmillan, 1916).

14 For more on the Wobbly conception of sabotage, see Elizabeth Gurley Flynn, Walker C. Smith, and William E. Trautmann, *Direct Action and Sabotage: Three Classic IWW Pamphlets from the 1910s*, ed. Salvatore Salerno (Oakland, CA: PM, 2014).

15 This work was eventually published; see David Montgomery, *Workers' Control in America* (New York: Cambridge University Press, 1979).

16 Brecher is referencing the section "The Era of People's History" in my article "Allan Nevins Is Not My Grandfather: The Roots of Radical Oral History Practice in the United States," *Oral History Review* 43, no. 2 (2016): 379–85 (which also appears in as a chapter in this volume).

17 W. Lloyd Warner, *Yankee City* (New Haven, CT: Yale University Press, 1963).

18 Robert Staughton Lynd and Helen Merrell Lynd, *Middletown: A Study in Modern American Culture* (New York: Harcourt, Brace & World, 1929).

19 For more on the project, see James Green, "The Massachusetts History Workshop: 'Bringing the Boundaries of History Closer to People's Lives,'" in *History Workshop Journal* 50 (Autumn 2000): 246–65.

20 Jeremy Brecher, Jerry Lombardi, and Jan Stackhouse, eds., *Brass Valley* (Philadelphia: Temple University Press, 1982); *Brass Valley*, directed by Jerry Lombardi, Jan Stackhouse and Jeremy Brecher (Stamford, CT: Color Film, 1984), DVD.

21 For more on Brecher's views of himself as pet outsider, see Jeremy Brecher, "How I Learned to Quit Worrying and Love Community History: A 'Pet Outsider's' Report on the Brass Workers History Project," *Radical History Review*, nos. 28–30 (1984): 187–201.

22 Jeremy Brecher, *Banded Together* (Urbana: University of Illinois Press, 2011).

23 Jeremy Brecher, *History from Below: How to Uncover and Tell the Story of Your Community, Association, or Union* (New Haven, CT: Commonwork, 1986).

PLACE-BASED PEDAGOGIES

ORIGINS OF PUBLIC HISTORY EDUCATION

The People's Camp

The Progressive Pedagogy of Camp Woodland

Rachel Donaldson

There is a certain irony in tracing the pedagogical origins of public history practice. Often, the taproot of the field of public history pedagogy is located in traditional classroom settings; after all, the historiography of public history largely begins with postsecondary education—when the University of California, Santa Barbara, began accepting students into its program in "public historical studies" in 1976. This may have been the first official public history program in higher education, but prior programs in areas including museum studies, historic preservation, and archival studies also set the stage for public history's pedagogical debut.[1] Yet while students may learn of the theories and methods that undergird the practice of public history in classrooms or in applied experiences that are tied in some way to classroom pedagogy in higher education (e.g., internships or class projects with community partners), these experiences do not *introduce* students to the ideas and concepts that have shaped the field. Rather, this introduction often happens, and historically has happened, much earlier and in nontraditional public settings such as museums, historic sites, and heritage tours. Removing the history of public history pedagogy from its classroom tether therefore not only challenges the traditional origin story but also provides greater insight into the historical development of the field itself, particularly into its radical origins.

One such nontraditional educative venue that played a key role both in introducing students to the theories and practices of public history and in shaping the field's political undercurrent was a left-leaning summer camp located outside the town of Phoenicia in the Catskill Mountains of New York.

Every summer, from 1938 until 1962, the staff at Camp Woodland taught campers how to conduct oral interviews, took campers on field trips to collect examples of tangible and intangible folk culture, and engaged the local community through public performances and a museum of work tools. Through these activities, Woodland introduced schoolchildren to the theories of applied folklore, material culture conservation, and oral history—all of which would become foundational for the emergence of the public history programs of the late twentieth century. The staff at Woodland interwove such values as racial inclusivity, internationalism, and an advocacy for political and social justice into the very fabric of the camp experience—values that are at the core of contemporary public history practice. Furthermore, some members of the first generation of public historians not only attended Woodland but also viewed their time at the camp as formative experiences.

The history of summer camps, particularly their political persuasions, is well-trod terrain. Historians have paid particular attention to northeastern camps like Wo-Chi-Ca (Workers' Children Camp), Camp Kinderland, and even Woodland because of their ties to radical politics but have paid far less attention to their pedagogical practices.[2] While many if not most camp directors and boards viewed their enterprises as pedagogical experiences that engaged students beyond the traditional classroom, education was a preeminent aspect of Woodland's mission; it was an education steeped in theories that would form the core of public history practice in the United States. For the twenty-four years of its existence, Norman Studer, an educator connected to left-wing progressive schools in New York City, was the driving force behind the camp. Because of his background, Studer ensured that the theories and practices of progressive education permeated almost every aspect of the Woodland experience. As an experiment in democratic living, camp activities were designed to educate students in civic engagement, a deliberately integrated camp experience exposed students to the theories of intercultural education, and every camp activity put the theories of applied learning into practice.

Progressive education models shaped the camp's instructional methods while progressive politics guided many of its programs and lessons in civic education. Although it was not directly affiliated with the Communist Party, as similar camps like Wo-Chi-Ca were, Woodland was clearly steeped in left-wing social politics. Woodland's radicalism manifested most clearly in the camp's staunch support of cultural pluralism, racial integration, and civil rights, issues that the camp continued to support throughout the 1950s when Cold War anticommunism made such positions politically perilous. Even though the camp suffered during the Red Scare, Woodland managed to survive the period intact and without ever compromising its mission to impart progressive social and political values. While this is noteworthy in itself, the fact that campers later recognized the significance of Woodland's political and social objectives and noted the influence it had on shaping their own public history careers further ties Woodland to the genealogy of the field, particularly in its political identity.

As an educational institution that promoted civic engagement and a radical (for its time) interpretation of American politics and civic ideals, Camp Woodland is situated well within the history of education and radical political culture in the United States during the mid-twentieth century. A key aspect of the camp that formed a nexus between political radicalism and public history pedagogy was its signature folklore program. As an avid folk enthusiast, Studer emphasized folklore in both his classroom and his camp. Yet rather than follow the path of academic folklore, which scholarly folklorists were in the midst of establishing as a field of study in its own right, Studer drew inspiration from the theories and methods of applied folklore. Emerging among folklorists that worked in the public sector during the 1930s, primarily in New Deal programs of the Works Progress Administration (WPA) or in other federal institutions such as the Library of Congress, applied folklorists directed their efforts in studying and conserving folk culture by learning directly from living informants (a precursor to the concept of shared authority) and disseminating what they had collected among a public audience. Unlike academic folklorists who focused on the *products* of folk culture like songs, stories, and crafts, applied folklorists focused on the *people* of folk communities and their cultural traditions. A core belief that many of these public folklorists shared was that products of folk culture were important not just in and of themselves but rather for the historical insight they provided into the groups that practiced them. Tangible and intangible folk traditions, they believed, provided a means to understand the social history of groups traditionally left out of the historical record. Examining the folklore program at Woodland, and the educative mission of the camp as a whole, reveals the early threads of civic engagement, political radicalism, and the practice of social history of underrepresented groups—all of which formed the foundation of public history theory and practice.

Camp Woodland and Civic Education

Like many camps of its era, Woodland employed a large staff and operated under the auspices of a board of directors. In 1941, Norman Studer founded the camp along with Rose Sydney, Regine Dicker (Ferber), Sara Abelson (Abramson), and Hannah Studer, his wife. While these figures all contributed to running the camp and designing the programs, Norman Studer provided much of the vision and direction for the entirety of its existence.[3] Studer had had several years of teaching experience prior to Woodland, but his participation in summer camp programming was far less extensive. Studer's first foray into camp leadership began in 1938 when he joined the staff of Camp Hilltop in New Jersey as head counselor. The following year, Hilltop was forced to relocate and Studer was among the leaders who selected a property in the Catskills as the camp's new home. When Hilltop moved to the site near Phoenicia in Ulster County, the camp's leadership shifted from Rose Snider, who had been the director, to Norman Studer and others who would begin Woodland. The camp retained the Hilltop name until 1941, when Snider officially transferred the camp's assets, marking the official beginning of Camp Woodland. The leaders of Woodland continued many of the programs that Hilltop had implemented, but their strong social, political, and educational values led them to reconceptualize the camp experience. Rather than simply a place for summer fun or even broad educational enrichment, Woodland became "a non-profit educational institution, with philosophy and structure similar to that of the best modern school. It is interracial and coeducational: children of all economic, cultural, and racial backgrounds live happily together." From the outset, the camp was a cooperative modeled after private experimental schools, with Studer in charge of directing the educational program.[4]

Studer was well suited for this role, for he had studied education under John Dewey at Columbia University and had been teaching at Little Red Schoolhouse, a progressive school in New York City, since 1933.[5] These experiences profoundly shaped his views on the educational potential of a summer camp. The idea of Woodland, he explained, developed during the later years of the Depression when "a new cultural movement born of the American democratic tradition" emerged, nurtured by trade unionists, civil rights activists, progressive historians, and encouraged by the federal government through WPA programs. Progressive educational reforms were another aspect of this "cultural movement," and the founders of Woodland were much influenced by these reforms.[6] While there was no fixed program of progressive education, a universal feature of all models was that of learning by doing, or applied learning. This idea could be manifested in child-centered programs that focused on the welfare of the individual child; in education that related to society, which sometimes included teaching children how to live in a large democracy; and in structuring the school as a small-scale democratic community. Indeed, progressive educators believed that places of learning should provide models for how to be active, engaged citizens by teaching civic values and developing the necessary skills for dealing with social issues, both in their contemporary lives and in their futures.[7]

A strong adherence to interethnic and interracial education was another key aspect of the kind of progressive education practiced at Woodland. Studer's approach embodied what was then referred to as "intercultural education." Stemming from the wartime necessity of national unity, intercultural or intergroup educational initiatives sought to unite Americans by overcoming ethnic and racial prejudice. Schools that adopted this program incorporated curricula on different ethnic groups and their historical backgrounds, organized cultural assemblies, and banned culturally demeaning books.[8] Intercultural educators believed that a core set of civic ideals formed the basis of American identity, one of which was cultural democracy. Cultural democracy stipulated that minority groups should not be forced to accept nor or expected to separate from mainstream culture, but neither should they retain traditional practices that were undemocratic; in all other circumstances the majority must respect their right to practice their own cultural traditions. Advocates of cultural democracy advocated a type of nationalism that defined America as "a plurality of sub-cultures bound together by a set of common ideals and practices." Emphasizing a "unity within diversity" view, intercultural educators rejected the forced conformity of assimilationist programs and celebrated cultural difference.[9]

During the mid-1930s, a group of left-wing progressive educators began a program of "social reconstruction through education," predicated on civic ideals.[10] These proto interculturalists balanced an appreciation of cultural difference with an interpretation of American history that emphasized democracy and highlighted movements for economic and political justice. As Studer explained, "For those of us who were beginning our teaching in the 30s and 40s, there was the challenge of creating a new synthesis to education, which would bring together the threads of revolt, and a reassertion of the American spirit. The white Anglo Saxon ethos, with its racial bias, its Horatio Alger mythology, was no longer viable."[11] Clearly, this belief placed him firmly in line with this leftist educational movement. Studer incorporated these historical lessons in his classrooms during the school year and at Woodland during the summer break. For the entirety of its duration, running "an intercultural educational camp that welcomed children of all races, religion, and economic levels and made them feel at home" ranked first among the camp's basic philosophical principles.[12]

The second guiding principle for the educational programming at Woodland was the progressive concept of the "community school." This idea emerged during the social and cultural shifts of the early twentieth century, wrought by heightened immigration (and the concomitant forced Americanization programs) and rapid rural-to-urban demographic shifts. The community school idea aimed to help children, both immigrant and native-born, grapple with the upheavals in their lives and in larger society. According to Studer's interpretation, this required transforming schools into "an embryonic community life, active with all types of occupations that reflect the life of the larger society, and permeated throughout with the spirit of art, history, and science." While community schools became holistic communities in themselves, students were also expected to go out and foster connections with members of a broader social network. Community schools essentially became "schools-without-walls, where students went out into the community, learned of its problems, and learned democratically," Studer explained.[13] While Studer clearly put his theory into practice when he became the director of the Downtown Community School in 1950, he also incorporated it into the structure of Camp Woodland.

Each summer, the programs at Woodland taught campers how to be engaged citizens in the camp community and in the larger community of the Catskills. The first part of this project was inscribed in the "community centered" structure of Woodland, which was predicated on the idea "that children from the very beginning live in a community. Their living is in relation to the group, and in an ever-widening degree in relation to a larger society. The community gives them their ideals, their values, their goals in living." The camp provided a very important lesson for the children it served, practically all of whom came from New York City: "Our children, being city children in the main, come from communities that are large and impersonal." Educating—and engaging—students in civic participation was difficult on such a scale. As a setting in which students lived and worked for two months of the year, Woodland created an atmosphere in which children could learn and practice civic participation to realize the goal of nurturing "citizenship of a concrete and living quality in a community that is cut to his size."[14]

The camp was divided into an upper camp, middle camp, and lower camp based on age. Each camper engaged in daily play, athletics, educational projects, and work; the activities of each category were designed to teach campers how to live and work collectively. For instance, the work category included anything from constructing trails, improving the campgrounds, assisting in the construction and maintenance of buildings and facilities, and cleaning the camp. As children aged, their responsibilities grew to the extent that the section for the oldest campers (ages fourteen to sixteen) was called "Work Camp."[15] Promotional literature emphasized the work involved in the camp's community school, as noted in an early brochure: "Upper camp is a little village in itself, designed to give real experiences in democratic living—with a weekly newspaper, a cooperative store, a post office and a camp council." Even children too young to perform much camp work were still able to participate in the community ethos during nightly and weekly group meetings: "At Sunday meetings and at campfires the children learn to express themselves and to participate in camp affairs. The aim is to make the camp itself a little community of work, play and cooperative learning—a laboratory in the democratic way of life."[16]

In addition to their work assignments and group discussions, campers participated in democratic living through their camp council. Every summer, the members of each bunk voted on one of their own to serve on the council, with the understanding that they would represent the concerns of their bunkmates. While Studer and the board were clear that the campers did not actually contribute to dictating the overall running of the camp, the directors worked to create an environment in which campers were encouraged to express their views and be heard by those in charge. From an early age, campers learned that in well-functioning democracies, all members must be able to contribute.

The lessons of citizenship and the importance of democracy were incorporated into the daily functions of the camp, but they were displayed most clearly during two camp-wide events: the annual Fourth of July program, which occurred almost immediately after the beginning of each summer, and World Youth Week, which typically occurred midseason. For the Fourth of July celebration, counselors were instructed on how this event set the stage for the rest of the camp season, as noted in their handbook from 1945: "Camp starts out on a high note of unity. The occasion also begins the season with an emphasis on the democratic philosophy of our nation, a way of life consciously followed at camp. . . . The basic framework of the program is a combination of past and present: we look back at some of the traditional episodes in the struggle to attain democracy and we also reflect the struggles on the immediate world scene. The keynote of our celebration was expressed in a song written by the children, 'We Sing a Song of Democracy.'"[17] This emphasis on exploring democratic struggles in the United States and abroad while simultaneously encouraging campers to participate in the camp community was also featured in the annual World Youth Week. Beginning after the end of WWII, for one week the camp invited children from other countries "who had been freedom fighters in their native lands," according to camper Paul Kantrowitz. The significance of World Youth Week was that students learned from people their own age who were "leading the struggle for freedom and democracy."[18] Moreover, campers did much of the planning for this activity, which further tied them to the operations of the camp itself. The event also educated campers about the global struggle for democracy and other civic ideals. Sometimes the campers put these lessons into practice, as they did during the 1947 season. During that summer, campers voted to forgo ice cream on one Sunday and send the money saved to a Chinese relief fund. During that same season, campers voted that money that some campers won at the annual Ulster County Fair should go to an anti-lynching fund (other options included the camp's scholarship fund, World Youth Week activities, Spanish relief, and camp improvements).[19]

Being an active and engaged citizen in local and global communities was one of the primary values that Camp Woodland sought to instill among its campers, and it was a value that lay at the core of the American left during this period. While there was nothing inherently politically partisan about progressive education reform, even within its intercultural wing, progressive educators in New York City often maintained left-wing social views. Norman Studer strongly sympathized with left-wing politics in the US, particularly the left's emphasis on social and economic justice issues. The camp directors, as well as involved parents, shared these views, which were manifested in a staunch advocacy for civil rights and democratic ideals, both nationally and internationally. In addition to lending support for political issues and groups connected to the left (e.g., educating students about Spanish relief and anti-lynching efforts), the camp also illustrated their directors' and supporters' political positions through a hallmark of the Woodland experience: the folklore program. Through applied folklore activities, the threads of progressive education, left-wing politics, and nascent public history practice and, especially, pedagogy, became tightly woven into the fabric of Woodland.

Folklore, History, and Public History

Like the progressive educators in New York City, the community of applied folklorists during the 1930s and 1940s was a small one, with many cultivating an educational emphasis in their work.[20] Throughout his career in education, Studer often collaborated with folklorists and incorporated aspects of their work into camp programs. Just as he was able to incorporate folklore into his classroom teaching, at Woodland, he infused it into the core of the camp's educational mission. With composers Herbert Haufrecht and then Norman Cazden serving as the camp's music directors, folklore became a vital part of the Camp Woodland experience. The purpose of the folklore program at Woodland was twofold: to teach social history through folklore and to give the music and lore students collected back to the community through public performances, publications, and a traveling museum exhibition. It is in these respects that Woodland epitomized the applied wing of American folklore practice and prefigured the pedagogical practices of public history.

The history of folklore study and practice in the United States is as complex as that of public history. From the founding of the American Folklore Society in 1888, folklorists differed on how to interpret the field. Folklorists in institutions of higher education sought to establish it as an independent scholarly discipline (although they differed as to whether to house it in the social sciences or humanities), while those working in the public often viewed folklore through lenses borrowed from literature, history, anthropology, and sociology. A broad difference between these two wings of the field pertained to their interpretations of folk culture: on the one hand, academic folklorists often studied folk traditions as cultural artifacts, with an emphasis on textual purity, and sought to protect them from becoming corrupted by the forces of mass culture. On the other hand, folklorists in the applied realm were generally unconcerned with determining the authenticity of folk traditions and rather turned their attention to understanding the function that they served in the communities that practiced them.[21] During the early twentieth century, the concept of applied folklore began to develop along various trajectories, as exemplified by John Lomax's books of cowboy songs and familial expeditions to collect prison songs, Olive Dame Campbell's published collections of Appalachian ballads, and Carl Sandburg's sing-along lectures and music books. These texts were filled with examples that only nominally qualified as "authentic" folk songs according to academic standards.

While the work of these modern public folklore pioneers helped shape the field, the idea of applied folklore took on new political meanings in the context of the Depression, particularly through liberal WPA programs and left-wing reform initiatives tied to the Communist Party of the United States of America (CPUSA).[22] Both the New Deal's populist celebration of the marginal and the Popular Front's radical Americanism required artists and intellectuals to go out and find "the people"—to discover the nation's cultural heritage and to employ the traditions of this heritage to aid Americans struggling through the Depression. Many key public folklorists of this era worked in New Deal agencies while maintaining left-wing political sympathies, views that shaped both their interpretation of folklore and their projects in public folklore. Regardless of position, they all maintained the dual desire to make folklore relevant to the people and to use it to educate Americans about their history and heritage—one that they argued was shaped by civic ideals of cultural pluralism, political democracy, and social justice. It was also an inherently diverse history because, as they argued, "national heritage" was actually a composite of myriad ethnic and racial groups from cities, towns, and rural areas across the country.

To applied folklorists, traditional music, stories, and handicrafts were historically significant because they reflected traditions that were handed down from generation to generation or that were created in response to specific historical conditions. As such, they lay at the core of American heritage and provided particular insight into the national past. Furthermore, this was a *people's* history because it came directly from the people, and the people with whom public folklorists were concerned were often the same groups that many public historians would come to engage—namely, those from politically disenfranchised and economically marginalized communities. Finally, folk culture represented a *living* history. Because local communities continued to practice traditions that passed from one generation to the next, these traditions had the ability to connect the past to the present. Rather than collecting folk traditions as cultural specimens to be preserved in the amber of academic archives, applied folklorists sought to infuse these traditions into mainstream culture in order to connect Americans to their local—and national—heritage. These protopublic folklorists encouraged people to find, record, and especially to practice the traditions of their local communities.

Each summer, the leadership and staff of Camp Woodland put the values of applied folklore into practice. Through field trips to different villages and hamlets in the Catskills, campers collected songs and stories and then returned what they collected from individual informants back to the community through dramatic performances, an annual folk festival, and a camper-staffed Museum of Work Tools. All of these activities contributed to the "camp's project of preserving and spreading enjoyment of the hitherto neglected folkways of the region . . . the folk culture of the people."[23] Furthermore, it was an effort that had an inherently radical bent: Woodland's folklore program "pioneered the effort to make American folk culture, particularly folk music, the basis for a radical political culture," according to historian Paul Mishler.[24]

As with almost all other aspects of the camp, the folklore program was steeped in progressive education. At the Downtown Community School and Little Red Schoolhouse, Studer emphasized teaching history through primary sources and firsthand experiences, an emphasis that became the hallmark of the folklore program at Woodland.[25] The first step of the program included community field trips, which became the "backbone of camp life." While traveling beyond the camp boundaries was common throughout the summer through hikes of varying lengths, the folklore field trips were specifically designed to teach students "first hand what life in the Catskills was like in the past, and what it is like now."[26] Studer argued that by learning the songs and stories—the living lore—of the region directly from local residents, students would be able to effectively connect the past with the present. Each camper was able to participate in two trips per summer, even when the number of campers reached upward of 250. Through these trips, campers explored the histories of neighboring towns as well as local communities that were no longer extant, like Shalom Hill, a utopian Jewish community that developed during the 1830s. In 1949, one of the field trips for group 8 of the work camp was to a town that was about to be flooded to create a new reservoir for New York City. According to a series of camper articles, they visited with the editor of the *Margaretville Daily News* to learn how local residents felt about being displaced.[27] Other field trips explored forms of labor in the region, such as dairying, lumbering, quarrying, and tanning. The emphasis on labor folklore, especially work songs, was common among both academic and applied folklorists of the era. One trip was to Chinchester, a town built around a furniture factory. In 1942, campers wrote a play about Chinchester based on the interviews they took with local resident Harry Haas and others, which they performed at that year's folk festival.[28]

Camp staff designed the field trips to engage campers in collecting folk songs and stories while conducting oral histories. Campers often relayed their experiences to the rest of the camp community in a weekly newsletter, *Catskill Caller*, and the camp yearbook, *Neighbors*, both of which the campers ran themselves. Through short articles, they wrote of what they learned and how conversations with local narrators shaped their views. The field trips illustrated both the applied learning model as well as the community idea. Studer recognized that, as a group of outsiders that moved into an area, Woodland was not an organic part of the local community. He therefore hoped that it would become "a camp that the community accepts but which represents something beyond what a community itself has achieved." The folklore program provided the cornerstone of this effort: by going out into the community the campers were forging strong connections with local residents. They continued this effort at the camp itself by inviting residents like George Van Kleek as callers at the weekly square dances. They also enlisted Orson Slack, an eighty-three-year-old lumberman, to help campers write and perform a play about Boney Quillan, "a folk hero of the rafting-lumbering days of the Catskills."[29]

Not only did collecting folk traditions tie Woodland to the surrounding towns, but it also illustrated a particular version of cultural conservation common among applied folklorists of the era. Many believed that local traditions were endangered as older generations passed away and younger generations either moved from the area or were more interested in pop culture. Studer therefore designed the folklore program with the express intention of generating local interest in regional traditions, explaining that through this effort, the camp could become "an instrument through which the people of a region become conscious of their folk traditions and of their local history" and that it would "give old people of the community a sense of dignity as transmitter of the heritage."[30] Applied folklorists and folk enthusiasts like Studer believed that local folklore could best be preserved by encouraging people from local communities to continue to practice those traditions rather than merely collecting them for the purpose of depositing them in institutional archives.[31] Furthermore, introducing the campers to folk culture could inspire a new generation to take up the mantle of preserving—and practicing—folk traditions. Folk music was therefore integrated into everyday life at Woodland, with singing folk songs around the campfire and weekly folk dances being regular features of the camp experience. Woodland also hired Pete Seeger to make an annual appearance and employed other folk singers like Bessie Jones, who taught songs from the Georgia Sea Islands.

The annual culmination of the folklore program was the Folk Festival of the Catskills. The festival, which was open to the community and often performed *in* the community at local centers like the American Legion Hall in Phoenicia, was divided into three parts. The first was a cantata that incorporated local history and folklore composed by a professional musician commissioned by the camp and performed by campers; the second was a series of performances by local musicians; and the third was a set of camper performances based in local folklore and music. Even this program had larger social objectives, especially during the camp's early years. The counselor's handbook of 1945 explained that the "basic purpose" of the festival was "to afford the children an opportunity to participate in a community project of social importance. [The] festival has for its purpose the building of unity between people of the city and people of the country, between people of various races, religions, and national origins."[32] Even in the appreciation of folk music, the larger civic mission of Woodland was strong.

In addition to the large festival, the camp sponsored smaller performances by campers throughout the summer. Again, these were events directed to local residents that campers created and executed. As with the festival, campers often performed these plays at community sites including American Legion Halls and Grange Halls. They also reached an even wider audience by recording broadcasts aired on a local radio station in the city of Kingston. During the summer of 1947, for example, students performed a play they wrote about the nineteenth-century Antirent War in the Hudson Valley. The play, *Down Rent*, was based on interviews campers conducted with local residents and research that they did at the town of Woodstock's library. Among the invited guests were members of the Historical Society of Woodstock.[33] That same season, the campers performed a play at the Mt. Tremper Church called *Out of the Valley*, which dramatized the plight of families being relocated from the Lackawack Valley for the impending reservoir.[34]

The third component of the folklore program at Woodland, what Studer referred to as the "heart" of the program, was the Museum of Work Tools that the students collected on their field trips from local residents and by donations. All the objects displayed were chosen because they "reflect[ed] the past industries of the Catskill region."[35] Even this effort exemplified applied learning, as older campers ran the museum as part of their work component, and interaction with the local community, because it was open to local residents throughout the summer. Studer sought to engage an even wider local audience by developing a mobile exhibit run by work campers that would travel to small villages in the Catskills in order to reach those who could not come to the camp to visit the museum.[36]

Studer's incorporation of folklore into camp programs dated back to his early days at Camp Hilltop in New Jersey. While serving as the head counselor there he also took students on field trips that were intrinsic to the camp's mission of being "a democracy of learning by doing," to teach children democratic values "by activities rather than by preaching or lecturing"—a mission that became the guiding principle of Woodland as well.[37] Through field trips, students were not just learning fun songs and stories but rather learning history, particularly the social history of people traditionally omitted from the historic record, long before academic and public historians would do so. For instance, when recalling one of the first times he took campers at Woodland to meet with a local resident, a resident whose stories and knowledge typified "the kind of oral history and folklore we used for the education of Woodland children," Studer wrote, "As Uncle Newt rambled on, one could see the history of a region unfold before one's eyes, the earthy history that is compounded of the experiences of the people. . . . Uncle Newt is a symbol of a type of history that has never been adequately known to Americans and never adequately utilized in education. He is a symbol of the social history that clings to the hills and rivers and the crossroads of America."[38] The heavy romanticism of this statement notwithstanding, it does summarize Studer's argument that folklore provided insight into local history. Indeed, if history educators recognized the significance of folklore as a historical resource they might be better able to construct a more socially inclusive narrative of the American past.

In connecting folklore and social history, Studer echoed a core tenet of applied folklore. In 1940, folklorist Benjamin Botkin argued that folklore was a useful, but often ignored, source of social and cultural history in an aptly titled essay, "Folklore as a Neglected Source of Social History." In this piece, Botkin called for historians and folklorists to overcome disciplinary boundaries and work together in using folklore to understand both the historical and contemporary circumstances of local communities. But rather than focusing on folklore of the distant past, as both had been doing, historians and folklorists should concern themselves with the traditions that were currently being practiced in local communities. This "living lore" or "folklore in the making," according to Botkin, "has a more direct relation to contemporary or recent social structure and is the expression of social change and cultural conflict."[39] Furthermore, because of the traditional emphasis on the historic deeds of famous men, the people of folk communities had been largely omitted from the historical record such that folkways provide one of the few means of accessing underrepresented histories. Botkin explains,

> If we admitted no impediments to a marriage of true minds between folklore and history, the product of their union would be folk history. This is history produced by the collaboration of the folklorist and the historian with each other and with the folk; a history of the whole people ... a history also in which the people are the historians as well as the history, telling their own story in their own words—Everyman's history, for Everyman to read.[40]

If there was a kind of history that was by the people and for the people, folk history was it.

After articulating the historical significance of folk traditions, Botkin continued to explain how applied folklorists interpreted folklore. Rather than simply being a product, folklore was a *process*; therefore, folk traditions were inherently dynamic, with each singer or storyteller leaving his or her stamp on various songs and stories. Again, Botkin explained, what makes a song or story folklore was "its history through diffusion and acculturation," meaning that even commercial songs could become folk traditions depending on how they were used. For example, the song "Oh Susanna," written by Stephen Foster, is not a folk song in its origin. But when miners of the Gold Rush adopted and adapted it, it *became* an example of a folk tradition. The significance of this song lay in the process of how it became a folk song: "Just why and how this song appealed to the miner in his particular socio-economic situation concerns the social historian as well as the folklorist."[41]

Midcentury public folklorists shared similar interpretations of, and objectives for, their work. As cultural conservationists, they argued that the best way to protect these traditions was to rekindle popular interest in them, which would save them from a fate of cultural oblivion. For this reason, many applied folklorists directed their efforts to children, encouraging them to learn the folkways of their communities.[42] For Woodland, this meant learning the folkways of the Catskills and situating these traditions within the context of local history and contemporary local practices. The field trips of the folklore program espoused Botkin's idea of living lore because they were expressly intended to educate the children in the fact that folk traditions remain vital components of contemporary culture. By taking campers out to learn of these traditions from residents, they "gave new impetus to the study of local life and history," Studer explained. He continued, "It was our aim to find the history on the landscape, and give our students the feeling of the humanity that is associated with places. We did more than try to establish what went on in the past: we also searched for the present. Our explorations led us off the main highways to the places where regional characteristics still remain, and regional difference can be enjoyed and cherished."[43] While these trips were designed to teach campers to appreciate and to better understand folk culture, they were also illustrative of the camp's community ethos. Even though the time that the campers spent living in the region was temporary, the folklore program reinforced the idea that the camp was part of that community—and thus the campers were as well.

The Radicalism of Camp Woodland

Besides sharing a common understanding of what constituted folklore and how it could best be preserved, many public folklorists of this era maintained similar political views and affiliations. These folklorists, especially those working in New Deal agencies, often turned their interest in recovering and popularizing the traditions of socially and economically marginalized Americans into advocating for social, political, and economic justice on their behalf.[44] Many of these folklorists believed that the infusion of folk traditions into the cultural mainstream would connect Americans to their cultural heritage while bringing the nation closer to achieving social equality. According to Charles Seeger, a composer and folklorist who served as a technical advisor in the Special Skills division of the Resettlement Administration, the folklorists working in federal agencies were social progressives who were boring from within through their work in New Deal projects. In this context, *boring from within* meant "getting as much consideration of the human being as a member of society, regardless of who he was or what he did, or how much money he had or anything else.... Wherever you had a chance to work for the view of things from below up, you would do it."[45] By protecting and valorizing the cultural traditions of folk groups, Seeger and others believed that New Deal folklorists would be able to act as advocates for these communities, working to fight their marginalization in the process.

Norman Studer and other leaders of Woodland were strongly invested in politically progressive causes from the time of the camp's founding. Historian Paul Mischler groups Woodland with other radical camps that emerged from the "Communist-oriented radical movement," which all shared a commitment to fighting ethnic and racial prejudice, "promoting interethnic and interracial cooperation," and supporting the labor movement. Camps of this ilk taught children values that were instilled at home but that were often marginalized in larger society.[46] Of all the political causes espoused by the left during the midcentury, the one for which the camp demonstrated unwavering support was civil rights and racial justice. Camp leadership infused civil rights advocacy into almost every aspect of the camp—from daily activities to the very design and structure of the camp itself.

What made Camp Woodland stand out among other summer camps of the era was that it was integrated from the outset and remained so for its entire duration.[47] This was not only a conscious decision but also something that camp directors consistently worked to achieve. Rather than simply being open to integration, camp leaders made deliberate efforts to recruit Black campers and staff members. While Woodland was a "pioneer in interracial camping," it took a significant amount of work on the part of camp leaders to recruit African American campers and to educate White parents on why this was a critical aspect of Woodland's social and educational mission. In a document titled "Camp Woodland's Designs for Integration," Studer noted that after WWII, the camp worked on strengthening its program of "intercultural, interracial education," even as the educational system started "backing off from its wartime concern with uprooting racism in schools." The leaders of Woodland were disturbed by this trend because they agreed with W. E. B. Du Bois "that the color line was the major issue of the twentieth century."[48] This would become another guiding principle for the next decade.

The initial rhetoric Woodland leaders used to explain the need for an integrated camp was steeped in the language of WWII-era intercultural education. This was especially apparent in an early description of how staffing decisions were made:

> There are a good number of Negro members of the staff, occupying all types of positions. Many of our white children who come from neighborhoods where Negroes are excluded except in the position of domestic workers, see Negro people occupying important positions of leadership at camp. Often the camp doctor is a Negro woman. Also on our staff may be Japanese or Chinese-Americans, Puerto Ricans and people of other backgrounds. When we celebrate our camp's traditional World Youth Week we can draw from our own staff for personal accounts of the life of young people in many parts of the world. Our staff is the living lesson of the One World idea. . . . With a deepening appreciation of each other comes a deeper understanding of the problems that face minority peoples.[49]

In addition to regular staff members, the camp reached out to African American folklorists to work with students and invited members of the student sit-in movement to work at the camp. In 1960, Angeline Butler, a former student at Fisk University and activist in the student sit-in movement, joined the staff at Woodland as a camp counselor.

Maintaining an integrated staff was a key aspect of establishing an interracial camp, but Woodland also needed to attract Black campers. Sometimes, this effort went hand in hand with the camp's emphasis on directly educating students about contemporary issues in the civil rights movement. In 1958, for example, Studer personally invited the nine students who participated in desegregating Central High School in Little Rock to attend Woodland for the summer. More typically, the camp worked locally, recruiting students from diverse backgrounds in New York City and surrounding areas with the incentive of financial aid. In order to maintain socioeconomic diversity, the camp's parent association raised money for a scholarship fund "to insure a democratic cross section of children from all racial, cultural and economic groups."[50] But inviting and financially supporting children from ethnic and racial minority groups to attend camp was only one aspect of achieving an interracial camp: the camp directors, all of whom were White, grappled with the difficulties of maintaining an integrated camp in a region that was predominantly White and segregated. A major problem that they faced was housing for visiting Black families. In 1949, most local boarding houses refused to serve African Americans, which prompted a concerted search for integrated facilities. The camp began to construct housing on campus to ease this burden, but in the meantime, the Intercultural Committee of the parent association issued a letter listing local resorts and hotels that would "welcome all our parents." Each year they updated the list; in 1949, there were only two; by 1960, that number had grown to thirty-seven. Rather than just directing this letter to Black parents, the Association expressly urged *all* parents to stay "*only* at places on the attached list." This was in keeping with the main reason they selected this camp: "We as parents chose Camp Woodland for our children because it affords them the opportunity to work, to grow, play and live with other children, regardless of race, color, or creed, in the atmosphere of democracy and equality. We do this consciously because we want our children to develop healthy social attitudes which can only grow from friendship and knowledge."[51] Efforts like this illustrated the camp's unwavering support for integration. Furthermore, it exemplified the progressive educational emphasis of learning by doing—of educating young campers through deeds as well as words.

Because the staff at Woodland centered integration in the Woodland experience, it is fitting that issues of racial justice were also intrinsic to the camp's folklore program. Group sing-alongs were an integral part of the folklore program and to the camp experience as a whole, and the camp directors made a point to include both Black and White musical traditions. African American folk singers like Bessie Jones taught the significance of Black folk songs for African Americans and the role they played in shaping American culture as a whole. Studer explained, "Black folklore had special meaning for the black camper. John Henry was more than a strong person: he was to the black child a symbol of inner strength and determination."[52] The Fourth of July celebration reinforced this view because it often focused on themes of freedom in American history; the performances always included at least one skit on the Black freedom struggle, in which the performers would link historical actions to present-day concerns. They also focused on leaders who played a significant role in the past like Frederick Douglass and Sojourner Truth, as well as contemporary figures such as Martin Luther King Jr. and Malcolm X. Woodland's exploration of the freedom struggle was not restricted to domestic issues but exposed campers to the global fight for racial justice as well.

By the 1950s, for instance, Pete Seeger began incorporating South African freedom songs in his annual visits to the camp.[53]

While campers were exposed to folk songs and stories pertaining to the Black freedom movement in the southern United States, Studer also wanted campers to draw connections to historical issues of inequality in the North and local civil rights efforts from the past and present. Even in the predominantly White region of the rural Catskills, there was a local figure who had been prominent in the abolitionist and women's suffrage movements: Sojourner Truth. Raised in slavery in Old Hurley, Truth had a strong connection to the area, but that connection was largely ignored in local history—something that the people of Woodland sought to change. Their effort to revive the memory of Truth began shortly after the end of WWII. One of the early field trips was to the town of Old Hurley to see the house where Truth was enslaved. Reviving her memory in local history was important because, Studer explained, "she belongs among the top rank of American leadership, and since her death has suffered the fate of our black leaders, of being blocked out and almost forgotten." In 1952, the camp commissioned a cantata about her life by Bob De Cormier; one hundred campers performed it at that year's Folk Festival of the Catskills, as well as at other performances in the town of Kingston and in New York City. Still another effort included organizing a committee of camp members and residents of Kingston and Old Hurley to create a memorial in her honor.[54]

The folklore program at Woodland emphasized the history and legacy of Sojourner Truth not only because of her importance to numerous rights-based causes but because her roots were in Ulster County, allowing the Woodland programs to emphasize her importance to both local and national history. She was also the ideal figure through which the camp could impart its educational message of teaching "black and white children a different set of values and attitudes from those traditionally taught. It was a program intended to produce the kind of democratic [person], who would in their lives carry out the ideals expressed by the founders of our country." Studer continued, "The story of Sojourner Truth was carried home in the hearts and minds of campers and counselors, and her courage gave many young people the strength to do [what] was needed to be done." This is precisely what happened to Jane Fourner, who played the role of Truth during the first performance of the cantata. According to a letter from her mother, the experience of learning about and playing the part gave her daughter the courage to pass picket lines of White residents protesting efforts to integrate the school she attended in Washington, DC.⁵⁵

Citizens with varying political positions and philosophies led the integration movement of the 1950s through '60s; it was not a movement born out of left-wing politics. However, in the context of the early Cold War era, during the midst of the second Red Scare, anticommunist crusaders often used citizens' support for civil rights as evidence of radical sympathies. Left-wing activists and sympathizers had supported civil rights since the early decades of the twentieth century, a fact that House Unamerican Activities Committee (HUAC) and other state and federal agencies used against suspected communists during loyalty investigations. Historian Zoe Burkholder explains that those called to testify often faced questions about their attitudes toward interracial mixing, specifically whether they "entertained individuals of another race at the home." To answer in the affirmative almost certainly meant being branded as a subversive.⁵⁶ While this kind of political atmosphere stymied some of the left-wing pro–civil rights activities that had flourished during the later years of the Depression, it did not dampen Woodland's pro-integration stance and civil rights advocacy. Perhaps because of the camp's staunch political progressivism, in 1956 the Joint Legislative Committee on Charitable and Philanthropic Agencies and Organizations of New York began investigating Woodland for communist indoctrination. A report from the investigation specifically identified Studer as a "longtime member of the Communist Party." Studer was even subpoenaed to testify, but no formal charges were filed against him or the camp.⁵⁷

In 1961, when the future of the camp was in jeopardy because of internecine fighting between Studer and three former board members, many former campers and their parents wrote in support of Studer, with several specifically commending the progressive values that the camp instilled in themselves or in their children. In one letter, former camper Katy Wechalen explained that her parents had been targeted by the KKK in Levittown, Long Island, when they openly supported the first African American family that moved into the community. Her parents wanted her to have a positive experience living in an integrated space, so they sent her to Woodland. Because they could not afford the fee, Wechalen was a beneficiary of the scholarship program. In the letter, she noted her love of learning about the folklore and history of the Catskills through the field trips that Studer led. Yet what truly made the Woodland experience remarkable, she explained, was the social and political awareness that the experience imbued among the campers: "Perhaps even more wonderful to me than the other things at the camp were the discussions we had on the important issues of the day. The oldest as well as the youngest groups in camp discussed these issues and put on skits expressing their feelings on the issues." This was a sentiment echoed by another former camper, Joanie Bernhard: "The two summers spent at Woodland are my ideal—in personal and educational values. Whenever I get disgusted with my present teaching situation I look back to Woodland and think of the place where I have lived and seen all my ideals in practice."[58]

The Woodland experience continued to shape former campers' lives and careers long after the camp closed in 1962. In 1997, the Hudson Valley Study Center at the State University of New York at New Paltz conducted a survey of former campers in connection to a Woodland reunion that they hosted. One of the questions asked whether attending camp at Woodland shaped former campers' career choices. One respondent, Karl E. Klare, a law professor at Northeastern University, stated that it influenced him "in a general way—e.g. a commitment to social justice."[59] This was a sentiment that many respondents echoed, noting that even while the experience may not have shaped their career paths, it did have a significant influence on other life choices. It is also a sentiment that Studer recognized during the rise of social activism during the 1960s: "In the integration struggle, in the effort to ban the atomic bomb, and in the struggles against the war in Vietnam, Woodlanders took heroic parts. They had learned at an early age that struggle for democratic rights was written into the history of this country from its birth."[60] While parents may have selected this camp because it fit their social and political views, the experience profoundly shaped campers' views as well.

The Woodland Legacy in Public History

In her genealogy of public history pedagogy, Rebecca Conard traces the institutional development of the field while exploring the shifting ideologies of public history theory and practice. Conrad explains that while "public history" became a catchall term for history outside of the academy by the late 1970s, during the following decade a cohort of public (and academic) historians pushed the social perspective in history even further to advocate for "people's history," emphasizing the histories of marginalized groups. While some of these scholars would go on to create the *Radical History Review*, others focused on injecting this perspective into traditional public history venues such as museums and archives.[61]

According to historians of public history, what is understood as public history in the United States—directing history to a public audience, incorporating the public into acts of history-making, and connecting the past to the present—largely emerged from the academic turns and social movements of the 1960s. Although historians had been working in the public realm over a century prior, the ideas that emerged from these midcentury movements helped form the theoretical and practical foundation of public history. Generating a socially and culturally inclusive understanding of the American past by incorporating the perspectives of groups traditionally ignored in academic history, enabling the people to speak for themselves in their own words, and using this history to change an unjust present were ideas incubated in the social and cultural upheavals wrought by the oldest of the baby boomers and their elder siblings.

In almost every respect, the programs at Camp Woodland set a precedent for the theories and practices that would come to shape public history pedagogy and practice well before the social movements of the 1960s. Steeped in the theories of applied folklore, and prior to the social turn in United States history, the folklore program used folk culture as a means to understand local history and the history of groups typically omitted from historical accounts. As the Oral History Research Office at Columbia University (the primary oral history project of this era) focused on collecting interviews with political leaders, Studer and other folklorists connected to Woodland fanned the region, seeking narrators among local residents. While this effort was akin to the kinds of interview projects that emerged from the populist, and leftist, milieu of Depression-era America, it also had the same kind of vision that would come to guide the Oral History Research Center at Indiana University, under the direction of John Bodnar, with its primary objective to "collect, preserve, and interpret twentieth-century history" through personal accounts.[62]

Furthermore, several former Woodland campers were among the first wave of public historians in the United States—a career path that they partially attributed to their camp experience. For instance, as Shari Segel Goldberg wrote in her own response to a survey from a reunion in 1997, Woodland had a direct effect on her becoming the Curator of Special Exhibitions at the Museum of Jewish Heritage in New York City. She received an MA in anthropology and spent ten years at the American Museum of Natural History as Margaret Mead's assistant, and her subsequent work in the "Museum Field can be seen as an extension of the collecting of artifacts and stories from the local Catskill Community."[63] She notes that campers in her cohort including

Nancy Foner and Richard Bauman followed similar paths. After the Woodland reunion in 1997, law professor Karl E. Klare wrote to the reunion organizers to express his gratitude for being able to participate in the event. Not only did it provide him with opportunity to reconnect with old friends, but it also reminded him of the ideals that the camp helped inculcate in him by providing an "opportunity to reaffirm the values Camp Woodland stood for, including a deep sense of community, a commitment to diversity, and particularly a commitment to recovering and celebrating the history and folk culture of the Catskill Mountains and the Hudson Valley regions."[64]

From the early years of formal public history pedagogy in the 1970s through contemporary practices of the twenty-first century, educators in the field have emphasized civic engagement, the progressive politics inherent in interpretations of history-from-below, the engagement of students in applied projects working in collaboration with local communities, and an inherently interdisciplinary historical perspective. These qualities were all inherent in the design and implementation of the annual summer experience at Camp Woodland. Institutions like this thus reveal the long progressive roots of both the practice and pedagogy of public history in the United States.

Notes

1. Rebecca Conard, "The Pragmatic Roots of Public History Education in the United States," *Public Historian* 37, no. 1 (February 2015): 106.
2. Notable scholarship in this area includes Paul C. Mishler, *Raising Reds: The Young Pioneers, Radical Summer Camps, and Communist Political Culture in the United States* (New York: Columbia University Press, 1999); and June Levine, Ronnie Gilbert, and Gene Gordan, *Tales of Wo-Chi-Ca: Blacks, Whites and Reds at Camp* (n.p.: Avon Springs Press, 2002).
3. Amy C. Schlinder, "How the Norman Studer Papers Came to the University at Albany," *Voices* 29 (Fall–Winter 2003), accessed July 19, 2016, http://www.nyfolklore.org/pubs/voic29-3-4/studer.html (URL invalid).
4. *Camp Woodland Brochure*, n.d., p. 1, series 4, box 1, folder 25; Norman Studer, "To Save the Woodland Idea," 1961, pp. 1–4, M. E. Grenander Department of Special Collections and Archives, University Libraries, University at Albany, State University of New York (known as the Studer Papers), series 8, subseries 1, box 2, folder 52. Unless otherwise noted, all other archival sources are from this archive.
5. In 1950, Studer became the director of the Downtown Community School, another progressive school in New York City. Studer would continue in this position until the school closed in 1971.

6 Norman Studer, *The Woodland Sampler*, ed. Joan Studer Levine, 1 (1987, 2001), series 4, subseries 3, box 6, folder 14.
7 Carleton Mabee, "Margaret Mead and a 'Pilot Experiment' in Progressive and Interracial Education: The Downtown Community School," *New York History* 65, no. 1 (1984): 11; Julia L. Mickenberg, *Learning from the Left: Children's Literature, the Cold War, and Radical Politics in the United States* (New York: Oxford University Press, 2006), 31.
8 James Banks, *Multiethnic Education: Practices and Promises* (Bloomington, IN: Phi Delta Kappa Educational Foundation, 1977), 8. Intercultural education efforts, however, did not continue past the 1950s, and they largely failed to become ingrained in mainstream education because they occurred in isolated pockets, largely in areas of high diversity, such as cities, rather than becoming a part of curricula across the nation.
9 James Henry Powell, "The Concept of Cultural Pluralism in American Thought, 1915–1965" (PhD diss., University of Michigan, 1971) 159–61, 163, 178. Powell notes that this theory was alternately referred to as "cultural democracy" and "cultural pluralism" during the years 1940–55.
10 Mischler, *Raising Reds*, 100.
11 Norman Studer, "Camp Woodland's Designs for Integration," n.d., p. 7, series 4, box 2, folder 1.
12 Studer, "To Save the Woodland Idea," 1.
13 Norman Studer, "Community Life—Chapter 1 Progressive Education: Beginnings," 1–2 series 8, subseries 1, box 1, folder 28.
14 Norman Studer, "Goals of Camp," n.d., p. 2, series 4, box 1, folder 27.
15 Work was a critical aspect of the camp experience because it was seen as a necessary condition for living in a society. Work, Studer later wrote, "was the activity that turned campers from being mere consumers into complete citizens, actively changing their life and conditions. Everybody works at Woodland because work is basic to life, and is an experience necessary for completion as a human being." Norman Studer, "The Woodland Story," chap. 2, series 8, subseries 1, box 3, folder 13. Campers at nearby radical camp called Wo-Chi-Ca also contributed to the construction of camp buildings, first because there were no buildings on the campsite, but then because work became integrated into the camp's ideology, "for it was thought that there was no better way to teach children the dignity of labor . . . than to make work one of the basic activities of the camp." Mischler, *Raising Reds*, 95.
16 *Camp Woodland Brochure*, 1.
17 *Camp Woodland Counselor's Handbook*, 1945, p. 2, series 4, box 1, folder 28.
18 Paul Kantrowitz, "World Youth Week," 1948, series 4, subseries 2, box 1, folder 11.
19 Camper Council Meeting "Accomplishments for the Summer" (August 24, 1947); "Report on Progress on Bunk Suggestions" (August 3, 1947) series 4, box 2, folder 2.
20 For instance, during this period, folklorist Benjamin Botkin wrote anthologies of folklore directed to adult and children audiences; Alan Lomax, another applied

folklorist, hosted a folk music educational program on CBS radio's *American School of the Air*; and record companies began issuing albums of folk music with a specific educative emphasis.

21. The academic/applied divide in folklore was bridged by scholars who used folklore in their research and pedagogy, even if they did not operate as strictly academic folklorists. For instance, Harold Thompson and Louis C. Jones at the New York State College for Teachers often engaged students in projects of collecting and interpreting folk materials. For a detailed and engaging exploration of their work, see William S. Walker, "Collecting Folk Histories: Harold W. Thompson and Student Field Research in the 1930s," *Public Historian* 37, no. 3 (August 2015). Notable University of North Carolina at Chapel Hill sociologist Harold Odum also based much of his work on folk material. For further information, see Howard Odum, *Folk, Region, and Society: Selected Papers*, ed. Katherine Jocher (Chapel Hill: University of North Carolina Press, 1964); Lynn Moss Sanders, *Howard W. Odum's Folklore Odyssey: Transformation to Tolerance through African American Folk Studies* (Athens, GA: UGA Press, 2003).

22. Woodland's first music director, Herbert Haufrecht, also worked in the Resettlement Administration as a field director in West Virginia.

23. *Camp Woodland Brochure*, 1.

24. Mischler, *Raising Reds*, 88.

25. Hudson Valley Study Center at SUNY New Paltz newsletter, Fall 1997, series 4, subseries 3, box 1, folder 4.

26. Norman Studer, "Camp Woodland Trips," n.d., series 8, subseries 1, box 1, folder 12.

27. Camper Writings, articles from 1949 *Neighbors*, series 4, subseries 2, box 1, folder 6.

28. "Possible Trips for Groups," n.d., series 4, subseries 3, box 2, folder 12; "Camp Woodland Trips," n.d., series 4, subseries 3, box 2, folder 13. Promotional literature explained this process: "Older children go on field trips to collect songs and stories, some of which were then turned into plays performed by younger children." *Camp Woodland Brochure*, 1.

29. "Camp Woodland Brochure #1," series 4, box 1, folder 25.

30. Untitled document, series 4, box 1, folder 27.

31. "Camp Woodland Brochure #1"; Norman Studer, *Camp Woodland and Folklore*, n.d., p. 1, series 4, box 2, folder 19.

32. Studer, 1; *Camp Woodland Counselor's Handbook*, 3.

33. Cut newspaper clipping on a radio talk given by Elizabeth Day on WKNY, Kingston, NY, transcript, August 17, 1946, series 4, box 1, folder 26.

34. Historical Society of Woodstock, letter to Norman Studer, August 21, 1947, series 4, box, 1, folder 26.

35. Studer, *Camp Woodland and Folklore*, 2.

36. Norman Studer, "New Directions," n.d., series 4, box 2, folder 19.

37. Studer, "Woodland Story," chaps. 2 and 6.

38. Studer, chaps. 2 and 11.

39 Benjamin Botkin, "Folklore as a Neglected Source of Social History," in *The Cultural Approach to History*, ed. Caroline F. Ware (New York: Columbia University Press, 1940), 308.

40 Botkin, 312. Botkin and Studer often crossed paths both professionally and personally. Botkin is credited in Studer's publication *Folk Songs of the Catskills*, based on songs collected by him, Cazden, Haufrecht, and campers. Botkin also recorded the 1944 Folk Festival of the Catskills for the Archive of American Folksong, and his children attended the camp in 1945. Furthermore, both he and Studer were active in the New York Folklore Society.

41 Botkin, 312.

42 The folklorist Alan Lomax provides a key example of this effort. In 1940, he published the article "Music in Your Own Back Yard" in *American Girl*, the magazine of the Girl Scouts, in which he encourages young readers to find and record the music of their own communities and, moreover, to practice singing the songs in order to preserve them. Alan Lomax, "Music in Your Own Backyard," *American Girl* (October 1940): 5–7, 46, 49. See also Ronald D. Cohen, ed., *Alan Lomax: Selected Writings, 1934–1997* (New York: Routledge, 2005), 47–55.

43 Studer, "Camp Woodland's Designs for Integration," 8.

44 Many of the New Deal public folklorists maintained progressive and left-wing social and political views. For further information, see Rachel Donaldson, *I Hear America Singing: Folk Music and National Identity* (Philadelphia: Temple University Press, 2014); Benjamin Filene, *Romancing the Folk: Public Memory and American Roots Music* (Chapel Hill: University of North Carolina Press, 2000), 133–82; Ron Eyerman and Scott Barretta, "From the 30s to the 60s: The Folk Music Revival in the United States," *Theory and Society* 25, no. 4 (August 1996): 501–43; Richard Reuss and JoAnne C. Reuss, *American Folk Music and Left-Wing Politics, 1927–1957* (Lanham, MD: Scarecrow, 2000).

45 Charles Seeger, interview, April 6, 1976, 32–33, David K. Dunaway Collection, American Folklife Center, Library of Congress, Washington, DC.

46 Mischler, *Raising Reds*, 88.

47 Woodland was not the only camp to promote interracial camping. Camp Wo-Chi-Ca was also integrated, but these two camps strayed far from the social norm of American camping.

48 Untitled document, series 4, box 1, folder 27; Studer, "Camp Woodland's Designs for Integration," 1.

49 "Goals of Camp," n.d., p. 12, series 4, box 1, folder 27.

50 "Goals of Camp," 13.

51 Camp Woodland Parents Association and Intercultural Committee, series 4, box 1, folder 29; Norman Studer, "Camp Woodland's Designs for Integration," n.d., p. 18, series 4, box 2, folder 1.

52 Here, Studer is referencing the song "John Henry." Folklorist Alan Lomax also specifically referenced this song to illustrate themes of interracial solidarity in American

folklore. In an article in the *New York Times Magazine* from 1947, Lomax highlighted the lyric "A MAN ain't nothin' but a man!," explaining that "in this sense America has reached out and welcomed the folklore of all the minority groups, racial and national. Jim Crow prejudice has been inoperative in folklore." Alan Lomax, "America Sings the Saga of America," *New York Times Magazine*, January 26, 1947, 41.

53 Studer, "Camp Woodland's Designs for Integration," 9, 11–12, 15.
54 Studer, 13. The memorial was never finished because the camp closed in 1962, prior to its completion. Official efforts to revival her memory began in 1970 when Ulster County officials declared March 12 Sojourner Truth Day.
55 Studer, 13, 14.
56 Zoe Burkholder, *Color in the Classroom: How American Schools Taught Race, 1900–1954* (Oxford: Oxford University Press, 2011), 151.
57 Peter Runge and Jodi Boyle, *Norman Studer Papers* (finding aid), Archives of Public Affairs and Policy, 2003, rev. 2012–13, http://library.albany.edu/speccoll/findaids/apap116.htm, accessed July 11, 2016. However, the camp lost advertising and received several pieces of hate mail.
58 Katie Wechalen, letter to Norman Studer, September 12, 1961; Joanie Bernhard, letter to Norman Studer, October 23, 1961, series 4, box 1, folder 26.
59 Karl E. Klare, letter to Roger W. Bowen (SUNY New Paltz president), October, 19, 1997, series 4, subseries 3, box 1, folder 4.
60 Studer, *Woodland Sampler*.
61 Conard, "Pragmatic Roots of Public History," 115, 117.
62 Conard, 117.
63 Shari Segel Goldberg, email to Neil Larson, Hudson Valley Study Center, October 31, 1997, series 4, subseries 3, box 1, folder 4. Many others who also responded that Woodland influenced their career decisions were primary, secondary, or postsecondary educators.
64 Klare, letter to Bowen.

Carter G. Woodson

A Century of Making Black Lives Matter

Burnis Morris

If a race has no history, if it has no worth-while tradition, it becomes a negligible factor in the thought of the world, and it stands in danger of being exterminated.

—Carter G. Woodson
"Negro History Week," 1926

Carter G. Woodson has a well-deserved reputation as a scholar who worked to commemorate Black achievement, and he founded and funded a research journal, initially from his meager earnings as a public schoolteacher in Washington, DC.[1] Along the way, an adoring public, especially the Black press, recognized his efforts, using terms such as *founder* and *father* to describe his relationship to Negro History Week and Black History Month. However impressive such terms of endearment, used without elaboration, they fail to capture the totality of what his life's work has meant for his profession, education, social justice movements, culture, and America.

Woodson's influence in the fields of history, public history, and African American history is simplified and marginalized by scholars and admirers who focus solely on his contributions to celebratory history-making, including those who favorably compare Woodson to other Black intellectuals[2] or support a museum created in his honor.[3] Woodson is not only the pioneer in Black history or a founder of radical public history. His life's work fundamentally altered America's understanding of history and brought it closer to truth.

Woodson's work involved more than memorizing dates and statistics, observing achievements one week a year or studying a single course in school.[4] He was driven by a deep concern about the devaluation of Black lives and culture, and he developed and carried out a program for restoration that envisioned Blacks overcoming the racist shackles of slavery and segregation. His vision for change was sweeping. Embracing the relationship between historical accuracy and social justice, Woodson led a revolution in education through which Black progress and respect would be achieved. In response to a colleague at a Black college who thought Woodson failed to recognize the progress his institution was making by offering Black history courses, Woodson explained why the institution's program was insufficient: "I have in mind the larger problem of the thorough education of the Negro in the light of what he is and what he hopes to be."[5]

Comparisons, understandably, will be made to other social justice causes the Woodson program antedates, particularly the Black Lives Matter (BLM) activism of recent years, which has campaigned against the murders of Black people, often at the hands of police. BLM's and Woodson's concerns may also be compared to those of journalist Ida B. Wells, whose opposition to White vigilante justice against Blacks in 1892 led to the vandalizing of her Memphis newspaper. She headed an international campaign against lynching and was a founder of the National Association for the Advancement of Colored People (NAACP) in 1909. Although she complained in her diary that Woodson did not acknowledge her work in this area, Wells was one of his supporters and attended at least one Negro History Club meeting in 1930.[6] Wells also was president of the Negro Fellowship League in Chicago, where she relocated after Memphis. Woodson spoke to the league in 1915 on his first book promotion.[7]

The NAACP estimated that 2,522 Blacks were lynched from 1885 to 1918,[8] but Woodson compared protests against lynching unfavorably to his cause. He used a racist education system as a metaphor for violence against Black minds, declaring his program was "much more important than the anti-lynching movement, because there would be no lynching if it did not start in the schoolroom. Why not exploit, enslave or exterminate a class that everybody is taught to regard as inferior?"[9]

Woodson's program itself was a Black-lives-matter cause, and it is better understood through its mission, which addressed the Black past and future, helped make American education more inclusive, and laid a foundation for the emergence of contemporary movements. Thus this notion of a Woodson century is explored using these trajectories: (1) Woodson's preparation for becoming a Black liberator, as he assumed the role of the century; (2) the state of Black historiography before Woodson, characterized by mis-education, misrepresentation, and omission of Blacks in history; (3) Black historiography during the Woodson years, a period in which he intervened to save Blacks from extinction or extermination, part of a multifaceted public education program for which he ultimately left academe to engage in full-time radical public history; (4) the intergenerational impact of Woodson's work involving history, Black rights, education, and a Woodson manifesto, issued with the publication of *The Mis-Education of the Negro*; and (5) the normalization of Woodson by political leaders and pop culture.

Role of the Century: Becoming a Liberator
Preparation for the role Carter Godwin Woodson would play as a Black liberator originated in rural New Canton, Virginia, where he was born December 19, 1875. He was the son of former enslaved parents James Henry Woodson and Anne Eliza Woodson, born when the Reconstruction era was concluding.[10] As a child, Woodson studied a William McGuffey fifth-grade reader and was obsessed with a character who studied hard, played hard, and was well liked by other boys—compared to another character who did not study before playing, was disliked by playmates, and was unsuccessful in life. The boy who impressed Woodson was successful in college and in later life—and Woodson decided to go to college and be like him.[11]

Woodson's illiterate father, a Civil War veteran, made the greatest impression on him, with Woodson inheriting his father's values of dignity and self-respect, despite hardship and other issues restricting Black lives. The young Woodson read newspapers to his father and to illiterate Black coal miners in West Virginia, where he worked as a miner himself for six years. It is within this environment that Woodson's world view began to take shape. He said one of the best-educated people he knew was Oliver Jones, an illiterate miner and Civil War veteran, who had an impressive library of books, newspapers, and magazines and compensated Woodson with food for reading to other miners. Jones had not been mis-educated because he had learned properly from what was read to him.[12] John Hope Franklin notes that the foundation of Woodson's advocacy of education and well-designed instructional materials meeting the specific needs of students was developed from such experiences.[13]

Woodson's father, a carpenter, helped build Huntington, West Virginia, after he moved the family from Virginia. The elder Woodson and several former enslaved people had assisted Collis P. Huntington in completing the Chesapeake and Ohio Railway in 1870, which was followed by establishment of the City of Huntington. The family moved back to Virginia in the early 1870s, before Carter Woodson was born, and returned to Huntington in the 1890s. The younger Woodson graduated from all-Black Huntington's Douglass School in 1896 and returned as its principal from 1900 to 1903.[14]

Woodson considered West Virginia the turning point in his life, but he expanded his world view after leaving Douglass. In 1903, he also graduated with the equivalent of a two-year degree from Berea College in Kentucky. That same year, Woodson heard educator Booker T. Washington, the undisputed leader of Black America, speak for the first time, in Lexington, Kentucky, and was awestruck by Washington's oratory. He also embarked on a new career as a supervisor of schools in the Philippines in 1903. He witnessed Filipinos being taught about other cultures but with no appreciation for their own circumstances, a situation he likened to the plight of Black education in America.[15]

After returning from the Philippines, Woodson earned undergraduate and graduate degrees in history at the University of Chicago, attended Harvard University for a doctorate in history, studied at the Sorbonne in Paris, and taught for ten years in the District of Columbia. Completion of his PhD in history, in 1912, made him the second African American recipient of that degree at Harvard, the first being W. E. B. Du Bois. Woodson also was the only person of former slave parentage who received a doctorate in history from any institution. His Harvard education also made possible his credentials for practicing the scientific method he advocated so zealously for historiography.[16]

Historiography before Woodson

University of Chicago professor Robert E. Park, a pioneer in urban sociology, sponsored two conferences in Chicago in 1915 to recruit students to the study of Negro folklore and expected the students to attend at their own expense. Recruits included Woodson, but he declined the invitation. He said he was not a folklorist, and the plan seemed unworkable.[17] That summer, Woodson was pursuing an idea more suited to his training, which resulted in his founding the Association for the Study of Negro Life and History (ASNLH), whose name was later revised to the Association for the Study of African American Life and History (ASALH).

Park, a former Booker T. Washington assistant, eventually joined forces with Woodson and became the only White president (1917–20) of ASNLH/ASALH.[18] The formation of the association, in 1915, is considered the launch of the Black History Movement, and for the purposes of the present argument, it also represents commencement of the Woodson Century of Making Black Lives Matter. The cause he pursued, like a general at war, offered freedom, empowerment, and optimism when few people outside Black America valued African American lives. Many within the Black community doubted he would succeed.

One of the historians Woodson mentored, Lawrence Reddick, curator of the Schomburg Collection at the New York Public Library, helped popularize the saying that "the history of Negro historiography falls into two divisions, before Woodson and after Woodson."[19] The fact that Woodson dominated the Black historiography field for so long (1915–50) lends credence to Reddick's claim. The first division, a period in which it was commonly believed Blacks had contributed little to society, was marked by systematic denial of their basic rights of citizenship, aided by biased, unsavory White historians. These historians were described by Franklin as "willing accomplices in the conspiracy to degrade a whole race of men."[20]

Racism and disrespect ran through all segments of White society during the pre-Woodson period, even among those not usually considered enemies of Black people. For instance, Theodore Roosevelt, who later would be both praised for his bravery and vilified for inviting a Black man, Booker T. Washington, to dinner at the White House, said in 1895, six years before his ascendance to the presidency, "a perfectly stupid race can never rise to a very high plane; the Negro, for instance, has been kept down as much by lack of intellectual development as anything else."[21]

Blacks were becoming a "negligible factor" in the world, Woodson said on numerous occasions.[22] He also repeated the point of view he had heard from Washington in Lexington: that conditions for African Americans were so dire they might be forced into serfdom. Woodson carried Washington's thought with him for decades and seemed motivated to avoid serfdom for Blacks and prevent their extinction.[23] As farfetched as it might seem today, Woodson's anxieties about the future of African Americans were not overblown. Franklin also discovered such sentiments among White historians in the nineteenth century: "In the generation following the Civil War several historians expressed the greatest grief that Negroes had been emancipated, for, they argued, it would only be a matter of time—a few decades at the most—and all Negroes would disappear. History, they claimed, clearly demonstrated that Negroes could not survive as free men."[24]

Woodson respected the works of several nineteenth-century writers of Black history who preceded him—including Booker T. Washington, William C. Nell, William Wells Brown, and George Washington Williams. Of Washington's *The Story of the Negro: The Rise of the Race from Slavery*, Woodson's *Journal of Negro History* stated the book was "one of the first successful efforts to give the Negro a larger place in history."[25]

Black intellectuals of the late nineteenth century, because they carried the burden of being Black, had much difficulty pursuing scholarship. Franklin found their qualifications and training were questioned at every turn.[26] The American Negro Academy was founded in 1897 and included Woodson as a member. The Academy sponsored forums and disseminated documents; however, there was nothing close to a history movement until Woodson set one in motion.[27]

Historiography after Woodson's Radical Public History Intervention

Officially, Woodson crafted an intervention program that began September 9, 1915, with the founding of ASNLH. This date represents the beginning of what Reddick considered the second division of Black historiography, when Woodson crusaded as teacher, scholar, and promoter, contradicting myths of Black inferiority and depictions of Black people as society's burdens. The Woodson cause "proclaimed as its purposes the collection of sociological and historical data on the Negro, the study of peoples of African blood, the publishing of books in this field, and the promotion of harmony between the races."[28]

Other early historians involved in the Black History Movement included Arthur Schomburg, founder of what became the Schomburg Center for Research in Black Culture in New York. Schomburg became an assistant editor of the *Journal of Negro History*, but he reportedly had responded negatively in his initial reaction in 1916 when Woodson founded the *Journal*. Schomburg had considered the publication a competitor "stealing our thunder in which we are pioneer."[29] John E. Bruce, a journalist, also was a Woodson ally. Bruce founded the Negro Historical Society of Brooklyn and was a life member of ASNLH.[30] Several individuals associated with the National Urban League and NAACP participated in the history movement, but ASNLH and Woodson were its cornerstone.

Having been trained as an academic historian, Woodson served short stints as dean at Howard University (1919–20) and the West Virginia Collegiate Institute (1920–22). However, for most of the four decades he spent pursuing the cause, Woodson was a radical public historian employed by no university or college. He had clashed with the president of Howard University, which led to his firing, but it worked out well because Woodson valued his independence and seemed to thrive in situations where he was in control. As his own boss, Woodson created the *Journal of Negro History* for scholarly research articles; Associated Publishers (1922), a book-publishing firm he founded because many book publishers would not publish manuscripts from Black writers; Negro History Week (1926); and *Negro History Bulletin* (1937), primarily for educators.

Ten years into his program, Woodson said, "It has made the world see the Negro as a participant rather than as a lay figure in history."[31] A decade later, Jackson found the first twenty years of ASNLH's activities should be separated into two periods: The first ten years (1915–25) involved ASNLH as a mostly scholarly organization behaving as most historical societies did. In the second ten years (1925–35), it played a unique, double-role addressing both scholars and general audiences. Jackson described ASNLH as an agency that had reached maturity: "Its influence has extended from Washington, DC, to every state in the union and to foreign countries. The Association, today, we must repeat, is a thing of the people."[32]

Public Education Program

The audience Woodson targeted required schooling in this new discipline; therefore, Woodson established a public education program, which essentially became the movement, incorporating his publications, Negro History Week, and outreach to schools. Negro History Week was the most conspicuous element of the overall education program, and Woodson believed the celebration was his most successful endeavor. The dates he chose for observance, the second week in February, coincided with the birthdays of abolitionist and diplomat Frederick Douglass and President Abraham Lincoln. Woodson explained Negro History Week: "It is not so much a Negro History Week as it is a History week. We should emphasize not Negro History, but the Negro in history. What we need is not a history of selected races or nations, but the history of the world void of national bias, race hate, and religious prejudice. There should be no indulgence in undue eulogy of the Negro. The case of the Negro is well taken care of when it is shown how he has influenced the development of civilization."[33]

Woodson functioned like a superintendent of schools. He created a home studies department with correspondence courses and awarded certificates. The department's faculty included distinguished scholars: Charles H. Wesley, instructor in history, who was the third Black student awarded a history PhD from Harvard and first Black Guggenheim Fellow; Alain L. Locke, instructor in African art, who was the first African American Rhodes Scholar, well-known for his association with the New Negro, or Harlem Renaissance; E. Franklin Frazier, instructor in sociology, who was a prominent Black sociologist; Luther P. Jackson, instructor in education, who was a Virginia State College professor and expert on Black history in Virginia; Charles S. Johnson, instructor in social psychology, who would become the first Black president of Fisk University in Nashville; and Woodson, instructor in anthropology.[34]

A publicity component of the education program led to larger exposure in Woodson's message-selling. However, the publicity on occasion conflicted with the overall mission. He oversold progress to motivate followers. Woodson hinted at this conflict in the draft of a 1946 report, when he stated objectives would take longer to accomplish than he had previously admitted, balancing optimism and pessimism in penciled revisions. He wrote that the "public has been encouraged to believe that the difficulties involved are being rapidly removed."[35] However, progress had slowed from delays in printing and the unavailability of records in Europe and Africa because of World War II.

Woodson became the world's major resource for Black history facts, responding to inquiries from across the globe. He also used his office like a university archive—collecting rare books and manuscripts—and he urged average people to document and preserve family histories for conveyance to him or the Library of Congress. He asked Black newspapers to preserve their files and turned to ASNLH members who were requested to "write the life histories of the 'near great' but useful Negroes of whom editors and authors take no account."[36]

Woodson himself was a newspaper columnist and pundit who used the press as a public education arm. Through much of the 1930s and 1940s, his columns promoted Negro History Week, supported civil rights issues, and attacked segregation, mis-education, Black leadership, and economic conditions. He embraced Africa against colonial powers and questioned America's ability to lead the world while holding down Blacks.[37]

In another aspect of Black life, Woodson was a strong supporter of the arts, imploring writers and actors to respect Black culture,[38] and he employed two Harlem Renaissance writers—Langston Hughes and Zora Neale Hurston—as assistants. Woodson's views about Black art seemed to conform to a philosophy Du Bois expounded during a 1926 speech at the NAACP ceremony where Woodson was awarded the organization's Spingarn Medal. Du Bois burdened artists with using truth "as the one great vehicle of universal understanding."[39]

Woodson was concerned, too, about whether White scholars would eventually respect African American lives. He found a little hope during his review of *Storm over the Land: A Profile of the Civil War*, a book by Carl Sandburg (1878–1967). Woodson wrote, "It is very much a humanized story. Even the Negro—something unusual for an American history—is made an actor in the drama. The Negro figures as a person rather than merely as a thing about which there was a much-regretted quarrel."[40]

In the 1940s, his final decade, Woodson reminded young people of his progress and seemed to warn future generations engaged in social justice movements not to lose ground: "These people whose civilization was marked by the kerosene lamp, the wash tub, the hoe, and the ox-cart disappointed the prophets who said they would be exterminated; and on the contrary they enrolled themselves among the great. What will you do in the day of the moving picture, the radio, and the aeroplane? If we do not take hold where they left off and advance further in the service of truth and justice, we are unworthy to claim descent from such a noble people."[41]

As he prepared to leave the stage, Woodson was incensed Negro History Week had become so popular that it was gaining interest among charlatans and exploiters who had different agendas, and for good reason.[42] Many Communist Party members in the 1940s tried to claim Negro History Week was the party's invention, and party members tried to seize control of several ASNLH branches in the late 1940s and early 1950s, when they openly competed with ASNLH in celebrating Negro History Week in New York.[43]

Gunnar Myrdal was a notable skeptic of Woodson's program. In *An American Dilemma: The Negro Problem and Modern Democracy*, Myrdal argued that many in the Black History Movement were engaged in propaganda activities, and he complained their enthusiasm in promoting Black accomplishments and racial pride was divisive.[44] Myrdal appeared to ignore the fact that on matters of race, the official US policy was divisive. Segregation was the law of the land until the US Supreme Court's decision in 1954, in *Brown v.*

Board of Education. Woodson wanted Blacks to make the most of the difficult hand segregation dealt them and to overcome the misinformation White historians, policy makers, and other dividers had forced on African Americans. Woodson observed that there was an abundance of propaganda, not from his movement, but from the side he was battling. He frequently referred to White historians as propagandists because they were often dishonest about African Americans.[45]

Woodson, in rejecting Myrdal's criticism, questioned the validity of Myrdal's research and methodology, noting the Swedish author had had few contacts with Blacks. Woodson also charged that Myrdal's study misinformed the public, and he challenged its thoroughness: "What the work contains has much value beyond the shadow of a doubt, but what it does not contain would have been a nearer approach to the truth. The world is suffering today from many ills which have resulted from the half truth."[46] *An American Dilemma* did not question Woodson's scholarship; Myrdal's landmark study clearly benefitted from Woodson's research, as a glance at Myrdal's list of citations indicated. Still, he ungenerously complimented Woodson, in a footnote, quoting the article by Reddick about Woodson's dominance in Black historiography.[47]

Another influential book, August Meier's *Negro Thought in America, 1880–1915* barely mentioned Woodson's program, but it did not ignore Woodson. The fact that Meier chose to conclude the period of his analysis the year Woodson founded ASNLH further bolstered Reddick's assertion about Black historiography and Woodson. Meier considered Woodson "less chauvinistic and far more scholarly" than the intellectuals who preceded him.[48]

The substance of the cause—scholarly research and education—was more important than public protest, which is evidenced by Woodson's comments, found earlier in this chapter, assigning less significance to the anti-lynching movement. Though he was an ardent supporter of civil rights, Woodson prided himself on avoiding the appearance of commingling research and social protest movements. He supported both, but separately, to avoid confusion. Woodson insisted his research associates maintain appropriate public distance from protests and politics, as he believed he did. He was critical of people he identified as "race leaders" and urged his associates to avoid the label, fearing their research would be compromised. He was especially tough on Jackson, the Virginia State College professor who skipped an ASNLH annual meeting in Detroit to make a presentation at an NAACP meeting. Woodson reprimanded Jackson, saying, "You made a mistake in not going. May God help you to repent! You are a historian, not a race leader."[49]

Woodson's Impact

Woodson's longevity on the public stage has allowed scholars to evaluate his work, from his contributions to historical research to his philosophical leanings, from a variety of perspectives. Franklin argued that Woodson's contributions to American historiography were "significant and far-reaching and that the program for rehabilitating the place of the Negro in American history has been stimulated immeasurably by his diverse and effective efforts."[50] Franklin argued that because of Woodson's work, "for the first time in the history of the United States, there is a striking resemblance between what historians are writing and what has actually happened in the history of the American Negro."[51]

Jacqueline Goggin found Woodson's success in correcting the historical record and his use of census data, marriage registers, birth and death certificates, letters, diaries, and oral histories in his research caused other historians to consider Woodson's approach. "Typically," Goggin wrote, "Woodson provided coverage on all aspects of the black experience."[52] Woodson was also a leader in publishing journal articles involving women. During the Woodson years, his *Journal of Negro History* published more articles by women writers and subjects about women than any other major historical journal, Goggin pointed out.[53]

Pero Dagbovie studied three intellectuals identified as twentieth-century iconoclasts: Woodson, sociologist E. Franklin Frazier, and cultural nationalist Harold Cruse, chosen because of their outspokenness and ability to challenge colleagues from within the intellectual group they critiqued. Dagbovie concluded that Woodson "was the only member of this iconoclastic cadre who attempted to solve the problems he described with concrete, practical programs."[54]

Daryl Michael Scott discovered a Woodson manuscript, lost since 1921, and found Woodson was far more sympathetic to Black elites in the newly found manuscript than he would become a decade later in *The Mis-Education of the Negro*.[55] Kelly Miller associated Woodson's philosophy with Marcus Garvey's race-consciousness and self-determination.[56] Tony Martin identified Garvey's school of thought as cultural nationalist, with group identity based on African heritage. Garvey, Martin said, "used history to establish a grievance, instill black pride, and point a way for eventual race emancipation."[57]

V. P. Franklin and Bettye Collier-Thomas associated Woodson with race vindication, citing his publication of the *Journal of Negro History* on behalf of the truth and evidence he provided about Black contributions in history.[58]

Dagbovie described Woodson's views as a "straightforward, bourgeoisie, economic nationalist platform,"[59] largely because he urged Blacks to buy from Black businesses and invest in and improve their communities. Gaines argued Woodson's philosophy was "a mix of subdued Black Nationalist and Social Reconstructionism," whose progressive proponents included Harold Rugg, George Counts, and William Watkins. Accordingly, Woodson tended to be more Black nationalist than two of his education contemporaries, W. E. B. Du Bois, a founder of the NAACP (which had a civil rights and social justice agenda), and Benjamin E. Mays, president of Morehouse College and the Atlanta Board of Education.[60] On the other hand, Scott argued that Woodson was not a nationalist but that he "spoke to the ethnic and racial underpinnings of black nationalism."[61]

Empowerment across Generations

Woodson's approach to history, Dagbovie observed, became "a practical tool of self-empowerment and liberation," and his contributions "served as useful object lessons for practitioners of the modern Black studies movement. Dimensions of Woodson's approach can be beneficially adapted to Black studies paradigms of the twenty-first century."[62]

Woodson has been praised for his work molding an understudy group of younger historians who followed him and made their own mark.[63] The most honored historian of this group, John Hope Franklin (1915–2009), was awarded the Presidential Medal of Freedom by Bill Clinton. Woodson's book *The Negro in Our History* dominated the Black history field for at least twenty-five years, until it was supplanted by a Franklin book, *From Slavery to Freedom: A History of African Americans*, first published in 1947. August Meier and Elliott Rudwick found that Woodson's dreams of greater recognition of Blacks in history by mainstream White historians and the enthusiastic embrace of history by Black people were both accomplished after his death.[64]

Beyond academe, Woodson had little trouble teaching audiences through the Black press, which followed the public education program in lockstep almost from the time the Black history movement began. Just before he died, *Ebony* magazine asked Woodson to name the fifteen outstanding events in Negro History from 1619 to 1940, which it published using pictorial reproductions in February 1950. The list covered the landing of the first Blacks in 1619 through the Great Migration.[65]

Woodson's lifelong focus on correcting and explaining history and saving African American lives, over time, was well received across the spectrum and across generations in the Black community. Black activists on all sides in the 1960s found the Woodson mystique appealing. Many were attracted by his attacks on establishment institutions failing their missions or profiting from segregation and other racist policies. His ability to speak out about race, without fear of retribution, was a source of racial pride.

Woodson was political but not partisan, a freethinker concerned about the human condition, rarely showing interest in any political dogma—other than truth and justice for people of African descent. Meier and Rudwick observed that Woodson avoided ideological controversy,[66] and Du Bois claimed Woodson never read Marx.[67]

Many audiences were receptive to Woodson's ideas, perhaps because he was encouraging commonsense values to save a race through popularizing the Black past and securing its respect. Still, messages of self-respect among Blacks and equality with Whites were radical ideas in the broader American public during the first half of the twentieth century.

Woodson was a symbol of the Black independence he advocated. The fact that he expressed pride in reporting that 97 percent of his support came from the Black community after the arrival of the Great Depression (when he lost support from White philanthropists) provided a certain cachet and bravado—an unconstrained Black man in an age of white supremacy. He was opposing segregation but demanding African Americans make the most of their situation.[68] He accused some members of Black leadership of being bought off by White politicians and asked Blacks to become politically and economically independent.[69]

The Woodson arguments were in step with rising aspirations in Black America, but progress did not follow a straight line. Meier and Rudwick suggested "a lost generation" or "generation gap" in Black scholars' output because of social changes after World War II that provided greater opportunities for African Americans.[70] However, Meier and Rudwick also found Black scholarly output sustained enormous growth beginning in 1960, and Black history became "fashionable" by the end of the decade, largely because of the civil rights movement.[71] Under these conditions, Woodson's work gained new relevance, and acceptance of his cause spanned the ideological spectrum.

Civil Rights

Many activists in the civil rights and social justice communities were among the history movement's strongest supporters. For instance, Malcolm X (1925–65) was among the leaders influenced by Woodson, disclosing in an autobiography that "Carter G. Woodson's *Negro History* [*The Negro in Our History*] opened my eyes about black empires before the black slave was brought to the United States and the early Negro struggles for freedom."[72]

The files of the Martin Luther King Jr. Center for Nonviolent Social Change show that Martin Luther King Jr. (1929–68) embraced Negro History Week as a young leader. King was the featured speaker at a Boston sorority's Negro History Week event and titled his address "The Negro Past."[73] Another speaking request included an invitation from Woodson's ASNLH and National Education Association (NEA) during a pre-history-week event on February 3, 1967, when ASNLH and NEA were to present a filmstrip about "The Negro in American History."[74] King's statements and speeches about Black history, especially about race relations and mis-education, often revealed his intellectual ties to Woodson. For instance, in a May 1967 address, King said, "The white majority has equally been harmed and reinforced in its prejudices by its ignorance of Negro history. In the operation of a system of segregation, whites had little personal communication with Negroes and without a literature that bridged the barriers, two peoples of the same nationality were substantially strangers to each other."[75]

Woodson and King had mutual friends who connected their movements, but it could not be determined whether the two men ever met. However, one of King's biographers was Reddick, the Woodson disciple, and Woodson was friendly with King's Morehouse College mentor, Benjamin E. Mays, himself a civil rights leader and influential educator. Woodson's work inspired other civil rights workers such as John Lewis (1940–2020), former chair of the Student Nonviolent Coordinating Committee (SNCC), later a US representative from Atlanta, who spoke fondly of Woodson at the opening of the National Museum of African American History and Culture in 2016. In 2015, Lewis was awarded the John Hope Franklin Lifetime Achievement Award by ASALH at its centennial meeting in Atlanta.[76] US Representative James Clyburn (1940–), the third-ranking Democrat in the House of Representatives and a former civil rights leader, was the keynote speaker at ASALH's Black history luncheon in 2017.

Mays (1894–1984) was influenced by Woodson's advocacy of Black history being taught in schools and believed it was fundamental for Blacks and Whites in having a well-rounded education.[77] He noted Woodson's death in a newspaper column.[78] In 1980, Mays addressed ASALH's annual meeting in New Orleans with a speech titled "I Knew Carter G. Woodson." Early in their relationship, Mays arranged for Woodson to speak at a meeting of the Florida Association of Social Workers in Tampa, but the executive director of the Welfare League and head of the Community Chest feared Woodson's statements on race relations would be unwelcome.[79] Mays tipped off Woodson to avoid trouble, and he recalled the moment Woodson began his address: "The first thing he said was, 'I want to set your minds at ease. We don't want your white women.' You could almost feel a moment of tension turn into a moment of relaxation."[80]

Black Panther Party

Links between Woodson's ideas and the Black Panthers' were as apparent as those between Woodson's thinking and King's. A Woodson philosophy of education, for instance, can be gleaned from the October 1966 Black Panther Party Platform and Program. Demand number five on the ten-point list stated,

> We want education for our people that exposes the true nature of this decadent American society. We want education that teaches us our true history and our role in the present-day society.
>
> We believe in an educational system that will give to our people a knowledge of self. If a man does not have knowledge of himself and his position in society and the world, then he has little chance to relate to anything else.[81]

Eldridge Cleaver, years before he joined the Black Panther leadership, displayed signs of a shared world view with Woodson in his first published essay, which criticized Blacks for defining culture and themselves through White standards.[82] In *Mis-Education*, Woodson had urged African Americans to develop their own standards and not imitate Whites' beliefs.[83] Cleaver's article—written while he was imprisoned in San Quentin, California, and before publication of his 1966 *Soul on Ice* classic—was published by Woodson's successors at the *Negro History Bulletin*. The article was critical of an American system that reinforced negative images of African Americans, views also represented in Woodson's works. Cleaver (1935–98) was known to have read well-known writers in prison.[84]

Mis-Education's message was closely studied by another leader of the Black Panthers, Huey P. Newton (1942–89), who was said to have had a literary connection to Woodson, Du Bois, and several other writers.[85] Matthew W. Hughey found that Newton, who urged his community college to teach a Black history course, "mourned" Woodson's mis-education, and his "discourse on education suggests he was carrying on a legacy from Malcolm, Du Bois, and Woodson."[86]

Woodson argued that many teachers were not equipped to inspire their students, but he urged the better-prepared among them to serve as constructive forces and motivate pupils. "Men of scholarship and consequently of prophetic insight," he said, "must show us the right way and lead us into the light which shines brighter and brighter."[87] Newton's early life appeared to reflect the failures of the education system Woodson described and tried to reform. An early passage in Newton's autobiography, *Revolutionary Suicide*, read like his personal experiences had been part of a Woodson anecdote: "During those long years in the Oakland public schools, I did not have one teacher who taught me anything relevant to my own life or experience. Not one instructor ever awoke in me a desire to learn more or question or explore the worlds of literature, science, and history. All they did was try to rob me of the sense of my own uniqueness and worth, and in the process they nearly killed my urge to inquire."[88]

Another Panther, Stokely Carmichael (Kwame Ture; 1941–98) who popularized the phrase *Black power*, was credited by the press in 1968 for a rising interest in Negro History Week.[89] One of the educators who influenced Carmichael was Sterling A. Brown (1901–89), who served as an honorary pallbearer at Woodson's funeral.[90] Brown's work as a scholar before 1950 has been credited with helping develop American studies and African American studies programs on college campuses.

The Manifesto

Two years before the publication of *The Mis-Education of the Negro* as a book, its debut was in condensed form, as an article on the pages of *Crisis*, the NAACP publication edited by Du Bois. It was spelled *Miseducation*, without the hyphen Woodson used in the book's title. An editor's note explained the occasion, saying that what Woodson had been saying in newspaper columns "has recently unsheathed his sword and leapt into the arena of the Negro press and splashed about so vigorously and relentlessly at almost everything in sight that the black world has been gasping each week."[91]

Mis-Education has joined Woodson's philosophy with other social justice and Black education themes since his death. It exemplifies what Jackson had in mind when he concluded that ASNLH had become a people's movement.[92] The book was intended for popular culture, and one publisher has estimated that more than five hundred thousand copies are in print, making it Woodson's most popular book by far.[93]

Woodson reserved his strongest criticism for education establishments that perpetuated racism. Woodson said he considered "the educational system as it has developed in both Europe and America an antiquated process which does not hit the mark even in the case of the need of the white man himself. If the white man wants to hold on to it, let him do so; but the Negro so far as he is able, should carry out a program of his own."[94]

The book was a call to action urging a revolution in education and rejection of old ideas. Woodson stated, "Only by careful study of the Negro himself and the life which he is forced to lead can we arrive at the proper procedure in this crisis. The mere imparting of information is not education. Above all things, the effort must result in making a man think and do for himself just as the Jews have done in spite of universal persecution."[95]

Gerald Early argued that *"The Mis-Education of the Negro* is probably the single most influential book by a black scholar for a black audience." Early found what Woodson asserted in *Mis-Education* about the connections between the study of Black history and the rise in Black political consciousness "was not exactly new. But no one had articulated it as a full-blown manifesto."[96]

The accumulative response to *Mis-Education* and Woodson's overall cause over several generations prompted *Ebony* magazine to associate Woodson's work with the entire century of Black progress. The magazine profiled Woodson in the lead article of a special section called "Giants of the Century: 1900–2000," which included King and Woodson's contemporaries Mary McLeod Bethune, the former president of ASNLH; Du Bois; and scientist George Washington Carver.[97] *The Mis-Education of the Negro* was named one of the "Great Black Books of the 20th Century." The opening lines of the lead article stated, "One of the most inspiring and instructive stories in Black history is the story of how Carter G. Woodson, the Father of Black History, saved himself for the history he saved and transformed."[98]

Normalizing Woodson

Woodson's ideas were normalized, and the transformation was in full view by the 1970s. Negro History Week was updated, and Gerald Ford began the US presidential tradition of embracing Woodson's objectives and proclaiming

Black History Month in 1976—coincidentally, the year of the nation's bicentennial. Reddick had recommended presidential proclamations soon after Woodson died.[99] Others in recent years have advocated, as Woodson had, that the study of Black history should be undertaken year-round.[100] The US Postal Service in 1984 unveiled a Woodson twenty-cent postage stamp just months after Ronald Reagan signed the bill establishing a federal holiday honoring King.

One of the strongest endorsements of Black history by a US president came in Bill Clinton's 1996 proclamation that acknowledged the cause, though not Woodson by name: "While previous generations read textbooks that told only part of our Nation's story, materials have been developed in recent years that give our students a fuller picture—textured and deepened by new characters and themes. African American History Month provides a special opportunity for teachers and schools to celebrate this ongoing process and to focus on the many African Americans whose lives have shaped our common experience."[101]

Barack Obama, the first Black president, proclaimed Black History Month his first February in office in 2009 and paid respect to Woodson by name: "Since Carter G. Woodson first sought to illuminate the African American experience, each February we pause to reflect on the contributions of this community to our national identity. The history is one of struggle for the recognition of each person's humanity as well as an influence on the broader American culture."[102]

Education and Black History

After King's assassination in 1968, collegiate departments offering Black history courses grew substantially. In American schools, Black History Month became a school-year fundamental. Sam Wineburg and Chauncey Monte-Sano found that "Black History Month still reigns as the crowning example of curricular change" and described Black History Month as a model for gaining access to curricula.[103]

Based on their survey involving students and questions about the most famous people in American history, Wineburg and Monte-Sano concluded, "Some eighty years after Woodson initiated Negro History Week, Martin Luther King Jr. and Rosa Parks have emerged as the two most famous figures in American history, with Harriet Tubman close behind."[104] Others in the top ten, in order, were Susan B. Anthony, Benjamin Franklin, Amelia Earhart, Oprah Winfrey, Marilyn Monroe, Thomas Edison, and Albert Einstein.

Separately, the *New York Times*, in a delayed obituary of Ida B. Wells, stated that many historians consider her the most famous Black woman of her lifetime,[105] and the Museum of African American History in Boston honored the memory of Frederick Douglass with an exhibit that named him the most photographed American of the nineteenth century.[106]

Researchers have recognized Woodson for his involvement in social studies and community engagement. LaGarret King, Ryan Crowley, and Anthony Brown argued that the "volume and significance" of Woodson's scholarship "should place him with the likes of scholars such as Harold Rugg, George Counts, and John Dewey" and urged "social studies educators to examine his pedagogical and curricular efforts as a guide for presenting diverse and rigorous content in classrooms."[107]

Woodson's ideas, of course, have not been universally followed. Just as Woodson and Newton experienced during their times, many educators have difficulty reaching minority students because they often fail to present lessons in terms that relate to their students' environments. Woodson addressed such problems in an allegory involving a businessman in the Philippines with no prior teaching experience, who, Woodson said, out-taught instructors from America's best schools:

> He filled the schoolroom with thousands of objects from the pupil's environment. In the beginning he did not use books very much, because those supplied were not adapted to the needs of the children. He talked about the objects around them. Everything was presented objectively. When he took up the habits of the snake he brought the reptile to the school for demonstration. When he taught the crocodile he had one there. In teaching the Filipinos music he did not sing "Come shake the Apple-Tree." They had never seen such an object. He taught them to sing "Come shake the Lomboy Tree," something which they had actually done.[108]

The Filipino example even today is applicable to learning in many classrooms and disciplines. Jeffery Menzise, for instance, suggested psychology professors should expose students to the works of Black scholars and studies involving Africa: "When studying Carl G. Jung, does the professor include Jung's studies in East African spiritual cultures, and his statements of the power and understanding he embraced because of these experiences? In this author's experience, it is rarely a part of this basis study [of psychology], yet, whenever it is included and given equal respect, the students of African descent benefit greatly."[109]

Pop Culture

The Woodson name has high recognition among Black intellectuals, educators, and opinion leaders, but it is not a name often recognized among the broad American public. Still, Woodson's ideas are popular.

In pop culture, Raymond Winbush found, Lauryn Hill's album *The Miseducation of Lauryn Hill* was an unambiguous, intergenerational reference to Woodson's *Mis-Education*. The phrase has come to symbolize people who have been misled, abused, or misguided. Winbush noted the album "echoes Woodson's central theme of how African American people are deliberately propagandized to unlearn their African self and to imbibe large doses of white supremacy in all that they do."[110]

Author Vashti Harrison was inspired by Woodson and her understanding of Black History Month to write the book *Little Leaders: Bold Women in Black History*. Harrison, in a television appearance, expressed her inspiration in a tone and style that would remind readers of Woodson urging members of ASNLH to write stories about "near great" Negroes.[111] She stated, "The theme of Black History Month when Carter G. Woodson started it was to highlight the stories that are not so big in the mainstream and often neglected throughout history."[112]

The National Museum of African American History and Culture opened with bipartisan support a century after first being proposed in 1916. Shortly before its opening, the museum's founding director, Lonnie Bunch III, elucidating like Woodson explaining how Black history is history,[113] stated, "This is not a *black* museum. This is a museum that uses one culture to understand what it means to be an American."[114]

Conclusion

As a pioneer in Black history and radical public history, Carter G. Woodson set out to reeducate America, return Black achievements to history books, and prevent Blacks from becoming extinct. Beginning more than a century ago, Woodson's cause, the rehabilitation of African Americans' image and an education system that did not serve them, has had profound effects on America's race relations, culture, and overall education. Woodson's resulting legacy also influenced contemporary movements—providing intellectual stimulation, advocating respect for humanity, and demonstrating how to effect change with a cause based on truth, practical ideas, and steadfastness.

The cause Woodson pursued, primarily as a radical public historian not directly affiliated with any academic institution, confronted conditions that endangered the well-being of generations of African Americans, and he sought redress with a well-designed public education program that continues to inspire African Americans and others. He expanded public knowledge about the Black past and weaponized ideas about the possibility of positive change.

Many activists and scholars from all sectors adopted Woodson's cause as well as his methods, which helped reshape American thought on race. Woodson's ideas also influenced curricular changes in the teaching of history in American schools—so much so that, in at least one study, schoolchildren named several Black figures as the most famous Americans in history, speaking volumes about the impact of Woodson's Negro History Week and Black History Month. Only infants among the more than three hundred million Americans today can escape annual celebrations of Black history—but not for long, because they will soon be introduced to Black history as students and media consumers.

A century ago, there was consensus that Black lives did not matter to mainstream America, and it was widely believed Blacks had not accomplished much throughout history. However, the force of a century of Woodson's ideas weakened such thinking. As a scholar and cheerleader, Woodson argued that Blacks had great achievements in the past, and everyone would learn about them when the truth is revealed. Unshackled, he argued, African Americans would prosper. When Woodson began the movement, few people could have imagined Black Nobel Prize winners, a Black president of the US, or a Black artist's painting being bought for $110.5 million.[115]

This chapter does not argue that Woodson and his movement solved America's race problems, but it does suggest Woodson helped provide African Americans and social justice movements with important tools. His work gifted them a script for arguing that Black lives matter and a road map to unleashing the power of grassroots organizing and opportunities for social change. To the history profession, which played a role in devaluing Black lives, Woodson left the possibility for redemption and atonement: he showed fellow historians how to rededicate themselves to truth.

Rather than disappearing after his passing, Woodson's ideas continued to flourish. The resulting stimulus provided by his ideas still resonate and have helped maintain his relevance. The seeds sowed during the first half of what should be called the Woodson Century of Making Black Lives Matter have provided a commonality and nexus that now run deeply through classrooms and American culture. They have brought him recognition among many mainstream historians and influencers whose ranks shunned him when he began prosecuting his cause. Even his old Washington, DC, home office—where he died on April 3, 1950, at seventy-four—has been restored as a National Historic Site, which was opened to the public by the National Park Service in 2017. Nearby is the Carter G. Woodson Memorial Park, which includes a bronze statue of his likeness.

The significance of Woodson's program—once considered unlikely to succeed because it was bold, inclusive, and radical enough to advocate that Black lives matter—now is widely accepted as both mainstream and inspirational.

Notes

1. Epigraph: Carter G. Woodson, "Negro History Week," *Journal of Negro History* 11, no. 2 (1926): 239, https://www.jstor.org/stable/2714171.
2. Michael Eric Dyson, "The Ghost of Cornell West," *New Republic*, April 19, 2015, https://newrepublic.com/article/121550/cornel-wests-rise-fall-our-most-exciting-black-scholar-ghost.
3. "Dr. Carter G. Woodson," Woodson Museum, accessed March 3, 2021, http://www.woodsonmuseum.org/about-us/#dr-carter-g-woodson.
4. Carter G. Woodson, *The Mis-Education of the Negro* (1933; repr., n.p.: Seven Treasures, 2010), loc. 101 of 2437, Kindle.
5. Carter G. Woodson, "Higher Education's Weaknesses Assailed," *Norfolk Journal and Guide*, April 18, 1931, 2.
6. Miriam DeCosta-Willis, *The Memphis Diary of Ida B. Wells* (Boston: Beacon, 1995), 12.
7. "Negro Fellowship League," *Chicago Defender*, July 25, 1915, http://ezproxy.marshall.edu:2048/docview/493321238?accountid=12281.
8. National Association for the Advancement of Colored People, *Thirty Years of Lynching* (New York: National Association for the Advancement of Colored People, 1919): 7.
9. Woodson, *Mis-Education of the Negro*, loc. 169.
10. Burnis R. Morris, *Carter G. Woodson: History, the Black Press, and Public Relations* (Jackson: University Press of Mississippi, 2017), 3–13.
11. Burnis R. Morris, "Carter G. Woodson: The Early Years," 2014, https://asalh.org/about-us/carter-g-woodson-the-early-years-1875-1903/.
12. Carter G. Woodson, "My Recollections of Veterans of the Civil War," *Negro History Bulletin* 7, no. 5 (February 1944): 116.
13. John Hope Franklin, "The Place of Carter G. Woodson in American Historiography," *Negro History Bulletin* 13, no. 8 (1950): 175.
14. Morris, "Carter G. Woodson."

15 Woodson, *Mis-Education of the Negro*, loc. 1849.
16 Morris, *Carter G. Woodson*, 3–13.
17 Carter G. Woodson, "Ten Years of Collecting and Publishing," *Journal of Negro History* 10, no. 4 (1925): 599, http://www.jstor.org/stable/2714140.
18 "University of Chicago Faculty, a Centennial View: Robert E. Park | Sociology," University of Chicago Centennial Catalogues, accessed December 3, 2020, https://www.lib.uchicago.edu/projects/centcat/centcats/fac/facch17_01.html.
19 Lawrence Reddick, "A New Interpretation for Negro History," *Journal of Negro History* 22, no. 1 (1937): 21, http://www.jstor.org/stable/2714314.
20 Franklin, "Place of Carter G. Woodson," 174.
21 John Hope Franklin, "The Dilemma of the American Negro Scholar," in *Black Voices: New Writing by American Negroes*, ed. Herbert Hill (London: Elek Books, 1964), 69.
22 Woodson, "Ten Years of Collecting," 600; Carter G. Woodson, "A Few Pointers on the Observance," *Norfolk Journal and Guide*, January 8, 1938, 9.
23 Carter G. Woodson, "Holding the Negro between Him and the Fire," *Louisiana Weekly*, December 30, 1933, 8.
24 John Hope Franklin, "The New Negro History," *Journal of Negro History* 42, no. 2 (1957): 91, https://www.jstor.org/stable/2715685.
25 "Notes," *Journal of Negro History* 1, no. 1 (1916): 98, http://www.jstor.org/stable/2713522.
26 Franklin, "Dilemma," 69.
27 Walter B. Hill, "Institutions of Memory," *Federal Records and African American History* 29, no. 2 (1997), https://www.archives.gov/publications/prologue/1997/summer/institutions-of-memory.html.
28 Woodson, "Ten Years of Collecting," 600.
29 Tony Martin, *Race First* (Westport, CT: Greenwood, 1976), 83.
30 "Notes," *Journal of Negro History* 9, no. 4 (1924): 9, http://www.jstor.org/stable/2713557.
31 Woodson, "Ten Years of Collecting," 598.
32 Luther P. Jackson, "The Work of the Association and the People," *Journal of Negro History* 20, no. 4 (1935): 385, http://www.jstor.org/stable/2714255.
33 Carter G. Woodson, "The Celebration of Negro History Week," *Journal of Negro History* 12, no. 2 (1927): 107, https://www.jstor.org/stable/2714049.
34 "Notes," *Journal of Negro History* 13, no. 1 (1928): 115, http://www.jstor.org.marshall.idm.oclc.org/stable/2713919.
35 Carter G. Woodson, "Annual Report," 1946, reel 3, Carter Godwin Woodson Papers, Manuscript Division, Library of Congress, Washington, DC.
36 "Notes," *Journal of Negro History* 13, no. 1 (1928): 110.
37 Carter G. Woodson, "Carter G. Woodson Earnestly Urges Union," *Philadelphia Tribune*, August 13, 1931, 9; Woodson, "Dangers of Political Leadership," *Cleveland Call and Post*, November 23, 1946, 4B.
38 Carter G. Woodson, "Negro Writers Loafing," *Atlanta Daily World*, November 17, 1932, 6A.

39 W. E. B. Du Bois, "Criteria of Negro Art," *Crisis* 32 (October 1926): 290–97, http://www.webdubois.org/dbCriteriaNArt.html.

40 Carter G. Woodson, review of *Storm over the Land: A Profile of the Civil War*, by Carl Sandburg, *Journal of Negro History* 28, no. 1 (1943): 90, http://www.jstor.org/stable/2714787.

41 Carter G. Woodson, "The Heritage of the Negro," *Negro History Bulletin* 3, no. 5 (1940): 78.

42 Carter G. Woodson, "Annual Report of the Director," *Journal of Negro History* 30, no. 3 (1945): 251–59, http://www.jstor.org/stable/2715110; Woodson, "Annual Report of the Director," *Journal of Negro History* 32, no. 4 (1947): 407–16.

43 Harold Cruse, *The Crisis of the Negro Intellectual* (New York: Morrow, 1967), 163.

44 Gunnar Myrdal, *An American Dilemma* (New York: Harper & Brothers, 1944), 751–54.

45 "Chicagoans Hear Dr. Woodson," *Chicago Defender*, February 17, 1940, 12.

46 Woodson, review of *Characteristics of the American Negro*, by Otto Klineberg, *Journal of Negro History* 29, no. 2 (1944): 234, https://www.jstor.org/stable/2715320.

47 Myrdal, *American Dilemma*, 751; Reddick, "New Interpretation for Negro History," 21.

48 August Meier, *Negro Thought in America, 1880–1915* (Ann Arbor: University of Michigan Press, 1963), 263.

49 Carter G. Woodson, letter to Luther P. Jackson, November 2, 1943, Luther Porter Jackson Papers, 1772–1960, Accession #1952-1 (35:988), Special Collections and Archives, Johnston Memorial Library, Virginia State University, Petersburg.

50 Franklin, "Place of Carter G. Woodson," 176.

51 Franklin, "New Negro History," 95.

52 Jacqueline Goggin, "Countering White Racist Scholarship," *Journal of Negro History* 68, no. 4 (1983): 360–61, http://www.jstor.org/stable/2717563.

53 Goggin, 365.

54 Pero Dagbovie, *The Early Black History Movement, Carter G. Woodson, and Lorenzo Johnston Greene* (Urbana: University of Illinois Press, 2007), 82.

55 Daryl Michael Scott, introduction to *Carter G. Woodson's Appeal: The Lost Manuscript Edition* (Washington, DC: ASALH Press, 2008), xxii–li.

56 Kelly Miller, "Carter Woodson Is Termed New Marcus Garvey," *Afro-American*, February 11, 1933, 22.

57 Martin, *Race First*, 85. Woodson on occasion seemed to personify such thinking, urging Blacks to establish ties to their African heritage, but he did not support Garvey's thinking on relocating Blacks to Africa. Woodson sought their full recognition as American citizens with equal rights. Woodson also did not use Black history simply to establish grievances; he brought social justice arguments against oppressors for valid reasons, and the sleights to Blacks in history he confronted were well researched.

58 V. P. Franklin and Bettye Collier-Thomas, "Biography, Race Vindication, and African American Intellectuals," *Journal of African American History* 87, no. 1 (2002): 160–74, http://muezproxy.marshall.edu:2130/stable/1562497.

59 Dagbovie, *Early Black History Movement*, 72.

60 Robert William Gaines, "The Educational Thought of Benjamin Elijah Mays" (PhD diss., University of Georgia, 2012), 298, https://getd.libs.uga.edu/pdfs/gaines_robert_w_201208_phd.pdf.

61 Scott, introduction to *Carter G. Woodson's Appeal*, xxv.

62 Dagbovie, *Early Black History Movement*, 62.

63 August Meier and Elliott Rudwick, *Black History and the Historical Profession* (Urbana: University of Illinois Press, 1986), 78, 94–95.

64 Meier and Rudwick, 1.

65 The fifteen events, in order, on Woodson's *Ebony* list are as follows: the arrival of Blacks at Jamestown, Crispus Attucks at the Boston Massacre, Peter Salem at the Battle of Bunker Hill, the passing of the Northwest Territory Ordinance of 1787, the Missouri Compromise, Nat Turner's insurrection, the growth of the abolitionist movement, the launching of the Underground Railroad, the 1850 omnibus bill, the Dred Scott decision, the Civil War; the Reconstruction era, the first Black exodus from the South (1877), the Booker T. Washington era, and the Great Migration. Morris, *Carter G. Woodson*, 118; Carter G. Woodson "The 15 Outstanding Events in Negro History," *Ebony* 5, no. 4 (1950): 42–46.

66 Meier and Rudwick, *Black History*, 280.

67 Dagbovie, *Early Black History Movement*, 23.

68 Woodson, "Dangers of Political Leadership."

69 Carter G. Woodson, "And the Negro Loses His Soul," *Atlanta Daily World*, June 27, 1932, 6.

70 Meier and Rudwick, *Black History*, 124.

71 Meier and Rudwick, 161.

72 Malcolm X, *The Autobiography of Malcolm X* (New York: Random House, 1964), 201.

73 Martin Luther King Jr., "The Negro Past," Dr. Martin Luther King Jr. Center for Nonviolent Social Change, accessed September 25, 2018, http://www.thekingcenter.org/archive/document/negro-past-and-its-challenge-future (URL invalid).

74 George W. Jones, letter to Martin Luther King Jr., December 30, 1966, Dr. Martin Luther King Jr. Center for Nonviolent Social Change, accessed September 25, 2018, http://www.thekingcenter.org/archive/document/letter-george-w-jones-mlk (URL invalid).

75 Martin Luther King Jr., "Importance of Negro History and Independence," May 1, 1967, Dr. Martin Luther King Jr. Center for Nonviolent Social Change, accessed September 25, 2018, http://www.thekingcenter.org/archive/document/importance-negro-history-and-independence (URL invalid).

76 John Lewis, "Grand Opening," September 24, 2016, YouTube, https://www.youtube.com/watch?v=HY3PUmwnheI.

77 Gaines, "Educational Thought of Mays," 286.

78 Benjamin E. Mays, "Mays: A Person like Dr. Drew," *Pittsburgh Courier*, April 29, 1950.

79 Benjamin E. Mays, "I Knew Carter G. Woodson," New Orleans, LA, October 18, 1980, Benjamin E. Mays Papers, Speeches box 10, Manuscript Division, Moorland Spingarn Research Center, Howard University, Washington, DC.

80 Mays.
81 Huey P. Newton, *Revolutionary Suicide* (New York: Harcourt Brace Jovanovich, 1973), 117.
82 Eldridge Cleaver, "As Crinkly as Yours," *Negro History Bulletin* 25, no. 6 (1962): 127, https://www.jstor.org/stable44215711.
83 Woodson, *Mis-Education of the Negro*, loc. 101.
84 *New World Encyclopedia*, s.v. "Eldridge Cleaver," last modified September 18, 2017, http://www.newworldencyclopedia.org/p/index.php?title=Eldridge_Cleaver&oldid=1006809.
85 Matthew W. Hughey, "The Pedagogy of Huey P. Newton," *Journal of Black Studies* 38, no. 2 (2007): 213, http://www.jstor.org/stable/40034976.
86 Hughey, 210.
87 Woodson, *Mis-Education of the Negro*, loc. 1762.
88 Newton, *Revolutionary Suicide*, 22.
89 Peniel Joseph, *Stokely: A Life* (New York: Basic Civitas, 2014), 239.
90 Encyclopedia.com, s.v. "Brown, Sterling," accessed March 3, 2021, https://www.encyclopedia.com/people/history/historians-miscellaneous-biographies/sterling-allen-brown#2871200013; "Honorary Pall Bearer," 1950, series 1, reel 1, part 2, Carter Godwin Woodson Papers, Manuscript Division, Library of Congress, Washington, DC.
91 Carter G. Woodson, "The Miseducation of the Negro," *Crisis* 38, no. 8 (August 1931): 266.
92 Jackson, "Work of the Association," 385.
93 The cover is from Khalifah's Booksellers and Associates' 2005 edition, available to view at https://devontekwatson.files.wordpress.com/2013/10/miseducation-text.pdf.
94 Woodson, *Mis-Education of the Negro*, loc. 139.
95 Woodson, 120.
96 Gerald Early, "The Invisible Intellectual," *New York Times*, April 14, 2002, https://www.nytimes.com/2002/04/14/education/the-invisible-intellectual-a-place-of-our-own.html.
97 "Giants of the Century," *Ebony* 54, no. 4 (1999): 162–83.
98 Lerone Bennett, "Carter G. Woodson, Father of Black History," *Ebony* 54, no. 4 (1999): 156.
99 Lawrence Reddick, "Twenty-Five Negro History Weeks," *Negro History Bulletin* 13, no. 8 (1950): 188, http://www.jstor.org/stable/44174932.
100 Carter G. Woodson, "How about Negro History Year?," *Norfolk Journal and Guide*, January 24, 1942, 8.
101 William J. Clinton, "Proclamation 6863—National African American History Month, 1996," January 30, 1886, available at American Presidency Project, https://www.presidency.ucsb.edu/node/223220.
102 Barack Obama, "Proclamation 8345—National African American History Month, 2009," February 2, 2009, available at American Presidency Project, https://www.presidency.ucsb.edu/node/286127.

103 Sam Wineburg and Chauncey Monte-Sano, "Famous Americans: The Changing Pantheon of American Heroes," *Journal of American History* 9, no. 4 (2008): 1187, https://www.hampshire.edu/sites/default/files/shared_files/Wineburg_Famous_Americans_JAH_1.pdf.
104 Wineburg and Monte-Sano, 1193.
105 Caitlin Dickerson, "Ida. B. Wells: Took on Racism in the Deep South with Powerful Reporting on Lynchings," *New York Times*, March 9, 2018, https://www.nytimes.com/interactive/2018/obituaries/overlooked-ida-b-wells.html.
106 *Picturing Frederick Douglass: The Most Photographed American of the 19th Century*, exhibition, Museum of African American History, Boston and Nantucket, accessed March 3, 2021, https://www.maah.org/exhibits_detail/Picturing-Frederick-Douglass.
107 LaGarret King, Ryan Crowley, and Anthony Brown, "The Forgotten Legacy of Carter G. Woodson," *Social Studies* 101, no. 5 (2010): 215, https://doi.org/10.1080/00377990903584446.
108 Woodson, *Mis-Education of the Negro*, loc. 1849.
109 Jeffery Menzise, *Dumbin' Down* (College Park, MD: Mind on the Matter, 2012), 133.
110 Raymond Winbush, foreword to Menzise, *Dumbin' Down*, i–iii.
111 "Notes," *Journal of Negro History*, 13, no. 1 (1928): 110.
112 Vashti Harrison, interview by Trevor Noah, *The Daily Show with Trevor Noah*, January 15, 2018, http://www.cc.com/video-clips/vfe5eo/the-daily-show-with-trevor-noah-vashti-harrison---sharing-the-triumphs-of--little-leaders--in-black-history---extended-interview.
113 Woodson, "Celebration," 105.
114 Vinson Cunningham, "Making a Home for Black History," *New Yorker*, August 29, 2016, https://www.newyorker.com/magazine/2016/08/29/analyzing-the-national-museum-of-african-american-history-and-culture.
115 Robin Pogrebin and Scott Reyburn, "A Basquiat Sells for a 'Mind-Blowing' $110.5 Million at Auction," *New York Times*, May 18, 2017, https://www.nytimes.com/2017/05/18/arts/jean-michel-basquiat-painting-is-sold-for-110-million-at-auction.html.

Louis C. Jones and the Cooperstown Model

Working at the Nexus of Public Folklore and Public History

William S. Walker

In the 1920s, the famed poet and popular historian Carl Sandburg brought American folk culture to thousands of eager audiences as he crisscrossed the country delivering his unique mixture of lecture, poetry recitation, and folk song performance. In the introduction to *American Songbag*, Sandburg's best-selling songbook, he wrote that he had visited "organizations as diverse as the Poetry Society of South Carolina and the Knife and Fork Club of South Bend, Indiana," as well as "about two-thirds of the state universities of the country." Through these performances, Sandburg showcased what he called the "human diversity of the United States."[1]

Not long after the publication of *American Songbag* in 1927, Louis C. Jones, a student at a small liberal arts college in upstate New York, witnessed one of Sandburg's performances. Two decades later, in 1947, Jones would become president of the New York State Historical Association (NYSHA) in Cooperstown, New York, and later, in 1964, the founder of the Cooperstown Graduate Program (CGP), the country's first master's program designed specifically to train professionals to work in history museums.[2] A literary scholar turned folklorist and public historian, Jones remembered that performance by Sandburg and his subsequent purchase of *American Songbag* as the beginning of a long career at the nexus of folk culture and social history.[3] In the latter half of the twentieth century, the marriage of folklife and history in Cooperstown that Jones cultivated would have a significant effect on the development of progressive public history practice. The fact that these two disciplines were so closely aligned at one of the key hubs for training history museum professionals influenced public historians to emphasize nonelite objects and narratives and present histories that complicated and challenged the status quo at a broad range of museums, historical societies, and historic sites throughout the United States.

For at least three decades, public history scholars and practitioners have recognized the significant intersections between the disciplines of folklife and history in the museum field, as well as the critical importance of public folklore in the development of contemporary public history practice. In the 1987 collection *Folklife and Museums: Selected Readings*, published by the American Association of State and Local History (AASLH), Jones, along with Candace T. Matelic, provided an introductory essay that touted the dual role of folklorists and social historians, beginning in the mid-twentieth century, in moving history museums and historical societies away from elitism and toward a focus on the "folkways" of nonelites.[4] Their essay argued that the rapid growth of outdoor living history museums in the United States

Louis C. Jones in the Folk Art Gallery of the New York State Historical Association, Cooperstown, New York, n.d. Courtesy of the Cooperstown Graduate Program.

in the mid-twentieth century was an important consequence of productive collaborations between folklorists and social historians. The Farmers' Museum in Cooperstown and Old Sturbridge Village in central Massachusetts, both of which opened to the public in the mid-1940s, were emblematic of the burgeoning popularity of folk-inflected museum experiences among history museum visitors. At both sites, staff members combined presentations of material culture with folklife, social history, and the history of technology to craft interactive programs designed to involve visitors in the everyday lives of nineteenth-century Americans. Their success inspired others to build on a model rooted in both social history and folklife research.

The role of folklorists in advancing public history practice accelerated in the 1960s and '70s with the opening of popular living history museums such as Iowa's Living History Farms, Prairietown at Indiana's Conner Prairie, and Old World Wisconsin, as well as the nationwide celebration of the bicentennial of the American Revolution, which was characterized by thousands of programs that centered on community histories, local traditions, and ethnic cultures.[5] This period also witnessed the founding of the annual Smithsonian Festival of American Folklife, which brought tradition bearers from all over the country and the world to the National Mall each summer to demonstrate their skills as well as to talk about their individual experiences and the histories of their communities.[6]

In the updated collection *Folklife and Museums: Twenty-First-Century Perspectives*, which AASLH issued in 2017, public folklorist Robert Baron argues that "three decades ago folklife anticipated issues and practices now more widespread among museums."[7] Smithsonian festival curators, for example, pioneered a collaborative and polyvocal model of exhibition that presaged the practices of community curation and dialogic programming that are common among contemporary public historians. Festival curators practiced what public historians and oral historians have labeled "shared authority": the idea that rather than monopolizing interpretive control, "experts" should craft historical narratives in dialogue with the "subjects" of their research—or, more radically, that they should facilitate the work of individuals and communities as they construct their own narratives and interpretations.[8] The festival continues to involve folklorists, historians, and other scholars, including anthropologists and musicologists, in developing programs on this model. Similarly, folklorists working elsewhere have enriched museums and historical organizations through exhibitions, digital projects, folklife demonstrations, and other public programs.[9] More important, they have brought their high-level skills as cultural intermediaries, or "culture brokers," to collaborative public historical work that involves cocuration and shared authority.[10]

In an essay in the foundational museum history collection *History Museums in the United States: A Critical Assessment*, published in 1989, Gary Kulik, an accomplished public historian who was at that time assistant director of the National Museum of American History, discussed how the intersection of folklife and history in Cooperstown had had a defining effect on public history. He emphasized Cooperstown's pioneering contributions to history museum practice and noted Louis C. Jones's "deep commitment to the history and culture of ordinary people." Kulik wrote of the New York State Historical Association and the Farmers' Museum under Jones, "It was among the very first museums to establish the importance of the commonplace and the everyday.... Through its seminars, its graduate program, and its presence in the profession, it exerted a strong influence."[11] Kulik recognized that the combination of social history and folk culture at NYSHA and the Cooperstown Graduate Program brought something to the field of history museums that was sorely lacking. "NYSHA established the importance of common people," he wrote, "in ways that few American museums ever had."[12]

Although it can be difficult to define the phrases *common people* and *ordinary people* (and as a result, contemporary historians often avoid them), Kulik clearly uses these phrases to refer to nonelites—individuals who, to that point, had not received much attention from historians or history museums. Although social history was not entirely absent from the mainstream of the field in the mid-twentieth century, most historians in this period focused on political history and most history museums were primarily concerned with objects associated with well-known historical figures. At the same time, art museums, most notably the Metropolitan Museum of Art in its American Wing, were interested in collecting and displaying examples of fine craftsmanship, evincing a connoisseur's approach to material culture rather than a social historian's interest in context. Folklorists were more expansive, and perhaps progressive, in their interests. By the mid-twentieth century, folklorists had extended their purview beyond the collecting of ballads that had migrated with Euro-American settlers from the British Isles to Appalachia and were beginning to embrace the concept of *folklife*, a more all-encompassing term than *folklore*, that included material culture, folk art, and performance, as well as songs and tales. Folklife scholars were drawn to things like household decorations, agricultural implements, and arts and crafts created by untrained artists, and they attempted to contextualize these things within broader social and cultural contexts. At NYSHA and the Farmers' Museum, for example, Jones used museum spaces to assemble farmers' and artisans' tools and folk artists' paintings and carvings and to showcase crafts demonstrations, all in the service of highlighting working people's lives and illuminating the social and cultural characteristics of central New York State in the mid-nineteenth century.

From his leadership position in Cooperstown, Louis C. Jones sought to radically transform history museums and public history training in the postwar decades by arguing that they must be more inclusive of a diverse range of people and histories and shift their focus away from elite narratives and elite material culture. Most of his work focused on displaying and interpreting the histories of White working people in nineteenth-century rural New York; however, he also spoke fervently about the need for museums and historical organizations to interpret the histories of other ethnic groups as well as people of color. In the 1950s, a time of anticommunist red-baiting and reactionary politics, Jones was a high-profile advocate for the museum field to become more inclusive of working people's histories, ethnic histories, and the histories of people of color. Later, in the 1960s, in a keynote address to the American Association of Museums, he would speak out strongly for the need to diversify museum staffs, explicitly arguing that museum training programs needed to train more people of color and museums needed to hire more people of color—battles that museum professionals continue to fight today.

Jones was an early prophet for the kind of inclusive field many progressive public historians continue to envision. His efforts were significant and unusual for the time but, ultimately, did not succeed in making historical organizations notably more diverse. The rising Black museum movement of the 1960s and '70s was far more successful in this regard, attracting talented Black scholars and activists to use museums as platforms to share African American histories and advocate for racial equality and social justice.[13] Nevertheless, within the historically White institutions of the public history field, Jones was a powerful voice for change. As a midcentury White liberal scholar, Jones's approach could be paternalistic at times; still, he was pushing the envelope in the field and his commitment to inclusive histories was genuine. His philosophy and approach emanated directly from the ways in which he saw folklife and social history as intertwined disciplines that were especially relevant to museums.

Understanding the relationship between history and folklife is not simply an exercise in enriching public history's genealogy; it has the potential to open productive collaborative pathways for contemporary public history practitioners and press them further in the direction of inclusivity. Public folklorists and public historians share many things in common and the close alliance between these disciplines in the past and present continues to offer transformative opportunities for history to demonstrate its relevance to society. Recognizing how the marriage of social history and folk culture has been critical to public history's development supports the broader goal of making history more inclusive, collaborative, and responsive to the needs of diverse communities in the United States and beyond.

Louis C. Jones's Background

Louis C. Jones had an unusual background for a state historical society director, and his perspective on the necessity of a new direction for history museums grew out of a generative mixture of folklore, history, and progressive politics. Jones came of age in a period that saw heightened interest in working people's stories in the public sphere, and he was fortunate to find positions at institutions that allowed him to pursue his interest in researching and disseminating such narratives. In some ways, the combination of folk culture and progressive politics in Jones's background is similar to that of better-known figures of the mid-twentieth century, such as Alan Lomax, Woody Guthrie, and Pete Seeger, yet unlike them, Jones was not a performer or public personality. He was, however, able to build a stable institutional presence at the New York State Historical Association and, consequently, had an important platform from which to share working people's stories and define public history practice for two and a half decades.

Prior to joining NYSHA as director in 1947, Jones's experiences as a student and young professor profoundly shaped his nascent perspective regarding the value of folk culture and social history and their role in transforming society. As a student in the late 1920s and early 1930s, Jones had a brief association with the radical left, specifically the Socialist Party. While he was an undergraduate at Hamilton College in Clinton, New York, in 1928, Jones reached out to the Socialist Action Committee in New York City as a representative of the college's Emerson Literary Society in an effort to secure "campaign material" that could be distributed, presumably among fellow students. In response, the committee sent fifty copies of their "national platform" and "Norman Thomas's Letter to Progressives."[14] As a doctoral student at Columbia University in the early 1930s, Jones joined the Socialist Party, which was one among several leftist organizations in this period that seized on the economic crisis to offer alternatives to a capitalist system that had seemingly failed to provide even a minimal level of protection to working people.[15] Many young people and college students were attracted to the radical left in this decade because of the economic ravages of the Great Depression as well as the significant cultural vibrancy of leftist-inspired artists, writers, and performers. Jones's direct commitment to the Socialist Party rather than the Communist Party suggests that he was, perhaps, more interested in seeing progressive reforms to the existing system than a revolutionary overthrow of capitalism. At the same time, his willingness to be a dues-paying member of the Socialist Party implies a certain level of commitment to radical politics that "fellow travelers" may not have evinced in this time. Beyond paying dues and distributing some printed materials, it is not clear what activities he undertook as a socialist, and his commitment does not appear to have lasted beyond his years in school. Nevertheless, it is clear that he identified as a liberal, progressive scholar and continued to display a strong interest throughout his career in the lives and cultures of working people, both past and present, and he would publicly describe NYSHA's audience and subject matter as working class. Thus although he may have later tempered somewhat the radical edge of his politics in order to function effectively in the conservative world of museums and postwar US society, he never abandoned his dedication to telling working people's stories. This deep commitment in his own work, and in the institutions he led, was the strongest legacy of his brief involvement with radical leftist politics.

After Columbia, Jones taught briefly at Long Island University and then moved to the New York State College for Teachers in Albany. Trained as a literary scholar, Jones gravitated to folklore as a young professor. This change of direction had much to do with an influential colleague in Albany, Harold Thompson.[16] Thompson had studied with George Lyman Kittredge at Harvard and was closely connected with John and Alan Lomax, providing the bibliography for the Lomaxes' *American Folksongs and Ballads* in 1934. In 1939, he published a popular work of regional folklore called *Body, Boots and Britches: Folktale, Ballads and Speech from Country New York*, which was widely read and well-reviewed in the *New York Times*. Later, he served as president of the American Folklore Society, and in 1944, he and Jones cofounded the New York Folklore Society.

It was Thompson's approach to teaching, however, that had the greatest influence on Jones's development. In the mid-1930s, Thompson began offering a popular undergraduate course on American folk culture, which covered everything from cowboy songs and outlaw tales to spirituals and the blues. Sandburg's *American Songbag* was the textbook, and students were encouraged to sing, dance, and recite poems aloud in class. The diversity of Thompson's content was striking and reflected his commitment to what today we would call multicultural education. Perhaps more significant, however, was the way Thompson empowered his students to become field researchers. Each time he taught the course, Thompson required them to collect folklore and local history from their families, friends, and neighbors. Over time, he built a large archive of student research, from both Albany and later Cornell, and he used their research as the basis for *Body, Boots and Britches*, as well as other projects, including radio broadcasts. Empowering students to conduct research in their home communities was a powerful way not only to gather excellent material from a wide geographical area but also to inspire active citizen engagement with local history and traditions. Thompson's collaborative approach to historical and folkloric research—over 1,600 students participated in research through his courses over more than two decades—offered a model for Jones that he would later adapt at the Cooperstown Graduate Program. By sending students into the field to do their own research, Thompson and Jones made history personal, relevant, and meaningful. This type of research required listening carefully to people's accounts of their lives and those of their families and communities and preserving stories that had not previously been part of traditional historical narratives.

When Thompson moved to Cornell in 1940, Jones took over his course at the New York State College for Teachers and so, for several years, he had the opportunity to adapt Thompson's model and make it his own. In 1946, Jones published "Folklore in the Schools: A Student Guide to Collecting Folklore," which offered practical advice for young people on how to conduct field research, suggesting both the types of materials they should look for as well as how to approach informants. Significantly, Jones recommended seeking out not only songs and tales—the traditional quarry of folklorists—but also "vernacular architecture," "folk art," and "narratives and folk history."

Clearly, he was already thinking broadly about the relationship between folklore, history, and material culture. Moreover, he was expanding the purview of folkloric research to encompass greater contextualization. "Learn as much as you can about each informant," Jones wrote, "where he was born, what kind of life he has lived, where he has lived, what work he has done, and where he learned the folklore you collect."[17] Jones was interested in having young people gather more than just snippets of folk songs or ballads; he was thinking about research in much the same way a social historian would.

While Jones was advocating for a more holistic approach to research that combined folklore, social history, and material culture, he was involved in a significant antidiscrimination project at the New York State College for Teachers. In 1945, White and Black students at the college formed a group to address issues of bias on campus. Subsequently, they invited some faculty members, including Jones, to join them and developed a campus-wide initiative called the "Inter-group Council." The New York State College for Teachers also became one of nine colleges involved in a national research project on intergroup relations sponsored by the National Council of Christians and Jews and the American Council on Education.[18] Both Albany's initiative and the national project corresponded well with the antidiscrimination message famously advanced in Gunnar Myrdal's landmark 1944 study *An American Dilemma: The Negro Problem and Modern Democracy*. Many liberal-minded scholars and educators in this period believed, perhaps naïvely, that increased education and moral suasion could ameliorate, if not eliminate, racial discrimination in the United States. The horrific example of the Holocaust had demonstrated what ethnic and racial bias could lead to, and consequently, liberal educators and social activists hoped that White Americans would recognize through concerted educational efforts the need to challenge discrimination in their own communities. The Albany group was dedicated to challenging all forms of discrimination, including racial discrimination.

Jones was not the leader of Albany's Inter-group Council, but he was on the "College Committee" and played a role in two projects that involved using folk culture to analyze and challenge racial and ethnic discrimination. One of the projects was a folk festival entitled "Out of Many Cultures—America," which included performances of folk dances and songs from various cultures and concluded with the singing of "The House I Live In," the anthem of postwar universalism popularized by Frank Sinatra.[19] The essential message of both the song and the festival was that although people may come from different places and have different cultural backgrounds, deep down they are all Americans and, therefore, share certain essential qualities. In other words, everyone is different, but everyone is the same. This type of universalism was common in the post–World War II era. Many people believed its message of essential commonality among all humans was a powerful remedy for sectarian hatred and ethnoracial bias. Critics would later argue, however, that in glossing over the differences among the world's cultures, universalism was simply another oppressive ideology that supported white supremacy. In this immediate postwar moment, however, the notion that all people, or at least all Americans, were basically similar was intended as a counter to racist ideologies that continued to envision a hierarchy of humanity with White Europeans and Euro-Americans at the top.

Jones's other project was a study of the "Use of Folklore in Intergroup Education," in which he explored how classroom teachers could utilize folklore to "help children from minority groups . . . overcome a sense of inferiority deriving from their chance of birth . . . [and] overcome their scorn and antagonisms for children from other minority groups." He also hoped to "discover if folklore can be used to ease intergroup tensions in the junior and senior high schools."[20] Although not a large study, it demonstrated that Jones saw potential for using folk culture to address social issues through education. In essence, Jones hoped that by stoking young people's pride in their particular cultures, they might be better equipped to succeed in US society. He maintained that collecting and sharing folk culture could generate pride and self-confidence in individuals from multiple backgrounds and demonstrate to broader society that all cultural groups should be valued. To be sure, this was an exceedingly optimistic, not to mention paternalistic, perspective, but it was one for which he had at least anecdotal proof, not only from his study but also from the research his students and Thompson's students had been conducting for over a decade.

Unfortunately, Jones did not stay much longer in Albany to continue this work; nevertheless, he carried into his next position the essential notion that folk culture could be a powerful tool in challenging discriminatory social attitudes. In 1946, Jones's growing success as a scholar of New York State folk culture led philanthropist Stephen C. Clark Sr. to offer him the directorship of the New York State Historical Association. Clark had been responsible for bringing NYSHA to Cooperstown from Ticonderoga, as well as founding the National Baseball Hall of Fame.[21] Relocating to Cooperstown in 1947,

Basket-making display in the Main Barn of the Farmers' Museum, Cooperstown, New York, 2011. Photograph by Aimee Dars Ellis. "Basket Making" by aimeedars is licensed under CC BY-NC-SA 2.0, https://ccsearch.creativecommons.org/photos/ca1c11cc-9e16-48d8-bd36-3e37a33bce7b.

Jones set about developing the historic infrastructure and collections of the Farmers' Museum as well as expanding the institution's other history and art collections. In this work, he brought his folklorist's perspective to historical interpretation, arguing that museums should focus on working people's narratives rather than the objects and stories of the elite.

The organization Jones came to was, in some ways, already moving in the direction of making history more inclusive. Dixon Ryan Fox, who was president of NYSHA from 1929 until his death in 1945, was a well-regarded social historian who had studied under Charles Beard at Columbia, published numerous books and articles on early American social history, and edited the twelve-volume *History of American Life* with Arthur M. Schlesinger Sr.[22] Fox also spearheaded the effort to publish a series of monographs entitled the *History of the State of New York*, which included Arthur C. Parker's pathbreaking volume *A Manual for History Museums*. Other NYSHA staffers—including Clifford Lord, Mary Cunningham, and Janet MacFarlane—pioneered outreach programming and disseminated New York's history to broad audiences across the state. Moreover, NYSHA served as the incubator for the New York Folklore Society, led by Thompson and Jones, which became a separate but still affiliated organization in 1944. Therefore, the organization that Jones took over was primed to lead a transformation in the way history museums approached interpreting the past and present of US society and culture.

Folk Culture's Potential to Transform Historical Organizations

In January 1950, in a keynote address to the annual meeting of the Minnesota Historical Society in Saint Paul, Jones illuminated the vital connection between folklore and history and its relationship to the public history community. In this speech, he made the case that museum professionals' embrace of folk culture and social history would be transformative for US museums and was an absolute necessity in a changing society. Jones prodded his colleagues, stating that the "historical societies of America must start thinking, in a way they have never thought before, about the workingmen and women who are the essential creators and defenders of our democratic faith, about the men and women who caught the later boats and whose children who stand among us as proud, full-fledged citizens."[23] He argued that the key to museums and historical societies remaining relevant and popular was by telling the stories of "the traditional ways of life among our people, and particularly among those classes of our society whose story has been neglected."[24] Working people, immigrants, and others whose stories historians had largely ignored should, he maintained, be the focus of a transformed public history.

Jones reiterated and expanded this message in two articles he published the same year in the brand new *American Heritage* magazine, published by the American Association for State and Local History. Founded in 1940, AASLH had emerged in response to the American Historical Association's neglect and mistreatment of historical societies and other non-university-based organizations. It became a critical professional resource for public historians as they sought to share resources and ideas with one another.[25] In his article, "Folklore in the American Heritage," Jones contended that presenting social, cultural, and labor histories of working people was an area where folklorists and historians could profitably collaborate. He made the case strongly that elite histories, which prioritized analyses of military and political events, were not connecting with the vast majority of public audiences and that instead, historians, folklorists, and museum professionals should work together to research and present working people's stories. At the Farmers' Museum and the New York State Historical Association in Cooperstown, Jones wrote, "We are trying to show with dynamic emphasis . . . that this country was made by the labor of its working people."²⁶ This approach, he maintained, had already shown its popularity with visitors: "The public which comes to us . . . is essentially a working class public, farm people and factory people. And one of the reasons that our visitors are increasing at the rate of 100% each year is, to my way of thinking, because we are interpreting the history of this country in terms of labor and labor is something that the great mass of our people understand."²⁷

In the next issue of *American Heritage*, Jones pressed his message even further. He not only emphasized the importance of working people's histories but directly attacked the exclusivity, elitism, and classism of historical societies across the United States, observing that "the racial complexion of the people [involved with historical societies] is almost entirely old stock Anglo-Saxon, and yet this is often in communities with large groups of people whose ancestors have come from southern and western Europe." Moreover, he wrote, "I have yet to see a Negro and seldom see a Jew attending one of these local historical society meetings, though certainly in some communities the Negro and Jewish families are among the most interesting in the town." Jones expressed his displeasure with this state of affairs, but he offered a rallying cry to the next generation of public historians: "I believe if we tackle this problem with imagination and with consciousness, we can interest the working men and women of all racial stocks in their local and state histories." The key, he contended, was to "shift our emphasis in our museums and in our programs so that their story is included."²⁸ The key, in other words, was to be more inclusive.

In the culminating paragraph of the essay, Jones laid out a statement of purpose, for both himself and the field, as it moved into the future. He argued that changing the focus of historical interpretation would make history and historical organizations more relevant "to the lives of the mass of the people themselves." He maintained that in order to accomplish this goal, historical organizations should present people's "work and the work of their ancestors" and communicate history that "represents America in terms which men and women can easily translate into the terms of their own lives." Such a transformation in public history was critical not only because "it promises . . . to make our historical societies stronger," but because "it promises to strengthen the moral and spiritual fibre of a country which must stand strong and free and filled with self-knowledge if we are to move out and beyond the realms of bickering nationalism which engulf us." Although it is difficult to parse exactly what he is referring to here, Jones appears to be simultaneously offering a critique of Cold War geopolitics and ethnoracial division. In this McCarthyite era, it is unsurprising that he is a bit coy about such a statement; nevertheless, the larger message about overcoming national chauvinism aligns with his central message of making historical organizations more inclusive and relevant to working people's lives. He reinforced this message with his closing lines: "We have here an opportunity to move forward into the second half of the twentieth century on a far broader program and with a far broader base that we have had before. Did I say an opportunity? I think we have an obligation." No longer could history museums and historical societies cater to a privileged few and showcase elite relics and expect to garner public support. With these public statements, Jones was calling for a transformation in public history's content and audience.

Reorienting the Training of History Museum Professionals

In May 1969, in a keynote address to the American Association of Museums meeting in San Francisco, Jones outlined his vision for museum studies and public history training. He stated bluntly that "the old assumption that anyone who is competent in an academic area will be an adequate member of a museum staff is outmoded" and chided scholars who saw the primary function of museums as research, asking, "If the first concern [of museums] is research unrelated to exhibits, why bother with the public?" Moreover, he remonstrated that "if we are going to let the people inside and even encourage their visits, then we must be prepared to communicate with them."[29] Jones hoped that the curriculum of the Cooperstown Graduate Program, which he had founded in 1964 as a partnership between NYSHA and the State University of New York at Oneonta, would create a new generation of museum professionals who were prepared to communicate effectively with broad audiences. His message had a progressive edge, making it more than simply a typical appeal for field-wide improvement and professionalization.

The relationship between folklore and history was critical to his vision of a fundamentally transformed approach to training. "Local history museums," he stated, "are really folk museums" and their collections are not at a "sophisticated or connoisseur's level" but rather a "folk or popular level."[30] In a field dominated by the aesthetics of elite connoisseurship embodied in the Metropolitan Museum of Art's American Wing, Jones's call to train students in how to interpret the material culture of ordinary people was provocative.

He offered a perspective on material culture that encouraged placing objects in social and historical context and, more important, relating them to the lives and work of nonelites. Beyond a focus on aesthetics and the particulars of materials and production, he encouraged students to analyze how people used material culture and explore the significance of objects in everyday life. Jones saw this approach as a critical move away from historical societies' and museums' almost universal focus on "the leaders and the rich" and the practice of choosing artifacts "on grounds of association, real or imagined, with them."[31] Rejecting the associational collecting that had long defined history museums' practices, a new generation of museum professionals would interpret material culture on the basis of objects' societal purposes and meanings.

Along with this shift in approach to material culture, Jones offered a strong statement in his 1969 American Alliance of Museums (AAM) keynote regarding the overwhelmingly White demographics of museum staffs and training programs. It echoed his critical comments almost two decades earlier about the racial composition of historical societies:

> Before we drop the subject of recruitment we had better take an honest look at the fact that there is a mere handful of Negroes working at a professional level in American museums. I visit about 40 museums a year in this country; I see thousands of black children; I see black janitors and guards; once in a while in the big city museums I see a black docent, but aside from that the jobs all belong to whitey. The logical point of entry to the profession is through graduate training programs. The jobs are opening up for Negroes, it is part of our responsibility to fill those openings with trained, young black professionals and to push for more openings. The truth of the matter is that the museum profession has failed to communicate with the whole college generation, black and white, and it is time we turned our minds and talents to that very pleasant duty.[32]

This statement, perhaps more than anything else he said that day, held the potential to radically transform the museum field. It was a message that museum leaders desperately needed to hear. In a paper delivered three years earlier at the 1966 AAM annual meeting, curator Keith Melder had written, "Historical museums in this country have treated the Negro as though he did not exist. It is little wonder that many Negroes are indignant at such treatment."[33] Outside of the relatively small but growing Black museum movement, little had changed by the time Jones spoke in 1969. In January of that year, the Metropolitan Museum of Art had opened the *Harlem on My Mind* exhibition with disastrous results, demonstrating vividly how White curators and administrators—even well-intentioned ones—could easily alienate and offend Black audiences. The Met's decision to feature photographs, music, and newspaper headlines about Harlem rather than the work of African American visual artists drew fire from critics and activists who protested outside the museum.[34] Around the same time, the Smithsonian was responding to criticisms that it had ignored African Americans in its museums. In this period, the Smithsonian's newly founded Anacostia Neighborhood Museum began creating important exhibitions that presented Black history as well as contemporary social issues relevant to Black communities. Moreover, the Anacostia museum was bringing a number of African Americans, including director John R. Kinard, on board as staff members. The institution's other museums, however, were much slower to change, and by 1969, virtually no progress had been made in incorporating African American historical narratives into the institution's larger museums.[35]

When he spoke at the AAM meeting in 1969, Jones was not a lone, or ignored, voice in the wilderness; he was clearly a leader in the museum field. Yet his vision was deeply challenging to the status quo of history museums and historical organizations. Nevertheless, as Jones's approach and philosophy spread across the country to hundreds of history museums, historic sites, and historical societies, his conception of the intertwined practice of folklife and history encouraged a community-based public history that emphasized the lives of working people and strove for inclusivity.

A critical partner for Jones at the Cooperstown Graduate Program was folklorist Bruce R. Buckley, who joined the faculty from Indiana University's famed folklore program. Buckley, however, was much more than simply an academic folklorist. In 1949, while in college in Ohio, he had hosted a radio show called *American Folkways*, which was picked up by the National Educational Radio Network. After college, he recorded an album of *Ohio Valley Ballads* for Folkways Records and continued to perform as he pursued advanced studies in folklore.[36] He also got involved with television programming, producing and hosting a television show also called *American Folkways*. According to Buckley, each show involved various performances and "had a theme of history, geography or human experiences."[37] In this period, Buckley also produced educational films as part of Indiana University's Educational

Media Department, developing "films for seventh grade social studies classes, using folklife and local history as a unifying theme."[38] By the time he came to Cooperstown in the 1960s, then, he had accumulated a wide range of experiences in public-oriented projects at the nexus of folklore and history. At its root, Buckley viewed his work as advocacy for subaltern peoples, writing "public folklore advocates for the goals and aspirations of voiceless groups struggling for recognition and equality. Its aim is the communication of the knowledge, attitudes and skills of a folk group to another group with the intent of changing the other group's perspective."[39] Although he had excellent academic training from Indiana's faculty, including Stith Thompson and Richard Dorson, Buckley's great skill was in the communication of folk traditions and local history to broad audiences, including children.

Another key faculty member was Per Guldbeck, who had come to Cooperstown after serving as archaeologist at Mesa Verde National Park and chief curator of the Museum of International Folk Art in Santa Fe. At the Farmers' Museum, Guldbeck was most responsible for the creation of an influential exhibition called *The Farmer's Year*, which chronicled rural agricultural life in great detail.[40] In his essay in *History Museums in the United States: A Critical Assessment*, Gary Kulik wrote that this exhibition had a tremendous impact on the field because of its thematic approach and engaging design. Combining material culture, paintings, and drawings, the exhibition presented a compelling narrative that simultaneously conveyed a key insight about farming—its seasonality. It was an exhibition that engaged visitors of all backgrounds, focused on working people's lives, and combined material culture, folklife, and social history. As Kulik notes, however, the exhibition was influential not only because of its quality, but because it became the model to many Cooperstown students of what a good museum exhibition should look like.

The student who best synthesized the melding of folk culture and history into progressive practice was the Cooperstown Graduate Program's most famous alumnus from its founding years, public folklorist Henry Glassie. A member of the program's first class in 1964–65, Glassie has recently commented that he "always had a vision of engaged scholarship, right from the beginning—a folkloristic version of public history."[41] It would be inaccurate to claim that Cooperstown was the only, or even the primary, place that pressed Glassie in this direction—he had formative experiences at the University of Pennsylvania as a doctoral student and elsewhere that surely contributed to his perspective on engaged scholarship. Nevertheless, the model of Jones,

Louis C. Jones with the first class of students at the Cooperstown Graduate Program, 1965. A young Henry Glassie can be seen at the center. Photograph by Milo Stewart. Image courtesy of the Cooperstown Graduate Association.

Buckley, and Guldbeck, and the practical training he received in Cooperstown undoubtedly contributed to his ability to work effectively outside the academic realm. In the late 1960s, one of his first projects after graduate school was documenting in-depth the Poor People's Campaign and creating a photography exhibition about it. Around the same time, he was involved in the founding of the Smithsonian's Festival of American Folklife, and as state folklorist of Pennsylvania, he worked with educators to create a "bibliography of ethnic culture for Pennsylvania."[42] Moreover, in the 1970s, he was a major consultant for Conner Prairie in Fishers, Indiana, and the Museum of American Frontier Culture in Staunton, Virginia.[43]

As a trailblazing expert in vernacular architecture, Glassie understood how examining folk culture, history, and material culture led to insights about social life and relationships of power. A 1971 essay, coauthored with Betty-Jo Glassie, made the case passionately for a more inclusive approach to public history: "Dingy industrial housing, cropper's shacks, bourgeois ranchers, vintage beatnik pads, New Mexican haciendas, Church of God of Prophecy store fronts—all manner of buildings deserve a place in the making of our past, not just those few which fit the going myth neatly. With most kinds of buildings gone, it will be easy to forget most kinds of people, the workaday farmers and factory hands, the people that old style historians are accustomed to call little."⁴⁴ Although Glassie was certainly an exceptional example, he was representative of a broader movement among young public historians toward engaged, pluralistic, and community-based scholarship and practice in this period.⁴⁵ The organic intersections between folklife and history were at the core of this transformation. Glassie and other students of this era maintained that history museums should no longer be bastions of elitism and that they had the potential to become sites where ordinary people could find their histories and communities represented and their stories told.

Conclusion

The current director of the Cooperstown Graduate Program, Gretchen Sullivan Sorin, enrolled in the program's history museum studies degree track in 1974. The program's first African American student, Sorin became a pioneering exhibitions curator and a powerful voice for diversity, equity, and inclusion in the museum field. As she prepared to graduate from Douglass College with a degree in American Studies, one of Sorin's professors recommended the program to her because a previous student had attended. At the time, Jones and the rest of the program's faculty did not engage in active recruiting of students of color. Although Jones hoped to diversify the field and preached the necessity of such work, he clearly had no idea how to go about it. According to Sorin, this was a major weakness of his approach to transforming museums and public history. Sitting and waiting for students of color to find Cooperstown was not going to make a significant dent in the overwhelmingly White demographics of the field. Thus although Jones, Buckley, and the other faculty welcomed Sorin and encouraged her aspirations to become a museum professional in the 1970s, she recognized when she became director of the program in 1994 that a much more concerted and active effort to identify, recruit, and retain students of color needed to be implemented. In addition, the curriculum needed to be adapted to reflect the true diversity of US society.⁴⁶ Building on and significantly expanding the inclusive spirit of Jones's original vision, Sorin has furthered the work of making public history inclusive and service-oriented and transforming it into a field that emphasizes narratives of the ignored or underrepresented.

Today, museums and other public history institutions strive to be relevant and responsive to their communities, public service-oriented, diverse and inclusive, and collaborative and multivocal. This is an ongoing project that remains, in many ways, incomplete. It is critical to recognize, however, that the paradigm shift in public history and museum practice of the late twentieth and early twenty-first centuries followed from the essential groundwork of influential public historians who brought social history, cultural pluralism, and working people's narratives to the center of US history museums, historic sites, and historical societies in the mid-twentieth century.

This narrative of public history's history counters the widely held perception that history museums and other historical organizations were backward, elitist, and conservative institutions until the "new social history" began to transform them in the late 1970s and '80s. The transformations often credited to the influence of the new social history were clearly well underway earlier. This popular narrative has privileged the influence of academic historians while erasing the pioneering contributions of public folklorists, public historians, and educators. Many scholars believed, and continue to believe, that museums and other history organizations needed to be saved, or redeemed, by enlightened scholars who had the true interests of the people at heart and offered critical rather than romanticized narratives of society and the status quo. The example of Louis C. Jones and Cooperstown suggests instead that it may be academic scholars who have something to learn from publicly engaged scholars working at the nexus of folklore and history.

Notes

1 Carl Sandburg, *American Songbag* (New York: Harcourt, Brace, 1927), vii, ix.
2 The Cooperstown Graduate Program was created through a partnership between the State University of New York at Oneonta and the New York State Historical Association in 1964. It included two tracks, or degree programs—one in history museum studies and another in American folk culture. It is important to recognize that the Winterthur and Hagley programs pre-date the Cooperstown Graduate Program by about a decade. Although both Winterthur and Hagley trained many students who went on to become distinguished museum professionals, their curricula focused primarily on decorative arts / material culture and business/technology history, respectively, rather than primarily the training of history museum professionals. In addition, New York University's Institute of Fine Arts, which was founded in 1932, has trained many successful art museum professionals. In addition, both Paul J. Sachs at the Fogg Museum at Harvard University and New York University's Institute of Fine Arts, which was founded in 1932, trained many successful art museum professionals.
3 Louis C. Jones, *Three Eyes on the Past: Exploring New York Folklife* (Syracuse, NY: Syracuse University Press, 1982), xii–xiii.

4   Louis C. Jones and Candace T. Matelic, "Folklife and Museums: How Far Have We Come since the 1950s?," in *Folklife and Museums: Selected Readings*, ed. Patricia Hall and Charlie Seeman (Nashville: American Association for State and Local History, 1987), 1–11. See also Jay Anderson, *Time Machines: The World of Living History* (Nashville: American Association for State and Local History, 1984). This marriage of folklife and social history in the United States drew inspiration, of course, from European open-air museums, especially Skansen.

5   Tammy Gordon, *The Spirit of 1976: Commerce, Community, and the Politics of Commemoration* (Amherst: University of Massachusetts Press, 2013).

6   William S. Walker, *A Living Exhibition: The Smithsonian and the Transformation of the Universal Museum* (Amherst: University of Massachusetts Press, 2013), chaps. 3–5.

7   Robert Baron, "Folklife and the American Museum Retrospective: Reflections and Reimaginings," *Folklife and Museums: Twenty-First-Century Perspectives*, ed. C. Kurt Dewhurst, Patricia Hall, and Charlie Seemann (Lanham, MD: Rowman & Littlefield, 2017): 28.

8   The phrase *shared authority* comes from Michael Frisch's 1990 collection of essays *A Shared Authority: Essays on the Craft and Meaning of Oral and Public History* (Albany, NY: SUNY Press, 1990).

9   See examples in Baron's essay, as well as folklorist Steve Zeitlin's discussion of City Lore's City of Memory project, "Where Are the Best Stories? Participation and Curation in a New Media Age," in *Letting Go? Sharing Historical Authority in a User-Generated World*, ed. Bill Adair, Benjamin Filene, and Laura Koloski (Philadelphia: Pew Center for Arts and Heritage, 2011), 34–43.

10 Richard Kurin, *Reflections of a Culture Broker: A View from the Smithsonian* (Washington, DC: Smithsonian Institution Press, 1997).

11 Gary Kulik, "Designing the Past: History-Museum Exhibitions from Peale to the Present," in *History Museums in the United States: A Critical Assessment*, ed. Warren Leon and Roy Rosenzweig (Urbana: University of Illinois Press, 1989), 24. Despite Kulik's forceful case for Cooperstown's significance to the field, subsequent scholars of public history's history have not paid much attention to Jones, NYSHA, or the Cooperstown Graduate Program. A common narrative of the origins of public history training identifies its genesis in academic history departments in the mid-1970s. In the widely read book *Museums, Monuments, and National Parks: Toward a New Genealogy of Public History* (Amherst: University of Massachusetts Press, 2012), Denise D. Meringolo helpfully expands and complicates the genealogy of public history; however, Cooperstown receives no mention. In the article "The Pragmatic Roots of Public History Education in the United States," *Public Historian* 37, no. 1 (February 2015), on the roots of public history education, Rebecca Conard broadens the genealogy of public history training to include a whole range of academic programs, including museum studies, archival science, historic preservation, material culture, historical administration, and applied history. Conard identifies the Cooperstown Graduate Program as the "first humanities-based museum studies program," a characterization which acknowledges the program's intertwining of history and

folklife. At the same time, Conard's description is somewhat misleading as it downplays the fact that Louis C. Jones created CGP specifically to train *history* museum professionals. Indeed, the degree it awarded to public historians was a master's in *history museum studies*, along with a separate track in American folk culture, and the vast majority of the program's alumni went on to work with historical organizations. It would be more accurate to write that CGP was the first history-based museum studies program. Conard also gives too much credit for the creation of the program to Fred Rath and shifts the focus away from Jones's role. As executive director of the National Trust for Historic Preservation in the 1950s, Rath was a key figure in the burgeoning historic preservation movement, and he was associated with CGP through his work as associate director of NYSHA. However, it is important to recognize that the Cooperstown Graduate Program was Jones's brainchild and other NYSHA staff and CGP faculty played a larger role than Rath in shaping the program's philosophy and curriculum.

12 Kulik, "Designing the Past," 24.
13 Andrea Burns, *From Storefront to Monument: Tracing the Public History of the Black Museum Movement* (Amherst: University of Massachusetts Press, 2013).
14 G. August Gerber (national campaign manager, Socialist Action Committee), letter to Louis C. Jones, October 13, 1928, Louis C. Jones Papers, Fenimore Research Library, Cooperstown, NY, box 9, folder 77, 410.9/77. Unless otherwise noted, all other archival sources are from this archive.
15 Cedric Fowler (treasurer, Socialist Party, Morningside Heights Branch), letter to Louis C. Jones, January 30, 1931; Margaret L. Lamont (treasurer, Socialist Party, Morningside Heights Branch), letter and receipt to "Comrade Jones," February 3, 1932; Julius Gerber (executive secretary, Socialist Party), letter to "Comrade," n.d., box 9, folder 77, 410.9/77.
16 On Thompson, see William S. Walker, "Collecting Folk Histories: Harold W. Thompson and Student Field Research in the 1930s," *Public Historian* 37, no. 3 (August 2015): 45–75.
17 Louis C. Jones, "Folklore in the Schools: A Student Guide to Collecting Folklore," *New York Folklore Quarterly* 2, no. 2 (May 1946): 148–53.
18 Louis C. Jones, memo to Dr. Frederick Bair, "Anti-discrimination and the Teachers College," n.d., box 20, folder 43, 410.20/43.
19 "Inter-group Council Presents Out of Many Cultures—America," April 6, 19[46?], box 20, folder 44, 410.20/44.
20 New York State College for Teachers, Albany, "Final Report on Studies and Projects Undertaken as the College's Part in the College Study in Intergroup Relations," February 14, 1946, box 20, folder 44, 410.20/44. Jones's report appears on pages 24–26.
21 Stephen C. Clark, letter to Louis C. Jones, September 3, 1946, box 10, folder 28. See also Kajsa M. J. Sabatke, "'Tremendous Possibilities': The Collaborative Partnership of Stephen C. Clark and Louis C. Jones at the New York State Historical Association, 1947–1960," (master's thesis, Cooperstown Graduate Program, SUNY

Oneonta, 2007); Erik A. Mason, "The History of the New York State Historical Association, 1899–1964" (master's thesis, Cooperstown Graduate Program, SUNY Oneonta, 1995).

22 Arthur C. Parker, "A Review of the Development of the New York State Historical Association, 1899–1946," *New York History* 28, no. 1 (January 1947): 10–21.

23 Louis C. Jones, "Folk Culture and the Historical Society," *Minnesota History* 31, no. 1 (March 1950): 12.

24 Jones, 13.

25 Rick Beard, "Creating a More Meaningful Past: A Short History of AASLH," *History News* 69, no. 4 (Autumn 2014): 22–27; see also Robert B. Townsend, *History's Babel: Scholarship, Professionalization, and the Historical Enterprise in the United States, 1880–1940* (Chicago: University of Chicago Press, 2013).

26 Louis C. Jones, "Folklore in the American Heritage," *American Heritage* 1, no. 2 (Winter 1950): 66–68, 72.

27 Jones, 72.

28 Louis C. Jones, "Folk Culture and the Historical Societies," *American Heritage* 1, no. 3 (Spring 1950): 55.

29 Louis C. Jones, "Twiggery and Tomorrow's Museums," keynote address, American Association of Museums annual meeting, San Francisco, May 26, 1969, Fenimore Research Library, Cooperstown, NY, 2, 4.

30 The Cooperstown Graduate Program's curriculum focused on everyday types of objects as well as the people who made and used them. Jane Spillman, interview by author, April 11, 2017.

31 Jones, *Three Eyes on the Past*, xxiv.

32 Jones, "Twiggery and Tomorrow's Museums," 16–17.

33 Keith Melder, quoted in Walker, *Living Exhibition*, 126.

34 Burns, *From Storefront to Monument*, 104.

35 Walker, *Living Exhibition*, 126–27.

36 Bruce Buckley, *Ohio Valley Ballads*, Folkways Records, 1955, http://www.folkways.si.edu/bruce-buckley/ohio-valley-ballads/american-folk/music/album/Smithsonian.

37 Bruce R. Buckley, "Forty Years before the Mast: Sailing the Stormy and Serene Seas of Public Folklore," *New York Folklore* 15, nos. 1–2 (1990): 6.

38 Buckley, 9.

39 Buckley, 1.

40 "Per Ernst Guldbeck," 1979, box 20, folder 22, 410.20/22; "Former NYSHA Research Associate Dies following Illness," *Freeman's Journal* (Cooperstown, NY), November 21, 1979.

41 Henry Glassie and Barbara Truesdell, "A Life in the Field: Henry Glassie and the Study of Material Culture," *Public Historian* 30, no. 4 (Fall 2008): 69. See also transcript of full interview, Henry Glassie, interview by Barbara Truesdell, March 13, April 4, April 24, April 30, May 7, May 10, May 29, June 6, 2007, Center for the Study of History and Memory, Indiana University, 18–20.

42 Glassie and Truesdell, 71, 73.

43 Glassie and Truesdell, 75.
44 Henry Glassie and Betty-Jo Glassie, "The Implications of Folkloristic Thought for Historic Zoning Ordinances," in *Papers on Applied Folklore*, Folklore Forum Bibliographic and Special Series 8 (Bloomington: Department of Folklore and Ethnomusicology, Indiana University, 1971), 31–37.
45 C. R. Jones, interview by William S. Walker, May 26, 2017. In addition, the author wishes to thank the numerous alumni of the Cooperstown Graduate Program who have shared their recollections of the early years of the program with him over the past decade.
46 Gretchen Sullivan Sorin, conversation with author, July 28, 2017.

The American Civilization Institute of Morristown

Education and Inclusive Community Building

Denise D. Meringolo

Public history as a field or track in higher education has multiple roots, but its origins are most often traced either to the creation of applied history programs during the early twentieth century or to the establishment of the first named public history program at the University of California, Santa Barbara, in the late 1970s. Applied historians of the earlier generation tended to emphasize the usefulness of historical research for policy makers.[1] Their goal was primarily to establish the legitimacy of their discipline—as natural scientists had in the previous generation—by connecting the study of history to the production and reproduction of formal state authority.[2] Applied history programs encouraged students and faculty members to conduct research that might benefit elected officials and civic leaders working to understand and solve social and political problems. Unfortunately, the establishment of applied history programs coincided with a period of discord among historians. Scholars in the American Historical Association doubted the intellectual integrity of historical narratives written for policy makers, and the discipline splintered. Because their subjects of inquiry originated in the political sphere, applied historians could not demonstrate their ability to achieve the ideal of objectivity. In the next generation, the founders of the original public history program at UC Santa Barbara did not attempt to challenge the emphasis on objectivity; they were not consciously working to develop a new discipline. Rather, Robert Kelley and G. Wesley Johnson, traditionally trained historians who had accumulated experience as expert witnesses and consultants, founded the program in response to a crisis in the academic job market. Kelley and Johnson believed public history education would create jobs for PhD-trained historians in public service where they would act as dispassionate advisers, not as advocates, activists, or policy makers.[3]

This standard origin story is simultaneously useful and limiting. On the one hand, it establishes public history as a legitimate field of academic inquiry, one that emerged during pivotal moments in the evolution of history as a discipline. On the other hand, by situating the roots of public history education inside both the academy and the discipline of history, this origin story has tended to restrict efforts to historicize and theorize a distinctive set of values, ethics, and practices that have shaped public history education over time. Measured against traditional standards, public history appears more pragmatic than intellectual. This criticism led many public history educators to occupy a defensive position, constantly emphasizing their disciplinary fitness rather than identifying their unique professional habits. Therefore, recognizing founders' emphasis on job development and their insistence on working toward the discipline's ideal of objectivity is valuable. It helps explain the tension many public historians experience while operating from inside academic departments of history. Unlike their colleagues, public history educators tend to emphasize methods and process over content and product, and they often struggle to find the right balance in their classrooms.

However useful this origin story may be, it does not explain the evolution of more radical practices and objectives that have arisen in public history education. Whether working with neighborhood associations, local museums, preservation organizations, or historical societies, many public history educators situate themselves and their students as advocates and activists. They emphasize the role that history-making processes can play in efforts to advance social justice and promote political change. While radical public history education often—perhaps even usually—involves the production of interpretive historical narratives, it may not. Sometimes public history educators and their students work with communities to develop archival collections, gather oral histories, and build local capacities without asserting interpretive authority.

Is there a different origin story for this kind of work?

We can open up more nuanced critical perspectives on public history education by identifying pedagogical approaches that took shape outside of university and college history departments in response to a wide variety of historical conditions. In this context, the American Civilization Institute of Morristown (ACIM) in New Jersey serves as a valuable case study. Established in the fall of 1965, the ACIM was a collaborative experiment in education that brought together students and faculty from Morristown High School and Fairleigh Dickinson University to work on a series of place-based research and collecting projects. As a precedent for public history education, the ACIM is significant because it adopted several learning innovations that have become commonplace in public history education. It provides an early example of community-specific service learning in the field of preservation and museum education. It represents an effort to establish student-focused, multidisciplinary, collaborative learning opportunities in which students analyzed the past in their hometown. The ACIM emphasized process over product and methods over content. Although founders tended to describe the ACIM as primarily vocational, closer examination suggests the project was designed as a creative response to a variety of local conflicts and opportunities. Placing these at the center of the ACIM history illuminates important questions about how and why public history education emerged in response to a complex social and political environment.

The idea for the ACIM was hatched in the spring and summer of 1964. This timing suggests growing public investment in collecting and commemorating the past had galvanized the project's founders. During the 1950s and 1960s, at least two state commissions encouraged the collection, preservation, and interpretation of New Jersey's history. Both projects sought to challenge exclusive interpretations of the past. The New Jersey Civil War Centennial Commission was the more overtly political of the two initiatives. The executive director of the state commission, Everett Landers, appointed an African American woman—former Democratic assemblywoman Madaline Williams—to serve as a delegate to the Civil War Centennial Commission. During the opening meeting of the national commission in South Carolina, Williams was refused a room at the conference hotel. The treatment of Black delegates became a point of serious debate, and it is likely Everett had appointed Williams purposefully to challenge the national commission's racist and exclusive perspective on the war. It is also clear that Williams's appointment had more local political motivations as well; state legislators and agencies were eager to demonstrate New Jersey's commitment to civil rights and to attract support from Black voters.[4]

While far less controversial, the second state history initiative also sought to democratize the past and to institutionalize community-based processes of history-making. State lawmakers established the New Jersey Tercentenary Commission in 1958 to develop projects of "enduring, rather than transitory worth."[5] Commission members encouraged local communities to participate in tercentennial efforts by assembling collections, preserving historic structures, publishing local histories, and developing public programs. In addition, members of the commission's advisory board on education advised college faculty and students to take the lead in identifying primary source material and making it broadly accessible.[6] Passage of the National Historic Preservation Act of 1966 may have encouraged the 1967 establishment of the New Jersey Historical Trust and the New Jersey Historical Commission, but both entities emerged in direct response to tercentenary initiatives designed to engage the public in historic preservation.

The ACIM founders clearly adopted the tercentenary commission's goals as the framework for their program, establishing an intersection between secondary school education and the rapidly professionalizing realm of preservation. On its most basic level, the ACIM was an experiment in applied learning that took advantage of a temporary intersection that had formed between history and policy. Morristown school district superintendent Harry Wenner, Morristown High School social studies teacher John "Jack" R. Stewart, and Morristown school board member Dorothy Harvey proposed using the Timothy Mills House, a mid-eighteenth-century, one-and-a-half-story house adjacent to Morristown High School, as a laboratory. There, history and science teachers could engage high school students "in the challenge and adventure of studying American civilization in depth through the reconstruction" of the house.[7] Following the advice of the commission's education advisory board, Wenner and his staff sought advice from faculty at Fairleigh Dickinson University. As a result, anthropologist Gene Weltfish, then on the Fairleigh Dickinson faculty, joined the ACIM project. Weltfish quickly became central to project planning and development. She and Harry Wenner shared leadership responsibilities, with Weltfish serving as academic director and Wenner as administrative director.[8]

Under Weltfish's guidance, the project team began planning. They reached out to the state field archaeologist Willard Schlosberg and the National Park

Superintendent Harry Wenner, Morristown High School yearbook photograph, ca. 1965.

Service, Northeast Region, archaeologist John L. Cotter, and they began to view the NPS history program as a model. Nineteen students and faculty from both the high school and the university traveled to Independence Hall in Philadelphia, where site historian Martin Yoelson and historical architect Norman Souder gave them a "very complete tour of the Park in terms of the

Jack Stewart, pictured after his promotion to vice principal, Morristown High School yearbook photograph, ca. 1965.

various phases of work and a thorough briefing in the problems involved in the work of historic reconstruction."⁹ They also took advantage of local expertise. They gathered at Morristown National Historical Park, where they met again with Cotter as well as the site's museum curator, Theodore Sowers, and NPS regional director Ronald Lee. By the time the project began in earnest in the fall of 1965, it had evolved into a multifaceted, multidisciplinary, locally designed project in which faculty and students took seriously state lawmakers' call to collect and preserve state history. Professors and students from Fairleigh Dickinson University acted as project leaders and mentors. Participating high school students encountered the project in courses as varied as social studies, art, home economics, and science. College students similarly entered into various phases of the project while studying history, chemistry,

The Timothy Mills House, HABS NJ-632, Historic American Building Survey, Library of Congress Prints and Photographs Division, Washington, DC.

Gene Weltfish, right, with her colleague Irving Herman Buchen from Farleigh Dickinson University. American Civilization Institute of Morristown, ca 1966.

and archaeology, among other fields. Weltfish and history professor Jack Fritz ran summer graduate seminars in which students conducted significant archival research "on the subject of the transfer of English institutions to the New World, making a close analysis of society on both sides of the Ocean during the Colonial Period."[10]

The ACIM faculty and students were not precisely starting from scratch, however. Morristown's ties to the Revolutionary War had stood at the center

Art teacher Vincent Butler, Morristown High School yearbook photograph, ca. 1965.

Science teacher Albert Caro, Morristown High School yearbook photograph, ca. 1965.

of the town's identity for at least a hundred years. Situated about thirty miles outside of New York City, Morristown's hills provided colonial forces with a clear vantage point from which to monitor British troops quartered in New York City. General George Washington established winter headquarters there twice, once in the winter of 1777–78 and again in the winter of 1779–80. During the second encampment, Martha Custis Washington and her two children accompanied her husband, and the family lived in a large home owned by Colonel Jacob Ford. Morristown was not the stage for any significant Revolutionary action. Indeed, bored troops suffering from disease and bitter cold constantly threatened mutiny. Nonetheless, the presence of Washington and his family became a source of civic pride for local residents and state officials alike. In 1874, these men established the Washington Association of New Jersey to purchase the Ford Mansion and acquire various sites associated with the troop encampments in order to ensure their preservation.[11] In 1933, the

Washington Association conveyed their holdings to the National Park Service, and Morristown National Historical Park became the first place designated as a national historic site by the NPS.[12]

Jack Fritz and his students did not seek to challenge the dominance of the Revolution in Morristown's past, but their work identified a broader global context and a deeper historical time line for understanding local history. Two of Fritz's graduate students established a residential research program at the Mills House. Morristown High School students joined them as researchers and, eventually, as docents and interpreters in a "junior museum." Together, students, teachers, and professionals completed a multiyear project to gather, study, and reinterpret the history of Morristown. The results of their work clearly met the official goals of the New Jersey Tercentenary Commission: They assembled archaeological and archival evidence as well as oral histories into collections that are still held by local institutions. They also established a variety of projects and educational programs to "make available to school children and to the public the results of the historical, educational, and preservation work accomplished by the organization and to allow the public to visit the reconstructed or restored buildings at reasonable times and for reasonable fees."[13]

Over the rather brief life-span of the project, faculty advisers produced annual progress reports and held at least one symposium during which over seventy high school and college students presented their research findings. These documents make clear that the ACIM was a point of origin in the development of public history education. It advanced service learning as a core method of teaching and learning. In some ways, it fits neatly into the traditional historiography of public history education. Like the founders of applied history programs and the UC Santa Barbara public history program, the leaders of the ACIM project tended to emphasize its practicality in preparing students for an evolving job market. Gene Weltfish explained in the first annual report, "The American Civilization Institute of Morristown, Inc., is an educational enterprise designed to close the gap between theoretical knowledge and applied skills so that we can prepare our young people educationally for a new age to come."[14] In several reports and presentations, she described the project as a remedy for youth unemployment and a rapidly evolving job market.[15] Undoubtedly, focusing on the pragmatic potential of the ACIM to train students for a postindustrial economy had immediate value. Weltfish and her colleagues successfully applied for funds from the Office of

Economic Opportunity in the United States Department of Health, Education and Welfare. In addition to supporting project administration, Weltfish and her colleagues used these funds to pay students for their work. "One of the reasons this project was set up as jobs for money," she explained, "is that we want to have a preamble, a preview to the possibility that these will be very important jobs in the future, and we wanted you to think of yourselves as . . . pre-professionals."[16]

At the same time, evidence suggests that the value of the ACIM projects transcended both the agenda set by state history commissions and the practical connection between education and job creation that Weltfish often emphasized. By the time the project ended in 1969, well over three hundred students had participated, and their voices are included in the formal project reports. While many offered narrow, concrete descriptions of their work, some reflected more critically on its value and meaning. Barbara Livingston, who worked in the loan department of the Junior Museum, thought the project had shifted her perspective on children: "I have tried for perhaps the first time in my life to put my mind on a different level of understanding and knowledge—namely, that of the grade school child. I have ceased to think of childhood as a mindless, obnoxious state of human existence."[17] Jessica Brambir, who participated in the summer work program at the museum, commented on the intellectual value of "vocational" education. She said, "In the academic world, actual experience is often divorced from the theoretical level. This is unfortunate because it leaves the person with a rather abstract frame of reference, which is of little use in guiding his life experiences as they occur. At the Museum, I found that there was an emphasis on . . . experience. The various artifacts that I handled became meaningful to me as I did research on them."[18] Emoke S. B'Racz reflected on the broader philosophical impact of the project, commenting, "Reconstruction of man's past is an activity of supreme importance to humanity, not least because in the collaboration of different individuals it holds the key to general interest and understanding. . . . As someone said, it is the most human of all sciences and the most scientific of all humanities; an opportunity for all to get to know one another on the best and easiest of terms."[19] By engaging students in a collaborative, real-world educational experience, the American Civilization Institute of Morristown facilitated emotional as well as intellectual and practical development.

The significance of the project is perhaps best understood by placing it within a local political context. The timing of the project's development and the composition of project leadership suggest the ACIM was designed, at least in part, as a tool to address deep and troubling rifts in the community. Like the members of the New Jersey Civil War Centennial Commission, the founders of the ACIM also intended their work to challenge racism and disrupt exclusive practices of community development. Examined from this angle, the ACIM comes into focus as an origin point for radical public history practice, a project developed as part of a larger response to local conflicts over social justice and inclusivity.

Morristown is a small urban municipality, just 2.9 square miles. It is completely surrounded by Morris Township, a largely residential suburban district measuring 15.7 square miles. The boundary lines distinguishing town from township are irregular and rather illogical, cutting across natural features and established streets.[20] The two jurisdictions originated as a single entity, but they were separated by petition to the state government in 1865. Popular histories commonly suggest the reasons for the separation between town and township are unknown and unknowable.[21] This is not the case. It is significant that Morristown "seceded" from Morris Township at the end of the Civil War. The state of New Jersey had long been divided over issues of slavery and emancipation, and those fissures transformed local politics in Morris County during the war and left powerful traces in the way race relations evolved in the state as a whole and in Morristown in particular.

After the Revolution, northern states abolished slavery gradually, and New Jersey was the last of these. The state legislature voted for gradual abolition in 1804, and many slaveholders took advantage of loopholes that enabled them to profit from enslaved people's labor well into the nineteenth century.[22] In 1830, 3,568 people were still enslaved in the North, and more than two-thirds of them were in New Jersey. While slavery was permanently abolished in the state in 1846, eighteen people were still categorized as "apprentices for life" at the start of the Civil War.[23]

During the war, so-called Peace Democrats dominated the New Jersey state legislature, which repeatedly passed resolutions denouncing the war as futile.[24] Party members in the state were hostile to abolition, and during the state convention of 1862, they condemned the preliminary Emancipation Proclamation Lincoln had issued in September. The Democrats in both the New Jersey state house and state senate were also opposed to the Thirteenth Amendment. This was particularly true in the New Jersey House of Representatives where Democratic members adopted the most extreme anti-Black arguments against emancipation, saying it would impose "negro equality" on the White majority and lead to "amalgamation of the races."[25] New Jersey failed to ratify the Thirteenth Amendment until 1866, when a postwar legislature dominated by Republicans took up the vote for a second time.[26]

George T. Cobb was a lone moderate in the state's virulently racist and antiabolitionist Democratic Party. Democratic leaders ejected Cobb from the party in 1862 because he had shown modest support for abolition. While it would be inaccurate to suggest he was a champion of African American civil rights, his position on slavery had begun to shift after the April 1861 attack on Fort Sumter.[27] When Confederate sympathizers fired on Union troops in Baltimore just a few days later, Cobb led a mass meeting in Morristown in which local residents vowed to provide material support to the Union.[28] Cobb was elected to Congress in 1861, where he supported emancipation in the District of Columbia and became an advocate of compensated emancipation.[29] He was the only New Jersey Democrat during the war to demonstrate any support for emancipation and among a minority who supported the war. During Cobb's tenure in Congress, another New Jersey Democrat, Andrew Rogers, wrote a new platform for the party in Cobb's home district, advancing a rigid antiemancipation stance. Cobb refused to sign it, and the party refused to nominate him for a second run for Congress. Rogers ran in his place and served in Congress from 1863 until 1867.[30] Cobb defected to the Republican Party and was elected to the New Jersey senate in 1865 and again in 1868.[31] In 1865, George T. Cobb led the successful effort to establish Morristown as a separate political entity.

These political machinations suggest that personal rivalries, framed by irreconcilable positions regarding slavery and emancipation, led directly to the separation of Morristown from Morris Township. George T. Cobb played a prominent role in nearly every philanthropic and economic initiative that took place in Morristown between the time he left the Democratic Party in 1862 and his untimely—and tantalizingly suspicious—death in a railroad accident in 1870. He served as mayor from 1865 to 1869. He donated land and $10,000 for the construction of a high school, which opened in 1869. He led the incorporation of the Morristown Bank in 1862, and after the passage of the 1864 National Bank Act, he was on the first board of directors of the First National Bank of Morristown. Active in the local Methodist Church, Cobb funded the construction of a new church building in 1866 and donated the building outgrown by the congregation to the members of the local African

Methodist Episcopal (AME) church.³² As Morristown grew into a financial and business district, the township remained a largely rural area, dependent on town services and on townspeople as customers.

In the years immediately following the Civil War, the African American population of Morristown remained small. Two hundred and ninety-three Black people lived in town in 1880. By 1900, migrants from Virginia and North and South Carolina had increased the Black population to 815. Irish and Italian immigrants also settled in the town. Although the overall population grew from 5,418 in 1880 to over 11,000 in 1900, the percentage of Black residents remained small—just around 5 percent in 1880 and 7 percent in 1900—until after the turn of the twentieth century.³³ While overall population numbers in Morristown grew steadily and consistently, averaging about 2,000 new residents per decade, racial diversity began to expand at a more rapid pace. By 1970, Morristown was home to 17,662 people, about 25 percent of whom identified as African American.³⁴ The number of Black residents in the surrounding district of Morris Township was always much smaller, and the population growth there fits the profile of a post–World War II transition from rural to suburban. In the last decades of the nineteenth century, Morris Township was sparsely populated. Indeed, after the Civil War, the district experienced a sharp drop in population. In 1880, it was home to fewer than 1,500 people, and the population fluctuated through the first half of the twentieth century, experiencing periods of minor growth and periods of decline.³⁵ This changed dramatically after World War II. Between 1950 and 1970, the population of Morris Township grew from 7,432 to 19,414.³⁶ But while overall numbers grew, diversity suffered. By the 1960s, Morris Township had evolved into a wealthy, White suburb, home to fewer than 1,000 African American residents. Morristown, in contrast, had evolved into a densely populated urban center, home to an economically and racially diverse community, including more than 4,500 African American people.³⁷

Differences—real and perceived—in the economic status and racial identifications in the town and in the township created unease and even hostility that influenced local decisions about education. Since 1865, the residents of the township had sent their children to school in Morristown, contributing some tax revenue to the maintenance of the school system. This arrangement met with little debate until the middle of the twentieth century. The 1954 Supreme Court decision in *Brown v. Board of Education* declared school segregation unconstitutional. In the South, this meant that the practice of formal segregation—the maintenance of entirely separate Black and White schools—became a flash point in civil rights activism. In the north, questions of racial imbalance created tension. Studies found that segregation or near-segregation were common in northern states, not only in large cities but also in small communities and in the suburbs. African American parents organized to protest these conditions. They made requests to transfer their children to different schools, petitioned school boards, and distributed fliers and pamphlets documenting unequal conditions and de facto segregation. Their efforts intensified during the 1963–64 school year with incidents of civil disobedience and increased policing of student behavior.[38] African American students staged sit-ins at predominantly White schools in Englewood, New Jersey, and boycotted predominantly Black schools in Jersey City, New Jersey.[39]

Similar unrest troubled the Morristown school district. When Harry Wenner arrived as superintendent in 1961, the two districts were renegotiating their relationship. Wenner advocated for a formal merger between the town and township educational systems, but residents of Morris Township had begun to press for the creation of a separate system. The two jurisdictions had agreed to a new ten-year contract in 1962, but their relationship was strained. Residents of Morris Township had begun to push for the creation of a separate high school. Although six of eight members of the township school board had expressed support for a formal merger of the system, pressure from township residents began to erode their commitment.

In the middle of all of this ferment, Harry Wenner met with Gene Weltfish to discuss the plans for the ACIM.[40] Although the notes from that first meeting are long gone, if they ever existed, it is evident that the two shared a commitment to inclusive community development, diversity, and antiracism. These beliefs stood at the center of both the ACIM development and the school district boundary fight. Gene Weltfish was a well-known, accomplished, and—in some circles—notorious anthropologist with an impressive intellectual pedigree. During the 1920s, she had studied with the progressive educator John Dewey, the rationalistic naturalist philosopher Morris Cohen, and the anthropologist Franz Boas. Under their tutelage, Weltfish developed a strong belief that intellectual inquiry must be relevant, grounded in contemporary life and politics. She joined the Columbia University graduate faculty as a contract lecturer in 1935. While there, she repeatedly connected her work as an educator and an anthropologist to a larger effort to challenge racism. In the early 1940s, she collaborated on the development of a high school science curriculum on heredity that called beliefs about racial difference into question. She was also quite active as a community organizer, helping create a conflict resolution center in the diverse neighborhood surrounding Columbia University, and working through the Chamber of Commerce, neighborhood associations, and a variety of city agencies to build cross-cultural understanding.

During the same period, she and her colleague, Ruth Benedict, coauthored a pamphlet *Races of Mankind*[41] that challenged contemporary beliefs about racial differences in intelligence, strength, and morals. For a brief time, the pamphlet was used by the War Department to educate soldiers, juxtaposing scientific evidence of human development against Nazi propaganda regarding white racial superiority. By 1944, the pamphlet had attracted ire from those who said it unfavorably compared the intelligence of White southerners to that of Black northerners, and it was banned from use. Immediately after the war, Weltfish's strong antiracist views and multifaceted efforts to organize communities and end racism combined with her participation in international feminist organizations attracted the attention of anticommunist politicians. She was called before Joseph McCarthy's Committee in 1952 and summarily dismissed from Columbia. Unable to find another faculty position in the Cold War climate, she turned full time to anthropological fieldwork and completed important studies of the Pawnee people. This work established her academic credentials, and Weltfish was hired in her first tenure-track position at Fairleigh Dickinson in 1961 when she was fifty-nine years old.[42]

Like Weltfish, Harry Wenner was committed to facilitating interracial cooperation and integration. He adopted as his guiding philosophy the key tenets of progressive education. Often criticized for its pragmatism, progressive education strives to make intellectual inquiry relevant in the lives of students from diverse backgrounds. For Wenner, this meant that "being born is enough of a passport to take you where your abilities should take you without any preconditions" and the role of education is to help all young people achieve their potential.[43] Born in Philadelphia, Wenner attended Northeast High School, a large, racially integrated, all-boys public high school. After completing a BA at Bucknell University, he taught biology and coached football at West Orange High School in New Jersey. While teaching, he pursued graduate studies at New York University and the Columbia University Teachers College. He was affiliated with the Teachers College research institute known as the Horace Mann Lincoln Institute of School Experimentation, which encouraged teachers to develop innovative classroom methods and to design curricula that was both responsive to student needs and encouraging of high student achievement.[44] Wenner may first have come into contact with Horace Mann Lincoln Institute leaders while teaching in West Orange. In 1952, the institute led a training session there for teachers interested in improving classroom discussion.[45]

Harry Wenner earned an ED in curriculum and teaching from Columbia Teachers College in 1956. His dissertation examined the impact school superintendents might have in establishing activities that might lead to program improvement. The study built on previous work that had established the importance of administrative leadership in program development by addressing the "need for evidence which can provide the basis for 'better preparation programs in educational administration in universities and improved educational leadership by superintendents and their associates in schools and communities.'"[46] While the timing of his degree makes it impossible for him to have worked with John Dewey—whose philosophies are the cornerstone of progressive education—it is possible that Wenner met Gene Weltfish during his studies; she remained at Columbia until the termination of her contract in 1953, and she had worked extensively with the Teachers College. In any case, after completing his degree, Wenner briefly served as superintendent of the Mountain Lakes school system in New Jersey, but he jumped at the opportunity to move to Morristown in 1961. Mountain Lakes was a predominantly White, middle-class area, while Morristown was a more diverse school district, similar to both West Orange and Philadelphia.[47] Wenner's son, Rolfe Wenner, recalled, "He viewed this as an opportunity to attempt to develop success in a diversified environment. There were many candidates who had more experience in terms of size and diversification of the community. However, during the interview process, his commitment and dedication to providing equal opportunities for success for all students plus demonstrated skill set in moving a district forward" earned him the position.[48]

Under the direction of Harry Wenner and Gene Weltfish, the ACIM directly challenged long-held ideas about the composition of the community. By demonstrating that the history of Morristown extended beyond long-revered historical and geographical boundaries, the ACIM project had not only established a strong intellectual context for disrupting the sense of "difference" between town and township but also encouraged a generation of students from town and township to recognize their mutual connections and responsibilities to one another. As Weltfish explained, "By taking a very limited area, this area here that is under our feet, a certain reality begins to grow up, not only about the past and its long time, but also about the possible long time of the future. That's the kind of future that we hope you will identify yourself with, the long time future that sees we have tried many things, we have survived many difficulties, and we move into the next step."[49]

Racial segregation was very much on the mind of Gene Weltfish as she celebrated the success of the ACIM during the student symposium. While Morristown High School itself was racially integrated, the project, apparently, was not. She challenged participating educators to address this directly. She said, "I have one more thing to say and that is, as I stand here and look around and I have been talking about it, I see on the whole that I address a middle-class White America and we should look at ourselves clearly and realize that in part this is the result of the nature of the senior research personnel who selected the apprentices for their work."[50] Weltfish's comments pushed symposium participants to think more broadly about issues of racial injustice. She said, "The trouble in White America comes from the middle class. . . . We are in need of assessing ourselves. We are the most in need of thinking about our values; we are the most in need of asking ourselves what American civilization really is. . . . Now we have to assess ourselves and hopefully the work we have done here will help us assess ourselves."[51] Weltfish believed that community based public history projects like those sponsored by the ACIM could provide necessary context and experiences for challenging White privilege and facilitating racial justice.

While Weltfish was challenging white supremacy and working to articulate connections between the ACIM work and a broader project of racial justice, Harry Wenner was working to disrupt perceived connections between geographical boundaries and community boundaries. Wenner hired an urban design firm led by Isadore Candeub to issue a report on the viability and benefits of a school merger.[52] Candeub's report challenged the validity of the boundaries between town and township, pointing to their irrationality and demonstrating that the two jurisdictions commonly shared municipal services. The report advanced a definition of community that rested on the maintenance of relationships, not on the respect for municipal boundaries. Candeub wrote, "We mean 'community' as describing the society of man occupying a given area within fairly definable boundaries, interacting within that area, with many interests in common despite differences and even antagonisms. If man is a social being, let's treat him as one and provide him with an environment in which he can function as a social being."[53] Candeub's report argued that a unified school system could facilitate the establishment of community connections across lines of race and class. Wenner picked up key points from the report, consistently using them as talking points at school board meetings and elsewhere. In particular, he championed the idea that a community shares a common sense of history and a common commitment to the creation and management of cultural institutions.[54] In the ACIM, Wenner and Weltfish designed an educational program that encouraged students to become active members of their community. They also clearly hoped the project would enable students and faculty to form relationships across lines of race and neighborhood, though Weltfish's pointed comments suggest they fell far short of this goal. Nonetheless, over the course of the short project life-span, strategies of civic engagement and concern for social justice shaped efforts to preserve and interpret historic places and to educate students in the broad realm of public culture. Student researchers established indigenous people as part of the evolution of the landscape and assembled collections of artifacts and oral histories that pointed to the importance of late nineteenth- and early twentieth-century industrial development in mapping the various relationships that defined Morristown over time. Their work lent credence to the idea that communities are made by human connections, not by municipal boundaries.

As the ACIM program took shape between 1964 and 1969, the school district dispute made its way through the New Jersey court system. The dispute hinged on competing understandings of the history and nature of community. In 1968, the township board of education held a nonbinding referendum, asking residents if they favored the creation of a separate K–12 system. Township residents voted 2,164 to 1,899 in favor of separation, and the township began to take steps to build a new, separate high school, including initiating a bond referendum.[55] When Wenner challenged the validity of this referendum, the state commissioner of education acknowledged that the vote was likely nonbinding and that the outcome would be to segregate the school districts, but he refused to act. The case eventually arrived in the state supreme court as *Jenkins v. Township of Morris School District*.

The New Jersey state supreme court decided the Jenkins case in 1971, declaring it the responsibility of the state commissioner of education to act to prevent segregation. The school district remained unified. In the aftermath of the decision, the Morristown unified school district experienced some minor incidents of racial unrest. Shortly after formal consolidation in 1973, scuffles between White and Black students drew both media and police attention, but they blew over quickly with no lingering legal ramifications for individual students or for the reputation of the school. Indeed, the district is among the most racially, ethnically, and socioeconomically diverse in the state of New Jersey, and Morristown High School has a record of high achievement for all of its students.[56]

The history of the American Civilization Institute of Morristown, New Jersey, suggests that public history education was not only an academic invention, designed to broaden job opportunities for history PhDs. Public history education has also been a broadly public invention, deriving radical intentions from the contexts in which it arose and from the individuals who gave it shape. It has been broadly interdisciplinary, approaching a study of the past from a variety of perspectives and areas of expertise. It was community-based, encouraging students and teachers to work together to collect and organize often overlooked forms of historical evidence—from material culture to oral history. It was inspired by state initiatives that sought to democratize the process of history-making and challenge racist and exclusive interpretations of the past. It was organized by two individuals with lifelong commitments to racial justice and diversity. It was temporary, designed to address a particular set of historical and political issues. In the end, the work of the ACIM engaged students, teachers, history buffs, and others in a process that made a legal and political philosophy of community into something concrete, measurable, and meaningful. And it has often fallen short of its most radical goals, forcing public history educators to question our determined belief that processes of historical inquiry can bridge stubborn barriers to inclusiveness and equality. The ACIM demonstrated that communities are made through shared experiences and shared spaces, and they cannot be contained by political or social boundaries. Surely, then, the ACIM emerges as a significant antecedent for radical public history education.

Notes

1 Benjamin Shambaugh coined the term *applied history* in 1910. See Rebecca Conard, *Benjamin Shambaugh and the Intellectual Foundations of Public History* (Iowa City:

University of Iowa Press, 2001); Rebecca Conard, "Shambaugh, Benjamin Franklin," in *The Biographical Dictionary of Iowa*, ed. David Hudson, Marvin Bergman, and Loren Horton (Iowa City: University of Iowa Press, 2008).

2 I wrote about this process earlier. See Denise D. Meringolo, *Museums, Monuments, and National Parks: Toward a New Genealogy of Public History* (Amherst: University of Massachusetts Press, 2012).

3 Robert Kelley, "Public History: Its Origins, Nature and Prospects," *Public Historian* 1, no. 1 (Autumn 1978): 16, 18; G. Wesley Johnson "The Origins of the *Public Historian* and the National Council on Public History" *Public Historian* 21, no. 3 (Summer 1999): 168.

4 Robert Cook, *Troubled Commemoration: The American Civil War Centennial, 1961–1965* (Baton Rouge: Louisiana State University Press, 2011), 90.

5 "New Jersey Tercentenary: For Three Centuries People, Purpose, Progress," *History News* 17, no. 6 (1962): 76.

6 "New Jersey Tercentenary."

7 American Civilization Institute of Morristown (ACIM), "ACIM So Far: A Progress Report," North Jersey History and Genealogy Center, Joint Free Public Library of Morristown and Morris Township, American Civilization Institute of Morristown Collection, box 1, folder 2.

8 Gene Weltfish, "American Civilization Institute of Morristown 2-Progress Report-1968," p. 13, North Jersey History and Genealogy Center, Joint Free Public Library of Morristown and Morris Township, American Civilization Institute of Morristown Collection, box 1, folder 5.

9 ACIM, "ACIM So Far," 3.

10 Gene Weltfish, "American Civilization Institute of Morristown 1-Statement of Purpose," North Jersey History and Genealogy Center, Joint Free Public Library of Morristown and Morris Township, American Civilization Institute of Morristown Collection, box 1, folder 5.

11 Edmund Drake Halsey, *History of the Washington Association of New Jersey* (Morristown, NJ: Washington Association of New Jersey, 1891). See also Governor Theo Randolph, "Letter to the Editor, Washington's Headquarters at Morristown," *Morris Republication*, reprinted from *Newark Advertiser*, September 9, 1873, Morristown National Historic Site Museum and Archives, Records of the Washington Association of New Jersey, 1824–2003, series 1, box 1, folder 12. While it was not atypical for men to work to preserve historic battlefields, it was unusual in the history of nineteenth-century preservation movements for a group of male volunteers to preserve and interpret a historic house.

12 Percy H. Stewart, A Bill to Provide for the Creation of the Morristown NHP in the State of New Jersey, H.R. 14302, 72nd Cong. (1933). See also Henry C. Pitney (secretary), "Special Meeting of the Trustees of the Washington Association of New Jersey," Morristown National Historic Site Museum and Archives, Records of the Washington Association of New Jersey, 1824–2003, series 2, box 15, folder 5.

13 "By-Laws of the American Civilization Institute of Morristown," North Jersey History and Genealogy Center, Joint Free Public Library of Morristown and Morris Township, American Civilization Institute of Morristown Collection, Box 1, folder 1.

14 Quoted in ACIM, "ACIM So Far."

15 For example, ACIM, "ACIM So Far"; Gene Weltfish, "American Civilization Institute Symposium," p. 5, North Jersey History and Genealogy Center, Joint Free Public Library of Morristown and Morris Township, American Civilization Institute of Morristown Collection, box 1, folder 9; Weltfish, "ACIM 1-Statement of Purpose."

16 Weltfish, "American Civilization Institute Symposium," 10.

17 Weltfish, "ACIM 1-Statement of Purpose," 19.

18 Weltfish, 23.

19 Weltfish, 26.

20 The governor of New Jersey established Morris County in 1739, and Morris Town and Morris Township operated there as a single jurisdiction until 1865. For more on this, see Charles A. Goodrich, "A Brief History of the Colony of New Jersey, 1664–1738," in *A History of the United States*, 1857, edited version available at http://www.celebrateboston.com/history/new-jersey.htm; Robert Hennelly "Secret History of a Northern Slave State: How Slavery Was Written into New Jersey's DNA," Salon, July 29, 2015, https://www.salon.com/2015/07/29/secret_history_of_a_northern_slave_state_how_slavery_was_written_into_new_jerseys_dna/; Douglas Harper, "Slavery in New Jersey" Slavery in the North, accessed March 3, 2021, http://slavenorth.com/newjersey.htm; Leonard L. Richards, *Who Freed the Slaves? The Fight over the Thirteenth Amendment* (Chicago: University of Chicago Press, 2015), 234–35.

21 North Jersey History and Genealogy Center, "A Brief History of Morristown," MorristownGreen.com, October 8, 2015, https://morristowngreen.com/2015/10/08/a-brief-history-of-morristown/.

22 Hennelly, "Secret History."

23 Harper, "Slavery in New Jersey."

24 Richards, *Who Freed the Slaves?*, 234.

25 Richards, 234–35.

26 Richards, 235.

27 Richards, 207.

28 Henry C. Pitney, ed., *A History of Morris County, New Jersey, Embracing upwards of Two Centuries, 1710–1913* (New York: Lewis Historical Publishing, 1914), 51.

29 Richard F. Miller, ed., *States at War: A Reference Guide for Delaware, Maryland, and New Jersey in the Civil War* (Lebanon, NH: University Press of New England, 2015), 4:575.

30 Richards, *Who Freed the Slaves?*, 207.

31 Miller, *States at War*, 4:575.

32 Pitney, *History of Morris County*, 90, 242.

33 State of New Jersey, Department of State, Census Bureau, *Compendium of Censuses 1726–1905: Together with the Tabulated Returns of 1905* (Trenton, NJ: John L. Murphy, 1906); Jenkins v. Tp. of Morris School Dist. and Bd. of Ed., 58 N.J. 483 (1971).

34 New Jersey Department of Labor (NJDOL), Labor Planning and Analysis, "Table 6: New Jersey Resident Population by Municipality: 1930–1990," NJ.gov, accessed March 3, 2021, https://www.nj.gov/labor/lpa/census/1990/poptrd6.htm; *Jenkins*, 58 N.J. 483.

35 United States Bureau of the Census, *Reports of the 13th United States Census*, vol. 3, *States with Statistics for Counties, Cities, and Other Civil Divisions, Nebraska-Wyoming, Alaska, Hawaii, and Puerto Rico* (Washington, DC: Government Printing Office, 1913), 127, https://www2.census.gov/library/publications/decennial/1910/volume-3/volume-3-p2.pdf; United States Bureau of the Census, *Fifteenth Census of the United States, 1930* (Washington, DC: Government Printing Office, 1931), 741.

36 NJDOL, Labor Planning and Analysis, "Table 6."

37 *Jenkins*, 58 N.J. 483.

38 "School Desegregation: 1954–1964," *CQ Researcher*, April 29, 1964, https://library.cqpress.com/cqresearcher/document.php?id=cqresrre1964042900.

39 "School Desegregation."

40 "Finding Aid to the American Civilization Institute of Morristown Records, 1965–1969," Morristown and Morris Township Library website, accessed March 3, 2021, https://mmtlibrary.org/HCFindingAids/AmericanCivilizationInstituteofMorristown.xml.

41 Ruth Benedict and Gene Weltfish *The Races of Mankind*, Public Affairs Pamphlet 8 (New York: Public Affairs Committee, 1943), available at https://babel.hathitrust.org/cgi/pt?id=mdp.39015035399206&view=1up&seq=3.

42 Ruth E. Boetcker, "Weltfish, Gene: Anthropologist and Human Rights Advocate," in *American National Biography* (New York: Oxford University Press, 1999); Juliet Niehaus, "Education and Democracy in the Anthropology of Gene Weltfish," *Visionary Observers: Anthropological Inquiry and Education* (Lincoln: University of Nebraska Press, 2006).

43 "A Tribute to Dr. Harry Wenner," December 13, 1981, North Jersey History and Genealogy Center, Joint Free Public Library of Morristown and Morris Township, Morris School District Records, 1851–2009, box 17, folder 12.

44 "Harry Wenner, 88, Important in Schools Merger," obituary, *New Jersey Hills Media Group*, February 1, 2006, https://www.newjerseyhills.com/harry-wenner-important-in-schools-merger/article_1afe4ce2-204e-5c76-9f49-f3ac2ec27ea3.html; "Tribute to Dr. Harry Wenner."

45 Ronald Doll et al., "An Experiment in Training Teachers for Discussion Group Leadership," *Educational Leadership* 10, no. 2 (November 1952): 112–17.

46 Harry W. Wenner, "The Relationship of Characteristics of the Superintendent of Schools to Group Program Improvement Activities—a Further Study" (PhD diss., Columbia University, 1956).

47 "Tribute to Dr. Harry Wenner."

48 Rolfe Wenner, personal email with author, July 8, 2016.

49 Weltfish, "American Civilization Institute Symposium."

50 Weltfish, 17.

51 Weltfish.

52 Candeub was born in Romania, and he was a 1943 graduate of the City College of New York. He attended graduate school at Columbia University, and received a master's degree in architecture and city planning from the Massachusetts Institute of Technology. He and Morris B. Fleissig established a community development and environmental planning firm—Candeub, Fleissig, and Associates—in 1953.

53 Isadore Candeub, "Urban Design Related to Social Needs," in *Planning Urban Education: New Ideas and Techniques to Transform Learning in the City*, ed. Dennis L. Roberts II (Englewood Cliffs, NJ: Educational Technology Publications, 1972), 103.

54 Harry Wenner, "Brief for Merger," North Jersey History and Genealogy Center, Joint Free Public Library of Morristown and Morris Township, Morris School District Records, 1851–2009, box 11, folder 18.

55 *Jenkins*, 58 N.J. 483.

56 Greg Flaxman et al., "A Status Quo on Segregation: Racial and Economic Imbalance in New Jersey Schools, 1989–2010," UCLA: The Civil Rights Project / Proyecto Derechos Civiles, October 11, 2013, https://escholarship.org/uc/item/59f9n7x7#author.

Radical Futures

Teaching Public History as Social Justice

Elizabeth Belanger

In his 2014 National Council on Public History (NCPH) presidential address, Robert W. Weyneth looked back at his career as a public historian, teacher, and scholar and identified two key themes shaping his work: "embracing a dark past" and "asking questions from the perspective of place." In Weyneth's call for public historians to look for the "pukas" or gaps in historical narrative, "for their presence usually signals there's a story that is absent," and to "cast their bucket where [they are]" working in local contexts and settings, one can see the tendrils of public history's radical past influencing its current practices.[1] As the chapters in this section attest, public historians as early as the Progressive Era sought out untold stories and voices, and worked in deeply local contexts. Yet for teachers of public history, Weyneth's address and his preceding writings on public history education do little to identify how to teach "chapters of history that are difficult, controversial, or problematical."[2] Working in and with community, seeking out untold and contentious stories, and teaching others to do the same creates a classroom that functions less like an objective space where students learn the history of the field and engage in the academic debates about key controversies, and more like what scholar Mary Louise Pratt describes as a "contact zone." In contact zones, learning becomes an "exercise in storytelling and in identifying with the ideas, interests, histories and attitudes of others." Contact zones are "experiments in transculturation and collaborative work . . . ways for people to engage with suppressed aspects of history (including their own histories)" in which students develop "ground rules for communications across lines of difference and hierarchy that go beyond politeness but maintain mutual respect."[3] Teaching public history for social justice is teaching our students the skills of the contact zone. It is fostering the skills—practical, cognitive, and affective—that allow students to work with community members and to uncover the untold stories in the community around them. Teaching public history is also acknowledging the discomfort such work engenders and bringing that discomfort back to the classroom, for only in wrestling with the feelings and emotions inherent in the work can we begin to reimagine a public history education that truly serves social justice ends.[4]

I would argue the skills of the contact zone are essential to public history and historians, yet with a few exceptions, most of the scholarship on the training of public history students focuses on either practical skills—grant writing, National Register of Historic Places nominations, digital history skills—or the cognitive dimensions of learning that take place in a public history classroom.[5] Since its inception as "applied history," educators have asserted that public history helps students develop critical thinking skills including problem solving, leadership, and team skills.[6] Yet as Weyneth's address hints, "embracing a dark past" locally requires not only the cognitive and practical skills public history educators call for but affective skills—empathy, awareness of self, mindfulness, and an openness in the face of work that is often uncomfortable, challenging and problematic. The classroom conditions that give rise to the affective dimensions of learning do not arise automatically. They require a pedagogy that nurtures the growth of these qualities, a pedagogy that public history educators might use but few describe in detail.

In what follows, I pull back the curtain on my own public history pedagogy and recount my efforts to address the nature and scope of affective learning in my classroom. As evidenced in their writings, it was not unusual for my undergraduate students to express a range of emotions engendered by their work in a community different from their own, emotions ranging from anger, fear, sadness, and frustration to pride and revelation. If I wanted my students to meet the course's social justice goal of examining systems of power and oppression and encourage them to create a project in the service of social change, I needed to directly address affective learning in my classroom. The affective domain of learning focuses on nurturing students' abilities to receive and tolerate new information, to respond to ideas, to be willing to stand up for those ideas, to organize their values and beliefs, and ultimately to practice and act on their values.[7] These skills were essential for my students whose privilege, for the most part, had shaped their previous values and beliefs. As researchers at the University of Indiana found, "Negative emotions, including sadness or defensive anger, may prevent them [students] from considering the intellectual issues central to a course."[8] Examining the place of those emotions in the classroom and focusing on how students' affective learning gains might further a social justice–oriented public history project became this study's central focus.

Given that current public history scholarship has so little to say about how teachers can address the feelings doing public history fosters in their students—feelings of anger, confusion, guilt, and frustration—I turned to the pedagogy and practices of community arts, a discipline that has long embraced affect as a central element in learning. This chapter theorizes what a public history pedagogy informed by community arts pedagogy should look like, exploring the tenets, beliefs, approaches, and philosophies central to community arts that foster the mission of public history pedagogy. It also describes how these pedagogies playout in a public history classroom, chronicling a four-month art/history collaboration between undergraduates and teens at an after-school club. Finally, it assesses the affective student learning outcomes in the course, examining evidence of students' emotional growth. In doing so, it articulates how the pedagogies of community arts and public history intersect in generative ways.

I've organized this chapter around four sites where community arts education intersected with public history's goals in ways that address the affective dimensions of learning: (1) The first intersection examines the ways in which community arts pedagogies focused on personal reflection can inform notions of reflection central to public history. Affective learning stipulates that in order for students to act on their values, they must first explore why they value certain things and not others. (2) The second asks how community arts pedagogies focused on collaboration can help public history educators interrogate notions of collaboration in ways that link it to social justice goals. Affective skills like listening, participating, and debating are central to an authentic collaboration. (3) The third looks at how community artists define knowledge and how those definitions help educators reimagine what public history teaching might look like. Viewed through the lens of affective learning, community-based epistemologies rely on students' ability to organize and act on a set of values derived from their community work. (4) Finally, I look to community arts to help rethink what success means and how to measure it in ways that acknowledge the transformative power of the work. At its highest level, affective learning is demonstrated by behavior that is consistent with a value system. To what extent did my students internalize a new set of values informed by their social justice work and how are those values exhibited in their final projects? In bringing these pedagogies into the public history classroom, I hoped to both address and utilize the affective dimensions of learning to serve social justice aims.

The lenses through which I framed my project speak to some of the core tenets that tie this project to the work of my public history educator forbearers. The pedagogies in this collection seek to uncover histories on the margins, stories that have been left out of conventional narratives. This choice of subject matter is a deliberate one, for these "pukas," as Weyneth terms them, challenge stereotypes, social inequalities, political agendas, and other forms of individual and systematic oppression. Teaching public history for social justice ends not only uncovers such stories but also places issues of power and privilege at the center of historical analysis.[9] In addition, these teachings prioritize the collective construction of historical narratives and recognize that such collaborative endeavors are central to radical work.[10] Finally, social justice public history practice and teaching are grounded in critical reflection. It requires a level of transparency that not only makes visible the process of history-making but asks students, teachers, and community members to acknowledge how systems of privilege and oppression operate both in their own lives and within the scope of the project. Such transparency is only possible through a careful examination of self. In defining radical pedagogy in a particular place at a particular time, my contemporary case study, in its own small way, provides insight into one set of contexts and conditions that foster radical practices.

Shared Histories

Collaborations between community artists and public historians are not surprising given public history and community arts' shared past. While some scholars have traced the roots of the two disciplines as far back as the early 1800s, their paths appear to cross in the early twentieth century and come to fruition at the turn of the century with the work undertaken in settlement houses, the village improvement movement, the city beautiful movement, cooperative extension service, and the outdoor art movement.[11] In these settings, practitioners came together in local community centers, schools, social clubs, and museums to work with the public in a variety of roles. Many of the individuals undertaking the work were influenced by John Dewey's writings on teaching and service. In works that echo public historians' call for "shared authority" and artists' calls for "collaborative" "participatory" and "dialogic" art, Dewey cautioned that "associations aimed at overcoming social divisions should be distributive, mutual, and reciprocal relationships, or they will by definition perpetuate the barriers they set out to destroy."[12] By the 1930s, the federal government supported a number of public art and public history initiatives. Under the New Deal, artists were encouraged to research and depict local history on post office murals and the Federal Writers' Project recorded hundreds of oral histories for the Slave Narratives collections. Teachers and intellectuals working in a variety of settings, including Harold Thompson and Lucy Maynard Salmon in higher education and Myles Horton at the Highlander Folk School, worked with students and community members to undertake grassroots history and art projects.[13] Public art and history organizations witnessed another renaissance in the 1960s and '70s. Organizations like the National Council on Public History and the National Endowment for the Arts reflected ideals advanced by civil rights movements, the Comprehensive Employment and Training Act, and critical pedagogy theories like those of Paulo Freire. In turn, they inspired more local efforts including the San Francisco Neighborhood Arts Program and the American Civilization Institute of Morristown.[14]

I call attention to the shared historical trajectories of public history and community arts because while few of these individuals and organizations deliberately engaged in interdisciplinary projects linking community arts and public history, these disciplines came of age together, influenced by the same radical and progressive impulses that shape much of their work today. Their shared time line speaks to the shared visions that animate their recent forms: civic engagement, a commitment to bringing forward the voices of underrepresented groups, and social justice.

Increasingly, public historians have been collaborating with artists especially on projects that address a "dark past."[15] The projects share a commitment to local history as a site of investigation, a desire to work with and not just for their community partners, and pedagogical practices that highlight the emotions, insights, and experiences of everyday people, including those of the students themselves. They also suggest that the power of public history extends beyond tangible outcomes like museum exhibits, historic preservation applications, and archives and can result in catalytic as well as conclusive results. My course was inspired by these collaborations and took its form from a series of questions they raised.

Background

A small liberal arts institution nestled on the shores of Lake Seneca in the Finger Lakes of central New York, Hobart and William Smith Colleges (HWS) enrolls over 2,600 students, the majority of whom reside at the colleges. As an upper-level course in American studies, Art, Memory and the Power of Place enrolled sophomores, juniors, and seniors from a variety of majors and minors including American studies, history, and social justice studies. Out of the thirteen students enrolled in the course, four were women, and two were students of color. I divided the course into four sections; in the first, the students explored issues of identity and bias. Next they examined how issues of power, privilege, and place and community voice shaped case studies of controversial public art and public history projects. The third unit focused on the history and current demographics of Geneva, where the school's campus is located. When students come to HWS, most travel to a city with demographics vastly different from their own: students of color make up 53 percent of students in the Geneva City Schools.[16] I believed it was important for students to know something about the community they lived and worked in. Students spent the remainder of the semester collaborating with teens in an after-school art program. The students worked with the teens to design and create a public art/public history exhibit for the city's monthly art event—Geneva Night Out. The collaboration resulted in two projects: *Behind the Walls*, a piece that explored "narratives of bullying and violence in Geneva," and *Diversity in Geneva*, a series of portraits and narratives of eight city residents.[17]

Intervention 1: Reflection and Public History

Reflection plays a prominent role in public history theory and practice. As the public history profession sought to define itself beyond the notions of applied history, historians like G. Wesley Johnson and Noel J. Stowe theorized that public history practice enabled historians "to work in a situation—to understand its values, construct, context, cultural overtones, and relevant social, economic and political facets."[18] Drawing from the emerging learning theories of Donald Schon, NCPH president Rebecca Conard encouraged public historians to adopt a method that encompasses both theory and practice and embark on a shared inquiry and modes of work in collaboration with the public to identify problems, ask questions, and offer interpretations.[19] The reflective practice of public historians, as Conard describes it, is not linear but iterative, as conversations with the public reveal new insights, reframe central questions, uncover new contexts, and ultimately influence the shape and scope of the project created.[20] In turn, with each new engagement, public historians are "rethinking intellectual, practical, and moral issues," and these techniques, public historians assert, distinguish public history from its counterparts.[21]

Given the field's focus on the public dimensions of history, it's not surprising that most conversations about reflective practice in public history have centered on reflection in action—the process of adjusting one's actions within the context of a collaboration. An expanded notion of reflection, however, might also ask how we train public history students to "know thyself." Self-reflection, a central element of community arts practice, encourages students to interrogate how their subjectivity and positionality influence their practice. As Michael Rohd, the artistic director for the Sojourn Theater, notes, individuals involved in community collaborations "need to explore their own vision and point of view. They need to be willing to have voice and also to negotiate voice/authority. And they need to utilize that set of skills to affirm what they know, and discard what they no longer know."[22] Drawing from community arts practice, I asked my students to reflect on how their history shaped their values. The assignment, adapted from a similar one community artist and educator Pepon Osario uses in his classes, asked students to situate themselves within their community of origin—a community they were born into based on ethnic, racial, religious background, or national origin.[23] The paper challenged students to explore how they define their community, how it has shaped their values, and how it has been affected by the dynamics of oppression in America.

Requiring students to connect with their own pasts helped them become more attuned to dynamics of power, privilege, and oppression in their own lives. One student shared their newfound awareness when describing growing up one of the few middle-class children in an urban setting: "Reflecting back on my childhood, I realize that I would go from a very diverse education setting to then being picked up and taxied fifteen minutes south to hockey practice with kids who seemed to look and be much more like me.

To a fifteen-year-old kid, it is sometimes hard to comprehend why you are going to school at a place so different than many of your athletic friends, friends who you find comforting and similar to you."[24] Another student noted, "It is hard to be uncomfortable in my community because our town is mostly White and upper class. As a kid I saw the resemblances of my family in other families and how their households are run. So to me, what I saw growing up made me think that my town and my family were 'normal.'" Self-reflection served as a way for students to make connections between personal history and viewpoints/biases that might shape their interactions with the community and their public work. Articulating when and why they felt comfortable in some settings and uncomfortable in others forced them to interrogate the deeply held but seldom named assumptions about whose family experience was "normal" and why some types of people and places were "comforting" while others caused anxiety.

For some students, the assignment also allowed them to express their feelings of guilt, anger, and resentment that accompanied critical reflection into the values, experiences, and beliefs they had experienced as "normal." "My boarding school" one student recalled "was the single most exclusive environment I have ever encountered—it is the school where every single girl aspires to own brand name leggings the second she steps onto campus. Everything is a competition between you and other students over things like who knows the most gossip, who has the most money, who is the most popular . . . It was a culture that didn't make me feel good about being on campus."
Another student confessed that she now seldom reveals where she grew up to her friends: "For the last few years I have been embarrassed about where I came from. I have struggled to speak out against the narrow-minded views of my peers and fit into social groups that disregard problems of social inequality at home." Still another student articulated, "If there is anything about my community that I resent, it is that it does not prepare its youth to integrate anywhere else." The assignment asked students to connect these personal histories to feelings of belonging and alienation through critical self-reflection.

The community of origin papers were not public, so while they encouraged self-reflection, they did so within an individual learner setting. In contrast, a second key activity I undertook, a "privilege walk" and reflection, fostered critical questioning of fixed ideas and identities and challenged stereotypical images within a group setting. The privilege walk activity made visible students' assumptions about classmates and revealed how categories of difference intersect with social power.[25] In order to ground the activity within the framework of power and privilege, I also had students read Peggy McIntosh's seminal work "White Privilege: Unpacking the Invisible Knapsack."[26] For many students, the combined reading and activity made them consider their own social location(s) in powerful ways. "When I read Peggy McIntosh's 'White Privilege,'" confessed one student, "I was shocked.... It forced me to be self-reflective and gain a better understanding of my place in society and others around me." Another student noted, "Before this week, I would try and avoid questions based on race." Many of my White students expressed shock and wonder at the different experiences their classmates of color had with the structures and institutions of US society. "Doing the privilege walk made me realize how one-sided my thinking was.... Growing up in a middle-class, mostly White suburb, lead me to think that everyone was just like me," wrote one student. For my students of color, the readings, activity, and discussion after affirmed their experiences of structural racism: "Most students here [HWS] seem to have the same idea of racism I had when I was younger. They understand racism as meaning an individual had their mind set on someone before knowing them because of the color of their skin. Racism isn't just personal. Why was the closest neighborhood to the 'bad' elementary school, the neighborhood with subsidized housing, made up of more people of color than the neighborhoods around the 'good' elementary school?" In order to illuminate the role privilege plays in history-making, I also asked a number of questions centered on students' experience of public history: step forward if you were taught history by a teacher who shared your ethnic/racial background; step forward if the stories of your ethnic/racial ancestors have been visible in history museums. These questions were also eye-opening to my students. "The privilege walk," one student commented, "made me wonder—what stories go untold in our museums and history markers?" Others acknowledged the lack of diversity among history teachers: "Despite my school being diverse, I cannot recall a time in which I had an African American teacher, not in elementary, middle, and high school." Perhaps equally telling was the same student's observation that the realization of the lack of diversity in history education was "deeply discomforting." These activities and reflections were not easy for my students, but in challenging students' deeply held assumptions about themselves and others, they formed the foundation for our collaboration with community members.

Community arts pedagogy contributes to public history education through a more fully realized notion of what learning looks like in a classroom where "dialogue" begins with self-reflection. Students' learning gains are centered on the affective domain, particularly in self-knowledge.[27] Educational psychologist Stephan Brookfield links these self-insights into a tradition of critical thinking that includes "uncovering and challenging assumptions that frame behavior and seeing familiar actions and ideas from a radically different perspective."[28] The pedagogy reframes notions of reflection in public history by creating spaces for students to consider how their own positionality affects their actions as public historians.

Within the context of our project in Geneva schools, personal reflection took a central role in my student's work. After brainstorming a number of issues the teens were concerned about as a larger group, the students and teens split up into two groups, one focusing on diversity in the city, the other focusing on bullying and violence. As the bullying and violence group came together to craft their required project proposal, which they submitted to the city's public art committee, my students found themselves at an impasse. What was their role in this project? Were they guides, participants, or both? The group had proposed a project that was deeply personal and reflective. Individual students would each craft a box that would explore the impact of bullying on their life. Filled with personal photographs, thoughts, and narratives, the students would then connect the boxes together to form a larger installation aimed at bringing awareness to the issue. Ultimately, my students chose to participate in the process, each making a box for the installation. Making their box, side by side with their teen collaborators, made visible the ways my student's privilege had shaped their connection to the issue. One of my students noted, "I experienced bullying, but my parents took me out of public school and enrolled me in private school to help. That doesn't seem like an option for many of these kids." Another observed, "At first I couldn't believe how many students said they had felt bullied and/or witnessed violence in their lives. . . . I guess I never really thought about who it [violence] happens to and why I wasn't aware of it growing up." Such reflection allowed my students to recognize and acknowledge the trappings of privilege in their own lives and gave them an outlet to address the feelings those revelations engendered.

In turn, reflections about privilege and power shaped my student's approach to the final elements of the exhibit. The first draft of the exhibit's brochure pulled together student research on violence and bullying. Written in the third person, the brochure summarized research on the impact of bullying on teens' self-esteem. It also included brief bibliographies of participants, highlighting accomplishments and noted students whose "art has been featured in local art shows" and "published in magazines."[29] The brochure shared the dispassionate academic tone of more conventional public history projects and a focus on the authors' "credentials" to legitimize their expertise and roles as creators. After looking over the first draft, I encouraged the group to reimagine the brochure not as an exhibit label but as an artist statement. I was immediately struck by how reframing the project's written elements as "artist statements" rather than "exhibit labels" seemed to provide my students with the opportunity to acknowledge the emotional and reflective aspects of their work. In the revised brochure, each member of the project, both college students and teens, reconfigured their biographies, focusing on a brief statement about what drew them to this project and their goals. Written in the first person, these statements highlighted how individual identities, experiences, and opinions had shaped their work. "I want to show people what occurs at school because sometimes I feel like you don't ever hear from the people being bullied," noted one teen, while another articulated, "This box says what I can't talk about—how bullying feels." The students placed individual narratives of the creators' motivations next to a rewritten project introduction that used the communal "we" to describe the overall goals of the exhibit. In their general introduction, the students wrote, "We hope our artwork will raise questions about the effects of bullying and violence on both personal lives and on our community. By looking at individual boxes, seeing how individual stories are also shared histories and bearing witness to the voices 'behind the walls,' we hope to inspire change." By moving between the individual and the shared as well as the personal and the communal, the final project made visible the students' understanding of how the intimate knowledge that they gained from personal reflection impacted their approach to the work. It also demonstrated how these personal narratives were in continual dialogue with each other. As one student wrote, the project revealed how "people have their own histories which are all smaller stories of the bigger experience." Visually expressing these histories provided students with a way to articulate and understand differing perspectives of a shared experience, both their own and those of their collaborators.

Intervention 2: Collaboration and Public History

Deep self-reflection also served as the foundation for our collaborative work. Since its inception, public history training has acknowledged the importance of collaboration. As public historian Rebecca Conard notes, collaboration separates out public history from public scholarship.[30] Within the field, theories of collaboration have focused on the notions of shared inquiry and shared authority. First coined by Michael Frisch in reference to oral history practice, *shared authority and inquiry* address the idea that public history projects, including oral history interviews, are shaped by both the historian and the community.[31] For public historians, both theories bring up important questions about power and agency within the collaboration. In practice, tensions sometimes emerge between the values that define the work of a "historian" and the work of a "public historian." Academic historians train their students to enter into the field as historians, objective, critical, and above all, unemotional.[32] Many of these values play a central role in undergraduate public history curriculums.[33] Yet dynamics of power inherent in traditional history training has profound implications for the trust building that is essential to collaborative public history work. As historian Barbra Franco notes, "It is a constant negotiation based on trust and mutual respect. . . . [In public history work] that seems far from the historical practices we have been trained to follow."[34]

As I considered how my undergraduate students were going to develop the bonds of trust essential to public history work, I turned to scholarship on public art. Community artists have different ideas about community collaboration and the role of the "expert." Both public artists and public historians observe that collaboration is a dialogical process, but public artists also acknowledge that the process "changes both the participants and the artist."[35] In public art practice, there is neither the desire nor the expectation for the artist to be dispassionate and removed from the community. As community artist Pepon Osorio observed about his classes, "The student learned that for each piece of information you gain you must share yourself personally. There is always a dual center of power in the relationship."[36] In descriptions of their work, public artists emphasize their role as caring participants in relationships built on empathy as well as reciprocity.[37]

In my course, students quickly realized that reading about community collaborations did little to prepare them for an environment in which they had to build trust with community partners. Within the first week of our collaboration, students articulated their challenges working with the teens. "It was difficult to establish a connection at first," a student wrote. "I didn't understand where this disconnect between us was coming from. The teens were very loud and outgoing, but incredibly reserved about their personal lives." Another commented, "I could sense a little bit of resentment in their body language . . . they were hesitant to trust us." Looking back at the collaboration's early struggles, a student reflected, "I think it is of huge importance to be able to create a community-like atmosphere with the teens, but it took time to build trust."

In the first weeks of the collaboration, I used various activities designed to make visible the shared experiences of my students and our collaborators. My students quickly identified the many ways our collaborators seemed "different" from themselves. As one student confessed, "It makes me nervous to start this [the collaboration] because I've only ever worked with kids with [a] very similar background to myself." In their journals, students commented on how activities like the privilege walk made shared experiences visible. "I have experienced bullying," one of my students remarked, "and I felt more comfortable knowing that I wasn't the only one that had to go through hard times during grade school. With this experience you get to share with everyone [and] I feel closer to the teens." Another commented, "I felt like through sharing our stories we were able to sympathize and understand each other's struggles. I left that day feeling like our group had just shared a special connection." In these reflections, students highlight feelings of closeness, comfort, and connection within the group and with individual teens. The feelings were valuable in my student's eyes because they served as the starting point for bonds of trust and respect that were central to the collaboration.

The influence of community arts pedagogy and theory on students' understanding of collaboration is most visible in the transformation of their thinking about their work with the teens over the course of the semester. In the beginning of the project, my students expressed frustration over what they viewed as the teens' unwillingness or inability to contribute to project brainstorming sessions. "Are they afraid to make a difference?" one student asked. "[Afraid] to be right or to have an opinion? Do they just not see community problems in Geneva?" Initial efforts to move past the early "icebreaker" activities and begin project planning were met with frustration. One student commented, "I feel awkward that we as HWS students are dominating the discussion." Another confessed, "I left kind of frustrated," adding, "It was hard to get the teens to talk and I feel like it [the brainstorming session] didn't push the class forward at all." Even in these initial stages, however, students were able to employ affective skills in empathy to reflect on project planning and how they might work with students. "I wonder," one student asked, "if that [teen participation] has something to do with comfort level?" Another remarked, "Since there was no baseline level of trust, we got very 'safe' ideas from the students," ideas that "did not require them to open up." Another student theorized, "I think they know more serious things happen in the community, but just don't feel comfortable enough to share certain experiences."

As the previous quotes suggest, for my students, foregrounding the importance of personal connections in the early stage of the collaboration helped them envision the project through the lens of dialogue. "Communication skills specifically, I felt were extremely important in this project," one student observed. The student continued, "When it comes to communication skills it does not exactly mean being able to talk constantly; it also means being a good listener. I realized that it was important to actually sit down and listen to what the teens had to say throughout the project. In order for them to feel comfortable with us, we had to be able to listen and get to know them." Others acknowledged how creating these personal relationships stretched their comfort level. "Through this class, I learned how integral it [dialogue] is to fostering a rapport within groups," a student commented. In addition, as evidenced in student reflections, honesty, not respect or consensus, became how my students defined the dialogue experience. "Because everyone was so honest we learned a lot about each other," commented a student. Another wrote, "I have learned to talk with many of the teens individually and honestly about who they are." Another explained, "Being honest, personal, and a listener is the best way to reach out to them in gaining input" because "if we want to create a meaningful project, both sides need to be honest with each other." In their highlighting of "honesty," the reflections speak to the ways in which the skills of the contact zone—"communications across lines of difference and hierarchy that go beyond politeness but maintain mutual respect"—became a means by which students assessed their own learning and the success of the project.[38] As one student commented, "[In traditional public history collaborations,] the role of the historian is to be a facilitator and they should not insert their voice into a project . . . What makes our project different is the honest stories of individuals." From the college students' reflections on the project emerge a tenet central to a social justice–oriented public history practice: the assertion that public history is a collaborative endeavor.

Intervention 3: Knowledge and Public History

As public history practitioners seek to incorporate voices from the margins of history, they struggle to reconcile radical impulses with deeply ingrained ideas about knowledge and the role of the expert within the historical profession. As historian Denise D. Meringolo points out, early public history programs "initially focused on the products of public history work, not the process. . . . Such an approach retained the expertise and authority of public historians."[39] Other scholars argue that not only does public history need to advocate for reflective public history "experts"; it needs to expand the definition of expert and reimagine their role. Equating expertise with authority and knowledge complicates public historians' efforts to work with communities.[40] In turn, expanding ideas about expertise to include the community also necessitates a reconsideration of what is considered knowledge in the field.

While notions of participatory museums and community-curated public history projects have garnered attention within the last ten years, community artists have a long tradition of working alongside community members and drawing from community expertise.[41] Perhaps because public historians are, more often than not, trained in the history profession with all its deeply rooted epistemologies, I turned to ways of knowing articulated in community arts to provide my students with frameworks for understanding how knowledge is created in a collaborative, nonhierarchical setting. These contemporary theories draw from the same historical well as public history.[42]

Framing students' work within the tradition of community arts helped them reenvision their role in the project. As they began to articulate the process of collaboration, my students located trust at the site of personal interaction, not expertise. As one student noted, "We can't take a top-down approach, where we think of the teens as more or less passive consumers, receivers of our expert wisdom. That approach goes again[st] our goal of creating a socially engaged project because it neglects their personal voice." Another student observed, "The project needs to engage in continual dialogue and create open relationships between our two groups." In emphasizing the importance of having the form and content of the project emerge out of a dialogue, students also articulated a collaborative public history practice that privileged everyday experiences and realities as ways of knowing. "In order for this project to work, it needs to include personal experiences," one student commented, "let the teens talk about what they want to talk about, and in a sense, let them create the project which shows their views accurately."

Another student observed, "An active part of this project is considering how information is collected through dialogue and presented through art. . . . In our project, active listening is extremely important, because that is how we get information."

In turn, teens involved with the project spoke to how they felt the project honored their voices and expertise: "The project talked about what a lot of us felt," wrote one teen. Another observed, "We all hear 'don't bully' and things like that, but you don't ever hear from the people who are bullied." One revealed, "I showed up because I found the topic really interesting." They continued, "A lot of people have been bullied, and it's something that we know." When asked to articulate what the teens felt that my students learned from the collaboration, a participant commented, "The college students learned that we are mature, we know school stuff."[43] The teens' comments also speak to how privileging everyday ways of knowing also served to decentralize authorship. Both the college students and the teens felt they had a stake in this project and could lay claim to project ideas.

Further, setting as the goal the creation of a dialogue-driven project, one viewed through the lens of community-based art, allowed my students to focuses on the process of creation rather than the product. "Again, it comes back to making a better effort of hearing all voices instead of getting impatient and suggesting my idea," articulated one student. Another observed, "I think I need to take a step back and lose my grip on the perfectionist inside of me. . . . Art embraces imperfections." Another noted, "I am realizing, that I cannot expect us to produce a beautiful work of art. It is more important in socially engaged art to make everyone's voices be heard, because in the past and currently, there are voices that are silenced in this community." A particularly reflective student offered this perspective on the collaborative process:

> Along with the idea of trust as a key theme, so was participation. I talked about "directed participation" in my journals and how that was the only thing that seemed to be occurring at first. We told the students what to do and they did it; there was no give-and-take of ideas. In fact, many of them asked us at first what they should put in their boxes. It was as though they needed our approval to feel like they could participate. Since we wanted these boxes to reflect unique and authentic voices, this was not the style of participation we were hoping for. However, as the project progressed, it became a very dynamic and joint project. They suddenly had no problem

abandoning our ideas for their own, and even became a bit defiant when they didn't like one of our suggestions. The fact that they were comfortable enough to challenge us means that they were comfortable with us in general. At the beginning of the semester, we couldn't pay them to challenge our ideas or us. However we now feel like their voices are in this project just as much as ours.

Participants' reflections reveal how knowledge emerged as a function of the collaborative process and a product of the group's discussions.

Focusing on the process rather than the product of the collaboration addressed important affective student learning outcomes. In their discussions, students grappled with both emotion and reason, pushing themselves and their collaborators to identify feelings, articulate choices, and express their vision for the project. Because this happened across lines of difference, the project participants also found themselves collaborating on shifting grounds, as group dynamics constantly changed. As one student commented, "Adjusting to this project was hard for all of us. Having to share ideas and discuss uncomfortable situations with the teens really contributed to the construction of community within our group." The teen's reflections supported my students' assessment of the importance of emotional awareness to fostering shared voice in the project. "I felt like the students who came from HWS wanted to talk with us," observed one teen. Another commented, "I love how we got to talk with each other and then decided to make two different projects." Questions of what elements to include in the piece, how to create an overarching narrative for the project, and how their understandings of the topic would be communicated in visual form were all determined and weighed among the group, making knowledge a function of community. As the quotes suggest, my students were also aware of what they gained through these interactions, a pedagogy that placed students in dialogue with individuals from different backgrounds supported the course's affective learning goals focused on empathy, openness to new ideas and different perspectives, and attentive listening.[44]

Intervention 4: Assessing Success in Public History Projects

Over the past twenty years, public historians have all struggled to define and assess success in their field. Contemporary definitions of success emerging from the field often focus on the content of a public history project: Did the project narrative balance multiple points of view? Did it incorporate relevant scholarship? Was it historically accurate?[45] As Cathy Stanton comments, "Public historians could attempt to understand much more clearly what the social consequences of these collaborations are" but often fail to do so because "this requires a set of skills that historians do not generally have, since the discipline is focused on the past and on the evidence of documents."[46] Little has been written about how to determine if a public history project engages with the affective dimensions of community work and the results of such engagement. Such assessment is vital for public history projects that operate on an emotional as well as a cognitive level. The absence of theoretical understandings of success that address the affective learning outcomes of public history projects pushed me to look to community arts to help rethink what success means and how to measure it in ways that acknowledge the transformative power of the work.

Scholars in community arts have put forth several useful models for assessing the success of their projects that directly connect their work to social justice goals. To begin with, community arts pedagogy compels us to consider not only the ways in which public history projects grapple with multiple points of view, understand community in context, and debate issues of voice but also how public history projects undertake such work within the context of social power. As community members and artists involved with the community arts group Appalshop note, art serving social justice ends "focus[es] . . . on how power is organized, used and shared in a community."[47] In doing so, community arts pedagogy pushes us to understand history's role as a technology of power and wield that power to create a counterdiscourse aimed at reclaiming dominant historical narratives. Community arts' focus on process over product also encourages public history educators to include community building in their definition of success. Finally, community arts practice urges us to consider the importance of transformation on an individual level measured by a growth in participants' critical thinking, affective skills, and self-definition. Community artist and educator Dudley Cook eloquently sums up the various intersections between these elements in his theory of social change: "Effective cultural organizing for social justice begins small, with the individual. First, one discovers his or her own truth of an issue, and then tests and develops that truth in dialogue with others. When this individual and collective learning process is multiplied, a national movement for reform develops and changes society. Such a movement can only be sustained when this grassroots process of individual and collective learning continues to inspire awareness and shape the actions."[48] As I turned to evaluating my student's collaboration on a project that was ephemeral and limited in its reach, I found such models useful for helping me consider how projects similar to my own in scale might measure success.

I examined both student reflections and the final products of the collaboration to assess how students grappled with multiple points of view, debated issues of voice within the context of social power, and articulated their growing understanding of the community. The *Diversity in Geneva* group decided their project would showcase eight city residents from a variety of backgrounds and ages. The project featured large portraits of community members with accompanying text from oral history interviews. This format emerged from conversations with the older teens at the after-school club who had shared their struggles growing up as children of color in Geneva. Perhaps as a response to my student's lack of awareness of communities outside the colleges, the teens spoke to community dynamics of visibility. Describing the origin of the project, one teen wrote, "I was just thinking about everyday life in Geneva and thinking about differences when I was in school and in the community as well. And I think it needs to be talked about more often, because we talk about diversity, but a lot of people don't really know what that means." Another noted, "I think most of [the] White people in Geneva doesn't notice the [racial] divides, but when you live in a neighborhood like mine, you notice it." In the brainstorming phase of the project, my students quickly embraced the teens' idea to focus the project on making the city's diversity more visible by printing large portraits. The size of the portraits, three feet by two feet, as well as the choice to display them outside in a public plaza, were deliberate decisions the students' and teens' made to achieve their larger goals. As one student observed, "A large part of the project for us is not the physical posters but how they will be displayed because it influences how the project is interpreted. By having all the posters next to one another, the audience is able to see the diversity in all the community members and compare and contrast them more critically. . . . I also think another valuable aspect of having the posters displayed together is it enhances the conversation and dialogue about diversity in the community that we hope will take place after viewing all the portraits." Likewise, the *Behind the Walls* project creators wanted their project to be something that made visible the hidden histories of bullying by showcasing the experiences of those who have been bullied.

The exhibit brochure claimed, "Through these boxes we have compiled a myriad of stories about the lives violence have touched... making visible the impact of bullying on individuals and the community as a whole." The groups' choice foreground these underrepresented histories in the exhibit, revealed their growing understanding of how individuals can be active agents in the creation of their own histories. As one student stated, "While it was surprising that so many of the kids had already experienced bullying... I think the more important takeaway was that they did all, in fact, have something to say."

Understanding their work in context also meant that the students and their projects grappled with questions of who and what represented community. "As we have seen in class, most of the people with the power to shape public art and history projects are still White and hold the purse strings," one student wrote. They continued, "When making public projects about 'the community' we need to ask, who are the people we are talking about?" Students worried about how to limit the scope of the project, some wanting to "make sure we have every group of people involved in the community," while others believed, "We need to focus on the voices of the kids and their experiences with diversity within their community and their opinions on what the Geneva community looks like." Questions over who to interview were complicated by my students' worries. Students and teens worked together to develop the scope and plan for the diversity project, but because teens could not leave the center, the actual interviewing was left to my students. They met this challenge with a range of feelings. "I do think we tried to get a diverse group of community members," explained one student, "but I will forever be slightly angst-ridden about how we went about collecting our interviews. How is this project influenced by the fact that we had to rely on the small number of people we already knew in the community to provide us with a way to be done with a project on time?" As they worked through these emotions in their groups, they acknowledged both their own positionality and the community context of their work. As one student commented, "I am happy that our project included voices from community members of color; however, I wonder if their responses were influenced by the fact that it was all-White HWS students interviewing them." Initial reflections about their own communities and identities helped students understand how their positionality in the Geneva community shaped their project.

In their questions of whose voices to include in their final projects, one can see students' and teens' warring desires to both celebrate Geneva's diversity and call attention to issues of racism and oppression. In a conversation with the group before opening night, the students and teens expressed their worries: "I hope it [the project] brings respect to people of color. I know coming from a low-income community of color, sometime you don't realize that White people are not the only ones who can be racist. I hope it really brings out the fact that we can all have prejudice and misperceptions," voiced one teen. One of the college students mused, "One thing that I am personally questioning is if we plan to celebrate the diversity in the community or start a dialogue about how the diversity can create divides. I feel that at first we wanted to celebrate the diversity in the community; however, working on this project has made me more aware of the issues that arise from it. One thing that has come to my attention just from the teens' comments is that people from different ethnic groups usually do not socialize." These tensions between a more celebratory message and a critical one are familiar to public historians like Linda Shopes, who observed that community history projects often celebrate imagined, nostalgic pasts, and rarely confront deeper historical contradictions.[49] Viewed through the lenses of Shopes's critiques, my student's public projects were perhaps not as radical as they could have been. In the narrative that accompanied the photographs, the *Diversity in Geneva* group acknowledged that "despite living in the same community, residents have a range of experiences and perspectives," and they pointed out that "interviews hint at the ways in which differences create divides." But their project did not call attention to systems of oppression that support racial divides and stereotypes in the community.[50] Likewise, the *Behind the Walls* group articulated their desire to "raise questions about the effects of bullying in both personal lives and on our community," but their narrative did not call attention to how structures and institutions silence narratives of bullying.

I would argue, however, the radical potential of the projects lay not in approaching the community from an oppositional stance but rather from an intentional practice of creating relationships. In their reflections on the final projects, both the students and teens spoke to their desire to create community through breaking down stereotypes and recognizing commonalities. Such work lies at the foundation of social transformation, for, as art educator Pablo Helguera points out, socially engaged art is assessed on its ability to create an "emancipated community. . . . This means that its participants willingly engage in a dialogue from which they extract enough critical and experiential wealth to walk away feeling enriched, perhaps even claiming some ownership of the experience or ability to reproduce it with others."[51] Both end projects sought to create community. "I think our project is powerful," commented one student, "because it starts a dialogue." They continued, "Our project seeks to raise awareness for violence and bullying by creating an art project where we are constantly talking and evoking conversation with the kids we are working with." Another student pointed out that "creating an environment where the kids are willing to talk about bullying and violence is extremely important because while it does not solve the problem, by bringing awareness to a critical issue, it can cause someone to help someone else that is a victim or a bully." Still another observed that while visitor numbers to the exhibit "weren't gigantic, I believe we were still successful. . . . We laid the foundation work for tools for social change. We completed the project, and the kids that helped us were proud of what they did. They brought their parents to the opening, and I overheard them talking to visitors explaining what it's [the exhibit's] about in hopes of starting talks about bullying."

Finally, student work speaks to how individual transformation should also be factored into definitions of success. A focus on the civic outcomes of collaborations overshadows the equally important personal transformation such work engenders. Community arts' focus on the process over the product suggests that evaluation of the capacity of the end product to enact social change is a limited perspective on success. As community artist Judith Baca explains it, "The process, that part, which is the ephemeral part of the work, . . . [is] probably the majority of the work. My work leaves a record of that process . . . in the two millimeters of paint. But previous to that, three quarters of the work is in the community cultural development work. The work in which the community has interacted with us, in which it participates to create the monument."[52] In the case of my students, the projects they created didn't result in tangible social change evidenced in fundamental changes to structures of oppression in the city, but the seeds for such changes lay in their understanding of the personal transformations they undertook in this course—their affective learning gains. Echoing the focus on process over product, students and teens wanted to "be judged on the personal impact rather than the art itself. If it affects peoples, their emotions, they are inspired and it makes them happy—then that is successful." They wanted to make "people in the project feel that they had a voice [in the project] and were able to speak to community members through a different venue" and spoke about the individual impact the work might have: "I'll be happy if it makes one person think. If they keep it with them while they are living." While, as one student observed, "there is no true way to measure whether or not that [social justice goal] is accomplished," it is clear from student and teen reflections that by the end of their collaboration, they viewed themselves as agents of social change. "You can't make every single person happy," one student remarked, "but you can get people to talk and that is what these projects did." The teens also expressed a sense of agency and empowerment as a result of participating in the project. One teen admitted, "I liked making the art and feeling like you were doing something for the community. It felt like we were making a difference."

Students also spoke to change within themselves. Through their connections with the teens and the larger Geneva community, students identified their need to rethink their own place(s) in the world, becoming more insightful and self-aware regarding the social contexts of their own lives and the lives of others. "I have never worked with anyone other than upper-class, White children," recognized one student. They continued, "To be thrown into a shared project with many different cultures and backgrounds was different than anything I have ever done. However, I think it was also the most rewarding of anything I have ever done. Between lessons of trust, participation, and voice, I will take away more than I thought I could from this class." Another noted, "This project was a learning experience for me in that I had to self-reflect on why I felt so uncomfortable at times. . . . In this class I had to push myself further and further outside my comfort zone it progressed. This course was more of a personal journey than I ever anticipated." For many, these personal transformations are what set this class apart from their other educational experiences. One expressed it this way: "As a White, middle-class college student it is easy to read about inequality and never take the time to learn about the social inequality in the community I live in. I spent last semester in courses focusing on social, racial, and gender inequality; however, I never applied that understanding to my daily life. I want to be more involved with the inequality that occurs around me daily." Students' learning outcomes came about through personal interactions and the work collaborative public history projects require. "Until this point," noted one student about a particularly meaningful conversation with a teen, "I had thought of our work as really just an art and history collaboration, but now I saw it transcend into a different level; one akin to friendship. I am not suggesting I will leave and become great friends with the kids, but I realized that while these kids may not remember us in five years, our impact for some may last a long time." In a field that teaches objectivity, placing awareness of self and others at the center of interpretation and critical skills is a radical proposition. Through a recognition of issues of power and privilege in the community, a focus on process over the product, and the students' and teens' personal transformations, these projects illustrate new affective learning outcomes for public history education that support larger social justice goals.

The Future of Public History Education

In 1987, G. Wesley Johnson and Noel J. Stowe looked back at the development of the public history field and argued, "To date, no one has articulated acceptable theoretical underpinnings for the teaching and practice of public history."[53] Twenty years later, NCPH president Rebecca Conard urged historians to "rethink public history education."[54] More recently Denise D. Meringolo has postulated that "we have not fully understood history as service, so we are not effectively training the next generation of public historians."[55] As the collection of chapters in this section suggest, perhaps the tools for reimagining public history education lie in its interdisciplinary and decidedly radical roots. In 1927, John Dewey reminded us that "the deepest and richest sense of a community must always remain a matter of face to face intercourse,"[56] and my study suggests that public history teachers might be well served by thinking carefully and critically about how we guide students through such intercourse. Pedagogical practices that foster self-reflection, emphasize collaboration, critique traditional forms of knowledge, and look for success in personal transformation are important training elements of teaching future public historians. I would argue that training in such affective skills are necessary if we want to keep public history relevant in a changing world. While the guidelines and practices developed in the years since Johnson and Stowe called for a new theoretical model for teaching public history speak to how public history teachers and programs have addressed the practical challenges of educating graduates and the cognitive learning outcomes of a public history degree, public history educators have failed to speak to affective dimensions of their work. If, as educator Julie Ellison claims, "the emergence of a new kind of public humanities registers most powerfully at the level of who we are," then focusing on how public history can help one get a job as a historian, or how it can provide a history department with a way to recruit more students to the history major, at best undersells the field and at worst runs the risk of creating a generation of public historians who reproduce the very power relations public history has the power to disrupt.[57] Training that teaches students to recognize history as a technology of power and provides them with the affective tools of empathy, awareness of self, and reflective judgment acknowledges not only the minds of our students but their hearts and souls as well. As bell hooks argues, "Dominator culture has tried to keep us all afraid, to make us choose safety instead of risk, sameness instead of diversity. Moving through that fear, finding out what connects us, reveling in our differences; this is the process that brings us closer, that gives us a world of shared values, of meaningful community."[58]

Notes

1 Robert W. Weyneth, "What I've Learned along the Way: A Public Historian's Intellectual Odyssey," *Public Historian* 36, no. 2 (May 2014): 9–25.
2 Robert Weyneth, "A Perfect Storm: Education, Employment, Profession, Training, Part 2," *History@Work*, September 6, 2013, accessed March 13, 2017, http://ncph.org/history-at-work/a-perfect-storm-part-2/.
3 Mary Louise Pratt, "Arts of the Contact Zone," *Profession* (1991): 34.
4 Denise D. Meringolo, "Learning to See What Service Learning Means," *History@Work*, March 22, 2012, accessed March 13, 2017, http://ncph.org/history-at-work/learning-to-see-what-service-learning-means/.
5 NCPH, for example, suggests, "Undergraduate programs that offer public history should keep the following four basic priorities in mind: (1) Provide students with strong training in the basic skills of the historian; (2) Provide students with a solid grounding in historical content; (3) Introduce students early in their studies to the wide variety of careers that incorporate some component of public history; and (4) Encourage students to participate in field-based research, service learning, and/or internships." NCPH Curriculum and Training Committee, "Public History for Undergraduate Students," October 1, 2009, http://ncph.org/wp-content/uploads/2010/08/Undergrad-Best-Practice.pdf.
6 See Barbara Howe, "Student Historians in the 'Real World' of Community Celebrations," in "The Field of Public History: Planning the Curriculum," special issue, *Public Historian* 9, no. 3 (Summer 1987): 126–37; G. Wesley Johnson and Noel J. Stowe, "The Field of Public History: Planning the Curriculum: An Introduction," in "The Field of Public History: Planning the Curriculum," special issue, *Public Historian* 9, no. 3 (Summer 1987): 10–19.
7 D. R. Krathwohl, B. S. Bloom, and B. B. Masia, *Taxonomy of Educational Objectives*, vol. 2, *Affective Domain* (New York: David McKay, 1964).
8 Joan Middendorf et al., "What's Feeling Got to Do with It? Decoding Emotional Bottlenecks in the History Classroom," *Arts and Humanities in Higher Education* 14, no. 2 (September 2014): 171. See also Chad Berry, Lori Schmied, and Joseph Schrock, "The Role of Emotion in Teaching and Learning History: A Scholarship of Teaching

Exploration," *History Teacher* 41, no. 4 (August 2008): 437–52; Baruch B. Schwarx and Tsafrir Goldber, "Looks Who's Talking: Identity and Emotions as Resources to Historical Peer Reasoning," in *Affective Learning Together: Social and Emotional Dimensions of Collaborative Learning*, ed. Michael Baker, Jerry Andriessen, and Sanna Jarvela (New York: Routledge, 2013).

9   Heather Hackman, "Five Essential Components for Social Justice Education," *Equity & Excellence in Education* 38, no. 2 (May 2005): 104.

10 As community scholar Dudley Cook remarks, "Those who directly experience a problem must make up the generative base for devising and enacting the problem's solution." See Jamie Half, "Voices from the Battlefront: Achieving Cultural Equity through Critical Analysis," Roadside Theater, accessed March 3, 2021, https://roadside.org/asset/article-voices-battlefront-achieving-cultural-equity-through-critical-analysis.

11 J. Ulbrich, "What Is Community-Based Art Education?," *Art Education* 58, no. 2 (March 2005): 6–12; Denise D. Meringolo, *Museums, Monuments, and National Parks: Toward a New Genealogy of Public History* (Amherst: University of Massachusetts Press, 2012); Arlene Goldbard, "Postscript to the Past: Notes toward a History of Community Arts," *High Performance*, no. 64 (Winter 1993); Rebecca Conard, "The Pragmatic Roots of Public History Education in the United States," *Public Historian* 37, no. 1 (February 2015): 105–20.

12 John Saltmarsh, "Education for Critical Citizenship: John Dewey's Contribution to the Pedagogy of Community Service Learning," *Michigan Journal of Community Service Learning* 3, no. 1 (Fall 1996): 13–21; Thomas D. Fallace, "John Dewey on History Education and the Historical Method," in *Education & Culture* 26, no. 92 (Fall 2010): 20–35; Patricia Goldblatt, "How John Dewey's Theories Underpin Art and Art Education," *Education & Culture* 22, no. 1 (Fall 2006): 17–34.

13 William S. Walker, "Collecting Folk Histories: Harold W. Thompson and Student Field Research in the 1930s," *Public Historian* 37, no. 3 (August 2015): 45–75.

14 Ulbrich, "What Is Community-Based Art?"; Goldbard, "Postscript to the Past."

15 Examples include the Poindexter African American Comin [sic] Home Festival described in Christopher Olubunmi Ajejumo, "Promoting Artistic and Cultural Development through Service Learning and Critical Pedagogy in a Low-Income Community Art Program," *Visual Arts Research* 36, no. 1 (Summer 2010); the Urban Bush Women Dance Troupe (https://www.urbanbushwomen.org/about-ubw) discussed in Sophia Chakos-Leiby, "Urban Bush Women and Community Engagement Pedagogy," *Community Arts Perspective* 2, no. 3 (November 2009); Maureen Mullinax, "Resistance through Community-Based Arts," *Transforming Places: Lessons from Appalachia*, ed. Stephen Fisher and Barbara Ellen Smith (Chicago: University of Illinois Press, 2012), 92–106; Laura Browder and Patricia Herrera, "Civil Rights and Education in Richmond Virginia: A Documentary Theater Project," *Transformations: The Journal of Inclusive Scholarship and Pedagogy* 23, no. 1 (Fall 2012): 15–36; Weeksville Heritage Center's FUNKGODJAZZ&MEDICINE project, described in Jennifer Scott, "Reimagining Freedom in the Twenty-First Century at a Post-Emancipation Site," *Public Historian* 37, no. 2 (May 2015): 73–88. See also Patrick Grossi, "Plan

or Be Planned For: Temple Contemporary's Funeral for a Home and the Politics of Engagement," *Public Historian* 37, no. 2 (May 2015): 14–26; Nicole King's work around neighborhood place making and historic preservation in P. Nicole King, "Preserving Places, Making Spaces in Baltimore: Seeing the Connections of Research, Teaching and Service as Justice," *Journal of Urban History* 40, no. 3 (January 2014): 425–49.

16 "Geneva City School District," Public School Review, accessed March 3, 2021, https://www.publicschoolreview.com/new-york/geneva-city-school-district/3611970-school-district.

17 *Behind the Walls*, Geneva, 2016, exhibit brochure.

18 Johnson and Stowe, "Field of Public History," 18.

19 Rebecca Conard, "Facepaint History in the Season of Introspection," *Public Historian* 25, no. 4 (2003): 9–24; Donald Schon, *The Reflective Practitioner: How Professionals Think in Action* (New York: Basic Books, 1983).

20 Rebecca Conard, "Public History as Reflective Practice: An Introduction," *Public Historian* 28, no. 1 (Winter 2006): 9–13.

21 Noel J. Stowe, "Public History Curriculum: Illustrating Reflective Practice," *Public Historian* 28, no. 1 (Winter 2006): 40.

22 Shannon Scrofano and Michael Rohd, "The Race: Collaborative Art-Making Meets Democratic Nation Making," *Transformations: The Journal of Inclusive Scholarship and Pedagogy* 20, no. 1 (Spring/Summer 2009): 44.

23 Pepon Osario, "Syllabus for Visual Studies: Community Arts Spring 2012," Steven Berkowitz, accessed July 2016, http://www.berk-edu.com/VisualStudies/syllabi/syllabus_1058_Osorio_Seminar_S12.pdf.

24 HWS student reflections were drawn from three sources: the community of origin paper assignment, weekly journal reflections, and a final paper. The study was approved by the HWS Institutional Review Board, and students gave consent for their work to be used anonymously. These writings have been lightly edited for publication.

25 In the version my students participated in, they were asked to form a line and step forward from that line if they agreed with the statement read. The statements, adopted from the textbook *Teaching for Diversity and Social Justice*, were designed to call attention to class, gender, racial, ethnic, and religious difference. For example, students were asked to step forward if their school holidays coincided with religious holidays they celebrated or if they attended grade school with people they felt were like themselves. Maurianne Adams, Lee Anne Bell, and Pat Griffin, eds., *Teaching for Diversity and Social Justice* (New York: Routledge, 1998).

26 Peggy McIntosh, "White Privilege: Unpacking the Invisible Knapsack," in *Race, Class, and Gender in the United States*, ed. Paula S. Rothenberg, 6th ed. (1988; repr. New York: Worth, 2004), 188–92.

27 See L. Dee Fink, "What Is 'Significant Learning'?," Western Carolina University, accessed March 3, 2021, http://www.wcu.edu/WebFiles/PDFs/facultycenter_SignificantLearning.pdf.

28 Stephan Brookfield, *Teaching for Critical Thinking: Tools and Techniques to Help Students Question Their Assumptions* (San Francisco: Jossey-Bass, 2012).
29 *Behind the Walls*, Geneva, 2016, exhibit brochure, first draft.
30 Conard, "Facepaint History."
31 See Michael Frisch, *A Shared Authority: Essays on the Craft and Meaning of Oral and Public History* (New York: State University of New York Press, 1989); Katherine Corbett and Howard Milled, "A Shared Inquiry into Shared Inquiry," *Public Historian* 28, no. 1 (Winter 2006): 15–38.
32 As public historian Benjamin Filene notes, "Professional historians have been trained to be wary of emotion. Years of graduate work and peer review inculcate the value of being dispassionate. We are supposed to gather evidence, evaluate preponderances, and track patterns, all with an eye toward creating balanced interpretations." See Filene "Listening Intently: Can StoryCorps Teach Museums How to Win the Hearts of New Audiences?," in *Letting Go? Sharing Historical Authority in a User-Generated World*, ed. Bill Adair, Benjamin Filene, and Laura Koloski (Philadelphia: Pew Center for Arts and Heritage, 2011).
33 The NCPH claims, "It is imperative that students get broad training in the theories, methods and content that provide the basis of a traditional undergraduate history education." NHCP Curriculum and Training Committee, *Best Practices in Public History: Public History for Undergraduate Students*, 2009, http://ncph.org/wp-content/uploads/2010/08/Undergrad-Best-Practice.pdf. Within the oral history field, interviewers are reminded to "work to achieve a balance between the objectives of the project and the perspectives of the interviewees," "participate in the interview without dominating it," and above all, remember "the ideal oral history interview is a guided monologue and not a conversation." "Principles for Oral History and Best Practices for Oral History," Oral History Association, October 2009, https://www.oralhistory.org/about/principles-and-practices-revised-2009/; Marjorie Hunt, *The Smithsonian Folklife and Oral History Interviewing Guide* (Washington, DC: Smithsonian Center for Folklife and Cultural Heritage, 2016), http://www.folklife.si.edu/the-smithsonian-folklife-and-oral-history-interviewing-guide/the-interview/smithsonian; Irene Reti, "Oral History Primer," University of California, Santa Cruz, last modified August 2013, https://library.ucsc.edu/reg-hist/oral-history-primer.
34 Barbra Franco, quoted in Corbett and Milled, "Shared Inquiry into Shared Inquiry," 20.
35 Jeff Kelly, "The Body Politics of Suzanne Lacy," in *But Is It Art? The Sprit of Art as Activism*, ed. Nina Felshin (Seattle: Bay Press, 1995), 232–33.
36 Amalia Mesa Bains and Pepon Osorio, "The Practices and Pedagogy of Pepon Osorio," *Community Arts Network Reading Room*, October 2008. Article is archived at https://apionline.org/community-arts-network/.
37 See Judy Baca's description of her process in her "Baldwin Park Press Release," SPARC, June 27, 2005, accessed March 3, 2017, http://www.sparcmurals.org/sparcone/. See also Pablo Helguera, *Education for Socially Engaged Art: A Materials and Techniques Handbook* (New York: Jorge Pinto Books, 2011), 49.

38 Pratt, "Arts of the Contact Zone," 34.
39 Meringolo, *Museums, Monuments, and National Parks*, xxi. See also Stowe, "Public History Curriculum," 46.
40 Kathleen McLean, "Whose Questions? Whose Conversations?," in Adair, Filene, and Koloski, *Letting Go?*, 72.
41 See, for example, Wing Luke Asian Museum's *Community-Based Exhibition Model Handbook* (Seattle: Wing Luke Asian Museum, 2006); see also Animating Democracy's *History as a Catalyst for Civic Dialogue* (New York: Americans for the Arts, 2005), which explored three case studies of history projects that explicitly engaged with the public with the goal of fostering social justice.
42 See Lynn Hershman, "Interview with Judith Baca and Suzanne Lacy," *Women Art Revolution*, July 7, 2004, accessed March 4, 2017, http://womenartrevolution.com/about_interviews.php; Bains and Osorio, "Practices and Pedagogy"; see also Bret Cook's work with elementary students, described in Tom Finkelpearl, "Interview with Bret Cook," in *What We Made: Conversations on Art and Social Cooperation* (Durham, NC: Duke University Press, 2013), 279. It was, after all, Myles Horton, founder of the Highlander Folk School, who noted, "My expertise is in knowing not to be an expert." Myles Horton and Paulo Freire, *We Make the Road by Walking: Conversations on Education and Social Change* (Philadelphia: Temple University Press, 1990), 128.
43 Teen comments were drawn from two sources: written reflections and a survey completed at the end of the project. The study was approved by the HWS Institutional Review Board, and administrators at the after-school organization gave consent for teen work to be used anonymously. These writings have been lightly edited for publication.
44 See Melanie Walker, "Making a World That Is Worth Living In: Humanities Teaching and the Formation of Practical Reasoning," *Arts and Humanities in Higher Education* 8, no. 93 (2009): 258.
45 See my discussion of public history assessment in Elizabeth Belanger, "Public History in the Classroom," *History@Work*, February 22, 2017, http://ncph.org/history-at-work/public-history-in-the-classroom/.
46 Cathy Stanton, "Outside the Frame: Assessing Partnerships between Arts and Historical Organizations," *Public Historian* 27, no. 1 (Winter 2005): 19–37.
47 Gwylene Gallimard and Hope Clark, "Principles of Working in a Community: Resources for Social Change," *Community Arts Perspective* 2, no. 5 (January 2010), accessed March 5, 2017, http://wayback.archiveit.org/2077/20100906201307/http://www.communityarts.net/readingroom/archivefiles/2008/09/principles_of_w.php (URL invalid).
48 Haft, "Voices from the Battlefront."
49 Linda Shopes, "Oral History and the Study of Communities: Problems, Paradoxes, and Possibilities," *Journal of American History* 89, no. 2 (2002): 588–98.
50 *Diversity in Geneva*, Geneva, 2016, exhibit brochure.
51 Helguera, *Education for Socially Engaged Art*, 13.

52 Hershman, "Interview with Baca and Lacy."
53 Johnson and Stowe, "Field of Public History," 12.
54 Conard, "Facepaint History."
55 Meringolo, "Learning to See."
56 John Dewey, *The Public and Its Problem* (1927; repr. University Park: Pennsylvania State University Press, 2012), 211.
57 Julie Ellison, "The New Public Humanists," *PMLA* 128, no. 2 (2013): 289–98.
58 bell hooks, *Teaching Community: A Pedagogy of Hope* (New York: Routledge, 2003), 197.

Radical Is a Process

Public History Pedagogy in Urban Universities

Rebecca Amato, Gabrielle Bendiner-Viani,
Dipti Desai, Denise D. Meringolo, and Mary Rizzo

The following edited conversation began as a working group at the November 2017 National Humanities Conference. We all teach at urban universities in the broad realm of public history and share a similar commitment to social justice pedagogy. We each have a different position within the academy—as tenure track and non-tenure track faculty, academic administrators, and a librarian—but we have a common interest in experiential learning. Our students work with community organizations on projects that respond to current political and social contexts. At our conference session, where we were joined by Heidi Cramer, assistant director for public services for the Newark Public Library, we shared our projects and talked about the discoveries and pitfalls that we encountered in planning, development, and implementation. Several key themes and questions emerged.

First, what do we even mean by the term *radical*? In many universities it is radical simply to believe in the potential of history and creativity to ignite positive change and to create opportunities for students to learn with and from nonacademic partners. This perspective tends to privilege the impact of our work on our institutions, our disciplines, and our students. But "radical" pedagogy should have broader significance. As educators, we have personal and political orientations that don't conveniently shut off when we are practicing our professions. Each of us has shared inquiry and interpretation with students and community members whose political beliefs are sharply at odds with our own. The negotiation and dialogue this requires is not detrimental to our projects; it is essential. We believe that honoring the messiness of humanity is a core value of the humanities. At the same time, it is crucial to practice humility when we imagine the value of our work to collaborators, stakeholders, and audiences. As public humanists, we bring particular skills to any task, including those related to archival study, critical pedagogy, oral history, theory, and analysis. But we must wield our scholarly authority lightly, if at all. Ultimately, we have all learned that people, particularly those who are continuously marginalized, ignored, violated, and drowned out, need us to listen far more than they need us to demonstrate our expertise. Recognizing and honoring that is radical.

Second, how do we do this work sustainably? All of us have embarked on long-term partnerships with community organizations. Generally speaking, universities don't actively support these kinds of partnerships, so how do we navigate university bureaucracies to get what we need for ourselves, our students, and our community partners? How do we create frameworks and processes that allow us to continue to do such work without reinventing the wheel every semester?

A major part of our job is managing relationships with and between at least two different groups: students and community partners. We have worked with undergraduate and graduate students from a variety of backgrounds, many of whom have had little knowledge or direct experience with the communities with whom we are working. As a result, we have had to temper our expectations regarding student engagement and learning, and that has shaped our approaches to both pedagogy and project management. We all agree that students must think of themselves as partners working with community members, not as experts who are informing communities about their own history and its meaning. Conflicts about terminology, memory, and perspective have spurred each of us to become especially reflexive about our teaching.

From the perspective of our community partners, we are representatives of our universities. Why do these partners trust us, especially when our universities have been catalysts for displacement and gentrification in their neighborhoods? Most of us agree that they trust us because we act in good faith. We listen. We work collaboratively. We don't steamroll. But even in the best marriage, there are going to be disagreements and hostilities. How do we deal with that? How do we handle the emotional toll of managing these partnerships?

Finally, it is notable that we are all women taking part in this conversation. This represents the continued problematic feminization of relationship management and emotional labor—one that historians working with the public and in the academy need to address.

The Projects

Denise D. Meringolo

DM: Preserve the Baltimore Uprising is a crowdsourced digital collection that enables local people to upload images, oral histories, audio files, video, and other materials directly to an Omeka-based website. I was driven by a sense of urgency to design the project over the course of a rushed weekend in April 2015. The national media was portraying protests and acts of civil disobedience in Baltimore as a "riot," minimizing the justified outrage of local residents who assembled to protest the death of Freddie Gray in police custody. I feared that the motivations, desires, ideas, and demands of people in the streets would be mischaracterized, minimized, and lost to history. I created the digital project as a way to make sure that the protesters could control their own message. And I modeled the site after projects like Documenting Ferguson and A People's Archive of Police Violence in Cleveland.

Dipti Desai

DD: The Community Book of Wellbeing was a collaborative project between our graduate students in the Research in Art + Education course at New York University in partnership with the Commission on Public Health Systems in New York City, an organization that advocates for people's right to access health care. **We were interested in using the arts to envision new ways of working within community settings to inspire dialogue about issues of concern to the community in order to initiate social change**.

This collaboration examined the way people in the Lower East Side and Chinatown neighborhoods of Manhattan see health and wellness in their lives and communities. We used art and other creative methods to collect stories from people in the Lower East Side and Chinatown regarding well-being. What is a healthy body? What does a healthy community or neighborhood look like? The Commission on Public Health Systems was interested in collecting stories in order to understand people's beliefs regarding wellness. Their ultimate goal was to advocate for changing public health policies, as existing policies do not meet the needs of many marginalized communities and many do not use public health services.

Our students facilitated several art workshops with elderly women at the University Settlement House to discuss well-being. In one session, they showed contemporary artworks to facilitate discussion about how the women understood well-being. In another session, participants drew or wrote on body maps to help them locate the places they felt discomfort and pain, as well as places they felt strong and healthy. This led to a lively conversation about home remedies from their cultures. They worked together to create a printed book about stories of well-being that included home remedies for various health problems that could be distributed to health clinics and ultimately inform public health policy.

Rebecca Amato

RA: The semester-long, undergraduate, community-engaged research course I teach at New York University is called (Dis)Placed Urban Histories. It is built on a partnership with the community-based organization Women's Housing and Economic Development Corporation (WHEDco) in the South Bronx.

Each year, our project takes a different form, but it is always history-based, always connected to neighborhood change, and always produced for the South Bronx community itself rather than a university audience. The work we do as a class is determined by WHEDco, though limited by the constraints of time and structure imposed by a semester. In spring 2017, our project was to create a digital archive and exhibit using the digital platform Omeka and to install a real-life exhibit that highlighted items from the archive. At the core of the exhibit were oral histories that students conducted with residents and workers who had a long engagement with Melrose, the South Bronx neighborhood we were studying. We recorded 19 oral histories and digitized and photographed

Students and residents visit the temporary exhibit at Boricua College in Melrose. The exhibit included biographical images, quotations, and materials donated to the class for documentation and display through both the digital and physical exhibits. Photographs by Rebecca Amato.

over 150 personal items from our collaborators. Dozens of residents visited the physical exhibit, which was on display at predominantly Puerto Rican Boricua College at its Bronx location. The final Omeka archive and exhibit has been used by WHEDco for planning reports and other materials intended to represent the neighborhood's interests in meetings with New York City officials, particularly around rezoning. In spring 2018, we mined the oral histories to identify places of significance to the local community, researched the sites, and created a Clio-based multimedia walking tour that invites residents to explore new pathways in their own neighborhood. This tour was integrated into the unveiling of the Bronx Commons and Bronx Music Hall in 2019, a mixed-use site that was proposed by a community plan more than twenty years ago. All the materials that came out of the partnership are now on the WHEDco website.

Mary Rizzo

MR: In fall 2016, students in my graduate seminar Place, Community and Public Humanities at Rutgers University–Newark partnered with the Newark Public Library, an advisory group made up of academic and community scholars, and an undergraduate class in Spanish and Portuguese studies to produce the exhibition *From Rebellion to Review Board: Newark Fights for Police Accountability*. Our topic was the long struggle for police accountability fought by generations of diverse activists in the city. It was timely. The Black Lives Matter movement had started a national conversation on police brutality in response to the killings of unarmed people of color by the police. Closer to home, two events happened. The Newark city council created a Civilian Complaint Review Board (CCRB) with supervisory power over the police. The city of Newark signed a consent decree with the Department of Justice for federal monitoring of the police after a report showed discriminatory policing practices. I was particularly interested in the creation of the CCRB. When the media covered it, they often talked about it in relation primarily to Black Lives Matter. In reality, Newark activists had been pushing for a civilian review board since the 1950s. All this made the topic ripe for a graduate-level public history class and an exhibition that would trace the history of police accountability.

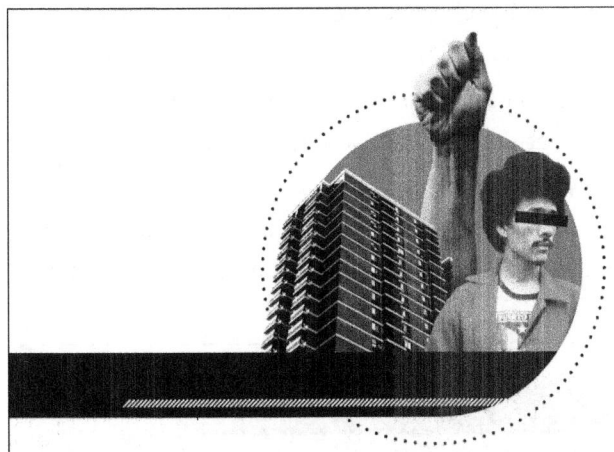

Photograph courtesy of Rutgers University–Newark. Graphic design by Eric Ng.

Prior to the semester's start, I developed three sets of collaborative relationships. I reached out to Heidi Cramer at the Newark Public Library about a partnership. The library's New Jersey room and the Hispanic Research and Information Center had significant archival holdings documenting activism. The library also agreed to host the completed exhibition. I utilized contacts at Rutgers and in Newark to identify people for a community advisory board who would ensure that the exhibit was factually correct and that it addressed community concerns. Finally, the undergraduate class worked on a complementary exhibit, *Accion Latina*, on Latinx "riots" in New Jersey entirely in Spanish. Both exhibits opened in December 2016 at the library.

Working with the historiography of Newark, the archivists, and the advisors, we devised three sections for the exhibit. The first would

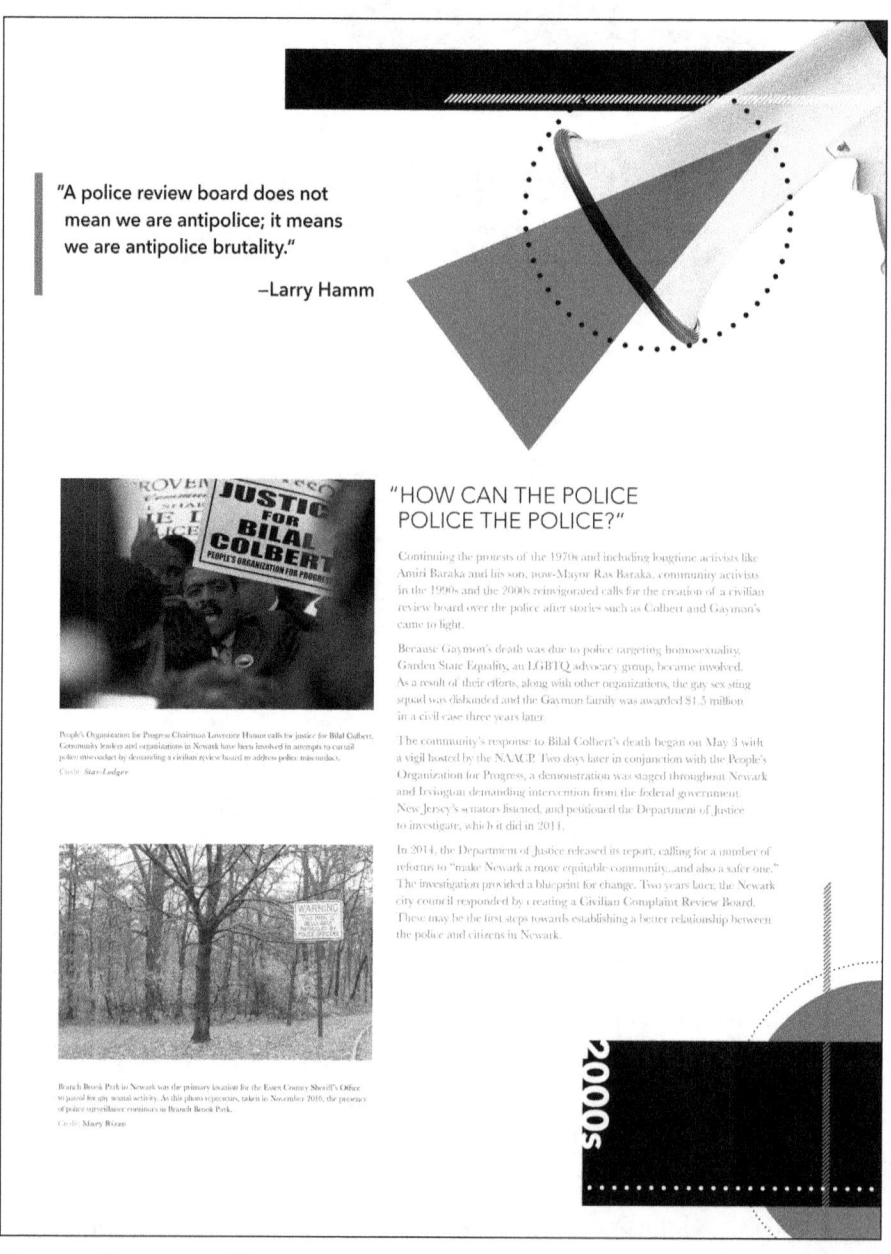

Photograph courtesy of Rutgers University–Newark. Graphic design by Eric Ng.

cover the lead up to and aftermath of the Newark rebellion, the civil disturbance that took place in Newark in July 1967. This mainly involved African American history. The second looked at the lead up to and aftermath of the 1974 Puerto Rican "riot" in Newark. Much less well known than the 1967 incident, there was little published material on it. Instead, my students used oral histories and archival sources to examine coalition building between Black and Puerto Rican activists in Newark, which led to the election of the first Black mayor of Newark, Ken Gibson, in 1970. The final section looked at the War on Drugs. How had the War on Drugs increased police surveillance over Black neighborhoods and, especially, young people? This section also dealt with overpolicing of the LGBTQ community by examining the murder of Defarra Gaymon, a Black man who was killed by Newark police while possibly cruising for sex in Branch Brook Park in 2010. His death ignited the LGBTQ community in New Jersey.

Gabrielle Bendiner-Viani

GBV: The Layered SPURA project was a five-year collaborative project between myself, more than fifty students in my regularly offered City Studio class at the New School, and several Lower East Side community-based organizations, primarily Good Old Lower East Side (GOLES) and City Lore. The collaboration was initiated through an existing collaboration that GOLES, City Lore, and the Pratt Center had begun and from which they had built a coalition, called "SPURA Matters."

The fourteen-square-block area of the Seward Park Urban Renewal Area on Manhattan's Lower East Side had been slated for demolition and "renewal" in 1967. For forty years, after buildings were demolished and almost two thousand families displaced—most of whom were people of low income and of color—very little had been built in the area. In that time, the site had been highly contested, often in bitter racially divisive community-level fights over affordable housing complicated by political corruption. The goal of the Layered SPURA project was to use art and public history practices to illuminate the many meanings of SPURA as a place, issuing a call to heed its history. In five years of community-based exhibitions, we sought to spur new dialogues to support a new planning process in which affordable

One installation from a Layered SPURA exhibition, consisting of panoramas of this portion of the Lower East Side neighborhood and a series of "viewers" that helped people see the many unbuilt plans, obscured cultures, and community desires of the Seward Park Extension Urban Renewal Area—an analog and participatory "augmented reality." Photograph by Gabrielle Bendiner-Viani.

housing could be built and in which those displaced might finally realize their long-promised "right to return."

The works in the exhibitions were cocreated by students and community members. The projects never suggested what a new plan might be—the neighborhood is weary of being told what to do—but rather used photographs, maps, oral histories, and tactile sculptural elements to present the SPURA site as a real place rather than as square footage of developable real estate. Over those five years, we exhibited in three different spaces: informal neighborhood spaces where people bumped into the work in the course of their daily lives and the more formal exhibition spaces of the Abrons Art Center at Henry Street Settlement and the Sheila Johnson Design Center at the New School. We also built partnerships with the Seward Park Area Redevelopment Coalition (SPARC), Jews for Racial and Economic Justice (JFREJ), and the Pratt Center for Community Development. I have written about the full evolution of the project and the SPURA site in my book, *Contested City*.[1]

The Students

DM: Until recently, my public history projects/courses were almost exclusively geared toward MA students who had opted for the public history track as part of their course of study. The Department of History created an undergraduate minor in public history in 2013, so now I teach a series of combined courses—upper-level undergraduate courses with a graduate section. Both graduate and undergraduate students are required to begin public history studies by taking an introductory course in which they learn about the values and essential methods of public history practice. I emphasize collaboration, shared inquiry, and shared interpretation, as well as historical research and writing. Students spend a significant amount of time analyzing the needs and interests of public history stakeholders and audiences, and examining relevant histories of the field, particularly those that have shaped historical landscapes, collections, and institutions. We also engage in lively discussions about the role public historians can—and often do—play in the realm of activism and advocacy. I often remind my students that public historians must be both responsible and responsive. We uphold the best practices of the discipline of history, and we actively include our audiences and stakeholders in processes of inquiry, research, and interpretation. Because our work stems from community relationships, we also strive for flexibility. We are attentive to the changing needs and interests of those we serve, and we can transform existing projects or begin new ones to address the social, political, or cultural environment. In order to practice these skills, we work with local partners on a variety of public history projects.

The challenge with public history education, however, is that there is little space between classroom-based theoretical exploration and real-world implementation. Students, accustomed to spending an entire semester working on a single paper, are sometimes daunted by the scope of research and compression of the time line necessary for producing even a fairly limited public history project. More seriously, however, my students struggle with issues related to power and privilege. First, many, particularly graduate students, resist embracing the notion of shared authority. They find it difficult to negotiate the space between "informing" an audience about the facts of history and "engaging" an audience in a discussion where history is at the center. Second, many of my students are uncomfortable with the political dynamics of public history practice. While a core group of graduate students in my Introduction to Public History class developed the ethical underpinnings of *Preserve the Baltimore Uprising*, **a small but vocal set of their classmates was uncomfortable with the project's political position**. Similarly—though perhaps less incendiary—other groups of students working to develop content for digital walking tours on the Explore Baltimore Heritage curatescape app have found it challenging to work in a collaborative fashion with the largely White, middle-aged, and elderly members of neighborhood associations and local historical groups. Some are reluctant to challenge our partners' nostalgia while others want to crush it with a sledgehammer. Finally, I have come to realize that many of my students do not immediately understand or trust the value of project-based learning until after they graduate and begin working in the field. This distrust manifests in several ways. Some approach the classroom as an entirely theoretical space and put minimal effort into the project work. Others develop somewhat dismissive attitudes toward our project partners, producing content that is informative but not engaging. Some embrace the process of project-based learning, but they are not quite successful in project implementation.

The biggest challenge for me has been to arrive at some level of acceptance. Student resistance, skepticism, and struggle are all part of the learning process. Projects are not "finished" at the end of a given semester. Rather, they are begun. Similarly, it is often at the end of a semester—or even later—that students arrive at a deeper understanding of public history as a social process.

MR: I have the privilege of teaching MA students in history and American studies and PhD students in American studies. Even though all of my students are in graduate school, their depth of knowledge, background, and training differ widely. Some are training for a career in public history, while others are hoping to land academic jobs, and still others are happy in the jobs they have and are earning credits for extra credentials. Many of my students work full or part time while going to graduate school. Understanding this has changed my expectations for my classes. When I was a graduate student at the University of

Minnesota, you were expected to devote yourself full time to research, reading, and writing. For my students, this is unrealistic. If we're serious about diversifying our graduate programs and the field of public history, then it's unrealistic for all of us. Of course, this doesn't mean that we can't expect rigorous work from our students. We simply have to be flexible. **For example, I learned that I couldn't expect that my students would be able to visit local archives that are only open during the day, because they are at work.** In my fall 2017 class, we used the Queer Newark Oral History Project, a born-digital audio archive, as our research base since these materials were available to everyone equally.

At the start of each semester, I tell the members of my class that they are both students in a graduate course and a collaborative team working together on a project. I try to model my classes as much as possible on how a team working together at a museum or nonprofit organization functions. On the first day, for example, I ask everyone to introduce themselves by giving their name, their program, and what special skills they have. I've had students tell me that their special skills are everything from being good at talking to strangers (an excellent skill when we're planning community meetings) to video editing (this student created a video loop of archival footage for an exhibit) to everything in between. Since most of my students have not had any previous training in public history, my goal is to make them see that they each bring skills with them into our project. This is one way that public history training differs from academic history training. Academic history requires a narrow set of skills (research acumen, interpretative ability, and strong writing). **Public historians work more broadly, so my classes become a way for students to explore their skills and figure out what kind of public history work might be best for them.**

I'm not sure what assumptions my students bring to my classes, but I suspect that they don't realize how much we will talk about process and how open our classroom will be to our community scholars and partners. Much class discussion time focuses on *how* we will take our research and translate it into an exhibit for public viewing. I emphasize that we're creating a narrative and that every narrative is ideological—it expresses a particular world view. It leaves out as much as it includes. At the same time, we can't let this paralyze us. We need to meet deadlines. Our collaborators—who we call community scholars—are critical to this process. We meet with them throughout the semester and give them the opportunity to criticize early drafts of our work. Unfailingly, students are anxious about this. Having a professor critique them is familiar terrain, but when community scholars come into class, students get really nervous, because they are so concerned that they are going to get something wrong or disappoint them. This sense of responsibility to the community is probably the biggest learning experience of the class.

RA: I teach undergraduates at New York University's Gallatin School of Individualized Study, an interdisciplinary program in which students design their own majors. Since Gallatin's core curriculum is composed of interdisciplinary seminars that are open to all undergraduate students at NYU, my course attracts students at all levels and from all disciplines. On the one hand, this means students come fresh to the topics I'm covering in class, so they are curious and eager to discuss our material. They also bring academic strengths in other areas into the class—creative writing, photography, ethnography, and literary analysis, among others—which encourages lively and wide-ranging discussion and provides useful skills for exhibit-making, while also keeping me on my toes.

On the other hand, **I am constantly surprised by how little US history my students actually know**. Placing a particular neighborhood's history in context always requires more background research than I expect. Nearly every year at the midterm, I realize that some percentage of the students in my class never grasped what the terms *urban renewal* or *deindustrialization* or *Great Society* meant, despite my referring to them regularly. We usually spend an entire class meeting with a "Twenty Questions"-type review in which the students write anonymous questions about historical terms on index cards and I answer them for the group.

Anchoring students in history is one important way of focusing us all on the objectives of the class. Challenging their reliance on critical and political theory is another. Gallatin students are particularly well trained in high-level theory early in their college education, so it can be a challenge to bring them back into the realm of empirical learning. As much as I embrace and am inspired by the works of theorists like Henri Lefebvre, Paulo Freire, and Antonio Gramsci, I often need to remind my students these thinkers insisted that knowledge exists in practice and in real encounters with actual people. It is not only in books or the classroom. **For that reason, they are asked to approach their projects in our course, particularly collaborative oral histories, as opportunities to listen, not occasions to collect case studies to prove their own emerging philosophies.**

When students enroll in my course, I think they are most excited to leave the classroom, talk about neighborhood change (particularly gentrification), and produce an exhibit. I don't think it occurs to them until a few weeks into the semester that this work will force them to consider their own positionality, assumptions, and responsibilities. Whether it has any lasting impact on how they engage with their studies or with their neighbors is impossible to know. But I do believe it humbles them a least a little bit. And if I can teach humility to college students at a private university, I think I'm doing pretty well.

DD: I teach the course called Research in Art + Education, which is half of a two-part, required capstone experience for graduate students in the Art, Education, and Community Practice program. This program attracts students from various backgrounds, including artists, designers, performers, filmmakers, and activists interested in the arts. All the students have a strong foundation in the arts, and some have experience teaching elementary- or secondary-school-aged students. Still others might have a minor or major in the humanities. Their academic backgrounds are varied and they bring this range of experiences to the course, which is really exciting. Although interested in artistic activism most of my students have little experience designing and enacting tactical art interventions in partnership with community organizations or in the public sphere.[2] This field-based course focuses on envisioning new ways of acting and thinking in our communities in order to create change. It deliberately challenges the notion that art practice, research, and social activism are discrete entities.

I have envisioned this class as a collaborative space where we first learn about different forms of artistic activist practices in a series of case studies—in order to analyze how artists and artist collectives

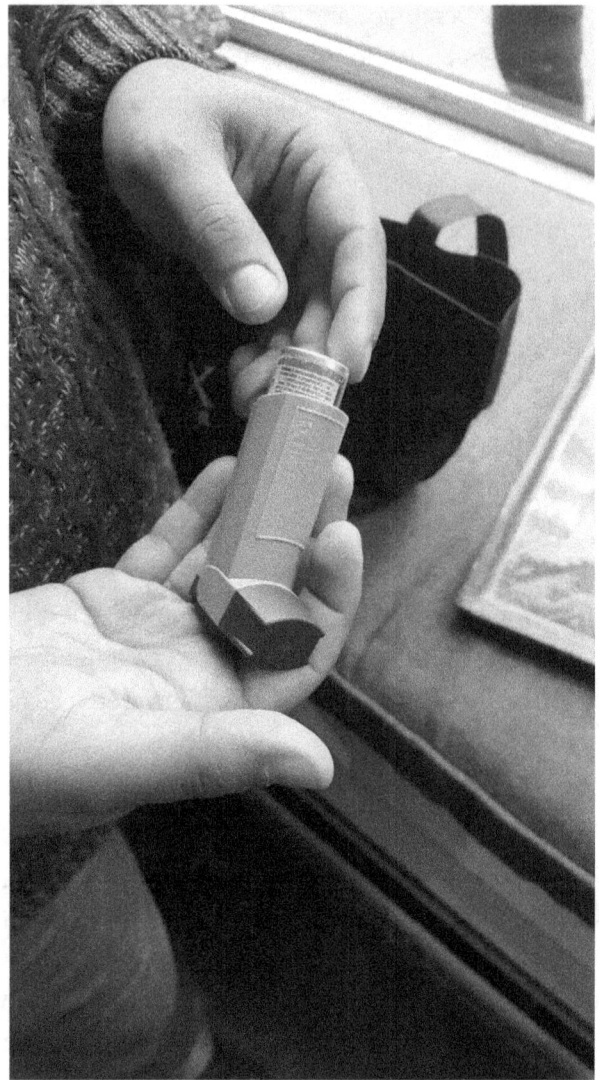

Student Diamond Naga Siu photographed the South Bronx resident and journalist Ed Garcia Conde holding his asthma inhaler. Up to 17 percent of South Bronx residents suffer from asthma, making it one of the worst neighborhoods in New York for respiratory health. Most people attribute the high rate to the car and truck traffic introduced to the area by the urban renewal era confluence of highways, including the Cross-Bronx, Major Deegan, and Bruckner. Photograph by Diamond Naga Siu, "Asthma Inhaler," (Dis)Placed Urban Histories: Melrose, accessed January 3, 2019, http://displacedhistories.hosting.nyu.edu/spring2017/items/show/86.

engage with communities, social movements, neighborhoods, and cities. Some of the research-based approaches we focus on are oral history, ethnography, archival research, community-based participatory action research, exhibition-as-research, and mapping as an activist intervention. The questions we explore in the course are, What does fieldwork mean in artistic activist practices? How do we learn to really listen to people and their concerns and then work together to enact interventions? How do artists and artist collectives organize, listen, collect stories, design tactical interventions, and document their process for critical reflection? Further, the collaborative nature of artistic activism requires us to continuously reflect on power, voice, and representation. Who speaks for whom and how? What does true collaboration look like and feel like? This exploration generates lively discussions on how to envision tactical interventions using the arts, but it is still theoretical.

The moment we move from this exploration to their own projects, students become uncertain about implementing their interventions in collaboration with an organization. This anxiety is not surprising as most of the students come from a traditional art background where their practice is studio-based and they have not learned about grassroots organizing. A majority of the class time focuses on how to design and implement projects in collaboration with their chosen organizations. **Learning to work in collaboration is new for many of them, as art practices are normally solitary practices. This collaborative practice forces them to think about how their position and location shapes their conversations. Their design of the intervention and the responsibility of working across differences is challenging yet ultimately rewarding when they see the effects of the art intervention on the people they work with.** I think humility and patience are two of the main takeaways for students, which are important dispositions they need in order to work toward social change.

GBV: I teach in the urban studies department at the New School, and I primarily work with undergraduates. The Layered SPURA class, and most of my engaged partnership classes, are geared toward juniors and seniors, but I also get sophomores and the occasional first year. My students often come from Eugene Lang College, the liberal arts undergraduate college of the New School, but I also always have design students from Parsons and nontraditional students from the bachelor's program at the School of Public Engagement. All of these institutions are part of the university of the New School. Hence my students are a range of ages and bring with them some widely varying backgrounds, experiences, and understandings of the city.

Most often, I need to give students a very deep and very rapid dive into the relevant urban context. For the Layered SPURA project, the first half of the semester was a crash course on histories of housing in New York. **This was something most students knew very little about beyond their own experience of overpriced apartments in gentrifying neighborhoods, an experience that made them keen to understand—and also wary of their own roles and positionality in the neighborhoods where we were working**.

Because the way I teach is always a hybrid of seminar and studio, and my classes demand rigor in critical writing and thinking as well as in creative practice, it is rare that any student will consistently operate within their comfort zone. Some students are very skilled with their visual work and exploration, but in-depth writing and research is new to them. Other students can research and write skillfully, but creating something in any other medium is a challenge for them. As a result, I often have students work together in teams—not so that one is designated the "designer" and then given all the visual work to do, but so that they each bring their individual strengths to the team and they can teach one other and learn how to create something together.

One perception that students typically brought with them to my SPURA City Studio classes was that the Lower East Side was a place for bars and nightlife or overpriced studio apartments, but not necessarily a coherent neighborhood. They might have a sense of its history as a center for immigration in the early twentieth century, but frequently their knowledge of the place did not extend beyond that. **The majority of my students also brought a political orientation with them. One that was often, though not always, strongly in support of community members and against displacement. They were primed to hear the story I had to tell them, even if they didn't always have the context for it**. They were also extremely sensitive to their own roles within the neighborhood and their crises over positionality, and the

City Studio students and community members working together at a SPURA community-visioning session, where students helped facilitate but also, more importantly, learned through practice about neighborhood histories, contemporary needs, and the depth of community members' knowledge and expertise in shaping their own futures. Photograph by Gabrielle Bendiner-Viani.

possibility that they might be part of the problem, raised important questions in our dialogues through the class. They were active parts of the conversation of "Why should people trust us as allies?" and asking that question was a crucial learning opportunity of the course.

Sustainability

DM: Here's a radical idea: depending on how you understand sustainability, I'm not sure it is really a valuable goal.

Very often, the more deeply institutionalized projects and courses become, the more "sustainable" we believe they are. Sustainable courses attract departmental funds. They get tied to programs of study. They may even achieve media attention. **But these forms of support can also disconnect projects and courses from the communities** they intend to serve. **They become sites for the reproduction of expertise and the assertion of authority** rather than spaces for dialogue, debate, and social justice action.

I have come to think that for projects and **courses to actually function in the realm of advocacy and serve social justice, they should be conceived of as temporary** and they should resist the kind of sustainability that comes from institutional acceptance.

Instead, we might begin to think of sustainability as something achieved through capacity building. If the goal of our projects and courses is to address immediate needs and advocate around pressing social and political issues, and if our premise is that public history methods can be understood as a set of tools we use to meet these goals, then our political aims are better served by working to build community-based capabilities to deploy these methods without us. Our work may be most successful when we become obsolete.

MR: What do we mean by sustainability? It is most important to nurture and sustain the relationships our work builds—between me and community leaders, between my program and external organizations, and between my students and their project partners inside and outside the university. While a specific project may end, I want the connections to continue. **I want those relationships to be sustainable; I don't want to "use them up" in a slash-and-burn way.** I've seen examples where public historians "burn out" their community partners because of mismatched goals, unreasonable demands for time or resources, or simply a lack of shared authority and expertise. Sometimes, public historians can run roughshod over the community. This is where a discussion of ethics is critical. How do we ethically work with communities? How do we ethically work with students on public history projects (which are still so outside the mainstream of undergraduate *and* graduate education)? Over the three years I've been teaching at Rutgers–Newark and leading classroom-based projects, I've ramped up my expectations from the students. At what point is it too much? How do we make sure that these ambitious classes are accessible to students who may be going to school part time while working?

I hope that I'm building and nurturing relationships with communities over time. My central relationship, however, has been with the

Newark Public Library, which is a great partnership, since we both are in the business of public engagement and share a language. Specific community partnerships grow out of this hub.

DD: My desire to develop long-term relationships with a few organizations in the Lower East Side for our program in Art, Education and Community Practice was based on my understanding that only **through consistent work within an organization rooted in a community will we be able to create real social change**. Otherwise, our tactical art interventions, whether in the public sphere or within a community organization may have a limited effectiveness in raising awareness about an issue, but fail to move people to take social action to create change. Even though my students were contingent labor that would move in and out of projects, I sought to maintain long-term relationships, becoming the glue that kept the partnership alive and healthy. A critical question that emerged from the Community Book of Wellbeing is, Who is being sustained, by whom, and for what purposes? And what are the power dynamics that come into play in relation to sustainability? These questions on sustainability lead me to think through how social change is understood in relation to art.

Social change in relation to socially engaged art moves across a spectrum from raising political awareness about a social issue to activating art as a political project to create social action. In this latter understanding, art is about organizing, which may be temporary and not necessarily about movement building. Art as organizing suggests that the goal is not necessarily to create a discrete art object that raises awareness about an issue. Rather, the art process involves understanding how and why we choose to work with people in the community and what kinds of networks of solidarity among people and organizations we can build, as well as asking at each stage of planning and implementation who the process serves, for what purpose, and how power dynamics play a role. It is through developing social relationships, alliances, and networks that we can create a cultural shift that precipitates change.

Although the Community Book of Wellbeing project did not lead to changing public health policy in NYC, it enabled privileged and sheltered students to build unexpected and mutually beneficial relationships with elderly, low-income, Dominican and Puerto Rican women in the Lower East Side community. This experience initiated a culture shift for my students that has the potential to mobilize change. These students have gone back to the University Settlement and visited the women a few times after the semester course was over and gave each of the women the book that they created together about what well-being means to them. **Sustainability in this context is both a process and a disposition that is cultivated rather than a goal to be achieved.**

RA: From my perspective, the sustainability of a community partnership, a project, or a campaign is almost always something that needs to be driven by my community partner. If an organization is fatigued or burnt out by working with my students and me—for any reason, whether it be lack of capacity or mismatched goals—I think the solution is an open-ended pause. Community partnerships have to be relationships built on integrity and mutuality. With my community partners in this and other projects, it has been essential that we communicate about changing goals and projects, and it is equally essential that we don't abandon one another *in medias res* when changes do occur. Like any potentially long-term relationship, there are moments of exciting activity, and there are lulls, and we have to be open to all of it or risk doing more harm than good.

But I do approach these partnerships as potentially long-term, which means I see them as an opportunity for coproducing meaningful social change, not as a precursor to institutionalization. My course is iterative, so each year we are building on work done in previous years. Ultimately, the historical research we've conducted will go public in ways that transcend the course I teach. That's the kind of sustainability I'm seeking beyond the community relationships I've built: public history that is usable, recyclable, and generative whether or not it is tied to my course, my students, or me. So the course itself is simply a vehicle for producing the research and, if I'm lucky, seeding a social justice orientation in my students. If it no longer serves those purposes, it is expendable.

GBV: I have some conflicting thoughts about sustainability. Having worked on a project for five years, with one main partner, I'm committed to the long-term trust that's built up through a long-sustained partnership. Yet I've also experienced the immense shift and change that every organization goes through over the years, and the need to shift and change that this engenders. People change jobs. An organization's priorities can pivot to new and pressing campaigns. What challenges does this pose for sustainability? This is also the case with politically shifting situations, in which we also often work. These changes mean that the project often needs to shift—and that is both important and very difficult, especially when bringing on fifteen to twenty new students each year. So what does flexibility look like within sustainability?

I am deeply committed to long-term partnerships, both because I think it's important for establishing and maintaining trust to keep showing up but also because I've seen so many times how partnerships can change and become something you never thought possible. Time allows for new possibilities to emerge—something that might surprise everyone—and that usually just is not evident in year one.

Sustainability to me also means recognizing that things end. No project needs to go on forever—nor should it, usually. But being thoughtful about "exiting" community (as the Urban Bush Women so helpfully put it) is not something we discuss a great deal. There are many reasons projects need to end—sometimes a new project becomes more pressing or even more useful for the neighborhood or community, sometimes funding ends, sometimes collaborators leave a job and no one is left to continue the partnership, sometimes faculty time becomes more limited than it was before. These are all normal things, not failures. **Without planning for these possibilities and then dealing with them, we risk the good that is done in projects by their precipitous end.**

Time is such an important aspect of this conversation. So is compensation, financial or otherwise. The sustainability of a project often depends on the project not, as Mary Rizzo says, "using up" anyone. It's important that partners' time is not monopolized for more than they can give and also that faculty, especially part-time faculty who often teach these classes, are not spending (inordinate) amounts of unpaid time on a project beyond "contact hours." It's just as important that students feel like the project works with the time that they have to give, as we increasingly work with students who have jobs, lives, families—other demands on their time beyond schoolwork.

Building Trust

MR: The biggest challenge to community partners trusting us is what our universities did to those communities! Rutgers–Newark, like many urban universities, displaced communities through eminent domain as it was expanding its campus in the 1960s. Now regularly regarded as having the most diverse undergraduate population in the country, there were few Black or Latinx students at the university before 1968. They fought to be admitted. The Black Organization of Students' takeover of Conklin Hall was the turning point for Rutgers–Newark development as a diverse and inclusive place. In the twenty-first century, the living memory of people who went through those experiences is merging with current concerns about the gentrification of downtown Newark, a process in which Rutgers is again implicated.

So with that backdrop, why does anybody in the community trust us? **Not to be flippant, but the simple answer is that they get some kind of material benefit out of working with us.** As public historians in the academy, we see very clearly what we get from working with communities (projects for our students, internships, publications based on this work, tenure and promotion, etc.), but we're less able to see the immediate value of this work from the point of view of our partners.

Members of the LGBTQ community working with Mayor Cory Booker and the Newark LGBTQ Community Center connected with Rutgers–Newark historians to create the Queer Newark Oral History Project because they recognized the importance of gathering and preserving the history of the community. They were especially concerned for LGBTQ youth: "This absence of a grounding history, and this sense that they are nowhere reflected in the history they learn in school, can add to the alienation that gay youth experience simply by virtue of growing up in heteronormative families, communities, and religious traditions."[3] The founders of Queer Newark were able to get funding from Rutgers for events, speakers, graduate students to conduct oral histories, community oral history training, and a multimedia exhibit about queer life in Newark. In this case, we have been leveraging Rutgers resources in support of the community.

Money isn't everything though. We need to treat our community partners as true partners, respecting their ideas and perspectives and also understanding that their involvement in these projects may wax and wane, while ours must remain consistent. One thing that does worry me, however, is that the qualities and skills that build trust—empathy, listening, compromise, and collaboration—are highly feminized. We know that the majority of public historians are women but that many public history institutions are run by men. Institutions may rely on community partners, but they may not appropriately value the labor that goes into maintaining these relationships. If women are being tasked with building community (because they're naturally "better" at it), does this mean we are not teaching *all* public historians the appropriate skills? Have we failed to recognize and teach our students—especially our female students—additional skills that might better position them to become cultural institutions' leaders in the future?

RA: It is certainly true that my university has made a deep emotional and physical impression on its surrounding neighborhood such that negotiating my own positionality as separate from that of the institution that employs me has been a big challenge. NYU's neighbors tend not only to have great antagonism toward the university—for many good reasons—but also toward its students and faculty, who are seen as individual agents of gentrification. In another research project I have been conducting on the nearby Lower East Side, some of our local participants refuse to set foot in an NYU building.

As my course has engaged with communities that are a little further afield from NYU, though, different issues arise. The organizations with whom we work and the neighborhoods where they are situated have predominantly Black and Brown populations with many residents who are more comfortable speaking in Spanish than English. My students, on the other hand, are typically (though not always) White and lacking Spanish-language skills. I, too, am White and speak only English. And while class status is often indeterminate for all of us, privilege is legible if only because we are affiliated with an expensive private university. Because of the ways in which gentrification is often visually codified by how people look, my students and I often present as "gentrifiers" and the subject of our study—neighborhood change—further emphasizes this. So I often wonder, why do our community partners trust us?

My answer, however incomplete or unscholarly, is that we claim no authority—or, put differently, we approach the partnership with humility. Different from a "shared authority" perspective, ours is that the community itself has the authority and experience to tell its own story. We are not amplifying so much as actually listening. And our job is to use the tools of history to labor on behalf of and use our resources toward the shared, mutually determined, social justice objective that animates the partnership in the first place. For the course, this objective has been to document the stories of long-time residents of changing neighborhoods and produce an archive of historical research that is available to our community partners. The social justice objective is for this research to make its way into community advocacy materials and to help with community building around self-advocacy in a neighborhood encountering increased displacement. That we are willing to and enthusiastic about doing this work as defined by our partner and without special gain for our own institutions has been, I think, central to building trust. I also think just being reliable, openhearted, and kind friends to our partners has been of incredible benefit—and it's genuine!

DD: The communities in the Lower East Side do not trust NYU given the ways it has treated its surrounding neighborhoods—contributing to gentrification and failing to promote goodwill with local residents. So it was initially difficult for me to enter these communities and indicate that we would like to work with them over a long period of time. I have been successful when I was able to begin with personal contacts that I had in the Lower East Side or an introduction from a colleague who knew a community member. Developing personal relationships was critical to build community trust and establish their willingness to work with us. When the director of the Commission for Public Health approached me to work with his staff to collect stories about well-being, he was very clear that it was not NYU that he was working with but rather our program, which he felt was different from NYU as an institution. He was very clear that he did not want NYU's medical school or its Global Public Health Initiative to know about this project or be involved in any way.

Humility is a key aspect of community-based pedagogy: we do not speak for the community; rather, they speak for themselves.

In our case we used art as the conduit to encourage people to talk about their experiences of well-being. The community trusted that we knew something about art and how to use it to facilitate dialogue. We have to build trust with people. It is always tenuous, and it takes constant attention and effort. It is by building long-term relationships and not through a single encounter that trust can slowly emerge.

DM: I tend to engage in projects that are not of my own design. I don't typically approach a community partner with research I'd like to conduct or a project I'd like to implement. Rather, I talk to potential community partners for a while before asking if there is anything my students and I might help with. In this scenario, I build a relationship with individuals and organizations first, then we develop a plan together.

That was not really the case with my current project, Preserve the Baltimore Uprising. Because I developed the digital, crowdsourced collection in response to a sense of urgency, I had to find partners and build connections retrospectively. Nonetheless, underneath the project are several key values that have helped me make connections and build relationships. **First, this is not my research. I am not seeking out partners to build the collection; I am asking potential partners if the collection might be useful for meeting their own goals. Second, this is not my project. I have created a framework for expanding the reach and use of the collection, but within that framework, there is significant flexibility.** I am grateful to have won a Public Engagement Fellowship from the Whiting Foundation to help build relationships and transform the collection into a truly collaborative space. With this support, during 2018–19, I worked with three Baltimore City high schools and several community-based partners—including a local culture organizer and a historically African American social club—to activate the collection. I provided training in collections development and oral history; what my partners actually did with that training was entirely up to them. The project looked quite different at each school and for each partner. Third, I work hard to remain aware of how, when, and with whom I deploy my authority. There are moments when asserting myself as Dr. or Professor Meringolo makes sense because it assists my partner in achieving a goal or gaining access to resources. There are moments when it can be a barrier to building trust. Learning to identify those moments is a lifelong process. Finally, while this is improving, most universities do not have a structure for bringing together faculty who are engaged in community-based work. Yet these structures provide a crucial support system. Working in isolation tends to magnify the challenges of building trust. Entering into dialogue with other public humanists and public historians helps illuminate our common experiences and identify best practices.

Candidly, the most difficult part of managing community relationships and building trust for me **is that I can be sensitive and very hard on myself. In any working partnership, there will be moments when trust is temporarily lost, when a partner feels slighted, when there has been a misunderstanding, big or small. When that happens, my first reaction is to believe that I have failed.** I have learned to acknowledge that feeling in myself but also to keep it to myself. Humility and honesty are key, but self-deprecation is not helpful. I personally find this difficult, but I am working on it—all the time!

GBV: Building trust often starts with overcoming our institutions' prior relationships with our partners or in the neighborhoods where we are working. While the New School doesn't have quite the real estate empire of other New York universities, it is growing, and it is certainly perceived as similar. In my experience working on the Lower East Side, people are both drawn to the possibilities, resources, or exposure that institutions can give them and are skeptical of being taken advantage of by those same institutions. Sometimes this skepticism originates from a general recognition of universities as agents of gentrification or displacement, but it also comes from much smaller, more personal experiences.

Too many times, I've found that in partnering with community organizations, which are almost always small and stretched, **I'm navigating the fallout and bad feelings engendered by some other class's or university's community-based project, in which community members felt taken advantage of, or where they felt their time was not compensated, or where they felt that students simply wanted them to do their schoolwork for them rather than treating them as experts or teachers.** In this context, I'm navigating my own relationships, histories, positionality, and institutional privilege, as well as issues of the larger field of community-engaged teaching, in which

For each year's Layered SPURA exhibition, they created a "newspaper" publication that exhibitiongoers could take. The first three are shown here. They included exhibition information as well as student-written guides demystifying the planning processes for city-owned sites like SPURA and mapping the considerable community assets of the Lower East Side. Photograph by Gabrielle Bendiner-Viani.

there are few agreed-upon norms about the ways that universities and classes engage with community partners. While there is a great deal of excellent discussion about community partners as coteachers, and those teachers and practitioners are the ones I like to engage, there are also classes in which the framework still hews too closely to a model of expertise held within the university and brought to the community, a model of "helping" rather than collaborating or learning together, and never enough recognition of the deep expertise held within communities, community organizations, and individuals.

In terms of overcoming some of this, I think time is crucial, both in the regularity of showing up and in allowing time for collaborations and projects to change and grow. This kind of time is challenged by the semester model in many ways—in particular by classes in which the idea that a "finished product" has to be created by the end of the semester. This can sometimes work, especially in multiyear projects, wherein a given "product" is building on past work, but it is often difficult, because the focus on the product too often leads people to forget that the process—in a class and in a collaboration—is primarily one of learning, not production.

In terms of what's worked for me, I'd echo one of Denise's points: I very frequently collaborate with organizations and communities that are already working on an issue or project, and then we think collaboratively about what an art or public history component could add. This is often a process of learning from both sides—not everyone is sure of what art or public history in the context of community activism can do, and I always need to listen deeply to understand what is at the core of the work we are embarking upon. The beginning of these collaborations requires that everyone comes to the table with some ideas to share as well as the willingness to change plans entirely, to make something new together. In the five years I worked on SPURA, primarily with GOLES, each year we made a community-based exhibition but the process was one of negotiating, reimagining, and experimenting about what an "exhibition" could do, what questions it could pose, who its audience might be, and what role it could play in the larger campaigns around affordable housing development at this site of inequity, displacement, and insufficient housing.

Radical Potential

DM: For Preserve the Baltimore Uprising, the radical potential resides, at least in part, in its potential to challenge systemic racism in the cultural sector.

Shortly after I built the project's Omeka site, the digital projects coordinator for the Maryland Historical Society approached me and proposed we work in partnership, and I agreed. **By locating the collection there, we are posing a direct challenge to the institutional structures that have led to the absence of urban history, African American history, and histories of unrest in the society's collections.** Materials uploaded to the site are not subject to the same collections committee review as three-dimensional or traditional archival materials, and contributors do not give up their ownership rights. This allows contributors to exert significant control over the way the collection represents the city, Freddie Gray's neighborhood, the African American experience, the parameters of community, and urban protest.

The radical potential of the project also resides, at least in part, in our efforts to ensure that more local people recognize and activate their ownership of the project. By facilitating the use of the collection by students, teachers, and others, with support from the Whiting Foundation Public Engagement Fellowship program, we sought to decentralize the project more fully.

DD: Using the arts to facilitate discussion as we did with the Community Book of Wellbeing is not new. What makes it radical is that, as a form of research, it is undertaken in a university by graduate students in collaboration with a community organization, the Commission for Public Health, and senior women with the goal of transforming public health policy. This visual research is meant to be useful to the community and social struggle—a critical aspect of what has come to be called "militant research." **The radical aspect of militant research is that through new ways of acting or embodied practice we learn to think in new ways or shape new knowledge.** According to the activist academic Andrea Smith, quoting her mentor Judy Vaughn, "You don't think your way into a different way of acting; you act your way into a different way of thinking."[4] Working across different forms (visual, writing, talking) and methods, then, is part of this process of using art to create social change—a form of militant research.

RA: Arguably, projects and courses like (Dis)Placed Urban Histories are not radical. **If they are, it is only because universities are reluctant to provide the support and flexibility necessary for instructors to develop courses that are driven as much by community needs as by academic objectives.** This is tied to questions of tenure, faculty course load, pay, accreditation, and sometimes even politics. (Many universities are reluctant to finance critiques of their own role in a neighborhood, for example.) At the same time, collaborations between historians and organizations that provide direct services to underserved communities are also disappointingly rare, and therefore their very existence is radical. As historians, we can and should be working with advocacy organizations that do the justice work we believe in. Organizations should know their own histories and the historical contexts that have shaped them. But perhaps more importantly, people who are served by these organizations, particularly when they are bound to a particular place, benefit from telling, hearing, and discussing one another's histories. **Community does not exist because people live near one another or have precisely the same experiences; it exists because people know and really listen to one another.** "Doing" history is a powerful way of building common cause. For organizations, like WHEDco, that aim to represent communities that have long been misunderstood and often neglected by government, a sense of common cause is crucial.

MR: For many people working in universities or public history organizations, just addressing the topics of police accountability and police brutality explored in *From Rebellion to Review Board: Newark Fights for Police Accountability* would have been radical. **But the meaning of *radical* is always "local."** Newark is a city with a long tradition of Black power and Black cultural nationalism, most famously through the work of poet and activist Amiri Baraka, whose son, Ras, is now our mayor. The only complaint I heard from a community member about the exhibit was that it was not radical enough.

I've thought a lot about what made this project radical. What I think is that we did something quite unique by weaving all of these

Student Brandon Crispin photographed this portrait of collaborator Sam Marquez during his years as a United States Marine. Marquez, a former New York Fire Department firefighter and longtime resident of Melrose, narrated his experiences during the 1970s when the South Bronx in particular experienced a surge in arson-related fires. Brandon Crispin, "Sam Marquez, USMC," (Dis)Placed Urban Histories: Melrose, accessed January 3, 2019, http://displacedhistories.hosting.nyu.edu/spring2017/items/show/71.

stories together into one narrative. The accepted narrative, the one that is repeated in academic and popular histories and in our local monuments and commemorations, positions the 1967 rebellion as *the* event of modern Newark history. In its shadow everything else lies. **By putting police overreach at the center of our exhibit, we connected together topics that had never been aligned in precisely the same way before**. This was particularly true in the inclusion of Defarra Gaymon's murder. Gaymon was shot by a police officer who was patrolling a county park where gay men cruised for sex. Was Gaymon cruising? It's unclear, but even if he was, his actions should not have warranted a death sentence. His murder started a public conversation about police relations with the LGBTQ community. Like many cities, Newark struggles with providing safe spaces for LGBTQ people. To position Gaymon's murder in the same story as the beating of John Smith by police (the event that started the 1967 rebellion) powerfully claimed space for gay men and lesbians in the history of Newark. Similarly, by discussing the successes and the challenges that came from the Black and Puerto Rican coalition, we helped bring the Puerto Rican community's story more fully into the narrative of Newark, known almost paradigmatically as a Black city. Did viewers recognize this renarrativization? I'm not sure. We certainly didn't proceed with that in mind so it's not made as an explicit point in the exhibit. But as someone who is training people to be scholars and public historians, I see this kind of broad perspective that allows stories from different communities and times to be brought together as our superpower.

GBV: One thing that made our approach in Layered SPURA radical was the extended time frame, which allowed the project to change over time in response to a volatile and very changeable political environment. As we were working on the project, the planning process for SPURA changed drastically, meaning that each semester's class was extremely different. Each class created their own exhibitions, but they also all built on the work that had come before. The other radical idea was not one that we identified from the outset—**it was that one of the greatest contributions of this project would be in the creation of a new kind of space in the neighborhood, outside of the battlegrounds of the community board meetings. We found that what**

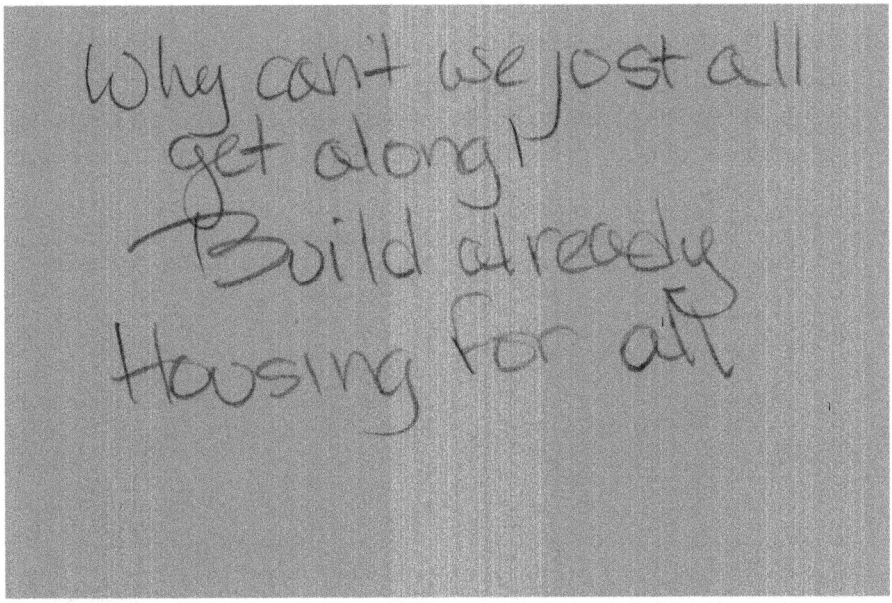

A heartfelt wish left by forty-year SPURA activist Lisa Kaplan at one of the Layered SPURA exhibitions. The exhibitions were always designed to incorporate multiple ways for viewers to participate in, touch, and contribute to the exhibitions themselves. Photograph by Gabrielle Bendiner-Viani.

exhibitions or creative practice can do is to bring multiple sides of an issue together in one space. Of course, it mattered what was on the walls, or in people's hands, as they engaged with the projects, but what mattered even more was the creation of a space—even a temporary one—that people could share. The possibilities for this work, and the challenging relationships they tackle, crystalized for me when, at the opening of our second exhibition, one of my partners, GOLES executive director Damaris Reyes, leaned over to whisper in surprise that she'd never before seen this group of people in the same room without screaming.

Notes

1 Gabrielle Bendiner-Viani, *Contested City: Art and Public History as Mediation at New York's Seward Park Urban Renewal Area* (Iowa City: University of Iowa Press, 2019).
2 For more on artistic activism, see Chantal Mouffe, "Artistic Activism and Agonistic Spaces," *Art & Research* 1, no. 2 (2007): 1–5, http://www.artandresearch.org.uk/v1n2/mouffe.html.

3 Darnelle Moore et al., "A Community's Response to the Problem of Invisibility: The Queer Newark Oral History Project," QED: A Journal in GLBTQ Worldmaking 1, no. 2 (2014): 2.
4 Natalie Bookchin et al., *The Militant Research Handbook* (New York: New York University Press, 2013), 4, http://www.visualculturenow.org/the-militant-research-handbook/.

SITES OF DISCORD AND DIALOGUE

MUSEUMS IN PROGRESS

Imperfectly Progressive

The Social Mission of Museums in the 1930s

Clarissa J. Ceglio

> Emerging from its chrysalis, the still [history] museum of the past will become active and to attain a commanding place in our community life. And in that day it will be said: "It is not what the museum has but what it does with what it has that counts in community value."
>
> —Arthur C. Parker (*Seneca*)
> "The Small History Museum" (1935)

Arthur Casewell Parker, director of the Rochester Museum of Arts and Science and a prolific author whose works include *A Manual for History Museums* (1935), had much to say on the matter of what collecting institutions ought to do with their historical artifacts and for their communities.[1] "Mr. Parker conceives of the history museum as neither a mausoleum nor warehouse," remarked one reviewer of the *Manual*, "but as an institution for service, a dispenser of ideas, a stimulus to social action."[2] In fact, as Parker himself declaimed, "A museum is a social service."[3] He did not stand alone in this conviction. Parker's museum contemporaries recognized him as a "trail blazer" during his lifetime.[4]

Indeed, the 1930s mark a period in the United States of America when a number of the field's practitioners advocated that museums, of all disciplinary stripes, become more actively involved in "the life of the people" through attentiveness to contemporary social concerns, adult-focused education initiatives, and narrative forms of object display.[5] More progressive spirits advocated that history as told through artifacts be treated as a resource from which communities could make decisions about the here and now—with a more knowing eye to the future. Such an idea finds resonance in Rebecca Conard's description of public historians' animating conviction: "At its core, the public history impulse springs from a fundamental belief in the utility of history and a persistent quest to apply historical knowledge to the contemporary needs of society."[6]

The decade, which falls within the longer arc of museums' institutional "paradigm shift" from "collection-driven" to "visitor-centered," also tracks with an important period in the genealogy of public history, as has been traced through the National Park Service and its museums by Denise D. Meringolo.[7] By taking the quest for public history's roots into the wider terrain of museums, the goal is to expand on the "proactive effort to historicize and theorize the attitudes and habits of mind that make public history distinctive" while being attentive to the impact that practitioners not academically trained in history have had in foregrounding values that activist public historians prize today, such as being of service to communities, connecting the past to the present, and using expressive communications methodologies that do not dismiss emotional connections as irrelevant or unprofessional.[8] Parker, who did not hold a degree in history, had come by his training in archeology and ethnography through informal apprenticeships, self-study, and the aid of mentors with museum connections.[9] This path, which landed him at the New York State Museum from 1906 to 1924, formed him equally into a self-described museologist. He went on to direct the Rochester Museum of Arts and Sciences for over twenty years.[10] Although not the only (nor a flawless) champion for the time, Parker advocated most consistently for the public place of history in the enterprise of more socially aware, community-focused museum work.

To understand why the idea of the museum as a social actor came to the fore as it did in leading-edge practice of the 1930s and how it shaped ideas about museum-based public history, one must look to the field's broader deliberations about the function of museums in civic life. These discussions played out in the professional literature, including some dozen books published (or in formation) during the decade. In their reflections and prognostications, museum observers paid special heed to the field's Progressive Era past as a touchstone for its new social-civic mission. From the mix of forces and debates that will be considered here, a reignited vision of the museum as both a "social movement" and a "social instrument" emerged.[11] But what did this vision look like in practice, particularly in the area of museum-based presentations of history for public audiences? Certainly, the age's aspirations lofted far above the realities of implementation. Exhibition and programming narratives very often remained bogged down in an evolutionary view of historical "progress," with its attendant racism, nationalism, and colonialism. Still, one sees within the literature some of public historians' hallmark concerns: acknowledging nonelites as historical actors, connecting interpretations to everyday life, and directing exhibition craft toward ends deemed socially progressive by those who created them.[12]

So to answer the question of what the social mission of museums in the 1930s looked like in practice, this essay draws out the arc of the field's major concerns and debates.[13] These frictions serve as the backdrop for two short profiles of work undertaken by the Charleston Museum and the Rochester Museum of Arts and Sciences, which appear as sidebars in this chapter. These snapshots suggest how localized factors, in the context of the field's bigger picture, gave shape to what "progressive" looked like when pursued by specific individuals, museums, and communities. More in-depth studies of the period are needed, of course, as underscored by the insights and lines of continued inquiry opened by Laura Schiavo's examination in this collection of the Jewish Theological Seminary's museum.[14] But whereas her work for this volume provides a much needed "alternative 'center,'" here we dive into the heart of the mainstream, Anglo-European-dominant museum culture during a period of introspective stocktaking.

Examining Museums' Foundations

> It has happened, time and again in the course of history, that museums have made their best progress when the foundations of things have been shaken.
>
> —Laurence Vail Coleman
> *The Museum in America: A Critical Study* (1939)

As the 1930s drew to a close, the American Alliance of Museums (AAM), supported by a grant from the Carnegie Corporation of New York, issued a landmark three-volume survey of the field: *The Museum in America: A Critical Study*.[15] In it the chief author and AAM's director, Laurence Vail Coleman, described American museums as a "Social Movement" gaining steam, fueled in part by their dramatically increased numbers.[16] New museums had appeared "at the rate of one a week," resulting in a fourfold increase from 600 institutions in 1910 to 2,480 by 1938.[17] Over roughly the same period capital investment in public museum facilities had increased some $144 million across the nation, with their estimated aggregate operating income growing from $2 million to "an all-time high" of $18 million.[18] These bullish comparisons did not, however, capture the Depression's deep trough years or its continued effects on institutional coffers. The field's income had dropped about 20 percent between 1930 and 1935.[19] Coleman acknowledged this statistical news of a one-fifth average decline might come as a "surprise" to those whose own institutions had seen "revenue cuts of 50, 60, 70, and even 80 per cent." No doubt the Grand Rapids Public Museum, which saw its municipal budget cut by 87 percent, would have been among the "surprised."[20] The economic rebound, as measured only by the fortunes of the nation's top one hundred "leading institutions," was a slender 3 percent.[21]

Still, despite such financial constraints, museums had, Coleman claimed, achieved "a more important part in the daily life of the people" as shown by the estimated 50 million visits a year.[22] By this accounting, up to 38 percent, or better than one-third, of the nearly 130 million people living in the US might have been to a museum in 1938.[23] Deeper within the study's pages, however, he admitted that attendance tracking methods, formulas, and discerning what the numbers said about a museum's success in reaching its community was not clear-cut. Almost as an aside, Coleman notes that some methods "used to bring on discussions" about whether to include the "negro population" in service calculations.[24] This, a reference to impact measures developed by the former director of the Charleston Museum, serves as a reminder that who counted as community (and who did not) and who constituted the public (and who did not) remained circumscribed by racism, classism, xenophobia, and other forms of prejudice operative at the national and local levels.

Despite their flaws, attendance figures still provided *some* measure of *some of* the public's interest; and this, the numbers said, had been falling off after a brief peak in the early 1930s.[25] Coleman pointed first to the slow financial recovery, which curtailed operating hours, staff, and programming capacity, as a cause. But he most strongly indicted overconservative minds among those who guided museum affairs. Trustees and others who held museums to be sanctuaries for the initiated or an amusement exclusive to "a little coterie," he argued, undermined progress by resisting museums' necessary expansion into fuller "community service."[26] He warned, "Although many museum boards still linger in the socialite spirit of yesterday, the narrow conception of the institutions' place is passing."²⁷ Not all board members obstructed progress, claimed Edsel B. Ford, who spoke at AAM on "The New Public Museum from the Standpoint of a Trustee." He lauded appointees from the modern corporate sector as the bringers of a "less passive and more positive participation" to institutional affairs. They brought something more than "moral and financial support" to their "adopted child," the museum.²⁸ He said, "Their close contact with the busy world about them enables them to sense the pulse of the public perhaps to a greater degree, than the somewhat absorbed and sequestered professional [museum] worker." Such modern trustees, Ford claimed, applied their business acumen in public relations and modern merchandising-display tactics to move their museums "in the direction of greater and greater service to the public." Providing popular educational service, he argued, was not negotiable. "The public museum of tomorrow may have to depend more and more upon governmental subsidy rather than endowments, if the earning power of its invested funds continues to shrink," Ford stated. "If the museum is to receive public financial support, it must play an essential part in the recreation and enjoyment of people who have ever more leisure."²⁹

With faith in endowment earnings shaken and the prospect of "great gifts" from the private sector slimmed, the field contemplated increased reliance on monetary support from municipal and federal sources as well as philanthropic organizations.³⁰ The fact that city appropriations, which weighed in as the field's second largest income source (19 percent) after endowment income (35 percent), had "only half recovered" from a 40 percent fall off during the Depression only heightened the abiding sense that public museums needed more than ever to prove worthy of their keep.³¹ Here, causes for optimism included efforts supported by the Works Progress Administration (WPA), which allowed museums to send exhibitions out to schools, settlement houses, public library branches, and other locations.³² The WPA, the Works Division of the Department of Public Welfare, and other government agencies also supported restoration and expansion of museum facilities, cataloging and care of collections, the installation of exhibitions, expansion of research and education activities, and generally, augmentation of existing staff so that long-deferred projects as well as ambitious new undertakings could be tackled.³³ The funds also supported work undertaken with communities, particularly in the arts.

ILLUMINATING VALUES: THE ROCHESTER MUSEUM OF ARTS AND SCIENCES AND THE SENECA ARTS PROJECT

"Your Museum of History, rather, must be a power station sending out a current that illumines the community and gives a clearer vision of social values," wrote Arthur C. Parker in his 1945 volume *A Manual for History Museums*.* The sentence implies that these community values are intrinsically present, even if dimly perceived. Born in 1881 on the Cattaraugus Indian Reservation to a mother of Anglo-European ancestry and a Seneca father, Parker's own personal and professional histories reveal values shaped by the complexities of navigating liminal spaces of belonging in multiple communities. The same man who tired of having "to play Indian in order to be Indian" and who in 1911 helped to found a national Native rights organization, the Society of American Indians, also advised in his *Manual* that "for an out-of-door play or pageant, there is scarcely any historical theme so effective as that of the Indian and pioneer."† That a man whose name was also Gáwasowaneh devoted six pages of "how-to" instructions to satisfying the White American penchant for "playing Indian" strikes modern eyes as a troubling concession to mainstream racism, an odd act of assimilation.‡ Why include this appendix to the book at all?

The first line of "How to Plan a Pageant" supplies its own answer and reveals a more subversive intention. Both word order and capitalization emphasize *whose* story commands this play of "the Indian and the pioneer." Indeed, of Parker's proposed twelve acts, "the coming of the white settlers" does not occur until the ninth. Act 10 completely inverts the story of postcontact assimilation by focusing on a White captive who, after tribal adoption, enjoys "adventures" with his new "People." The two concluding acts, as well as the first eight, focus squarely on the

---

* Arthur C. Parker, *A Manual for History Museums*, New York State Historical Association Series 3 (New York: Columbia University Press, 1935), 19.
† Parker, quoted in Joy Porter, *To Be Indian: The Life of Iroquois-Seneca Arthur Caswell Parker* (Norman: University of Oklahoma Press, 2001), xvii; Parker, *Manual for History Museums*, 169.
‡ On the history of such practices, see Philip J. Deloria, *Playing Indian* (New Haven, CT: Yale University Press, 1999).

Indians' telling of their "discovery and settlement of the region," self-government, and lifeways. Parker's further instructions foreground the need to strive for historical accuracy even in the fanciful realm of reenactment. Here, Parker's mission as a sometimes radical public historian comes to the fore. He names a dozen Indigenous leaders (many of who resisted land theft and dispossession)—from Osceola to Red Cloud (Maȟpíya Lúta)—as historical figures to be included and delineated with the same care and fullness as "pioneer fathers" William Penn, George Washington, Daniel Boone, and Sam Houston.

Would-be pageant planners are also admonished to give care to the accuracy of dress, avoiding "fancy store blankets with pseudo-Indian designs" and to "get the facts from a recognized historian or museum curator."* In the passage, Parker resists pernicious stereotypes while also reinscribing racial categories. Indian men and women are not, he warned, to be referred to as "bucks" and "squaws." The latter, he wrote was particularly "insulting": "It is an evil term, and one not to be used by the government in its dealings with red people. Avoid it as you would wench, wanton or huzzy as applied to a good woman of modern times."

At the time of *A Manual for History Museums*' publication, Parker and staff had embarked on two museum-community collaborations, known collectively as the Seneca Arts Project, with residents of the Cattaraugus and Tonawanda reservations. Funded first through the Temporary Emergency Relief Administration and subsequently by the Works Progress Administration, craftspeople and project supervisors in the communities earned a nominal wage for their labors. For its part, the Rochester Arts and Sciences Museum provided work benches, tools, other resources, and guidance in the form of reference books, materials, photographs, and drawings from the museum's and other institutions' ethnographic collections representing earlier periods of Iroquois (Haudenosaunee) production. The museum would also gain artifacts, some replicating mid-nineteenth-century materials it had lost to a fire, for its collection and for trade with other institutions. Parker described the museum's primary aims as a corrective to cultural repression, noting that "long had they been taught to imitate all the cultural

---

* Parker, *Manual for History Museums*, 172–73.

patterns of the European. Native thinking, native art, native creative ability practically had been crushed out. . . . The result has been anything but beneficial."* Writing from the vantage point of community member and a Tonawanda project supervisor, Cephas Hill credits the community's own experts with providing knowledge and guidance. "Old Seneca residents at Tonawanda visit the project and offer suggestions and criticisms to the younger workers," he noted. "We discuss legends, traditions, and customs and we find in them material which we put to use."†

The project did not, however, result in an immediately sustainable channel for the reservations' economic development. Such "Indian New Deal" efforts, which aligned with the US federal government's Indian Reorganization Act of 1934 and the 1935 formation of the Department of Interior's Indian Arts and Crafts Board, were both leveraged and resisted by Native peoples. Where some saw a useful conduit to reclaiming threatened traditions, others pushed back against the narrow premodern framing of Indigenous possibility. In fact, a core grievance among resistors was the reduction of Indigenous training and work prospects to limited preindustrial forms of production that served to reinforce a colonialist vision of Native peoples as inhabiting a "past" space—a space the White market for these craft commodities could imagine as free of the state-imposed political, human, and economic costs of reservation life.‡ In Parker's time, as now, public history collaborations undertaken as a means to illumine community and social values often prove most valuable in bringing difficult-to-face shadows to light.

The combination of support for populist outreach and fiscal pressure to provide clear community value gave the more socially progressive voices of

---

* Arthur C. Parker, "Museum Motives behind the New York Arts Project," in *Indians at Work* (Washington, DC: United States Bureau of Indian Affairs, 1935), 11.
† Cephas Hill (Seneca) and William F. Fenton (an ethnologist), "Reviving Indian Arts among the Senecas," in *Indians at Work*, 13.
‡ See Porter, *To Be Indian*, 208–9; Jennifer McLerran, *A New Deal for Native Art: Indian Arts and Federal Policy, 1933–1943* (Tucson: University of Arizona Press, 2009), 84–93.

the field, such as museum educator Theodore L. Low, cause to believe museums might be pushed into change:

> Since the fateful events of 1929, which in many ways can be considered a blessing, the ideas of [John Cotton] Dana have been cropping out again and have finally been accepted by many museum men and educators. The old guard still clings to its sheltered concepts but others have realized that museums need a transfusion of blood and thought if they are to take their rightful place in society today. In short, they recognize that the only real justification for the existence of a museum lies in its degree of usefulness to society as a whole and that museums today are failing miserably to attain the standards necessary for continued life.[34]

The larger writings of Low, Coleman, and Ford reveal that even those in agreement on the ethical and financial need for museums to assume greater involvement in civic affairs did not necessarily align on the details. Debates about the nature of museums' social mission and how best to pursue it impacted every level of museum work. In fact, AAM's Committee on Education found it necessary, with support from both the Rockefeller Foundation and Carnegie Corporation, to research and "correlate the vast amount of controversial literature" that had been published in the 1930s.[35]

Ironically, the resulting volume, *The Museum as a Social Instrument: A Study Undertaken for the Committee on Education of the American Association of Museums* (1942), written by Low would itself become a source of controversy.[36] Central questions dealt with how museums, as democratic institutions, might better equip the public to navigate society's considerable changes. These included adults unmoored from work routines and in need of tools for self-advancement, the dulling effects of mass communication techniques on the public mind, propaganda in its political and corporate manifestations, the growing complexity of social and technological issues with which citizens needed to contend, and the implications of brewing European tensions and jingoism. The answers to serving as well as wooing an expanded public required, many thought, not only a resurgence of the Progressive Era social reform spirit but an embrace of contemporary mass communications techniques in service to popular education for adults.

Popular Education as Democratic Social Instrument

> The democratic ideal of equal cultural opportunities for all citizens is, after all, the heart and backbone of the adult educational movement. When groups possessing social or economic power fail to fulfill their educational responsibilities to the common man, democracy is betrayed to the extent of their neglect.
>
> —Thomas Ritchie Adam
> *Civic Value of Museums* (1937)

As Coleman described it, "The thing that educators mean now by 'adult education' is only about a decade out of its Cradle. It is a movement to get as many people as possible self-consciously improving themselves as a regular custom through the whole span of their years."[37] The contemporary movement to which he referred emerged with the formation of the American Association for Adult Education (AAAE) in 1926.[38] As other scholars have noted, the AAAE championed adult education as a democratic means to "create informed citizens, promote tolerance and understanding of differences, and maintain social stability."[39] Educating Americans throughout adulthood had become a topic of national focus due to the spreading phenomenon of "leisure" time in the laboring classes. Causes for this included the comparatively shorter work week of the twentieth century, the Depression's widespread unemployment, and the National Recovery Administration's curtailment of work hours.[40] Many museums already had formal educational programs in place, of course, but the greater number focused on schoolchildren. Lectures, exhibitions, and offerings for the older set happened as a matter of course but not as a field-wide initiative to popularize museums' educational approaches to adults. A 1934–35 assessment of museums' adult education activities conducted on behalf of the Rockefeller Foundation found the following: "Many of them, judged by standards of museum work in the past, seem relatively progressive and satisfactory activities. Judged by newer concepts of museum function and a growing interest in and demand for popular adult education, they appear halting and inadequate."[41] Given their shared interests, AAM and AAAE leadership soon sat on one another's committees, spoke at one another's meetings, and shared ideas in print. Commissioned by AAAE, Thomas Ritchie Adam, a professor of political science, wrote *The Civic Value of Museums* (1937) and *The Museum and Popular Culture* (1939).[42] Adam, an admitted amateur on the topic of museums as he approached the 1937 volume, did not always grasp the "internal complications" that made some of his proposals "facile" from the perspectives of those in the trenches.[43] Nonetheless, on the larger issues of adult education and the expanded roles museums might play in a democratic society, practitioners found much of merit.[44]

What emerges in Adam's volumes and similar writings is a reweaving of older strands of Progressive thought on museums' educational roles with concerns particular to the 1930s. Ideas such as improving workers' lot in an industrialized democracy, which were in force before the Great War, mingled with aspirations pursued in the 1920s, such as outfitting corporate producers for international competition and preparing the public for consumer citizenship.[45] These now intermixed with the populist ambitions of the New Deal and a worry-tinged interest in the ability of popular mass communication and advertising techniques to capture the public imagination. Here, Adam and others of the age feared that the undereducated working and middle classes would lack the criticality of mind needed to sift the wheat from the chafe of the media buffet. As with the AAAE generally and some in museums as well, Adam was wary of educational interventions and institutions that relied too heavily on government funds as the answer.[46] These might become beholden to political influence. Here, he pointed to cultural dictatorships in Europe and Asia as evidence of the abuses that could result—and to underscore the necessity of a well-informed polity capable of independent, critical thought.[47] Museums with their collections, he argued, could be precisely the "trustworthy authority accessible to the common man" *and* source of "scholarly" information that popular education needed.[48]

While AAAE pondered museums' roles in popular education from without, many within the nation's institutions had already begun to put such ambitions into wider practice. Low and Grace Fisher Ramsey, associate curator of education at the American Museum of Natural History (AMNH), stood among these activists. Ramsey, author of *Educational Work in Museums of the United States: Development, Methods, and Trends* (1938), pointed to purpose-trained museum educators, capable of inspiring learning from objects, as the essential drivers of a transformation wherein museum collections and exhibitions might finally "serve as free and informal universities."[49] Instructors whose sole purpose was to provide education could earlier be found within the field.[50] In most cases, however, curators or other museum staff handled whatever educational activities were undertaken, doing so in tandem with their primary responsibilities and often approaching public learning with different sensibilities and priorities than the professional class of educators who would follow. The writings of educator, philosopher, and psychologist John

Dewey, whose work inspired the adult education movement, also influenced Progressive Era museum leadership directly, and perhaps none more so than John Cotton Dana, founding director of the Newark Museum. He, director Laura Bragg of the Charleston Museum, and others not only embraced the idea that popular education had the power and the duty to serve social and political ends but also formed the training programs from which many museum educators of the 1930s emerged.[51]

> ### CONCEPTUALIZING COMMUNITY AT THE CHARLESTON MUSEUM
>
> Contemporaries of Paul Marshall Rea (1879–1948) and Laura Bragg (1881–1978) would have counted them as among the spectrum of progressive-minded museum professionals of their day. This said, looking at their bodies of work illuminates the importance of parsing the individual as well as collective boundaries of the social movement within museums in any time period but, certainly, as it existed in the twentieth century prior to World War II. The two worked together at the Charleston Museum in South Carolina. When Bragg came to the museum at Rea's invitation in 1909, he had been its curator since 1903 and then, through a negotiated title change, its director. Rea, an academic biologist by training, had transformed the languishing Museum of the College of Charleston into simply the Charleston Museum. This shift to becoming a community-focused entity involved a move off campus as well as the new name.* Assuming the title of librarian (later changed to "Curator of Books and Public Instruction"), Bragg quickly expanded the museum's services for and engagement with the area's segregated public schools, both Black and White.
>
> Still, as reflected in its 1915 municipal charter of incorporation as "a general museum and library of art, science, and industry," Jim Crow politics held sway, spelling out in writing that White citizens constituted the public to be served.† Nonetheless, Bragg, Rea, and

---

* The College of Charleston was but one of the museum's many homes and incarnations since its 1773 founding as an endeavor of the Charleston Library Society.

† Louise Anderson Allen, *A Bluestocking in Charleston: The Life and Career of Laura Bragg* (Columbia: University of South Carolina Press, 2001), 56.

museum trustees chipped away at the restrictions in a gradualist fashion. By 1917, policy extended admission to teacher-accompanied Black school groups—a loophole that Benjamin F. Cox, the Fisk University–educated principal of the nearby Avery Normal Institute, wasted no time in leveraging.* Bragg assumed the directorship after Rea's departure in 1920. Within her first year, and with municipal support, she instituted Saturday afternoon hours for Black visitors, where previously only those—adult or child—associated with pre-arranged school visits could gain entry. Others have highlighted Bragg's multiple radicalities as an educator, woman director, possible lesbian, and individual who since childhood dealt with profound, progressive hearing loss.† They have dealt, too, with her privileges as a Northern-born, Simmons College–educated White woman undertaking social welfare work in a community to which she was an outsider.

Among the issues bearing deeper scrutiny, however, is the role Cox and others within the local Black community played in bringing about these changes. Likewise, Rea's later reflections on Black museumgoing underscore limits to the vision of museums as social instruments. In 1932, Rea, now the director of the Cleveland Museum of Natural History, published a statistical study commissioned by the Carnegie Corporation and its Advisory Group on Museum Education (to which Rea served as a consultant).‡ The Carnegie Corporation hoped to provide funders like itself, museum directors, trustees, and others, including municipalities, with a quantitative means of assessing "the museum-community

---

* Allen, 63.

† See the online *Journal of the American Association for the Advancement of Curriculum Studies* 3 (February 2007) for the following articles: Louise Anderson Allen, "Reinterpreting Laura Bragg: How Deafness, Feminism, and Maternalism Defined Her Actions as a Progressive Educator and Curriculum Worker," https://ojs.library.ubc.ca/index.php/jaaacs/article/view/187655; Douglas McKnight, "The Discourse of Educational Professionalization and Laura Bragg," https://ojs.library.ubc.ca/index.php/jaaacs/article/view/188580; William F. Pinar, "Religion, Love, and Democracy in Laura Bragg's Boxes," https://ojs.library.ubc.ca/index.php/jaaacs/article/view/187656/185759.

‡ Rea also had deep ties with the American Alliance of Museums. He had been present at its establishment in 1906, assumed its secretaryship in 1907, and from 1919–21 was its director.

relation."* With such metrics in hand, leaders could rely on sound social science, rather than "blind guesswork," to steer their museums along a path of increased public usefulness.†

The matter of who "the public" excluded came to the fore in Rea's description of Charleston. He called it an aberrant city, lacking a "normal" suburban population to counterbalance the fact that Whites accounted for only about half of its urban demographic.‡ He deemed the "large negro population" a "handicap" in determining the Charleston Museum's efficacy in serving its constituency. Not only did the African American population reportedly attend the museum rarely and in small number, "the white population" paid "nearly all the taxes" that supported the institution. To resolve the quandary, Rea reported two sets of figures: one calculated using the total census and another featuring a refined Whites-only subset to reflect a truer measure of the museum's service. The text did not in any way consider how segregation, the deep scars of slavery, or the museum's own shifting admission policies affected these statistics. Similarly, neither Rea nor the volume's reviewers commented on whether this excluded audience merited museums' attention.§ In essence, by tacit agreement, the public and Whiteness remained synonymous throughout much of the literature, as well as much of the practice, of those who were, nonetheless, pushing socially progressive agendas.

Other museum functions also underwent professionalization during this period. A number of art historians who completed a course of study at Harvard University's Fogg Art Museum took up positions as directors and curators at leading institutions.[52] The differences in training sometimes served to place

---

* Paul Marshall Rea, *The Museum and the Community, with a Chapter on the Library and the Community; a Study of Social Laws and Consequences* (Lancaster, PA: Science Press, 1932), iii.
† Rea, 19.
‡ Rea, 41–42.
§ Though, as George E. Hein, notes in *Progressive Museum Practice* (163–65), Rea's data on branch museums may ultimately have helped paved the way to the later advent of the Anacostia Neighborhood Museum. See also Hein's profile of Bragg (87–95).

scholarly connoisseurship in opposition to public education. As Coleman put it, the sore point had become, "Are museums primarily educational, or are they for only such educational work as can be carried on without limiting the curatorial function?"[53] He further noted, "The real question now is whether the two different roles will tend to differentiate museums of two classes—the collectors of objects and the leaders of people, with scholarship given to the one and recreation to the other, and with education divided between them according to its nature, and theirs."[54] While Coleman imagined this divide as sorting museums into different classes, it had the effect, in some cases, of pitting staff in the same institution against one another as exhibitions, education, and other public-directed functions received greater shares of limited budgets and internal resources. Ramsey's own institution, the AMNH, experienced such a row when modernization of displays brought accusations from research staff of a flagging commitment to scholarship.[55] Low noted that professional "jealousies" had the "devastating result" of dividing museums generally so that "scholars have come to look with disdain upon popular education and popular education has, in turn, come to decry the narrow-minded haughtiness of the scholars."[56] The solution, according to Low, was for all to agree that "the purpose and the only purpose of museums is education in all its varied aspects from the most scholarly research to the simple arousing of curiosity."[57]

For the task of stimulating a curiosity for learning among adults, museums of the 1930s grew increasingly interested in adapting to their purposes the display tactics of merchandisers and narrative formats familiar to the public from contemporary mass media. The impulse, with its echoes of John Cotton Dana's praise for department store display practices, was not a novel one.[58] But it did gain renewed traction within the field as well as investment from philanthropic groups. The Rockefeller Foundation, for example, sponsored in-depth studies of 1939's Golden Gate International Exposition and New York World's Fair. These resulted in two books detailing the exhibition practices corporations and countries used to attract, engage, and impart information to a wide public.[59]

Didactic Exhibitions: Information or Indoctrination?

> An exhibition of symbols—conveying what somebody *thinks* about something—is a break with custom.
>
> —Laurence Vail Coleman
> *The Museum in America: A Critical Study* (1939)

In rethinking their roles and reach in society, museums also rethought how human-thing interactions produced knowledge and conveyed meaning.[60] At the vanguard were pointedly didactic exhibitions conceived of as immersive narrative encounters that engaged museumgoers as sensory, embodied beings in order to inspire civic spirit and even social action. The same year that AAM published *The Museum in America*, some two hundred of its members convened in San Francisco for its annual meeting, which took the theme "Interpretation through Exhibits" and included sessions held within the Golden Gate International Exposition grounds.[61] Many of these, from museums of various types, considered "the didactic functions of museum display in relation to other purposes and functions of exhibits."[62] Of the many talks later distributed in print, perhaps it is one given on "The Place of the Museum in Adult Education" that most strongly hints at the double-edged sword that this trend in exhibition craft presented. Arranging objects so that they told "a definite story" by "synthesiz[ing] basic facts into a dramatic unity" provided a compelling way to attract museumgoers' attention and communicate a "main idea" such that they not only grasped that idea but also made some connection between it and their "daily life and well-being."[63] The dilemma was this: how to use the persuasive communications strategies that made mass media messaging and even political propaganda emotionally resonant and compelling for the accomplishment of democratic social agendas without also becoming agents of indoctrination.

In that AAM presentation, Morse A. Cartwright, executive director of the AAAE, pointed to political events in Europe and described popular education as a bulwark against fascism.[64] He called on museums "to assume their proper and rightful educational role in the developing culture of the democracy."[65] Failure to "meet the challenge of that opportunity," he said would leave museums and other agencies for adult education "to suffer the general fate that will sweep away all our democratic institutions when the totalitarian state prevails" or, perhaps worse, leave them to an "inglorious sentence of serving in perpetuity as propaganda arms of the government in power." Certainly, museum professionals did not need to look far to see the dangers of exhibition craft bent to the state's will. For example, Hitler's ousting of disfavored staff in German museums soon after his rise to power—along with the 1937 Munich showing of *Entartete Kunst* (Degenerate art), which reportedly drew twenty thousand spectators a day—gave cause for alarm.[66] Likewise, Italy's *Mostra della rivoluzione fascista* (Exhibition of the fascist revolution;

1932) deepened concerns in some quarters over talk that US museums might increase their reliance on government funding and thereby open the door to unwanted state influence.[67]

The matter of how democratic forms of persuasive education could be advanced without veering into the territory of political propaganda generated much debate. Within the Rockefeller Foundation, for example, some felt "a democracy-enhancing balance between education and propaganda" might be achieved in films and other tools designed to shape public opinion.[68] In parsing the period's museum literature, it is important to understand that the term *propaganda* carried a broader meaning than is common today. The older, ecclesial sense of the word, "to disseminate or propagate," often functioned as a value-neutral shorthand for contemporary public relations and marketing strategies. That said, US opinion leaders and the public alike viewed the suite of persuasive communications techniques bundled under the term *propaganda* with "morbid fascination."[69] Concerned with its abuses during the Great War and uses in the rising field of advertising, they worried over who in the US had mastery of such tools and to what ends they would be used.[70] Passages such as the following from Edward L. Bernays's *Propaganda* (1928), one of the better-known texts among corporate readers, seemed to underscore the stakes: "Those who manipulate this unseen mechanism of society constitute an invisible government which is the true ruling power of our country.... It is they who pull the wires which control the public mind."[71]

Bernays, a self-proclaimed propaganda counselor and pioneer in the new field of public relations (who would speak at AAM in 1942), held that the masses looked first to a "trusted leader" when "making up its mind."[72] For its part the AAAE hoped to ensure public institutions, such as museums, libraries, and schools, did not cede that leadership to government or industry. Adam, in *The Museum and Popular Culture*, again urged museums to redouble popularizing and extending their adult education efforts because, in his assessment, public ignorance made it possible for small factions to manipulate opinions and thereby rise to power.[73] Indeed, some museums, by adapting persuasive communications techniques to object display, likewise hoped to more vigorously participate in the marketplace of ideas competing for the public mind.

The catch for those practicing this still nascent style of exhibition craft was the need to reconcile purposive education with social aims and the mandate that museums ought to "speak about objects, not about notions *symbolized* by objects."[74] Here, Coleman wrote with specific concern for the use of "models, charts, and objects that stand for sophisticated concepts," a practice most evident in industrial and social museums. "An exhibition of symbols—conveying what somebody *thinks* about something—is a break with custom," he warned. The goal for museums, Coleman cautioned, was to inform minds, not produce actions. Among the offending exhibitions to which he referred might have been 1934's Housing Exhibition of the City of New York at the Museum of Modern Art.[75] This show, sponsored with the museum by the New York City Housing Authority and other agencies, positioned architectural design as an essential tool of social reform. Through blueprints, statistical charts, architectural models, enlarged photographs, and even a flat reassembled from a demolished old-law tenement house, it presented the case for slum removal.[76]

This effort and others like it echoed civic exhibits organized in the Progressive Era by government agencies, professional associations, museums, and other civic groups, sometimes in cooperation with one another, and that tackled such topics such as child welfare, city planning, health, worker safety, and other problems of modernity.[77] Those in Coleman's camp not only found the presence of a social directive to be a disconcerting diversion from the purpose of museums but also expressed valid worries over museum exhibits that lacked in the stabilizing anchor of artifacts' objective truths:

> This method of display has its values and its dangers. It is thoughtful and awake. It can narrate—which is an important point for history museums. But also it falls easily into making what is little more than an illustrated book—big and cumbersome and looking like an exhibit, but really a book all the same. This practice can lead on to indoctrination. It gets away from what museums are for—to give evidence, primarily. Perhaps, when the dust of rapid change has settled—in museums of history, and of industry and science too—there will be a picture book in the hands of the visitor and museum material in museum cases.[78]

The interpretive ambiguity—the rupture in the vision of objective (as in object-derived) artifact-inherent meaning cracked open by the trend toward narrative, storytelling frameworks—only exposed what had always been true of taxonomies and exhibition craft: that arrangements, inclusions, gaps, and omissions all constituted a material rhetoric of "what somebody *thinks* about something."

Culture History in Museums Rewrites "The Material Story"

> The historical museum has, as a main objective, the presentation of its subject in such a way as to visualize the history of the past so that it may serve a useful purpose in the present.
>
> —Institute for Research, Chicago
> *Careers in Museum Work* (1939)

Arthur Parker would have seen his own words mirrored back at him in this definition of the history museum put forth by *Careers in Museum Work*. It neatly echoed his own thoughts from 1935's *A Manual for History Museums*, in which he stated, "Our purpose is to re-visualize the past for the benefit of the whole community, thereby making the values of the past potent to the present."[79] Coleman's *The Museum in America* offered a similar take: "One purpose animates museums of history. This is to recreate the past in the minds of the living. Any history museums that are themselves dead are victims not of their concern with the past but of their unconcern about the present."[80] Culture history, all agreed, provided the chief intellectual framework whereby artifacts, from the size of a button to the scope of a house and its outlying grounds, could create the vivid impressions capable of popularizing study of the past by making it relevant and alive to the public.

Culture history for these authors meant the study of ordinary people through the material items they made, owned, and used. "The spirit in which local history is approached by museums is close to that of the modern historian, interested increasingly in culture history," observed Coleman in his analysis of current trends. "Scholarly interest has shifted during recent years from political and military affairs, from the lives of leaders to the life of all the people . . . by increased attention to objective evidence."[81] He singled out Arthur M. Schlesinger Sr. and Dixon Ryan Fox as leaders in this approach through their History of American Life book series.[82] Within museums that employed it, the framework breached disciplinary boundaries, as dictated by the nature of an institution's holdings. For museums of varied collections, "the interpretation of art, history, anthropology, and applied science—all together as culture history" might provide a unity purpose, said Coleman.[83] The approach did remain tethered to notions of history as a tale of evolution and progress, however, as witnessed by this summation: "The duties of the curator of culture history are to approach history from the standpoint of the evolution of material culture. Culture, it should be understood, is a term applied to things mankind makes or does to modify natural things and materials. The term does not mean 'polite culture.' The curator of this division of museum activity should have specialized in history, social studies, ethnology, and art. Most successful history museums are in fact museums of culture history."[84]

Fox, no stranger to the work of museums, had earlier written the introduction to Parker's *A Manual for History Museums*, which the New York State Historical Association commissioned in hopes of bringing a greater degree of professionalization to this sector of the field.[85] Parker himself had agitated for such a manual some ten years earlier. The Carnegie Corporation provided a subvention to make the book affordable to workers in small local institutions and to encourage broad circulation as "an indirect but potent aid to adult education."[86] Institutionally, then as now, the term *history museum* applied to a wide range of collection-holding institutions: from open-air sites to houses and other preserved structures, from the department in a "general" museum or the room or building under the aegis of a historical society, to "special history" museums devoted solely to golf, road building, crime, or some other human activity.[87] So by AAM's 1938 accounting, 1,235 of the tallied 2,489 museums in the US could be classified in part or in whole as history museums.[88]

Coleman summarized the sector thus: "More places have history museums *of some kind* than have science or art museums, but very few places have *good* public history museums." Their chief sins, to paraphrase Coleman, consisted of meddling with natural history, taking in everything "dumped upon them" by donors, and attempting to show it all without attention to meaning, organization, or historical merits.[89] Both Parker and Fox agreed, adding that such flaws, particularly among historical society and small local museums, stemmed from the fact that they had "never been given over to the administration of trained museum men and women."[90] Custodians without a trained eye for culture history remained so "engrossed in written records" that they neglected modernizing their use of the object collections that "made them wealthy beyond dream."[91] Parker's own training in archaeology no doubt accounted for his confidence that history could be not only read from objects but written with them as well.[92]

On the debatable question of how objects told "the material story" of culture history, Parker had no qualms about making his views clear.[93] "With ideas first in mind as the function of the institution, one may work and plan for the materialization of ideas," he counseled in his *Manual*, further emphasizing,

"First get your ideas, *ideas are to be presented, not specimens.*"[94] Such an exhibition, if well executed, would, its curators hoped, effectively act upon "the intellect and the emotions."[95]

The field's deeper struggle lay not in whether museum education should provoke thought and action but the degree to which it sought to channel those impulses. In a time with greater faith in the possibility of neutrality, tensions focused on whether exhibitions were to give evidence or exposition for public benefit. On the matter of historical artifacts, the principle at issue was whether they constituted a "usable past" in terms of equipping members of the public to engage in civic life, contend with the day's issues, and shape a better future.[96] For adherents of philosophies like Parker's, the purpose of history for the public was to connect the past and present in meaningful ways in order to illumine future possibilities and paths.[97] For the most part, this meant putting history before the public, be it at the museum, in shop windows downtown, in schools, or at other community sites. It is in Parker's views of what small and local history museums *might* become that glimpses of courting public participation in the work of history are seen. He envisioned "active committee chairmen" seeking out counsel to "relate the work of the museum to the needs of the community," and the making of museums into places where an institution's visitors and neighbors might "form the nucleus of community projects for the interpretation of history."[98] History museums' work might also touch upon matters of citizenship, familiarizing people with the functions of local government and hosting events where museumgoers met with public officials.[99] For others, to carry on such work within the history museum went beyond the pale: "The responsibility to the living carries an obligation to teach only the truth. Training in citizenship and moralizing from the past for the future is foreign to this duty."[100]

Conclusion

> It is in activity that the museum succeeds; it is by ideas and not by visible storage that it lives; it is by touching the lives of the people with values that it gives inspiration.
>
> —Arthur C. Parker
> "The History Museum—an Opportunity" (1934)

Although none claimed the title of public history for their work, museum practitioners of the 1930s who dealt in interpreting and presenting the past still grappled with concerns familiar to our field: who is "the public"; what does it mean to place history in service to contemporary civic issues; and how are collections useful to communities?[101] Deeper exploration of the gap between the visionary rhetoric and workaday realities of implementing new practices is needed. Also needed is attentiveness to the longer arc of time over which efforts to make museums socially progressive recur. As recounted here, the museum as a social movement, a social instrument, arose in a historically specific set of circumstances but also drew inspiration from the work and writings of an earlier generation—some whose lifetimes spanned the social, economic, and political changes informing conceptions of museums' roles in civic life. And even before *The Museum in America: A Critical Study* was published, national security interests and the coming of war amplified existing tensions within the vision of the museum as a social instrument. This led to its derailment, for a time, from the center stage of discussions of museum practice.

A chief reason this essay focuses on ambitions ultimately diverted by World War II is that histories focused on trends that persisted in the long-term tend to obscure experimental practices and institutional forms.[102] Also a critical reexamination of exhibition work that is dismissed today as mere propaganda is in order. First, the distinctions that practitioners themselves made between biased or misleading forms of persuasion and their own purpose-driven exhibition craft and educational programs merit new consideration. To ignore these is a form of misrecognition that makes little allowance for the fact that activist public history and museum practice, even in our own times, seek quite often to advance social agendas through some of the same means: didactic exhibitions conceived of as immersive narrative encounters that engage museumgoers as sensory, embodied beings. The aims are similar too: to create deeper, more compelling understandings and to guide the embodied museal encounter toward socially relevant and useful ends. This is not to suggest false equivalencies between the past and present but to urge greater historical introspection within our practice.

More important than broad-brushed censure (or naïve reclamation) is the task of examining the ways in which earlier individuals and institutions struggled to make the museums of their time more accountable, more meaningful, and more useful to a broader public. It is important to recognize these steps along the path, even in their imperfectly conceptualized and realized aims—not least of all for how they can lead us to ask different questions of our own work. And as I have argued elsewhere, divorced from a deeper historical knowledge of itself, the museum field is prone to patterns of immediacy and reinvention when confronted with local and national crisis points.[103] This is a blind spot we can ill afford—least of all now.

HISTORICALLY SIGNIFICANT MUSEUM STUDIES BOOKS AVAILABLE THROUGH HATHITRUST

Adam, Thomas R. *The Civic Value of Museums*. Studies in the Social Significance of Adult Education in the United States 4. New York: American Association of Adult Education, 1937. https://hdl.handle.net/2027/mdp.39015067063803.

———. *The Museum and Popular Culture*. Studies in the Social Significance of Adult Education in the United States 14. New York: American Association of Adult Education, 1939. https://hdl.handle.net/2027/uc1.$b45863.

Berkeley, William Noland. *The Small-Community Museum; Why It Is Entirely Feasible; Why It Is Extremely Desirable*. Lynchburg, VA: J. P. Bell, 1932. http://hdl.handle.net/2027/mdp.39015035858763.

Careers in Museum Work. Report no. 91. Chicago: Institute for Research, 1939. https://hdl.handle.net/2027/mdp.39015084384174.

Ramsey, Grace Fisher. *Educational Work in Museums of the United States: Development, Methods, and Trends.* New York: H. W. Wilson, 1938. https://hdl.handle.net/2027/wu.89090364522.

Rea, Paul Marshall. *The Museum and the Community, with a Chapter on the Library and the Community; a Study of Social Laws and Consequences*. Lancaster, PA: Science Press, 1932. https://hdl.handle.net/2027/uc1.b4579533.

Notes

1 Epigraph: Arthur C. Parker, "The Small History Museum," *New York History* 16, no. 2 (April 1935): 195.

   Arthur C. Parker, *A Manual for History Museums*, New York State Historical Association Series 3 (New York: Columbia University Press, 1935). Parker (1881–1955) was born on the Cattaraugus Indian Reservation to a Seneca father and a mother of Scots-Irish ancestry. With no matrilineal Seneca tie and a father who was also of mixed heritage, Parker remained outside tribal enrollment until his adoption into the Seneca Bear Clan around age twenty-two. On the many ambiguities, contradictions, and maturing of Parker's positions with regard to his own heritage and assimilation as a strategy for Native advancement in American society, see Joy Porter, *To Be Indian: The Life of Iroquois-Seneca Arthur Caswell Parker* (Norman: University of Oklahoma Press, 2001); and Chip Colwell, *Inheriting the Past: The Making of Arthur C. Parker and Indigenous Archaeology* (Tucson: University of Arizona Press, 2009).

2   Herbert Gambrell, review of *A Manual for History Museums*, by Arthur C. Parker, *Pennsylvania Magazine of History and Biography* 61, no. 2 (April 1937): 225.

3   Quoted in Terry Zeller, "Arthur Parker and the Educational Mission of American Museums," *Curator: The Museum Journal* 32, no. 2 (June 1, 1989): 117.

4   Frank DuMond, quoted in Zeller, 120. DuMond was a director of the Grand Rapids Public Museum and well-known voice of the period among his contemporaries.

5   Laurence Vail Coleman, *The Museum in America: A Critical Study*, 3 vols. (Washington, DC: American Association of Museums, 1939), 1:18.

6   Rebecca Conard, "The Pragmatic Roots of Public History Education in the United States," *Public Historian* 37, no. 1 (February 2015): 119.

7   Gail Anderson, "Introduction: Reinventing Museums," in *Reinventing the Museum: Historical and Contemporary Perspectives on the Paradigm Shift*, ed. Gail Anderson (Walnut Creek, CA: AltaMira, 2004), 1–7; Denise D. Meringolo, *Museums, Monuments, and National Parks: Toward a New Genealogy of Public History* (Amherst: University of Massachusetts Press, 2012). On the shift of scientific discovery from museums to universities and the impact of this on museums' conceptualizations of their place in society, see Steven Conn, *Museums and American Intellectual Life, 1876–1926* (Chicago: University of Chicago Press, 1998).

8   Meringolo, *Museums, Monuments, and National Parks*, xxvi; Rachel Donaldson, "Summer Camp and the Radical Roots of Public History Pedagogy," in this volume. On valuing "emotional connections to the past," see, for example, Benjamin Filene, "Passionate Histories: 'Outsider' History-Makers and What They Teach Us," *Public Historian* 34, no. 1 (February 1, 2012): 11–33; and Marianne Babal, "Sticky History: Connecting Historians with the Public," *Public Historian* 32, no. 4 (November 1, 2010): 76–84.

9   For details on Parker's training, work, and life, see Colwell, *Inheriting the Past*; Joy Porter, "Arthur Caswell Parker, 1881–1955: Indian American Museum Professional," *New York History* 81, no. 2 (April 2000): 211–36; and Terry Zeller, "Arthur C. Parker: A Pioneer in American Museums," *Curator: The Museum Journal* 30, no. 1 (March 1, 1987): 41–62.

10 When Parker came on board, the institution was called the Rochester Municipal Museum; he succeeded in changing its name to the Rochester Museum of Arts and Sciences in 1930.

11 Coleman, *Museum in America*, 1:5; Theodore L. Low, *The Museum as a Social Instrument: A Study Undertaken for the Committee on Education of the American Association of*

Museums (New York: Metropolitan Museum of Art for the American Association of Museums, 1942).

12 Meringolo, *Museums, Monuments, and National Parks*, 168. The "populist shift" of 1930s public history (understood as history presented to a public) and the "redefining [of] American history as something that included common people as historical actors" is briefly noted in Michael Wallace, "Visiting the Past: History Museums in the United States," *Radical History Review* 1981, no. 25 (January 1, 1981): 79.

13 Clarissa J. Ceglio, *A Cultural Arsenal for Democracy: The World War II Work of U.S. Museums* (Amherst: University of Massachusetts Press, forthcoming), treats the decade's developments and their impact on museum activities in the war years in greater detail.

14 Laura Schiavo, "What to Do with Heritage: The Museum of Jewish Ceremonial Objects, 1931–1943," in this volume.

15 Epigraph: Coleman, *Museum in America*, 1:3.

  AAM itself relied on the philanthropic organization for almost 45 percent of its operating budget in 1939 according to fiscal year 1938–39 and 1939–40 data reported in American Association of Museums, "Cash Statement: General Fund," January 31, 1939; and "Cash Statement: General Fund," January 31, 1940, Smithsonian Institution Archives, American Association of Museums, 1906–85, RU 7450, series 2 "general correspondence: 1942–46," box 15, folder "Council 1939–1940 to 1946–7."

16 Coleman, *Museum in America*, 1:3.

17 Coleman, 1:4, 44.

18 Coleman, 1:18; "Museum Income Last Year at All-Time High of Eighteen Million," *Museum News* 17, no. 6 (September 15, 1939): 1–2. Coleman notes that the "figures take account of new museums as well as changes in older museums." It remains unclear, given increase in number of museums between 1910 and 1938, if the increase in aggregate operating income also corresponds to an increase in the average income per institution, nor is it clear if his figures account for changes in the dollar's value overtime.

19 Coleman, 1:180.

20 Frank L. DuMond, "Presenting the Museum to the Community," *Museum News* 18, no. 13 (January 1, 1941): 10.

21 Based on a comparison of aggregate operating incomes for 1930 and 1938. "Museum Income Last Year," 1.

22 Coleman, *Museum in America*, 1:44, 2:298. Coleman's vague wording does not indicate which twelve-month span or the source of this number.

23 Coleman's figures, an aggregate, do not separate unique single visitors from repeat visitors. "Historical National Population Estimates: July 1, 1900, to July 1, 1999," Population Estimates Program, Population Division, US Census Bureau, June 28, 2000, http://www.census.gov/population/estimates/nation/popclockest.txt. The national population estimate for July 1, 1938, was 129,824,939.

24 Coleman, *Museum in America*, 2:298. One approach of the time for calculating a museum's reach within its community was to divide the year's total attendance by

the local population and use the resulting percentage as a measure of effectiveness. See the Charleston Museum vignette for additional details on how racism factored into these equations.

25 Coleman, 2:297–99. He does not provide numbers and, in similarly vague terms, notes that London's national museums were also seeing "disquieting decline," which, he thought, might be due to the automobile affording access to other attractions.

26 Coleman, 1:182.

27 Coleman, 1:9. Although Coleman made this statement with regard to art museums, the predominant and most prestigious form of museum at the time, the lesson he wished to impart had broader resonance.

28 Although Ford's description of museums as the adopted children of their trustees conjures a tender paternalistic relationship, it is a relationship with clearly defined dominant-subordinate positions.

29 Edsel B. Ford (president, Arts Commission of the City of Detroit), "The New Public Museum from the Standpoint of a Trustee," *Museum News* 18, no. 5 (September 1, 1940): 9, from a paper read at the annual meeting of the American Association of Museums in Detroit, May 22, 1940, as part of the session "The New Public Museum—an Orientation for the Years Ahead from Five Points of View."

30 Coleman, *Museum in America*, 1:182.

31 Philip N. Youtz, "Museums among Public Services," *Museum News* 11, no. 6 (September 15, 1933): 6.

32 Richard F. Bach, "Neighborhood Circulating Exhibitions," *Museum News* 14, no. 12 (December 15, 1936): 7–8, from a paper read at the annual meeting of the American Association of Museums at New York, May 11–13, 1936. Particular effort was made to reach immigrant groups by sending word of the exhibits to the foreign-language press. By teaming with the host organizations' educators, the museum offered study groups, classes, and lectures in conjunction with the exhibits.

33 "WPA Provides Museums with 2,774 Workers," *Museum News* 15, no. 18 (March 15, 1938): 4; Ellen S. Woodward (assistant administrator, Works Progress Administration), "WPA Museum Projects," *Museum News* 15, no. 13 (January 1, 1938): 7–8.

34 Low, *Museum as a Social Instrument*, 12. John Cotton Dana is recognized for insisting that museums be made more useful to a broader public. Several of his books have been reprinted and are still in use today, including *The New Museum* (Woodstock, VT: Elm Tree Press, 1917).

35 Francis H. Taylor (chairman, American Alliance of Museum's Committee on Education; director, the Metropolitan Museum of Art), foreword to Low, *Museum as a Social Instrument*, 3.

36 At the time AAM contracted Low to write *The Museum as a Social Instrument*, he had served as a part-time museum educator at the Metropolitan Museum of Art, was a graduate student in art history at Harvard University, and was also pursuing adult education at Columbia University's Teachers College. He went on to serve as director of education at the Walters Art Gallery / Walters Art Museum from 1946–80.

On the volume as a source of lingering controversy, see George E. Hein, *Progressive Museum Practice: John Dewey and Democracy* (Walnut Creek, CA: Left Coast, 2012), 128–29, 138–39.

37 Epigraph: Thomas R. Adam, *The Civic Value of Museums*, Studies in the Social Significance of Adult Education in the United States 4 (New York: American Association of Adult Education, 1937), viii.

   Coleman, *Museum in America*, 2:317. One author's sardonic, winking piece, which touts museums' offerings, rightly suggests that the fear of wrongly occupied time was a more a preoccupation of the classes accustomed to spare time than it was of the average worker; see Lincoln Heights Recreation Corporation, "New Leisure Will Not Catch New York Citizens Unawares: The City Is like a University, Equipped with Plants for Study and Play and Full of Occupation for Spare Time," *New York Times*, April 15, 1934, XX9.

38 An outgrowth of the Carnegie Corporation of New York's mission to promote "the advancement and diffusion of knowledge and understanding," the AAAE claimed a longer history for itself, one rooted in the democratic impulse to self-enlightenment that resulted in the Junto clubs of Benjamin Franklin's era and the lyceum movement of the early 1800s. See, for example, Morse A. Cartwright (executive-director, American Association of Adult Education), "The History of Adult Education in the United States," in "Adult Education for Negroes in the United States," *Journal of Negro Education* 14, no. 3 (Summer 1945): 283–92.

39 Harold W. Stubblefield and Patrick Keane, *Adult Education in the American Experience: From the Colonial Period to the Present* (San Francisco: Jossey-Bass, 1994), 194.

40 Coleman, *Museum in America*, 2:318.

41 Leonard Outhwait, "Museum Survey. Activity of Museums in Adult Education. January–March 1935," 1, Rockefeller Archive Center, RG 1.1, series 200 "U.S.," box 252, folder 3005.

42 Adam, *Civic Value of Museums*; Thomas R. Adam, *The Museum and Popular Culture*, Studies in the Social Significance of Adult Education in the United States 14 (New York: American Association of Adult Education, 1939). Among the cited shortcomings of Adam's first book was that he based his firsthand assessments on just a handful of institutions, all from the New York City area. He remedied this for the 1939 study by casting a wider geographical wider net, visiting more museums, and talking to more active practitioners in order to gain a fuller awareness of current trends.

43 Adam, *Civic Value of Museums*, v; Low, *Museum as a Social Instrument*, 13.

44 On the volumes' merits, see Low, *Museum as a Social Instrument*, and Henry C. Shetrone, "Review of Diagnosis and a Remedy: The Civic Value of Museums," *Journal of Higher Education* 9, no. 4 (April 1938): 232–33.

45 On the tensions and contradictions within the Progressive Era as a whole and within the museums that embraced its spirit of reform, see Jeffrey Trask, *Things American: Art Museums and Civic Culture in the Progressive Era* (Philadelphia: University of Pennsylvania Press, 2012); Ezra Shales, *Made in Newark: Cultivating Industrial Arts*

and *Civic Identity in the Progressive Era* (New Brunswick, NJ: Rivergate Books, an imprint of Rutgers University Press, 2010); and Carol Duncan, *A Matter of Class: John Cotton Dana, Progressive Reform, and the Newark Museum* (Pittsburgh, PA: Periscope, 2009).

46 One who outlined the possible pressures that increased reliance on municipal funding and governance might bring was Ira Edwards (director, Milwaukee Public Museum), "The New Public Museum from a Directors Viewpoint," *Museum News* (September 1, 1940): 10–12, from a paper read at annual meeting of the American Association of Museums in Detroit, May 22, 1940, as part of the session "The New Public Museum—an Orientation for the Years Ahead from Five Points of View."

47 Adam, *Civic Value of Museums*, vii, 20–23.

48 Adam, 50, 61.

49 Grace Fisher Ramsey, *Educational Work in Museums of the United States: Development, Methods, and Trends* (New York: H. W. Wilson, 1938), 18, 254. Ramsey conducted her research, which she described as involving interviews with directors and educators from more than 140 museums, between 1936 and 1938 for her doctorate, which she earned from New York University while working at AMNH.

50 Lisa C. Roberts, *From Knowledge to Narrative: Educators and the Changing Museum* (Washington, DC: Smithsonian Institution Press, 1997), 33.

51 The Newark Museum's apprenticeship program, for example, began in 1925 with support from AAM, and the Buffalo Museum of Science inaugurated a sixteen-week course in 1929. Ramsey cites these as the first museum training programs to provide students grounding in museum teaching and adult education, specifically (*Educational Work in Museums*, 212–16). For details of the Newark Museum apprenticeship program, see Hein, *Progressive Museum Practice*, 69–95. In the 1920s, Bragg's contributions to the professionalization of museum work, particularly for women, included developing and teaching a museum training at Columbia University, which ran for several summers. See Louise Anderson Allen, *A Bluestocking in Charleston: The Life and Career of Laura Bragg* (Columbia: University of South Carolina Press, 2001), 140–48.

52 Sybil Gordon Kantor, *Alfred H. Barr, Jr. and the Intellectual Origins of the Museum of Modern Art* (Cambridge, MA: MIT Press, 2002), 36–85; Sally Anne Duncan and Andrew McClellan, *The Art of Curating: Paul J. Sachs and the Museum Course at Harvard* (Los Angeles: Getty Research Institute, 2018). Ramsey, in her volume *Educational Work in Museums*, claimed Sachs's museum course included "very little of the educational work in museums" (214).

53 Coleman, *Museum in America*, 2:319.

54 Coleman, 1:81–82.

55 Karen A. Rader and Victoria E. M. Cain, "From Natural History to Science: Display and the Transformation of American Museums of Science and Nature," *Museum and Society* 6, no. 2 (2008): 152–71; Victoria Cain, "The Art of Authority: Exhibits, Exhibit-Makers, and the Contest for Scientific Status in the American Museum of Natural History, 1920–1940," *Science in Context* 24, no. 2 (June 1, 2011): 215–38.

56 Low, *Museum as a Social Instrument*, 20.

57 Low, 21.

58 John Cotton Dana, *The Gloom of the Museum* (Woodstock, VT: Elm Tree Press, 1917), 23–24. On earlier museum borrowing of inspiration from commercial endeavors, see Neil Harris, "Museums, Merchandising, and Popular Taste: The Struggle for Influence," in *Material Culture and the Study of American Life: A Winterthur Book*, ed. Ian M. G. Quimby (New York: W. W. Norton, 1978), 56–81; and Victoria Cain, "'Attraction, Attention, and Desire': Consumer Culture as Pedagogical Paradigm in Museums in the United States, 1900–1930," *Paedagogica Historica: International Journal of the History of Education* 48, no. 5 (2012): 1–25.

59 Carlos Emmons Cummings, *East Is East and West Is West: Some Observations on the World's Fairs of 1939 by One Whose Main Interest Is in Museums* (East Aurora, NY: Buffalo Museum of Science, 1940); *Exhibition Techniques: A Summary of Exhibition Practice Based on Surveys Conducted at the New York and San Francisco World's Fairs of 1939* (New York: Museum of Science and Industry, 1940).

60 Epigraph: Coleman, *Museum in America*, 1:99.

The object-based epistemology of the late Victorian era as described by Conn had not altogether vanished in the 1930s; rather, it often stood in tension with the narrative or "communicative turn" in exhibition practice described by Manon Niquette and William J. Buxton, "'Sugar-Coating the Education Pill': Rockefeller Support for the Communicative Turn in Science Museums," in *Patronizing the Public: American Philanthropy's Transformation of Culture, Communication, and the Humanities*, ed. William Buxton (Lanham, MD: Lexington, 2009), 153–93. These authors do not, however, give sufficient credit to earlier narrative-style exhibition forms, such as those described by Deborah Martin Kao and Michelle Lamunière, eds., *Instituting Reform: The Social Museum of Harvard University, 1903–1931* (Cambridge, MA: Harvard Art Museums, 2012); Julie K. Brown, *Health and Medicine on Display: International Expositions in the United States, 1876–1904* (Cambridge, MA: MIT Press, 2009); and Brown, *Making Culture Visible: The Public Display of Photography at Fairs, Expositions, and Exhibitions in the United States, 1847–1900* (Amsterdam: Harwood Academic, 2001).

61 "San Francisco Program to Include Day of Visits," *Museum News* 17, no. 1 (May 1, 1939): 1.

62 "San Francisco Program."

63 *Exhibition Techniques*, 16.

64 Morse A. Cartwright, "The Place of the Museum in Adult Education," *Museum News* 17, no. 8 (October 15, 1939): 10–12, from a paper read at the annual meeting of the American Association of Museums at San Francisco, June 26–28, 1939.

65 Cartwright, 12.

66 Bruce Altshuler, *The Avant-Garde in Exhibition: New Art in the 20th Century* (New York: Abrams, 1994), 136–46. Of course, *Entartete Kunst* (Degenerate art) had debuted earlier. It was the evident popularity of the 1937 show that increased alarm among museum professionals.

67 Jeffrey T. Schnapp, "Epic Demonstrations: Fascist Modernity and the 1932 Exhibition of the Fascist Revolution," in *Fascism, Aesthetics, and Culture*, ed. Richard Joseph Golsan (Hanover, NH: University Press of New England, 1992), 1–37.

68 Brett Gary, *The Nervous Liberals: Propaganda Anxieties from World War I to the Cold War* (New York: Columbia University Press, 1999), 111.

69 Allan M. Winkler, *The Politics of Propaganda: The Office of War Information, 1942–1945* (New Haven, CT: Yale University Press, 1978), 4.

70 Gary, *Nervous Liberals*, 2–3.

71 Edward L. Bernays, *Propaganda* (New York: H. Liveright, 1928), 9–10.

72 Bernays, 50–51.

73 Adam, *Museum and Popular Culture*, 142.

74 Coleman, *Museum in America*, 1:99.

75 This exhibition is sometimes called *America Can't Have Housing*, after an accompanying volume edited by Carol Aronovici: *America Can't Have Housing* (New York: Committee on the Housing Exhibition by the Museum of Modern Art, 1934).

76 For descriptions of the exhibition, see Mary Anne Staniszewski, *The Power of Display: A History of Exhibition Installations at the Museum of Modern Art* (Cambridge, MA: MIT Press, 1998), 196–99; and Joan A. Saab, *For the Millions: American Art and Culture between the Wars* (Philadelphia: University of Pennsylvania Press, 2004), 121–27.

77 On this topic, see Kao and Lamunière, *Instituting Reform*; Brown, *Health and Medicine on Display*; and Brown, *Making Culture Visible*.

78 Coleman, *Museum in America*, 2:265.

79 Epigraph: Institute for Research, Chicago, *Careers in Museum Work* (Chicago: Institute for Research, 1939), 13; Parker, *Manual for History Museums*, 15.

80 Coleman, *Museum in America*, 1:60.

81 Coleman, 1:50.

82 History professor Lucy Maynard Salmon pioneered decades earlier the use of material culture in the college classroom and urged history museums to abandon ill-fitting scientific taxonomies in favor of chronological display schema. See Conard, "Pragmatic Roots," 106–8.

83 Conard, 116. As others have noted, museums with self-taught as well as academically trained specialists allowed interdisciplinary minglings. See, for example, Sally Gregory Kohlstedt, "History in a Natural History Museum: George Brown Goode and the Smithsonian Institution," *Public Historian* 10, no. 2 (1988): 7–26. Writers of the age were also aware of how anthropology, for example, was influencing historians practice: Harry Elmer Barnes, "Some Contributions of Anthropology to History," *Journal of Social Forces* 2, no. 3 (March 1924): 362–73.

84 Institute for Research, Chicago, *Careers in Museum Work*, 14.

85 Dixon Ryan Fox, foreword to Parker, *Manual for History Museums*, vii–x.

86 Fox, x.

87 See Warren Leon and Roy Rosenzweig, introduction to *History Museums in the U.S.*, xvi–xviii. Both "general" and "special" museums are categories used in *The Museum*

in America, while reference to the types of special history museums extant in 1938 is found at 1:63–64.

88 Coleman, *Museum in America*, 1:61, 3:663.
89 Coleman, 1:62, 64–66.
90 Arthur C. Parker, "The History Museum—an Opportunity," *New York History* 15, no. 3 (July 1934): 331. Parker, who sent a questionnaire to two hundred small history museums, reported that "only one out of four local museums had a paid or volunteer curator, but 70 percent of them had definite plans for the future. With county historical societies it was found that only half of them rendered any service to the schools and only half of them made any attempt at arrangement of material. Only 20 percent of these societies actually emphasized museum objects or had period rooms," though 80 percent were active publishers of work. See Parker, "Small History Museum," 191. For his part, Fox found the "half-trained, part-time caretaker" inadequate to "the important matter" of "*how* they [artifacts] are displayed." Fox, foreword to Parker, *Manual for History Museums*, viii.
91 Parker, 331.
92 Arthur C. Parker, "History Is Written in Objects," *Regional Review* 1, no. 6 (December 1938): 21, available at http://npshistory.com/newsletters/regional_review/vol1-6h.htm.
93 Parker, *Manual for History Museums*, 55, 64.
94 Parker, 55, 63–64 (emphasis in original).
95 Parker, 18.
96 Van Wyck Brooks, "On Creating a Usable Past," *The Dial* (April 11, 1918): 337–41, http://www.archive.org/stream/dialjournallitcrit64chicrich#page/338/mode/1up.
97 Parker, *Manual for History Museums*, xv; Parker, "History Museum—an Opportunity," 328.
98 Parker, "Small History Museum," 194, 192.
99 Parker, *Manual for History Museums*, 114.
100 Coleman, *Museum in America*, 1:60.
101 Epigraph: Parker, "History Museum—an Opportunity," 330.
102 I take this idea from Julie K. Brown, "The Chicago Municipal Museum," *Museum History Journal* 3, no. 2 (July 2010): 231–56.
103 Clarissa J. Ceglio, "Case Statement," National Council on Public History, February 2016, http://ncph.org/phc/ncph-working-groups/museums-civic-discourse-2016-working-group/ceglio-case-statement/. This was written for Museums and Civic Discourse: Past, Present, and Emerging Futures, a 2016 NCPH working group. Work on this project with fellow editors Jennifer Scott, Elena Gonzales, Nicole Ivy, and Robin Grenier is ongoing and pursues the aims described in "Museums and Civic Discourse: Past, Present, and Emerging Futures—2016 Working Group," National Council on Public History, accessed March 4, 2021, http://ncph.org/phc/ncph-working-groups/museums-civic-discourse-2016-working-group/.

What to Do with Heritage

The Museum of Jewish Ceremonial Objects, 1931–43

Laura Schiavo

A potsherd, a piece of clay or stone, a crude design of primitive man . . . become at once priceless treasures to the scholar. The potsherds or stones are the plots for the future romances written by historians about ancient peoples; their life, their culture and their art. . . . To the curator of a museum, a piece of parchment with faded writing, a torn piece of material, a chip of metal or stone are inspirations for minute study which inspire a delving into the past. . . . The curator is able to clothe them with flesh, to cover them with skin, and breathe life into them, though they have been lying dead for centuries and millennia.

—Paul Romanoff, May 3, 1935

Our museum has become a medium for inter-racial tolerance and understanding.

—Paul Romanoff, May 10, 1939

As curator of the Museum of Jewish Ceremonial Objects in New York City (now the Jewish Museum), Paul Romanoff made these two claims about the significance of material culture in the interpretation of life, culture, and art, and about the social value of the museum.[1] The largely overlooked Romanoff was the first full-time curator appointed to one of the first culturally specific museums in the United States. His relatively brief career (from 1931 until his untimely death in 1943) has gone almost completely unnoticed in the annals of the Jewish Museum.[2] Similarly, the history of smaller museums is often absent from the grand narrative of museum history, including the "golden age" of the American museum from the late nineteenth and early twentieth century.³ This chapter looks at Romanoff's career and his ideas about objects, meaning, identity, and publics to ask, What are we missing when the history we tell about museums is focused on large national museums as sites of power and knowledge rooted in hierarchies of race and nation? What sites of resistance do we omit when we depict museums as the ultimate imperial project that helped constitute a citizenry imagined as White and Protestant? What of the early identity museum that by its nature acknowledged difference and asserted positionality? By their very nature and existence, museums like these called in some way for decentering the dominant culture. The example of the Museum of Jewish Ceremonial Objects begins to lay out the possibility that when we broaden and deepen conventional museum history we discover places that we might label, if not radical, at least resistant to hegemony.

"Identity museums" (a shorthand I use here for museums dedicated to depicting the history and culture of a specific race, religion, ethnicity, or community, created by that identity group) are a crucial component of museum work that defies the dominant narrative. If we understand any radical efforts within the museum to be pushing back against the centering of the dominant culture not only as the objective norm, but even more problematically as the epitome of that which is significant, beautiful, and worthy of exhibition, then the identity museum surely presents an important alternative framework. As mainstream museums began to engage with the potential for civically engaged practice in the late 1990s and early 2000s, Ellen Hirzy, in the landmark *Mastering Civic Engagement* (2002) by the American Association of Museums (AAM), urged museum staff to "learn from their colleagues at ethnic and community-based museums, which have set the standard by establishing deep and meaningful civic involvement as their founding principle."⁴ Hirzy's statement positions ethnic museums as exemplifying work that potentially supplants an interpretation of history and culture whose assumed audience is the general (White) public and whose relation to those visitors is objective and distant.

Yet identity museums have a longer history than is often acknowledged. Scholars who discuss the history of identity museums in the United States typically locate their origins in the victories of the civil rights moment, when ethnic groups established local museums in an effort to preserve their heritage and cultural knowledge.⁵ In one of the most concise presentations of the relationship between "the museum" and "the public," Stephen Weil denies even these postwar developments when, in the broadest of strokes, he contrasts the museum "in its earliest days" with "the museum of the near future." The earlier model is "grand and imposing" in which, quoting Charles Callahan Perkins in 1870 regarding the plans for the Museum of Fine Arts, Boston, "There exists a modicum of capacity for improvement in all men, which can be greatly developed by familiarity with such acknowledged masterpieces as are found in all great collections of works of art."[6] From there, Weil shifts abruptly to "the museum of the near future" in which "it will be primarily the public, and not those inside museums" who will decide what is important and what "stance the museum may take."[7] In fact, there was clearly much more nuance occurring in the late nineteenth and early to mid-twentieth century, developments that those who participated in the post–civil rights frenzy of identity-museum-making were aware. In her account of the early work of the international Afro-American museum movement, Andrea Burns describes how, as Margaret T. G. Burroughs began considering opening a museum devoted to African American history in Chicago in 1960, she visited "small ethnic museums," including the Jewish Museum and the Polish Museum of America in Chicago.[8] As Burns's historical account indicates, the civil rights–era museum movement acknowledged earlier attempts, forays into doing identity work in the museum that have largely gone unstudied.

There is a certain irony in making claims for the counterhegemonic character of an identity museum given the reactionary tendency inspired by much ethnic heritage practice. In one of the only full-length studies of ethnic museums, Rosa Cabrera describes the function of these institutions as providing a space where adherents to a culture can "recall their homeland" and preserve a cultural identity, including passing cultural heritage on to a new generation.[9] Such institutions might default to notions of essentialized ethnicity, ignore differences within that identity, and commit themselves to the celebration of a simplified past—or present. In this, heritage practices would almost in any case fail to look to the future. They would naturally, it may seem, celebrate a static, bounded culture rather than invest in theories of change. Yet late twentieth-century and twenty-first-century identity museums—the National Museum of the American Indian perhaps most notably—provide a sense of the much broader possibilities than the confines of such conservative frameworks allow. NMAI's critics, however, might second the allegation of a celebratory inclination and a simplified notion of identity.[10]

Presaging these negotiations regarding the exhibition of identity and the assertion of difference, the Museum of Jewish Ceremonial Objects in the 1930s exhibited the material culture of a nonmajority culture in a way that provided an alternative "center." These were "Jewish things" presented with honor and respect in an age of widely held anti-Semitism. This was an identity museum established by Jews in the era of the Immigration Act of 1924, when the wisdom and feasibility of assimilation were debated among Jews and in the wider intellectual world. These objects belonged to a global diasporic religion and culture in an age when nation was the most salient context in many museums and most international expositions.

Looking back at one of the earliest examples of identity museums might thus be useful in considering heritage work in an institutional setting. This investigation allows for the exploration of the relationship between the impulse to decenter the dominant culture and a tendency toward the celebration of heritage, as well as the possibility for doing socially instrumental work with cultural heritage. As I will explore, Paul Romanoff's decade of museum work demonstrates that identity museum professionals struggled to make sense of a specific culture's material evidence and to figure out how to make objects and their interpretation accessible to a wide audience. From his hiring in 1931, Romanoff advocated for and championed the collections, asserting the value of the museum in reaching various audiences. He was determined to create a museum that could communicate across communities and confront bigotry, work that received little support from his superiors. I argue that Romanoff's belief in the value of sharing Jewish history and religion with Jewish and non-Jewish audiences alike to forge understanding and improve relations was productive civic engagement. Romanoff's ideas—clearly articulated in his views about outreach to the Jewish community and beyond—might provide a model for thinking about relationships among objects, identity, community, and communication that continue to perplex us today.

My aim is not to establish a genealogical through line of identity museums from the 1930s through today. Rather, I highlight a moment in which a museum presented a story driven neither by nationalism nor by the desire to assert white, Anglo-Saxon, Christian superiority (although, as we will see, not wholly divorced from claims for a shared Judeo-Christian tradition). Finally, this work suggests that it might be a radical act in the historiography of museums and public history to bring the story of the early decades of the

Jewish Museum out from the history of Jewish cultural practice and into the narrative of museums and public history. By doing so, we can decenter the story of museums, shifting focus away from White Protestant curators at the American Museum of Natural History and the Metropolitan Museum of Art. This is a narrative of a Jewish immigrant exhibiting the material culture of his heritage to his New York neighbors—Jew and gentile, young and old, native-born and immigrant.

"A More or Less Fixed Thing": The Possibilities and Limitations of a Collection

The roots of the Jewish Museum date to 1904, although it would be decades before the establishment of a museum space, and nearly a half century before the creation of the Jewish Museum in its current form. That year, book collector and Philadelphia judge Mayer Sulzberger gifted a book and manuscript collection to the library of the Jewish Theological Seminary (JTS) in New York City.[11] Sulzberger's donation was predominantly paper materials (7,500 Hebrew books and books related to Judaism and 750 manuscripts) and a small collection of twenty-six ceremonial objects.[12] The inclusion of three-dimensional objects along with the research materials served as a "suggestion" by Sulzberger about the future "establishment of a Jewish museum in connection with the library."[13]

At the National Museum (Smithsonian Institution), another collecting initiative was already in process under the guidance of Cyrus Adler, who would later become Romanoff's boss. Adler, the first person to earn a PhD in Semitic studies from a US university (Johns Hopkins University, 1887), advised the Smithsonian on its collection of Near Eastern antiquities and encouraged the National Museum to add to its assemblage of biblical artifacts and eighteenth- and nineteenth-century ceremonial objects related to Judaism.[14] As early as 1902, Adler was already involved in the administration of the Seminary, splitting time between the school and the Smithsonian.[15]

There was also international precedent for collections of Judaica and written materials related to the ancient and modern tradition. Jewish museums (and exhibits of Jewish materials within larger international exhibitions) had been founded in large European cities in the late nineteenth and early twentieth century within the context of the wider culture's desire to preserve the past and develop sanctioned narratives of place (bounded by nation-state and city) in the face of modernization and urbanization.[16] Just what a "Jewish museum" would collect was likely not much debated, but in hindsight, it is clear they collected and exhibited that "elusive entity that can be best encapsulated by a general definition as that 'that which reflects Jewish experience.'"[17]

At the Jewish Theological Seminary in New York, the efforts first concentrated in the realm of rare books and manuscripts in the original library setting. The realization of Sulzberger's "suggested" museum was limited, with no dedicated curator for more than two decades after the original donation. A single case for objects stood in the library, and one of the star artifacts—an ark for storing Torah scrolls from Urbino, Italy—was displayed in the library's manuscript room.

Seminary chancellor Solomon Schechter did support the substantial growth of the books and manuscripts collection. Librarian Alexander Marx produced exhibitions, although they were not well-developed installations. Marx referred to the first of these, a commemoration of the biblical commentator Moses Maimonides on the seven hundredth anniversary of his death in 1905, as "a small number of rare books and Mss . . . arranged on a few tables in the Lecture Hall of the old Seminary building."[18] By 1914, the research library included 44,000 printed volumes and 1,700 manuscripts.[19] The

Library reading room, Jewish Theological Seminary, early 1920s. Photograph by Peyser and Patzig Industrial Photographers. Courtesy of the Library of the Jewish Theological Seminary.

collection came to include an extensive catalog of biblical editions in Hebrew, Arabic, Aramaic, Spanish, and Italian, among other languages; Torah scrolls from around the world from China to the Middle East; illuminated manuscripts; prayer books; and works of Hebrew grammar. The book- and paper-based exhibitions at the library in the 1910s and 1920s included a show of biblical manuscripts (1913), an exhibition of multiple editions of the Hebrew Bible (1914), and one on Hebrew printing in Asia and Africa (1924).[20]

After Schechter's death in 1915, Cyrus Adler became chancellor. Adler initially provided more support for the museum concept for professional—and likely personal—reasons. Adler was a second cousin of Sulzberger, the original donor. More significantly, as noted previously, beginning in the late 1880s, Adler had consulted for the collection and organized exhibitions on biblical and "Oriental" content at the National Museum (as honorary assistant curator of the "Section of Oriental Antiquities" and then as curator of historic archaeology and historic religions) and published on biblical antiquities and

The Museum of Jewish Ceremonial Objects, first floor of the Schiff Library, 1940s. Photograph by Virginia F. Stern. Ratner Center. Courtesy of the Library of the Jewish Theological Seminary.

Jewish ceremonial objects. His Smithsonian association positioned him to lead the development of the ethnography exhibits at the 1893 World's Columbian Exposition, with an eye to those assembled collections ending up at the Smithsonian at the fair's conclusion.[21]

Despite Adler's experience exhibiting objects related to Jewish culture and the history of ancient Israel, it was not until 1930, when the Seminary moved around the corner to Broadway and West 122nd Street (from its original building on West 123rd Street), that a separate space was allocated for the newly named Museum of Jewish Ceremonial Objects. The new museum was dedicated in November 1931. Soon after, Adler hired Paul Romanoff as curator.[22] Romanoff had emigrated from Poland and received a PhD in Palestinian topography at Dropsie College for Hebrew and Cognate Learning in Philadelphia, where he met Adler, the school's first president.[23] In 1931, at the time of his hire, Romanoff had most recently been associated with Yale University as a research fellow in biblical and Semitic languages.[24]

Newly arrived in New York, Romanoff knew no one except Adler, but in his new boss, he failed to find a kindred spirit.[25] From the time of his hire, Romanoff frequently wrote to Adler (and eventually to Louis Finkelstein, who succeeded Adler as president of JTS in 1940). His written correspondences evidence the formality of the working relationship between curator and seminary president and clearly document Adler's frequent refusal to support Romanoff or even directly communicate with him face-to-face. Romanoff's letters make two consistent appeals: more support for the museum and more dependable income. He requested to keep the museum open in the summer, for financial support for outreach activities, and for moral support by his superiors by way of acknowledgment of the museum's positive impacts. His letters also include increasingly desperate pleas for a raise.

Between 1931 and 1940, Romanoff was finding it nearly impossible to support himself (and later his wife, Bertha Blum, whom he married in 1937). In one particularly compelling letter, dated May 19, 1932, as his first summer in New York approached with no promise of salary or lodging if the museum were to be shuttered seasonally as Adler intended, Romanoff wrote to Adler from Brush Dormitory, where he was living at Broadway and 122nd Street. The letter, written at the end of May, establishes what would become a pattern in his correspondence: the linkage of his fate to that of the museum:

> As far as I am personally concerned, the closing of the Museum will leave me destitute and homeless. While I was employed here I lived at the

Dormitory. After the end of this month I have practically nowhere to go and nothing to do. I could not very well save anything out of my meagre salary, having had to spend two-thirds of it for my room and meals in the Dormitory and to use the remainder to send to my close relatives abroad to save them from actual starvation. I am now confronting a very desperate situation indeed, and very much against my will, turn again to you for advice in my hour of need.[26]

Along with that letter, Romanoff sent a report of visitors to the museum. Adler never encouraged Romanoff, and in only a few instances granted him a raise.

When Romanoff grew ill in the late 1930s, Adler increased his pay by ten dollars per month, but it was never clear how long that support would last. A particularly harsh response to yet another request came during the summer of 1938 from Adler's summer vacation in Woods Hole on Cape Cod:

I told you on several occasions, and rather emphatically, I thought, this winter in a talk that was interrupted that there was no real place at the Seminary for you. I told you that I regarded the little museum as a more or less fixed thing. I have no desire to build up a great museum nor have we the means. The post there is that of caretaker and whatever your merits, does not justify in the present condition of the Seminary, a salary for a man with a family. . . . At all events, I think the kindest thing I can say to you is that you ought not look to the Seminary for any real position for your future.[27]

Romanoff's understandably pained response came eleven days later: "Both the content and your indifferent attitude surprised and shocked me."[28]

It is difficult to account for Adler's dismissal of the promise and future of "the little museum." In her study of Adler's role in the Smithsonian Judaica collections, Grace Cohen Grossman briefly attempts to account for Adler's lack of support for him or the museum. "Although it is possible that the visionary who pioneered the use of exhibitions of Judaica for education had a change of heart in his final years, it is more likely that the financial constraints brought about by the Depression of the 1930s shaped his response."[29] By exploring Romanoff's museum activities in more detail, the variances between his viewpoint and Adler's priorities come into clearer relief, suggesting more than budgetary concerns. Despite Adler and Romanoff's shared interest in ancient languages and ceremonial objects, the break may have been between their philosophies of the museum. In the only full-length exploration of the early history of the Jewish Museum, Julie Miller and Richard Cohen assert that Romanoff was "the first to define what the museum's public mission should be."[30] What that public mission was, and Adler's repeated dismissal of Romanoff's advocacy for it, is the subject of the rest of this paper.

Jewish Archaeology and Cultural Pluralism

The building of a Jewish museum was, by its very nature, a political act. Collections assembled in Europe in the late nineteenth century promoted Jewish consciousness and pride. Artistic production was increasingly understood as a basic element of a modern nation, an idea reflected in what sociologist Tony Bennett has termed the "exhibitionary complex" of museums, expositions, and other nineteenth-century displays. In visual extravaganzas—including "museums, panoramas, Mechanics' Institute exhibitions, art galleries, and arcades"—curators and exhibitors put hierarchies of nation on display for the edification and civilization of the citizenry. These exhibitions and expositions became "annexed to national histories as, within the rhetorics of each national museum complex, collections of national materials were represented as the outcome and culmination of the universal story of civilization's development."[31] In this scenario, "museums became one of the institutions and practices associated with modernity, part of the checklist for being a nation."[32]

This assertion of a kind of Jewish nationalism spoke back to the potentially anti-Semitically tinged denotation of the "Jewish race." Indeed, examples abound of the New York collection as a point of pride for Jewish visitors. Romanoff's records allow a glimpse into the reaction of the majority-Jewish audience (Jews made up roughly 80–85 percent of museum visitors in the years for which statistics are available). The Hebrew Tabernacle Sisterhood, for example, noted after a visit, "We can well be proud of our Jewish history and I feel the future ever holds glorious things for us Jews," an oddly optimistic reaction given the approximate date in the late 1930s. For the visitors from Temple Israel in New York, the museum "opened their eyes to the antiquity and beauty of the various collections, and that [they] have an art to be proud of," and the National Council of Jewish Women reported being already "familiar with every-day Jewish life" but unaware of the "wonderful works of art."[33]

Uncovering and acknowledging a Jewish visual heritage through the act of collecting and interpreting thus asserted legitimacy and value on its own terms. The museum stood in contrast to a trope of difference and exoticism that would have framed exhibitions of Jewish culture in mainstream institutions or in the Hebraic sections of international exhibitions. This claim for a relevant and admirable material past, although cast in the terms of the Jewish "nation" and appealing in some sense to such conventions, also flew in the face of the national imaginary associated with the modern state. In an identity museum like the Museum of Jewish Ceremonial Objects, the parameters of engagement and inclusion were, by contrast, global and diasporic. They presented an alternative narrative to national identity and perhaps to nationalism, one that opened the possibility of an affinity with—and roots in—an ancient culture rather than identification with the more arbitrary modern nation.

Integrally related to the founding of Jewish museums was the developing field of Jewish archaeology—the scholarly pursuit of the ancient remains of the Greco-Roman period. Romanoff was an avowed participant in the field, reviewing notable books, doing research, and publishing books and articles. He and Adler shared this interest. Romanoff's 1937 book on ancient Jewish topography and his articles based on archaeological material published between 1931 and 1944 (the last published posthumously) all documented and interpreted the visual, artistic, and iconographic record of ancient Jewish culture.[34] Jewish archaeology, including Romanoff's research, was concerned with the "placement of Jewish artifacts in dialogue with ancient Jewish literature, in the hopes of understanding more about Jewish culture than either the extant literary texts or excavated artifacts could yield on their own."[35]

This scholarly inquiry put material culture on a playing field with text, a somewhat revolutionary act given the reputation of Jewish culture, fostered by both some Jewish scholars and others as well, as an "aniconic" religion, devoid of a history of artistic production. Given that the existence of a national art was an essential feature of nineteenth-century romantic nationalism, Jews committed to the maintenance of Jewish peoplehood looked to provide evidence of the existence of a strong and vital "Jewish art."[36] Romanoff's "The Discovery of Jewish Art," for example, one of two articles in a 1935 issue of the journal the *Reconstructionist* dedicated to the arts in the Jewish tradition, discussed the human figures in frescos in the third-century synagogue of Dura-Europos (a Hellenistic, Parthian, and Roman border city built on the bank of the Euphrates river in today's Syria). These scholarly efforts thus mirrored the intent of the founders of Jewish museums to show that "Jews, like all other nations, created beautiful and exciting art throughout their long history" and to create a "positive national Jewish identity."[37]

In the popularization of this intellectual thread linking contemporary Judaism with biblical Hebrews, public intellectuals like Adler and Romanoff relied on historically specious claims. Adler wrote about the contemporary practices of the inhabitants of Palestine as "living archaeology," "as if the way of life in those areas had survived without change since antiquity and therefore could be treated as if it were directly linked to ancient times."[38] Similarly, eighteenth- and nineteenth-century Jewish ceremonial objects on display at the Museum of Jewish Ceremonial Objects were exhibited as links in an unbroken chain between the practices of biblical Hebrews and contemporary Jewish people. While contemporary Jews may descend from ancient Hebrews, the Jewish religion is based on scriptural and textual rabbinic tradition that postdates the biblical era. As Grossman points out about Adler's interpretation, his "rather unscientific link between those who lived in the 'Bible lands' in his own time and their ancient Semitic ancestors" was an ahistorical, if enticing, interpretive hook. The same could be said of Romanoff's work. To combat anti-Semitism in the modern age, one could prompt non-Jewish audiences about the endurance between Judaism and the world of the Old Testament they venerated. As Grossman writes, "The concept of this unbroken continuity of practice would subsequently become Adler's rationale for using Jewish ceremonial objects of the eighteenth and nineteenth centuries in an exhibition of Biblical archaeology."[39]

In addition to establishing an ancient past as a viable and legitimate source of identity formation, Romanoff also used the collection to assert Jewish influence in the Americas and thus the possibility of the Jewish American or American Jewish identity.[40] A 1937 exhibition in honor of Columbus Day included the almanac by Jewish astronomer Abraham ben Samuel Zacuto that had been used by Columbus on his voyage.[41] Romanoff also showcased the first Hebrew grammar books published in the United States.[42] These objects suggested the potential of a lasting religious and cultural Jewishness alongside national citizenship. By 1939, there was a gallery devoted to such objects, the "American Room."[43] Some historians have suggested that these themes were intended to Americanize the seminary's (mainly foreign-born) rabbinical students and, through them, their immigrant congregations.[44] However, the hyphenated nature of American Jewish identity can go both ways. Jews could become American, but also "America" could be, in part, Jewish. Although surely never expressly spoken in an exhibition label, this narrative implicitly decentered Protestantism as the unnamed "default" American religion and resisted the narrative of the United States as a Christian nation.

The museum might be seen within the early to mid-twentieth century debate about assimilation.[45] Over the course of the 1910s, Jewish scholar Horace Kallen published a series of articles proposing a vision for American democracy and identity in the face of massive immigration. Kallen challenged the idea of "Americanization" as necessitating the "adoption of English speech, of American clothes and manners, of the American attitude in politics" and the "fusion of the various bloods, and a transmutation by 'the miracle of assimilation' of Jews, Slavs, Poles, Frenchmen, Germans, Hindus, Scandinavians into beings similar in background, tradition, outlook, and spirit to the descendants of the British colonists, the Anglo-Saxon stock."[46] This, Kallen asserted, was antithetical to the spirit of democracy. We might thus imagine the Jewish Museum as an instantiation of melting-pot-defying "cultural pluralism." Romanoff was a one-man show, curating exhibitions, writing interpretive materials, cultivating collegial relationships in the collecting community, giving public talks, pursuing research and publishing articles, and cultivating a far wider audience than was of interest to his bosses, as we shall see.

Audience and Publics

Romanoff's efforts resulted in a steady rise in yearly attendance from December 1931 (shortly after his hire) through the first half of 1941.[47] The outlier of a huge spike in late 1934 / early 1935 coincided with the opening and run of a very popular Maimonides exhibition about the twelfth-century biblical commentator. During that exhibition, the museum was open extra evenings to accommodate the large crowds.[48] Likely out of a sense of self-preservation, Romanoff felt compelled to explain to his superiors that the museum was doing good work both within and beyond the Jewish community—and could do more if properly supported. He sent reports about his attempts to cultivate and broaden his audience, visitor statistics, and hand-drawn infographics with a breakdown of the audience by religion, sex, and type of group (including women's groups, refugee organizations, Hebrew schools, church groups, labor unions, and educators). Romanoff compiled excerpts from the many visitor letters that attested to the power of the objects in the collection to tell the story of Jewish culture and history and touted the curator's skills as a teacher, lecturer, and guide. The record of Romanoff's work surely suggests that the curator was far more committed than his superiors—whose attention and respect seem to have been impossible to earn—to addressing the question of who comes to a museum and what might be accomplished there.

The number and nature of the groups who visited—Jewish and non-Jewish, adults and children, residents of the New York area as well as visitors to the city—was a source of pride. In 1932, less than a year after his arrival, the curator noted attendance by not only members of the local Jewish community but "visitors from other cities." He reported with interest changes in the percentage of Christians among total visitors. (In 1940, 20 percent of visitors were Christian, including six church groups, but only 15 percent the following year.) He commented on the various types of visitors—students,

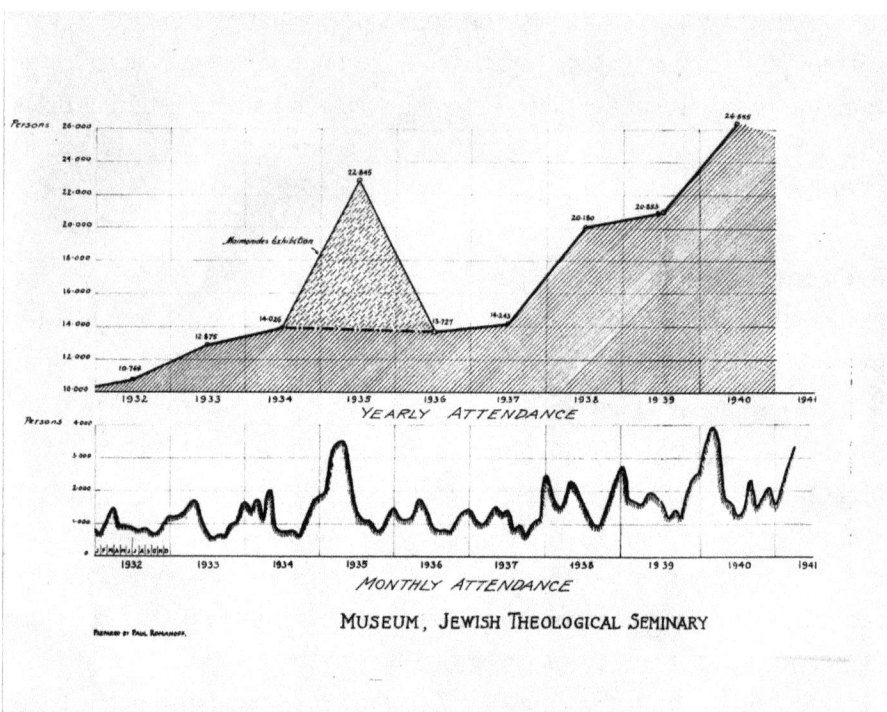

"Museum, Jewish Theological Seminary of America, Attendance, December 1931–April 1939," prepared by Paul Romanoff, JTS, RG 1, series A, box 22, folder 39. Courtesy of the Library of the Jewish Theological Seminary.

ministers, co-religionists, artists—and their different reasons for visiting, from doing research to seeking inspiration, including "themes for artistic pursuit and advice about how to beautify and prepare for the holidays and festivals."[49]

Romanoff thought carefully about how to increase attendance by appealing to a variety of inclinations, including attracting those with a casual interest in Jewish culture. He noted to librarian Alexander Marx, "Our Museum differs somewhat from other museums in the city in that it has its own seasons during our [Jewish] holidays.... But the attendance is also dependent on the communal life of the city," including American holidays and festivals that brought people to the city and granted New Yorkers more leisure time. Preeminent among the events was the New York World's Fair. Romanoff advocated placing advertisements in guide books for the 1939 event "if we wish that our Museum and Institution should become known to the millions of visitors which the Fair will bring to New York."[50] In May 1939, at the start of the fair (which ran from April 30, 1939, through October 27, 1940), the curator noted an increase in attendance by individuals and groups. That report also indicated an increase in foreign visitors likely with no connection to the fair, including German refugees and visitors from Palestine, suggesting the role of New York and the museum in formulating a diasporic Judaism.[51]

Communication skills were clearly important to Romanoff, who made great effort to bring the seemingly esoteric within reach of his audience. In 1937, he completed a glossary to acquaint visitors with the terminology on the labels, a project that must have gone through a series of revisions. Eighteen months later, he was again requesting permission to complete a "dictionary-list of the Hebrew names and titles that appear on the cards and a brief description of their meaning and usage" as an aid to improving visitor experience.[52] One of Romanoff's most accessible published contributions to Jewish archaeology was his "The Discovery of Jewish Art" in the journal the *Reconstructionist*. This article about the decoration in a third-century synagogue is notable for its placement in a publication meant for a general audience.[53] The readership for the *Reconstructionist* were not archaeologists and historians, and the accessible tone presumes no expert knowledge. Romanoff authored at least one article in Yiddish, "Formen un simboln in der arkhiṭeḳṭur funm Beysàmigdesh" (Architectural forms and symbols of the Temple), widening the readership for his scholarship among immigrants.[54] The same accessibility was evident in a syndicated series Romanoff wrote for the national Jewish press. An article from 1935 about Maimonides, corresponding with the exhibition at the museum, began with an invitation to consider "the human side" of texts. "I shall," he wrote, "therefore, take you with me on a trip to look into a manuscript and to search for the story behind it."[55]

As another way to broaden the audience to people who for reasons of geography or interest would not have visited, Romanoff inaugurated and administered a loan program. He lent objects to the Temple of Religion at the 1940 Golden Gate International Exposition in San Francisco; Bamberger's department store; the Reformed Church of Bronxville, New York; branches of the New York Public Library; and other institutions and events.[56] This type of outreach suggests, if not firsthand knowledge of similar practices premiered by museums like the Newark Museum, at least a similar inclination toward outreach and audience expansion.[57]

Romanoff understood and embraced the potential of personal as well as written communication and acted as docent as well as curator, giving hundreds of tours of the collections, noting these efforts in his memos to his supervisors. Visitors noted the power of his tours and wrote to thank him and elaborated on their museum experience. One correspondent wrote that he had studied theology previously but stated, "Your [Romanoff's] interpretation of the various exhibits in your Museum cases helped to throw light on things which I know only in part."[58] An excerpt from a letter from the Seward Park Branch of the New York Public Library read, "I want to tell you how much the Seward Park Mothers' Club enjoyed their visit to the Museum. It was a great day in their lives and there were full of enthusiasm and appreciation.... You gave them a most enjoyable afternoon and they came away with many things to think about." Given the location of this branch library on the Lower East Side, most of these visitors were likely immigrants. Good reviews, dispersed by word of mouth among educators, spread Romanoff's positive reputation around the city. An undated compilation of comments received by Romanoff after his tours includes that of the director of the field laboratory of the Child Education Foundation, who reported that his class considered Romanoff's lecture on the history of prejudice "of great value to them," noting, "We are glad our students will have the opportunity to hear you."[59]

In addition to teaching the teachers, Romanoff also considered tours for children an important part of his practice. Roughly 16 percent of the visitors to the museum in 1940 were children and 28 percent were in the first half of 1941.[60] He taught many Hebrew School and Yeshiva groups (117 Hebrew school groups and 2 Yeshiva groups in 1940; 74 Hebrew school groups and 3 Yeshiva groups, from January to May, in 1941).[61] He had a good rapport with children despite what, in the hands of others, might have been an inaccessible topic. A teacher who had visited with students from a Brooklyn synagogue commented on his "pleasant demeanor toward the children."[62] In the winter of 1939–40, Anna Wright, a teacher from St. James Church School in Montclair, New Jersey, wrote with her appreciation of the curator's ability to communicate with her high school students. She describes her students as "entranced" by Romanoff's two-hour tour. Considering how difficult is it to "hold the attention of a class of that restless age" for even a half hour, she noted that Romanoff's "gift" in being able to present a subject in a manner suitable to various ages "borders on true genius!"[63] In the first few months of 1935, Romanoff did three radio talks in Yiddish and Hebrew. His outreach to the wider community paid off. In a November 12, 1936, memo to Adler, Romanoff reported his invitation to deliver an illustrated lecture at the Metropolitan Museum of Art on "The Symbols in the Synagogue and Christian Art."[64] In one of his 1937 memos to Adler, Romanoff described his interest in starting a regular series of public lectures every second Sunday, explaining that such offerings were successful in other museums in the city. The answer came from Adler three days later: a curt no.[65]

Why would Adler have been so dismissive? Adler had worked steadfastly on public exhibitions of biblical archaeology and Jewish ceremonial objects in the 1880s and 1890s. A report on a March 1890 exhibition at the National Museum, which included objects lent and donated by Adler's extended family (including Mayer Sulzberger, whose donation was the first to the Jewish Theological Seminary), described the "collection of objects used in connection with the public and private ceremonies of the Jews" as "intended to illustrate Jewish ceremonial and worship."[66]

Yet the extent of the public-facing element of Romanoff's work and his active outreach likely tipped the scales for Adler. Adler gave voice to the dual role of the museum in his address to the Congress of Anthropology in Chicago in 1893, but his efforts were more solidly devoted to historical and scientific study of religion than to popular education. The mandate of the Section of Oriental Antiquities (also, the Department of Biblical Archaeology) that Adler curated was to build a scholarly audience. In the 1889 annual report, Adler wrote about the potential of the collection to broaden *scholarly* interest in the museum—in his words "to interest a large number of scholars not hitherto specially attached to the institution." Adler made a point of inviting "accredited Orientalists" to visit the museum.[67]

In addition, Romanoff's outreach efforts would have had little application to Adler's commitment to a "scientific" approach to the classification of religion. The questions Adler asked of objects were more about whether and how material culture could support theories of civilization rather than about how they might serve as popular educators about world religion.[68] In this, Adler was a man of his (museum) times. He was a curator of religion in the way that others were curators of anthropology, applying concepts developed in the natural sciences to create taxonomies of peoples, progress, and civilization. His comparative methods would have had no place in the Museum of Jewish Ceremonial Objects. Adler was committed to a scientific approach and the establishment of a historical context for religion, locating the academic possibilities of objects in a category apart from their theological or doctrinal meaning. Despite his own traditional religious beliefs, in this work, Adler operated as a scholar, not a Jew. In an intellectual move that was broad-minded in its embrace of material culture for the study of religious history, and in his insistence on a historical, scientific approach to religious history, Adler appeared to have little interest in reaching across religious groups to build relationships *as* religiously affiliated people in the way Romanoff sought to do at his "little museum."

"A Medium for Inter-racial Tolerance and Understanding"

As we have seen, Romanoff was interested in using the museum to cultivate a sense of pride in "the Jewish race," but this inclination coexisted with another impulse to use the museum and its collections as a way to model a better future. Romanoff consciously made connections between the past and the contemporary moment. Unlike the first book exhibit at the Seminary in 1913, his blockbuster 1935 installation celebrating the birth of Maimonides was a monthlong celebration that emphasized the relevance of the medieval scholar to contemporary issues.[69] Romanoff wrote enticingly about the artifacts for the press, and the museum produced supporting printed materials. One pamphlet noted, "During these days when Jewry is especially conscious of the oppressive measures directed against it in many lands, the observance will serve to emphasize the spiritual and cultural achievements of the great Jewish minds, in spite of the persecution they have always been forced to face."[70]

Romanoff's interest in an expanded role for the museum was very much a part of professional discourse on museums, adult education, and audience in the 1930s. Indeed, as Clarissa J. Ceglio found during her research for the article in this collection, from 1932 to 1942 (almost the exact years of Romanoff's tenure at the Jewish Museum), "eleven new books dealt in some way with the past, present, and prospects of museums with the goal that they become better equipped to play a more dynamic role in contemporary civic life." In its newsletters, the American Association of Museums engaged questions about the responsibility of museums as democratic institutions in preparing the public to confront rifts in the "social and political fabric."[71] In his 1939 *Critical Study of Museums in America*, Laurence Vail Coleman recounted how museums had "gained a recognizable place in communities" and assumed "a more important part in the daily life of the people."[72] While evidence of the import of museum visits on people's lives is hard to discern, the aspirational norm among museum thinkers was shifting away from a satisfaction with the status quo of museums as elite institutions "unsullied" by and untethered to contemporary issues.

Romanoff appears to have been in tune with this broadening sense of the purpose of a museum. As the decade advanced and the situation in Europe grew ever more urgent, Romanoff described his vision to use the museum and its collections to "help bridge the gap of ignorance that lies between Jew and Christian. I am sure you will see the need to do all in our power toward such an end." He explained his efforts to bring "Christian children knowledge of the beauty, moral and cultural value of the Jewish religion and history."[73] "Our museum," Romanoff wrote in 1939, "has become a medium for interracial tolerance and understanding."[74] Late in 1939, Romanoff made what was likely his most desperate plea to connect the museum to the European crisis in the utopian language of the New York World's Fair: "We serve as a medium for better understanding and have become the place where one can learn of the beauty of our rituals and holidays, and of the common background of all faiths. . . . The Christian children of today are the Christian men and women of tomorrow. We owe to posterity every effort toward making the World of Tomorrow a better place to live in. We can do this by encouraging more Christian groups to visit us."[75] That same year, a local teacher requested a museum visit with the same purpose in mind. Dorothy Wright wrote to Romanoff, explaining that she was an instructor for eight- and nine-year-olds in Garden City, New Jersey. She was looking for, she said, "the kind of information about the Jewish people that I can give these children to help in creating attitudes of appreciation and understanding" for her students "who know nothing whatever of the Jewish people or their religion." The materials "would aim to produce in these children the feeling that they hold much in common with those of the Jewish faith, to stress likenesses in people rather than differences, and to give them an admiration for those things which are beautiful and of moral and cultural value in the religion and history of the Jewish race." Wright was well aware of the climate: "Children hear so much that is negative today, and I'm sure there are many teachers like myself who wish they could help in combating ignorance and intolerance with more positive constructive material than we have found available." She hoped to bring her students to see the museum one Sunday morning and asked if someone would be available to answer questions "about the things in [the] Museum and explain them to the children."[76]

Two incidents of other children visiting the museum make clear that Romanoff was able to provide the kind of experience Wright sought. The first incident occurred among literal neighbors. In 1939, Romanoff entertained a prolonged series of visits with the nuns who taught at the school associated with neighboring Corpus Christi Church located around the corner from JTS.[77] Prior to this extended engagement, the seminary building had been "continually annoyed by the children of the neighborhood, the Museum especially, by the throwing of pebbles at the windows, sometimes breaking panes of glass, or while visiting the Museum the children would mutilate the labels on the objects or carry them away or leave the place untidy, particularly the American room."[78] As Romanoff reasoned to Finkelstein, "The children are not bad," but rather "social conditions and their ignorance of our Institution are to blame. In view of the fact that [Father Charles E.] Coughlin[79] meetings are constantly being held on the street corners near the Seminary, all this feeling has been intensified." Romanoff hosted the nuns for multiple visits and "lectured for several hours" about the objects and Jewish customs. Following this elaborate tour for the educators, several groups of children visited. They were reportedly, Romanoff said, "interested in the meaning of the objects as never before, asking proper questions, as I explain the beauty and symbols of the collection."[80] The vandalism stopped.

Around the same time, Anna Wright, the previously mentioned teacher from St. James Church School, wrote to Romanoff to extol the combination of the objects and context provided in Romanoff's talk. She explained that they were so moved by his presentation that they had gathered money to send to the museum: "They suggest that if it is not feasible for you to use the money in some way toward the museum itself, you pass it on, if that seems best, toward Jewish Refugee relief or anything else according to your judgment for your people,—not that the money in itself is much but the feeling which prompted offering it was truly heartfelt."[81] Although it is difficult to parse the longer-term outcome from museum visits, their interest in sending support suggests that an empathy-building experience had occurred. The connections Romanoff's talk helped them make between objects in a museum and the humanity of a people compelled the students to action, as seen in their desire to dedicate funds for refugee relief.

Museum educator Theodore Low also proposed an expanded role for museums. *The Museum as a Social Instrument*, written for the American Association of Museums and published by the Metropolitan Museum of Art in 1942, described the potential for museums to "become social instruments and communicate values."[82] Now celebrated for his "forward thinking ideas" and populist approach to museum accessibility, Low, like many museum critics in this period, was also a product of the Progressive Era, including its racial politics. As Ceglio's work for this volume makes clear, the broader public imagined for museums was tacitly understood as racially white and could be limited in terms of class.[83] Low described the role of museums in "strengthening that thing which we like to call 'the American Way of Life.'"[84] To "American," we might add "Christian." If museums were expected to help constitute a democratic citizenry, perhaps one of the more radical notions of the Museum of Jewish Ceremonial Objects in the 1930s was to constitute a politically or socially engaged citizenry in a way that made fewer assumptions about a citizen's ethnic and racial identity. The public Romanoff imagined was less homogenous, less nationalist, and distinctly less Protestant than Low might have fantasized.

One limitation to this broad engagement with audience is detectable in the particular ways that Romanoff understood the educational value of the collection for Christian scholars and laypeople. When recounting his work with Corpus Christi Church, Romanoff explained that he was compelled not only to explain Jewish objects and customs but also to explore, as he put it, "the origins of many of their ceremonies . . . in our ritual, and that the Bible, New Testament and many of their customs could be visually illustrated by the objects in our Museum."[85] After a visit to the museum, a Christian theology student reported, "I was wishing that I had been able to benefit by a course on Jewish customs and beliefs at the hand of a Hebrew Scholar in advance rather than to have been dependent solely on what I had gained through a study of Old and New Testament teaching at the hand of one of our teachers. If this had been the case I could have then interpreted the New Testament more successfully."[86] The historic roots of Christianity in Judaism, as Romanoff must have experienced while studying religion at Yale, were of great interest to practicing Christians and to theologians and historians. In using Jewish ceremonial objects and texts to illuminate Christianity, Romanoff responded to a desire from Christian visitors and correspondents for a deeper understanding of the roots of their faith. However, he was also taking advantage of this angle to align his institution with the powerful majority. In this interpretive approach, the understanding sought by Christian visitors was linked to a shared Judeo-Christian history rather than an appreciation and respect for difference. In making Judaism available in the service of Christianity, Romanoff might have participated in the process of claiming "Whiteness" for the Jewish "race" by establishing a commonality with the dominant, White, Christian culture. While a reasonable intellectual approach to the material due to historical connections, and a smart strategy for outreach given the population of a country (if not a city) with such a small percentage of Jews, the forming of bonds over a shared history, by intent or not, would exclude adherents to religions other than Judaism and Christianity. It normalized a shared Judeo-Christian core to the exclusion of other faith traditions. As Eric Goldstein recounts in his book-length study of Jews becoming White (after long being considered an unassimilable other, including being ascribed a physical and cultural likeness to African Americans at the turn of the century and beyond), "Claiming the status of 'whites' in America was far from simple for Jews. It involved a complex emotional process in which conflicting desires for acceptance and distinctiveness often found no easy balance."[87]

"A More or Less Fixed Thing"

Given their lack of support for Romanoff's work, it appears that the curator's superiors were either unaware of or unconvinced by the arguments about the productive nature of interfaith dialogue based in museum collections. Adler's, and later Finkelstein's, reluctance requires additional explanation because the Seminary did not shy away from the connections between an ancient religion, contemporary practice, and modern life. A declaration of the rationale for the JTS Social Justice Committee, launched in 1933, read,

> These are times when social and economic problems force themselves with greater compulsion than ever upon the attention of spiritual leaders. We do not have to go out to look for them. They are right at our doorstep. . . .

Not only are the questions of world peace, social and economic justice, and the relationships between religious and racial groups within our land, so pressing and circumambient, that only those can remain aloof who are deliberately and willfully neglectful, but the determination of many of these questions is actually in the balance.[88]

In his extramuseum activities, Adler was an activist on behalf of Jewish causes, and Seminary initiatives instituted by Finkelstein sought to establish intercultural dialogue.[89] So what, in addition to the explanations previously explored, might account for Adler and Finkelstein's resistance to the curator's ideas? Miller and Cohen suggest that Adler never imagined this would be Romanoff's lifelong career, assuming he would move on after finding his footing in the United States. They write that Adler understood himself to be helping "a poor scholar by offering him a temporary job."[90] Like Grossman, they saw the stresses of the Depression as an influence on Adler's resistance to investing in the museum.[91] A 1938 letter from Arthur Oppenheimer to Adler supports this understanding of the museum as a distraction to the underlying mission: "The salary which we pay him was all that the position was worth to us."[92] There may also have been a personal disconnect for which it is difficult to uncover direct evidence in the historical record. The Romanoffs may have been too solicitous or seemed too uncouth to Adler and Finkelstein, who were more socially established—evidence of the cultural divide between the immigrant Paul Romanoff and the American-born chancellors.

A more broad-reaching explanation might well be a difference of opinion about the mission of a museum. Wedded to an older object-driven model of collection and preservation, neither Adler nor Finkelstein was concerned with reaching new audiences, building relationships between museum and community, or engaging with the role of the museum that Romanoff proposed and enacted. They were either not able or not willing to imagine how the interpretation of material culture could actively inform a social agenda, even one advanced by the Seminary in other programs. That they did not see a role for the museum, or its object lessons, in the Seminary's work is what Adler likely meant in his dismissive and cruel letter to Romanoff: "I told you that I regarded the little museum as a more or less fixed thing." While Adler, unlike Schechter before him, might have appreciated the idea put forward by the field of Jewish archaeology that objects have something to add to the textual record, what to do with that heritage and how it might be useful on the front lines of building relationships across community seems to have held little interest for Adler. It was Paul Romanoff alone at the Museum of Jewish Ceremonial Objects—scholar, published author, docent, lecturer, marketing facilitator, and outreach coordinator—who was in tune with the idea of the museum as a "social instrument."

The back-and-forth between Romanoff and his superiors took on a heartbreaking urgency midway through 1939 as his health diminished (according to his account in his letters) due to malnourishment from a diet too reliant on starchy (we can assume inexpensive) foods.[93] In March the following year, he wrote to Finkelstein, after the chancellor granted a small raise:

> Since you were kind enough to evince a material interest in my welfare, I am sure you will be pleased to know that the temporary interest you allowed me has really started me on the road to good health. Obviously, if this increase is withdrawn, I would soon find myself in perhaps a worse condition than heretofore. My physician tells me that my illness is the result of malnutrition and complete lack of vitamins. Returning to those conditions responsible for my illness may prove fatal.[94]

In December 1943, Bertha Romanoff buried her husband, who had died at the age of forty-five, in Congregation Mishkan Israel Cemetery in New Haven, her hometown.

Shortly after, in January 1944, philanthropist Frieda Schiff Warburg made what was most likely an unsolicited donation of her mansion on Fifth Avenue and Ninety-Second Street to the Seminary as a new home for the museum. Romanoff had died less than a month before, but it is unlikely that Finkelstein would have considered him an appropriate curator for the new museum. In fact, at the opening of the museum in 1947, the press coverage mentioned only the newly appointed curator, art historian Stephen Keyser, and librarian Alexander Marx as the keepers of the collection until that point, deleting any record of Romanoff's years of dedicated service.[95] The hiring of Keyser signaled a new direction for what would henceforth be called the Jewish Museum. The new location provided the opportunity to more easily draw an audience from the non-Jewish world. To do so, the museum would turn its attention to collecting and exhibiting contemporary art (mostly but not exclusively by Jewish artists) to establish itself as a "museum among museums, rather than a Jewish institution among other Jewish institutions" (although it would retain and still holds an outstanding collection of ceremonial objects to this day).[96] Now the answer to the question of what this Jewish Museum would and should exhibit became more complicated; mission statements made claims about universal aesthetic standards. By its second anniversary, the Jewish Museum had attracted 175,000 visitors.[97]

The editors of the aptly named anthology *Museum Frictions* describe the tensions that still exist within museums and thus the faulty logic that approaches any particular institution as a single text.[98] Similarly, in her article about Historic Weeksville—the African American site in Brooklyn, New York—Jennifer Scott documents the loss of momentum for particular agendas with staff changes.[99] These two examples suggest that perhaps institutions themselves are never radical, but rather supply a shifting ground on which forces so inclined may or may not activate their radicalism. Institutions, it seems, if we understand Adler's phrase somewhat more optimistically, are *either* a *more* or a *less* fixed thing. With that in mind, we might consider how to revise the history of museums by looking not only at the interpretation and practices that have won out but also at individuals who have seen the potential to use a museum space to advance visitors toward a more peaceful, respectful, or multivalent world view. Paul Romanoff's tenure of thirteen years at the Museum of Jewish Ceremonial Objects provides us with one such case study.

Notes

1. In 1947, the trustees of the museum's parent organization, the Jewish Theological Seminary, shifted the focus to contemporary art and moved to new, grander quarters in the Fifth Avenue mansion where the Jewish Museum exists to this day.
2. The significant exception to this erasure is the only full-length article on the history of the Jewish Museum, Julie Miller and Richard I. Cohen, "A Collision of Cultures: The Jewish Museum and the Jewish Theological Seminary, 1904–1971," in *Tradition Renewed: A History of the Jewish Theological Seminary of America*, ed. Jack Wertheimer, 2 vols. (New York: Jewish Theological Seminary of America, 1997), 2:311–61. I draw largely on Miller and Cohen's work in this article. However, because Miller and Cohen's article treats a longer span of time, only nine of its fifty pages are dedicated to the 1930s. The article situates the Jewish Museum in the context of its parent organization, the Jewish Theological Seminary, not the history of American museums. Other treatments of the museum's early decades exclude Romanoff entirely. See Brett Drucker's unpublished thesis, "Two Visions, Two Publics: The Jewish Museum and the Skirball Jewish Center" (master's thesis, University of Southern

California, 2008). Drucker only discusses Cyrus Adler, Seminary chancellor and Romanoff's boss.

3 Among treatments that focus only on the larger institutions are Edward Alexander, *Museums in Motion: An Introduction to the History and Functions of Museums* (Lanham, MD: AltaMira, 1979); Tony Bennett, *Birth of the Museum: History, Theory, Politics* (London: Routledge, 1995); and Steven Conn, *Museums and American Intellectual Life, 1876–1926* (Chicago: University of Chicago Press, 2000). An exception is Michael S. Shapiro, "The Public and the Museum," in *The Museum: A Reference Guide*, ed. Michael Shapiro (Westport, CT: Greenwood, 1990). Shapiro considers the range of exhibitionary spaces, including coffeehouses, proprietary museums, and commercial galleries.

4 Ellen Hirzy, *Mastering Civic Engagement: A Challenge to Museums* (Washington, DC: American Association of Museums, 2002), 10.

5 Fath David Ruffins refers to the "thirty-year-old ethnic museum movement." Ruffins, "Culture Wars Won and Lost: Ethnic Museums on the Mall, Part I: The National Holocaust Museum and the National Museum of the American Indian," *Radical History Review* 68 (1997): 79. Similarly, Anastasia Loukaitou-Sideris and Carl Grodach, in 2012, describe how, "as many mainstream museums have struggled to transform from exclusive temples to inclusive public forums, new types of museums have also emerged. Over the last three decades, there has been a tremendous rise in the US and Canada of ethnic museums." Loukaitou-Sideris and Grodach, "Displaying and Celebrating the 'Other': A Study of the Mission, Scope, and Roles of Ethnic Museums in Los Angeles," *Public Historian* 26, no. 4 (Fall 2004): 52. Graham Black's *Transforming Museums in the Twenty-First Century* identifies museum work by and with "communities" as a late-twentieth-century development. Black, *Transforming Museums in the Twenty-First Century* (London: Routledge, 2012), 202–39. Rosa M. Cabrera, in 2008, dates their proliferation to the "last three decades." However, she notes, "the concept of ethnic-specific museums can be traced to the arrival of major waves of immigrants from Europe to the United States before the Second World War." Cabrera, "Beyond Dust, Memories and Preservation: Roles of Ethnic Museums in Shaping Community Ethnic Identities" (PhD diss., University of Illinois at Chicago, 2008), 47.

6 Stephen Weil, *Making Museums Matter* (Washington, DC: Smithsonian Institution Press, 2002), 197.

7 Weil, 199. Weil's reading is based on the Boston Museum of Fine Arts, Metropolitan Museum of Art, South Kensington Museum, British Museum, and in a nod to historic sites in the United States, Mount Vernon.

8 Andrea A. Burns, *From Storefront to Monument: Tracing the Public History of the Black Museum Movement* (Amherst: University of Massachusetts Press, 2013), 18.

9 Cabrera, "Beyond Dust," 47.

10 On the range of critical reception to the National Museum of the American Indian, see Amy Lonetree and Amanda Cobb, eds., *The National Museum of the American Indian: Critical Conversations* (Lincoln: University of Nebraska Press, 2008). See

also Joanne Barker and Clayton Dumont, "Contested Conversations: Presentations, Expectations, and Responsibility at the National Museum of the American Indian," *American Indian Culture and Research Journal* 30, no. 2 (2006): 111–40.

11 The Jewish Theological Seminary, founded in 1886, ordained Conservative rabbis in order to preserve the knowledge and practice of traditional Judaism outside the confines of the Orthodox movement. See Wertheimer, *Tradition Renewed*.

12 On the early collections, see Miller and Cohen, "Collision of Cultures," 312–19; and Drucker, "Two Visions," 4–8. A 1914 account in the *New York Times* reported 3,000 rare books and 400 manuscripts, and an additional gift of 5,000 books and 200 manuscripts. "Almost Unrivalled Collection of Jewish Manuscripts Here," *New York Times*, April 5, 1914, SM6.

13 Miller and Cohen, "Collision of Cultures," 312.

14 This position became official when Smithsonian secretary Samuel P. Langley hired him as a librarian at the National Museum in 1892. Adler later became assistant secretary and advised the museum about the Judaica collection through the 1920s. Grace Cohen Grossman with Richard Eighme Ahlborn, *Judaica at the Smithsonian: Cultural Politics as Cultural Model* (Washington, DC: Smithsonian Institution Press, 1997), 28, 36, 24–26. On Adler and the collection, see chaps. 3–8. For context, see chap. 2, on ethnographic collections at the National Museum.

15 Grossman, *Judaica*, 25. In 1908, Adler became the first president of Dropsie College for Hebrew and Cognate Learning in Philadelphia, where he worked until coming to the Seminary as acting president seven years later. Ira Robinson, "Cyrus Adler: President of the Jewish Theological Seminary, 1915–1940," in *Tradition Renewed*, 1:10.

16 For a history of European collections, see Barbara Kirschenblatt-Gimblett, "Exhibiting Jews," in *Destination Culture: Tourism, Museums and Heritage* (Berkeley: University of California Press, 1998); Richard I. Cohen, "Self-Image through Objects: Toward a Social History of Jewish Art Collecting and Jewish Museums," in *The Uses of Tradition: Jewish Continuity in the Modern Era*, ed. Jack Wertheimer (New York: Jewish Theological Seminary of America, 1998); and Grossman, *Judaica*, chap. 1. Grossman's chapter describes the establishment of Jewish museums and collections in Europe and Palestine.

17 Richard I. Cohen, *Jewish Icons: Art and Society in Modern Europe* (Berkeley: University of California Press, 1998), 7.

18 Alexander Marx, "The Library," in *The Jewish Theological Seminary of America, Semi-Centennial Volume*, ed. Cyrus Adler (New York: Jewish Theological Seminary of America, 1939), 117, as quoted in Miller and Cohen, "Collision of Cultures," 314.

19 "Almost Unrivalled Collection," SM6.

20 On the development of the collection, see Miller and Cohen, "Collision of Cultures," 312–19.

21 For a treatment of Adler's approach to ethnographic and religious objects, and his articles on the topic, see Barbara Kirschenblatt-Gimblett, "Exhibiting Jews," in *Destination Culture*, 78–128. The discussion of Adler's work for the Smithsonian is on

pages 88–106. Also see Grossman's discussion in *Judaica at the Smithsonian* of the World's Columbian Exposition (chap. 6) and Grossman's bibliography for a selected list of Adler's publications.

22 On Adler's recommendation of Romanoff, see Paul Romanoff, letter to Cyrus Adler, December 22, 1931, Jewish Theological Seminary (JTS), RG 1, series A, box 22, folder 39.

23 The 1940 US census reports Romanoff's place of birth as Poland, although Miller and Cohen identify his country of origin as Russia (Miller and Cohen, "Collision of Cultures," 319). This may be due to the annexation of the territories of Poland by Germany and the Soviet Union in the late 1930s, perhaps suggesting that Romanoff's hometown (which I have not been able to discover) was in the eastern area of Poland annexed by Russia.

24 In New Haven, he likely met his future wife, Bertha Blum, who was living there with her mother. In 1930, Blum (variously recorded as being born in New York and Connecticut) was the sole support for her widowed mother, Sophia, with whom she lived at 47 Orange Street. She was thirty years old and working at a finance company. "1930 United States Federal Census. Connecticut. New Haven District 0050," US Census Bureau, 1930, accessed through Ancestry.com, March 8, 2021, https://www.ancestry.com/imageviewer/collections/6224/images/4531880_00338?ssrc=&backlabel=Return.

25 Miller and Cohen, "Collision of Cultures," 319.

26 Paul Romanoff, letter to Cyrus Adler, May 19, 1932, JTS, RG 1, series A, box 22, folder 39. According to census records, in April 1935, the bachelor Romanoff was living at 502 W. 122nd Street, apartment 298, down the street from the Seminary. Five years later, Paul and Bertha were married, living in the same apartment, paying $45 in rent per month. The $540 annual expense for housing would have eaten up 32% of the $1,700 annual salary that Romanoff reported making as a curator. He also reported having some additional sources of income, but they must have been minimal. "1940 United States Federal Census for Paul Romanoff. New York. New York 31-1170 (Enumeration District) (Image 30 of 40)," US Census Bureau, 1940, accessed through Ancestry.com, March 8, 2021, https://www.ancestry.com/imageviewer/collections/2442/images/m-t0627-02652-00295?usePUB=true&_phsrc=tLT1&_phstart=successSource&usePUBJs=true&pId=5875891.

27 Cyrus Adler, letter to Paul Romanoff, July 6, 1938, JTS, RG 1, series A, box 22, folder 39.

28 Paul Romanoff, letter to Cyrus Adler, July 17, 1938, JTS, RG 1, series A, box 22, folder 39.

29 Grossman, *Judaica*, 55.

30 Miller and Cohen, "Collision of Cultures," 321.

31 Tony Bennett, "The Exhibitionary Complex," *New Formations* 4 (1988): 74, 89.

32 Ivan Karp et al., eds., *Museum Frictions: Public Cultures/Global Transformations* (Durham, NC: Duke University Press, 2006), 3. For an elaboration of this argument, see Bennett, *Birth of the Museum*.

33 Comments from Temple Israel and National Council of Jewish Women, Passaic, NJ, in "Comments on Dr. Romanoff's Lectures," n.d., JTS, RG 1, series A, box 22, folder 39.

34 Steven Fine places Romanoff within this scholarly field in Fine, *Art and Judaism in the Greco-Roman World* (New York: Cambridge University Press, 2005), 8, 32, 219n50. Romanoff's only book-length work was *Onomasticon of Palestine: A New Method in Post-biblical Topography* (New York: Jewish Publication Society, 1937). He published articles and book reviews in journals including *Jewish Quarterly Review*, *Biblical Archaeology*, *Journal of Biblical Literature*, and *Proceedings of the American Academy for Jewish Research* on topics ranging from biblical illustration, to archaeological evidence of ancient synagogues and geological causes of the biblical flood. His articles included "The Fox in Jewish Tradition," in *Review of Religion* (New York: Columbia University Press, 1942), 184–87; and a three-part series, "Jewish Symbols on Ancient Coins," published in *Jewish Quarterly Review* in 1942, 1943, and posthumously in 1944. His "The Discovery of Jewish Art" was one of two articles in a special 1935 issue of the journal the *Reconstructionist* devoted to art in the Jewish tradition.

35 Fine, *Art and Judaism*, 1.

36 Fine.

37 Deborah Waxman and Joyce Galpern Norden, "The Challenge of Implementing Reconstructionism: Art, Ideology, and the Society for the Advancement of Judaism's Sanctuary Mural," *American Jewish History* 95, no. 3 (September 2009): 210.

38 Grossman, *Judaica*, 38.

39 Grossman, 37.

40 On the question of hybridity in a contemporary European Jewish museum, see Jackie Feldman and Anja Peleikis, "Performing the Hyphen: Engaging German-Jewishness at the Jewish Museum Berlin," *Anthropological Journal of European Cultures* 23, no. 2 (2014): 43–59.

41 "Astronomy Book Shown: Jewish Museum Has 1496 Edition, Same as Columbus Used," *New York Times*, October 11, 1937, 19. Also in Miller and Cohen, "Collision of Cultures," 316.

42 Miller and Cohen, 316.

43 Romanoff references the "American Room" in Paul Romanoff, letter to Louis Finkelstein, November 24, 1939, JTS, RG 1, series A, box 22, folder 39.

44 Romanoff.

45 I am grateful to Rachel Donaldson for suggesting this context for Romanoff's curatorial work.

46 Horace Kallen, "Democracy versus the Melting Pot," *Nation* 100 (February 18–25, 1915): 190–94, 217–20, reprinted at http://pluralism.org/encounter/historical-perspectives/the-right-to-be-different/.

47 Attendance in 1932 was 10,673, with annual totals for the following years recorded at 12,375 (1933), 14,026 (1934), 22,345 (1935), 13,727 (1936), 14,243 (1937), 20,180 (1938), 13,840 (1940), and 6,700 (January–May 1941). "Museum, Jewish Theological Seminary of America, Attendance, December 1931–April 1939" and

"Museum, Jewish Theological Seminary, Attendance, 1940/1941," JTS, RG 1, series A, box 22, folder 39.

48 Miller and Cohen, "Collision of Cultures," 317.

49 Paul Romanoff, letter to Alexander Marx, May 18, 1939, JTS, RG 1, series A, box 22, folder 39.

50 Romanoff.

51 Romanoff.

52 The glossary is described first in a memo from Romanoff to Adler dated November 2, 1937, and then again on May 18, 1939. JTS, RG 1, series A, box 22, folder 39.

53 Paul Romanoff, "The Discovery of Jewish Art," in *Reconstructionist* (Wyancote, PA: Reconstructionist Rabbinical College, 1935), 1:13–16. Deborah Waxman and Joyce Galpern Norden mention Romanoff briefly in "Challenge of Implementing Reconstructionism," 210.

54 The article was published in a Yiddish periodical in 1936. Information on this article is included in the Center for Jewish History database of publications.

55 Dr. Paul Romanoff, "The Tale of a Letter by the Rambam," *Detroit Jewish Chronicle*, May 3, 1935, 4.

56 *Jewish Register*, 1934–35, 1942–43, as quoted in Miller and Cohen, "Collision of Cultures," 317n20.

57 On the Newark Museum and lending, see John Cotton Dana, *The New Museum* (Woodstock, VT: Elm Tree, 1917), 16.

58 Comment from J. L. Moulton, Club Executive Committee, New Haven, CT, in "Comments on Dr. Romanoff's Lectures."

59 Comment from Child Education Foundation, NY, in "Comments on Dr. Romanoff's Lectures."

60 "Museum, Attendance, 1940/1941," hand drawn chart prepared by Paul Romanoff, May 1941. JTS, RG 1, series A, box 22, folder 39.

61 "Museum, Attendance, 1940/1941."

62 Comment from Cong Shaari Israel of Brooklyn, NY, in "Comments on Dr. Romanoff's Lectures."

63 Anna Wright, letter to Paul Romanoff, December 5, 1939, JTS, RG 1, series A, box 22, folder 39.

64 Paul Romanoff, letter to Cyrus Adler, November 12, 1936, JTS, RG 1, series A, box 22, folder 39.

65 Paul Romanoff, letter to Cyrus Adler, December 13, 1937; Adler, letter to Romanoff, December 16, 1937, JTS, RG 1, series A, box 22, folder 39.

66 *Annual Report of the Board of Regents of the Smithsonian Institution for the Year Ending June 30, 1890*, in Grossman, *Judaica*, 39.

67 Grossman, *Judaica*, 37.

68 Years after the Columbia Exposition, Adler considered how the Section of Historic Religious Ceremonials was developed for the fair. He explained, "There was doubt, however, in the minds of many as to whether the abstract ideas which group themselves about the word 'religion' could be adequately or even fairly portrayed through

ceremonial objects, numerous as they might be." Grossman, *Judaica*, 49. Quotation is from Cyrus Adler and I. M. Casanowicz, "The Collection of Jewish Ceremonial Objects at the United States National Museum—No. 1630, September 28, 1908," *Proceedings of the United States National Museums* (Washington, DC: Government Printing Office, 1908), 34:701–46.

69 Marx, "Library," as quoted in Miller and Cohen, "Collision of Cultures," 314.
70 Alexander Marx, ed., *Celebration of the Eight Hundredth Birthday of Moses Maimonides*, Maimonides Octocentennial Series (New York: Jewish Theological Seminary of America, 1935).
71 Clarissa J. Ceglio, from an earlier draft of "Imperfectly Progressive: The Social Mission of Museums in the 1930s," in this volume. My discussion of the museum literature of the 1930s and 1940s is indebted to Ceglio's synthesis of interwar professional museum publications.
72 Laurence Vail Coleman, *The Museum in America: A Critical Study*, 3 vols. (Washington, DC: American Association of Museums, 1939), 1:4, 18, as quoted by Clarissa J. Ceglio in this volume.
73 Paul Romanoff, letter to Cyrus Adler, March 22, 1939, JTS, RG 1, series A, box 22, folder 39.
74 Paul Romanoff, letter to Cyrus Adler, May 10, 1939, JTS, RG 1, series A, box 22, folder 39.
75 Romanoff, letter to Adler, March 22, 1939 (reference to the New York World's Fair); Romanoff, letter to Marx.
76 Dorothy Wright, letter to Paul Romanoff, March 14, 1939, JTS, RG 1, series A, box 22, folder 39.
77 The stationary lists the church's address as 529 West 121st Street.
78 Paul Romanoff, letter to Cyrus Adler, November 24, 1939, JTS, RG 1, series A, box 22, folder 39.
79 Adler references the right-wing, anticommunist Father Charles E. Coughlin who hosted a popular radio program in the 1930s. Coughlin used his magazine, *Social Justice*, to spread support for fascism and defame a host of perceived threats to American liberty. Among his targets were individual Jewish leaders and Jewish institutions, which would explain why his followers congregated on the corner outside JTS. By 1938, Coughlin had developed the Christian Front, a mouthpiece for anti-Semitic propaganda and a philosophy of isolationism.
80 Romanoff, letter to Finkelstein, November 24, 1939.
81 Wright, letter to Romanoff, December 5, 1939.
82 Quoted in Shapiro, "Public and Museum," 36, 248.
83 On the connection to the Progressive Era museum, see Ceglio, "Imperfectly Progressive," in this volume.
84 Theodore Low, "What Is a Museum?," in *Reinventing the Museum: Historical and Contemporary Perspectives on the Paradigm Shift*, ed. Gail Anderson (New York: AltaMira, 2012), 34–47. Reprinted from *The Museum as a Social Instrument: A Study Undertaken for the Committee on Education of the American Association of Museums*,

published in 1942 by the Metropolitan Museum of Art for the American Association of Museums.

85 Romanoff, letter to Adler, November 24, 1939.

86 "Comments on Dr. Romanoff's Lectures."

87 Eric L. Goldstein, *The Price of Whiteness: Jews, Race, and American Identity* (Princeton, NJ: Princeton University Press, 2006), 3. For a full treatment and analysis of this process, see Eric L. Goldstein and Karen Brodkin, *How Jews Became White Folks & What That Says about Race in America* (Livingston, NJ: Rutgers University Press, 2010).

88 "Social Justice Committee," n.d., JTS, RG 1, series A, box 22, folder 39.

89 On Adler, see Grossman, *Judaica*, 29. For Finkelstein's era, see Miller and Cohen, "Collision of Cultures," 325–27. See also Jeffrey Shandler and Elihu Katz, "Broadcasting American Judaism: The Radio and Television Department at the Jewish Theological Seminary," in *Tradition Renewed*, 2:365–401. The Institute for Religious and Social Studies (IRSS), open to clergy of all faiths, used culture to bridge religious as well as cultural divides. The Conference on Science, Philosophy and Religion ran meetings for scholars in the sciences and humanities. By 1944, the IRSS had also established a weekly radio show, *The Eternal Light*, produced by the Seminary and broadcast over NBC, which aimed to increase "understanding among people, knowing that tolerance, understanding, and peace go hand in hand."

90 Miller and Cohen, "Collision of Cultures," 320.

91 Miller and Cohen, 319–20.

92 A[rtheu] O[ppenheimer], letter to Cyrus Adler, August 24, 1938, JTS, RG 1, series A, box 22, folder 39, and also in Miller and Cohen, 320n35.

93 Romanoff, letter to Adler, May 10, 1939, JTS, RG 1, series A, box 22, folder 39, RG 1, series A, box 22, folder 39.

94 Paul Romanoff, letter to Louis Finkelstein, March 1939, JTS, RG 1, series A, box 22, folder 39.

95 "Jewish Museum to Open: Collection of Ceremonial and Art Items on View May 7," *New York Times*, February 16, 1947, 46.

96 Miller and Cohen, "Collision of Cultures," 327.

97 "Jewish Museum Event: It Will Celebrate Its Second Anniversary on Monday," *New York Times*, May 11, 1949, 31.

98 Karp et al., *Museum Frictions*, 1–3.

99 Jennifer Scott, "Reimagining Freedom in the Twenty-First Century at a Post-Emancipation Site," *Public Historian* 37, no. 2 (May 2015): 87.

Exhibiting Ourselves

The Making of a Community Museum in a National Institution

Michèle Gates Moresi

The black public sphere—as a critical social imaginary—does not centrally rely on the world of magazines and coffee shops, salons and highbrow tracts. It draws energy from the vernacular practices of street talk and new musics, radio shows and church voices, entrepreneurship and circulation. Its task is not the provision of security for the freedom of conversation among intellectuals, as was the case with the bourgeois public spheres of earlier centuries. Rather, it marks a wider sphere of critical practice and visionary politics, in which intellectuals can join with the energies of the street, the school, the church, and the city to constitute a challenge to the exclusionary violence of much public space in the United States.
—the Black Public Sphere Collective, April 1995

This description of a Black public sphere captures the essence of the early years of the Anacostia Neighborhood Museum at the Smithsonian Institution.[1] In 1967, as an experiment to reach underserved minority audiences in Washington, DC, the Smithsonian opened a storefront museum in the economically depressed and predominantly African American neighborhood of Anacostia, four miles distant and separated from the National Mall by the Anacostia River. The young museum's staff, together with local residents, created exhibition language and visual representation that consistently challenged the validity of dominant portrayals of Black people, both past and present. Anacostia Neighborhood Museum (ANM) exhibitions focused on contemporary urban problems relevant to current community concerns and intended to educate its audience, although not in a didactic manner. Some exhibits, such as *The Rat* and *Lorton Reformatory*, were directly relevant to the situations and everyday experiences of the neighborhood residents and, in this sense, spoke the vernacular of the street. The exhibit creators—museum staff and community members—were engaged in an intellectual endeavor to overtly politicize the museum, as demonstrated by the museum's first pamphlet in 1968: "Dear Friend, Welcome to the Anacostia Neighborhood Museum. You have just entered an institution that is your own. You and your family are welcome seven days a week. The director and his staff are at your disposal, and urge you to voice praise or criticism of what you see here.... THIS IS YOUR MUSEUM."[2] The words are welcoming and inviting, which foregrounds the museum's mission to extend itself to a community usually ignored by the museum world. More than public outreach, however, the museum staff actively engaged their audience to participate in museum planning. Not a passive audience, Anacostia residents took part in the brainstorming, creation, and implementation of exhibits and programs. ANM staff consciously conferred power to their primary audience.

Initially, the new museum's goal was to bring the Smithsonian *to* the people. Through their efforts to collaborate with local residents, the director and staff transformed the ANM into a museum *of* and *for* the people. Emerging in the midst of the Black power movement, ANM manifested one of the ways that ideals of racial pride and control over representations of Black people's past, present, and future could be realized. With the prestige of being a Smithsonian museum, ANM not only provided a successful model for the community-based museum but also signaled to the museum world a change in the way that museums could represent and relate to minority communities through active engagement and shared authority.

This community-focused museum of Black history and culture was not something Smithsonian administrators and officials ever envisioned. An African American museum stood in stark contrast with previous Smithsonian positions that asserted national, holistic representations, and avoided specialization in any one ethnic or racial group. The ANM had begun as an outreach program and was originally envisioned as a children's science museum that would serve as an arm of the Smithsonian and encourage Anacostia residents to visit other Smithsonian museums on the Mall. Under the direction of John R. Kinard, with the influence of participating residential committees, and in the culturally radical climate of the late 1960s, the ANM became instead a highly successful community-run museum that advanced Black consciousness and pride.[3] However, by the ANM's fifth-year anniversary in 1973, the staff, particularly the director, began to reconsider the museum's direction and its place within the Smithsonian family. Marginalized by both its location and its philosophy, the museum needed to evolve in scope and vision in order to survive. In 1987, the word *neighborhood* was dropped from the museum's official name as part of the initiative to broaden its range. Although the Anacostia Neighborhood Museum served to ameliorate some of the tensions about exhibiting African American history and culture in the 1960s, its evolving mission ultimately contributed to the Anacostia Museum's continued marginalization in the national narrative.

Black Power and the American Museum

The Anacostia Neighborhood Museum was at the cusp of a growing movement to democratize and politicize the museum. The conferring of power to the museum audience was a transformation of the original outreach program idea that occurred in the intensifying atmosphere of the Black power movement and the antiestablishment activism of the era. The consciousness raising of various activist groups such as those involved in the civil rights movement, those opposed to the Vietnam War, and advocates for Black power all contributed to intense criticism of American cultural institutions, which were seen as upholding the status quo.[4]

Until the late 1960s, museums had professed a position of neutrality in social and political matters.[5] However, activists turned their attention to supposedly neutral cultural institutions and pointed to the role of museums in sustaining the oppressive ideologies of the dominant culture. In 1970, the American Association of Museums' annual meeting in New York was disrupted by protestors from the New York Art Strike and Art Workers' Coalition—an alliance of artists, feminists, and various minority groups—which criticized museums for ignoring the social crises of the times. The speaker, Ralph Ortiz, director of Museo del Barrio, accused museums of "complicity in the atrocities of our day through their failure to take a stand on the vital issues of our times."[6] The American Association of Museums passed some of the strikers' demands in a resolution, which recognized "racism, sexism, and repression as the most pressing social issues of the day" and resolved to work to end them.[7]

The Anacostia Neighborhood Museum was one of very few major museums to take on the challenge of the new demands of a changing audience. While the number of local museums, historical societies, children's museums, and various outreach programs dramatically increased between 1960 and 1980, very few museums attempted to broach topics that were contemporary or controversial before 1970.[8] The Metropolitan Museum of Art has been identified as the major art museum to produce an exhibition addressing the social concerns of its day: *Harlem on My Mind*, in 1969.[9] The exhibition displayed photographs documenting the artistic, intellectual, and social institutions of Harlem since the turn of the century. The Metropolitan's new director, Thomas Hoving, had embraced the show because he had believed in the art museum's role "to relate art to practical life, and practical living to art."[10] Hoving and the exhibition's curator had expected the show to be condemned by art critics as "not art" and politically motivated. However, the heated controversy and protests to the show took them by surprise. Black artists picketed the museum in protest of the museum's display of African Americans as subjects and its failure to exhibit art by African Americans. Newspapers, radio, and television broadcast the controversy, which intensified when the Jewish Defense League objected to the exhibition's catalog because they claimed it contained anti-Semitic remarks. The criticism and public controversy it generated seemed to confirm some people's view that museums are and should be above politics.[11]

As protesters articulated and ANM staff were aware, the museum was indeed a site of political contention regardless of the content of exhibits. The representation of a dominant and mostly elite culture by the country's most prestigious museums reified the social and economic status quo in terms of "culture." Indeed, there is a dramatic contrast between the blockbuster style of exhibition of the Metropolitan Museum of Art's *Harlem on My Mind* and ANM's community-based approach. Despite their best intentions to heed the call of protesters, curators of *Harlem on My Mind* in effect treated the subject of their art exhibition as an abstract group to study and display. ANM staff cultivated the desires and point of view of the subject, engaged them along the way in the exhibition process, and subsequently, developed a new model for museum exhibition practice.

As a minority community with recognition by the nation's official repository of national culture, the people of Anacostia gained a platform on which to negotiate these political and cultural issues in their own terms.

African Americans were not regular visitors to Smithsonian museums on the Mall, and this was one of the reasons frequently cited to create a neighborhood museum in the first place. Reflecting upon why African Americans did not visit Smithsonian museums on the Mall, John R. Kinard stated, "The problem was that the black man did not see himself in those jobs or in those exhibits, so he wasn't going to embarrass himself by paying respect to what essentially represented cultural pressure."[12] To relieve that cultural pressure, the people of Anacostia demanded a museum that was relevant to their circumstances and to their developing notion of African American culture.

This desire for self-definition was the point at which varied groups of the Black power movement converged. William Van Deburg has demonstrated the centrality of the cultural sphere to Black power advocates' call for the power to define themselves. Whether adhering to a strict separatist doctrine, seeking peaceful coexistence within a culturally diverse society, or some other variant of Black power ideas, all proponents looked to a revision of history and culture as a crucial step toward real change.[13] They all believed psychological oppression to be as potent as political and economic oppression. Therefore, psychic liberation depended on revisiting the past to acknowledge Africa as a rich, dynamic culture and to reveal African Americans as not merely victims of American injustice but as a resilient community with its own traditions and triumphs. The building of pride in an ancestral Africa and a valued African American culture was key to a Black power agenda of community empowerment.

As one scholar has noted, for African Americans, a pride in Blackness was a way to deal with the dilemma of integration: while integration through legal avenues sought to rectify injustices of inequality, it did not directly address the problem of cultural negativity that sustained portrayals of Black racial inferiority.[14] Within the Black community, writers, artists, and activists identified Black self-hatred as part of the problem.[15] A heightened awareness of systematic oppression and a newfound pride in "Blackness" were a counter to the feeling that assimilation would compromise one's ethnicity and self-identity; they were a response to accusations of wanting to "become White" and identifying with the source of one's oppression.[16]

In resisting and turning on its head racist ideology that depicted Black bodies as unattractive and less than ideal, the "Black Is Beautiful" mantra countered such negativity. People celebrated Black skin color and "going natural" became at once fashionable and political. Black pride and a heightened sense of the need to assert Black culture and history became widespread in all facets of society. From the mid-1960s to the mid-1970s, the Black Arts movement flourished and cultural activists, especially those in drama, poetry, and music, founded Black repertory theaters and organizations across the country. In an effort to define Black art and affect the consciousness of Black people, artists rejected Western standards, which often applied a strict dichotomy of art and politics, and instilled their work with messages of Black pride and unity. Described as the "spiritual sister" of Black power, proponents of a Black aesthetic emphasized the function of art to transform the artistic sensibilities of African Americans away from a demoralizing "White aesthetic" to a self-affirming Black one. People applied the creative sentiments of Black power often by performing them in conjunction with street rallies and demonstrations, blending the worlds of creative arts and political activism.[17]

African American writers disseminated messages of Black power to take psychic control of their lives and their culture. In his autobiography, Malcolm X demonstrates his own self-loathing, his alienation, and how, as Detroit Red, he aspired to "become White." Malcolm X exhorts readers to know themselves, to know the truth about African American culture through African history and religion.[18] Playwrights, poets, and magazine writers aimed their works directly to the Black community, and a proliferation of bookstores and sales indicates that Blacks were reading their messages. The Black Academy of Arts and Letters formed in 1969 in order to give recognition to Black artists and scholars such as Amiri Baraka, W. E. B. Du Bois, Paul Robeson, and George Jackson.[19]

Militant student activism was widespread and encompassed an array of social concerns; increasingly in the late 1960s, African American students participated in campus protests that called for Black studies programs and more Black representation within university infrastructure. In many universities, students demanded and faculty agreed that traditional curricula needed to be reformed.[20] By 1970, more than 170 colleges and universities established Black studies programs that ranged from several courses to entire departments.[21]

The Black power movement and its widespread manifestations in art, theater, literature, and the academy alienated most Whites. Generally, it conjured feelings of reverse racism for White people, who often accused Blacks of failing to remain "objective." Historian Daniel J. Boorstin, for instance, commented on the effect of Black power on contemporary scholarship: "Future Historians will doubtless begin to be wary of the books on the history of the Negro in the United States when they find the word 'Negro' being displaced by

Black Creation 1, no. 1 (1970). The sentiments of Black power applied all aspects of culture—including art, literature, and fashion aesthetics—that celebrated and dignified Blackness. Copyright Institute of African American Affairs. Collection of the Smithsonian National Museum of African American History and Culture.

the word 'Black.' . . . The 'Black Studies' movement has tended to inflame the subject without proportionately illuminating it, and has become the Trojan Horse of a new racism."[22] Such sentiments advanced by leading academics shaped views and raised doubts for some Smithsonian staff regarding the scholarship of ANM projects.

Whether in the realm of arts, academics, or politics, there were some basic interrelated tensions that existed in demanding and implementing an emphasis on African American culture in the museum: there was always the question of autonomy or control over an event or program, the need to establish legitimacy, and the issue of political (rather than apolitical) motives. These issues shaped the mission and identity of the Anacostia Neighborhood Museum as it changed over time.

From New Idea to New Museum

By 1966, the Smithsonian's newly appointed secretary, S. Dillon Ripley, sought to enliven the institution's mission by expanding the museum audience and reaching out to communities traditionally neglected by museum programs. In a speech presented at the American Association of Museums meeting

Carver Theater, first home of the Anacostia Museum, 1967. The Smithsonian's secretary, S. Dillon Ripley, sought to reach a neglected audience by creating a new museum in a rented theater that had closed in the Anacostia neighborhood of Washington, DC, about four miles from the National Mall. Smithsonian Institution Archives, Image #92-1790.

during the fall of 1966, Ripley had suggested that museums make the leap to reach broader audiences by renting buildings in low-income neighborhoods and installing exhibits that could be touched and operated. The Smithsonian held informal exploratory meetings with various community representatives and reached an agreement with the Greater Anacostia Peoples' Corporation, a nonprofit civic group, to open the experimental museum in the old Carver Theater on Nichols Avenue in Anacostia.[23]

In the fall of 1966, Ripley issued an institution-wide call to curators and division heads for ideas about exhibits for an experimental storefront museum. The initial concept was for "a small, neighborhood museum that people who do not normally visit our museums could use easily and casually." In addition, many believed that a storefront museum would be filled with artifacts that could be touched and handled by the visitor. Exhibits would be unstructured and simplified, and objects were to be self-explanatory: "We feel that such a 'drop-in museum' should be very low-keyed, without a formal theme or structured program or elaborate exhibits."[24] The imagined visitors were primarily youth who came from economically depressed and educationally disadvantaged backgrounds. Many suggestions for exhibits drew on children's museums and hands-on science museums for their inspiration.[25] Other suggestions proposed something like a "curiosity shop." The hope was that people would become interested, engaged, and excited enough about museums so that they would be encouraged to venture to the Smithsonian museums on the Mall.

Early in the first planning stages of the ANM, neighborhood residents and Smithsonian staff formed the Anacostia Advisory Committee and met weekly. Smithsonian representatives—such as John Anglim, chief of the Office of Exhibits, Ben Lawless, chief of exhibits for the Museum of History and Technology (MHT), and Keith Melder, curator of political history at MHT—met with interested residents of Anacostia regularly to discuss everyone's expectations for the new museum. The advisory committee had no formal structure in order to avoid slighting anyone, although a chairman and vice chairman were selected.[26] Meetings held in the summer of 1967 were open to all residents of the neighborhood, and the participation rate was high. In an era when community activism was dynamic and people felt their participation might be effective, Anacostia residents did not hesitate to join in the meetings. One participant observer recalled, "It was early summer. The airconditioning wasn't working, so the doors were wide open and anyone could walk in, sit down, and take part in the discussion. . . . No formal notices were sent out; the message spread by word of mouth. Most of the time, from 35 to 50 people met every week to plan for a museum that would be the first of its kind in the world."[27]

Planning for the museum required community engagement, and all aspects of the project were open for discussion and negotiation. Contrary to Ripley's account of the first consultations that led to the agreement, neighborhood residents were at first doubtful and a little suspicious of the Smithsonian's efforts.[28] Some felt unsure that a museum would be truly helpful to the community, and some even thought that a museum would be irrelevant to their immediate concerns. Anacostia residents also felt apprehension about how a museum, particularly a traditional museum, might treat the culture and lifestyle of the neighborhood. Nonetheless, residents entrusted their community leaders with the final decision to accept the Smithsonian's proposal.[29] In the evolution of the idea about how ANM would actually operate and the kinds of exhibits it would produce, residents eventually shifted the focus of a "touching museum" to projects that dealt with local urban problems and, more broadly, African American history and culture.[30]

The experimental museum's first staff members consisted of just four people. The director, John R. Kinard; Zora B. Martin, an educator; Edgar Tyler; and William Wilson. Six additional people served as "special assistants" and all, except the museum director, were employed on a temporary basis for the first year. Larry Erskine Thomas joined the team as a researcher and designer shortly after the museum first opened.[31] As one of the major concerns expressed by the community had been about whether the museum would provide jobs, Smithsonian officials (such as Charles Blitzer) promised that museum positions would be filled by residents whenever possible. Six of the initial museum team, including Kinard and Martin, were local residents.[32]

The Anacostia Neighborhood Museum opened September 15, 1967, to the music of multiple bands and a block party accompanied by speeches and klieg lights. In the months leading up to the opening day, neighborhood residents had been the primary drivers of the museum's planning and implementation. While Smithsonian curators, designers, and engineers had enthusiastically worked to renovate the building and plan exhibitions, residents were the mainstay of the museum's implementation. The neighborhood advisory committee, youth groups, and passersby picked up paintbrushes and brooms

Opening of the Anacostia Neighborhood Museum, 1967. Residents were involved in readying the museum building for its grand opening and continued to influence its exhibits and programs in collaboration with museum staff. Smithsonian Institution Archives, Image #91-517.

to refurbish the old building that would become the museum. The empty lot next to the refurbished theater had been turned into a garden by the Trailblazers, a work-recreation-beautification program, along with other local youth organizations, who also painted a new mural along the property edge. The museum's first displays drew from the resources of the Smithsonian, especially the Museum of History and Technology and the National Zoo, with a setting that showed astronaut suits and a space capsule, an 1890s country store, and a petting zoo. In addition, museum planners set up a hands-on science corner and artist workbenches for working with paint and clay.[33]

From the outset, Smithsonian museum planners expected that Anacostia exhibit displays would be touched and handled by visitors. Curators from across the Smithsonian Institution frequently provided objects to the ANM that were expendable because they understood they would be frequently handled and feared they would vulnerable to vandalism.[34] While on-site staff generally agreed that some objects would be vulnerable, there was some resentment that this was always expected to be the case.[35]

During the early months of collaboration with Smithsonian curators and outside consultants, assumptions about the audience created some of the tensions that would strain communication and understanding between established Smithsonian curators and the new Anacostia staff. For some Smithsonian curators and administrators, there was a basic underlying notion that people who lived in slum areas were of a different world and spoke a different language. Some curators assumed that the urban slum dweller lacked "a sense of process" and the experiences of the "physical commonplaces," such as how to operate a wheelbarrow, play in the bath, or ride a bike.[36] There was a sense of a wide gulf of different and unknown experiences that the typical museum person did not and could not understand about the people who lived in Anacostia.[37] Given these institutional biases and misconceptions, the Anacostia museum staff believed there needed to be constant and open communication with the residents. They understood that respect and sensitivity to the audience's opinions and ideas were essential to the success of the experiment.[38] ANM staff had to negotiate this mix of condescension and respect. At times offended by the assumptions made about poor people, staff also adapted the various ideas to overcome barriers of communication with local residents and to develop new and different kinds of exhibits. Most of all, the Anacostia staff learned to listen to their audience and to respond positively to their demands. Although Ripley's initial idea for an outreach museum to poorer sectors of the city had not imagined it, the ANM on-site staff developed processes for sharing authority with Anacostia residents.

Very quickly, it became clear to the small ANM staff that the community felt personally invested in the museum and believed strongly that they should take extensive part in the development of exhibits. While hands-on science was interesting and engaging for youth, it lacked any sense of cultural relevance to the wider community. They found that exhibits focusing on Black achievements were the most popular. At the request of community members and visitors to the museum, the Anacostia Advisory Committee "agreed to design future exhibits and programs . . . to include, whenever and wherever possible, themes, artifacts and educational materials that would contribute to the understanding and knowledge of Negro history and culture."[39] Such exhibits were intended to not only correct the traditional omission of Black history and culture in museum representations but truly represent American history with a fully integrated portrayal.[40] A holistic and integrated narrative, however, was overshadowed by the representation of racial and cultural difference.

Creating Exhibitions

The Anacostia Neighborhood Museum's opening exhibitions were largely interactive displays adopted from the children's museum model. Residents selected exhibition topics in public meetings, choosing from numerous suggestions offered by Smithsonian staff from other museums. The Neighborhood Museum's first major display was a Project Mercury space capsule equipped with working gadgets. Other hands-on activities included a "bone room" where skeletons could be taken apart and reassembled, a closed-circuit television and monitor, and "shoebox" activities, where children could encounter and handle objects. The museum's first art show was a display of sculpture by a local artist in November of 1967. Called *Doodles in Dimension*, the exhibition showed the artist's three-dimensional rendition of doodles made by President Kennedy. While ANM staff and press coverage were positive and enthusiastic about the show, some observers remained critical and were concerned about the museum's future direction.[41]

Questions about the "museum quality" of ANM exhibits reflected tensions around the staff's effort to design a new kind of museum, one that actively took on current and sometimes controversial issues. Traditionally the Smithsonian had sought to eschew questions of immediate political import, but the Anacostia addressed them directly. The informal structure of the satellite museum allowed for a more fluid and organic process for the creation of exhibits and made it possible to plan and implement them without the presence of a curator on staff.[42] Exhibition planning flowed from the museum's advisory committee. Residents and activists pushed for exhibits and programs relevant to the lives of local people.

As the staff began to recognize the need to create immediately relevant presentations, a confluence of circumstances and events stimulated the development of the museum's first "urban problem" exhibition. The museum maintained a permanent, small zoo for children, and this had elicited some criticism from both staff and visitors. The animals, including birds, snakes, squirrel monkeys, gerbils, hamsters, and small mice, were said to be "noisy, dirty," and smelly. Children wanted to retain the small zoo at the museum and compromises made it possible. Nonetheless, many visitors remained wary of the rodents that stayed in the museum, and when a donated pair of laboratory rats went on display, someone poured a can of paint over them. Residents of Anacostia struggled with serious problems regarding rat infestation, the subject of many horror stories among community residents. Likely the protest and vandalism upon the small zoo's rodents "reflected the deep, abiding hatred that people who live with rats develop for rodents."[43] Based on these exchanges and events, Zora B. Martin researched and developed the exhibition *The Rat: Man's Invited Affliction*, which went on display from November 16, 1969, to January 25, 1970.

Both Kinard and Martin made note of skepticism from neighborhood residents and museum colleagues alike, but they believed the support and enthusiasm from some members of the community, especially youth, warranted its production. Anticipating criticism of the show, Kinard asserted, "The Museum does not wish to be a prophet of doom nor is this exhibit designed to lower the morale of the community.... The Neighborhood Advisory Committee of the Museum has decided that we cannot afford to present exhibits that deal only with life in the past. Such exhibits must have some relevance to present-day problems that affect the quality of life here and now in Anacostia."[44] The

The Rat: Man's Invited Affliction, November 16, 1969. The Anacostia Neighborhood Museum developed exhibitions and programs relevant to resident's experiences. Smithsonian Institution Archives, Image #2004-63044.

exhibition sought to educate people and dispel misconceptions about urban rats. It examined the ecological and historical significance of rats while focusing on contemporary means of dealing with them in urban areas. The displays included a simulated rat environment in a backyard to demonstrate "how they [rats] exist and survive, their destructiveness, and disease-carrying potential."[45] Associated programs included a television segment, "Who Do You Kill?," which dramatized life in the ghetto; an original skit called "RATS" by a local group of young people; and seminars and demonstrations that discussed pest control, housekeeping, and the psychological impact of living with pest infestations.

Another exhibition that dealt with contemporary issues was the show *Lorton Reformatory: Beyond Time*, which went on display in October 1970. In cooperation with men at the Lorton prison facility, ANM created a slide, audiotape, and photograph show about life behind bars. The exhibition was "presented to promote an understanding and appreciation of how the men at Lorton 'spend the time' during their sentences" by displaying artwork and crafts by inmates. A recent debate about the future maintenance of Lorton Reformatory was the apparent catalyst to create the exhibition. Congressional hearings had been held to consider transferring the correctional facility from the district to the federal government because of, in part, charges that the facility was wrought with problems. Proponents argued that the district could not handle basic prison operations. Security and discipline were lax. Prisoners were idle without a useful industrial program. Narcotics and alcohol were rampant. Prison guards were harassed by prisoners and had difficulty in dealing with "a new breed of inner-city inmate who has brought with him 'militant ideas.'"[46] Yet proponents overlooked advancements at the facility. Expanded rehabilitation programs had recently made academic courses accessible to inmates through a local college. New vocational training programs had been put in place as well.

The Lorton Reformatory exhibit embodied the principles of Black power and reflected the Anacostia Neighborhood Museum's focus on urban issues. The goal was to create a forum for discussion and to create a space to hear the voices of the inmates, mostly African Americans from the district. The museum director explained, "A discussion on the causes of crime, on the meaning of justice and penal reform is of paramount importance to all of us. After all, our concern is not for strangers, unknown to us, but for our neighbors—for those related to us by blood and marriage—in a word—our concern is for our brothers."[47] The museum held a "rap session" in which men without prison records met with former prisoners to discuss and evaluate the programs at Lorton. Live performances and public programs during the exhibition included singing groups, an instrumental band, and a speech-writing group. Thus the exhibition allowed for an alternative view on the experiences of men at Lorton, revealing their creativity, motivation, and hope.

In addition to producing exhibitions about contemporary community issues, the Anacostia Neighborhood Museum quickly broadened its programs to focus on the broader history and culture of Africans and African Americans. Although the museum's constituents had asked for and appreciated shows dealing with relevant questions, they also felt an aversion to focusing too heavily on problems.[48] Residents expressed their desire for shows about "our Negro heritage."[49] In response, the museum mounted a number of exhibitions about Black culture and history. For example, *Negro History* (February 1968), displayed during what was then called Negro History Week (now Black History Month), included material from the Harmon Foundation Collection held by the Smithsonian's National Portrait Gallery.[50] The exhibit included twenty-eight paintings and two sculptures, as well as a life-sized farmhouse built to represent one in which Benjamin Banneker, the eighteenth-century astronomer and mathematician, might have lived. Martin commented on the exhibition: "As one child was later to say, 'I've never seen so many Negroes in one place in my whole life.' And this was true. For the first time in the lives of many blacks they were completely surrounded, engulfed, and inundated by images of blackness—Harriet Tubman, Aaron Douglas, Alain Locke, Harry T. Burleigh, Arna Bontemps, and so many others."[51] It was tremendously important at that moment to many African Americans, especially youth, to see these large, beautiful paintings of distinguished Black Americans. The desire to present African American heroes and role models in history was an intricate part of Black empowerment. The Harmon Foundation Collection had been displayed years earlier at the Smithsonian. Originally intended to inspire racial harmony through the display of Black artists' achievements in the arts, their inclusion in this exhibition functioned as a source of self-esteem and appreciation for African American heritage.[52]

Another exhibit, *Africa: Three Out of Many, Ethiopia, Ghana, Nigeria* (September 15–December 26, 1973), displayed woodwork sculpture, such as masks, from three African nations. In contrast to the Herbert Ward African Collection on display in the Natural History Museum, the Anacostia exhibition presented the continent as a country of diverse peoples with varying cultural traditions and vibrant artistic creativity. Anacostia's *Africa* show displayed African art as a source of ethnic and racial pride. In an introduction to the 1973 exhibition, Kinard wrote, "What is displayed here represents the artistry, the religious inspiration, and the history of a people whose culture has been too long denied. Each object, from the simplest tool to the most elaborate work of art, embodies the best that is within the people who created that culture so that Africa comes alive and speaks to us in a way all men can understand."[53] Kinard's statement echoes the sentiments of Black power and avoids the extreme position of Black separatism. African Americans, omitted from representation in American culture and portrayed as disconnected from African cultures, could come to the ANM and witness a great artistry identified as their own heritage. At the same time, non–African Americans would benefit from learning about the long-misrepresented history of Africa and African culture. Thus the exhibit functioned as a resource both for the community to learn about some African heritage and for a broader audience to recognize African culture as worthy of recognition and praise.

During the 1970s, American museums experimented with numerous forms of outreach programs.[54] As a leader of the community-based museum movement, the ANM pioneered activities for outreach to people who still did not walk through the front doors. The museum created a Mobile Division to "take the Museum to the people." A bright-blue van made the rounds in the neighborhood, carrying portable versions of exhibitions and bringing lecturers to local schools. Fletcher Smith, head of the Mobile Division, described the significance of his work: "What was so unique about this concept? Certainly the idea of taking such a service to the people was relatively new. But even more stimulating was the delivery of an intangible item that many label 'pride.' Through such exhibits [on Black history and culture], a river of strength flowed. Young as well as old could begin to drink from the waters of self-worth, a thirst long denied."[55] Smith's words epitomize the goals of cultural empowerment advocated by Black power. The Anacostia Museum's Mobile Division transformed the initial Smithsonian goal of outreach to a distant constituency and advanced the museum as part of the social-political activism of the moment. In responding to the demands of its audience, ANM became a source for creating a sense of an American heritage and identity that did not simply "include" Black people but asserted racial pride and cultural distinctiveness.

The community museum directly challenged the tradition of major museums to present their shows as "apolitical" and above the politics and racial tensions of the day. What many activists argued and the ANM epitomized in its practices was that culture was politicized. Embracing this concept, the Anacostia Neighborhood Museum openly and assertively declared the representation of African American culture as a political endeavor necessary to change social and economic conditions.

Black Culture and Legitimacy in the Museum

The experiences of developing and implementing exhibits in intimate cooperation with the target audience gave ANM staff insight into the workings of a neighborhood museum. One staff member noted that the staff could not plan for its constituents but needed to plan *with* them. In order to do that effectively, the staff of the neighborhood museum needed to be "sensitive and responsive to the need to understand, analyze and creatively change that which seemed changeless in the minds, spirits—and environments—of those they serve."[56] The original effort to create engaging exhibits evolved into a larger effort to design programs that spoke to the community's problems, piqued their curiosity, and helped them recognize the vital role they could play in a larger intellectual and cultural world.

In conjunction with exhibit displays, ANM conducted educational workshops, demonstrations, dramatic presentations, and music and dance programs to "bring life" to the traditional exhibit mode of display. Kinard explained the philosophy behind ANM exhibitions to one colleague:

> What we do here at Anacostia arises out of the desires and interests of this community and these can be limitless and varied. This adds zest and enthusiasm to the activities. Exhibits are not just something the staff decided would be worthwhile. It has been our experience that when exhibit ideas and the way they should be displayed come from the community, and neighborhood people are involved in the plans as well as the production, the exhibit conveys a sense of truth that cannot be achieved in any other way. This by no means lessens the quality but strengthens it.[57]

Kinard needed to defend the Anacostia Neighborhood Museum's approach because prioritizing the demands of their audience had led some to doubt the legitimacy of ANM exhibition practices. Some viewed the exhibitions as undermining expertise and lacking objectivity. The ANM was criticized by Smithsonian curators for its lack of organization and for its emotional connections to exhibit topics.

Tensions between the ANM staff and other Smithsonian Institution curators became evident as early as the summer of 1968, during planning for "Negro History" week. During the previous ten months, the museum had mounted numerous small displays and programs leading up to a major exhibition: Benjamin Banneker was featured in *Moments in History* in January 1968, and portraits from the Smithsonian's Harmon Foundation Collection had been displayed in February. In March, drawing upon the creativity of the local community, the museum invited school groups and art students to develop panel discussions and perform Negro folk music, and the museum also hosted a poetry reading by Sterling A. Brown.[58]

But exhibition script development exacerbated tension in the relationship between the Anacostia Neighborhood Museum and the Museum of History and Technology. Input and support from Smithsonian curators and administrators, especially from MHT, had been a typical part of the ANM's exhibition development process. Left out of the process, Smithsonian curators and administrators questioned the expertise of the selected scriptwriter, Larry Thomas, who had been hired not as a historian but as a designer at the museum.[59] The Smithsonian curators argued that only a trained historian with expertise in African American history was qualified for the work. This question regarding expertise was intimately tied to issues of control over exhibition content and process. One Smithsonian administrator addressed the issue: "Any remarks [that criticize the choice of scriptwriter], no matter how mildly phrased, receive an immediate response from John Kinard that bristles with defensiveness. It is understandable that the Anacostia people would want to be in complete control of such a project, but I think there is a danger that this exhibit could become a mish mash of unrelated ideas, mistaken emphasis, and errors that will not reflect credit on either Anacostia or the Smithsonian."[60] What we might dismiss as intellectual disagreements became more intense in the aftermath of the Martin Luther King Jr. assassination riots in April 1968. The heightened emotions and sense of urgency among ANM staff made interactions with other Smithsonian staff extremely difficult. Non-African American staff felt the need to move forward with caution and not be swept up by the intensity of the political moment. In sharp contrast, African American staff members at ANM felt a need to assert control and self-determination for their institution and for constituency. Their arguments in favor of moving forward echoed those of Black separatists and mirrored debates about rebuilding the damaged city after the riots.[61]

In spite of skepticism from some curators and staff, the highest ranking officials at the Smithsonian Institution continued to support the Anacostia Neighborhood Museum and to encourage its independence. Dedicated to letting the experiment run its course, Frank Taylor, director of MHT, and Charles Blitzer, assistant secretary of the Smithsonian, insisted that curators and administrators allow the ANM staff to determine how much and what kind of assistance was appropriate.[62]

A Museum of the Moment

The Anacostia Neighborhood Museum achieved a worthy goal, even if it was not the one originally intended. Secretary Ripley wanted to serve the interests of the Smithsonian Institution by bringing underrepresented audiences to the National Mall. Instead, the members of that target audience influenced and transformed the museum medium, creating an institution that served their own interests. ANM reflected the impulses and desires of engaged, forward-thinking professionals of the times. While not explicitly professing Black power militancy, museum staff of the ANM embraced the spirit of Black power ideals: shaking off the mantel of Western cultural traditions that rendered darker peoples inferior and invisible and instead expressing the desires and asserting the voices of African Americans in the neighborhood. By implementing the "critical practice and visionary politics" of the street, ANM staff listened to, engaged with, and collaborated with neighborhood residents to realize a museum that reflected its primary audience. In doing so, the ANM made it possible to share authority with residents and create new narratives.

By 1975, the museum had grown beyond just a neighborhood operation and, nationally and internationally, came to be recognized as a venue for Black history and culture. Various museum and community representatives looked to the ANM as a model museum that facilitated the cultural life of its immediate constituents and actively worked with young people.[63] Yet Kinard had begun to express dissatisfaction with the way Anacostia was viewed by many, both within the Smithsonian and without. Primarily, its location in Anacostia and in the old theater building fostered a wider perception that the neighborhood museum was solely local in scope. This view hampered the possibilities for ANM to be seen for its national impact and in line with the prestigious position of other Smithsonian museums.[64]

Although Kinard hoped to mainstream the scope and purpose of the Anacostia Neighborhood Museum, he also held fast to the vision of a museum that served a specific community. In this sense, he aimed to have ANM make a unique and significant contribution to the museum field. In 1972, Kinard stated, "There are far too many museums whose exhibits say nothing at all to far too many people. They fail to create a special mood or feeling. There is no soul or even heartbeat—no social consciousness or historical continuity. They cater to the interests of a select few and the so-called mighty, assuming to know what everyone wants, when actually the interest of the masses of the people and the various minorities who make up that larger group have never been considered."[65] Kinard implicitly critiqued the content and activities of the traditional museum and other Smithsonian museums. The museum must move, touch, and be relevant to a broader audience, Kinard argued, rather than educate at a distance. Placing the Anacostia Neighborhood Museum on the vanguard, he sought to push the Smithsonian as a whole in a new direction that would lead the museum world.

For some Smithsonian curators, however, the very existence of a museum dedicated to African American history and culture was anathema to the integrationist commitments of their own work and what they believed to be integral to the Smithsonian's larger mission as an arbiter of the nation's culture. For instance, the Smithsonian's Museum of History and Technology selectively avoided racial and ethnic-specific history.[66] The atmosphere of the late 1960s made a focus on African American history problematic. The development of the Anacostia Neighborhood Museum at once made it easier for the Museum of History and Technology to avoid producing its own work about African Americans while confirming some people's fears that the topic would only politicize museum activities.

The creation of the Anacostia Neighborhood Museum was a unique moment of potential transformation for the Smithsonian. In its early years, the ANM created a space that challenged the Smithsonian to be more responsive to criticism from those ignored by traditional museum practices. The Smithsonian's experimental museum allowed for a venue that was intimately connected to place and community, a museum that worried less about an "official" narrative and more about its primary constituents, the neighborhood residents. However, the museum's founding director had noticed the effect of physical marginalization (located off the Mall) and psychologically (outside the Smithsonian "family"). Thus Kinard pushed to have the ANM recognized as a unit of the Smithsonian's Art and History Museums division, rather than as a bureau in the Public Programs division, in 1985.

The ways that the sentiments of Black power had influenced and shaped ANM programs made for a successful experiment. However, to move beyond the experiment and continue to grow as a Smithsonian entity, the ANM would shift its persona to look more like a traditional museum. It moved out of its remodeled storefront and into a new building built for its museum purposes. The new look reflected new practices as well, including hiring a professionally trained staff, starting a collection program, and creating public programs that addressed a broader national (and later even an international) audience.[67] Nonetheless, into the 1980s, as a separate, Black museum, the Anacostia Museum would continue to serve a targeted audience that did not feel welcome or respected in mainstream museums, even when those museums made efforts to tell stories about Black history.[68] At the same time, although an emphasis on Black history and culture was crucial to the early development of ANM, the rhetoric of Black pride had ultimately and ironically undermined the integrationist aspect of its mission.

Notes

This article is revised from Michèle Gates Moresi, "Exhibiting Race, Creating Nation: Representations of Black History and Culture at the Smithsonian Institution, 1895–1976" (PhD diss., George Washington University, 2003), chap. 4, "Exhibiting Ourselves: Self-Representation in a National Institution, 1967–1975."

1 Epigraph: Black Public Sphere Collective, ed., *The Black Public Sphere: A Public Culture Book* (Chicago: University of Chicago Press, 1995), 3.
2 Museum pamphlet, n.d., Smithsonian Institution Archives (SIA), Exhibits Department, Anacostia Neighborhood Museum Records, 1967–84 (hereafter cited as Exhibits ANM), RU 378, box 3.
3 John R. Kinard (1936–89) was the director of ANM from 1967 until his death in 1989. He was a native Washingtonian and cultivated a career in community service. See John R. Kinard, interview SIA, 1987, John Kinard Oral History Interview, RU 9538.
4 Terry Zeller, "From National Service to Social Protest: American Museums in the 1940s, '50s, '60s, and '70s," *Museum News* 75, no. 2 (March/April 1996): 48–59.
5 Zeller, 49–52.
6 Quoted by Zeller, 56.

7 Zeller.
8 Andrea A. Burns, *From Storefront to Monument: Tracing the Public History of the Black Museum Movement* (Amherst: University of Massachusetts Press, 2013), 72–105.
9 Zeller, "From National Service," 54–55.
10 Thomas P. F. Hoving, preface to *Harlem on My Mind: Cultural Capital of Black America, 1900–1968* (exhibit catalog; 1968; repr. New York: New Press, 1995).
11 Allan Schoener, introduction to *Harlem on My Mind*; Zeller, "From National Service," 55; Burns, *From Storefront to Monument*, 104. Incidentally, before opening the show, the Metropolitan Museum of Art invited the Smithsonian to consider the exhibition for their galleries. However, the potential cost prevented the Smithsonian from making any commitments and the notion was suspended. Thus the Smithsonian was never involved in the controversy generated by the show. S. Dillon Ripley, letter to Thomas G. Hoving, June 4, 1968; Robert W. Mason, memo to Ripley through Mr. Warner, cc: Messrs. Anglim, Blitzer, Kinard, Taylor, and Mrs. Marsh, October 2, 1968; Ripley, letter to Charles Blitzer, October 3, 1968, SIA, Assistant Secretary for Public Service, RU 145, box 2.
12 Kinard, interview SIA, 13.
13 William L. Van Deburg, *A New Day in Babylon: The Black Power Movement and American Culture* (Chicago: University of Chicago Press, 1992). Van Deburg presents the various tactics and ideologies among pluralists and nationalists in the Black power movement (25–26, 112–91). For discussion on the role of Black power ideals in burgeoning Black museums, see Burns, *From Storefront to Monument*, 4–10.
14 Robert Blauner, *Black Lives, White Lives: Three Decades of Race Relations in America* (Berkeley: University of California Press, 1998), 16.
15 In the 1960s, E. Franklin Frazier's study of the Black middle class, *Black Bourgeoisie* (New York: Macmillan, 1957), was cited frequently.
16 Blauner, *Black Lives, White Lives*, 16.
17 Van Deburg, *New Day in Babylon*, 181–83.
18 Malcolm X with Alex Haley, *The Autobiography of Malcolm X* (1965; repr. New York: Ballantine Books, 1992).
19 Alphonso Pinkney, *Red, Black, and Green: Black Nationalism in the United States* (New York: Cambridge University Press, 1976), 80.
20 Van Deburg notes that as a record number of Blacks entered colleges during 1964–70, increasingly in mainstream colleges, more protests occurred in nonsegregated facilities and focused on institutional change well beyond the issue of desegregation. Van Deburg, *New Day in Babylon*, 65–68. For an analysis on the roots and development of Black studies in colleges and universities, see Peniel Joseph, "Black Studies, Student Activism, and the Black Power Movement," in *The Black Power Movement: Rethinking the Civil Rights—Black Power Era*, ed. Peniel E. Joseph (New York: Routledge, 2006).
21 Robert Blauner, *Racial Oppression in America* (New York: Harper & Row, 1972), 288. Blauner points out that institutional resistance to the independent programs was

strong. Opposition was not directed at the idea of curricular reform. Rather, debated centered on the programs' form, focus, and status.

22 Daniel J. Boorstin, *The Americans: The Democratic Experience* (New York: Random House, 1973), 648; Richard Dudman, "The Nomination of D. J. Boorstin: Reflections of Racial Reservations," *Post Dispatch* (St Louis, MO), July 13, 1975.

23 S. Dillon Ripley (1913–2001) was appointed the eighth secretary of the Smithsonian in 1964 and served a twenty-year tenure. Ripley's address to the Association of American Museums in Aspen, Colorado, reportedly appeared in Washington newspapers, November 1966. Robert Kinard, "The Making of a Museum," n.d., SIA, Exhibits ANM, RU 378, box 4. The Greater Anacostia People's Corporation formed in 1965, shortly after an incident in which some young people of the neighborhood had a clash with the police, in order to bring community concerns to the attention of the press and the public. Esther Nighbert, "The History of the Museum," in *Anacostia Museum, Fifth Anniversary* (Washington, DC: Anacostia Neighborhood Museum, 1972), 3.

24 Charles Blitzer (director, education and training), memo to "Heads of Bureaus, etc.," October 21, 1966, SIA, Assistant Secretary for Public Service, RU 145, box 2. The concept of a drop-in museum had been proposed at a conference on museums and education that was sponsored jointly by the Smithsonian and the US Office of Education in August 1966. Caryl Marsh, "A Neighborhood Museum That Works," *Museum News* 47, no. 2 (October 1968): 11.

25 Walter Male, memo to Charles Blitzer, October 25, 1966; Frank A. Taylor, memo to Charles Blitzer, October 27, 1966; Richard H. Manville (director, Bird and Mammal Laboratories), memo to Charles Blitzer, October 27, 1966; C. Malcolm Watkins, memo to Charles Blitzer, November 3, 1966; Waldo L. Schmitt (research associate), memo to Charles Blitzer, November 9, 1966, SIA, Assistant Secretary for Public Service, RU 145, box 2.

26 Anacostia residents Alton Jones Stanley Anderson served as chairman and vice-chairman, respectively. Nighbert, "History of the Museum," 5.

27 Nighbert.

28 S. Dillon Ripley, *The Sacred Grove: Essays on Museums* (New York: Simon & Schuster, 1969), 106; Portia James, "Building a Community-Based Identity at Anacostia Museum," *Curator* 39, no. 1 (March 1996): 21.

29 James, 21; Kinard, interview SIA, 13.

30 Kinard, 12.

31 Nighbert, "History of the Museum," 6. As the museum's success became apparent and federal monies were increased, more of the staff were employed full-time and still more joined the team with support from grants and private funds. By the fifth-year anniversary, ANM listed twenty-one people on its staff.

32 Nighbert, 4.

33 For descriptions of the opening day of ANM and its preparation, see Ripley, *Sacred Grove*, 108; Marsh, "Neighborhood Museum That Works," 12; Nighbert, "History of the Museum," 5–6.

34 Beverly Hall, memo to Dr. [Charles] Blitzer et al., January 16, 1967; Philip S. Humphrey, memo to Charles Blitzer, November 25, 1966, SIA, Public Service, box 2. Other concerns included available funds, time taken from current projects and staff, and the reputation of the Smithsonian.

35 Repeatedly, advocates of ANM stated that incidents of theft and vandalism were nonexistent and indicated that this was overlooked. Marsh, "Neighborhood Museum That Works," 13.

36 Michael Butler, letter to Charles Blitzer, September 18, 1967, SIA, Office of the Director, National Museum of History and Technology, RU 265, box 3; C. Malcolm Watkins, memo to Charles Blitzer, November 3, 1966, SIA, Assistant Secretary for Public Service, RU 145, box 2. Michael Butler, a sociologist, served as a consultant to the Smithsonian Institution regarding the Anacostia Neighborhood Museum.

37 Michael Butler, letter to Charles Blitzer, April 3, 1967, and September 18, 1967, SIA, Office of the Director, Anacostia Neighborhood Museum, RU 265, box 3.

38 Keith Melder, memo to Charles Blitzer, November 10, 1966, SIA, Public Service, box 2; Michael Butler, letter to Charles Blitzer, September 18, 1967, SIA, Office of the Director, Anacostia Neighborhood Museum, RU 265, box 3.

39 John R. Kinard (director, ANM), memo to James Bradley (assistant secretary), July 23, 1968, SIA, Public Service, box 2.

40 John R. Kinard, report to ANM Exhibits and Youth Advisory Committees, June 27, 1968, SIA, Exhibits ANM, box 4.

41 The local artist was Ralph M. Tate. Brownlow Speer described the Tate exhibition as "a good beginning with a brilliant success" for a WTOP Radio editorial on November 23, 1967. Clipping included in SIA, Assistant Secretary for Public Service, RU 145, box 2. However, another review questioned the artistic quality of the sculpture and the reflection of such a show for a Smithsonian endeavor. Jack [Anglim], memo to Zora Martin, n.d., SIA, Assistant Secretary for Public Service, RU 145 box 2.

42 Portia James, "Building a Community-Based Identity at Anacostia Museum," in *Heritage, Museums and Galleries: An Introductory Reader*, ed. Gerard Corsane (New York: Routledge, 2005), 339–56.

43 *The Rat: Man's Invited Affliction* (exhibition booklet), November 1969, SIA, Exhibits ANM, box 3. In the summer of 1969, the DC health department reported that the infestation level in Anacostia was 67 percent, more than four times the recognized "critically high" level. Zora B. Martin, "A Guide for the Teacher in the Urban Area," n.d., SIA, Exhibits ANM, box 3.

44 *Rat* (exhibition booklet).

45 *Rat* (exhibition booklet).

46 *Lorton Reformatory: Beyond Time* (exhibition booklet), October 1970, SIA, Exhibits ANM, RU 378, box 3.

47 *Lorton Reformatory*.

48 Kinard, interview by SIA.

49 Marsh, "Neighborhood Museum That Works," 12.

50 The Smithsonian received nine hundred works of art—only a small portion of which are paintings—as a gift from the Harmon Foundation in 1967, shortly after the philanthropic organization had closed down.
51 *Anacostia Neighborhood Museum* (fifth anniversary booklet), September 15, 1972, p. 14, SIA, Assistant Secretary for Public Service, RU 145, box 2.
52 See Gates Moresi, "Exhibiting Race, Creating Nation," chap. 2.
53 *Africa: Three Out of Many, Ethiopia, Ghana, Nigeria* (exhibition pamphlet), n.d., SIA, Exhibits ANM, box 3.
54 Zeller, "From National Service," 54. The art mobile concept, in which a mini gallery traveled to local communities in a trailer, had taken off in the 1960s, and the Smithsonian's National Collection of Fine Arts (NCFA) proposed such an endeavor in 1964. See *The Mission and Projects of the National Collection of Fine Arts*, report, 1964, SIA, Central Administrative Files, NCFA, 1908–74, RU 313. Notably, NCFA had been circulating traveling exhibits since 1952, when the Smithsonian Institution Traveling Exhibit Services (SITES) was established. The scope of SITES exhibits expanded into crafts, history, technology, science, and education in 1966.
55 Fletcher Smith, "The Wheels of Self Worth," in *Anacostia Neighborhood Museum* (fifth anniversary booklet), 17.
56 John Kinard, memo to Dr. R. S. Cowan, September 2, 1968, SIA, Public Service, box 2.
57 John R. Kinard, memo to Douglas E. Evelyn (administrative officer), National Portrait Gallery, October 6, 1972, SIA, Exhibits ANM, box 6.
58 John Kinard, memo to Dr. R. S. Cowan, September 2, 1968, SIA, Public Service, box 2.
59 Anacostia exhibits schedule, minutes, August 2 and 19, 1968, SIA, Public Service, box 2.
60 John E. Anglim (chief, Office of Exhibits), memo to Mr. Frank A. Taylor (director, MHT), August 19, 1968, SIA, Public Service, box 2.
61 Howard Gillette Jr., *Between Justice and Beauty: Race, Planning and the Failure of Urban Policy in Washington, D.C.* (Baltimore: Johns Hopkins University Press, 1995), 180–81.
62 Frank A. Taylor (director, MHT), memo to Mr. Anglim, August 23, 1968, SIA, Assistant Secretary for Public Service, RU 145, box 2.
63 The ANM is described as a successful neighborhood museum in Edward Alexander, *Museums in Motion: An Introduction to the History and Functions of Museums* (Lanham, MD: AltaMira, 1979), 224–25. Its wider impact on the museum world is discussed in Kenneth Hudson, *Museums of Influence* (Cambridge: Cambridge University Press, 1987), 179–81. John R. Kinard met with museum heads from Europe and Africa to discuss the goals and activities of the museum, such as when Tongolese officials met with Kinard in 1975.
64 John R. Kinard, memo to Charles Blitzer, February 6, 1974, SIA, Exhibits ANM, box 4. In 1987, the ANM changed its name to the Anacostia Museum and opened

in a new structure located in the middle of a landscaped public park, one mile from the Carver Theater building and next to its laboratory-research center, which had been built in 1975.

65 *Anacostia Neighborhood Museum* (fifth anniversary booklet), 2.
66 See Gates Moresi, "Exhibiting Race, Creating Nation," 136–38.
67 James, "Building a Community-Based Identity," in *Heritage, Museums and Galleries*.
68 Burns, *From Storefront to Monument*, 139–40.

Crossing the Gentrification Frontier

The Lower East Side Tenement Museum and the Blind Spots of Social History

Rebecca Amato

In the fall of 2000, the Lower East Side Tenement Museum's most-valued artifact—a pre-law[1] tenement located at 97 Orchard Street—suffered worrying damage as a result of construction taking place at a privately owned tenement directly next door at 99 Orchard Street. Both 97 and 99 had been constructed by the same builder and landlord in 1863. The two were considered "sister" buildings and shared a party wall at 97's northern side and 99's southern side such that, whatever building work was done to, one could not help but have an impact on the other.[2] The damage to 97 Orchard Street, according to a March 20, 2001, report from the New York City Department of Buildings, consisted of a crack to the plaster in the cellar wall, as well as some bulging.[3] While no major structural damage was discovered, an engineer hired by the museum suggested that these issues may be a result of the building settling as construction continued (often without a permit) next door.[4] Such settling had the potential to irredeemably harm 97 Orchard Street and cost the museum tens of thousands in repairs, launching the museum into a battle with its neighbors that would challenge its reputation and reorient its relationship with its own social justice mission. This chapter examines the ways in which a mission-driven museum, anchored in traditions of social history and equipped with a civic agenda, grappled with its role both as a preserver of what was then an underrepresented history and as an unintentional agent on the Lower East Side's "gentrification frontier."

To borrow from Denise D. Meringolo's definition of *radical* in the introduction to this volume, the Tenement Museum's practice of public history was officially "committed to the advancement of social justice" and the "creation of a more inclusive material record." This was true at a time when museums generally were excused from community engagement outside of their conventional education programs. While it would not take long for the American Alliance of Museums (AAM) to call for greater civic engagement among their members with its formation of the Museums & Community Initiative in 1998, the Tenement Museum had already adopted these strategies when it was established ten years earlier. Its original mission in 1988 was "to promote tolerance and historical perspective through the presentation and interpretation of the variety of immigrant and migrant experiences on Manhattan's Lower East Side, a gateway to America."[5] This mission was accomplished through permanent exhibits inside 97 Orchard Street—the interpreted apartment homes of immigrant families who had actually lived in the building—and through temporary exhibits, performances, and educational and community programs. Among the programs were "Around the Kitchen Table" (later "Kitchen Conversations"), a facilitated discussion about the content of tours of 97 Orchard Street, as well as contemporary issues related to immigration; "Familiar Strangers" (later reinvented as a series of workshops called "Shared Journeys"), an ESOL (English to Speakers of Other Languages) class offered at 97 Orchard Street with support from University Settlement; and an ongoing partnership with the Immigrants' Theatre Project, a Brooklyn-based theater company dedicated to staging new work about the immigrant experience produced by immigrant playwrights. By 2001, the museum had been recognized by a number of organizations in the museum and preservation fields, including the Rudy Bruner Foundation for Urban Excellence (via its 2001 silver medal award), the National Park Service, and the National Trust for Historic Preservation. Scholars in public history, museum studies, anthropology, and urban studies had written about the museum as an "agent for social inclusion," a model for public pedagogy, and a museum that had fully embraced its public service orientation. In many ways, the Tenement Museum was becoming a game changer regarding what it meant to successfully interpret social history for a broad audience while also playing a civic role as a site for discussing social policy, particularly around immigration.

Facade of 97 Orchard Street, ca. 1994. Collection of the Lower East Side Tenement Museum.

At the center of the museum's growing reputation was 97 Orchard Street, which had been ordained as an icon of the substantial part immigration had played in American history; it had been declared both a National Historic Site by the National Park Service and a landmark site of the National Trust for Historic Preservation in 1998.

The preservation of 97 Orchard Street—a kind of vernacular building that, for the previous hundred years, nearly every planner and reformer sought to destroy—was deeply radical. Indeed, halting the destruction of the material remnants of immigration was one of the driving forces behind the museum's mission: "When, even with the best intentions, we destroy every shred of physical evidence of a widely shared cultural memory, we suggest that neither that memory nor the people who experienced it are worthy of inclusion in the historical record."[6] So while the cost of repairing the party wall of 97 Orchard Street was one matter for the museum's staff, the harm done to a national landmark was another. In other words, damage to the tenement was not just damage to the Lower East Side Tenement Museum; it was officially considered a direct threat to the nation's heritage. For this reason, by the end of 2001, the museum decided to work with its allies in state government to have 99 Orchard Street condemned through the process of eminent domain. As the museum's founder and executive director Ruth Abram explained, this action was necessary to protect 97 Orchard Street from further damage. More importantly, however, it was also an inescapable responsibility, since "safeguard[ing] a national landmark" was now central to the museum's status beyond the Lower East Side.[7]

Abram's leadership of the Tenement Museum, including the option to entertain the notion of lobbying for state condemnation of a private tenement, benefited from her own deep ties to power brokers in the private and public sectors. Born in 1945 and raised in Atlanta, Georgia, Abram's father, Morris B. Abram, was a celebrated civil rights lawyer who had served in presidential administrations from Kennedy's to Bush Senior's. He was general counsel to the Peace Corps, US representative to the United Nations Commission on Human Rights under Johnson, and vice-chairman of the US Commission on Civil Rights under Reagan, among other posts. In the mid-1960s, Morris Abram was also elected president of the American Jewish Committee and, from 1968 to 1970, was president of Brandeis University.[8] Ruth Abram, for her part, was educated at Westminster Day School in Atlanta, followed by Sarah Lawrence College and then Brandeis, where she pursued a graduate degree in social welfare policy. Her early career extended the legacy her father had already established, although with a second-wave feminist slant: she held positions with the NAACP Legal Defense Fund, the American Civil Liberties Foundation, and the Women's Action Alliance. She also served as president of the New Israel Fund and cofounded Mazon: A Jewish Response to Hunger. Finding herself unfulfilled by these positions, she paused in the 1980s to pursue a master's degree in history at New York University, where she began to imagine a new project to combine public history and social work. While the museum came to be only years later, Abram often credits her graduate work in history as the turning point in her career. Yet it was not just a passion for a "usable past" but the social capital she had acquired growing up among world leaders and occupying positions of prestige in politically liberal nongovernmental organizations that allowed her to catapult the Tenement Museum into its own position of prestige. Without her social status and personal charisma, the museum might have gone the way of countless other house museums that too often limp along with shrinking budgets, volunteer staff, and sparse attendance.

The decision to pursue eminent domain launched the Tenement Museum full force into the center of spatial politics in the Lower East Side, an area that had been battling with what many scholars call *the gentrification frontier* for decades.[9] In the early 1980s, both celebratory and embittered cries of impending gentrification peppered the public discourse around the East Village and Lower East Side, such that US-based scholarship on the gentrification frontier was often derived from studying the area. In 1984, art historians Rosalyn Deutsche and Cara Gendel Ryan published a now well-known essay in the critical theory journal *October* titled "The Fine Art of Gentrification." In it, they argued that the development of an art "scene" on the Lower East Side—as punctuated by galleries such as Fun Gallery, Civilian Warfare, Gracie Mansion, and 51X—was aided by a grander municipal vision of transforming the area into a middle-class residential feeder district for the advancing FIRE (finance, insurance, real estate) economy of New York City. The new class of Lower East Siders would, the vision went, walk to their jobs in the nearby Wall Street area and replenish the city's coffers with new economic and social capital. Artists and curators were complicit in this process of gentrification not just by "pioneering" the area for bourgeois resettlement but by aestheticizing its poverty: "In addition to the economic impact . . . the art world functions ideologically to exploit the neighborhood for its bohemian or sensationalist connotations while deflecting attention away from underlying social, economic, and political processes."[10] Four years after Deutsche and Ryan's article was published, the Tompkins Square Park "riot," in which anti-gentrification protesters were beaten by police, pitted the city and middle-class newcomers against the poor and homeless residents of the Lower East Side. By the 1990s, the "gentrification frontier" had been drawn even as its geographical boundaries shifted and moved farther into the southern end of what constituted the historical Lower East Side neighborhood. As geographer Neil Smith wrote in 1996 in reference to the area, "Gentrification portends a class conquest of the city. . . . Physical effacement of original structures effaces social history and geography; if the past is not entirely demolished it is at least reinvented—its class and race contours rubbed smooth—in the refurbishment of a palatable past." The argument was peculiarly prescient.[11]

The Tenement Museum's founder and board of trustees were not unaware of this discourse, although they remained publicly silent about the displacement that accompanied the acceleration of gentrification. Indeed, the museum's leaders kept a trained eye on fluctuating real estate values as a matter of realpolitik. Ideologically, the museum was both a leader and supporter in efforts to preserve the neighborhood's built environment and defy developers who saw greater financial gain in the process of demolition and new construction than in the careful restoration of historical structures. In later years, the museum would spearhead the proposal of a Lower East Side Historic District to be designated by the city's Landmarks Preservation Commission.[12] At the same time, however, the Museum benefited directly from the introduction of a new middle and upper class on the Lower East Side. The cafés, restaurants, boutiques, and galleries that replaced shuttered storefronts and aged retailers drew tourist dollars and real estate hounds to the museum's surrounding blocks, enhancing the nearby leisure options for visitors interested in exploring the area. Financial reinvestment also meant an investment in safety, as policing increased and crime—already falling throughout the city—decreased dramatically.[13] One local Orchard Street retailer—Joe Cohen, owner of Joe's Fabric Warehouse—even credited the museum for the revival of the Lower East Side: "Since they [the Tenement Museum] came to the neighborhood, the area has new life." Similarly, Buddy Fishkin of Fishkin Knitwear Co. Inc. argued, "The LES Tenement Museum has had only a positive effect on my business. Over half of my customers remark that they've either just taken a tour or are due to join one. They have done a great deal for this neighborhood."[14] With friends in the business community and government, as well as among preservationists, the museum very often trod lightly on the question of gentrification. The only oblique reference to it in its tours was through the acknowledgment of neighborhood change and the frequent need for new populations to repurpose older structures for more immediate needs.

While ambivalent about the gentrification frontier, the museum was forthright about the idea of an "urban frontier," complete with "urban pioneers." The origins of this language were not in gentrification, but rather in the stories of immigration the museum sought to tell. The museum rewrote the established narrative of the Lower East Side as a slum by embracing its inhabitants as Americans-in-the-making and its environment as a totemic backdrop to the Americanization process.

Indeed, in Abram's words, "The pioneer spirit that built this country, its cities, its businesses, its schools . . . was alive and well at 97 Orchard Street," and its immigrant residents ought rightly to be seen as "urban pioneers on the municipal frontier."[15] In this way, Abram hoped, the nation's immigrant

The Rogarshevsky family outside 97 Orchard Street, ca. 1910–25. Images like these helped bring the social history of the immigrant working-class to life by personalizing it as one lived and produced by real, relatable people. Museum Visitors Collection of the Lower East Side Tenement Museum.

forebears might be included among the wagon trains and overland explorers that were so embraced in American national mythology. The Lower East Side could also be recast not as an urban wasteland, but as a "gateway to America." In other words, while speculators saw a Lower East Side replete with undervalued and underutilized land, the Tenement Museum's narrative provided the neighborhood with cultural capital that could be repurposed for the growth of economic capital as well.

The immigrants to whom Abram referred, however, were themselves a select group. Soon after its purchase of 97 Orchard Street, which had been sealed for residential use since 1935 because of the Multiple Dwellings Law of 1929, the Tenement Museum's leadership made the decision to interpret the lives and experiences only of the immigrant families who had once lived in the building.[16] This would allow the museum to be "specific, detailed, convincing and clear—rather than generalized, or 'generic,'" but it also effectively cut off significant exploration of the Chinese, Central American, and Ukrainian immigration, as well as the Puerto Rican and African American migration, that characterized the Lower East Side after the mid-twentieth century.[17] Over the years, the museum's long-term planning vision made the preservation and interpretation of 97 Orchard Street its main priority, with temporary and supplementary programming addressing more recent immigration.[18] Therefore, the stories of four, notably "White ethnic" families—the Gumpertzs (German Jewish), the Rogarshevskys (Eastern European Jewish), the Confinos (Sephardic Jewish from Turkey), and the Baldizzis (Italians)—would form the core of the permanent exhibits.[19]

Significantly and in keeping with the pioneer spirit, each of the family stories revealed a version of pluck and determination that eventually led to an exodus from the Lower East Side, assimilation, and a shift into the rising middle class. The German Jewish Gumpertzs moved to the more salubrious Yorkville in the 1880s, while the Sephardic Jewish Confinos changed their first names and relocated to the new, more spacious residences of East Harlem in the 1910s. The Rogarshevskys became the Rosenthals, with all but the matriarch finding homes outside the Lower East Side by the start of World War II, and the Baldizzis found reliable employment after the Great Depression, eventually moving to Brooklyn.[20] This winning story line highlighted the assertion Abram would make again and again that more contemporary Americans could trace their origins to late nineteenth- and early twentieth-century immigration than to the log cabins and colonial manses of traditional

Image of the Baldizzi apartment kitchen, ca. 1995. Collection of the Lower East Side Tenement Museum.

American lore. Through assimilation, as well as the established route of hard work and an entrepreneurial spirit that were the pillars of the "American dream," immigrants like those at 97 Orchard Street conquered the urban frontier. Whatever poverty or uneasiness one suffered along the way were merely a consequence of growing pains and dues-paying, never a long-term sentence. And anyway, the narrative went on, the struggle was worthwhile because the rewards of American citizenship lay at the end of the journey.

While perhaps unintentional, such descriptions of exalted and temporary poverty and upwardly mobile, assimilating immigrants contrasted with the entrenched poverty and increasing segregation of the Lower East Side's contemporary ethnic and immigrant poor. That these more recent residents of the Lower East Side were included in the museum's narrative in mostly parenthetical ways only heightened the dissonance. Puerto Rican leaders such as Chino Garcia, one of the cofounders of the Puerto Rican community and arts center Charas / El Bohio, had long been wary of this kind of comparison. As historian Liz Ševčenko noted, with "an explosion of writing by social scientists and political commentators condemning the failure of the new immigrants to assimilate and advance in comparison to their European predecessors" in the 1970s and 1980s, linkages between past immigration and present ethnic groups were rarely complimentary.[21] Indeed, Garcia and poet Bimbo Rivas, a prominent member of the Nuyorican movement, invented the term *Loisaida* to both embrace and revise the Lower East Side's immigrant heritage. Still claiming themselves and other ethnic immigrants and migrants as inheritors of this legacy, *Loisaida* activists offered a narrative counter to the one presented at the Tenement Museum. To them, poverty was the result of a voracious and possibly racist capitalist system, not a measure of personal determination. Poor immigrants were simply pawns in the same political economy. Therefore, while "a belief in the past, present, and future probability of upward mobility underlies a sense of common destiny [at the Tenement Museum]," as anthropologist Jack Kugelmass argued, upward mobility was not necessarily within reach of all its neighbors, particularly the ethnic poor of color.[22] American character and citizenship, according to this counternarrative, could not be defined by hard work, desire, and personal integrity so much as by economic and political opportunity and a structural revolution.

Acknowledgment and discussion of such critiques, however, were not within the scope of the museum's mission. Nor was it inclined to challenge the political status quo. As Jack Kugelmass observed, any political radicalism on the part of the museum had the potential to undermine funding, particularly from government supporters.[23] Likewise, with real estate and financial executives such as Peter B. Madoff and Raymond O'Keefe on its board, the museum's leadership was not in a position to critique the city's power structure.[24] Even if, in Abram's words, the museum's premise was to "[preserve] the past as a road map to our future" because "a successful future requires an appreciation of diversity in all its forms and a commitment to democracy," the museum's execution of this goal was primarily a sentimental one.[25] Less interested in citizenship as a set of political, economic, and social rights, the Tenement Museum viewed its work as a step toward cultural citizenship for its immigrant heroes and heroines. As Abram put it, "The intimate stories of the people who rerooted themselves in America . . . together form our collective memory. To understand this history is to understand ourselves . . . as individuals, as members of communities, and as a Nation."[26] The immigration stories, humble and compelling, were, therefore, a key to connecting a more diverse set of Americans to their forefathers and mothers. Through

Fannie Rogarshevsky on the roof of 97 Orchard Street. Images like these helped bring the social history of the immigrant working-class to life by personalizing it as one lived and produced by real, relatable people. Collection of the Lower East Side Tenement Museum.

a sense of shared history—particularly one that merged the pioneers of the Western frontier with those of the nation's cities—Americans might renew a sense of common purpose.

To enhance this interpretation of cultural citizenship, Abram borrowed from historians such as Daniel Boorstin and Arthur Bestor, whose aphoristic writing she often quoted in articles and speeches. Boorstin, who taught history at the University of Chicago for twenty-five years and then served as Librarian of Congress, was prolific in his analysis of American national character. His neoconservative politics made him a notorious target of the political left, but his agility in producing a grand narrative of American history through the three-volume opus *The Americans* (1959–74) elevated his public stature. Abram found his faith in history particularly appealing, quoting Boorstin as saying, "Planning for the future without a sense of history is like planting cut flowers." "Planting Cut Flowers" would serve as the title of her 2000 article for the American Association for State and Local History, and the quotation would appear in a handful of Abram's public addresses.[27] In the same vein, she would turn to Bestor, a constitutional historian who wrote about citizenship and social studies education, to support her claim that inclusion of a larger body of Americans in the national narrative was key to democratic strength. An uncited quotation from Bestor—"Deprive me of my historical consciousness, and in the most literal sense, I do not know who I am"—would appear in remarks Abram gave at the National Trust for Historic Preservation in 1997, "Planting Cut Flowers" and a 2008 Japan Society symposium on preservation campaigns in Kyoto in which she participated.[28] Through quotations like these, Abram sought to affirm that historical understanding was a requisite for national membership. Thus cultural citizenship, in the form of inclusive national history, was attainable through the kind of preservation and storytelling the Tenement Museum represented.

Yet Abram's idea of cultural citizenship was not in dialogue with other public historians such as John Kuo Wei Tchen and Rina Benmayor, whose definition of the term had a far more radical agenda. Tchen and Benmayor defined cultural citizenship as "an identity that is formed not out of legal membership but out of a sense of cultural belonging" linked to greater political agency.[29] This kind of citizenship was a two-way street, with history perhaps providing roots for contemporary experience, but with contemporary experience highlighting the unfinished business of history as well. As both scholars and their fellow collaborators in the Inter-university Program for Latino Research would assert, "The key element of cultural citizenship is the process of 'affirmation,' as the community itself defines its interests, its binding solidarities, its boundaries, its own space, and its membership—who is and who is not part of its 'citizenry.'"[30] For Benmayor, Tchen, and other scholars working in the public humanities, then, cultural citizenship was not only about finding a secure place in the established American mythology, as Abram's immigrant story did, but also about challenging that mythology by claiming political agency and defending separate cultural territories. In other words, Benmayor's and Tchen's were not stories of linear assimilation so much as claims to alternative spaces for the critique of the dominant (read: White) culture.

Against this complex and layered backdrop of encroaching gentrification, narrative distance between the stories of immigration the museum would tell and those of the surrounding community, as well as competing interpretations of cultural citizenship, cracks—both literal and figurative—appeared in the party wall between the tenements at 97 and 99 Orchard Street. While the height of the battle would take place toward the end of 2001 and into early 2002, the tense relationship between the Tenement Museum and the owners of 99 Orchard Street could be traced back years earlier, when the museum began to work on expanding its programming and purchasing another building. In some ways, expansion held the promise of a more in-depth examination of the contemporary immigrant and migrant experience. If the museum hoped to stay committed to the idea of interpreting only the stories of those who had dwelled in its buildings, then the addition of a new tenement that had housed residents *after* the Great Depression could connect the museum to the histories of the Lower East Side's more recent immigrants.[31] In addition, expansion would allow for more classroom and office space, as well as a better opportunity for the proper preservation of its growing collections. After 97 Orchard Street was designated a national landmark by the National Trust for Historic Preservation in October 1998 and declared an affiliated site of the National Park Service in November, expansion would also satisfy the federal requirements for a General Management Plan detailing the museum's future growth.[32] The potential for compliance with the Americans with Disabilities Act through the construction of ramps and elevators in a new, unlandmarked building, as well as more space for the tens of thousands of additional visitors the museum expected, were also desirable.

Before 97 Orchard Street was ever designated, however, Abram and the museum's board functioned in accordance with a "grow or die" ethic. Keen though it was on protecting its tenement, which made the bordering tenements particularly attractive, the museum's leadership also simply viewed expansion as a necessary and inevitable long-term objective. The first attempts to buy 99 Orchard Street, then, took place in the fall of 1997—a year before 97 Orchard Street earned its landmark designation. In a memo addressed to board member John Samuelson from October of that year, Abram was direct: "I believe we should try our best to obtain this building. We don't need space (except storage space) immediately, so, we can take our time as long as we have an agreement."[33] Two and a half months later, in January of 1998, the museum's Real Estate Committee began to formulate an offer to the owners of 99 Orchard Street, one of whom, Rita Eckhaus, a seventy-year-old retiree, demonstrated interest in selling. By June, the museum was ready to acquire the building for an estimated cost of $600,000 to be paid out over seven years. During the seven-year stretch, the museum planned to rent out the ground floor of the tenement for its own needs and allow Eckhaus to remain as a renter in the upper floors for a term of eighteen months.[34] The building at 99 Orchard Street had been Eckhaus's primary residence for years, and it had been in her family for almost a century. This last detail alone would cast a long shadow on the Tenement Museum's expansion goals.

But 99 Orchard Street was not the only building the museum was eyeing. The one at 95 Orchard Street, located to the south of the museum's landmark, was also tempting. The building, owned by the Belov family since the 1890s, was not for sale, but the museum's Real Estate Committee believed "Mrs. Belov" (or "Beloff") might be willing to reconsider her position after she began to receive violation summonses for renting her space to a welding company in November of 1998. "It might be an opportune time to discuss the sale of 95 with Mrs. Belov," the committee's minutes detailed, "after the various NYC departments had completed their inspections of the property." Belov stood her ground, however, even accusing the museum of drumming up the inspections for its own benefit.[35] No sale was in the offing. Other nearby owners also felt the museum's aims were not in step with those of property holders. Randy Settenbrino, owner of 100 Orchard Street, considered selling his property to the museum in November of 2000 but felt the museum was undervaluing the market price. "I was dismayed by the content and tone of your letter," wrote Settenbrino to the museum's leaders. "It is not my priority to sell the building to the museum or anyone else for that matter."[36] Meanwhile, ambitious attempts to expand to the southern section of the Essex Street Market on the former Seward Park Extension Urban Renewal Area through a city-run Request for Proposal (RFP) process were also rebuffed that year.[37] It was evident by 2000 that 99 Orchard Street was the museum's best bet for expansion.

Rita Eckhaus, however, could not sell the building alone. She shared ownership of 99 Orchard Street with her nephew, Lou Holtzman. Eckhaus's father (Holtzman's grandfather) had purchased the building in 1910, and four generations of the family had continued to live there, including Eckhaus and her sons, as well as Holtzman and his wife, Mimi, through the 1990s.[38] Holtzman also operated a sound studio out of the building starting in 1972, just as a spate of tenement abandonments throughout the Lower East Side began. Notably, despite the blight surrounding them, the Eckhaus/Holtzman clan never completely left their property. As Holtzman's personal website highlighted, his son Joel went to the same public school—PS 42 on Hester Street—that his mother had attended years before. His mother, for her part, worked in a shop in 99 Orchard Street through the 1980s.[39] In Holtzman's narrative, his family had worked to maintain businesses on the Lower East Side for decades, particularly, as he put it, "when the Lower East Side wasn't the most popular neighborhood."[40] His grandfather had owned a dairy restaurant on Delancey; his parents had met at the Loew's Delancey movie theater in the 1940s.[41] Family portraits taken in front of the tenement—his mother, grandmother, grandfather, and aunts—captured scenes similar to those the Tenement Museum would show of its own alumni.[42]

This shared history initially built a sort of kinship between Holtzman and the museum. In 1988, when the museum opened next door, Holtzman "compiled an exciting montage of sounds: the clopping of horse hooves, the cries of street vendors and the singing of his father, a Cantor who had lived on Orchard Street his entire life" for its inaugural ceremonies.[43] With the museum's early attempts to purchase 99 Orchard Street in 1997, however, the relationship turned cold. Even if Eckhaus was ready to sell her share of the family's tenement to the museum, Holtzman was not. Offers from the museum culminated in a final attempt in late 1999 to buy out Holtzman for $1 million cash. This offer, too, was rejected.[44] Soon after, however, Holtzman partnered with local businessman Peter Liang who presumably purchased Eckhaus's shares. Their plan was to renovate 99 Orchard Street through Liang's own construction company, Sun Sun Construction. On the ground floor, they would open an extension of the small Chinese restaurant next door at 101 Orchard Street, and on the upper floors, they would rent out apartments

To support his own claim to the Lower East Side's immigrant and working-class history, Lou Holtzman, co-owner of 99 Orchard Street, posted photographs of his family on his anti–Tenement Museum website, http://tenementnauseum.com. This photograph of his mother, Frances, was taken outside 99 Orchard Street in 1939 and recalls similar images of Tenement Museum "alumni." Courtesy of Lou Holtzman.

at market rate. Sun Sun began work in the fall of 2000 and finished in July of 2001. That summer, Congee Village restaurant, which was immigrant-owned and immigrant-staffed, opened at the Allen Street entrance of 99; in the renovated, 325-square-foot apartments above, fifteen tenants moved in, paying a then-exorbitant rent of more than $1,600 per month.[45]

What damages were made and the extent to which they threatened 97 Orchard Street remain a matter of debate. Four "stop work" orders were issued over the months of construction at 99 Orchard Street, but the museum contended that construction continued in violation of each one.[46] Both the architect in charge at 99 Orchard Street and the engineer hired by the Tenement Museum to examine the damage agreed that cracks had appeared in the party wall by December of 2000, but neither was able to determine the degree of harm 97 Orchard Street sustained.[47] Nevertheless, as the museum, the National Trust, and the National Park Service would soon point out, any damage at all was alarming for a landmarked building. Abram, in the meantime, reached out to Community Board 3 (a community-based advisory board within New York City government), as well as local political supporters, to both enforce the stop work orders and identify a plan of action for the acquisition of 99 Orchard Street. "We fear if we do not," wrote Abram to Martha Danziger of Community Board 3, "the Museum will have constant difficulty insuring [sic] the safety and enjoyment of its visitors as well as the physical integrity of its land marked tenement."[48]

Despite efforts from the community board, local council members, and state senators to broker a fair mediation between the museum and the owners of 99 Orchard Street, the bad blood continued. "As a last gasp effort," Abram explained in a public statement, "the Museum appealed to the State. It responded through the Empire State Development arm," eventually voting "to initiate eminent domain proceedings" against 99 Orchard Street.[49] Holtzman and Liang were furious, of course, but they were not alone. By the time the museum and its supporters—as well as Holtzman, Liang, and their supporters—appeared before the Lower East Side's Community Board 3 for a condemnation hearing on January 9, 2002, the entire skirmish had become a touchpoint on the gentrification frontier. What the museum's leadership learned at that hearing, however, was perhaps unanticipated: *they* were considered the gentrifiers, while Holtzman and Liang were embraced as humble and bullied Lower East Side loyalists.

Buoying this configuration was not the legality or the ethical scaffolding behind either side's behavior. With smear campaigns emerging from both Holtzman (through a website, newspaper interviews, damning signage that could be seen by museum visitors, and a conversation with then mayor Rudolph Giuliani on a call-in radio show) and the museum (through fierce accusations about Holtzman's improper use of permits, licensing, and residency requirements at 99 since the 1970s), neither side was angelic in this contest. Rather, the most vicious obstacle the museum faced was its long, lingering inattention to its surrounding community. So determined had the museum's leadership been to secure the cultural citizenship of long-ago immigrants, to create a more diverse and inclusive national narrative that re-created the Lower East Side as a "gateway to America," that the museum neglected its own neighbors. Misdiagnosing the battle lines on the gentrification frontier, the museum found itself with few local allies as it lumped in Holtzman and Liang with the rent-gouging developers elsewhere in the area. More importantly, the museum lost control of the narrative of the Lower East Side. Perhaps it could be honored for its immigrant past, as the museum did so well, but it could not be "set in amber" as a space set apart from the burgeoning and wealth-producing city, as Holtzman insisted. "I want to be the first in four generations of my family," Holtzman declared, "to make money out of this building."[50] Sociologist Christopher Mele, who had studied the century-long history of real estate on the Lower East Side, summarized the situation well when he was interviewed by the *Los Angeles Times* about the controversy: "It's easy to sympathize with the two sides, so the question is, which view of the Lower East Side do you embrace? Is this area a gold mine of immigrant history that should be preserved? Or is it a living, breathing place filled with new and older immigrants who should be protected?"[51]

At the January 2002 hearing, the crux of the museum's argument had been that "97 Orchard Street symbolizes our nation's debt to immigrants past and present and our appreciation that our diversity made us great." To follow, Abram listed a series of reasons why acquisition of 99 Orchard Street would serve this larger purpose: the museum needed 99 to protect 97; 99 Orchard would allow for an interpretation of contemporary immigrant experiences, compliance with the Americans with Disabilities Act, more classroom space, additional exhibition space, and "community meeting spaces"; and the museum would be able to accommodate an estimated two hundred thousand more visitors.[52] The museum's supporters, too, spoke of the importance of nineteenth-century immigration to the nation's history, the desirability of tourism in Lower Manhattan (particularly after the attacks of September 11, 2001), the need for more programming at the museum, and the necessity for building "tolerance through history."[53] All of these criteria were also cited in the resolution of the Empire State Development Corporation, New York

State's economic development agency, to condemn 99 Orchard Street as a "civic project" on behalf of the Tenement Museum.[54]

None of this reasoning, of course, addressed what condemnation through the state's use of eminent domain would do for the people of the Lower East Side. Writers for *Tenant/Inquilino*, a newsletter published by the tenants' rights organization the Metropolitan Council on Housing, asserted that "eminent domain abuse" of this kind was one strategy behind "both primary and secondary displacement . . . often disguised by schemes to 'revitalize' or 'restore' neighborhood through tourism, arts, sports and economic development." Though the newsletter's authors acknowledged the "good work" the museum had done in its historical interpretation, they also argued that use of eminent domain "would hurt the very neighborhood whose values it seeks to extol."[55] In other words, the authors suggested, eminent domain condemnation "for the public good"—a favorite method of Robert Moses during the urban renewal era fifty years before—was only another way to develop and gentrify a neighborhood.[56] Similarly, Martha Danziger of Community Board 3, to whom Abram had written for support two years before, was offended by the introduction of the Empire State Development Corporation in this neighborhood battle. "The irony just smacks you in the face," she told the *Los Angeles Times*. "They want to create a virtual tenement museum in a neighborhood that already has tenements."[57] Danziger's colleague on the board Harry Wieder agreed. An advocate for the disabled himself, he argued, "The museum needs to deal with its access issues themselves" rather than expanding through the antagonistic process of state condemnation.[58] Barden Prisant, another board member concurred: "I think there's a certain unseemliness about bringing in the bully of the state to solve this construction problem."[59] Moreover, as Holtzman and his supporters would underline again and again, condemnation of 99 Orchard Street in early 2002 would result in the eviction of tenants, as well as the elimination of immigrant jobs. Eric Li, the new manager of Congee Village and an immigrant from China who had recently earned his citizenship noted, "Everybody is really scared. Restaurant jobs are really hard to find now, especially downtown and especially for immigrants." Li himself had lost his previous job at Windows on the World after the World Trade Center towers fell.[60] Other workers had endured months of unemployment before finding jobs at Congee Village.

Such local public relations snafus for the Tenement Museum finally resulted in loss of support elsewhere. By March of 2002, a mortgage from

Amalgamated Bank, which was supposed to help finance the museum's purchase of 99 from the Empire State Development Corporation after condemnation took place, was withdrawn. The city, which had promised $2 million to help the museum purchase 99, also began to hesitate on its disbursement of funds because of its own budget constraints. That month, as well, Empire State Development Corporation chair Charles A. Gargano voted against the condemnation he had previously approved. At the same time, city councilmember Sheldon Silver, Manhattan Borough president C. Virginia Fields, state senator Thomas Duane, city councilmember Alan Gerson, and Community Board 3 all publicly opposed the condemnation.[61] A rally outside 99 (and, therefore, 97) Orchard Street took place in April of 2002, where reference was made to a petition against the museum signed by 1,500 protestors.[62] Within months, the entire deal had disintegrated. The Tenement Museum staggered on, publicly wounded and bereft, at least in 2002, of a new building. Later, it would take a more traditional route by purchasing buildings that were already for sale. These offset the museum's legitimate expansion needs but did not fully repair its reputation among its neighbors.

In the heat of the battle between the Tenement Museum and Lou Holtzman, the *New York Daily News* shared one unnamed Lower East Sider's

Protestors lined up outside 97 and 99 Orchard Street during the eminent domain battle. This rally included many of the employees of Congee Village, the restaurant on the ground floor of 99 Orchard Street. (The entrance of the restaurant faces Allen Street.) Courtesy of Tenant.net.

straightforward analysis: "It's the immigrant museum vs. the immigrants, the newcomers vs. the old-timers."[63] As the situation unfolded, it became evident that despite Ruth Abram's efforts to avoid being viewed as an "intrusion of 'uptown' interests on the Lower East Side," as she phrased it early in her engagement with the area's preservation campaigns, she and her museum were still considered outsiders with a mission of conquest. The homemade signs Lou Holtzman posted outside his building and at the April 2002 protest he organized blasted slogans such as "Eminent Domain Abuse," "Hell No We Won't Go," "Don't Replace Living History with Artificial History," and "The Museum Will Not Take My Home."[64] For anyone who had been following the spatial politics of the Lower East Side for the previous two decades, such sentiments were eerily similar to the messages of antigentrification activists in the 1980s: "This Land Is Our Land" and "Speculators get out!," they wrote on signs, sidewalks, and lampposts from Fourteenth Street to the Brooklyn Bridge, the Bowery to the East River.[65]

Until then, the Tenement Museum seemed to attempt to bypass local politics. While its mission could not be divorced from the preservation of the Lower East Side and stories of the immigrants who had lived there, the museum had aspirations that were unbounded by the neighborhood's geographies. The Tenement Museum's "urban pioneers" were crossing national frontiers, not local ones. And leaving the Lower East Side was a key part of

Lower East Siders organize in the empty lot at Fifth Street and Avenue C in 1988 to protest rising speculation and gentrification. Courtesy of Marlis Momber.

this achievement. In the meantime, the museum neglected its impact on the gentrification frontier that plagued its environs.

The case raises questions about the political role of an urban museum like this one in an era of accelerated urbanization marked by reinvestment in the urban core, high-end real estate development, and the displacement of the economically, politically, and racially marginalized. At what point should aspirations to improve the national conversation around salient and underexamined histories—such as those of immigration, poverty, labor, and housing—eclipse the material needs of a local population? At what price should a landmarked building be protected from minor damage when its neighbors are suffering under skyrocketing rents, landlord harassment, evictions, disappearing community resources, and a neoliberal city government that is eager to sell off public assets?

There are no easy answers, but there may be guiding principles. No museum or historic site is free from responsibility toward its geographical neighborhood no matter how laudable its message and meaning. Like the art galleries Deutsche and Ryan discussed in their 1984 essay, museums are not cleansed of their own political meaning—or, indeed, real estate value—because they are committed to art and culture. Museums must align their political positioning in their neighborhood with the values they publicly defend in their interpretive work, even if it means sacrificing their own growth. This is particularly true of those sites that signify radicalism in their subject matter, community engagement, and form. In the case of the Tenement Museum—which oriented itself toward affecting social policy; embraced a despised, urban vernacular building (the tenement); and adopted a storytelling mode that personalized the poverty and struggle of immigrants—the choice to bring state and national interests into its local dispute smacked of hypocrisy. This could have been avoided had the museum paid closer attention to its local context rather than focusing on its own national significance.

There is more at stake than this, however. What the Tenement Museum's embattled eminent domain campaign also demonstrates is that "historical perspective," as the museum's mission put it, is not neutral territory. It is part of a knowledge economy like any other that is molded by power relations as they are articulated through, among other social categories, class and race. Whose history is told, how that history was and continues to be recorded, and who has the authority to interpret it are direct reflections of the dynamics of economic and racial dominance and repression. Social history of the kind the

Tenement Museum embraced came out of a historical moment in the 1960s and 1970s that made these dynamics more transparent and aimed to make the everyday experience of those least reflected in the historical record more available. Thus a museum dedicated to the immigrant experience that recreated the lifestyles and practices of the poor advanced the cause of democratizing the official stories we tell about ourselves and our nation. Yet social history had another concern—that of the role of the state and capital to determine human potential—that the Tenement Museum did not critically address and, in practice, directly avoided when it came to the persistence of structural racism. This intersected directly, much as gentrification does in the United States, with the everyday privilege and material wealth that the museum was able to rely on as an institution associated with Whiteness—not only that of its board and staff but that of the menagerie of its immigrant subjects who, if they had not already done so, were poised to achieve Whiteness.[66] Whether intentional or not, the museum's historical perspective affirmed a social history of Whiteness that failed to critique the ways in which the state and capital construct Whiteness itself at the expense of racial others, the very people whose histories were not fully interpreted at the museum in 2002. It is, therefore, incumbent upon museums and historic sites that aim to radically change our national conversations to also radically admit to their own limitations, privileges, failures, and shared authority with those whose histories are still being told. Otherwise, we reproduce unjust silences and frontiers rather than occasions to listen and build solidarity.

Notes

This essay is revised from Rebecca Amato, "Alien Spaces: Planning, Reform, and Preservation on the Lower East Side, 1880-1920" (PhD diss., City University of New York, 2013), chap. 4 "Settling the Urbran Frontier."

1 *Pre-law* describes tenements built prior to the Tenement House Act of 1879.
2 Andrew Dolkart, *Biography of a Tenement House in New York City: An Architectural History of 97 Orchard Street* (New York: Center for American Places, 2008), 17.
3 New York City Department of Buildings, "Memo from Engineers to Department of Buildings Executive Offices re: 97–99 Orchard Street," March 20, 2001, RG 2.10, Lower East Side Tenement Museum Archives, New York, box 1, folder 2. Unless otherwise noted, all other archival sources are from this archive.
4 Anthony Guidice, letter to Judith Saltzman (Li/Saltzman Architects PC), December 4, 2000, RG 2.10, box 1, folder 3.

5. This mission statement was revised in the early twenty-first century. The new language can be found on the museum's website. Tenement Museum, accessed April 4, 2020, https://www.tenement.org/about-us/.
6. Ruth J. Abram, "Urban Pioneers" (speech), November 9, 1992, p. 16, JTS, RG 1.2.1, box 1, folder 11.
7. Ruth J. Abram, public statement to Community Board 3, "A National Treasure," January 9, 2002, RG 2.10, box 1, folder 3.
8. Sharon Udasin, "A Preservationist, Moving On," *New York Jewish Week*, June 4, 2008; Elaine Woo, "Morris B. Abram; Jewish Leader Was Longtime Human Rights Advocate," *Los Angeles Times*, March 17, 2000. See also Daniel E. Lowe, *Touched with Fire: Morris B. Abram and the Battle against Racial and Religious Discrimination* (Omaha: Potomac Books, 2020).
9. See, for example, Neil Smith, *The New Urban Frontier: Gentrification and the Revanchist City* (London: Routledge, 1996); Gordon C. C. Douglas, "The Edge of the Island: Cultural Ideology and Neighbourhood Identity at the Gentrification Frontier," *Urban Studies* 49, no. 16 (December 2012): 3579–94; Nicholas Blomley, *Unsettling the City: Urban Land and the Politics of Property* (London: Routledge, 2004).
10. Rosalyn Deutsche and Cara Gendel Ryan, "The Fine Art of Gentrification," *October* 31 (Winter 1984): 91–111. It must be noted that the municipal agenda Deutsche and Ryan described did not originate in the 1980s. Indeed, the 1929 Regional Plan and local advocacy in the late 1920s through the East Side Chamber of Commerce promoted similar visions.
11. Smith, *New Urban Frontier*, 25.
12. Alyssa Giachino, "Back the Future of L.E.S.; District Plan Revives," *Villager* 76, no. 51 (May 16–22, 2007), https://www.amny.com/news/back-to-the-future-of-l-e-s-district-plan-revives/; Max Page, "The Gerrymandered Lower East Side Historic District," op-ed, *New York Daily News*, April 26, 2001. For more on the East Village / Lower East Side Historic District, see the Greenwich Village Society for Historic Preservation website at https://www.villagepreservation.org/2012/10/17/your-east-village-historic-district-guide/.
13. Amy Ellen Schwartz, Scott Susin, and Ioan Voicu, "Has Falling Crime Driven New York City's Real Estate Boom?," *Journal of Housing Research* 14, no. 1 (2003): 101–35.
14. Ruth Abram, remarks re: 99 Orchard Street; statements made at public hearing (ESDC), RG 2.10, box 1, folder 5.
15. Abram, "Urban Pioneers."
16. Center for Urban Real Estate at Columbia University, "Policy Brief: A History of the Far Limitation under the New York Multiple Dwelling Law" (New York: Trustees of Columbia University, 2015), https://d37vpt3xizf75m.cloudfront.net/api/file/seK91Cu3Qr2NBDe1q1yp.
17. American History Workshop, "AHW Conceptual Plan," 1990, RG 1.4.1, box 1.
18. Board of Trustees, Real Estate Committee, Long Range Planning Committee presentation, December 4, 2003, RG 1.1.14, folder "Board of Trustees: Long Range Planning

Committee Presentation, December 4, 2003." Of "low priority" were "participation in community fairs/events" and "establish[ment of] platforms for contemporary immigrant/migrant voices."

19 This was the case until 2002, when the Levine family apartment also opened. The Levine's were also of Eastern European Jewish origin. In 2008, the Moore family apartment—Irish Catholic immigrants who lived at 97 Orchard Street in the 1860s—opened. In 2012, the "Shop Life" exhibit was unveiled, interpreting the story of German immigrant entrepreneurs John and Caroline Schneider, who ran the saloon on the basement level of 97 Orchard Street.

20 Dolkart, *Biography of a Tenement House*, 15, 64, 65, 68.

21 Liz Ševčenko, "Making Loisaida: Placing Puetorriquenidad in Lower Manhattan," in *Mambo Montage: The Latinization of New York*, ed. Agustin Lao-Motes and Arlene Davila (New York: Columbia University Press, 2001), 297.

22 Jack Kugelmass, "Turfing the Slum: New York City's Tenement Museum and the Politics of Heritage," in *Remembering the Lower East Side*, ed. Wenger, Shandler, and Diner (Bloomington: Indiana University Press, 2000), 197.

23 Kugelmass, 198.

24 Peter B. Madoff is the brother of Bernard Madoff, principal of Bernard L. Madoff Securities. Both brothers were investigated and convicted of running the largest Ponzi scheme in history. Raymond O'Keefe was a member of the board of directors for Cushman and Wakefield, a commercial real estate firm, as well as former president of Grubb and Ellis NY, also a major player in commercial real estate.

25 Ruth J. Abram, "Remarks to National Trust for Historic Preservation," March 6, 1997, RG 1.2.1, box 1, folder 27. In the fall of 2004, the museum would introduce a radical new program to begin this kind of democratic exchange of ideas, particularly about race, ethnicity, and immigration. That program, "Kitchen Conversations," is detailed in Ruth J. Abram, "Kitchen Conversations: Democracy in Action at the Lower East Side Tenement Museum," *Public Historian* 29, no. 1 (Winter 2007): 59–76.

26 Ruth J. Abram, "Founding Day Speech," July 1988, RG 1.2.1, box 1, folder 1.

27 Ruth J. Abram, "Planting Cut Flowers," *History News: The Magazine of the American Association for State and Local History* 55, no. 3 (Summer 2000): 4–10.

28 Abram; Ruth J. Abram, speech to the National Trust for Historic Preservation, March 6, 1997, RG 1.2.1, box 1, folder 27; Machiya Preservation Project, November 5, 2008, Symposium, Japan Society, New York.

29 Inter-university Project for Latino Research, Hunter College, working group concept paper, 1988, quoted in Dolores Hayden, *The Power of Place: Urban Landscapes as Public History* (Cambridge, MA: MIT Press, 1995), 8-9. It is worth noting that the New York Chinatown History Project—later the Museum of Chinese in America in New York—was codeveloped by Tchen in 1980 and grew out of The Basement, an arts organization partnered with Charas / El Bohio through the Seven Loaves coalition. See Mario Maffi, *Gateway to the Promised Land: Ethnicity and Culture in New York's Lower East Side* (New York: New York University Press, 1995), 26.

30 Rina Benmayor and William V. Flores, eds., *Latino Cultural Citizenship: Claiming Identity, Space, and Rights* (Boston: Beacon, 1998), 13.

31 In fact, this is precisely what the museum eventually did. In 2007, it purchased 103 Orchard Street at the corner of Orchard and Delancey Streets, and in 2017, it launched the new exhibit *Under One Roof*, which details the stories of a Puerto Rican migrant family, Chinese immigrants, and Jewish Holocaust survivors. See "Under One Roof, 1950s–1980s," Tenement Museum, accessed March 4, 2021, https://www.tenement.org/tour/under-one-roof/.

32 The details of the proposed relationship between the National Park Service and the museum are outlined in Ruth J. Abram, "Our Relationship with the National Park Service," memo to Capital Campaign Planning Committee, November 9, 1998, RG 1.1.14 Real Estate Committee, folder "Board of Trustees: Real Estate Committee Minutes, November 9, 1998."

33 Ruth J. Abram, to John Samuelson, October 15, 1997, RG 2.10, box 1, folder 1.

34 Ruth J. Abram, memo to Lou Holtzman and Rita Eckhaus, 99 Orchard Street, June 16, 1998 (draft), RG 2.10, box 1, folder 1 "Correspondence Possible Purchase of 99 Orchard Street, 1998."

35 Handwritten note (unknown author), August 10, 1999; minutes, November 9, 1998, RG 1.1.14, folder "Board of Trustees: Real Estate Committee Minutes, November 9, 1998."

36 Randy Settenbrino, letter to Renee Epps, November 8, 2000, reposted at http://www.tenementnauseum.com/99orchard/Randy-Museum.jpg.

37 Minutes of Real Estate Committee, August 10, 1999, RG 1.1.14, folder "Board of Trustees: Real Estate Committee Minutes, November 9, 1998."

38 Clyde Haberman, "Your Tired, Your Poor, Your Building?," *New York Times*, February 13, 2002.

39 Lisa Keys, "Immigration Museum Called Bad Neighbor in Expansion Battle," *Forward*, February 6, 2002.

40 John Lehmann, "Museum in Bizarre Bid to Wreck Building," *New York Post*, January 4, 2002.

41 Keys, "Immigration Museum."

42 Lou Holtzman, "Tenement Museum: The 'True' History: Family Album," Tenement Nauseum, accessed March 4, 2021, http://www.tenementnauseum.com/album.htm.

43 Keys, "Immigration Museum."

44 Minutes of Real Estate Committee.

45 Jennifer Jensen, "Neighbors Fear Museum Will Make Them History," *Villager*, January 9, 2002.

46 Robin Marcato, email to "John" from Tenant.net, ca. late 2001 / early 2002, RG 2.10, box 1, folder 2 "99 Orchard Street Correspondence 2002"; Ruth J. Abram, "Saving a National Treasure," RG 2.10, box 1, folder 3 "99 Orchard Street Correspondence and Related Docs Re: Code Violations 2002."

47 New York City Department of Buildings engineers, letter to Department of Buildings executive offices re: 97–99 Orchard Street, March 20, 2001, folder 2 "99 Orchard

Street Correspondence 2002," box 1, RG 2.10; collection of memos from Department of Buildings, Sun Sun Construction, and Anthony DelGiudice to Ruth Abram, November–December 2000, RG 2.10, box 1, folder 3 "99 Orchard Street: Code Violations 2002"; Abram, "Saving a National Treasure."

48 Ruth J. Abram, memo to Martha Danziger, November 28, 2000, RG 2.10, box 1, folder 3 "99 Orchard Street Correspondence and Related Docs Re: Code Violations 2002."

49 Abram, "Saving a National Treasure."

50 Brian Kates, "Immigrant Museum vs. Locals: Lower East Side Divided," *New York Daily News*, April 28, 2002.

51 Josh Getlin, "Museum Plan Hits Too Close to Home," *Los Angeles Times*, April 18, 2002.

52 Abram, "Saving a National Treasure."

53 Michael Adlerstein (National Park Service), Susan Chin (New York City Department of Cultural Affairs), Frank Sanchis (executive director, Municipal Art Society), Catherine Cullen (Henry Street Settlement), testimony, RG 2.10, box 1, folder 5 "Remarks made by Ruth Abram re: 99 Orchard Street; Statements made at Public Hearing (ESDC)."

54 Charles A. Gargano, "Subject: New York (New York County)—Lower East Side Tenement Museum Expansion Civic Project," memo to "The Directors" (Empire State Development Corporation), August 23, 2001, available at http://www.tenant.net/alerts/lestm/lestm.pdf.

55 "Eminent Domain Abuse Has the Potential to Disrupt Tenants and Neighborhoods on a Scale Not Seen since Robert Moses Evicted 500,000 Tenants," *Tenant/Inquilino*, April 2002.

56 Analyses like these attempt to trace the consequences to the built urban environment of neoliberal policies. For an excellent examination of similar forces of gentrification, cultural investment through museums, and the marketing of ethnicity, see Arlene Davila, *Barrio Dreams: Puerto Ricans, Latinos, and the Neoliberal City* (Berkeley: University of California Press, 2004), particularly chap. 3.

57 Getlin, "Museum Plan."

58 "Tenement Museum Wants Tenement Next-Door," *New York Observer*, February 4, 2002.

59 Jennifer Jensen, "Board 3 Committee Critical of Museum Expand Plan," *Villager*, January 16, 2002.

60 Kates, "Immigrant Museum vs. Locals."

61 "Campaign Components—Draft," RG 1.1.14 Real Estate Committee, folder "Board of Trustees: Real Estate and Campaign Planning Committee Minutes and Memoranda, March 2002."

62 "[NYtenants-online] Sunday Rally to Support LES Tenants—Oppose Eminent Domain Abuse," Tenant.net, April 28, 2002, available via the Wayback Machine, https://web.archive.org/web/20020604035139/http://tenant.net/pipermail/nytenants-online/2002-April/000141.html.

63 Kates, "Immigrant Museum vs. Locals."
64 "Rally at 99 Orchard St.—April 28, 2002," Tenant.net, accessed January 4, 2021, http://tenant.net/alerts/lestm/rally.html.
65 Janet L. Abu-Lughod, "Money, Politics, and Protest: The Struggle for the Lower East Side," in *From Urban Village to East Village: The Battle for New York's Lower East Side*, ed. Janet L. Abu-Lughad (Cambridge, MA: Blackwell, 1994); Sarah Ferguson, "The Struggle for Space: 10 Years of Turf Battling on the Lower East Side in Patterson," 81, 146; Ševčenko, "Making Loisada," 314.
66 For a pointed critique of the museum's recent exhibition, *Under One Roof*, in the context of its real estate dealings, see Andrew Urban, review of *Under One Roof*, *Public Historian* 40, no. 4 (2018): 169–76, https://www.muse.jhu.edu/article/742287.

Recollections on Interpreting Slave Life and Falling into Your Purpose

Nicole A. Moore

"How did you get into interpreting slavery?" My path into interpreting the lives of the enslaved came after years of rebelling against doing something, anything, related to African American history. It came from often being the only Black person in a history class. It came after years of teachers telling me what I needed to do, who I needed to study, and what I needed to talk about. I arrived on this path to interpreting slavery only reluctantly, after years of challenging others' assumption that I was the content expert for all things Black and the spokeswoman of the Black experience.

I hated it.

The color of my skin did not make me an expert in anything related to the African American experience. It did not make me the scholar on all things Black. I was not your Encyclopedia Black-tannica. I wanted to learn about the second rising of the Klan—what triggered this intense campaign against Black bodies? I wanted to know the plight of the poor yeoman farmers, White plantation mistresses, free Blacks, and overseers. I wanted to get to know the people who were hidden in the pages of our history books, not the usual actors we were introduced to. I was sitting in a graduate course at the University of North Carolina at Charlotte when all of that changed. John Flower unknowingly managed to do what many had tried. He offered a simple assignment in my digital history class. It was something along the veins of finding how history was discussed on the internet and write about it. Suddenly, I wanted to know how slavery was being talked about in the digital world. Who were the thought leaders around the study of slavery in 2006? The assignment led me down a rabbit hole of PBS documentaries and historic sites. I wasn't completely satisfied with what I found and wanted to make sure that more was being done. Without that assignment, and the freedom to do whatever I wanted, I would not be here interpreting the lives of the enslaved and telling the stories that I resisted for so long.

The examination of narratives regarding the enslaved at historic sites, and the history of slavery at them opened my eyes to the amount of work public historians had and still have in front of them. Discovering that there were places more focused on architecture than on the labor that had crafted it was a bit bothersome. More so, the unchallenged suggestion that plantation owners planted two hundred acres of cotton, created by the omission of stories about the people who actually toiled in the fields, was downright disturbing. Yet this was the common visitor experience. The lack of stories and other representations of Black bodies was not so much disturbing as it was sadly expected. Who in their right mind would want to "act like a slave" all day for the amusement of some and education of others? I did not realize it at the time, but I was looking at my future as a public historian. Finding the answers to all those questions has been my work ever since. And to the "acting like a slave" question? Here I am.

It would be easy to say that I was made for this work, but I was not. I had to be comfortable in my own skin and comfortable in the history of my ancestors. When the history of slavery is presumed to interest you only because of your skin, it can be discouraging and dismissive. Some say they are called to do this work. I don't know if I was called to do this, but I feel like it is the best way for *me* to discuss history with others. You have to be comfortable being uncomfortable. I like to think that I am helping people deal with a discomfort that seemingly cloaks discussion of slavery in the United States. While I know many wonderful first-person interpreters like Dontavius Williams, who performs the Chronicles of Adam, or Cheyney McKnight of Not Your Momma's History,[1] I am served best doing third-person interpretation. By addressing visitors in the third person, I am able to meet them where they are and to help them make meaningful connections. Popular culture often provides a common ground for working with visitors to achieve a new level of understanding. The popularity and long history of "Moonlight and Magnolias" tours, which have represented slave owners as gentle and enslaved people as docile—even grateful, has proven to be a challenge for helping visitors recognize the full and complicated experiences of the men, women, and children whose labor not only built the sites but also created wealth for those who claimed ownership of their bodies.

Colonial Williamsburg took a radical approach to interpreting the lives of enslaved men and women in 1994 when the staff and committee on African American Interpretation and Presentations reenacted a slave auction. Then director Christy Coleman defended the decision to hold the reenactment, stating, "The legacy of slavery in this country is racism, and until we begin to understand the horrors that took place, people will never come to understand what's happening in our society today."[2] Making both staff and visitors face the horrors of slavery head-on, while traumatic, can be extremely impactful and important in discussing one of the most painful moments of our nation's past. Today, visitors to Williamsburg can see the lives of African Americans by exploring the Peyton Randolph House, where you can "gain knowledge of the early African American experience . . . and discover how the enslaved members of the household struggled to find their own roads to freedom,"[3] or by walking through Great Hope Plantation to engage in southern plantation life. The Slave Dwelling Project, headed by historian Joseph McGill, seeks to "identify and assist property owners, government agencies and organizations to preserve extant slave dwellings."[4] The project also has a living history arm, Inalienable Rights: Living History through the Lives of the Enslaved. The program, first funded by a grant from the South Carolina Humanities in 2016, assembles living historians who participate in cooking demonstrations, blacksmithing, or storytelling.[5] Each Inalienable Rights experience includes an overnight stay at the site, which must include an extant slave dwelling. These overnights are not your typical sleepover. Often the public is invited to participate in a deep conversation about racial tensions of the past and today and what ways the country can learn from the past for reconciliation in the present and future. These conversations are meant to challenge how we view current issues regarding race in a space that was created by systemic racism. Now in its third year, this small ensemble, of which I am a part, continues to change the narrative of the enslaved population at historic sites. With a multifaceted approach, visitors are able to see first-person interpretation in storytelling, third-person interpretation in cooking, and receive a history lesson in Gullah-Geechee culture. By offering various methods of interpretation,

Inalienable Rights and the Slave Dwelling Project push the envelope, changing the narrative around what the interpretation of slavery should look like while reclaiming often forgotten spaces that represent an often forgotten population. Through the work of these sites and organizations and individuals like Dontavius, Cheyney, and James Beard Award–winning author and food historian Michael Twitty, the public has the opportunity to see the humanity in a community whose members were considered three-fifths of a person. While my story starts with a class assignment in graduate school, the education really began once I got into the field and put in hours of work. It started simply enough with an internship and has been a state of constant evolution ever since.

Taking the Plunge into the Past
The first time I stepped on a plantation to do work was when I interned at Historic Latta Plantation in Huntersville, a suburb of Charlotte, North Carolina. Built in the late eighteenth century by Scottish merchant James Latta, Latta Plantation is a Federal-style plantation home in Mecklenburg County.[6] It is now a living history museum that offers tours of the historic house and grounds, as well as educational programs for students, but was once home to thirty-three enslaved men and women, along with Latta; his wife, Jane; their daughters, Nancy, Polly, and Betsy; and a young son, Ezekiel. What drew me to the site was that it was local and somewhat hidden; many visitors did not even realize the plantation was there, hidden in the Latta Nature Preserve. The history of slavery is similarly hidden in Charlotte. Nonetheless, Latta Plantation and the Latta Nature Preserve are popular with school groups and casual site visitors often respond positively to "discovering" the plantation. In addition to its educational programming, Latta hosts numerous special events, including Civil War reenactments. I was impressed that the site acknowledged the thirty-three enslaved men, women, and children by name—it was the first time I'd seen the population recognized in this way. My research focused on all thirty-three, but I was intrinsically drawn to Sucky, who by all accounts was the cook and Jane Latta's personal slave. I was able to track her whereabouts after the family left the plantation because she accompanied Mrs. Latta to Mount Mourne after Mr. Latta's death. I'm not sure why I was so drawn to her, but Sucky—who was always listed with a child—may have been the reason I've taken such a personal approach to telling the story of the enslaved. Her journey stood out to me, and I wanted to

tell her story. Since then, I have made it a point to speak for those like her and give them the voice history books have, until now, silenced.

During my time at the Latta Plantation, I observed visitors when I was not researching the enslaved. I watched them listen to the tour guides and be amazed at the house but ignore the ditch in the doorway possibly caused by the server who, after bringing food from the kitchen into the house, would stand there until called upon. The tour spoke mostly to the house and the Latta family, and not many visitors asked about the labor. Since the tour was only of the homestead and not of any other buildings, questions seemed to focus on the construction of the home, the rooms, and what the family would be doing in the space. I wondered how the staff would have interpreted the living space of the slaves and talked about the list of names. How would they discuss Peter, who ran away from the plantation in 1826?[7] How would they explain the sale of slaves at the time of Latta's death? The thoughts I had while observing visitors' reactions to the physical structure of the home helped me begin to imagine how to structure a tour that featured the experiences of the enslaved. Watching helped me understand why people come to plantations, and it also showed me how easy it was for a site to ignore its history: visitors weren't asking about the enslaved population.

Based on these observations, I created several interpretive components for the site as a part of my thesis project.[8] One of those components was an educational tour that focused on the lives of the enslaved. When I observed tours, I noticed that visitors connected to the history of the site best when hearing stories about the family. Why couldn't a tour that focused on stories about Sucky; her child, Peter; and the others create similar connections? The perfect place for this interpretive approach was the reconstruction of a slave cabin that had housed the thirty-three men, women, and children who were enslaved by the Latta family. I spent a lot of time in that space, envisioning what the landscape looked like when the Latta family lived there. The slave cabin was a home, something that all visitors could relate to. The tour I designed helped visitors recognize that enslaved people occupied every space on the plantation, from the home to the kitchen to the fields, both public and private spaces. I wanted the tour to introduce visitors to the enslaved population as a community of people who created a world within a world, and who had thoughts, emotions, desires, and skills not unfamiliar to most visitors. One school lesson I created highlighted the impact that the Latta family's economic decisions had on enslaved families. After Mr. Latta's death, his will distributed property—including enslaved people—among his children and to settle his debts. This meant that enslaved people saw their families broken up, as children were sent to live and work on other plantations. I also designed a permanent exhibit installed inside of the walls of the cabin—a time line detailing the history of the enslaved people on site. It spanned forty years and began with two unnamed slaves listed on the 1800 census and ended with the twelve slaves named in court documents detailing James Latta's estate.

My time at Latta proved to me that this was a line of work I was willing to do. I wanted to break down the walls that made history seem boring to average people. These were powerful stories, and I knew they could make history interesting and meaningful for visitors. I also wanted to make sure site interpretation demonstrated respect for the lives of enslaved people. But questions remained. While I was an intern at Latta, I was somewhat removed from visitors. I designed interpretive materials, but I did not do the interpretation myself. I conducted the research and left the difficult work to others. I wasn't sure I was willing to put myself on the frontline.

The Brattonsville Experience

My first professional experience as an interpreter began when I went to work at Historic Brattonsville. This was the first time that I worked at a site in costume, telling the story of the enslaved and really implementing the work I had imagined in my thesis. I encountered many guests who were frequent visitors. They had become accustomed to hearing about White families as the defining residents of plantation homes, and they were often apprehensive about interacting with interpreters who focused on the "hidden population." These visitors were sometimes facing the reality of slavery at these sites

Nicole Moore in costume at Historic Brattonsville. Courtesy of Nicole A. Moore.

for the first time, and I was fully invested in finding ways to open up their understanding. I actively challenged the absence of interpretation about slavery and the enslaved community by finding ways to humanize the experience and connect with even the most reluctant visitors.

Historic Brattonsville is a 775-acre historic site that tells the story of three generations of the Bratton family, located about thirty miles south of Charlotte in McConnells, South Carolina. First settled in the mid-1700s by Colonel William Bratton, the landscape includes three homesteads and historic structures dating from the 1760s through the late nineteenth century.[9] Two locations on the property were particularly well-suited for interpreting slavery, but doing so challenged long-held beliefs and romantic stories associated with the Bratton family.

At the Colonel William Bratton House, located on the eighteenth-century side of the site, the story of Watt proved particularly difficult to overcome and transform in my efforts to interpret the history of slavery. Watt was an enslaved man owned by the colonel and his wife, Martha. Over time, Watt came to represent a romantic view of the relationship between slave owners and enslaved people. According to family lore, Watt "saved" the family during the Battle of Huck's Defeat (1780). Watt supposedly alerted Col. Bratton, a leader of the New Acquisition Militia, about the presence of British captain Christian Huck at his home. Watt's warning enabled the colonel and his group to surprise Huck and deliver a striking blow to the British Army during the Revolutionary War. Watt was rewarded for his loyalty. Though never freed by the Bratton family, he was supposedly never asked to work again. He and his wife are the only persons enslaved by the Brattons whose graves are marked. The tombstone is engraved as follows: "Sacred to the memory of WATT, who died December 1837. During the War he served his master Col. W. Bratton faithfully and his children with the same fidelity until his death. Also Polly, his wife who died July 1838 who served the family with the same faithfulness."[10]

The story of Watt is complicated. On the one hand, I found it rewarding to have a "hero" figure to highlight for visitors. On its surface, the story of Watt is the story of a brave man who, rather than running away, decided to save the family responsible for his enslavement. Watt understood the danger posed by the arrival of the British. He could have aided them in attacking the Bratton family. He could have grabbed his wife, Polly, and run away as the British "searched" for the colonel, securing freedom. On the other hand, I also had to explain why, in return for such bravery, the Bratton family did not grant

Watt his freedom. The idea that Watt remained a "loyal slave," satisfied with "never having to work again," made it appear that the colonel and his wife were benevolent owners. In truth, the story itself is questionable. The only documentation we have is the tombstone and receipts from its purchase. We do not have any direct evidence of Watt's actions or his motivations. Some oral histories suggest Watt did not live a life of leisure. Instead, he was moved to the position of overseer, responsible for forcing other enslaved people on the plantation to perform difficult work over many hours. Yet over time, the romantic version of the story has become central to the site interpretation and the visitor experience. It has shaped their understanding of the Brattons as "good" slave owners. But both the construction of the story through selective use of evidence and the serious questions raised in the story as told point to the need for deeper interpretive inquiry. Can first-person interpretation invite visitors to interrogate how meaning has been created and for what purpose? Ending the site tour with this "feel-good" story always left me a little unsettled. I never successfully reconciled the interpretation. Watt's story provides a window into the constrained choices available to enslaved people trying to make an unbearable situation marginally better. Watt's story might tell us something about his effort to claim some agency by taking a risk on the family that owned him. Perhaps he knew that the family valued loyalty more than anything else, and he understood that his loyalty would be rewarded in some fashion. Was this a way to keep his family together? Was the story false? Was it merely an interpretive trick to make slavery palatable for visitors? In hindsight, I do wish that I engaged visitors with more discussion around Watt's actions and raised questions about the conversations he might have had with Polly or other members of the enslaved community, especially after he learned of his "reward." The story of Watt represents a crossroads where many enslaved men and women arrived: duty to owners or duty to self? Exploring more deeply the diversity of enslaved people's experiences may have helped visitors understand why some ran away while others stayed put.

Visitors also encounter the history of slavery at Historic Brattonsville in the 1820s buildings associated with Col. Bratton's son, Dr. John S. Bratton. Dr. Bratton's home has been restored along with various outbuildings, including a reproduction brick kitchen, original and reproduction brick slave cabins, wooden barns, and workspaces. At the time of his death in 1843, Dr. Bratton held 139 men, women, and children in bondage.[11] I interpreted their lives, stationed in the reproduction brick slave cabin. My job was made more challenging by a variety of inaccuracies on the landscape. For example, the reproduction cabin was constructed with bricks. It had raised wooden floors, whitewashed walls, and glass windows. The average visitor walking into this space is surprised; this is not the wooden cabin with a dirt floor one tended to associate with the experience of slavery. By comparison to that stereotype, the cabins on the Bratton property suggested to visitors that the family must have been benevolent. I explained that it was economics, not benevolence. The Brattons had a brickyard on site, so bricks were plentiful and inexpensive. The Brattons likely ordered construction of brick cabins around the main house because it was more aesthetically pleasing and because the brick cabins demonstrated their wealth. Further, the fact that bricks were not a common material used to construct quarters provided me with an opportunity to discuss the variety of accommodations inhabited by enslaved people, not just on the plantation but also throughout the southern states. Describing who lived in the brick cabins at this particular site allowed me to talk about the roles and living conditions of domestic and skilled slaves as opposed to those who performed agricultural work.

The presence of the cabins did create other opportunities for me to make the experience of enslaved people more visible on the landscape. Using documents and past interpretive history, I discovered that the brick cabins more than likely had small plots for gardening. I asked for permission to create an interpretive garden, growing vegetables that might have been present in a slave garden. In the process of tilling the plot of land for the garden, we found a few bricks buried that had the handprints of the individual who made them. It was a powerful discovery. Indentations like this gave me and visitors direct material evidence of the Black people who had lived, worked, gardened, and made homes on this landscape. Between the bricks and the vegetation, this space became the place where my best interpretation occurred and where interactions with visitors flourished. I was able to talk about the diet of the enslaved. I recall talking to a brother and sister who were interested in what I was doing but were very nervous to talk to me. I engaged the parents with an overall description of the different vegetables that were growing and asked the kids if they liked to eat their vegetables. I explained how the children their age that might live in the cabin next to the garden may not have had vegetables to eat and were given rations of pork and cornmeal. The children would be excited to have something different to go with their pork and cornmeal and probably valued what could be done with vegetables. This opened the eyes of the visitors and helped them think about how important variation to the slave diet was. Conducting interpretation in the third person was crucial because it allowed me to find ways to relate the past to the present, whether by describing the possibility that enslaved people could have visited family on the weekends or by working in the garden. I could break down historical barriers and make it possible for the visitor to be engaged with me in the present as I explained the past.

Working in the garden, I was able to make connections with visitors based on what was growing. It was easiest when a visitor who loved gardening approached me. They often wanted to know not only what I was growing but also about methods of pest control and other techniques of gardening. Many talked about the various deer repellants, electric fences, and sprays they used to keep animals away from their plants, and I described historical techniques for protecting the garden. Creating connections between the work of the enslaved and the hobbies of visitors allowed those coming to the site to recognize the slave community as human and relatable. It helped break down monolithic views of slavery as cotton fields and brutality and opened up opportunities to describe slaves as people operating within a system of oppression. I had similar experiences during cooking demonstrations, whether I was preparing food over a fire outside the cabin or in the brick kitchen at the hearth. During cooking demonstrations, visitors were able to make connections not just to the food but to everyday experiences related to domestic labor and family. Visitors asked about methods of cooking, and those who enjoyed camping were particularly interested in preparing food over a fire. Others marveled at the necessity of preparing food without a recipe and with heavy tools such as cast-iron pots and Dutch ovens.

Most of the visitors with whom I interacted were members of school groups from the surrounding areas of North and South Carolina. The educational programming at the site was designed to supplement classroom lessons on the Revolutionary War, the history of Scotch-Irish settlers in the area, and the antebellum South. While textbooks and teachers tended to associate slavery with cotton, I found that students were quite willing to learn about the complexity of slavery, and they responded to my interpretation with appropriate questions and respectful curiosity. Only a few instances made me pause, like when one African American girl, about nine years old, asked me to speak in dialect. For the most part, however, students understood the deep injustice of slavery and the lack of rights for the enslaved. They could handle nuanced conversations about those who lived on the property, including three generations of slaveholders. Sitting in the reproduction brick cabin, the students heard about varying living conditions for those who worked in and around the main house and those who worked in the fields (and in the "stereotypical" log cabins). They learned about the responsibilities of the enslaved cook and her likely morning routine as well as the responsibilities of a blacksmith, farmhand, and fieldworker. By the time students left the site, they had arrived at a deeper understanding of slavery, what it meant for not only those who lived through it but those who came after them. It gave them a look into the issues of our country that they might not get from home, school, or the news and it was the type of education I hoped that more sites would provide as the narrative around slavery changed.

However, not all the interpretive experiences created successful moments of connection. Often I had to navigate a landscape that included racism that manifested itself largely because of what I was interpreting and where I was doing the work. Visitors asked if they could "buy" me, and they inquired about my skill set in order to put a price on me. Some insinuated that I should be in the kitchen making food for White patrons or that I should be serving visitors when I was on-site doing general interpretation. Even more disturbing were the comments I received from some volunteers when I entered the homestead through the front doors instead of going around to the back. One colleague was against my having receipt books or site information on the grounds because "slaves could not read." My White coworkers were discouraged from assisting me in the slave garden because it would not be "historically accurate" to have someone White working alongside a slave. These things occurred despite the fact that we were doing third-person interpretation on site. I was told that only African Americans should talk about slavery and anything to do with African Americans on the site. I once had to apologize to a visitor who a coworker sent across the plantation to ask me about my clothes, despite the fact that I was wearing the same thing she was. These micro- and macroaggressions didn't make it difficult to do the work, but they did make it infuriating to work collaboratively with my White colleagues. There were very few whom I could sit side by side with anywhere on site to do necessary sewing or cooking, or to generally interact with without feeling as if they were wishing I was their property. It became infuriating to work with colleagues who were unwilling to talk about the slave population because they insisted it was a job only I could do. Meanwhile, I was required to know the entire history of the Bratton family, as well as the history of their enslaved population. Eventually the attitudes of these staff members and volunteers made me decide that I didn't need to work in a racist environment that was not open to fully inclusive interpretation.

Every experience, though, is an opportunity to learn and explore the challenges and wins in the interpretation of slavery, so while things may have been difficult toward the end of my time at Brattonsville, I was able to take those experiences and use them as a framework for helping other sites improve their interpretation of slavery. A few things became clear to me. First, it is crucial for staff and administrators to fully integrate the interpretation of slavery; the work should not fall solely on African American interpreters. Second, site directors must be sensitive to the fact that the history of slavery has a particular emotional weight, and African American interpreters need support, particularly in our current political climate. While I did have support from my leadership team at Brattonsville, there was no direct effort to address the use of racially insensitive language by coworkers and volunteers. Strong leadership can help change the culture on site. Third, regular staff training is essential for creating a sense of command and comfort necessary for interpreting difficult narratives. Before my departure, I asked for and received permission to create and conduct interpretive training for my White colleagues. I walked them through a newly created site tour that focused on the experience of African Americans. The tour looked at slavery in both the colonial and antebellum periods and touched on the difference between the two eras. It was designed to guide interpreters in discussing the slave population with visitors, whether they were officially giving a tour or not. The interpretive guide included information about how to have appropriate interactions and how, specifically, to work with students. After I left the site, I remained in contact with coworkers who had been supportive of me and had been willing to expand their interpretive "territory." They shared with me their experiences in interpreting the slave stations during field trips. I am proud to know that they continued to engage students especially in the interpretation of slavery. They did not report any incidents of visitors taking offense, nor have they been asked about their ability—as White people—to interpret slavery.

It would have been possible for an interpreter to leave a position at the site without offering a suggested solution to the lack of Black interpretive staff. But I felt a sense of mission and commitment to the site's history, to the enslaved men, women, and children I had represented, to their descendants (who are still connected to the site), and to the countless visitors who had asked me questions about the enslaved people who lived there. I was worried about what would happen to the interpretation when I left, especially because my mentor on site, Miss Kitty Wilson Evans, had retired shortly after I arrived. She too was concerned about what would happen to the interpretation. She knew that the story had to continue to be told. I was happy to be able to carry on her legacy and to provide a way for the story to continue after my departure.

On My Own

When I left Brattonsville, I continued to work to improve the interpretation of slavery by maintaining a blog and by doing freelance consulting. I also became an active and frequent presenter on the subject of slavery interpretation at various conferences, including the National Council on Public History and the American Association of State and Local History. This work led to my involvement in both organizations as part of various committees. I also began to network with other people dedicated to changing the narrative. Kristin Gallas and James DeWolf Perry invited me to be an author in the book *Interpreting Slavery at Museums and Historic Sites*. I wrote about the role that race and perception play in how interpretation is given and received. I have consulted with sites looking to expand their interpretation as well as train

Courtesy of Nicole A. Moore.

staff on interacting with visitors as these changes take place. I find the most joy in doing presentations and training simply because I've been there, and I understand some of the struggles as well as some of the joyous moments where interpreters share the wins they've had. Whether it's the guest who decided to challenge everything the interpreter says until they've been presented with information so intriguing they are rendered speechless or those moments when descendants stop by and share family history—all of it makes this job of sharing a "difficult narrative" worth it.

Recently, I have had the honor of being a part of Inalienable Rights: Living History through the Eyes of the Enslaved. I first met Joseph McGill when he wanted to conduct a Slave Dwelling stay at Historic Brattonsville in 2011. Brattonsville would be the first time that he connected with the descendants of the enslaved and told them of the project and why he wanted to honor their ancestors in this particular way. We have been finding ways to work together ever since. Inalienable Rights participants accompany Joe during some of the many sleepovers he holds across the country where a slave dwelling is present. While I do not work for a living history site anymore, participating has allowed me to take part in interpretive demonstrations, educating the public on the lives of the enslaved one site at a time. My role as a cook has allowed me to connect to a variety of audiences—surprisingly, many young White males, who are captivated by my cooking over a fire. They can relate to the methods from their camping trips with either family or scout troops and are often interested in the foodways of enslaved African Americans simply because the food had to be done over a fire. They're interested in the utensils used, from knives to the wooden spoons; the dishes we eat off; and the meats that are prepared because they can relate to working under similar food circumstances. For older southerners, the use of fatback reminds them of their grandmother's kitchen, and for those who grew up not having a lot monetarily, the meager rations of the enslaved echo many a meal for them. Most of these audience members openly admit to not knowing much about the enslaved other than what they might have seen on television or learned about in school, and when they watch a demonstration, they see that to an extent, their life experiences mirror those of the enslaved. No longer is this population less than human; they are very real and the history becomes tangible, and the walls that create "othering" come down. As a member of the board of directors for the Slave Dwelling Project, it's my self-imposed duty to ensure that the interpretive work continues to be a large part of what we

Nicole Moore, costumed cooking demonstration. Courtesy of Nicole A. Moore.

do as an organization while conducting the moments of reflection and reconciliation that take place during every overnight stay.

Taking Care

Despite all the joy that being a public historian who gets to actually do the work of their thesis brings, there is the very real side of knowing when to take a break and take care of yourself. Embodying slavery and interpreting it in various forms takes a very real toll on you mentally. Beginning this work when Barack Obama was newly in the White House was interesting enough—having to hear from people who said, "We have a Black president, is this necessary?"—and in the era and immediate aftermath of the Donald Trump presidency, it can feel like this work is a matter of life or death. There is a real danger in doing this work now because you have no idea who you're going to get or what reaction you're going to get. However, now more than ever I find it important to challenge those who want to ignore this facet of history as we hear rhetoric that historically has had dire consequences for people of color. But the mental health of all who take part in this work has to come first.

When working with sites now, for those that do have African Americans carrying this load, I remind their White colleagues that they need to be the ones to step in and protect their coworkers from abusive visitors and to check their own privilege. It's so easy to go home at night when you do not physically reflect the enslaved community, yet for those of us who wear this costume called the skin I'm in, some days can be demoralizing. At the 2017 Carolina Lowcountry and Atlantic World Conference, I had the pleasure of participating in a panel discussion featuring three other African American women, all of us public historians. Dr. Ashley Bouknight, Elon Cook Lee, Sara Daise, and I discussed the struggles we've encountered in this profession—the resistance to change, the micro- and macroaggressions we've faced from colleagues, blatant racism, and the pain that comes from doing this work. Yet we all are still very much dedicated to recognizing and teaching our history. The session, for me, ended up being the therapy I needed. I had no idea how much I had been holding in, the hurt I'd experienced, and the abuse that I'd dismissed. I realized that I had been used by other public historians who looked to promote themselves but hesitated to give the same energy, effort, and resources to those they drained in the process. It also gave me the sense of community that I missed out on during my tenure as an on-site interpreter. Elon felt it was necessary for Black interpreters to have a space to call their own where we could connect, talk, vent, or just uplift one another, and she had the foresight to create the Black Interpreters Guild, a community on Facebook that has included Google Hangouts, conference meetups, and sincere good vibes. She described the group as "a space for Black/African American museum, historic house or historic site interpreters to learn, share stories and resources, encourage each other and build a supportive nationwide community. We are not alone."[12] It has been so important for many of us to have this community in which to share our experiences and come together, especially when it is very easy to feel alone.

From an unexpected beginning in a simple class assignment, I have built a career that I don't see slowing down any time soon. I can affirmatively say that I don't regret my earlier decision to not fully study slavery when teachers kept insisting I do it. Coming into the subject in my own time and my own way has kept me open to learning more while doing the work necessary to educate the public. Even as my day job at the National Center for Civil and Human Rights pulls me into the twentieth and twenty-first century, I have not stopped consulting with sites or presenting on this extremely important work. I don't think

I'll stop doing the work until sites like Whitney Plantation in Louisiana—where the story of enslaved people is at the center of site interpretation—are the rule and not the exception and until Black interpreters aren't largely the only ones responsible for sharing the narrative. I was meant to do this, and finding purpose in the work has allowed me the opportunity to not just engage thousands of people over the years but truly appreciate who I am, whose I am, and where my own history lies. This descendant of slaves will continue to interpret slave life and tell the stories that are finally being heard.

Notes

1. The Chronicles of Adam, accessed March 4, 2021, https://www.facebook.com/TheChroniclesofAdam/; Not Your Momma's History, accessed March 4, 2021, http://www.notyourmommashistory.com/.
2. Anders Greenspan, *Creating Colonial Williamsburg* (Washington, DC: Smithsonian Institution Press, 2002), 163.
3. "Freedom's Paradox Tours," Colonial Williamsburg, accessed March 4, 2021, https://www.colonialwilliamsburg.org/events/freedoms-paradox/; "The Peyton Randolph House," Colonial Williamsburg, accessed March 4, 2021, https://www.colonialwilliamsburg.com/locations/peyton-randolph-house.
4. Joseph McGill, "About Us," Slave Dwelling Project, accessed March 4, 2021, https://slavedwellingproject.org/about-us/.
5. Joseph McGill, "Inalienable Rights: Living History through the Eyes of the Enslaved," *Slave Dwelling Project Blog*, March 27, 2016, http://slavedwellingproject.org/inalienable-rights-living-history-through-the-eyes-of-the-enslaved/.
6. Nicole A. Moore, "Presenting Slave Life: The Interpretation of Slavery and Its Place in Public History and at Historic Latta Plantation" (master's thesis, University of North Carolina at Charlotte, 2008).
7. James Latta, "Ten Dollar Reward," *Western Carolinian*, August 29, 1826, http://libcdm1.uncg.edu/cdm/ref/collection/RAS/id/1846.
8. Moore, "Presenting Slave Life."
9. "History," Culture and Heritage Museums, accessed May 16, 2018, http://chmuseums.org/history-hb/.
10. "African American History," Culture and Heritage Museums, accessed May 16, 2018, http://chmuseums.org/african-american-history-hb/.
11. "The Brattons, a Family of Physicians," Culture and Heritage Museums, accessed May 16, 2018, https://www.chmuseums.org.
12. Black Interpreters Guild, accessed on May 16, 2018, https://www.facebook.com/groups/BlackInterpretersGuild/.

PUBLIC HISTORY FROM THE GROUND UP

CULTURAL HERITAGE AS COMMUNITY BUILDING

Unintentional Public Historians

Collective Memory and Identity Production in the American Indian and LGBTQ Liberation Movements

Lara Kelland

Introduction

We all draw on a wide variety of sources to make narratives about the past. Each day, throughout the day, we understand our present experiences in the world based on our knowledge of past events. The social movements of the latter half of the twentieth century sparked a powerful transformation in the consciousness of subjugated peoples. African Americans, women, gays and lesbians, Native Americans, Chicanos, and other marginalized groups transformed their communities into much more forceful political presences, but along the way, their efforts also inspired a desire for identity-based history. Movement participants found that their new consciousness led not only to the call for social and political equality but also to a longing for narratives of collective struggles and successes, both present and past.

This chapter considers efforts made by two social movements to author their own history.[1] Alongside their comrades in other movements, both American Indians and LGBTQ activists identified a need for new collective memory forms. Three significant cultural interventions emerged from this: (1) the development of new political identities based in historical narratives that served the movements internally; (2) establishing the groundwork for the demands of community-authored history and heritage practices that underpinned the culture wars of the 1980s and 1990s; and (3) revised dominant historical narratives that ignored or stigmatized marginalized communities.

Individuals came to movement-based collective memory work from a variety of backgrounds. In most cases, activists within various movements tended to be community organizers first and cultivators of collective memory second. Although some gay liberation activists had a connection to academic history (people like John D'Emilio and Gregory Sprague worked simultaneously to bring LGBTQ studies into the ivory tower at the same time that they also developed community resources), still others—like Joan Nestle, Deb Edel, and Jonathan Ned Katz—worked entirely outside of academic institutions to promote popular historical consciousness within the community.[2] American Indian activists usually emerged as community-based intellectuals, as they sought to reclaim historical and cultural authority away from the federal government. They did this through the development of autonomous educational institutions, the symbolic and physical reclamation of place, and the production of pan-tribal cultural traditions. Some Native activists working in the American Indian Movement (AIM) and larger red power initiatives cultivated tribal colleges to repair the cultural damage wrought by a century of church- and government-controlled boarding schools, while others claimed entitlement to and authority over historically significant spaces and practices like tribal lands and spiritual and dance traditions.

The emergence of the gay liberation movement in the aftermath of the 1969 Stonewall riots shifted queer memorial practices away from simple reclamation of famous figures and moved it toward the exploration of a more populist and broad-based gay and lesbian history. As activists devoted to this work began to seek out narratives that would represent a wider array of past experiences, LGBTQ history mirrored the new social history by attending to the experiences of everyday same-sex-loving people. By the mid-1970s, activists and scholars, working both independently and in community organizations, developed a variety of queer memorial practices, including slide show lectures, conferences, films, and other programming to bring the new scholarship to the community. Many community historians developed their projects into books, videos, and exhibits, while others organized community archives and developed more institutionalized history projects.

Similarly, the red power movement deployed a variety of methods toward intertwining collective memory with political identities and movement initiatives.[3] Place held a particular significance for Native activists, and many political actions comingled historically meaningful locations with actions and demands for contemporary community needs. Additionally, a significant portion of red power activism sought policy solutions, a distinction from other movements due to tribal relationships with the federal government.[4]

Additionally, the production of a politicized pan-tribal identity remained a critical tactic, and much of the cultural activism involved strategies for producing and securing a pan-tribal consciousness. The demand for self-determination and cultural autonomy in religion and other cultural practices proved a fundamental part of this work. Prior to this era, dominant US culture had used American Indian culture and heritage in exploitative ways, especially in matters of heritage tourism, and as such, part of the struggle sought to reclaim interpretive authority over cultural forms like powwow dances and historical narratives tied to heritage tourism.

Separatism and Self-Determination
As one of the more significant cultural interventions of this era, activists from both movements worked against the silencing effects of what one historian has called "archival power."[5] To counteract narratives that told a history of inferiority, inconsequence, and nonexistence, movement historians created new methods for researching their pasts, at times relying on nontraditional sources, reading archival traces against the grain, and collecting documents that mainstream archives and historians had ignored or overlooked. Recognizing the discursive power of archival collections, community historians often modified more traditional archival practices, including materials that represented the experiences and lives of the marginalized and also broadening the array of possible sources of historical information. Social movement leaders understood that the institutional ownership of historical narratives was another form of imperial power and subjugation and that demanding cultural ownership of such was a critical act in their own liberation.[6]

Cultural, educational, and historical separatism was a central goal for the red power movement. Educational institutions had been a deeply subjugating force in Native communities throughout the nineteenth and twentieth centuries, as Indian boarding schools served as a fundamental link between US federal government paternalism and the project of cultural repression. Some private and some Bureau of Indian Affairs–facilitated boarding schools removed indigenous youth from their tribal and familial contexts and sought to enculturate the next generation of Native communities in the ways of hegemonic American society, oftentimes through significant brutality and neglect. Boarding school policy prohibited the use of tribal languages, and school leadership usually understood that part of their institutional mission was to eradicate the traditional cultural practices of Native communities.

As such, boarding schools increasingly became a target of Native activism during the twentieth century, and the schools served as both a potent symbol of the need for self-determination and cultural autonomy and a touchstone for the cultural activism engaged in this chapter.

For American Indian activists like Raymond Nakai and Jack Forbes, one of the major strategies for cultivating a greater awareness of Native heritage was in the development of tribal colleges. These community-controlled institutions were envisioned as an alternative to mainstream colleges and universities, which had embraced a curriculum that was either silent on Native issues or represented indigenous cultures, experiences, and histories in a woefully inadequate manner. As a correction to this, the plan for tribal colleges sought to shift control of Native education back to the tribal communities as well as incorporate indigenous culture into all aspects of postsecondary learning.

Beyond the production of identity, movement leaders envisioned tribal colleges as a space in which to cultivate the next generation of tribal leadership, both as a general preparatory experience that built character and leadership skills and also as professional development for specific fields. Planners asserted that it was very important to have "strong programs in Native American history, anthropology, religion, [and] folklore" to facilitate the general development of students.[7] Part of the reason these fields were underscored was their significance to cultural heritage, but they were also seen as opportunities to rewrite dominant narratives about indigenous cultures, as "some of these fields have been dominated by an Anglo-American point of view, often to the detriment of the Indian community."[8]

In 1968, the Navajo Nation established the Navajo Community College (NCC) in Tsaile, Arizona, and by early 1969 offered classes and an associate degree. The first of its kind, other tribal colleges and universities (TCUs) shortly followed, including United Tribes Technical College in North Dakota (1969), the Cankdeska Cikana Community College in North Dakota (1970), the Sinte Gleska University in South Dakota (1970), the D-Q Community College in California (1971), the Oglala Dakota College in South Dakota (1971), Turtle Mountain Community College in North Dakota (1972), Nebraska Indian Community College (1973), Sitting Bull College in North Dakota (1973), and the Blackfeet Community College in Montana (1974). By the twenty-first century, there were over thirty such institutions granting degrees across tribally held lands located in the US. TCUs were founded to address a decades-long desire for American Indians "to achieve participation in and control over their educational systems."⁹ Although the ideological underpinnings for TCUs could be linked to early and mid-twentieth-century conversations and organizational work, serious efforts emerged in the mid-1960s toward institutionalized tribal control over education at the primary, secondary, and postsecondary levels.

In a brochure, NCC explained its purpose as an important step toward political self-government, recognizing its status as the first college to be located on a reservation, the first to be controlled by an Indian board of regents, and the first institution to be developed for the sole purpose of fulfilling the educational needs of young Native Americans. The brochure also educated its readers on the importance "that these educational systems be directed and controlled by the society it is intended to serve."[10] In fact, activists would settle for no less than complete control over the tribal college.

NCC was an endeavor to create an educational environment that sustained tradition but also reformulated it for the contemporary needs of the red power movement. Rather than seeking to transmit Native traditions in a static manner, administrators recognized that education needed to be relevant to immediate needs within the community by observing that, within the Navajo community, "in between the spectrum of both the traditional and progressive Indian lies the majority of the Navajo, the moderate Indian, who has embraced a portion of the Indianness and white man's way of life."[11] The vision for this balance emerged from debates that included the perspective of young Indians. In 1969, students responded to the heavy emphasis on history and culture within the curriculum: "Teaching us Navaho history, religion, and culture is good, but [not] trying to convert us back to real traditional Navahos, to the extreme. We can learn the old Navaho ways, but not stuff it down the student's throat in terms of helping them find their identity.... This is a different generation with a different environment."[12] It is clear that the students' concerns impacted administrators, as just a few years later the accreditation report directly discussed making such changes.[13] Ultimately, although the preservation of traditional culture was fundamental to the project of tribal colleges, a younger generation of activists ensured that these initiatives were constantly in touch with contemporary political struggles while also ensuring community control over historical narratives and cultural preservation.

Queer Separatism

Like their Native activist counterparts, the establishment of archives and the development of research networks within the gay liberation movement proved an important strategy in claiming and owning LGBTQ history. Early efforts at finding archival sources for same-sex-loving experiences in the past proved to be daunting. Yet one of the first researchers to undertake a sizeable gay history research topic, Jonathan Ned Katz, remembered not a dearth of sources but rather other mainstream institutional barriers that silenced love letters and buried other traces of queer history. Although often closeted themselves, queer librarians and archivists also proved quietly useful in the early days of Katz's research, as they would surreptitiously point him toward appropriate boxes.[14] Early scholars working on LGBTQ history topics shared information with one another on both methods and resources. Gregory Sprague corresponded with a variety of researchers regarding his projects to "hit pay dirt" as he mined what he could from traditional archives. Grassroots lesbian historian Judith Schwarz also corresponded with Jonathan Katz, alerting him to archival items in the FBI files at the National Archives that documented numerous lesbians who had not yet been written about.[15] Suggestions and hints regarding how to locate sources were passed back and forth in letters between individual scholars doing research for books, slide shows, films, and community history courses. These letters illuminate the creative strategies necessary for LGBTQ historians working within an archive organized by forms of knowledge that did not recognize nor document gay and lesbian historical experiences.[16]

Although many LGBTQ researchers began to develop LGBTQ historiography as they learned to work within existing mainstream repositories, other activists began to cultivate separatist organizations, providing community-controlled archival spaces for those seeking to learn more about queer history. One of the oldest and most significant lesbian feminist history organizations in the United States, the Lesbian Herstory Archives (LHA), emerged out of the young Gay Academic Union proceedings in late 1973 / early 1974. Women members of the GAU who felt a need for a women-only space formed a consciousness raising group to address both a political need for self-determination and a cultural need for lesbian history and representation. As the group focused its efforts more on the collective queer women's past, its members began to pool their personal collections and actively collect additional materials pertaining to same-sex women-loving experiences.[17]

For members of the LHA collective, the personal commitment to archival work did not end, however, with the donation and collection of materials. Rather, many of these women began to commit their own labor and much of their leisure time to the project. Perhaps most notably, founding member Joan Nestle cared for the entire archives in her Upper West Side apartment from 1974 to 1991. During the years that Nestle maintained the collection in her apartment, the holdings grew from a few boxes to an archive filling several rooms. Women from all over the world began to travel to the archives, and Nestle and other volunteers welcomed them, offering research support, camaraderie, and warm mugs of tea.[18]

As LHA grew, members of the collective fiercely held to their commitment of being a grassroots, community-held organization in the service of lesbians across the world. To this end, in a conversation with other LGBTQ historians, Nestle underscored the importance of keeping the archives entirely separate from a patriarchal institution, insisting, "[Lesbians] should be in control of our own materials, our own history."[19] Similarly, the Archives prohibited men from using the space and collections, a policy that lasted through the 1970s and well into the 1980s.[20] The archives also maintained a strict commitment to a nonelite atmosphere in order to guarantee accessibility for all lesbians. Policies such as these produced an archival space that was as much a community center as it was a repository for historical materials. Throughout its organizational history, collective members remained committed to the archives as "a cultural institution which, though it plays a dynamic role in the Lesbian community, is, at its core, a safe, nurturing environment, a mixture of library and family album."[21] This commitment led to the organization not simply serving as a historical resource for lesbians, but as a social and political organizing space as well.

Although community archival projects flourished during the 1970s and early 1980s, movement historians diverged over whether to keep the historical assets in the community or to bring LGBTQ history into mainstream repositories. While frustration with mainstream archival practices led members of the Canadian Gay Archives, the organization that published the *Gay Archivist* newsletter, to argue for community-held repositories,[22] others felt that keeping such historical materials out of mainstream institutions was a disservice to the history and the community.

Beyond the question of ownership of materials, LGBTQ archivists passionately debated one another over issues of access and collections control. Such conversations took place in a professional space that encompassed both self-trained community historians and professionally trained gay and lesbian archivists. Deborah Edel, an activist first and archivist second, lamented that some authors and artists in the community, although otherwise very supportive of LHA, deposited their own papers at a mainstream institution. Some of these women thought that their papers would receive a higher level of preservation care and were also desirous of the legitimacy bestowed by prestigious mainstream archives.[23] Another reason to entrust LGBTQ historical materials with mainstream institutions was articulated by Chicago GAU member Jim Monahan, who urged gay historians "to integrate the past into [mainstream] historical thinking."[24] Although Monahan recognized the importance of early archival activism in the hands of the community, he argued vehemently against keeping such materials in separatist organizations: "The only separation and faction this archival movement can tolerate is one that allocates tasks, and divides the labor required to bring the gay archives into, and thereby creating, the major research centers that hold them."[25] While Monahan advocated for sensitivity and security for LGBTQ historical materials, his main concern was the consolidation of gay materials into one or a few centrally located repositories within academic libraries.

In response, Joan Nestle came out against the removal of local and community control of historical materials. The occasion gave Nestle the opportunity to put forth a practice she termed *radical archiving*. Applied to the Lesbian Herstory Archives, radical archiving called not only for community ownership but also for community responsibility for the archives:

> 1. All lesbian women must have access to the Archives; no academic, political or sexual credentials may be required for usage of the collection; race and class must be no barrier to the use or inclusion. 2. The Archives will collect the prints of all our lives, not just preserve the records of the famous or the published. Every woman who has had the courage to touch or desire another woman deserves to be remembered here. 3. The Archives shall be housed within the community, not on an academic campus which is by definition closed to many women, and shall be curated and maintained by lesbians. 4. The community should share in the work of the Archives. 5. The Archives shall be involved in the political struggles of all lesbians. 6. Archival skills shall be taught, one generation of lesbians to another, breaking the elitism of traditional archives. 7. Funding shall

be sought from within the communities the archives serves, not from the government or mainstream financial institutions.[26]

For Nestle, the practices connected with maintenance of the archives were woven into the daily fabric of the community and as such were intertwined with the political struggles and other needs of that community. To this end, the lesbian community had an obligation to share in the work and financial well-being of the institution, and in return, the community had a stake in a cultural organization that was open and available to all members as a cultural, historical, political, and social resource.[27] Although both Monahan and Nestle wanted LGBTQ history to serve the community, their significant disagreements illustrate the tension between using LGBTQ history for community building and identity-making, and the effort to gain mainstream acceptance through claiming a place in the national historical narrative.

Movement Education

While movement members held that cultural separatism was an important goal, they also worked to infuse historical narratives into movement rhetoric and culture, both to cultivate new political identities and to contextualize movement efforts in a history of struggle. For Native American activists, such work often took place under the auspices of tribal colleges. For queer activists who were beginning to build community institutions, alternative forms of community education served as a primary means of narrative sharing and identity building.

Educational activists sought to rectify centuries of cultural damage wrought by boarding schools through the promotion of multicultural curriculum, active engagement with tribal languages, school calendars that honored holidays that were significant to Native populations while disregarding US dates, fieldwork that cultivated pan-Indian consciousness by bringing students into other tribal contexts, school space designed by Native architects, and a history curriculum that was organized around, in part, the political narrative of US-Native conflict.[28] From the preschool through postsecondary years, Native educators cultivated educational experiences that fulfilled the cultural, spiritual, and political needs of Native students.

For American Indian activists, the higher educational institutions failed to serve the needs of indigenous communities. To rectify this, educational activists envisioned that the colleges would conserve individual tribal traditions but also nurture pan-tribal consciousness and movement building. Planners like Jack Forbes sought to "do more than merely 'preserve' tribes . . . [but also] be the means for educating large numbers of Indians in an environment suitable for the development of self-confidence, both individual and collective."[29] Native education activists, like their contemporaries in other movements, recognized the importance of identity development in both creating stable individuals and an empowered community. In fact, tribal colleges were categorically charged with the task of assisting "students [with] their [college] orientation by developing a pride in the Native American heritage."[30] From their first encounter with tribal institutions, students would receive messages that directly contradicted the false stories about Native culture, history, and identity that they had received from dominant society.

From its inception, Navajo heritage was envisioned as a critical component of the curriculum at NCC. Furthermore, it was "absolutely necessary for every individual to respect and understand his culture and his heritage," and this knowledge was intimately tied to the future of the tribe.[31] Here the tension between the pan-tribal impulses of the larger red power movement and the desire of some activists to focus their efforts within tribal bounds emerges most clearly. For many NCC leaders, the preservation of Navajo traditions superseded the development of pan-tribal movement building.

NCC organizers were mindful that their new college emerged as part of a national and even international push for cultural ownership over education and the transmission of heritage. As students staged sit-in protests to establish Black studies programs on campuses across the country and women were also beginning to demand courses that addressed gender issues, administrators contextualized NCC within the larger milieu of both radical educational reform and the larger social movements that gave birth to such. As Navajo tribal chairman Raymond Nakai identified, recent activism "has called to our attention the very real fact that we cannot ignore the minorities in our land—whether they are housed in ghettos, in the cities, or reside on reservations. The minorities, regardless of race, color, creed, and their convictions, are praying, pleading, and protesting to make their hopes and dreams known."[32]

Curricular goals also echoed the causal relationship between autonomous tribal education and the production of new political, heritage-based identities for Native youth. This correlation could be seen most clearly in the objectives for the Native studies major, which sought to inculcate students with "respect [for] Navajo history, culture, and language" and pride for being both Navajo and Indian, working toward "Indian unity and cooperation" and engaging "sacred and historical places important to Navajo culture."[33] Curriculum planners also saw the major as providing a significant foundation for the entire curriculum at the college, as it would prepare students with a fundamental knowledge of their history, culture, and the contemporary issues facing the tribe.[34]

Like other movement educational initiatives, the curriculum at NCC somewhat mirrored those of mainstream colleges but was also understood as in service to the larger needs of the political movement. Historical and cultural narratives served as instructional examples but also as models for the kind of leadership needed by the red power movement:

> The history, tradition and culture of our Indian heritage are full of the tales of brave, proud men who led our people in peace and in war. Today, we face a new kind of battlefield, the battlefield of the dominant culture. Many of our reservations, our pueblos, our Indian communities are desperately in need of positive change. On every front we face crises, including education, housing, health care and economy. We worry that our culture will be lost, our young people will join the mainstream, our identity disappear.[35]

Here activists make clear that their educational initiatives are squarely in service of larger movement goals, and that cultural and linguistic preservation was intertwined with other key issues of the movement.

US national holidays like the 1976 bicentennial provided an interesting opportunity for the school. While acknowledging the complexity of engaging with the origin narrative of settler colonialism, Navajo Community College's presidential newsletter laid claim to a part in that narrative:

> Indians are very much a part of this nation's history. . . . We were Americans for thousands of years before Europeans came to our land and eventually built a United States in it. The most distinctive thing about America are Indian—from the agricultural and medical contributions of our ancestors, to the fact that we have no peasants in America. Without Indian corn, tobacco, potatoes, beans, tomatoes, chocolate, cotton, and rubber, more than half of the US agricultural income would not exist.[36]

Although tribal college leadership devoted significant energy toward decolonizing Native collective memory, they also recognized that there was power in connecting the narrative to commemoration in mainstream culture. By resisting historical erasure in the national narrative, activists generated pride based on their role in larger historical forces such as agricultural development and the cultivation of foodways.

Movement education in the LGBTQ communities emerged out of community archiving projects but also had more informal qualities than other movements' educational efforts. LGBTQ activists who worked on the cultural front of the movement were passionate about sharing the collective past with other queer folk. These movement historians held dear the intimate connection between identity and history and eagerly sought to return their research to the community. Out of this desire, LGBTQ historians developed community-based slide shows that were joyfully delivered and eagerly received. As improvised community centers filled to capacity with cheering crowds, young gays and lesbians coming of age during the 1970s and 1980s received an informal education in their own histories. Documentary films that attended to the historical experiences of same-sex-loving folks such as *Word Is Out* and *Before Stonewall* also blossomed during this period, further generating interest in LGBTQ history. As queer historians reached out to the community through their educational efforts, they extended the larger movement goal of crafting a new political identity to the individual members of the movement.

Beyond LHA, many other community historians and activists in LGBTQ history projects utilized the communicative power of the slide show. On a given Friday or Saturday night during the mid-1970s to the mid-1980s, queers in towns across the country could take in a traveling slide show on an impressive array of same-sex-loving topics. Some shows were part of what would turn into scholarly research projects; some came out of the collective efforts of community history projects. Yet others were simply labors of love for a gay or lesbian individual who felt passionate enough about an LGBTQ historical topic to undertake research and produce a visual narrative. A number of the shows focused on simple historical inquiries bounded by space and time, such as *Lesbians and Gay Men in Early San Francisco, 1849–1880*; *Our Boston Heritage*; *From the Gay and Lesbian Rights Movement to the Holocaust, 1860–1935*; and *100 Years of the Lesbian in Biography*. In other cases, slide show content reflected the growing transnationalism of the LGBTQ movement, covering topics as broad as *African Women in Antiquity: Lesbian Themes among the Amazons*, *Mayan and Mexican Goddesses*, and *Gay Germany*. Topics that echoed gynocentric themes flourished within the lesbian community, including *The*

Goddess and the Witch, *The Mother Goddess*, *Lesbian Erotica by Women Artists*, and *Yantras of Womenlove*. Cultural history themes also proved quite popular, including *What the Well-Dressed Dyke Will Wear—Dyke Fashion, 1900–Present*; *Gay Science Fiction*; *Lesbian Masquerades*; *Lesbian Pulp: Twilight Tales*; *Styles of Being Lesbian, 1890–1945*; *Lavender Letters: Lesbians in Literature*; and *The Captive* (1922). Still others underscored the importance of community to earlier generations, some examples of which were *A Family of Friendship—Portrait of a Lesbian Friendship Group*, *Marching to a Different Drummer*, *From Boston Marriage to the Tell-All '70's*, and *The Heterodoxy Club of Greenwich Village*.[37]

Identity Cultivation

For activists of the 1970s, creating new political identities based on narratives of the past served as a key cultural strategy for movement building. For American Indians, this entailed rebuffing negative stereotypes and dispelling the myth that by the twentieth century, Native culture had been assimilated into mainstream US society. For LGBTQ activists, this entailed new research strategies and sharing narratives through print and visual forms.

One of the more interesting examples of the redefinition of identity through heritage is the evolution of powwows. The history of powwows is a complex one and echoes larger themes in twentieth-century American Indian history: namely, the resistance to both assimilation to and the exoticization that came from dominant US society. One scholar of Native American history and culture has called powwows "one of the most powerful expressions of identity in the contemporary Indian world."[38] Powwow gatherings were a contested space, cultivating group and individual identity and simultaneously providing White audiences with a screen on which to project their racialized ideas of the American Indian.

The rise of powwows in post-WWII America is noteworthy as an expression of a new pan-tribal consciousness, but it's also a culmination of decades of resistance to policy that sought to repress dancing traditions. The first significant suppression of dancing culture came in the late 1880s, as the Ghost Dance ritual emerged, a new religious practice embraced across tribal lines.[39] In 1890, the Wounded Knee Massacre emerged out of, in part, policy makers and Bureau of Indian Affairs (BIA) officials' fear of the practice, and the ensuing slaughter of over two hundred Lakota people reflected the growing federal discomfort with Native cultural expression. BIA staff often sought to control tribal dances, and during the 1920s, some agents created "The Secret

Dance File," a collection of reports on dancing traditions gathered under the leadership of BIA director Charles Burke, intended to help staff recognize and suppress cultural expression.[40] These documents denounced dancing practices as amoral and identified them as a barrier to the assimilation envisioned by Burke's administration.[41] Despite this repression, powwow traditions emerged, echoing many different tribal war dances and even the Wild West shows of the late nineteenth and early twentieth centuries.[42] Dances increasingly appeared in local fairs across the West, and one particularly well-institutionalized example was the fifty-year powwow that took place in Flagstaff, Arizona.

In 1929, a group of Flagstaff city boosters seized upon local tribal cultures as both a tool for economic development and an attempt at cultural inclusion with the numerous tribes from the area. Although the event was envisioned to support a cross-cultural exchange, there were no Native participants in planning or producing the event. The powwow's 1939 brochure details the "Indian Village," inviting White participants to visit the space and purchase handiwork from Native residents, calling the opportunity to buy authentic crafts a "golden opportunity." In fact, the village itself was billed as an attraction, alerting White spectators to the fact that during the social dances held there, they were free to watch and even join in.[43] By the 1960s and 1970s, the tone of the descriptions of the Indian Village had much more fully developed objectification as a part of the festival experience, and festival planners found themselves increasingly confronting rising red power activism.

Powwow events like the Flagstaff festival held a complicated place within the growing American leisure culture in the twentieth century. Such events served as a space where racialized views of Native Americans were produced and reinforced, but they also provided spaces for the nurturing of Indian pan-tribal identity and culture. By capitalizing on the fascination and exotic lure perpetuated by dominant society, they reinforced ideas of Native communities as primitive and subordinated. But they also challenged the idea that warfare and other policies had eradicated Native cultural expression and gave dancers the opportunity to craft a new sense of self that transcended the bounds of individual tribes while also celebrating Indianness. Although the AIM protests sought to reclaim Native dancing culture from White boosters and spectators, their own political consciousness was built, in part, on the changing definition of community nurtured by powwow culture.

On July 2, 1972, under a clear, cool summer sky in Flagstaff, Arizona, an audience waited with excitement for the Navajo-Yei-Be-Chai dancers to take the stage. Instead, a group of American Indian Movement activists took over the announcers' booth and flooded the stage just as the dancers began to move into the arena. The demonstrators encircled the dancers as they began their ritual movements, and off-site, other activists cut the power to the PA system. The audience became aware of a scuffle in the announcers' booth, and an audience member yelled, "Let him speak!" One of the protestors stepped forward in the booth and, in a projecting voice, declared that "the Indian people should not have come to the Pow Wow and performed sacred ceremonies for money," suggesting instead that participants needed better housing, food, educational opportunities, health services, and jobs. After a number of activists were arrested, many remained, maintaining a protective circle around the dance.[44] For these activists, Native heritage was not an object to be commodified or to serve as amusement for White audiences but rather a sacred practice that should be for tribal sustenance. AIM continued to make cultural interventions by crafting a new pan-tribal identity through movement literature and the tactical occupations of sacred space, including sites like Alcatraz Island, the Pine Ridge reservation, and Ellis Island.

For LGBTQ activists, the construction of a new political and explicitly public identity was at the very core of their work, for if the general public didn't understand themselves as queer, there would be no movement. As such, a claim to the past was especially integral to developing a shared identity that was based on visibility and resiliency. As many LGBTQ people had been disowned by biological family and thus estranged from more traditional forms of heritage, the need to craft a new lineage was fundamental to the success of the movement. Queer activists wove historical themes into movement writings and events to cultivate queer identity that was based on narratives of resilience and resistance.

By asserting the endurance of same-sex-loving practices and individuals, activists crafted both an internal sense of self and an external community image that linked resilience and strength to the LGBTQ community. In 1979, historian and gay studies pioneer Jonathan Ned Katz saw an explicit connection between the movement's struggle to shrug off the pathologizing narratives of psychiatry while finding a place for gay and lesbian experience within the American past. Katz described the quest for origin stories as "an important contribution to our current struggle to dispossess the professionals and repossess ourselves" while simultaneously "finding spiritual nourishment in knowledge of our historical foremothers and fathers."[45] To this end, laying claim to the past provided not only the legitimation of both presence and precedence but also contributed to the building of a proud identity inspired by those that came before.

Shortly after publishing *Gay American History* in 1977, Jonathan Ned Katz reflected on how political consciousness and a desire for history were inextricable from one another: "Only recently have lesbians and gay men begun to think of ourselves in time, as a long-oppressed and resistant social group. This new consciousness of ourselves arises from our recent political organization and activity. . . . Previously, deprived of our history, we were made one-dimensional, diminished, trivialized. Without serious research into our history we made do with silly gossip. Learning our history gives us a deeper, more rounded, complex picture of ourselves. It tells us who we've been, so that we more clearly perceive who we are now, and who we could be in the future."[46] For Katz and others, to seek a past went far beyond a recreational desire for history; rather, the on-the-ground political work and cultural production reproduced one another. At the core of Katz's and others' sentiments was a desire to redefine their identity, to create a public, collective side that claimed full citizenship and celebrated difference. In this way, gay liberation activists were like their counterparts in the red power movement: all recognized the import of the cultural to such a goal.

Beyond written communications, activists also used history in gatherings to nurture new political identities. In May 1975, members of the Lesbian Herstory Archives participated along with other lesbians from across the country in a consciousness raising event organized by West Coast lesbian activists outside of Los Angeles. The Lesbian History Exploration event, claimed as the "first national lesbian separatist event," drew women from across the country for a weekend of festivities focused around building lesbian historical consciousness.[47] Event planners gave careful consideration to the use of *history* versus *herstory*, ultimately settling on what some considered a masculinist word. The collective produced an invitational packet that included an explanation of several paragraphs on the Greek origins of the word, arguing that it in fact did not come from the masculine pronoun but rather from *istor*, meaning "knowledge or learning." To this end, planners rejected the increasingly popular *herstory*: "We plan to include in the Exploration some way for women to give words to each other, to invent and share new words, and to reclaim lost woman-words. But we don't want to discard words at face value. We want to take our own history seriously, and we want to take seriously the history of the words we use."[48]

Planners imagined a wide array of uses for lesbian history within the lesbian feminist movement, from the embracing of the difficulty of historical lesbian struggles to the development of a future political strategy of the movement as a whole. To this end, Jan Oxenberg, an organizer and filmmaker, acknowledged that a full understanding of historical lesbian struggles might prove unpleasant: "This event has to do with pain, incredible pain and rage. What we're doing is just dredging up crumbs from the past . . . like dragging the lagoon for dead bodies. What I really want from this event is *catharsis*."[49] While most of her peers in gay liberation talked about using the past as a means to build a proud identity, this comment marks a distinct new use of the past as a means to process suffering and loss through a shared history marked by oppression and erasure. Still others strove to use such narratives as a means to political reinvigoration. Exploration participant Jo Hyacinthe, for example, was driven by past oppression to organize for change: "We're changing our scripting, we've always been scripted to lose, now we're gonna be scripted to win. I see a lull in lesbian feminist politics, it's not the time for marches or rallies—that was just the beginning—it's time now to create theory, get facts, [determine] where we're coming from, why, [and] where we're going."[50] This expansive, and at times unpleasant, engagement with the past contrasts sharply with the Daughters of Bilitis's reclamation of famous and laudatory figures. In only a decade or so, lesbian activists greatly expanded the utility of the past as both a process of healing and a tool for political mobilization to connect it to the current goals of the movement.

Conclusion

The cultivation of identity within the gay liberation movement functioned similarly to that of the red power movement in that it served to mobilize members and recast centuries of negative messages from dominant culture. By rewriting pathologizing narratives, social movements cultivated new collective identities that operated to create pride within movement membership and refute stereotypes in mainstream society. Native activists refuted the notion that Indians were lazy, drunk, or simply gone by building separatist educational systems that nurtured existing tribal traditions and cultivated pan-tribal customs. through powwow festivals and red power movement culture. LGBTQ activists negated the perception that they were mentally unwell by changing perceptions of the community within academic discourse and by demonstrating historical precedence and survival. Such identity-building goals certainly required a somewhat selective, even celebratory historical revision, but this period of hagiographical history-making was a necessary phase that led to more balanced historical writing and paved the way for the demands on mainstream cultural organization that fueled the culture wars of the 1980s and 1990s.

By the height of the culture wars, LGBTQ folks and American Indians had made significant progress toward authoring their own histories. In 1990, and in response to years of pressure from indigenous activists, the federal government passed the Native American Graves Protection and Repatriation Act (NAGPRA), a far-reaching piece of legislation that required that cultural organizations collaborate with Native communities and return cultural artifacts and ancestral remains to their tribal origins. By the mid-1990s, mainstream cultural organizations were increasingly engaging LGBTQ communities as well, a move pioneered by the New York Public Library's exhibit *Becoming Visible: The Legacy of Stonewall* in 1994. By the end of the century, identity-based groups had played a key role in the democratization of cultural institutions in America and as such must be understood as contributors to the field of public history as we now know it.

In both social movements, the past had not been entirely passed but was rather a route to future possibilities. In some cases, and in other comparable social movement work, movement historians' efforts directly led to what we would now call public history projects, like the establishment of interpretive visual programs like the gay liberation slide shows. In others, the reclamation of heritage served toward movement-building strategies, like the development of a pan-tribal identity and the intervention in the narratives of mainstream heritage tourism. By insisting on articulating their own histories, social movement activists laid groundwork for more democratic, evidence-based, and culturally sensitive history-making. And they proved beyond a doubt that the useable past is indeed relevant, meaningful, and transformative.

Notes

1 This chapter draws on sources and arguments that appear more fully in Lara Kelland, *Clio's Foot Soldiers: Twentieth-Century U.S. Social Movements and Collective Memory* (Amherst: University of Massachusetts Press, 2018).

2 John D'Emilio became a preeminent academic professor, while Gregory Sprague, Joan Nestle, and Deb Edel served in leadership roles in Chicago's Gerber-Hart

Library and the Lesbian Herstory Archives, and Jonathan Ned Katz authored numerous queer history books as an independent scholar.

3   Although sometimes conflated in popular culture, the red power movement encompasses mid-twentieth-century activism, usually pan-tribal in nature, that arguably began in the 1940s with the establish of the National Congress of American Indians. The American Indian Movement is a subset of the red power movement, as AIM stands as a discrete American Indian advocacy organization founded in 1968 in Minneapolis, Minnesota.

4   Although the civil rights movement also worked on the policy level, the interdependent relationship between the Bureau of Indian Affairs and tribal governments meant that red power activists had a particularly strong focus on policy work.

5   Michel-Rolph Trouillot, *Silencing the Past: Power and the Production of History* (Boston: Beacon, 1995), 57.

6   Although the struggles against imperialism were more direct in the red power movement, activists within all of the social movements of the 1960s and 1970s borrowed language and interpretation from the anticolonialist struggles across the globe.

7   Jack Forbes, "American Tribal Higher Education Proposal," n.d., p. 5, National Indian Youth Council (NYIC) Records, Center for Southwest Research, University Libraries, University of New Mexico, box 6, folder 21.

8   Forbes.

9   Patricia Locke, "Education as War: American Indian Participation in Tribal Education," unpublished white paper, October 1974, Michael Taylor Papers, Alfred M. Bailey Library and Archives, Denver Museum of Nature and Science, box 7, folder "Indian Education Resources Center."

10 Navajo Community College (NCC) brochure, 1969, p. 1, Navajo Community College Vertical Files, Northern Arizona University.

11 Draft copy of accreditation report, March 9, 1971, p. 1, Peter Iverson Collection, Arizona State University, box 13, folder 2.

12 Article from *Navaho Diary*, student newsletter, November 4, 1969, Peter Iverson Collection, Arizona State University, box 16, folder 12.

13 Draft copy of accreditation report, p. 1.

14 Jonathan Ned Katz, interview with author, March 23, 2011, New York.

15 Judith Schwarz, letter to Jonathan Ned Katz, October 28, 1997, Jonathan Ned Katz Papers, Humanities and Social Sciences Library, New York Public Library, Manuscripts and Archives Division, box 9.

16 See correspondence files in Gregory Sprague Papers, Chicago History Museum, Chicago, and Jonathan Ned Katz Papers, Humanities and Social Sciences Library, New York Public Library, Manuscripts and Archives Division.

17 Deb Edel, "Building Cultural Memories: The Work of the Lesbian Herstory Archives," in *Our Right to Love: A Lesbian Resource Book*, ed. Ginny Vida (New York: Prentice Hall, 1978), 270–72.

18 Joan Nestle, interview with author, March 25, 2011, New York.

19 "Gay History Meeting at Jonathan Ned Katz's Apt. in Greenwich Village," January 28, 1978, Jonathan Ned Katz Papers, box 41, Manuscripts and Archives Division, Humanities and Social Sciences Library, New York Public Library, New York.
20 As lesbian separatism diminished in favor within the movement in the 1980s, LHA began to relax the policy. During the 1970s, a few gay male researchers were occasionally allowed to conduct research at the archives, including John D'Emilio and Jonathan Ned Katz. While most archives volunteers had some separatist tendencies, most cultivated alliances with gay men who were sensitive to gender issues within the movement. When the archives opened the new building in Brooklyn, male researchers with a clearly defined research query were permitted.
21 Edel, "Building Cultural Memories," 270.
22 "Problems with Research of Gay History," *Gay Archivist* 1, no. 1 (May 1977): 2.
23 Deb Edel, interview with author, March 23, 2011, New York.
24 Jim Monahan, "Considerations in the Organizations of Gay Archives," *Gay Insurgent* 5 (1978): 9.
25 Monahan.
26 Maxine Wolfe, "The Lesbian Herstory Archives: A Passionate and Political Act," Maxine Wolfe Papers, box 1 "1995," Lesbian Herstory Archives, Brooklyn, NY.
27 Joan Nestle, "Radical Archiving: A Lesbian Feminist Perspective," *Gay Insurgent* 5 (1978): 9.
28 Patricia Locke, "An Ideal School System for American Indians—a Theoretical Construct," n.d., pp. 4, 7, 8, 12–13, 17–19, Michael Taylor Papers, box 7, folder "Indian Education Resources Center."
29 Forbes, "American Tribal Higher Education Proposal," 2.
30 Forbes, 6.
31 Navajo Community College brochure, pp. 5–6.
32 Raymond Nakai, chairman's speech given at Navajo Community College, October 14, 1968, Raymond Nakai Papers, Northern Arizona University, box 6, folder 52.
33 Navajo studies brochure, Navajo Community College Vertical Files, Northern Arizona University.
34 Navajo studies brochure.
35 "NCC Program Teaches Leadership Skills," Navajo Community College newsletter, March 1971, Virginia Brown, Ida Bahl, and Lillian Watson Collection, Northern Arizona University.
36 Navajo Community College, special president's newsletter in honor of the bicentennial, July 1976, Navajo Community College Vertical Files, Northern Arizona University.
37 Fliers for various slide shows, Topical Files "History Projects" and "Slide Shows," Lesbian Herstory Archives, Brooklyn, NY.
38 Clyde Ellis, "The Sound of the Drum Will Revive Them and Make Them Happy," in *Powwow*, ed. Clyde Ellis, Luke Eric Lassiter, and Gary H. Dunham (Lincoln: University of Nebraska Press, 2004), 11.

39 For more on the development of the Ghost Dance, see Louis S. Warren, *God's Red Son: The Ghost Dance Religion and the Making of Modern America* (New York: Basic Books, 2017).

40 Clyde Ellis, *A Dancing People* (Lawrence: University Press of Kansas, 2003), 14–15.

41 Tisa Joy Wenger, *We Have a Religion: The 1920s Pueblo Indian Dance Controversy and American Religious Freedom* (Chapel Hill: University of North Carolina Press, 2009), 152–54; Ellis, *Dancing People*, 14.

42 Ellis, *Dancing People*, 17.

43 1939 program brochure, p. 2, All Indian Pow Wow Records, Cline Library, Special Collections and Archives Department, Northern Arizona University, box 3, folder 10.

44 "AIM Leaders Threaten More Protests," *Arizona Daily Sun*, July 3, 1972, 1.

45 Jonathan Ned Katz, "Why Gay History?," *Body Politic* 55 (August 1979): 19–20.

46 Katz, 19.

47 Barbara J. Love, "Nancy L. Toder," in *Feminists Who Changed America, 1963–1975*, ed. Barbara J. Love and Nancy F. Cott (Urbana: University of Illinois Press, 2006), 464.

48 "Lesbian History Exploration Invitational Packet," November 1, 1974, p. 3, Lesbian History Exploration Collection, box 1, Lesbian Herstory Archives, Brooklyn, NY.

49 Jan Oxenberg, quoted in transcript of Lesbian History Collective meeting notes, May 13, 1974, "Lesbian History Exploration Invitational Packet" Lesbian History Exploration Collection, Lesbian Herstory Archives, Brooklyn, NY (emphasis in the original).

50 Jo Hyacinthe, quoted in transcript of Lesbian History Collective meeting notes.

Reflections on Black Public History

Past, Present, Future

Pero Gaglo Dagbovie

Throughout my career as a professional historian, I have sought to make the study of history, specifically African American history, relevant to the present and accessible to and digestible by nonacademic audiences, especially millennials and learners from the hip-hop generation and Gen Y and Z. I appreciate the fundamental values of applied history ("a term used synonymously and interchangeably with public history for a number of years"[1]). For more than a decade, I have also had the good fortune of working on a range of public history projects with the Charles H. Wright Museum of African American History in Detroit, Michigan; the US Department of Education; the Michigan Department of Education; the National Park Service; and various foundations, organizations, and communities. My early research focused on Carter G. Woodson and the early Black History Movement that he created and sustained for more than three decades during the era of Jim Crow segregation. Though I did not forthrightly situate the early Black History Movement within the expansive context of the American public history campaign or expressly identify it as being a Black *public* history crusade, Woodson (the "Father of Black History") could indeed be labeled a Black *public* historian of some sort and the movement that he vigorously led certainly constituted an early Black *public* history movement. My training, experiences, and research do not qualify me to claim the designation of being a public historian.

Still and all, I have attempted to practice some of public history's basic tenets and have learned immensely from my collaborations with public historians, government historians, museum professionals, historic preservationists, and grassroots Black history aficionados and by, more recently, familiarizing myself with snippets of public history scholarship, theories, and methodologies. The following thoughts that I modestly offer are in no way intended to be authoritative. My assessments represent a semioutsider's, or self-taught public historian's, impressions of Black public history's past, present, and future. In this think piece, I share some of my interpretations of Black public history within the context of the broader US public history enterprise, focusing on how Black public history—including features of its history—has been and can be conceptualized as well as how Black history functioned wholly as an expression of public history prior through the era of Jim Crow segregation. Though I recognize that many have contributed to the study of Black history, I concentrate on African American historians and chroniclers and popularizers of the Black past.

When the American Historical Association (AHA) earnestly began collecting data on US historians' areas of specialization in the mid-1970s, the identified fields of expertise were quite broad-ranging and conventional (i.e., cultural, social, intellectual, economic, political, military, diplomatic/international, religious, etc.). While women's and/or gender history was identified as an emerging topical specialty in the AHA's 1975–76 *Guide to Departments of History*, Black history and public history (not to mention Black public history) were not.[2] In distinctly different manners, Black history and public history were at that time in the process of becoming "legitimized" in the US historical profession. During these fields' formative years in the 1970s, practitioners in both specialties were obliged to demonstrate the academic rigor required for their work. The legacies of these struggles for recognition in the US historical profession and academia are evident. In some cases, elements of these undertakings have endured. It is also important to acknowledge that Black history and US public history both have deep and rich, yet often underappreciated, historical roots that reach back long before the mid- to late 1970s—all the way back to the nineteenth century, more than half a century before the academic study of history underwent professionalization in the United States. As recognized fields in the mainstream American historical profession during the last four and a half decades or so, Black history and public history have also undergone significant transformations within relatively brief periods of time. Moreover, based on its dual thrust of challenging White racism (academic and popular) and empowering African American communities, much of Black history, though it is a distinct field and discipline in its own right, could be considered public history.

Since the field of public history, or what Denise D. Meringolo has called the "academic public history movement," formally emerged in the United States academy during the mid- to late 1970s, practitioners have unsurprisingly offered countless definitions for this utilitarian and increasingly popular and important historical enterprise. Debates about the field's meaning, scope, methodologies, and nomenclature abound. Even the meaning of the descriptor *public* has been contested. As former president of the National Council on Public History (NCPH), Robert Weible, commented about the field a decade ago, "Perhaps it is fruitless to seek consensus on a single definition."[3] Nevertheless, it seems that most in the field would agree with the basic premise that while public historians—like all types of historians—are indeed ideologically diverse, have different sets of priorities, operate in a range of spaces and venues, and employ a wide array of approaches and strategies, public historians are all in some way concerned with how the general public perceives history. In various degrees, these practitioners also advocate engaging directly with the public, shaping how the general public practices "thinking historically," and making history and the study of the past usable and relevant outside of the ivory towers of the academy. Several decades ago when she was executive director of the Historical Society of Washington, DC, Barbara Franco described what public history could entail in a straightforward manner that, by virtue of its simplicity, should not engender too much debate. "Public history can mean history *for* the public, *of* the public, *by* the public, and *with* the public," suggested Franco.[4]

Those in the Radical Roots Collective, many of whom have contributed to this project *Radical Roots: Civic Engagement, Public History, and a Tradition of Social Justice Activism*, endorse "radical public history," a form of public history that explicitly links the study of the past with social activism and the fight against multiple forms of social injustice. Such a framing of public history is especially pertinent to Black history and more specifically Black public history. For most of its history, the African American historical profession (shaped most by an assortment of African American intellectuals) has expressly employed interpretations of the Black past to give substance to Black humanity and refute racist historical discourse. Black history, therefore, has been primarily directed at different publics. In a recently published accessible volume on public history, historians Cherstin M. Lyon, Elizabeth Nix, and Rebecca K. Shrum offer a provocative and revisionist reconceptualization of public history. For them, public historians produce history for a range of public audiences (largely nonacademic audiences); collaborate with the public, stakeholders, and other scholars from a wide array of disciplines; and deeply contemplate strategies for democratizing the study of history. Most importantly, these scholars embrace "progressive public history"—a form of public history that overlaps with and can change the normative historical profession, is explicitly activist in orientation, strives to change society for the better, and empowers "everyday" people. "Progressive public history," they note, "can harness the innate sense people have of themselves as historical interpreters, working with them to uncover liberatory tools in their lives, communities, and nation."[5]

Such aforementioned conceptualizations are germane to the understudied history of Black public history. Before, during, and a bit following the era of Jim Crow segregation, diverse groups of scholars, activists, and amateur and professionally trained African American historians practiced Franco's basic notion of public history as well as the convictions of "radical" and "progressive" public history. Foremost, their versions of "radical" and "progressive" public history were guided by a commitment to antiracist activism. For many African American historians, educators, social reformers, activists, and history aficionados who were active prior to the integration of the study of African American history into the mainstream academy sometime during the 1960s and 1970s, the study and practice of Black history was inherently political and oppositional, challenged anti-Black racism, and was unambiguously "people's history." More often than not, for African American chroniclers of the past, it seemed that civic engagement and grassroots community-centered history was a priority, that the struggle for social justice was paramount, and that the use of Black history to promote social change was a guiding principle. More than many of those who write the histories of other groups in the United States, those who write Black history have been, and in some sense still are, compelled to produce history that is pertinent to the public.

Tracking down scholarship on Black public history is a bit onerous in part because the moniker *Black public history* has not been commonly used. It seems that discussions of the history of Black public history—what was initially called "Afro-American public history"—first surfaced beginning sometime during the 1980s, when its history and evolution was dubbed "little-known."[6] Initiated by Earl E. Thorpe's pathbreaking *Negro Historians in the United States* (1958), a robust body of work on the activism, scholarship, and contributions of Black historians (amateur and professionally trained) now exists. As this historiography reveals, for more than a century, African American historians vindicated "the race," released narratives for public consumption, worked with and for their communities, and strove to make the study of Black history part of the general Black public's collective identity and culture. The scholarship on African American historians, however, does not directly situate these efforts within the context of *Black public history*, per se.

In one of the first detailed, thoughtful, and often cited accounts of Black public history, published more than three decades ago, Black studies scholar and public historian Jeffrey C. Stewart and historian and curator Fath Davis Ruffins provided a historically grounded overview for various expressions and practitioners of Black public history. At the same time, they equated "Afro-American public history" with the field of African American history in general. That is, they did not really draw clear distinctions between Black public history and, for lack of better terminology, conventional academic Black history. This tendency to use *Afro-American public history* interchangeably with *Black history* was the result of their focus on the field prior to the mainstreaming of Black history and the post–civil rights movement increase in the number of PhD-holders in the field.

For Stewart and Ruffins, "Afro-American public history" dates back to the 1820s, had "an oppositional character" (that is, it debunked White racism), transformed over time and was molded by broader trends and turning points in the Black historical experience (it surveyed the evolution of "Afro-American public history" from the early nineteenth century through the Black power era), and "was powerfully shaped" by "the mass" Black audience.[7] Stewart and Ruffins underscore,

> Afro-American public history arose out of the desire to promote a positive racial identity among blacks, to preserve a history in danger of being lost, and to challenge racist stereotypes and myths pervasive in American popular culture. For most of its two hundred years, Afro-American public history has been supported by a black audience, since black history and black historians were excluded from mainstream public and academic institutions before the 1940s. Thus, Afro-American public history has tended

to serve the external and internal needs of the black community. Afro-American public history has played a role in both the cultural self-defense of the black community and the debate over the merits of integration and separation.[8]

Notwithstanding the significance of Stewart and Ruffins's essay and the more recent scholarship on the Black historical profession and Black historians as well as important African American oral history projects and publications, it could be argued that the most identifiable body of scholarship on Black public history focuses on African Americans and museum culture.[9] Furthermore, following the publication of *Slavery and Public History: The Tough Stuff of American Memory* (2006, edited by James Oliver Horton and Lois E. Horton), discussions of the place of slavery in US public history and memory have proliferated. During the "age of Obama," US slavery was perhaps most profoundly introduced to the general American public not by slavery historians, but by Hollywood films like Quentin Tarantino's *Django Unchained* (2012) and Steve McQueen's *12 Years a Slave* (2013), and the 2016 *Roots* miniseries reboot produced by Mark Wolper.

In the years since, several important books have been published on Black public history, studies that specifically identify expressions of Black public history by name. For instance, in *From Storefront to Monument: Tracing the Public History of the Black Museum Movement*, Andrea A. Burns explores what she calls "the black museum movement" that spanned from the early 1960s until the founding of the African American Museum Association (now the Association of African American Museums) in 1978.[10] Shaped by the activism of the civil rights and Black power movements, during this period, more than a few major and pioneering African American museums were founded. The struggle to create, maintain, and publicize early African American museums mirrored the efforts of historians and scholars—many of whom were African American—to integrate the study of Black history and Black studies into the mainstream academy during the 1960s and 1970s. At the same time, as Burns convincingly argues, public history in the form of museum work has been practiced by self-taught African American historians and intellectuals since "at least the early nineteenth century."[11]

Like the recently opened National Museum of African American History and Culture in Washington, DC; the Legacy Museum in Montgomery, Alabama; and the Mississippi Civil Rights Museum, the purpose of African

American museums has historically been to educate and entertain the general public about African American history and culture. Especially beginning in the late twentieth century, the curators of African American museums have been challenged to portray the Black historical experience to multiple publics, recognizing that the general Black public interprets the history of their ancestors in distinctly different manners than most (White) Americans do. Because the vast majority of African Americans were denied their most basic human and civil rights during nearly 80 percent of the total Black experience, the curators of Black museums face a significant quandary: how to offer a snapshot of the African American experience that tactfully balances the prevailing themes of victimization and perseverance. In the late twentieth and twenty-first centuries, this issue has preoccupied those involved in working with displaying Black history. "African American history does contain certain difficult, controversial, and sensitive topics—as does all American history," president of Engaging, LLC, Max A. van Balgooy observes echoing many of his fellow museum professionals. "As historical museums and historical sites, we have a great responsibility to share all of the lessons of history, whether it moves through successes and failures, tragedy and delight, laughter and sadness. Favoring one without the other can mislead our listeners, giving them only an incomplete understanding of our past and present."[12] Some African American museums have been more successful than others in this realm. Unlike James Cameron's America's Black Holocaust Museum (ABHM) in Milwaukee, Wisconsin (that currently exists as an online virtual museum), most do not radically reenvision how African Americans were mistreated in the past and seek to satisfy the needs of multiple publics. It could be argued that some recently founded African American museums do not prioritize Black publics as those founded during the Black power era did.

In *Black Public History in Chicago: Civil Rights Activism from World War II into the Cold War* (2018), one of the first major historical accounts of a distinct Black public history movement in the United States, historian Ian Rocksborough-Smith examines how a group of African American Chicagoans, leftists and activists, used public history "for explicitly political ends." Highlighting the contributions of Margaret T. G. Burroughs (artist, activist, teacher, and founder of the DuSable Museum of African American History, founded as the Ebony Museum of Negro History and Art) and other African American activists inspired by Woodson's early Black History Movement, Rocksborough-Smith provides us with a template of some sort for how historians can understand and examine Black public history activities in other major cities during the first half of the twentieth century.[13] More historical studies of this nature are needed to not only help us understand the historical antecedents of African American public history but also to contextualize the twenty-first-century African American museum movement. Even so, Rocksborough-Smith does not offer extended theoretical discussions that can be readily used to theorize the history of Black public history.

Those active in the field of mainstream US public history have been delinquent in analyzing and even acknowledging the approaches and contributions of Black public historians who were active in public history from the professionalization of the US historical profession through the founding of the NCPH. Though the well-rounded edited volume *Presenting the Past: Essays on History and the Public* (1986) did include several intriguing essays that explored dimensions of Black public history (most importantly, the previously mentioned think piece by Stewart and Ruffins), later state-of-the-field anthologies on public history have tended not to be as inclusive, and it was not until the 1990s that the leading public history journal, the *Public Historian* (founded in 1978), included articles on African American public historians.[14] The Black "pioneers of public history" whose ideas and contributions were first explored in the pages of the official scholarly forum for the NCPH in 1995 and 1997, respectively, were Black women Dorothy Burnett Porter Wesley (librarian, bibliographer, author, and longtime curator of what is now called the Moorland-Spingarn Research Center at Howard University in Washington, DC) and DuSable Museum of African American History–founder Margaret T. G. Burroughs.[15] While these Black women are not usually included in the traditional pantheon of trailblazing US public historians, both were advocates of "radical" and "progressive" public history in their own ways. Most importantly, both believed that African American history should be accessible to those outside of the traditional, elitist academy and linked to the struggle for African American identity formation and civil rights and the liberation of African-descended peoples. Though they were not doctorate holders in history, Porter Wesley and Burroughs participated in the Black History Movement that was shaped most profoundly by Carter G. Woodson, from the founding of the Association for the Study of Negro Life and History in 1915 until his sudden death in 1950.

Prior to the institutionalization of public history in the United States during the 1970s that coincidentally coincided with the protointegration of the study of African American history into the Whitestream US historical profession, there existed an identifiable, vibrant, and influential tradition of "radical" and "progressive" Black public history. They shared with their White colleagues a commitment to making history relevant to "the masses," to their respective general publics. Yet African American advocates of Black public history also challenged how the White public portrayed and perceived African American history—a history that, according to much of White America, was devoid of significant contributions to American culture and civilization, thereby justifying their often violent repression. For African Americans who were historians by vocation and hobby, until the founding of the NCPH, history *was* in a sense oftentimes inherently "radical" and "progressive" public history.

Before W. E. B. Du Bois became the first African American to earn a PhD in history (Harvard University, 1895), a group of antebellum-era amateur Black historians practiced elements of "radical" and "progressive" public history. Writers like Benjamin Lewis, William Cooper Nell, James C. Pennington, William Wells Brown, and others not only were abolitionists but produced scholarship for a literate Black public and a broader educated White public. They sought to empower the former with celebratory and vindicationist accounts of their peoples' past accomplishments and prove to the latter that African Americans had a rich and glorious past, a past that in these writers' minds had biblical and African antecedents. These amateur historians' main goal was to dispel the notion that African Americans were inferior and destined to be enslaved. In part because history as a discipline had not yet been professionalized, they generated historical narratives for the public, Black and White, and believed that Black history was a tool for Black liberation. Furthermore, because the literate Black population was very small during the antebellum era (approximately 5 to 10 percent of African Americans were literate at the time of emancipation), early Black writers of history often wrote for themselves and the White public. Their efforts were mainly corrective in nature.

During the postemancipation period through the early years of the Progressive Era, the "nadir" of the African American historical experience as historian Rayford W. Logan dubbed it, a new generation of amateur Black historians and reformers published more scientific historical scholarship that was targeted at Black and White literate publics. George Washington Williams's two-volume *A History of the Negro Race in America from 1619 to 1880* (1882) adhered to the contemporary standards of the US historical professor and, in his words, "contributed to greater effort in the struggles of citizenship and manhood." However, books like Edward Augustus Johnson's *School History of the Negro Race in America from 1619 to 1890* (1891), John Stephens Durham's 1897 *To Teach the Negro History: A Suggestion*, Leila Amos Pendleton's *A Narrative of the Negro* (1915), and others were produced to educate the general Black public, including African American youth. Similarly, during this period, Black historical societies and associations throughout the nation, like the Bethel Literary and Historical Association, practiced public history by popularizing Black history, encouraging civic engagement, and amassing historical records with and for their communities.

During the era of Jim Crow segregation, Carter G. Woodson and his coworkers in the Association for the Study of Negro Life and History (ASNLH) were at the forefront of the early Black History Movement that could at various levels be considered a Black public history movement. Central to Woodson's and his ASNLH colleagues' approach was legitimizing the academic study of Black history in the US academy, demonstrating to White America that Black people had a history, and popularizing and democratizing the study of Black history within Black publics. In this sense, Woodson connected traditional academic history to public history. Woodson's philosophy of public history was rooted in an academic and fact-based approach to the Black past and he refused to sacrifice the rigor of his craft when popularizing it. He used different mediums and approaches when delivering history to Black publics and scholarly communities. Woodson routinely reminded those in the ASNLH, especially during annual Negro History Week celebrations from 1926 until 1950, that they needed to fully engage with the general Black public in particular. "Let the public know about it," Woodson commented in reference to Negro History Week in 1940. "Convince the public first of all that it is not an effort restricted to the seven days concentrated on for special exercises from February 9 to 16. . . . One of the best ways to set the celebration before the public is to interest the local librarian."[16]

While Woodson and his PhD-holding disciples published rigorous scholarship and sought to legitimize what was then called "Negro history" in the mainstream US academy and historical profession, they also created practical programs and produced accessible scholarship that catered to the general Black public who were unaware of academic discourse. Woodson and the ASNLH took Black history to the public and collaborated with them in many ways and with various vehicles. Without detailing these strategies and measures, which several historians have thoroughly unpacked, these numerous efforts included Negro History clubs; Negro History kits; the publication of accessible and popular books like *The Negro in Our History* (first published in 1922), other books published by the ASNLH's Associated Publishers, Inc., and the *Negro History Bulletin* magazine that collectively reached hundreds of thousands of Black people; "Extension Courses in Negro History" through a home study program; and most importantly, Negro History Week. Woodson also created a collection at the Library of Congress and even had plans to open a Black history museum. In part because the study of Black history was excluded from the US historical enterprise, those active in the early Black History Movement focused their energy on packaging African American history in a manner that would be most useful to the general Black public. The professionally trained historians in the ASNLH (it should be noted that there were only fourteen African American PhD holders in history by 1940) understood that laypersons had their own interpretations of history. They, therefore, adjusted their writing and activities to meet their needs.[17]

It is not an overstatement to conclude that Woodson's death in 1950 significantly impacted the early Black History Movement as well as the ASNLH and its public history focus. In many ways, Woodson *was* the early Black (public) history movement. In the years following his death in 1950, the ASNLH continued to carry out their public history programs. However, it seems that there was some concern about the association's position vis-à-vis the public. For instance, in a paper that he delivered at the 1953 annual ASNLH convention entitled "The Association and the Public," Charles H. Wesley lamented that African American scholars and historians suffered from the "ivory tower complex" and needed to seriously contemplate and improve how they interacted with the public. For him, the ASNLH needed to be "a servant to the people." Wesley pled his cause:

> It is not difficult, however, to have the Association gain a larger position in the public mind and to meet the responsibility which rests upon it for the dissemination of this knowledge among the people. In order to achieve this purpose, we must plan to close the disparity between the accumulation and publication of knowledge and the development of understanding through the spread of information to the public. Scholarly associations, institutions and organizations must extend their teaching increasingly to the public if they are to be effective in their relationships. . . . Our Association can be a learned society but it must be more than one of these. For it has a public to serve and this is beyond the province of most

societies of scholars. . . . Our public, then, cannot be described with any singular definition. There is no one public but there can be a number of publics.[18]

When Wesley stated his case, the situation might not have been as bleak as he intimated. There were still those who were committed to the Black public history ethos promoted to Woodson, his colleagues, and their predecessors. There were grassroots and amateur writers of history who were publishing Black history books and organizing Black history programs. Professionally trained historians like John Hope Franklin, who in 1947 first released his famous and accessible *From Slavery to Freedom*, were still attempting to reach nonacademic audiences with their scholarship. As an editor for the popular and widely read *Ebony* magazine, Lerone Bennett Jr. began writing essays and books with the Black public in mind. During the ensuing civil rights movement and the Black power era (that coincided with the first major "Black museum movement" led by activists, curators, and Black museum professionals), activists in a range of organizations—from the Black Panther Party to the Republic of New Africa to the US organization and others—enlisted an approach to Black history ("people's history"). This proved an important dimension of the Black (psychological) struggle for liberation. From the mid-1970s until the 1990s, many subfields in African American history were established, and even though the distinct field of Black public history was not one of the more popular specializations, some African American historians continued to situate what they did within the context of a broader general Black public.

At the same time, it does not appear that Black public history has developed into a specialization in the same manner that US public history in general has. Though Wesley's plea is now more than six decades old, archaic in fact, it can still be instructive to today's African American historians, especially those of us who were born during and following the second part of the Black power era—those of us who are hip-hop generation and millennial African Americanist historians. Today, there are graduate students specializing in African American public history at institutions like Howard University (whose history department has a strong tradition of training graduate students to work in historical preservation and in archives). There are also Black historians who are acting as public intellectuals—working on public history projects with museums, the National Park Service, and historical societies, and publishing popular books with major trade presses for the general public (e.g., in 2016, historian Ibram X. Kendi won the National Book Award for Nonfiction for his *Stamped from the Beginning: The Definitive History of Racist Ideas in America*). Nonetheless, it is also true that contemporary African Americanist historians do not seem to be as concerned as their pre–Black power era predecessors were with writing for and collaborating with the general Black or White public. This shift is in part an unfortunate by-product of the post–Black power era mainstreaming of the study and teaching of African American history in higher education.

It is obvious that Black historians no longer face the challenges that their pre–Black power era predecessors did. In spite of the erroneous twenty-first-century attacks on Black studies, African American history as a field no longer needs to be justified or legitimized in the US academy. Yet given the fact that during "the era of the digital echo," public knowledge and understanding of African American history has been profoundly shaped by museums, filmmakers, politicians, journalists, and bloggers, conventionally trained African American historians should, in my estimation, attempt to participate in the academic Black public history movement. Those of us without specific training and expertise in Black public history and those of us who are not historical consultants, museum professionals, curators, or historic preservationists should, in whatever ways we can, seek to make Black history both relevant to the present and this-worldly in orientation.

In the early years of the new millennium, journalist Paul Ruffins suggested that historians of the Black past should consider careers in public history because "the number of jobs in museums and other public history ventures is growing." There was, in his mind, a dramatic increase in public history in "minority communities" that would provide alternative paths to what he called "the publish or perish environment of academia." He also suggested that "the importance of good storytelling represents the widest philosophical difference between academic history and public history."[19] While I understand Ruffins' enthusiasm about the "resurgence of black history museums" and appreciate his celebration of African American doctorate holders who left the academy for museum work, I disagree with the distinction that he makes between "academic" and "public" Black history and his suggestion that employment in Black public history ventures was less stressful or easier to come by than jobs in academia.

Several years ago, Denise D. Meringolo indicated that the number of "public history tracks and programs in departments of history" has grown and "has had a measurable impact on the broader discipline."[20] This is promising for the practice of public history in the US academy. Yet at the surface level, it appears that the cause of Black public history may not be making the advances that the US public history that Meringolo describes is. On the bright side, there is a noticeable trend among younger Black historians to become more relevant outside of the academy and in the public sphere. However, being a Black public intellectual historian is not the same, of course, as being a Black public historian. Though multidimensional and diverse in orientation, Black public history as a whole has its own distinct methodologies, goals, and strategies that should be learned by its practitioners during graduate training. Nevertheless, the desire of many young African American historians to become public intellectuals is a small step in the right direction in the broader quest to help popularize Black public history.

Let me conclude with a statement from Elizabeth Clark-Lewis, the director of the public history program at Howard University, pertaining to the relevance of Black public history:

> If you really want to understand the difference between having a career as a traditional university-based historian and working in a public history setting such as a museum, think about this. At some time in their careers, most academic historians reach a point where they stop and worry whether anyone outside of a very small circle of scholars and graduate students will ever really care about their articles or publications. However, when you meet a family who has driven miles to visit a museum exhibit for the third time because it has a photo of their great-uncle, you realize that public history really can touch ordinary people's lives. And this is particularly true for Black people who are hungry to have their historical experiences publicly acknowledged.[21]

Notes

1. For a brief discussion of public history and its relationship with applied history, see "How Do We Define Public History?," National Council on Public History, accessed on June 24, 2018, http://ncph.org/what-is-public-history/about-the-field.
2. See Robert B. Townsend, "What's in a Label? Changing Patterns of Faculty Specialization since 1975," *Perspectives on History: The Newsmagazine of the American Historical Association*, January 2007, https://www.historians.org/publications-and-directories/perspectives-on-history/january-2007/whats-in-a-label-changing-patterns-of-faculty-specialization-since-1975.

3 Robert Weible, "Defining Public History: Is It Possible? Is It Necessary?," *Perspectives on History: The Newsmagazine of the American Historical Association*, March 2008, accessed on June 17, 2018, https://www.historians.org/publications-and-directories/perspectives-on-history/march-2008/defining-public-history-is-it-possible-is-it-necessary.

4 Barbara Franco, "Public History and Memory: A Museum Perspective," *Public Historian* 19 (Spring 1997): 65.

5 Cherstin M. Lyon, Elizabeth M. Nix, and Rebecca K. Shrum, eds., *Introduction to Public History: Interpreting the Past, Engaging Audiences* (New York: Rowman & Littlefield, 2017), x.

6 For early usage of the concept of Black public history, see Jeffrey C. Stewart and Fath Davis Ruffins, "A Faithful Witness: Afro-American Public History in Historical Perspective, 1828–1984," in *Presenting the Past: Essays on History and the Public*, ed. Susan Porter Benson, Stephen Brier, and Roy Rosenzweig (Philadelphia: Temple University Press, 1986), 307–38.

7 Stewart and Ruffins, 307–8.

8 Stewart and Ruffins, 334.

9 See, for instance, Bridget R. Cooks, *Exhibiting Blackness: African Americans and the American Art Museum* (Amherst: University of Massachusetts Press, 2011); Mabel O. Wilson, *Negro Building: Black America in the World of Fairs and Museums* (Berkeley: University of California Press, 2012); Andrea A. Burns, *From Storefront to Monument: Tracing the Public History of the Black Museum Movement* (Amherst: University of Massachusetts Press, 2013). There is also a collection of recently published books that discusses the National Museum of African American History and Culture in Washington, DC.

10 See Burns, *From Storefront to Monument*.

11 Burns, 7.

12 Max A. van Balgooy, introduction to *African American History and Culture at Museums and Historical Sites*, ed. Max A. van Balgooy (New York: Rowman & Littlefield, 2015), xiv.

13 See Ian Rocksborough-Smith, *Black Public History in Chicago: Civil Rights Activism from World War II into the Cold War* (Urbana: University of Illinois Press, 2018).

14 To be fair, during the new millennium, the *Public Historian* been much more generous in its treatment of Black public history. Since the early 2000s, the journal has published a group of excellent articles dealing with African American historical subject matter (e.g., slavery, African American museums, Black national historic sites).

15 See Avril Johnson Madison and Dorothy Porter Wesley, "Dorothy Burnett Porter Wesley: Enterprising Steward of Black Culture," *Public Historian* 17 (Winter 1995): 15–40; John E. Fleming and Margaret T. Burroughs, "Dr. Margaret T. Burroughs: Artist, Teacher, Administrator, Writer, Political Activist, and Museum Founder," *Public Historian* 21 (Winter 1999): 31–55.

16 Carter G. Woodson, "How to Make Negro History Week Count," *Negro History Bulletin* 4 (December 1940): 72.
17 I have written extensively about this in Dagbovie, *Early Black History Movement*.
18 Charles H. Wesley, "The Association and the Public," *Negro History Bulletin* 17 (January 1954): 75, 76.
19 Paul Ruffins, "Embracing Public History," *Black Issues in Higher Education*, February 14, 2002, 32, 33, 34.
20 Denise D. Meringolo, *Museums, Monuments, and National Parks: Toward a New Genealogy of Public History* (Amherst: University of Massachusetts Press, 2012), xv.
21 Ruffins, "Embracing Public History."

What Happens Next?

Institutionalizing Grassroots Success in Selma, Alabama

Abigail Gautreau

In 2013, the Selma Civil Rights Movement (1865–1972) Multiple Property Submission (MPS) was accepted to the National Register of Historic Places. This document represents a significant contribution to understanding the local experience of the movement and in particular of the role local Selmians played in the events leading up to and following Bloody Sunday and the March to Montgomery.

Like all such projects, this achievement was the result of months of research and years of grassroots advocacy and planning. It is perhaps the nature of historic preservation to occupy these liminal spaces between intuitions and grassroots efforts; the selection of a site and the decision to save or preserve it is local and grassroots, while the technical work requires navigating institutional and legal frameworks. Historic preservation's origin story in the United States, which often includes Ann Pamela Cunningham's campaign to save Mount Vernon from a slow death by neglect, tells a similar story. While there was of course no National Register or other national body overseeing historic buildings in 1850, Cunningham formed an institution, the Mount Vernon Ladies' Association, in order to restore and protect the site in perpetuity. In order for the preservation process to go on beyond the life- and attention span of those who began the project, historic preservation requires an institutional approach.

In describing what public history is, public historians often fall back on examples of the products of public history work—an archive, exhibit, or interpretive material. Among ourselves, however, we generally conceive of the discipline methodologically, unified by the process of creation through shared authority, self-reflection, and audience engagement rather than the results of those efforts. This reflects a tension in the field between the professional and academic branches, where academic public historians are often pressured to define and explain the work and its intellectual merit to skeptical administrators and traditionally minded colleagues who may be inclined to view that work as service rather than scholarship.

The addition of public history to the university in the late 1970s, along with the creation of the scholarly journal the *Public Historian*, also led to a push for work dealing with the field's history and historiography, due in no small part to a need to legitimate public history in the eyes of traditional historians. There is a considerable body of work dedicated to teasing out the origins of public history, but until fairly recently, much of this work focused on contextualizing it alongside traditional historiography. Consequentially, much of the existing work on the history of public history echoes the erasures of traditional historiography. In order to address these silences, it is critical that public historians reexamine the ways in which the creation myth(s) of public history serve to reinforce structural biases that favor Whiteness, heterosexuality, patriarchy, and ableism.

The object of the *Radical Roots* project is to reevaluate the origins of public history and broaden our sense of where the field came from and where it might go. Grassroots public history is at the heart of the practice and history of public history in general; the vitality of the field derives from its continuous creation and re-creation by individuals and communities who do the work and bring their own voices and perspectives to it. This case study addresses this complex process by examining a grassroots preservation project that became an institution (the Alabama Black Heritage Council) and that institution's ongoing role in advancing grassroots efforts to preserve the voting rights landscape in Selma.

In 1978, a tornado touched down in Selma, Alabama, and severely damaged First Baptist (Colored) Church. It destroyed the spire, part of the roof, and brought down two walls, leaving only the shell of the once impressive Gothic Revival edifice and community landmark. First Baptist has deep roots in Selma. Samuel Phillips, a freeman, started the congregation in the 1840s. It met in the same space as the White Baptist congregation until shortly after the Civil War, when the White congregation bought out the Black congregation's interest (though accounts differ on how exactly that came about). The

Black congregation built a church on St. Phillips Street and from that location helped found Selma University, a Black college and theological school that served as one of the handful of (private) Black colleges offering secondary education to African American students. By the late 1880s, the congregation had outgrown its building and commissioned locally prominent Black architect and contractor Dave Benjamin West to design a new building at the corner of Sylvan Street (now Martin Luther King Jr. Street) and Jefferson Davis Avenue (now J. L. Chestnut Avenue). Completed in 1894, the new First Baptist Church was hailed by an early church historian as "the finest colored church edifice in Alabama" and quickly became a local landmark.[1] The church served both the congregation and the community, hosting concerts as well as city and county high school graduations into the mid-twentieth century.[2] In the 1960s, it became the site of mass meetings associated with the voting rights movement and provided office space for members of the Student Nonviolent Coordinating Committee (SNCC). In March 1965, would-be marchers underwent physicals in First Baptist's basement to ensure that they were healthy enough for the March to Montgomery.

Louretta Wimberly was a lifelong member of the First Baptist Church when the tornado struck and, as one of the only 156 African Americans who were registered to vote in Dallas County in 1962, an activist in her own right.[3] That disaster would launch her career as a self-described grassroots historic preservationist. Unwilling to allow her church to fall into disrepair or be demolished, she rallied the congregation and reached out to the Alabama Historical Commission (AHC) for help. The AHC nominated the church to the National Register of Historic Places and helped them secure grants to repair the roof and stabilize the structure. Though the restoration was not fully completed, the congregation was able to return to the sanctuary in 1982. Wimberly's experience and the relationship she developed with the AHC launched her into the world of historic preservation and led to the institutionalization of Black preservation in Alabama. Wimberly became a leader in assisting individuals and local organizations to preserve sites associated with Black history across the state. Many of these sites had been protected through informal, grassroots efforts, but there was no cohesive program to provide guidance and support for these organizations or to make them aware of the resources that existed to help them. By extension, there was no dedicated effort at the state level to ensure that resources and funding were made available to projects related to African American history.[4]

In Alabama, as in many states, state-level grants and matching funds for preservation are available only to sites listed in the National Register of Historic Places. The National Register, which is managed federally by the National Park Service and overseen by the Keeper of the National Register, lists sites that are nominated by the State Historic Preservation Officer (SHPO). In Alabama, the SHPO operates out of the Alabama Historical Commission; thus the AHC serves as a gatekeeper to preservation resources, one that continues to be led and staffed primarily by White people.

Following her success in saving First Baptist, Louretta Wimberly embarked on a second career advocating for historic preservation in Black communities, which included attending meetings and training workshops organized by the National Trust for Historic Preservation. By the early 1980s, the leadership at the AHC became increasingly aware of the need for deliberate, focused outreach to African American communities. In 1983, the AHC founded the Black Heritage Council Task Force, the precursor to what would become the Black Heritage Council (BHC). Wimberly was a founding member, helping shepherd the disparate grassroots efforts at preservation into the state-run institution.

The goal of the BHC was to increase the number of sites associated with Black history on both the state-wide Alabama Register of Landmarks and Heritage and the National Register of Historic Places, because inclusion on the National Register in particular would make these sites eligible for grants and funds. Then-executive director Larry Oakes hoped that the work of the BHC would draw attention to the resources available through the AHC so that "if money becomes available, local-level concerns like affiliates of the BHC will have knowledge of grants available, understand them and have applications and information necessary to apply."[5] In reviewing the task force meeting minutes, it is clear that the AHC was aware of the limitations of their current outreach and knowledge and believed that the BHC would be an important institution for engaging with individuals or groups attempting to preserve sites associated with Black history.

The question of awareness was central to the discussion and purpose of the BHC. Grassroots efforts and unofficial campaigns to preserve cultural heritage associated with Alabama's Black history needed to be aware that there were funding and other forms of support available to them. The AHC needed to know what sites existed in order to list them. While publicly owned buildings are fairly straightforward to include, privately owned properties may only be listed on the National Register with the explicit consent of the owner. This means that the process for listing is usually initiated by the owner, who would then approach the AHC; if local organizers were unaware of the existence or availability of the AHC, then properties would remain in limbo. Larry Oakes suggested that the BHC "begin a comprehensive identification of projects and groups involved with resources related to our entire program" to help the AHC identify likely partners.[6] Richard Dozier would expand this call at the first BHC meeting on January 16, 1985, asking for a statewide survey of sites significant to Black history along with their condition so that state review board members evaluating National Register nominations could compare the list of properties up for review against the list of Black cultural heritage sites awaiting recognition.

Dozier proposed a five-point strategy for stimulating awareness across the state that included

A. Networking/making contacts
B. Locating, assessing and collecting resources (local libraries/librarians; histories/historians; urban planners/planning projects; etc.)
C. Expand membership/community outreach
D. Community Education (local workshops/seminars)
E. Publicity-Visibility-Publicity (APTV [Alabama Public Television], newspapers, etc.)[7]

The first point in particular speaks to the importance of the BHC's role in connecting the AHC (a state-run institution) with existing and potential grassroots efforts. While the BHC as part of the AHC became an institution, BHC members like Louretta Wimberly did not suddenly develop amnesia in regard to their experiences as grassroots organizers operating outside of the institution of which they were now a part. Wimberly was in a unique position to shape the institution she helped create in ways that would make it more accessible and useful to those outside of it. She knew how to identify the keepers of Black cultural heritage and how to reach out to them based on her own lived experience. At the same time, she and other BHC members learned more about the (traditionally White) institutions of historic preservation. They attended meetings of the National Trust for Historic Preservation, and Wimberly attended national and regional preservation workshops. At these events, the Alabama BHC developed relationships that laid the groundwork for the eventual creation of a network of Black Heritage Councils across the southeast that operated for ten years.

By 2002, the BHC had nearly doubled the number of African American history sites included on the Alabama and/or National Register.[8] From 1965 to 1984, only 64 African American history sites were listed. Between 1985, the year of the BHC's founding, and April 2002, 108 more were added. In 1996, Congress passed legislation designating the Selma to Montgomery National Historic Trail, protecting the US highway that marchers followed in 1965. In 2004, the National Register listed the Birmingham Civil Rights (1933–79) MPS. In 2013, the National Register listed the Selma Civil Rights (1865–1972) MPS. Furthermore, within the AHC itself, the BHC operates an internship program specifically focused on involving African American students in historic preservation work, and the AHC staff has included more people of color in nonclerical positions since its creation.

Perversely, the BHC's success may also be measured by the pushback the Alabama state legislature has meted out against the AHC in recent years. Following the 2008 recession, the conservative legislature imposed a series of austerity measures aimed at balancing the budget, including significant budget cuts at the AHC and an unsuccessful attempt in 2015–16 to break up the commission itself, putting the SHPO back under the Department of Archives and History and moving the AHC's historic sites to the Department of Conservation and Natural Resources.[9] It is also worth noting that in 2015, the state legislature also passed a budgetary measure closing thirty-one part-time driver's license offices that served rural and predominantly Black counties shortly after passing a voter ID measure. Swift backlash led to an agreement to open the offices one day a week, which did not prevent an investigation by the US Department of Transportation. The DOT investigation found in December 2016 that the closures disproportionately hurt the state's minority population and violated the Civil Rights Act of 1964.[10]

As part of a state agency, the BHC has become itself an institution and is no longer, in the strictest sense, a grassroots organization, but its origins as the product of a grassroots movement make it uniquely situated to serve as an intermediary for groups that may be reluctant to work directly with the state. At the same time, its position as part of a state agency gives it the ability to influence and change the state's focus, as evidenced by the significant increase in the inclusion of Black heritage sites on the Alabama Register. While becoming a state institution is not necessarily a desirable outcome for all grassroots movements, the establishment of the BHC created a stable infrastructure for protecting Black cultural heritage sites that were at risk or overlooked (deliberately or not) by the predominantly White preservation community. The end result has been a much stronger preservation outcome for Alabama history, ensuring that the state's cultural landscape reflects the diverse experiences of those who lived there.

By 2011, Louretta Wimberly was chair emerita of the Black Heritage Council and refocused her energy on her hometown. Wimberly envisioned a National Voting Rights District for Selma, a comprehensive preservation project that would protect Selma's historic Black neighborhoods as well as the smaller churches, schools, and businesses whose role in the movement was often overshadowed by the focus on King and the marches. Selma's existing preservation landscape as of 2012 mainly included four historic districts concentrated in the downtown area, one of which (the Ice House District) focused on a historical Black neighborhood.

Early nominations for other districts primarily focused on the architectural significance of the sites, overlooking their importance to the history of civil rights, and very much reflect the time in which they were written. The nomination document for the Old Town District from 1978 is an excellent example of this. Much of the downtown area falls under this district overlay, including the Dallas County Courthouse, which played a significant role during the voting rights campaign as it was the location of the voter registration office. Between 1963 and 1965, multiple protests focused on this ostensibly public space that served as ground zero for preventing the city's Black citizens from exercising their rights. Photographs and newsreel footage show people lined up waiting to register, and multiple confrontations with the city's White authority, Sheriff Jim Clark, took place here, including Clark's assault on Annie Lee Cooper and his televised attack on C. T. Vivian after Vivian confronted him on the issue of voter registration. The statement of significance in nomination includes exactly one line referring to the voting rights campaign: "In the mid-1960's Selma became the focus of national attention for the Civil Rights movement, and events there led to the passage of the Voting Rights Act of 1965."[11] It is worth pointing out that the authors at the time did find space to discuss the supposed abuses of federal troops during the Civil War and to highlight the "resiliency of a citizenry who rebuilt from the rubble."[12]

There are multiple explanations for this type of bias in the nominations. The National Register discourages the inclusion of properties whose significance falls within the last fifty years, though sites of exceptional significance can be included.[13] It is worth noting that the National Register Bulletin on the subject includes as its cover image a photo of Little Rock High School, site of one of the first school desegregation crises. This bulletin was not published until 1979, after the Old Town District nomination, and the nomination is best understood as a product of its time and reflective of the biases inherent in the National Register system, which favors older properties (perceived as being at higher risk) and is itself a tool that has long been used to protect particular historical narratives that legitimize existing (White, patriarchal, heteronormative, ableist, etc.) power structures.

While older nominations can perhaps be excused, there were other gaps in Selma's preservation that were more difficult to explain. As of 2012, only First Baptist Church and Brown Chapel AME Church were listed for their civil rights significance. The Edmund Pettus Bridge, one of the most iconic structures in the civil rights movement and the starting point of 1965's Bloody Sunday (a riot perpetrated by police and a deputized posse of white men against nonviolent demonstrators intent on marching to Montgomery), was not listed in any capacity. In 2013, just ahead of the fiftieth anniversary of Bloody Sunday, the National Park Service made the bridge a National Historic Landmark.

With the fiftieth anniversary looming, and growing concern about the steady deterioration of Selma's vernacular architecture, Wimberly contacted the Center for Historic Preservation at Middle Tennessee State University to see about securing a Certified Local Government (CLG) grant from the Alabama Historical Commission to tackle a large-scale preservation project related to Selma's Black history and the voting rights movement.[14] Wimberly chose to work with the center based on a prior partnership with the organization and its director, Carroll Van West, to complete the Birmingham Civil Rights Movement (1933–79) MPS and because of the center's community-driven approach to preservation (meaning that projects must be initiated and advocated for by the communities themselves). Here again, Wimberly's background and training helped her both identify a likely institutional partner and take advantage of the grant process.

The process of developing what became the Selma Civil Rights Movement (1865–1972) MPS to the National Register of Historic Places began with a community meeting to gauge interest at the end of 2011. A larger follow-up meeting took place in 2012 to share the idea for the project, answer questions about the National Register, and ask community members what they thought was important about Selma's voting rights history and which places should be included. In addition to leadership, staff, and graduate assistants from the Center for Historic Preservation and Wimberly, the meeting also included representatives from the AHC, BHC, city government, and rangers from the National Park Service Selma to Montgomery National Historic Trail.

The meeting had two significant outcomes. First, it was clear that despite Wimberly's interest in a more aggressive approach, the temporal and financial restriction of the grant meant that a smaller project was in order. The best use of resources would be to create an MPS to the National Register of Historic Places for Selma as a whole and complete one nomination to go with it. Although Multiple Property Submissions do not list any of the properties they mention on the National Register, they provide a statement of significance and establish the eligibility of properties linked under a common theme. The MPS for Selma includes a narrative of the movement in Selma, grounded in local history with clear references to the built environment and cultural landscape in which events took place. Later nominations of districts or individual properties can then refer back to the larger document without repeating the same information or doing the same research. It provides a foundation from which other groups can act without having to generate the same level of resources. Along with the MPS, the Center for Historic Preservation would also complete a nomination for Tabernacle Baptist Church, a historically and architecturally significant church that hosted Selma's first mass meeting on voting rights in 1963.[15]

The second major outcome of the meeting was the exposure of significant generational tension over the memory and commemoration of the movement. Those who had been teenagers and students felt that their experiences had been sidelined or glossed over in favor of a narrative focused on Martin Luther King Jr. and the adult leadership. The younger generation's stories included significant personal trauma that was not resolved by the legislative achievement of the Voting Rights Act of 1965. Those who had been adults during the movement were protective of their legacy and in particular of their associations with King, whose role they viewed as integral to the success of the movement. The MPS would have to include a narrative that met the technical requirements of the document while honoring the overlapping and sometimes contradictory experiences of the community.

After several months of research and numerous field visits, the Center for Historic Preservation completed a document that attempted to meet these goals. In addition to grounding the story of Selma's voting rights movement in the cultural landscape, the center attempted to address the generational tension in how it grouped buildings. Rather than categorizing them by their intended purpose as schools, churches, and so on, the center created categories like "strategy centers," "conflict centers," and "reconciliation centers." "Strategy centers," for example, includes properties "where prominent persons who represented local, state, or national institutions and organizations held meetings and strategy sessions both in support of, and in opposition to, the Civil Rights Movement."[16] This category includes sites like Brown Chapel AME, where King spoke at mass meetings as well as R. B. Hudson High School, where students planned walkouts and from where they departed for demonstrations. By including spaces where youth activists met and made plans alongside those where adults operated, the MPS highlights the significance of both groups and the messiness of the movement's origins.

The story of the Black Heritage Council and the process of creating the Selma MPS illustrate the complicated relationship between institutions and grassroots efforts in historic preservation. The partnership that developed from a grassroots activist, engaged community members, and thoughtful institutional partners generated positive preservation outcomes for the community. The relationship also led to a more nuanced understanding of the experience of the voting rights movement and a warning about how celebration, rather than commemoration, can silence and reinforce past trauma.

Is it fair to call a project conceived of by the chair emerita of the Black Heritage Council of Alabama, run by a regional institution like the Center for Historic Preservation, and funded by the Alabama Historical Commission a "grassroots effort"? Maybe not. It is also difficult, however, to describe it as a purely institutional effort. In the United States, the meager protections of the National Register are only available to sites that both meet the criteria and have institutions dedicated to protecting them. The Black Heritage Council began as a grassroots effort and became an institution in order to develop the resources to protect Black cultural heritage in Alabama specifically because the existing historic preservation structures in the state (and elsewhere) did not address these needs. The story of the BHC shows how firmly embedded Whiteness is in historic preservation as a field. The story of the Selma MPS, which would not exist without the BHC, illustrates how essential this cultural heritage is to understanding US history as well as the present. When preservationists and public historians describe the history of historic preservation as a tidy narrative from Ann Pamela Cunningham to the National Historic Preservation Act, they erase organizations like the BHC and reinforce the field's Whiteness through that absence.

It is possible to see the dramatic evolution of historic preservation since the 1970s simply by looking at old nominations; the Old Town Selma nomination, for example, would not pass muster by the increasingly professional standards of the field. While this professionalization has resulted in much better-quality nominations that can serve as resources in their own right, it also means that nominating a property requires significantly more resources, time, and training than it once did. At the same time, many states like Alabama have cut funding for state historic preservation offices, meaning that these organizations have fewer resources to assist in the preparation of nominations, much less the grant money necessary for preservation firms to complete those nominations. In order to save a building, as Louretta Wimberly did when the tornado struck First Baptist, communities and individuals must have considerable resources to pay for the work themselves or figure out the bureaucratic and technical grant application process. The Black Heritage Council of Alabama plays a critical role in this process, fighting for Black cultural heritage from the inside.

The history of historic preservation is not the history of the National Register of Historic Places; it is a history made up of all sorts of formal and informal organizations, some of which endure and others whose nature is inherently ephemeral, forming to save a building and dispersing when it is stable or destroyed. Few of these organizations have the resources to dedicate to archiving and publishing their own institutional history. Thus the burden is on the part of the field with adequate resources to find new ways to conceive of our history that acknowledge its messy, complicated nature and open the door to a future of historic preservation that challenges rather than reinforces dominant cultural narratives.

Notes

I would like to express my gratitude first and foremost to the Black Heritage Council of the Alabama Historical Commission, particularly Frazine Taylor, Dorothy Walker, and Louretta Wimberly. It has been an honor to work with you all and tell this small part of the BHC's story. Thank you as well to the Alabama Department of History and Archives for providing access to and assistance in locating the BHC's records. Finally, my sincere thanks to my reviewers at all stages. Your feedback clarified and improved this work immeasurably. Any remaining errors or shortcomings are strictly my own.

1. Ellen Mertins, "The First Baptist Church," *National Register of Historic Places Inventory/Nomination Form*, September 20, 1979, Alabama Historical Commission, Montgomery https://npgallery.nps.gov/NRHP/GetAsset/NRHP/79000383_text.
2. Louretta Wimberly, conversation with author, October 10, 2016.
3. Those 156 registered Black voters represented just 0.9 percent of eligible Black voters.
4. Tuskegee University became the first Black college to be listed as a National Historic Landmark in 1966, but this is very much the exception rather than the rule.
5. Black Heritage Council Task Force minutes, March 30, 1984, 2, unprocessed collection box "Alabama Historical Commission, Black Historic Council (sic)," folder "Meeting Agendas, Minutes, and Packets, 1993-2001," SG037323.
6. Black Heritage Council Task Force minutes, 1.
7. Black Heritage Council Task Force minutes, 2.
8. Black Heritage Council of the Alabama Historical Association, "Alabama's Historic African American Places," April 2002, available via the Wayback Machine, accessed March 8, 2018, https://web.archive.org/web/20030307104159fw_/http://www.preserveala.org:80/BHC/AA_properties_registers.htm.
9. Mike Brantley, "Alabama Historical Commission Suspends New Landmark Listings," AL.com, September 1, 2009, https://www.al.com/live/2009/09/alabama_historical_commission.html; John Archibald, "Alabama Legislature's Yard Sale Is Littered with the State's History," AL.com, May 12, 2015, https://www.al.com/opinion/2015/05/alabama_legislature_forget_his.html.
10. Associated Press, "Feds: Alabama to Expand Driver's License Office Hours after Probe," AL.com, December 28, 2016, https://www.al.com/news/montgomery/2016/12/feds_alabama_to_expand_drivers.html.
11. Nancy N. Holmes and Nicholas H. Holmes, "Old Town Historic District," *National Register of Historic Places Inventory/Nomination Form*, November 23, 1976, Alabama Historical Commission, Montgomery, available at https://npgallery.nps.gov/NRHP/GetAsset/NRHP/78000486_text.
12. Holmes and Holmes.
13. Marcella Sherfy and W. Ray Luce, "Guidelines for Evaluating and Nominating Properties That Have Achieved Significance within the Past Fifty Years," US Department of the Interior, National Park Service, 1979 (revised 1990, 1996, 1998), available at https://www.nps.gov/subjects/nationalregister/upload/NRB22-Complete.pdf.
14. I was a graduate research assistant at the Center for Historic Preservation and worked extensively on this project, including attending community meetings and eventually serving as a community liaison in Selma.
15. Jessica French, Carroll Van West, and Elizabeth Moore Humphreys with the assistance of Tabernacle Baptist Church History Committee, "Tabernacle Baptist

Church," *National Register of Historic Places Registration Form*, February 5, 2013, available at https://www.nps.gov/nr/feature/places/13000469.htm.

16 Carroll Van West with research from Amber Clawson, Jessica French, and Abigail Gautreau, "The Civil Rights Movement in Selma, Alabama, 1865–1972," *National Register of Historic Places Multiple Property Documentation Form*, received May 10, 2013, 51, available at https://www.nps.gov/nr/feature/places/64501182.htm.

Getting to the Heart of Preservation

The Place of Grassroots Efforts in the Contemporary Preservation Movement

Kristen Baldwin Deathridge

Introduction

Too often contemporary preservation work has been accomplished by playing almost exclusively to economic interests. History, the stories of why places matter, has been secondary to this process. As business investors and governments have tended to varying degrees toward austerity in spending, preservationists have necessarily justified projects by emphasizing their economic potential. Although preservationists did this with the best of intentions, hoping to save more historic places, this course of action has had a variety of unintended consequences. At its worst, leaning purely on the economic value of preservation can lead to extreme displacement. In contrast, the work of preservation can balance economic potential with the interests of resident communities and honor history as a source of meaning. Under these ideal circumstances, preservation can function to promote more just, equitable, and inclusive distribution of benefits—both economic and intangible. This article analyzes two case studies to explore the conditions and circumstances under which preservation might serve social justice.[1]

The first of the case studies focuses on the fight to save Japantown's Bush Street Temple in San Francisco, California. The Bush Street Temple began as a synagogue and ultimately served as a Buddhist temple and, temporarily, an African American church during Japanese American internment in the Second World War. Ultimately, it returned to service as a Buddhist temple that briefly shared space with a western-facing Zen Center. Now the building provides income-restricted housing as an assisted living facility. When the site became a focal point for preservationists in the early 2000s, the project leaders' main goals were to encourage people to return to living in the community and to preserve the space; although economics was not a primary consideration, the project remains economically successful.

The second study highlights efforts by African American alumni and other supporters to preserve Lincoln Heights Rosenwald School in North Wilkesboro, North Carolina. Their effort to protect the site and promote its story was tireless in its effort to win support and has continued for twenty years. While the association with Rosenwald and his eponymous fund helps attract attention to the project, group leaders are more interested in preserving the community that formed around the school. They want their experiences remembered and feel preserving the school is an important element of preserving their memories. They aren't looking for an adaptive reuse that provides a financial return on investment; they want to preserve their school, which is now a community center.

Neither of these groups labels themselves preservation activists, though they are clearly engaging in work that falls into that category. Rather, these examples emphasize the significance of community-based, or grassroots, efforts for shaping a social justice orientation in the contemporary preservation movement.

Traditionally marginalized communities, including African Americans as well as immigrants and first-generation Americans, have had to work outside of the formal preservation system to control their stories. Some have reluctantly partnered with preservation organizations or worked within government structures when their local efforts were in danger of failing. By describing two counternarrative preservation projects and exploring their ultimate financial benefits, this article makes the case for balancing the economic interests with community efforts to protect history and create meaningful collective space.

One note on terminology: I argue that the term *grassroots* should be reserved for preservationists who consciously work to preserve the history of their own communities, even those who choose to partner with government or entrepreneurial entities. Because so much preservation work is locally based, it can be tempting to call any locally driven work "grassroots preservation."[2] In addition, there's a sense in which all historic preservationists might be considered activists in their work to save structures and districts from destruction, whether they are lobbying local government, writing editorials, making use of social media to draw attention to their cause, or researching and writing formal reports to help preserve places. However, not all local groups are accurately described as working from and for the grassroots. Many are working on behalf of government; others are business owners who will personally benefit from the gentrification that can follow from preservation. Activists of this sort are working from a middle-class perspective, trying to make their neighborhoods more beautiful.[3] It is therefore important to reserve the term *grassroots* for less-privileged groups who are working not to make a profit or appeal to investors but to preserve a sense of coherent and connected community in the face of demographic change. For the purposes of this piece, then, the term *grassroots* applies to people who lack authority, power, or connections that may allow them to shape public discourse and who are working to preserve their own community's spaces and stories.

Economic Considerations: A Necessary Evil

Most current preservation efforts rely on convincing business owners and lawmakers that preservation makes money. Groups like the National Trust for Historic Preservation's Green Lab and consulting firms like Donovan Rypkema's PlaceEconomics connect the preservation and reuse of historic buildings to both environmental sustainability and economic development.[4] There is no doubt that these are valid and necessary arguments. The movement toward green construction has created unexpected opposition to preservation. Older buildings can contain environmental hazards including lead paint or asbestos. Preservationists have worked to articulate the environmental benefits of rehabilitation. Preservation recognizes the embodied energy in historic buildings—the energy used to make the bricks, cut the timber, work the metal, and get all the building fabric to the site has already been expended—and argues that reusing historic structures can be one of the most "green" building efforts around.[5]

Although adaptive reuse of historic structures is essentially a form of recycling, it is often an economic argument that focuses only on selling certain benefits of preservation to community leaders. The underpinnings of the economic argument for adaptive reuse are reflected in the audience Rypkema and others target for their publications that demonstrate to local governments the ways that preservation quite literally pays.[6] For example, PlaceEconomics worked with the Historic Savannah Foundation to publish *Beyond Tourism:*

Historic Preservation in the Economy and Life in Savannah and Chatham County in 2015. This important study compiled data to record the economic impact of historic preservation for those living and working in Savannah, not just for tourists or those directly in the tourism industry. Evaluating historic districts, construction, property values, density, livability measures, and jobs, the report argues that not only is preservation good business for tourism; it is good business for Savannah's daily economy and quality of life. Because preservation organizations require governmental support, they tend to focus on these economic benefits.

Crucially, Rypkema and his devotees are not wrong. Preservationists can be as high-minded as they like, but without proving to those that hold the purse strings (and set the zoning laws) the economic gains that result from taking the time to repurpose and rehabilitate older buildings, much less preservation would occur. The efforts that work to convince folks of both the ecological and economic benefits of preservation are immensely important. In fact, these efforts can and should be increased, as too many town planners and entrepreneurs remain unaware of these benefits. In *The Past and Future City: How Historic Preservation Is Reviving America's Communities*, Stephanie Meeks and Kevin C. Murphy drive these benefits home and combine them with the argument that, essentially, people love old places. Nor are they the first to make that argument. Jane Jacobs made it in the 1960s, and Stewart Brand made it again in the 1990s.[7] One thing that all preservationists can agree on is that people must continually argue its merits.

However, Americans' collective experience of our hometowns tells us that markets change and few businesses last forever. Many of today's preservationists spend much of their time and resources convincing one investor to rehabilitate one property for one new purpose. We rejoice when a place like Pullman, the community planned to house those who built the company's sleeping cars, becomes a National Monument and is saved, and we mourn when a place like Bertrand Goldberg's brutalist Prentice Women's Hospital and Maternity Center is lost.[8] But not every historic place can become a national monument or historic house museum, and many institutions have technological needs that outstrip some older buildings.[9] Many historic buildings, then, are adapted and reused as new businesses. But how long does that last? What happens in five, ten, or twenty years when that business is no longer sustainable? Neighborhoods shift and change as people move around, following careers and affordable housing. The folks who fought for that old mill (so many places have these old mills!) and remembered it with fondness will not always be around. A strictly economic, or even ecological, argument in favor of saving a historic place remains a short-term solution. How will the new neighbors learn what makes these places special? Some will fall for the beauty of architectural lines, and after all, aesthetics is what we are told drove early American historic preservationists. Early and mid-twentieth-century preservationists fought for laws that would recognize the United States' built legacy precisely because they realized that beauty is not enough to persuade folks that newer is not always better when it comes to buildings and that the natural resources of the US were not as unlimited as it often seemed.[10]

The people who worked in Charleston to create the first legal historic district in the 1930s and those who fought for the passage of the National Historic Preservation Act of 1966 did not include *historic* by accident. Contemporary preservationists often, of seeming necessity, leave the historic out of the narratives they use to convince business leaders to preserve special places. The assumption—and maybe it is correct—is that the developers do not need to hear the story of a place; they only require information that affects their bottom line. The focus on the financial is inherently conservative, whereas the urge toward historic preservation in the United States has often been about something much more radical—the desire to connect the personal to the political.

Where Is the Story?

Historic preservation has not always emphasized the bottom line. The historic preservation field's origin story in the United States often begins with the Mount Vernon Ladies' Association (MVLA) and its sister organizations. These groups emphasized the emotional connection people felt to places associated with (White) men who played a significant role in the nation's history.[11] Founders of various female-led preservation groups from the mid- to late nineteenth century and the early twentieth century occupied an uneasy cultural space. They were simultaneously elite because they occupied positions of cultural authority based on the wealth and stature of their husbands or fathers and disenfranchised because, as White upper-class women, they were traditionally confined to private, domestic spaces. Their preservation efforts helped them expand their own sphere of influence, but their preservation agenda was not designed to create a more inclusive historic landscape. Rather, it was designed to cement the social, cultural, and political influence of White, middle- and upper-class people. While all this is true, contemporary community leaders who want to protect places that are important to them are much more aligned with the motives of someone like Ann Pamela Cunningham—founder of the MVLA, who emphasized the emotional and moral value of historic places—than they are with preservationists who craft financial justifications for their work. While fiscal responsibility might justify preservation to a local government or to a property developer, marginalized communities have watched governments at all levels use fiscal conservatism as a tool to erode the resources available to the economically disadvantaged. Communities do not protect historic buildings because doing so will balance the budget; they protect historic buildings because they are places that matter to them. For them, preservation is about the story or stories of what happened there; it is about securing a place in the public memory. By reducing preservation to its quantitative value, we strip it of its meaning and power.

Case Study 1: Bush Street Temple

The Bush Street Temple served as a cornerstone of San Francisco's Japantown for decades. While even a quick review of the structure's history reveals a story of displacement and injustice, community members sought to frame it as a representation of community-making and survival. Built as a synagogue in 1895, the temple's use shifted as neighborhood demographics changed.[12] Teruro Kasuga purchased it in 1934, transforming it for Zen Buddhist observances. It became known as the Soto Mission. During World War II, an African American congregation rented the building from its Japanese owners during their internment.[13] In this case, the owners were able to retain the title to the building and were able to return to it after internment ended. Membership in the Buddhist Soto Mission (Sokoji) grew to 250 in the postwar years. In the late 1950s and early 1960s, residents of San Francisco's Western Addition (the part of the city that includes Japantown and the adjacent predominantly African American Fillmore neighborhood) experienced massive dislocation and destruction of their neighborhoods as a result of federal urban renewal programs.[14]

For a few years in the 1960s, Soto Mission shared the Bush Street Temple space with the Zen Center, which trained Zen priests working with non-Japanese people.[15] Through the Zen Center, Sunryu Suzuki brought Zen Buddhism to a diverse group of people, and its popularity spread throughout the United States from San Francisco and the Bush Street Temple. By the 1970s, members of the Sokoji Soto Mission bristled at the use of their space

Exterior of the Kokoro Assisted Living building, formerly the Bush Street Temple, February 2012. Photograph by Kristen Baldwin Deathridge.

by non-Japanese and also longed for a more architecturally traditional worship space, something Bush Street could never provide.[16] They built a new space nearby, on Post Street.[17]

A local redevelopment agency purchased the building in 1973 and leased the building to the San Francisco Go Club. Although the go club hosted

Japanese cultural games and showed samurai movies in the space, the Bush Street Temple remained largely empty for twenty-five years.[18] Beginning in the 1980s, Felix Warburg, a prominent Jewish businessman, began campaigning to save the Bush Street Temple. By this time, Japantown had fewer Japanese residents. As often happens, the Japanese community had moved out to the suburbs in search of lower rents and more space. However, many people still returned to the area at least once a week for shopping, restaurants, and beauty parlor appointments. An interfaith organization, the Japanese American Religious Foundation (JARF), worked to keep former residents of Japantown connected and aware of their common interests.[19] While Warburg was trying to raise funds to purchase Bush Street Temple in the late 1980s and early to mid-1990s, many Japantown advocates, including those connected to JARF, saw the building as essential to their plans for the revitalization of the neighborhood.

Members of JARF recognized the significance of the Bush Street Temple, in all its incarnations, for Japantown, and they wanted to ensure it could continue to serve the community. After many public meetings, they decided that the building should be adapted for use as income-restricted apartments for retirees. The group saw this as a way to encourage the return of former Japantown residents, a shift that could help reclaim the neighborhood's residential history. Significantly, neighbors of non-Japanese descent supported this idea. Warburg became a vocal supporter of the project once the rehabilitation plan included preservation of the Jewish sanctuary. The redevelopment agency opened the property to bids in 1996, and they selected JARF's plan.[20] Major renovations were required due to the dilapidated state of the building, but Kokoro Assisted Living opened in 2003.

From the planning stages onward, those involved with the Kokoro project wanted to honor the history of the place and incorporate it into the new use. The members of the board and other supporters, including Warburg, saw history as an essential part of what made the Bush Street Temple a keystone in the community. Those involved wanted to ensure the story remained; they had already seen changes in the demographics of the neighborhood and knew this would continue, but they wanted to include this part of Japantown's legacy.[21] They wanted to work to reverse some of the economic displacement in the neighborhood, and also to serve people who were economically precarious.

Preserving the sanctuary space ensures that everyone who comes inside the building can see its former religious purpose. It is important to be clear

Interior of Kokoro, former Bush Street Temple worship space, February 2010. Photograph by Kristen Baldwin Deathridge.

that the space has been restored most closely to its period of use as a synagogue, with little trace of its uses either as an African American Christian church or as Soto Mission. The use of the space during WWII years by Christians has proved nearly impossible to track, and more should be done in this direction. However, the folks at Kokoro talk often about the building's uses by the Japantown community, despite the fact that this is not reflected in the architecture. It remains obvious to Westerners upon entering that the room was a religious space of some variety. Today, the space is used for a variety of events: mealtimes, activities, and musical performances, as well as religious services. In keeping with the multireligious history of the Bush Street Temple and the wider neighborhood, services rotate among various religions and denominations, including all those that have historically practiced in the space. There are also reproductions of several images from the Magnes Collection of Jewish Art and Life at the Bancroft Library in the lobby and entry hallway, which tell part of the story of the building's original use.

Kokoro administrators provide limited interpretation of the historic temple. There is information about the history of the Bush Street Temple both on the website and in the brochure for Kokoro. By necessity, the public has limited access to the former sanctuary. Because public funds were accessed for completion of this project, general public access is required. The facility's bylaws state that anyone can access the space, provided they call ahead, but few individuals actually do so unless they are visiting a resident. There are frequent, specific opportunities for community members to access the space. At the grand opening ceremony, eight ministers, including Felix Warburg, provided the traditional blessing of their faiths to the space.[22] Twelve churches, members of JARF, mainly located in the surrounding neighborhood, use the sanctuary space for events. The public funds also require that Kokoro provide its tenants with moderate-income pricing rather than market rental rates for the area.

In an interview, former JARF and Kokoro board member Steven Suzuki noted, "Culture is the fabric of neighborhoods."[23] The San Francisco Redevelopment Agency, which had purchased the Bush Street Temple, and members of various local communities worked together for the adaptive reuse of the building. Japantown supporters and activists see the former temple building as literally holding down the corner of their neighborhood, and they wanted to continue using the space for worship and community events as much as possible.[24] These same advocates acknowledge that many in the Japanese American community have little interest in saving a building for its own sake.[25] Linda Jofuku, director of the Japantown Task Force, said in an interview that folks worked hard to reuse Bush Street Temple as Kokoro Assisted Living to help restore "the psyche of a culture."[26] Kokoro has become self-sustaining and can be termed an economic success, but the primary driver for the project was preserving the history and restoring the residency of the community. These activists committed to saving the space not only for aesthetic or economic reasons; cultural significance was the driving factor.

Case Study 2: Lincoln Heights Rosenwald School
Meanwhile, on the other side of the country, in the small town of North Wilkesboro, North Carolina, a group of concerned citizens has been trying to save their former school, Lincoln Heights. During the Progressive Era, separate did not often mean equal in any sense of the word. Booker T. Washington (1856–1915) was well aware of this fact and convinced Julius Rosenwald (1862–1932) that he could do something to improve education for Black southerners. Eventually, Rosenwald funded over 5,300 school buildings, teacherages (residences for teachers), and workshops across the South.[27] During the 1920s, local people worked to replace the traditional but outdated one-room schools in Wilkes County, North Carolina, with larger schools, better reflective of Progressive Era attitudes toward education. By the late 1930s, all the one-room schools had been closed. While several consolidated schools were built for White students in the area, Lincoln Heights was the only school for Black children. The project was driven by local African Americans and funded by a combination of money from the Rosenwald fund, Wilkes County, and local families. During the planning stages, prospective students sold "bricks" for twenty-five cents each to raise the community's portion.

Originally established as Wilkes County Training Center, the community changed the name to Lincoln Heights because they had designed it as a state-of-the-art school at which students could "reach the heights of Lincoln."

Lincoln Heights opened in 1924 with six classrooms and an auditorium. Students came not only from Wilkes County but also from the surrounding counties of Alleghany, Ashe, Caldwell, and Surrey. It was similar to schools built for Whites in the area. The bathrooms were outdoors, students brought water in from a well, and there was no gymnasium. Rooms were heated using potbellied stoves. At the same time, while Lincoln Heights represented an improvement in local African American education, it still did not provide Black students with an education fully equal to that White students received. Students at Lincoln Heights used outdated textbooks, handed down from White schools. Several students had to commute long distances. Commuters came to North Wilkesboro for the week, rooming with local families, and only returned home on weekends. Particularly in later years, there were subjects offered at the White Wilkes Central High School that were not available either at Lincoln Heights or in other, more rural, White schools.

By the 1950s, Lincoln Heights had several outbuildings, including a gymnasium, and it had been expanded twice. Elementary and high school students were bused in from five surrounding counties. In 1965, more than a decade after the Supreme Court's *Brown v. Board of Education* decision, the state of North Carolina sought to comply with desegregation by implementing a "Freedom of Choice" plan. Parents could continue to send their kids to segregated schools or they could choose to integrate their children into local White schools. Most parents in the region served by Lincoln Heights chose to send their children to more convenient and more modern schools that had previously served only White students. Lincoln Heights closed in 1968.

Nonetheless Lincoln Heights School remained a source of pride for those who had attended as well as for other members of the local Black community. Elizabeth Ann Parks Grinton galvanized a local effort to preserve the building and retain it for use as a community center. The school had long been a center of neighborhood life. Local people had attended performances,

Lincoln Heights School, current front entrance (this was the rear of the building when it was a school), September 2015. Photograph by Kristen Baldwin Deathridge.

dances, meals, parades, and other events there. Under Grinton's leadership, they formed the Lincoln Heights Recreation Corporation (LHRC), an alumni group, to manage the property.

Members of the LHRC understood the value of Lincoln Heights history. The school is a reminder of life in the Jim Crow South, but it is also a symbol of the community's effort to transcend the limits imposed by segregation by providing Black children with the best possible education. Alumni feared that young people did not understand the significance of this school to the community. They began to reach out to traditional preservation groups in North Carolina, wanting to gather information about how formal organizations could help them share their story and repair the building for ongoing use.[28]

The LHRC found creative and practical ways to keep the structure as a living part of the community. They leased space to a local Masonic Lodge, hosted fish frys and bingo nights, and rented the building for celebrations by a variety of groups and individuals, including members of the local Hispanic community. I first encountered this project as part of my role as an assistant professor teaching public history at Appalachian State University. In 2015, my students and I began working with LHRC board chair Brenda Dobbins to have the property listed on the National Register of Historic Places. The LHRC recognized that listing the site on the National Register would help prove its significance both to a broader local community and within the context of a larger national history. They also hoped that recognition of this nature would help them access grant funds for repairs.

The students met with the board and worked in teams to complete several significant tasks that the board requested. They completed a draft nomination to list the main building on the National Register of Historic Places. They conducted a landscape survey to determine if any of the other buildings formerly associated with the campus could be nominated. They developed an exhibition proposal. They compiled a list of grants that might help fund renovations to the structure. They wrote a historic structure report on the main building, detailing its current condition and listing priorities and strategies for rehabilitation.[29] The students also created a plan that included suggestions for including more young people in work to meet the goals of the Lincoln Heights Recreation group. The members of the LHRC board want young people to recognize their story and become involved.

The next semester, another a group of public history graduate students from Appalachian State and I worked with the LHRC to develop a website

Members of the LHRC, students in an Introduction to Historic Preservation graduate course, and Kristen Baldwin Deathridge, with "This Place Matters" flag from the National Trust for Historic Preservation, September 2015. Courtesy of Kristen Baldwin Deathridge.

so that they could share their story and solicit input from the wider community. The site did not see much traffic at first, but the group turned its attention to other, more pressing matters, including the completion of a grant proposal to fund repair of the school building roof. In December 2016, we received a National Endowment for the Humanities Common Heritage grant. This grant enabled us to host a one-day event where members of the community brought photographs, artifacts, and other items to be scanned or photographed on-site. Community members received digital copies of their scanned or photographed items on USB drives at the event, and we created a digital collection that is linked to the LHRC website as well as to the Appalachian State University Library's digital special collections.[30] The day featured public programming, including talks from alumni of the school, screening of the 2015 documentary *Rosenwald*, and a talk by Mary Hoffschwelle, author of the 2006 book *Rosenwald Schools of the American South*. This event helped with the LHRC's goals of publicizing their story and preserving it for the future.

Collaboration between Appalachian State University students and the LHRC served a larger purpose. It revealed the commitment and activity of the Lincoln Heights group over the years, and it also created a bond between the organization and the students. They enjoy working with young people and sharing their story with anyone who will come and listen. The members of the LHRC board and the students genuinely appreciate each other. The building's preservation requires funding beyond the immediate reach of the Lincoln Heights alumni and friends, and the students were able to help them find and win grants to help. At the same time, projects like these bring prestige to the university and the public history program, as well as providing essential training for students. On one hand, university partnerships provide a great way to overcome economic hurdles for grassroots groups, but on the other, the unequal balance of power in these agreements can prove problematic. Regardless, Lincoln Heights alumni continue working to preserve and restore their building, not to turn a profit (though of course they want to be able to afford upkeep without going into debt) but to share their story.

Who Gets to Be Considered a Preservation Activist?

Both the members of the group that worked to save the Bush Street Temple and those working to save Lincoln Heights know about preservation. They have learned the term in order to reach their goals, but very few would call themselves preservationists or activists. I suspect that some readers might wonder why this question matters. To the community members themselves, perhaps it does not matter much.[31] But it matters to our broader understanding of preservation as a potential tool for establishing healthy and self-determined communities. The members of each group were collecting histories and shaping their own narratives, just as the best public history work helps communities do, and they used preservation to achieve their goals. In an environment where some of the most powerful preservationists heavily utilize economic arguments, groups that foreground community history and address local needs may appear radical to the traditional preservation community. They seem this way because, despite many public history-trained preservationists recognizing that work should be done with and for locals, most preservation processes, particularly laws around preservation, are not set up to prioritize working that way. These cases show that radicalism in preservation can manifest simply in the insistence that the historic meaning of a place is more important than its potential future economic benefit.

The work at Bush Street was done long before I came to study it for my doctoral dissertation, though those responsible for its preservation were happy to talk with me and very generous with their time. I spoke at length with Steven Suzuki, who had been a board member of JARF and of Kokoro, as well as meeting with members of the Japantown Task Force, who were moving forward with plans to continue revitalizing their neighborhood and telling the stories of its former residents. They certainly did not need my help, though it must be acknowledged that the city of San Francisco has prioritized this sort of neighborhood redevelopment. The members of the LHRC asked for help with their projects, but they already had specific goals in mind. They'd been doing their own historical research for years and had reached out to the State of North Carolina's Natural and Cultural Resources Department for assistance.

The answer to the question "Are these groups examples of grassroots preservation activism?" is a clear yes because each community drove their projects. Both JARF and the LHRC have worked to save special places and to share those stories with their wider communities. Kokoro has been economically successful, and the folks at Lincoln Heights are still working to get more of a financial investment to continue using their former school as a community center. Both groups' passion for these places shines through. How can preservationists engage in the necessary work of demonstrating the economic viability of their work without losing the heart and soul of the work itself? There may not be a singular answer that applies in all contexts, but we must remember that people want to preserve places *because* of their histories in order to better strike this balance. Preserving places costs money, but it is the stories that show why places should be saved.

Those who live in, work at, and visit Kokoro Assisted Living recognize that it is a special place; they are drawn to the deep history of community events and worship that took place in the building. Speaking on a similar theme, Elizabeth Ann Parks Grinton said, "Lincoln Heights has never been an empty place. It has served its purpose and continues to serve the children of this county. As long as a human being lives in this area, it will go on because Lincoln Heights means so much to many people." Lincoln Heights "was not only a place of learning, but a reminder of black students' history and the black community effort to provide quality education to its children."[32]

Notes

For their time, comments, and discussion, I am grateful to those who have reviewed this piece in the years it has taken to bring this piece to publication. Thanks so very much to Denise D. Meringolo, for her dedication and skill as editor of *Radical Roots*.

1. The displacement of communities in Brooklyn, New York, due to some of the negative effects of gentrification is so well-known as to be played for laughs. For an example, see the TBS show *The Last O.G.* (2018–), in which the main character is released from prison after fifteen years, "returning to his newly gentrified Brooklyn neighborhood" ("The Last O.G.," TBS, accessed March 4, 2021, https://www.tbs.com/shows/the-last-og). However, in recent years, people such as Justin Garrett Moore, executive director of the NYC Public Design Commission, have been working for citizen-led, inclusive approaches to planning in Brooklyn and elsewhere. Moore's work does not particularly integrate stories, but it does show the best of planning and preservation that considers people first. New York City has developed the *NYC Neighborhood Planning Playbook* (available at https://www1.nyc.gov/site/hpd/services-and-information/nyc-neighborhood-planning-playbook.page), and Moore's Indianapolis-based Urban Patch is a group doing similar work. See Justin Garrett Moore, "Making a Difference: Reshaping the Past, Present, and Future toward Greater Equity," *Forum Journal* 31, no. 4 (2017): 19–26.
2. The authors in this section participated in many conversations about the meanings of *grassroots*, during our collaborative research process. We have had long discussions in an effort to pin down a specific meaning. Ultimately, we concluded that it was necessary for scholars to define the term as it relates to their own work, as I do in this paragraph.
3. This isn't a bad thing! See the introduction to Stephanie Meeks and Kevin C. Murphy's *The Past and Future City: How Historic Preservation Is Reviving America's Communities* (Washington, DC: Island Press, 2016), 1–24, for more on the appeal of historic preservation to a variety of people and why they don't always recognize their work as preservation.
4. There are a variety of publications available at these groups' websites that explore both economic output and environmental sustainability. Preservation Green Lab, *The Greenest Building: Quantifying the Environmental Value of Building Reuse* (Washington, DC: National Trust for Historic Preservation, 2011); Donovan Rypkema and Briana Paxton, *Beyond Tourism: Historic Preservation in the Economy and Life in Savannah and Chatham County* (Savannah, GA: Historic Savannah Foundation, 2015), would be excellent places to begin.
5. The Leadership in Energy and Environmental Design (LEED) Green Building Rating System was made available to the public beginning in 2000 and has undergone several changes since that time. Initially, only one of the six available classifications applied to historic buildings, but that "Existing Buildings" category is for

maintenance, not for adaptive reuse of historic buildings. In 2006, the National Trust for Historic Preservation, working with other interested groups, began lobbying the US Green Buildings Council (the organization that evaluates and issues LEED certifications) to consider historic buildings in new ways. LEED 2009 included some updates that helped adaptive reuse and historic projects to earn the certification. Barbara A. Campagna, "How Changes to LEED Will Benefit Existing and Historic Buildings," *Forum News* 15, no. 2 (November/December 2008), https://forum.savingplaces.org/viewdocument/how-changes-to-leed-will-benefit-ex. Historic Preservationists have continued to push the US Green Buildings Council to go further, and LEEDv4, released in 2013, addressed more of their concerns. With LEEDv4, buildings listed on the National Register of Historic Places, their state register, or a local register automatically get 5 points toward certification; this is an improvement because rather than looking at a percentage based on how much building fabric is reused in a project, it considers the cultural relevance and incorporates historic standing. Barbara A. Campagna, "Raising the Bar for LEED," *True Green Cities* (blog), July 22, 2013, http://barbaracampagna.com/category/leed-v4/page/4/.

6 Such as Atlanta-based Presonomics.
7 Jane Jacobs, *The Death and Life of Great American Cities*, vintage ed. (1961; repr. New York: Random House, 1992); Stewart Brand, *How Buildings Learn: What Happens after They're Built* (New York: Penguin, 1994).
8 Both are in Chicago. The Pullman Historic District was designated a national monument by President Obama in February 2016. It is also the first National Park Service unit in Chicago.
9 As happened with Prentice. It was part of Northwestern University's medical campus, and they could not justify keeping the historic building that they believed could not be retrofitted to support the technology needed for medical research. Preservationists argued this point, but the university would not be moved. This happens. Not all preservation fights can be won.
10 Special Committee on Historic Preservation, United States Conference of Mayors, *With Heritage So Rich* (1966; repr. Washington, DC: Preservation Books, 1999).
11 Ann Pamela Cunningham created the Mount Vernon Ladies' Association in 1853 to save George Washington's home in the mid-nineteenth century. This was the first of several "ladies' associations," including the Ladies' Hermitage Association, founded in 1889 to preserve Andrew Jackson's home, and these were joined by the Sons and Daughters of the American Revolution (founded 1889 and 1890, respectively). For more information about the traditionally accepted origins of historic preservation, see Norman Tyler, Ilene R. Tyler, and Ted J. Ligibel, *Historic Preservation: An Introduction to Its History, Principles, and Practice*, 2nd ed. (New York: W. W. Norton, 2009), esp. 29–30 on APC and associations; William J. Murtagh, *Keeping Time: The History and Theory of Preservation in America*, 3rd ed. (Hoboken, NJ: Wiley & Sons, 2006), esp. 14–16 on APC and associations.

12 Their congregation was the Ohabai Shalome Temple, but folks began calling it Bush Street almost immediately. It was called this throughout its religious use, regardless of which sect was using the building at the time.

13 According to the 1913–50 Sanborn Fire Insurance Map, the congregation was called Macedonia Methodist. A 2003 *San Francisco Chronicle* article and the collection summary from the Magnes Collection of Jewish Art and Life both call it "Macedonia Missionary Baptist." Gerald D. Adams, "Tug of War over Old S.F. Synagogue Building Ends: Jewish Architectural Heritage to Coexist with Asian American Center," *San Francisco Chronicle*, September 2, 2003; "Magnes Collection on Congregation Ohabai Shalome, 1871–1975," Magnes Collection of Jewish Art and Life, accessed January 24, 2012, http://www.magnes.org/collections/archives/western-jewish-americana/magnes-collection-congregation-ohabai-shalome-1871-1-0.

14 Japantown Task Force, *Draft Japantown Better Neighborhood Plan* (San Francisco: San Francisco Planning Commission, 2009), 18.

15 Landmarks Preservation Advisory Board, *Final Case Report: Bush Street Temple (Soto Mission) 1881 Bush Street*, 1975, p. 2, available at http://sfplanninggis.org/docs/landmarks_and_districts/LM81.pdf.

16 The preferred style would likely have been Zenshuuyu, a Japanese architectural style based on the style that came with Zen Buddhism from China to Japan. Mary Neighbor Parent, "Zenshuuyu," *Japanese Architecture and Art Net User System*, accessed January 5, 2018, http://www.aisf.or.jp/%7Ejaanus/deta/z/zenshuuyou.htm.

17 Donna Graves, *Japantown, San Francisco, California: Historic Context Statement* (San Francisco: Page & Turnbull, 2009), 37.

18 Adams, "Tug of War."

19 This organization had been established in the 1950s.

20 Steven Suzuki, interview by author, San Francisco, February 1, 2012.

21 Suzuki.

22 Suzuki.

23 Suzuki.

24 Suzuki.

25 The Japantown Task Force report, which discusses the community heritage of the neighborhood, lists "physical heritage" (including buildings) last among five cultural resources. People, including those of Nikkei cultural identity and other groups with roots in the area, are listed first, followed by customs, events, and the arts; businesses that contribute to cultural lifeways; and community service groups. Japantown Task Force, *Draft Japantown Better Neighborhood Plan*, 15.

26 Adams, "Tug of War."

27 Rosenwald (an owner in Sears, Roebuck, and Co.) served on the board at the Tuskegee Institute. The Rosenwald Fund provided partial funding, building plans, and sometimes educational materials to communities throughout the South. For more on Rosenwald and the schools, see Mary S. Hoffschwelle, *Rosenwald Schools of the American South* (Gainsville: University of Florida Press, 2014); Mary S. Hoffschwelle,

Preserving Rosenwald Schools (Washington, DC: National Trust for Historic Preservation, 2012); Aviva Kempner, *Rosenwald: The Remarkable Story of a Jewish Partnership with African American Communities* (Washington, DC: Ciesla Foundation, 2015), DVD.

28 Material summarized from author's attendance at several LHRC board meetings in the course of their work with the board.

29 The North Carolina Department of Natural and Cultural Resources hired Cheri Szcodronski and Heather Slane to complete National Register nominations for seven Rosenwald schools throughout the state, including Lincoln Heights. They used the students' draft as research for the project. Lincoln Heights was listed on the National Register of Historic Places in September 2018.

30 Mrs. Grinton donated her papers to the Appalachian State University library on her passing. They are not fully digitized, but there's an exhibit highlighting them; see the Elizabeth Ann Parks Grinton Papers in the Appalachian State University Libraries Digital Collections (https://omeka.library.appstate.edu/exhibits/show/elizabeth-ann-parks-grinton-pa). See also Ashlee Lanier et al., Lincoln Heights Rosenwald School website, Spring 2016, accessed March 4, 2021, https://lincolnheightsrosenwald.org. That site does not have the storage space to host the resulting collection, but it is linked there, and the LHRC has digital copies. The entire collection is available at "Preserving and Sharing the Story of the Lincoln Heights Rosenwald School," Appalachian State University Library Digital Collections, accessed March 4, 2021, https://omeka.library.appstate.edu/collections/show/86.

31 At least, this was the case when last we spoke; things may have changed, particularly in Japantown, since early 2012. Personnel has certainly shifted.

32 Elizabeth Grinton, quoted in Fay Byrd, *Wilkes County Bits and Pieces* (Wilkesboro, NC: Wilkes County Community College, 2011).

Philadelphia's Original Social Justice Warriors

The Little Big Story of Germantown and the Germantown Mennonites

Craig Stutman

Germantown Past and Present

On July 8, 2017, on a hot and sunny day in the Germantown section of Philadelphia, the neighborhood's multicultural spirit and history were on full display. The Universal African Dance & Drum Ensemble was dancing and drumming to West African rhythms and beats on a stage that was located directly in front of the Deshler-Morris House, otherwise known as the "Germantown White House," a National Register of Historic Places–designated site built in 1752 where George Washington lived during extended stays in 1793 and 1794.[1] The occasion for the celebration on this particular summer day was the Germantown Festival, a relatively new collaborative event organized by the Germantown United Community Development Corporation (GUCDC) and Historic Germantown with the aim of attracting community members and other visitors to celebrate the neighborhood's historic sites and support an array of local businesses located along Germantown Avenue. The GUCDC declared in its 2011 mission statement its intention to "promote and facilitate the revitalization of Germantown's business corridors through a sustainable, creative, and community-driven approach to economic development." Its partner on this afternoon, Historic Germantown, is a nonprofit, community-based umbrella organization, whose aim is to oversee and assist, both directly and indirectly (through programming, grants, and/or best practices), a loose confederation of sixteen National Register of Historic Places sites, all located within a National Historic District along Germantown Avenue.[2]

The Universal African Dance & Drum Ensemble at Germantown's Second Saturday Festival, July 2017. Photograph by Craig Stutman.

As a spectator during this vibrant event, I was painfully aware of the irony as I watched the Universal African Drum & Dance ensemble perform in front of George Washington's former home. Here we were—men, women, and children of all ethnicities, religions, and sexual orientations—celebrating peace, love, and diversity on a street abounding with numerous African American-centered economic and historic enterprises. Yet the revelries took place in front of George Washington's Germantown White House; The very same George Washington who was the "owner" of hundreds of enslaved men, women, and children and who was an advocate for a strong federal fugitive slave bill.[3] Most of us who were there that afternoon also knew something else about the neighborhood's history. We knew that this was a special place where Black and White Philadelphians had challenged this kind of morally corrupt ideology for over three hundred years. We knew that it was home to centuries of antislavery and abolitionist protests. We knew that it had been part of an active corridor that housed many stops on the Underground Railroad during the nineteenth century. We knew that this was a place where the oldest petition against slavery ever brought forth by a religious institution in the British colonies was signed: the 1688 Mennonite and Quaker petition against slavery. All these stories have been continually memorialized and celebrated for hundreds of years within Philadelphia's Germantown. Past and present. Present and past.

Among the various musical, dance, and poetry performances that had taken place on the central stage that afternoon, and amid the numerous food trucks and the thousands of revelers, were the tables and booths set up and manned by people who represented an assortment of Germantown's community organizations, agencies, businesses, and historic sites. I was stationed at one of these tables. It was a stall set up for the Germantown Mennonite Historic Trust (GMHT), an organization that was founded in the early 1950s by congregation members who desired to oversee and maintain their historic church, built in 1770, as well as its grounds, archives, and cemetery. As a board member for GMHT, I was at the Germantown Festival that afternoon serving as a volunteer. My job for the day was not only to give a brief history of our site to those who visited our booth but also to assist the many parents who came over to us with their children on an arts and crafts endeavor that we had set out on our table. Replicating what is a fairly common children's art activity, we had laid out strips of construction paper (different colors) as well as latticed, square-cut paper templates (also different colors) so that children or adults who wanted to participate could "weave" together the thin strips of paper into the paper-lattice templates, thus creating "miniquilts" that became their takeaway gift.[4]

A few blocks away from the central plaza where the Germantown Festival was held sits the 1770-built, 1973 National Register of Historic Places–designated, and 1935 Historic American Buildings Survey (HABS)–surveyed Germantown Mennonite Meetinghouse.[5] Specifically located at 6133 Germantown Avenue, the church rests along a corridor that for a few hundred years was referred to as "Main Street" and before that was an active Lenape Indian trail. The 1770 church was not the first church built on the property; that honor is given to a rustic log cabin that is no longer in existence and which dates back to 1708. William Rittenhouse, the founder of the first paper mill in North America, preached his first sermons in that original church to the earliest German and Dutch Mennonite immigrants. The congregation's size ebbed and flowed for approximately three hundred years until the mid-1980s, when the Germantown Mennonites relocated their worship services to a site around the corner on Washington Lane (formerly known as "Keyser's Lane," the name of a prominent Germantown Mennonite family).[6] Consequently, the current structure that the trust oversees today is no longer an active church but instead serves as a historic site that is administered by an executive director, a few staff members, and a board.[7]

Throughout Germantown, radical approaches to public history have taken shape over the past few decades. This can be seen in the growth of a number of innovative and/or reimagined historic sites, freshly interpreting the 335-year history of the community from the colonial era to the present.[8] Included in this group are Vashti DuBois's Colored Girls Museum, whose founder describes its confines as "a memoir museum, which honors the stories, experiences, and history of Colored Girls"; the Aces Museum, a former Black USO establishment and ballroom that operated during World War II and is now designated as "a museum that pays tribute to Minority Veterans"; and the Black Writers Museum, which, located in Germantown's Vernon Park, is headquartered at the historic colonial Vernon House and was founded by Supreme D. Dow, who organizes events such as the People's Poetry & Jazz Festival.[9] These projects and others like them are "radical" because they have disrupted unexamined ideas about which stories are central and which are marginal in both local and national history. History on the avenue had, in the past, been based on a top-down, static, colonial-architectural-historical narrative. Today, it is re-created and reimagined by African-centered, interracial, class-informed, gender-informed, and LGBTQ storytellers.[10]

These trends are not simply recent. A tradition of grassroots history-making that rests on the community's independence of thought runs deep in local history. The legacy of slavery, slaveholding, and abolitionism are critical themes that tie together the community's Mennonite history and its contemporary public history landscape. These subjects have saturated Germantown's history from the founding years of the colony through to the present day. Cliveden, a National Historic Trust site, has been commemorated for over 240 years as the locale for the Battle of Germantown during the American Revolutionary War. Recently, Cliveden has begun to interpret the story of Quaker lawyer Benjamin Chew's connections to slavery, both directly as a slaveholder at his Germantown estate and as an absentee plantation owner in Delaware as well.[11] But Germantown residents find more meaning in the

1770 Germantown Mennonite Meetinghouse just a few blocks away. The site emphasizes the signing of the 1688 Mennonite petition against slavery. As forerunners of the American antislavery movement, these early German (and perhaps Dutch) residents of Pennsylvania[12] wrote a petition that was delivered to several local and regional Quaker meetings condemning slaveholding as an immoral, abhorrent institution that went directly against the Bible's golden rule. Essentially falling on deaf ears, this measure was not endorsed by the Quaker Church as a whole until 1756, which only then would censure slaveholders. It also foreshadowed the state of Pennsylvania's gradual abolition of the institution in 1780.

This essay traces the evolution of both the historical interpretation and the memory of this antislavery protest, from 1688 to the present, observing how the petition has been commemorated over time and how we tell the story today. Although incongruities abound as we follow this time line forward, there is also significant consistency in the emphasis that has been placed on this event. Protest against slaveholding was embraced not only in the Germantown community for hundreds of years but also by German Americans in general, whose immigrant communities in the late nineteenth century happily connected their origin story to both the founding of Germantown and the signing of the petition against slavery. Although the significance of the petition changed over time—sometimes it was highlighted and sometimes it was de-emphasized—the preservation of this document and its memory allowed a powerful possibility to remain part of Germantown public history. A belief in the importance of protest and social justice has shaped local identity and public history. Through storytelling, pageantry, festivals, anniversaries, memorials, historic markers, and sculpture, Germantown is united by the common threads of both honoring and celebrating diversity, elevating stories of social justice, and remembering and learning from the unexpected stories of our country's immigrant past.

Historic Context: Germantown's Mennonite Past and the Writing of the 1688 Petition

In October of 1683, only two years after William Penn had established the proprietary colony of Pennsylvania, a group of thirteen German Anabaptist families arrived at the port of Philadelphia. They disembarked from their ship, the *Concord*, and made their way up to the northwestern outskirts of the colony's capital, where they established homes and businesses. Hailing from the town of Krefeld (which was situated in the western portion of modern-day Germany close to the Rhine River to its east and the Netherland's border to its west), they had made the months-long trek across continental Europe and over the Atlantic Ocean because of a promise made to them by one of William Penn's most trusted land agents and confidants, Francis Daniel Pastorius. Pastorius, a lawyer, educator, and Lutheran Pietist, who would later become memorialized as the "Founder of Germantown," roamed the Palatinate region of the Rhineland at William Penn's urging, looking for religious dissidents and refugees who would benefit from Pennsylvania's "Holy Experiment." Pastorius assured the thirteen Krefeld Anabaptist families that Pennsylvania was a haven for religious tolerance, a place where they would be safe to worship as they pleased.[13]

Germantown Mennonite Meetinghouse in the 1950s. Courtesy of the Germantown Mennonite Historic Trust.

The Krefelders had suffered significant religious persecution while searching for a home in Europe. Disciples of Ulrich Zwingli, Conrad Grebel, and perhaps most notably, Menno Simons (hence the name Mennonites), the Krefeld Anabaptists had belonged to a sect that formed in the 1530s in Switzerland, only a few years after the Protestant Reformation.[14] They rejected what they saw as too much formality within the Catholic Church and within Martin Luther's new Protestant church. They rejected several of the Lutheran Church's policies, angering leadership. In addition, their antiwar stance and their rejection of infant baptism and an adherence instead to an adult "believer's baptism" led the dissidents to become anathema among both European Catholics and Protestants alike, a dilemma that forced them to wander the continent looking for a place free from persecution.[15] The Anabaptists had recorded and graphically illustrated the persecution they had suffered. Known as the *Martyr's Mirror*, these books were first published in Europe in 1660 and arrived among the possessions of many Anabaptists in The New World. Eventually, they were printed in the American colonies. The early effort to print the *Martyr's Mirror* was accomplished under the direction of Jacob Gottschalk, the third pastor of the Germantown Mennonite Church (from 1702 to 1725), after he left the settlement and moved to the Ephrata Cloister in the 1740s. Several copies of the Gottschalk volumes are on display in the back room of the Germantown Mennonite Meetinghouse.[16]

Perhaps because they had been victims of persecution and violence, the Germantown Mennonite's actively opposed acts of oppression against other groups of people. The community adopted an antislavery position, and in 1688, the members of the community authored the first formal protest against slavery in British North America. This protest was significant not only because it predated by more than a century the rise of the organized abolitionist movement but also because its authors insisted that there be consequences for members of Anabaptist sects and other Christians who held slaves. The Quakers rejected the measure, which was presented in succession to the monthly, quarterly, and annual meetings of the Friends, but the issue split congregations down the middle. Neither the New Jersey nor the Pennsylvania annual meetings adopted the policy of censuring slaveholders and condemning the transatlantic slave trade until the 1750s.[17] The protest occupies a central place in the local identity of Germantown today, and it is vigorously shared and interpreted throughout the community as a solidarity-building story of social justice. The Germantown Mennonite Historic Trust displays a 1901 memorial to the signing of the petition, which is on loan

A 1901 marker created by the Germantown Site and Relic Society (now the Germantown Historical Society) commemorating the 1688 antislavery petition. Photograph by Craig Stutman.

from the Germantown Historical Society. The GMHT also displays a facsimile of the actual petition (the original sits in the Swarthmore College Archives).

Visitors to the Meetinghouse hear selections from the original 1688 protest text.[18] Scholars argue that the text is significant because it was the first to emphasize the incompatibility of slavery with Christian values.[19] For example, both the members of the Anabaptist community and the broader community of Christian believers would have recognized references to the golden rule, such as this one: "There is a saying that we shall doe to all men like as we will be done ourselves; making no difference of what generation, descent or colour they are." But the document goes further, arguing that enslaved people had a moral right to revolt and that Christians could not oppose the fight for freedom while still claiming to uphold the tenets of their religious faith.[20]

Scholars' focus on the protestors' use of literal and figurative symbolism as literary devices in the attempt to make their argument persuasive, which is important, but the authors of the protest also do this with other powerful deployments of language and reasoning. They drew attention to the hypocrisy of Christians who might claim to uphold the Ten Commandments while also committing the atrocities of the slave trade. For example, some claim to uphold the commandment against adultery, yet they "do commit adultery, in separating wives from their husbands and giving them to others; and some sell the children of these poor creatures to other men." The petitioners also accused Anabaptist slaveholders of bringing shame to their community, committing persecution that far surpassed any perpetrated against them by European governments, some of which did not practice human bondage. They wrote, "You surpass Holland and Germany in this thing. This makes an ill report in all those countries of Europe, where they hear of, that ye Quakers doe here handel men as they handel there ye cattle." While some Germans, including Lutherans, were guilty of enslaving people, "Germans made up the first, and probably the most vehement group opposing slavery," and "their opposition appears to have been based on both religious and moral grounds, as well as a predisposition toward self-reliance and independence." In fact, few Germans had held slaves and they began protesting the institution of slavery soon after their arrival in Pennsylvania.[21] The stridency of German American antislavery activism is therefore central to the history of the German community more broadly and to Germantown specifically.

Historical Memory and the Germantown Mennonite Experience

The Mennonite community has been central to Germantown's grassroots expressions of heritage since the nineteenth century, but that community's history also became significant in the construction of a larger German American identity over the course of the twentieth century. By observing the evolution of commemorative activities, we can recognize subtle shifts in this identity at the local, state, and national levels over time. At first, commemorations portrayed the Germantown community as "pioneers," highlighting stories of migration and survival. On September 29, 1883, a syndicated column appeared in the *St. Louis Post Dispatch* describing the upcoming celebration of the Germantown settlement's bicentennial that was to occur in Philadelphia the following week. The article connected the city's burgeoning German immigrant population (many of whom had populated that region and arrived throughout the Midwest in the millions after the failed revolution of 1848) to "the pioneers who settled Germantown . . . in Philadelphia on October 6th of 1683" and reminded them, "It is this day which the Germans of the United States propose to celebrate." The author described these first German immigrants, drawing attention to their Mennonite theology and antiwar principles, and citing the community's first minister and printmaker, William Rittenhouse, for building "the first American Paper Mill in 1690, on a branch of the Wissahickon." Perhaps most significant, the article highlighted the 1688 Mennonite protest against slavery. The author emphasized the significance of celebrating such an event, asserting that "the two hundredth anniversary of the Germantown settlement will be celebrated by millions of American Germans."[22]

Local newspapers also covered the celebration. An article in the *Philadelphia Times* covered the preparations that were underway for a "large-scale and well-funded event" to celebrate the founding of Germantown. The plans finalized by the German American Pioneer Jubilee committee included an opening day concert at the Philadelphia Academy of Music. Speeches would be made "in both English and German." Invited guests would listen to a Mozart-composed, German librettist (Emanuel Schikaneder) version of "The Magic Flute," as well as hear selections from Felix Mendelssohn. The speaker of honor at the next afternoon's events was to be Carl Schurz. Schurz had been a major general for the Union during the Civil War, a United States senator supporting Reconstruction after the war, and secretary of the interior under President Rutherford B. Hayes.[23] The *Philadelphia Inquirer* ran a series of stories about the bicentennial. One article speculated, "If Pastorius, the founder of Germantown, were living now, his simple and loyal heart would be gladdened by ocular proof of the fact that 'young generations' look more than kindly upon the little Mennonite Colony of which he was the guiding spirit." The *Inquirer* also noted that one of the keynote speeches would be given by Samuel Pennypacker, the soon-to-be governor of Pennsylvania, "whose publications on the early history of Germantown have made him well known in literary circles."[24]

Bicentennial celebrations of the founding of Germantown and its Mennonites also took place in Europe. Correspondence from Germany appeared in the November 12, 1883, edition of the *Philadelphia Inquirer*, under the heading "Germantown: Its Bi-centennial Celebrated in Germany." Written by "a correspondent in Berlin," the piece excitedly announced that "besides the splendid festivals which have been celebrated in Germany within the last two months . . . there was a modest anniversary held at Crefeld[25] in commemoration of the two hundredth return of the day on which the first association of German emigrants departed for the present United States." The author suggested that had it not been for William Penn, the "thirteen Quaker and Mennonite families" would never have been able to settle peaceably in the New World "for conscience sake." The celebration in Krefeld included an "exhaustive sketch of the political and religious causes which drove these Crefeld linen weavers" across the sea. But what most struck the foreign correspondent and the German revelers was their former countrymen and women's role in the 1688 protest against American slavery: "As an immortal memorial of them be praised that glorious protest which, as early as April 1688, was made by those against human slavery, and which places them on the same platform with the noblest abolitionists of our day."[26]

If German people were proud to claim the migrants as part of their own history, American attention to the celebration signifies the crucial place that Germantown's history began to occupy in German American identity. Carl Schurz's presence at the Philadelphia celebration is a significant indicator of this. As a German immigrant who had arrived after the 1848 revolution, Schurz believed not only in overthrowing monarchy but also, more broadly, in protecting civil liberties and promoting personal and religious freedoms. Because he was on the losing side of the revolution, he was also among the millions of refugees who made their way to the United States, and the Midwest in particular, to start a new life. Schurz served the Union during the American Civil War and as a Radical Republican during Reconstruction, passionately advocating for the civil and political rights of African American people. Many of Schurz's fellow refugees had strongly supported the antislavery movement before the war and civil rights (at least based on race) after its conclusion. These values, virtues, and ideals matched their fellow countrymen's quest for freedom and human rights. Celebration of the connection between antislavery activism and German American history would last well into the next century.

By the early twentieth century, festivals commemorating "German American Day" became ubiquitous in a number of American cities. An October 1910 celebration in Lincoln, Nebraska, was typical: it included parades, pageants, and tableaux depicting German emigration, history, and accomplishments. The *Lincoln Star* ran a large banner entitled "Spectacular Pageant in honor of German Day." In a front-page article, the author claimed that "the realization of a mighty influence which has helped to make America great among the nations was brought home to thousands of people who thronged the streets of Lincoln today and witnessed the passage of the German Day parade." Among the floats to make the several-mile journey during the pageant was a representation of the *Concord*, the ship that had brought Germantown's Mennonite families to colonial North America.[27]

The popular festivals and parades represent a process by which German American communities adopted the history of Germantown as part of their own identity. But festivals are temporary, so their messages and meaning are mutable. The establishment of Germantown as historically and culturally significant entered a new phase in the first decades of the twentieth century, one with more permanent implications for German American public history: monument building. The *Lincoln Star* article reported that German American benevolent societies in Lincoln had made an appeal for donations to support the construction of a monument dedicated to Daniel Pastorius and the thirteen Krefeld Mennonite families who had founded Germantown. Further, not only had the committee recommended that the German American Alliance of Nebraska help fund "the erection of a suitable monument in honor of Daniel Pastorius," but a congressmen in DC had already "made an appropriation of $30,000 for this purpose upon condition that the national German-American Alliance appropriate a like amount."[28] This proposal began a process in which commemorations of Germantown moved toward enshrining particular aspects of the story as meaningful not only to the community but to the nation. The German American Alliance of Nebraska was likely aware that a project to construct a monument to Francis Daniel Pastorius had been in the works for several years. The idea had been originated with Charles J. Hexamer, president of the National German American Alliance.[29] Hexamer recruited sculptor Jacob Otto Schweizer, a member of the German Society of Pennsylvania, to design a cornerstone to be laid in Germantown's Vernon Park on October 6, 1908, at the 225th anniversary of Germantown's founding. In a letter dated July 17, 1908, Richard J. Austin, the treasurer of the German Society of Pennsylvania and Chairman of the finance committee for the founder's day celebration in Germantown, confirmed there would be installed "in Vernon Park the cornerstone of a monument which they will erect to commemorate the landing of Francis Daniel Pastorius and the band of German emigrants who settled in Germantown in 1683."[30]

It was not until 1910, however, that the drive for the construction of a monument really began to take off, as Philadelphia congressman J. Hampton Moore got explicit support from Washington for a monument to be installed in Vernon Park.[31] Moore's Bill (HR 9137) provided for a $25,000 federal grant and required the National German Alliance to provide matching funds for the design, construction, and installation of the monument. In a speech to Congress advocating for this cause, Moore proclaimed that the funds were to be used to help build "a monument in historic Germantown, Philadelphia, to memorialize the first settlement of Germans in what is now the United States." Moore had to address the clamor that such a memorial might fail because it "propose[d] to memorialize a certain class of citizens." Moore argued, "That noble band of scholars and industrialists made so deep an impress upon the American character that is questionable whether we owe less to it than to the martial heroes whom we so cheerfully celebrate upon battlefields and in city squares." Moore placed particular emphasis on the community's role in antislavery activism, arguing, "German Americans have always shown good common sense and a just appreciation of the personal rights of others," and "the first successful German Colony, at Germantown (now the twenty-second ward of Philadelphia), in 1688 drew up a remonstrance against slavery—the first of all such protests."[32]

The start of World War I in Europe impacted the construction of the monument and shifted its messages in subtle but important ways. Although the appropriation bill eventually received the necessary support from Congress the timing for creating a monument to German immigration to America was unfortunate. Germany's role as aggressor during the war spawned widespread suspicion and hostility toward Germans, German Americans, and German history and culture. This was the case despite the fact that the political and communal beliefs of the earliest German Mennonite settlers and those of the later German Lutherans and Catholics placed many German Americans in opposition to the German government, especially German policies of imperialism. The monument's unveiling, originally scheduled May 28, 1917, was canceled or postponed a number of times because "relations between the

A 1908 letter describing the plans for founder's day celebrations, including the plans to lay a cornerstone for a monument to Pastorius. Courtesy of the Germantown Historical Society / Historic Germantown.

country and Germany" were "strained."[33] The sculpture, created by Albert Jaeger, was stored away for two and a half years before its eventual unveiling. The local press covered the controversy, and in 1919, there was still a hesitancy to fully support the unveiling of the monument. For instance, in June of 1919, the *Philadelphia Public Ledger* asserted that "despite its designer's plea that Germania is not represented in his handiwork, the Pastorius monument in Vernon Park, Germantown, which is scheduled to be unveiled, is still the target for attack." The Twenty-Second Ward's Council of the Stonemasons Fellowship objected to the fact that the monument would be "unveiled in spite of objections by Germantown residents." They argued that the monument "spread German propaganda . . . to retard the progress of the United States," and were angered that it was "not a memorial to Pastorius but . . . a memorial to German arrogance."[34] Similarly, a September 1919 *Philadelphia Public Ledger* article reported that "a committee representing various secret societies of Germantown has undertaken to bring about the removal and destruction of the founders' monument, in Vernon Park, which has been the cause of controversy because it is supposed to be tainted with Germanism and which is now enclosed in a box and under the control of the war department." Among the committee's "resolutions" was that "the secretary of war [should] be authorized and directed to remove and destroy this evidence of German propaganda, and place on the base or platform two or more captured German cannon."[35]

Virulent anti-German sentiment led German American communities across the nation to more carefully define and defend their commitment to American ideals. In spite of vocal opposition to the project, the monument was finally unveiled in November 1920, bearing both the name and image of Pastorius as well as the names of the thirteen Mennonite families who settled Germantown in 1683. The images on the monument seemed to establish the Germantown community as quintessentially American by depicting the settlers as hardworking farmers and weavers. The prominent attention to the community's antislavery stance simultaneously honored Germantown's local pride and integrated German immigrants into the center of American history. One panel included an inscription commemorating "the protest of the Germans of Germantown against slavery" but its iconography reflected popular depictions of White Americans as the saviors of weak and powerless African Americans; it included an image of an enslaved individual being liberated by a female emancipator. Such imagery established the Germantown community not necessarily as Germans with a unique culture, but as Americans, committed to the nation's economic and political ideals.

The unveiling ceremony further emphasized connections between the Germantown community and American identity. J. Hampton Moore featured prominently on the program. By then, he was mayor of Philadelphia and had ushered the monument legislation through Congress and proved himself a steadfast ally to the National German American Alliance. The opening prayer was given by Bishop N. B. Grubb, the current pastor of the Germantown Mennonite Church. His presence ensured that the original congregation remained central to the commemoration of German American

Pamphlet for the dedication of the monument to Francis Daniel Pastorius and the founders of Germantown. Courtesy of the Germantown Historical Society / Historic Germantown.

Monument to Francis Daniel Pastorius and the founders of Germantown, located in Vernon Park, Philadelphia, Pennsylvania. Photograph by Craig Stutman.

history. Finally, a direct descendent of Francis Daniel Pastorius, Mr. Samuel N. Pastorius, was present to introduce the mayor. According to reports from the event, "Col. Laude (from the War Department) formally turned over the memorial to the city. Mayor Moore in his acceptance promised that the city would care and protect it. The young daughter of the president of the Crefeld

Side relief of Pastorius monument, representing the 1688 antislavery protest. Photograph by Craig Stutman.

Society, which is composed of descendants of the original settler families, then pulled the cord releasing the drapes concealing the statue."[36] The combined participation of federal and local government officials, descendants of Pennsylvania's founder, and leaders of the Germantown community located the original community members and their antislavery protest as significant by placing them within a complicated matrix of national, state, and local identities.

The creation and dedication of the monument during World War I pushed German Americans to claim their patriotism even as they celebrated their German identity. The years leading up to World War II made their efforts to balance German and American cultural influences even more difficult. In 1933, Germantown was set to celebrate the 250th anniversary of its founding. The festivities were scheduled to take place between October 20 and 22. However, a disturbing incident clouded anticipation for the event. On Friday, October 6, German American Day, the German ambassador to the United

States, Hans Luther, refused to make his scheduled speech because there was no swastika adhered to the podium. Instead, Luther stood up and saluted Hitler in front of the stunned organizers.[37] There is no record of the stance Germantown's German population took regarding the Third Reich and its treatment of Jews.[38] But the Germantown Mennonites of the 1930s, like the German, Dutch, or English Quakers before them, were pacifists by tradition. The antiwar tenants of their faith were as significant a part of their theological principles as was the prohibition against child baptism. Many American Mennonites, including several from Germantown, had been conscientious objectors during World War I. But World War II was different. Photographs from the Germantown Mennonite Historic Trust archives indicate that the church displayed American flags both inside and outside and hosted USO dances as well.[39]

The German community's perceived ambivalence about the rise of Hitler combined with general distrust of conscientious objectors made German Americans in general and pacifist religious communities in particular vulnerable during the war. As a result, it is not surprising that planners of the 250th anniversary of Germantown shifted focus away from Germantown's founding, the Germantown Mennonite community, and the significance of the antislavery protest. Instead, the event focused heavily on the Revolutionary War–era Battle of Germantown. The 250th anniversary of Germantown is significant because it is the moment during which the battle, which had taken place on October 4, 1777, began to take center stage in Germantown's history. Today, the battle and its reenactment remain a popular draw both for local people and for heritage tourism.

The guidebook prepared by the 250th anniversary planning committee for an open house walking tour of Germantown emphasized sites associated with the Battle of Germantown. Cliveden occupied a prominent position in the story because "in the battle of Germantown, October 4, 1777, a small force of the British occupied the house, converting it into a fortress, and all efforts of the Americans to dislodge them were futile." The Revolutionary War's significance at most other sites in Germantown is less well documented and more anecdotal, but the guidebook emphasized them nonetheless. For instance, St. Michael's Lutheran Church is appropriately identified as the oldest Lutheran establishment in Philadelphia, but instead of exploring that connection fully, the guidebook focuses on Revolutionary War connections: "In the churchyard are the graves of Christopher Ludwick, 'Baker General' in the American Army of the Revolution, and Major James Witherspoon, who was killed in the battle of Germantown." Similarly, the Johnson House listing provided no context regarding its Quaker occupants' lives or the site's role on the Underground Railroad. Rather, the text indicates that "the house bears marks of the battle of Germantown, severe fighting having occurred hereabouts."[40] This wartime shift overshadowed the radical potential of Germantown's history, replacing stories about protest and social justice with stories about American patriotism, and allowing national interests and concerns to overshadow locals' sense of identity.

1983, 1988, and Beyond

What impact did late nineteenth- and early twentieth-century celebrations, commemorations, and monuments have on shaping radical public history practices in Germantown? How has the Germantown Mennonite Historic Trust worked to promote social justice, and how have its efforts connected to the changing demographics of the community in the late twentieth century and beyond?

It is crucial to acknowledge that the Germantown Mennonite community's celebration of its abolitionist tradition coexisted with its acceptance of segregation through most of the twentieth century.[41] Black people neither worshipped alongside White in the church building nor were they buried in the church cemetery. African American people across the country recognized the Germantown Mennonites' significant role in antislavery activism, however. During the early twentieth century, they organized commemorative events to celebrate the 1688 protest. In 1914, for example, an African American newspaper in Iowa, the *Des Moines Bystander*, picked up a report from the *Pittsburgh Dispatch* that congregants from Germantown's African American churches had organized a celebration in the Mennonite Church: "The old church was selected for the reason that the communion table in that church is said to be the table upon which the Germantown pioneers of 1688 wrote the first public protest in America against human slavery."[42] Such commemorative moments may have been overlooked by the White press, but they are crucial in the history of the community. Eventually, separate acts of remembrance by Black and White people became a bridge for establishing radical public history practices in Germantown and for building a tradition of interracial cooperation, multicultural collaboration, and civic engagement. But that tradition would not begin to take root until the midcentury American civil rights movement, and it would not become a celebrated part of local heritage until the late twentieth and early twenty-first centuries. Over time, the 1688 protest had become a pillar of Germantown's identity. Beginning in the 1980s, the centrality of that story would help drive a significant commitment to social justice by the city's public history leaders.

In 1983, preparations for the 300th anniversary celebration took a marked turn away from the troubled and ultimately conservative one of 1933.[43] The Germantown Mennonite Historic Trust board members focused less on parades or monument building, and more on the collection, preservation, and interpretation of abolition and African American history in Germantown. Their efforts marked a return to the community's original sense of heritage and functioned to untangle the nationalistic and white supremacist narrative that had taken over local history during World War II. The program of commemorative actions included plans to restore the Johnson House, a site that the trust had purchased from the city several years earlier. Between 1983 and 2003, the GMHT oversaw the rehabilitation of the structure, successfully lobbied for a State History Marker that emphasized the original owner's role in the Underground Railroad, and won National Historic Landmark Status. Most importantly, these efforts were guided by an insistence by the trust that "the interpretation of the house will emphasize the contributions of blacks and immigrant groups to Germantown history, as well as testifying to the faith of the Mennonites and Quakers who have owned the land."[44]

Commemoration of Germantown's 300th anniversary also included the creation of an archive. The members of the board invited broad participation by the local religious community, explaining, "Mennonites could become involved in Germantown by helping to create a Germantown Archives, where such valuable family papers as exist might be housed, where black history materials, church records, etc. might be kept, and where historical research can be undertaken in the context of the town which produced the materials." While this was an ambitious plan, the GMHT successfully gathered and organized these materials, and the organization was awarded a 2015 Hidden Archives Initiative grant to improve the archives' accessibility. Today, the trust has two partners in their effort to preserve Mennonite history: the Germantown Historical Society Archives and Library, and the Mennonite Heritage Center Library and Archives in Harleysville, Pennsylvania. The anniversary plans also called for the trust to create or partner with projects that might help animate Mennonite values. To this end, the board proposed to organize a

"Peace Church" interpretive slide show to serve as a counternarrative during celebrations of the Battle of Germantown.[45]

The Germantown Mennonite Historic Trust also envisioned the anniversary as a way to provide meaningful service to the members of the broader Germantown community. They imagined establishing a preservation corps that would "provide a pool of trained persons in building repair and maintenance to give low cost repair services . . . which could be combined with an apprenticeship program for Germantown youth." They also unsuccessfully proposed establishing a local Ten Thousand Villages craft store in Germantown to connect local craftspeople with international artisans, empowering both through fair-trade arrangements. Ten Thousand Villages was created by Edna Ruth Byler, a Mennonite from Kansas, who had imported goods from Puerto Rican artisans after traveling with the Mennonite Central Committee in the 1940s. The Mennonite Central Committee did indeed open a Ten Thousand Villages store within the region in the 1990s, but it was in the Chestnut Hill neighborhood of Philadelphia. Nonetheless, the GMHT recognized the potential of businesses like Ten Thousand Villages to create meaningful local opportunities. The trust was notably cognizant that economic revitalization can sometimes have unintended consequences, such as inflating prices and property taxes. Even as the board looked for ways to revitalize the community or design any project, they insisted that "any implementation should be done in consultation" with local residents. They insisted that any economic enterprise must not "displace present merchants—small enterprises of the Mom and Pop variety—but rather that our resultant business community contain a mix of proprietors, goods and services, and types of businesses."[46]

Once the 300th anniversary of Germantown approached, however, the board planned several events that combined the very principles that they hoped to advance, especially in terms of social justice education and activism. For example, the trust, working with Quaker congregations across the Northwest, organized an antiwar event called "October 6 Witness: Friendship without Missiles." As part of this event, the Germantown Mennonites released a lengthy and powerful political statement, connecting the founding of Germantown to the principles of pacifism, racial equality, and poverty relief. The statement began, "On October 6, 1683, the boat Concord landed at Philadelphia, carrying with it the first German immigrants who planned a German settlement. . . . They were a mixture of Mennonite and Quaker peoples who were . . . firm believers in the way of peace." And it concluded with a reaffirmation of their commitment to these values: "We are witnessing on October 6th because this is the day which belongs to us, the day of the landing of the Concord. We are witnessing to the values and faith of those original settlers and residents of Germantown: friendship without weapons, equality of all people, and concern for the poor and homeless."[47]

Speakers at the witnessing included General Gert Bastian, a Green Party member of the West German Parliament; Sister Falaka Fattah of the House of Umoja, an organization from West Philadelphia dedicated to ending gun violence; renowned Mennonite scholar, pastor, and college president Myron Augsburger; and United States representative and civil rights activist Ron Dellums from California. Envisioned as an act of public art as well as one of public protest, the event was advertised at various venues. The Philadelphia Museum of Art distributed a flyer explaining the event's goal to "oppose deployment of the Cruise and Pershing II missiles in Europe; to celebrate German-American friendship and the powerful heritage of Germantown; and to highlight the social, economic and racial injustices caused by the arms race. A note on the bottom of the flyer read, 'Let's tell Bush and Reagan: Employment not Deployment!'"

At the rally, Myron Augsburger appealed for "a network of people around the globe . . . a community of people committed to the way of love and nonviolence."[48] West German president Karl Carstens was a surprise attendee. The *Philadelphia Daily News* reported that he had been visiting with President Ronald Reagan, and "flew in from Washington to commemorate the 300th anniversary of the arrival of the first Germans to settle in the United States."[49] According to Susan Reed of the *Germantown Courier*, President Carstens also visited the Germantown Historical Society, though "Germantown residents, cordoned behind a police barricade set up across the street from the Historical Society, had to settle for a fleeting glimpse of Carstens' arrival and departure amid a swarm of police and Secret Service escorts." The *Courier* also reported that "seven members of the Philadelphia Women's Peace Encampment, two of them from Germantown," were arrested protesting outside of the state dinner and German-American Tricentennial Banquet at the Franklin Plaza Hotel that was attended by both Carstens and Vice President George Bush.[50]

Highlights of the 1983 celebration undoubtedly included the unveiling of a Pennsylvania Historic and Museum Commission State Marker commemorating the "First Protest against Slavery," and the opening of an exhibit tracing the history of Germantown, the Germantown Mennonites, and Germantown's

African American history. The exhibit was prepared by GMHT member and historian Bob Ulle. Local students from Germantown Friends, Wister Elementary, Pickett Middle School, and Germantown High School unveiled the marker, and the Talented Black Souls Drill Team led a procession to Wister Street where students then read aloud from the original proclamation. Among the speakers was Charles Blockson, an archivist, activist, and the founder of Temple University's Blockson Library. Blockson had led a movement to place Black history markers in Philadelphia during the 1980s and 1990 and beyond. At the unveiling, he echoed the words of Martin Luther King Jr.: "We are coming to the mountaintop," but we "still have slavery in this country . . . the slavery of ignorance."[51]

The historical exhibit was a massive time line affixed to a wall in the basement of a nineteenth-century Victorian house, adjacent to the 1770 Meetinghouse, that the trust had purchased in the 1950s. During the 1970s, the basement had been transformed into the Mennonite Information Center and operated as a small museum of Germantown Mennonite History. The exhibit covered four themes: the history of the Germantown Mennonites, the history of Mennonites in America, the history of African Americans in Germantown, and the history of African Americans in the United States. It was an incredibly ambitious, albeit straightforward and inexpensive, venture, but it connected the Mennonite role in the antislavery protest to the rise of Richard Allen's African Methodist Episcopal (AME) church in Philadelphia and beyond.

Bob Ulle, the board member and historian responsible for the exhibit, also organized a Black history panel, held at the closing of the tricentennial celebration. Shirley Parham alongside Ulle. Parham was a historian and the education director for the Afro-American Historical and Cultural Museum of Philadelphia that had opened in 1976 (now known as the African American Museum of Philadelphia). The panel's aim was to change how Germantown history was taught.[52] Parham suggested that change had to begin with challenging the belief that Germans were the only ones responsible for the development of Germantown. Parham also sought to temper the praise that White Germantown residents heaped on themselves related to the 1688 protest that she said had been "staged on the basis of economic rather than strictly moral concerns."

An opportunity to begin to transform the memory of the protest arrived five years later, during the 1988 tricentennial commemoration of the protest. Preparations for the occasion began in 1987. Shirley Parham and Charles

Blockson were members of the planning committee, which also included members of the GMHT and a number of other local and city historians. The first meeting was held at Trinity Lutheran Church in Germantown. Blockson's voice emerged as the most authoritative. Blockson argued that the commemoration of the protest was nationally significant, in part because of Germantown's well-established national significance. He was also cautious, however, about overstating Germantown's history of interracial cooperation. He reminded the committee that "it wasn't until the 1950s that all kinds of blacks moved into Germantown, many coming from the south, that Germantown took on a multiracial character—although blacks were certainly here along with Native Americans from the very first days."[53] In addition, Blockson argued, "We are taught that William Penn was a great man. That he established a colony and called it a 'Holy Experiment' with liberty and freedom [for] all, but not for blacks. Many Quakers owned slaves, including Penn. But those who hold the pen of history have left out women, Native Americans, and blacks." For these passionately argued reasons, Blockson suggested, celebrating such an occasion was vital. He said, "Throughout our history, there are many incidents recorded of people of other races and creeds who stood up for us. Our liberty and so-called freedom came about through centuries of agitation by blacks and whites. . . . Therefore, we too must have an integrated history."[54] Blockson's position was influential. Correspondence between William Grassie and Markus Miller leading up to this event indicate that both men identified four themes for the event: to "Protest Injustice—Then and Now; Build Community; Take Responsibility; and Revitalize Our Neighborhoods."

Events held to commemorate the protest during March and April of 1988, included a lecture series entitled "Mid-nineteenth Century Slavery and the German Americans," moderated by Villanova University professor James Berquist; a talk on "Quakers and Anti-slavery in the Eighteenth Century," by Patricia Reifsnyder; and the opening of an exhibit located at both the Johnson House and the Germantown Mennonite Church entitled *The Johnsons and the Underground Railroad in Germantown*. In addition, a panel discussion was held at the Germantown Friends Meeting entitled "Afro-American Perspectives on the 1688 Protest," with Shirley Parham, Charles Blockson, and Leroy Hopkins all as panelists.[55]

Conclusion

On June 16, 2018, several hours before Executive Director Cornelia Swinson and her associates at the Johnson House were to begin their annual Juneteenth Parade and Celebration, I participated in a meeting at the Germantown Mennonite Historic Trust with Board Chair Dave Hersch, Krefeld textile engineer Eduard Loers, Krefeld resident Werner Daniels, and German Society of Pennsylvania president Tony Michels. The German Society of Pennsylvania and Philadelphia City councilman Al Taubenberger had invited these individuals to march in the parade. They had carried with them a banner that read "1688 For Emancipation of Slaves," which had, according to Michaels, recently been found in the archives and had been apparently used in nineteenth-century abolitionist parades by Germans in Philadelphia sympathetic to the cause of antislavery. The five of us met around a table in the back room of the GMHT. Several members of the Germantown Mennonite Church congregation joined us, as did a docent from the Johnson House. A lively conversation took place, in which Eduard Loers expressed his excitement over being at the site where his former countrymen had made the journey to America over three hundred years before. His family research connected him to the Jan Luckens family, who were among the first thirteen families to migrate to Germantown in 1683.

Another conversation centered around a question from Toni Michels. He asked how the Quakers had claimed authority for the antislavery heritage of the Anabaptists when most of the men who had signed the petition, with the

Members of the Germantown Mennonite Historic Trust pose with historic banner while preparing for Juneteenth celebration, 2018. Photograph by Craig Stutman.

This photograph from the 2017 Juneteenth celebration shows the connection that the Germantown Mennonite Historic Trust has built with the broader movement for racial justice. Photograph by Craig Stutman.

exception of Pastorius, were Mennonites when they disembarked from the *Concord*. We talked about the fluidity of the religious traditions of those who migrated to Germantown. Many worshipped together until they had built churches. Once established, congregations changed over time. We spoke of the fact that the Lutherans and Mennonites, enemies in Europe during the sixteenth and seventeenth century, had formed friendly relationships in Germantown around their common German culture. We discussed the fluidity of the Rhineland area as well; Dutch and German, Mennonites and Quakers all emigrated to American and to Germantown, contributing to the complexity of the story. And we of course talked about the protest against slavery. Michels agreed that the German abolitionist spirit, especially among those in the Palatinate region, seemed to be strong among immigrants arriving in North America from the colonial era through to the mid-nineteenth century.

Throughout the meeting, I couldn't stop thinking about how our guests were absorbing the aesthetics of our 1909 Sunday school room annex. Folding tables and chairs set up for community and board meetings sat in the center of the room, and its rectangular perimeter was lined with display cases holding *Martyr's Mirror*s, German Bibles, Frakturs, and silk samples from Krefeld. One large windowsill held a facsimile of the 1688 protest. On the center wall hung a 1901 Site and Relic Society Wooden Marker commemorating the signing of the 1688 protest as well. I also wondered what they thought about our Historic Germantown exhibit, *Petitions for Social Justice and Change*, a large monolithic structure outfitted with the language of the protest draped around its body. Historic Germantown commissioned the artist Ben Volta as part of Historic Germantown's Elephants on the Avenue: Race, Class and Community in Historic Germantown series. Volta used the petition as a platform rather than a relic, and he designed a project in which local people could participate and "draw from the powerful words found throughout the 1688 petition to create our own historic artifacts that document the times." He explained, "These collaborative and individual artworks will serve as contemporary petitions for equity and justice that speak to our current climate of social change."[56]

After the meeting ended, we all went over to the Johnson House and waited for the parade to begin. Eduard, Tony, and Michel then went onstage with Cornelia Swinson and Al Taubenberger, where they joined Philadelphia mayor Jim Kenney, who had come to the festival to speak about the importance of the event and the significance of the 1688 petition: past and present, present and past.

Notes

1. Washington, and many others who could afford it, came to Germantown during those two years in particular to either escape the yellow fever epidemic (1793) in Philadelphia or flee the city's heat wave (1794). The 1752-built house was donated to the National Park Service in 1948 and placed on the National Register of Historic Places in 1972. See also "Germantown White House," National Park Service, last modified May 16, 2018, https://www.nps.gov/inde/learn/historyculture/places-germantownwhitehouse.htm.

2. Germantown United Community Development Corp, accessed March 4, 2021, http://germantownunitedcdc.org/; Historic Germantown: Freedom's Backyard, accessed March 4, 2021, http://www.freedomsbackyard.com/. The event also took place in a central plaza in front of the Colonial Revival–built headquarters of Historic Germantown, in which the Germantown Historical Society also operates its museum, library, and archives. The story of the 1960s and early 1970s colonial Germantown group's intention to build a central plaza as an anchor for Germantown's historic sites was controversial and did not work, although the plaza has been reincorporated into Historic Germantown's and GUCDC's (among other groups) current plans for Germantown.

3. The city has, although not without controversy, addressed the "Washington and his slaves" story with the Washington's house memorial in front of the Liberty Bell. This at least begins to tell the story about the paradox of having men who relied on enslaved labor build a new nation on the premise of liberty, equality, and freedom.

4. One might wonder what a weaving project has to do with the Germantown Mennonites. Well, contrary to the age-old mythology of Mennonite émigrés to colonial America being predominantly farmers, the Germantown Mennonites, who arrived in colonial Pennsylvania in 1683, were mostly weavers and paper-makers by trade, not farmers. Although many of these Germantown Mennonites certainly possessed either farming or husbandry skills, later generations of German and Dutch Mennonite immigrants actually comprised the communities of farmers that dotted the landscape of rural America, spreading out from points north and west of Germantown.

5. "HABS PA, 51-GERM, 51- (Sheet 2 of 7)—Mennonite Meeting House, 6119 Germantown Avenue, Philadelphia, Philadelphia County, PA," Library of Congress: Prints and Photographs Online Catalogue, accessed March 4, 2021, http://www.loc.gov/pictures/item/pa1000.sheet.00002a/; "Mennonite Meeting House," National Register of Historic Places: Digital Archive, accessed March 4, 2021, https://npgallery.nps.gov/NRHP/AssetDetail?assetID=773d66df-3da0-43df-b38f-38003a2a67ff.

6. This occurred during the same period that saw the GMHT's purchase of several additional historic properties. These included the Johnson House, a Quaker Underground Railroad site that was next door to a Mennonite homestead known as the Peter Keyser house, and Historic Rittenhouse Town, named for the William Rittenhouse. Both sites' relationship with GMHT will be discussed at length later in this essay.

7 As of the fall of 2018, there is no longer an executive director, as the board of the trust is now weighing the economic feasibility of the position against the consequences of not having a centralized figure to direct or delegate responsibilities.

8 At first glance, the story of Germantown, Philadelphia, appears to have followed a familiar American trajectory. A group of seventeenth-century religious dissidents—in this case German and Dutch Mennonites and Quakers from the Palatinate region of Germany—accepted an offer to settle on a plot of land on the outskirts of the capital of William Penn's "Holy Experiment." They gradually displaced the Lenape Indian population. During the late eighteenth century through to the mid-nineteenth century, wealthy city dwellers began to appear in the area, venturing out of the city to build their country homes and estates. And by the turn of the twentieth century, Catholic and Jewish migrants from southern and eastern Europe—many of whom were looking for work in the industrial mills of southeastern Pennsylvania—joined the fray. By the late nineteenth and well into the twentieth centuries, African Americans, many of whom who had been living in small enclaves nearby, began to set up larger, more intentional communities within the town's confines (which had been incorporated into the city of Philadelphia in 1854). During the Great Migration, many African Americans from the southern states relocated to Germantown, increasing the size of Black educational, religious, and cultural institutions. By the middle of the twentieth century, Germantown could be described, in the words of Frank X. Delany, as "a physically, socially and economically diverse community." Delany has argued that the neighborhood's development was shaped by its dual identity; it evolved as both "a mill town on the one hand and . . . a garden suburb on the other." Unfortunately, racially-based economic and cultural segregation grew alongside the town's increasing class and ethnic diversity. Segregation in churches, recreational facilities, and other social and economic institutions became the norm.

9 The Colored Girls Museum, accessed March 4, 2021, http://www.thecoloredgirlsmuseum.com/; The Aces Museum, accessed March 4, 2021, http://www.acesmuseum.online/; Supreme D. Dow, "About Us: Word from the Founder," Black Writers Museum, accessed March 4, 2021, http://blackwritersmuseum.com/about.html#mission; see also Andrea Burns's *From Storefront to Monument: Tracing the Public History of the Black Museum Movement* (Amherst: University of Massachusetts Press, 2013) in order to better understand how this movement was already part of the African American public history experience and discourse since the mid-twentieth century.

10 This is a bit of a paradox, however, because telling these colonial peoples' cultural, social, economic, religious, and architectural histories is also vitally important to preserving both the neighborhood's ethos and its built environment as well, a point that will be noted throughout this essay. But what is not up for debate is the centuries-old practice in the humanities and in the social sciences of neglecting, denigrating, or flat-out erasing histories.

11 "The Truth about Cliveden: The Chew Family Had Slaves and It's Time to Talk about It," WHYY, June 6, 2012, https://whyy.org/articles/clivedens-new-campaign/. Cliveden's programming has also been mentioned in Kristin L. Gallas and James DeWolf Perry's *Interpreting Slavery at Museums and Historic Sites* (Lanham, MD: Rowman & Littlefield, 2014). See also Donna McDaniel and Vanessa Julye's *Fit for Freedom, Not for Friendship: Quakers, African Americans, and the Myth of Racial Justice* (Philadelphia: Quaker Press, 2009), which has only quite recently looked at exploding the myth of Quakers, abolitionism, and slaveholding—a topic that will be examined in more detail later on in this essay.

12 An active debate exists within the historiography regarding who authored the protest—whether they were Mennonites, Mennonites and Quakers, or just Quakers.

13 E. Hocker, *Germantown 1688–1933* (Germantown, PA: Author, 1933). The heads of these thirteen original families were Dirk, Herman and Abraham Isaacs Op den Graff; Tunes Kunders, Johannes Bleikers, Lenart Arets, Peter Keujrlis, Wilhelm Strepers, Reinert Tisen, Jan Lense, Jan Simens, Abraham Tunes, and Jan Luken.

14 Harold S. Bender, *Conrad Grebel, 1498–1526: The Founder of the Swiss Brethren Sometimes Called the Anabaptists* (Goshen, IN: Mennonite Historical Society, 1958), 108–20; Johann Loserth, quoted in John Horsch, *Mennonites in Europe* (Scottdale, PA: Mennonite Publishing House, 1942), 298.

15 C. Henry Smith, *The Story of the Mennonites*, revised and enlarged by Cornelius Krahn, 3rd ed. (Newton, KS: Mennonite Publication Office, 1950), 67–87.

16 C. Henry Smith, "Mennonites in America" (PhD diss., University of Chicago, 1909); Smith, *The Mennonites: A Brief History of Their Origins and Later Development in Both Europe and America* (Berne, IN: Mennonite Book Concern, 1920); Leonard Gross and Jan Gleysteen, *Colonial Germantown Mennonites* (Telford, PA: Cascadia, 2007).

17 McDaniel and Julye, *Fit for Freedom*.

18 There are many reprints of this document, including "Resolutions of the Germantown Mennonites; February 18, 1688," Yale Law School Lillian Goldman Library: The Avalon Project, accessed March 4, 2021, http://avalon.law.yale.edu/17th_century/men01.asp. It also appears in a variety of historic and contemporary publications, such as in Samuel Whitaker Pennypacker's *The Settlement of Germantown, Pennsylvania* (Philadelphia: William Campbell, 1899) and Leon Higganbotham Jr.'s *In the Matter of Color, Race and the American Legal Process: The Colonial Period* (New York: Oxford University Press, 1978).

19 Brycchan Carey, "Inventing a Culture of Anti-slavery: Pennsylvania Quakers and the Germantown Protest of 1688," in *Imagining Transatlantic Slavery*, ed. Cora Kaplan and John Oldfield, 17–32 (New York: Palgrave Macmillan, 2010).

20 Higganbotham Jr., *In the Matter of Color*, 377–79.

21 Higganbotham Jr., 293.

22 *St. Louis Post Dispatch*, September 29th, 1883, 11. Most likely, the anonymous author who composed the piece had gleaned his or her ideas from the writings of Daniel Cassel and Samuel Pennypacker, including their Mennonite histories, written during

the 1870s and 1880s and encompassing the Germantown part of the story. Such articles that would detail Germantown over the next few decades pretty much followed the same narrative.

23 "German Bi-centenary," *Times*, October 6, 1883, 3.
24 "Bi-centennial: How the Founding of Germantown Will Be Commemorated," *Philadelphia Inquirer*, October 6, 1883, 3.
25 Historical records include two spellings for the name of the town of Krefeld. Until 1925, it was common to see "Crefeld," particularly in English-language sources. In Pennsylvania, some locations and businesses—including the Crefeld School—still use the older spelling.
26 "Germantown: Its Bi-centennial Celebrated in Germany," *Philadelphia Inquirer*, November 12, 1883, 7.
27 "Spectacular Pageant in Honor of German Day," *Lincoln Star*, October 6, 1910, 1.
28 "Spectacular Pageant."
29 Gordon J. Howard, "The First Germantowners Memorialized," *Germantown Crier* 64, no. 2 (Fall 2014): 27–44.
30 "Founder's Day Celebration in Germantown," letter, folder "Pastorius Monument," Germantown Historical Society, Philadelphia.
31 He became mayor of Philadelphia in 1920.
32 J. Hampton Moore, "Monument at Germantown: Speech of J. Hampton Moore of Pennsylvania in the House of Representatives," February 7, 1911, Germantown Historical Society, Philadelphia.
33 "Pastorius Statue Dedication Halted," *Philadelphia Inquirer*, April 25, 1917, 2.
34 "Protest on Monument," *Philadelphia Public Ledger*, June 9, 1919, 11.
35 "Would Destroy That Monument," *Philadelphia Public Ledger*, September 1919 (no specific date—in clippings file for the Germantown Historical Society, Philadelphia, under "Pastorius Monument").
36 Howard, "First Germantowners," 41.
37 "Swastika Absent, Dr. Luther Balks at Address Here," *Philadelphia Inquirer*, October 8, 1933, 25.
38 This subject would require further research.
39 "25 War Objectors Given Furloughs: Camp Meade Officials Believe Quakers and Mennonites Better at Farming," *Philadelphia Inquirer*, July 17, 1918. See also Richard Lichty, *An Increase in Time: Story Lines of Germantown Mennonite Church and Its Historic Trust, 1683–2005* (Elkhart, IN: Institute of Mennonite Studies, 2015), 110–11.
40 "250th Anniversary of the Settlement of Germantown," program, 1933, Germantown Mennonite Historic Trust Archives (hereafter cited as GMHT Archives). The Johnson House is next door to the Keyser house, which was not even on the list of sites to visit.
41 Unfortunately, this was an occurrence at many Quaker churches until the early twentieth century as well. See McDaniel and Julye's *Fit for Freedom*; Devin C. Manzullo Thomas, "Mennonites," in *The Encyclopedia of Greater Philadelphia*, http://philadelphiaencyclopedia.org/archive/mennonites/.

42 "Afro-American Cullings," *Des Moines Bystander*, November 6, 1914.
43 In 1983, the organization was called the Germantown Mennonite Church Corporation. For clarity and brevity, I am continuing to use the contemporary name of this organization, the Germantown Mennonite Historic Trust, to describe this group.
44 "Germantown: 1683–1983, Mennonite Roles for Celebration," GMHT Archives, folder "1983 Celebration."
45 "Germantown: 1683–1983."
46 "Germantown: 1683–1983."
47 "October 6 Witness: Friendship without Missiles," GMHT Archives, folder "1983 Celebration."
48 "Protest Challenges U.S. Policy," *Germantown Courier*, October 12, 1983, 2.
49 "President Makes It a Bonn-y Day Here," *Philadelphia Daily News*, October 7, 1983, 40.
50 "West German Prez Comes to Germantown: Carstens Stops to Mark 300th Birthday at Historical Society," *Germantown Courier*, October 12, 1983, 3.
51 "Anti-Slavery Ceremony: Marker Honors 1688 Protest," *Germantown Courier*, October 12, 1983, 1.
52 "Black History Here Revealed," *Germantown Courier*, October 12, 1983, 1. In reference to the contested memory over the ownership of the protest that Dr. Parham alludes to, here is a summary.

A number of nineteenth- and twentieth-century historians and publications indeed refer to the protest as a "Mennonite protest against slavery," including Samuel Pennypacker, Leon Higginbotham, and the *Philadelphia Tribune* (the longest continuously running Black newspaper in the United States—from 1884 to today—which for at least three decades beginning in the 1970s ran advertisements on what Black history sites could be visited in Philadelphia and had on their list both the Johnson House and the 1770 Germantown Meetinghouse, as well as an anecdote about the Germanton Mennonite protest against slavery). However, there has also been confusion or disagreement over the faith of the German Germantown residents who signed and put forth the petition.

In the 250th anniversary book that was previously discussed, there is a short essay entitled "The Religion of the Founders" that essentially encapsulates this entire debate. The anonymous author of that essay wrote that "some of the original settlers had been Mennonites in Europe, but all the thirteen 'heads of families' from Crefeld arriving on October 6, 1683, became members of the Society of Friends, except for Jan Lensen, who remained a Mennonite." The problem that scholars have with this logic is that several of the signers, including Abraham Op De Graef, are buried in Mennonite cemeteries in Montgomery County, and it does not take into account the fact that most of the thirteen families' ancestors remained Mennonites.

It appears that the story got co-opted—though most likely for benign reasons. Nathaniel Kite, self-described as a "Quaker antiquarian," "discovered" the original document protesting slavery in 1844 and immediately wrote about it in the *Friends Journal* and deposited the document in a Swarthmore library. But Kite's ideas (and those of the dozens of others who followed him) on why the Mennonites became

Quakers might be due to a simple stumbling block: because there was no formal Mennonite meetinghouse until 1708, Mennonites worshipped in the homes of early settlers, and both the Quakers and Mennonites often worshipped together. Additionally, because of this and because of the fluidity of Germantown's early residents to change denominations (such as Anabaptists to Anabaptist, Mennonite to Brethren, Mennonite to Quaker, Quaker to Mennonite, Mennonite to Lutheran, etc.), the story gets a bit muddled.

But it may have also been wrongly attributed to Quakers because of how and why the protest was signed in the first place. Because a number of prominent Quakers owned slaves, including William Penn, the petitioners brought forth their protest to Quaker meetings, pleading with the supposedly social-justice-conscious churchgoers to end the practice of slaveholding among Quakers first and foremost. As such, appearing then in front of the Quaker monthly meeting in Dublin, Pennsylvania, and then to the quarterly and annual meetings in Philadelphia, to object to this practice does not show membership but instead a belief that as allies, both communities should work together to end slaveholding.

To be most accurate, therefore, it is perhaps best to call the protest a Mennonite and Quaker protest at the least, and a Mennonite protest at best, but not a Quaker protest. This subject deserves an article or a book of its own.

53 "Minutes from the Planning Meeting for the 300th Anniversary of the First Protest against Slavery in North America," April 21, 1987, GMHT Archives, folder "1988 Protest Anniversary."
54 "Minutes from the Planning Meeting," 4.
55 "The 300th Anniversary of the Germantown Protest: Calendar of Events," pamphlet, GMHT Archives, folder "1988 Protest Anniversary."
56 ttps://www.pewcenterarts.org/event/elephants-avenue-petitions-social-justice-change-benjamin-volta-2017-05-13-000000?page=1.

Conclusion

The Uneasy Relationship between Civic Engagement and Social Justice

Denise D. Meringolo

The essays in this volume demonstrate that a commitment to social justice has shaped the broad field of public history and that individuals have been willing to explore connections between political activism and intellectual practice even at some risk to their own professional stature and personal security. Some practitioners have actively reflected on this problem. Gene Weltfish regularly risked censure for her vocal commitment to antiracist action. She criticized fellow participants in the American Civilization Institute of Morristown for paying insufficient attention to white supremacy. Paul Romanoff literally gave his life to establish the role of his collections in challenging anti-Semitism and creating cross-cultural understanding. At the same time, the essays in this volume raise questions about the sustainability of radical practices. Sometimes, social consciousness breaks under the weight of professionalization and institutional development. The Tenement Museum, in its effort to expand both interpretively and spatially, became implicated in processes of gentrification. Carter G. Woodson's work to promote Black pride and Black consciousness has been watered down—though not entirely lost—by the broad institutionalization of Black History Month in educational and cultural institutions.

As we uncover the potential of public history to serve social justice, it is also crucial that we recognize the qualities and conditions that limit this potential. Throughout this inquiry, participants have understood that the effort to identify the radical roots of public history was not designed to help create a list of heroes. Rather, we aimed to identify these radical roots in order to develop a more historically well-grounded critique of radical practices, a more clearly articulated set of ethical principles, and a flexible series of best-practices guidelines. Recognizing the impact that historical trends have had on the development of radical forms of public history—from progressive education, to New Deal–era social experimentation, to late twentieth-century identity politics—provides us with a clearer view of both the promise and the shortcomings of politically engaged historical work.

In this vein, there remains a deep contradiction at the center of this volume. The practices the contributors have placed at the center of their collaborative inquiry—a community focus, an emphasis on problem solving, a preference for shared inquiry and collaboration—are recognizable as elements of what is often labeled as "civic engagement." Each contributor has benefitted, directly or indirectly, from the relatively recent rise of civic engagement as a recognized set of strategies that can demonstrate the broad public value offered by cultural institutions and universities. Indeed, the ubiquity of civic engagement as an ideal lent immediacy to our research. The term dominates mission statements, long-range planning documents, and best-practice guidelines. However, we quickly discovered that there is no one generally agreed-upon definition of *civic engagement*. For political scientists, the term describes any activity that promotes democracy by expanding citizen participation in decision-making. Public historians and academics have used it more broadly to describe any effort to include audiences, stakeholders, and local people in research and interpretation as part of a larger process to address the social, cultural, and/or political conditions of everyday life.[1] But the practice of civic engagement in this context has been insufficiently historicized and theorized. Indeed, the historiography of civic engagement is at least as problematic as the broadly accepted historiography of public history our work sought to address.

Throughout the existing literature, the contemporary emphasis on civic engagement in higher education is most often traced to the 1990s, when then secretary of Housing and Urban Development Henry Cisneros created an Office of University Partnerships to help colleges and universities develop practical solutions to the problems of poverty and injustice in urban America. Through strategies such as service learning, collaborative research, and university-community partnerships, faculty members and administrators sought to be more responsive to the communities that existed outside the walls of the academy.[2] By the first decade of the twenty-first century, there had been a sharp increase in the number of faculty committees, administrative offices, and bureaucratic systems dedicated to promoting community-centered research and teaching.[3] Perhaps as a reflection of this trend, the Carnegie Foundation established an elective "community engagement" classification in 2010 to draw attention to the value that civic engagement has for institutions of higher learning. During the same period, museums also turned toward civic engagement. The American Alliance of Museums, the leading professional association for museums in the United States (then called the American Association of Museums), initiated a challenge for museums to become better connected with underserved communities.[4] The timing of these trends indicates they were, at least in part, a response to the late twentieth-century culture wars. During the 1980s and 1990s, politicians and citizens alike questioned the use of public funds to support cultural institutions and the arts, and they vilified scholars, curators, and others who advanced controversial interpretations or promoted offensive works of art and history.[5] Civic engagement strategies provided a way for museums and universities to demonstrate their broad public value and bolster their image.

The emphasis on this recent historical context is relevant. It may explain why the assessment of cultural and educational programs aimed at civic engagement has been focused on internal institutional impacts. Experts on pedagogy have analyzed the value of civic engagement for improving students' political awareness, empathy, and interpersonal skills.[6] Experts on museums and other cultural institutions have accepted civic engagement as an essential component of best practices and a tool for diversifying audiences, enhancing the relevance of museums, and illuminating new perspectives on the past.[7] City administrators tout the value of civic engagement for improving fiscal management and promoting urban development.[8] All these outcomes are undeniably positive for universities, public history sites, and government entities, but there has been insufficient effort to identify and analyze external impacts. In other words, while the literature indicates that civic engagement can serve as a positive response to institutional crises, it is less clear how well these strategies have benefitted the communities themselves.

The contributors to *Radical Roots: Civic Engagement, Public History, and a Tradition of Social Justice Activism* argue that radical public historians developed and advanced the practices that compose civic engagement as strategies for advancing social justice, advocating for marginalized communities, articulating the root causes of pressing political issues, and promoting change. The use and adaptation of these practices over time by individuals connected through social and political networks is the thread that ties past to present, establishing a recognizable genealogy for radical public history. At the same time, without rigorous critical analysis and focused attention on their ongoing use and development over time, it is possible for both civic engagement and public history to lose their radical potential. In order for strategies of shared inquiry, collaboration, dialogue, and other practices of civic engagement to serve a social justice agenda, practitioners must turn their attention outward. Has civic engagement been successful in advancing justice by enabling communities to build stronger platforms from which to influence politics or transform their own social and cultural environments?

The goal of this volume is to begin to allow those invested in advancing social justice to more adequately and accurately recognize and address the potential shortcomings of their work. In turn, this may also allow for the development of a more honest and appropriate approach to self-reflection and assessment. Civic engagement has become implicated in the neoliberalization of both the education and culture sectors; it attracts funding and positive media attention at the same time that it depends on a tremendous amount of unrewarded and unrecognized labor. Further, civic engagement is often marginalized: as "service" rather than scholarship, "outreach" rather than interpretation, "visitor services" rather than the cocreation of knowledge. Yet as this volume seeks to illuminate, professors, museum professionals, oral historians, preservationists, and others who have fully integrated shared inquiry, dialogue, self-reflection, and collaboration into their various modes of inquiry have often activated elements of civic engagement as strategies for addressing issues of injustice and inequality. Paying close attention to the contradictions and conflicts the contributors to this volume have identified may help practitioners develop new strategies for reclaiming and energizing the radical potential of civic engagement, public history, and other forms of community-engaged practice.

Notes

1 For more on the various definitions of *civic engagement*, see, for example, Richard P. Adler and Judy Goggin, "What Do We Mean by 'Civic Engagement'?," *Journal of Transformative Education* 3, no. 3 (July 1, 2005): 236–53; Ben Berger, "Political Theory, Political Science, and the End of Civic Engagement," *Perspectives on Politics* 7, no. 2 (June 2009): 335–50; Thomas Ehrlich, ed., *Civic Responsibility and Higher*

Education (Lanham, MD: Rowman & Littlefield, 2000); "Indicators of an Engaged Campus," Campus Compact, accessed March 4, 2021, https://compact.org/initiatives/advanced-service-learning-toolkit-for-academic-leaders/indicators-of-an-engaged-campus/; Stephen Long, "Practicing Civic Engagement: Making Your Museum into a Community Living Room," *Journal of Museum Education* 38, no. 2 (2013): 141–53; Aaron Smith, Kay Lehman Schlozman, Sidney Verba, and Henry Brady, "The Internet and Civic Engagement: The Current State of Civic Engagement in America," Pew Research Center, September 1, 2009, https://www.pewresearch.org/internet/2009/09/01/the-current-state-of-civic-engagement-in-america/; Elizabeth Theiss-Morris and John R. Hibbing, "Citizenship and Civic Engagement," *Annual Review of Political Science* 8 (June 2005): 227–49. See also Denise D. Meringolo, "Civic Engagement," Inclusive Historians Handbook (cosponsored by the American Association for State and Local History and the National Council on Public History), May 23, 2019, https://inclusivehistorian.com/civic-engagement/. This post was grounded in my research and editorial work for *Radical Roots*.

2 Tracy Soska and Alice K. Johnson Butterfield, eds., *University-Community Partnerships: Universities in Civic Engagement* (New York: Routledge, 2004).

3 Penny A. Pasque et al., eds., *Conference Proceedings: Higher Education Collaboratives for Community Engagement and Improvement* (Ann Arbor: National Forum on Higher Education for the Public Good, University of Michigan, 2005).

4 American Association of Museums, *Mastering Civic Engagement: A Challenge to Museums* (Chicago: University of Chicago Press, 2002).

5 See, for example, Barbara Gamarekian, "Corcoran, to Foil Dispute, Drops Mapplethorpe Show," *New York Times* June 14, 1989, https://www.nytimes.com/1989/06/14/arts/corcoran-to-foil-dispute-drops-mapplethorpe-show.html; Andrew Guilford, "Visitors Respond: Selections from 'The West as America' Comment Books," *Montana: The Magazine of Western History* 42, no. 3 (Summer 1992): 77–80; Michael Kimmelman, "ART VIEW: Old West, New Twist at Smithsonian," *New York Times*, May 26, 1991, https://www.nytimes.com/1991/05/26/arts/art-view-old-west-new-twist-at-the-smithsonian.html.

6 Susan Benigni Cipolle, *Service Learning and Social Justice: Engaging Students in Social Change* (Lanham, MD: Rowman & Littlefield, 2010); Christine M. Cress, Peter J. Collier, and Vicki L. Reitenauer, *Learning through Serving: A Student Guidebook for Service-Learning and Civic Engagement across Academic Disciplines and Cultural Communities* (Sterling, VA: Stylus, 2013); Barbara Jacoby et al., *Civic Engagement in Higher Education: Concepts and Practices* (San Francisco: Jossey-Bass, 2009).

7 Gail Anderson, *Reinventing the Museum: The Evolving Conversation and the Paradigm Shift* (Lanham, MD: AltaMira, 2012); Viv Golding and Wayne Modest, eds., *Museums and Communities: Curators, Collections, and Collaboration* (New York: Bloomsbury Academic, 2013).

8 Roger L. Kemp, ed., *Town and Gown Relations: A Handbook of Best Practices* (Jefferson, NC: McFarland, 2013).

Further Reading

This list of projects, sites, and publications provides a glimpse into a growing and diverse body of work that continues to compose and advance radical public history practices.

Antonovich, Jacqueline, et al. Nursing Clio. Accessed November 11, 2020. https://nursingclio.org/about.

Ater, Renee. Contemporary Monuments to the Slave Past. See particularly the "Statement of Principles." Accessed November 11, 2020. http://slaverymonuments.org/statement_of_principles.

Beyond Kin Project. Accessed November 11, 2020. https://beyondkin.org.

Big Door Brigade. Accessed November 11, 2020. https://bigdoorbrigade.com.

Casey, Jim, and P. Gabrielle Forman. Colored Conventions Project. See especially the data use guidelines in "Introduction to CCP Corpus." Accessed November 11, 2020. https://coloredconventions.org/about-records/ccp-corpus.

Chinook Story: A Chinook Nation-Portland State University Collaboration. Accessed November 11, 2020. https://chinookstory.org.

Clark, Meredith, Bergis Jules, and Trevor Munoz. Documenting the Now. Accessed November 11, 2020. https://www.docnow.io.

Climates of Inequality. Accessed November 11, 2020. http://www.climatesofinequality.org.

Drake, Jarrett M. "Diversity's Discontents: In Search of an Archive of the Oppressed." *Archives and Manuscripts* 47, no. 2 (March 2019): 270–79.

———. "'Graveyards of Exclusion': Archives, Prisons, and the Bounds of Belonging." *Medium*, March 24, 2019. https://medium.com/community

-archives/graveyards-of-exclusion-archives-prisons-and-the-bounds-of-belonging-c40c85ff1663.

Equal Justice Initiative. National Memorial for Peace and Justice. Accessed November 11, 2020. https://museumandmemorial.eji.org/memorial.

Erickson, Ansley, and Ernest Morrell. Harlem Education History Project. Accessed November 11, 2020. https://harlemeducationhistory.library.columbia.edu.

Georgia Public Broadcasting. "An Exploration of Antebellum Savannah through the Owens-Thomas House and Slave Quarters." Accessed November 11, 2020. https://www.gpb.org/education/virtual/owens-thomas-house.

Greenfield, Briann. Harriet Beecher Stowe Center. Accessed November 11, 2020. https://www.harrietbeecherstowecenter.org.

Guantanamo Public Memory Project. "Project Principles." Accessed November 11, 2020. https://gitmomemory.org/about/principles.

Hughes-Watkins, Lae'l. "Moving toward a Reparative Archive: A Roadmap for a Holistic Approach to Disrupting Homogenous Histories in Academic Repositories and Creating Inclusive Spaces for Marginalized Voices." *Journal of Contemporary Archival Studies* 5 (2018), article 6. https://elischolar.library.yale.edu/cgi/viewcontent.cgi?article=1045&context=jcas.

International Coalition of Sites of Conscience. Accessed November 11, 2020. https://www.sitesofconscience.org/en/home.

Jennings, Gretchen. "The Zeitgeist of Tyranny: What Should Museums Do?" Museum Commons, March 2, 2020. https://museumcommons.com/2020/03/the-zeitgeist-of-tyranny-what-should-museums-do.html.

Monroe and Florence Work Today. Accessed March 4, 2021. https://plaintalkhistory.com/monroeandflorencework/.

Ramey, R. J. "The Profundity of Your Archive Doesn't Want to Live in Boxes Anymore: An Introduction to *Monroe Work Today*." *Preservation, Digital Technology, and Culture* 48, no. 2 (July 2019): 61–69.

Relevancy and History Project. Accessed November 11, 2020. https://www.parks.ca.gov/?page_id=29393.

Remer, Ashley E. Girl Museum. Accessed November 11, 2020. https://www.girlmuseum.org.

Reser, Anna, and Leila McNeill. Lady Science. Accessed November 11, 2020. https://www.ladyscience.com.

Ševčenko, Liz. Humanities Action Lab. Accessed November 11, 2020. https://www.humanitiesactionlab.org.

SNCC Digital Gateway. Accessed November 11, 2020. htttps://snccdigital.org.

States of Incarceration: A National Dialogue of Local Histories. Accessed November 11, 2020. https://statesofincarceration.org.

Traditional Knowledge (TK) Labels Project. Accessed November 11, 2020. https://localcontexts.org/labels/traditional-knowledge-labels/.

Utah American Indian Digital Archives and Utah Indian Curriculum Project. Accessed November 11, 2020. http://utahindians.com.

Whitney Plantation. Accessed November 11, 2020. https://www.whitneyplantation.org.

Contributor Biographies

Rebecca Amato is Director of Teaching and Learning at Illinois Humanities and former Associate Director of the Urban Democracy Lab at New York University, where she was also Associate Faculty.

Kristen Baldwin Deathridge is an Assistant Professor of History at Appalachian State University.

Elizabeth Belanger is an Associate Professor of American Studies at Hobart and William Smith College. Her teaching and research interests include public humanities, critical pedagogy, and historical geographic information systems (GIS).

Gabrielle Bendiner-Viani is an urbanist, curator, and artist pioneering public arts and urban research for community engagement. She is the author of *Contested City: Art and Public History as Mediation at New York's Seward Park Urban Renewal Area*. She teaches Urban Studies and Public Art at the New School and is Principal of Buscada, an interdisciplinary studio on place and civic dialogue.

Shane Bernardo is a life-long resident of Detroit involved in social justice, primarily food justice issues. His current role is Training Facilitator for Uprooting Racism Planting Justice. Shane is also a member of the Detroit Asian Youth Project, the Detroit Food Justice Task Force, the People's Platform Detroit, Equitable Detroit Coalition, and Groundswell, and a fellow with the Detroit Equity Action Lab and Stone Barns Center for Food and Agriculture.

Clarissa J. Ceglio is Assistant Professor of Digital Humanities and Associate Director of Research for Greenhouse Studios | Scholarly Communications Design at the University of Connecticut.

Maria E. Cotera is an Associate Professor in the Departments of American Culture and Women's Studies and Director of the Program in Latina/o Studies at the University of Michigan.

Pero Gaglo Dagbovie is a University Distinguished Professor in the Department of History and an Associate Dean in the Graduate School at Michigan State University.

Dipti Desai is Professor of Art and Art Education and the Director of the Art + Education program at New York University, which is grounded in contemporary art, critical pedagogy, and social activism.

Rachel Donaldson is an Assistant Professor of History at the College of Charleston.

Fernanda Espinosa is an independent oral historian, artist, and cultural organizer. She is part of the Andean diaspora in the New York area, and her practice is embedded in interrogating colonial standards and forms. She is the Cofounder and Coordinator of Cooperativa Cultural 19 de enero (CC 1/19), an oral transmissions and visual arts collaboration.

Michèle Gates Moresi is Supervisory Museum Curator of Collections at the Smithsonian National Museum of African American History and Culture. She assists in identifying and obtaining collections for the museum, oversees collections acquisition and management activities, and participates in exhibition development.

Abigail R. Gautreau is Assistant Professor of History at Grand Valley State University.

Judith Jennings is an independent scholar who writes primarily on abolitionism in Britain and also has deep roots in the life and culture of the eastern Kentucky coalfields.

Lara Kelland is the E. Desmond Lee Endowed Professor in Museum Studies and Community History at the University of Missouri–St. Louis, where she directs the Museum Studies, Heritage, and Public History MA program.

Daniel R. Kerr is Associate Professor of History and the Director of the Humanities Truck Project at American University. He is the Vice President of the Oral History Association.

Kristen Ana La Follette lectures in oral history, creative writing, and service learning at California State University, Monterey Bay. She also creates verbatim theater.

Denise D. Meringolo is Associate Professor of History and Director of Public History at the University of Maryland, Baltimore County.

Nicole A. Moore is a public historian and Director of Education at the National Center for Civil and Human Rights in Atlanta, Georgia.

Burnis Morris is the Carter G. Woodson Professor of Journalism and Mass Communications and Cofounder of the Dr. Carter G. Woodson Lyceum at Marshall University. He taught journalism history courses for more than three decades and created the Fourth Estate and the Third Sector, a national training program for journalists who cover tax-exempt organizations and philanthropy that was funded by Knight Foundation. He is author of three published books, including *Carter G. Woodson: History, the Black Press, and Public Relations*.

Mary Rizzo is Assistant Professor of History at Rutgers University–Newark, where her work focuses on inclusive public history, digital humanities, and urban studies.

Laura Schiavo, a curator at heart, is Assistant Professor of Museum Studies at the George Washington University, where she focuses on the study of museums and identity.

Amy Starecheski is the Director of Columbia University's Oral History MA Program and Codirector of the COVID-19 in New York Oral History Project.

She is a cultural anthropologist whose research focuses on property, value, and the production of history in cities.

Craig Stutman is an Associate Professor of History and Public Policy at Delaware Valley University. He is the Chair of the Toni Morrison Society's Bench by the Road Project and is a working board member at both the Germantown Mennonite Historic Trust and Eden Cemetery, a historic African American Cemetery in Collingdale, Pennsylvania.

Anne M. Valk is Professor of History and Executive Director of the American Social History Project / Center for Media and Learning at the City University of New York Graduate Center.

William S. Walker is Associate Professor of History at the Cooperstown Graduate Program. He is the author of *A Living Exhibition: The Smithsonian and the Transformation of the Universal Museum* and a lead editor of *History@Work*, the blog of the National Council on Public History. An active public historian, Professor Walker oversees *CGP Community Stories*, an ongoing oral history project that uses recorded narratives to initiate public dialogue programs on critical social and environmental issues.